F. Max Müller

A Sanskrit Grammar for Beginners

Salzwasser

F. Max Müller

A Sanskrit Grammar for Beginners

1. Auflage | ISBN: 978-3-84605-010-1

Erscheinungsort: Frankfurt, Deutschland

Erscheinungsjahr: 2020

Salzwasser Verlag GmbH

Reprint of the original, first published in 1870.

A

SANSKRIT GRAMMAR .

FOR BEGINNERS,

IN

DEVANÂGARÎ AND ROMAN LETTERS THROUGHOUT,

BY

Fⁿ MAX MÜLLER, M.A.,

FOREIGN MEMBER OF THE FRENCH INSTITUTE,

ETC.

SECOND EDITION, REVISED AND ACCENTUATED.

LONDON:

LONGMANS, GREEN, AND CO.

1870.

PREFACE

TO THE FIRST EDITION.

THE present grammar, which is chiefly intended for beginners, is believed to contain all the information that a student of Sanskrit is likely to want during the first two or three years of his reading. Rules referring to the language of the Vedas have been entirely excluded, for it is not desirable that the difficulties of that ancient dialect should be approached by any one who has not fully mastered the grammar of the ordinary Sanskrit such as it was fixed by Pâṇini and his successors. All allusions to cognate forms in Greek, Latin, or Gothic, have likewise been suppressed, because, however interesting and useful to the advanced student, they are apt to deprive the beginner of that clear and firm grasp of the grammatical system peculiar to the language of ancient India, which alone can form a solid foundation for the study both of Sanskrit and of Comparative Philology.

The two principal objects which I have kept in view while composing this grammar, have been clearness and correctness. With regard to clearness, my chief model has been the grammar of Bopp; with regard to correctness, the grammar of Colebrooke. If I may hope, without presumption, to have simplified a few of the intricacies of Sanskrit grammar which were but partially cleared up by Bopp, Benfey, Flecchia, and others, I can hardly flatter myself to have reached, with regard to correctness, the high standard of Colebrooke's great, though unfinished work. I can only say in self-defence, that it is far more difficult to be correct on every minute point, if one endeavours to re-arrange, as I have done, the materials collected by Pâṇini, and to adapt them to the grammatical system current in Europe, than if one follows so closely as Colebrooke, the system of native grammarians, and adopts nearly the whole of their technical terminology. The grammatical system elaborated by native grammarians is, in itself, most perfect; and those who have tested Pâṇini's work, will readily admit that there is no grammar in any language that could vie with the wonderful mechanism of his eight books of grammatical rules. But unrivalled as that system is, it is not suited to the wants of English students, least of all to the wants of beginners. While availing myself therefore of the materials collected in the grammar of Pâṇini and in later works, such as the Prakriyâ-Kaumudî, the Siddhânta-Kaumudî, the Sârasvatî Prakriyâ, and the Mâdhavîya-dhâtu-vṛitti, I have abstained, as much as possible, from introducing any more of the peculiar system and of the terminology of Indian grammarians* than has already found admittance into our Sanskrit grammars; nay, I have frequently rejected the grammatical observations supplied ready to hand in their works, in order not to overwhelm the memory of the student with too many rules and too many exceptions. Whether I have always been successful in drawing a line between what is essential in Sanskrit grammar and what is not, I must leave to the judgment of those who enjoy the good fortune of being engaged in the practical teaching of a language the students of which may be counted no longer by tens, but by hundreds†. I only wish it to be understood that where I have left out rules

---

* The few alterations that I have made in the usual terminology have been made solely with a view of facilitating the work of the learner. Thus instead of numbering the ten classes of verbs, I have called each by its first verb. This relieves the memory of much unnecessary trouble, as the very name indicates the character of each class; and though the names may at first sound somewhat uncouth, they are after all the only names recognized by native grammarians. Knowing from my experience as an examiner, how difficult it is to remember the merely numerical distinction between the first, second, or third preterites, or the first and second futures, I have kept as much as possible to the terminology with which classical scholars are familiar, calling the tense corresponding to the Greek Imperfect, Imperfect; that corresponding to the Perfect, Reduplicated Perfect; that corresponding to the Aorist, Aorist; and the mood corresponding to the Optative, Optative. The names of Periphrastic Perfect and Periphrastic Future tell their own story; and if I have retained the merely numerical distinction between the First and Second Aorists, it was because this distinction seemed to be more intelligible to a classical scholar than the six or seven forms of the so-called multiform Preterite. If it were possible to make a change in the established grammatical nomenclature, I should much prefer to call the First the Second, and the Second the First Aorist; the former being a secondary and compound, the latter a primary and simple tense. But First and Second Aorists have become almost proper names, and will not easily yield their place to mere argument.

† In the University of Leipzig alone, as many as fifty pupils attend every year the classes of Professor Brockhaus in order to acquire a knowledge of the elements of Sanskrit, previous to the study of Comparative Philology under Professor Curtius.

or exceptions, contained in other grammars, whether native or European, I have done so after mature consideration, deliberately preferring the less complete to the more complete, but, at the same time, more bewildering statement of the anomalies of the Sanskrit language. Thus, to mention one or two cases, when giving the rules on the employment of the suffixes *vat* and *mat* (§ 187), I have left out the rule that bases ending in *m*, though the *m* be preceded by other vowels than *a*, always take *vat* instead of *mat*. I did so partly because there are very few bases ending in *m*, partly because, if a word like *kim-ván* should occur, it would be easy to discover the reason why here too *v* was preferred to *m*, viz. in order to avoid the clashing of two *m*'s. Again, when giving the rules on the formation of denominatives (§ 495), I passed over, for very much the same reason, the prohibition given in Pân. III. 1, 8, 3, viz. that bases ending in *m* are not allowed to form denominatives. It is true, no doubt, that the omission of such rules or exceptions may be said to involve an actual misrepresentation, and that a pupil might be misled to form such words as *kim-mán* and *kim-yati*. But this cannot be avoided in an elementary grammar ; and the student who is likely to come in contact with such recondite forms, will no doubt be sufficiently advanced to be able to consult for himself the rules of Pânini and the explanations of his commentators.

My own fear is that, in writing an elementary grammar, I have erred rather in giving too much than in giving too little. I have therefore in the table of contents marked with an asterisk all such rules as may be safely left out in a first course of Sanskrit grammar *, and I have in different places informed the reader whether certain portions might be passed over quickly, or should be carefully committed to memory. Here and there, as for instance in § 103, a few extracts are introduced from Pânini, simply in order to give the student a foretaste of what he may expect in the elaborate works of native grammarians, while lists of verbs like those contained in § 332 or § 462 are given, as everybody will see, for the sake of reference only. The somewhat elaborate treatment of the nominal bases in *i* and *á*, from § 220 to § 226,

---

* In the second edition all these paragraphs are printed in smaller type.

became necessary, partly because in no grammar had the different paradigms of this class been correctly given, partly because it was impossible to bring out clearly the principle on which the peculiarities and apparent irregularities of these nouns are based without entering fully into the systematic arrangement of native grammarians. Of portions like this I will not say indeed, μωμήσεταί τις μᾶλλον ἢ μιμήσεται, but I feel that I may say, यत्ने कृते यदि न सिध्यति कोऽत्र दोष: ; and I know that those who will take the trouble to examine the same mass of evidence which I have weighed and examined, will be the most lenient in their judgment, if hereafter they should succeed better than I have done, in unravelling the intricate argumentations of native scholars *.

But while acknowledging my obligations to the great grammarians of India, it would be ungrateful were I not to acknowledge as fully the assistance which I have derived from the works of European scholars. My first acquaintance with the elements of Sanskrit was gained from Bopp's grammar. Those only who know the works of his predecessors, of Colebrooke, Carey, Wilkins, and Forster, can appreciate the advance made by Bopp in explaining the difficulties, and in lighting up, if I may say so, the dark lanes and alleys of the Sanskrit language. I doubt whether Sanskrit scholarship would have flourished as it has, if students had been obliged to learn their grammar from Forster or Colebrooke, and I believe that to Bopp's little grammar is due a great portion of that success which has attended the study of Sanskrit literature in Germany. Colebrooke, Carey, Wilkins, and Forster worked independently of each other. Each derived his information from native teachers and from native grammars. Among these four scholars, Wilkins seems to have been the first to compose a Sanskrit grammar, for he informs us that the first printed sheet of his work was destroyed by fire in 1795. The

---

* To those who have the same faith in the accurate and never swerving argumentations of Sanskrit commentators, it may be a saving of time to be informed that in the new and very useful edition of the Siddhânta-Kaumudî by Sʹrî Târânâtha-tarkavâchaspati there are two misprints which hopelessly disturb the order of the rules on the proper declension of nouns in í and ú. On page 136, l. 7, read स्त्रीयत् instead of स्त्रीवत्; this is corrected in the Corrigenda, and the right reading is found in the old edition. On the same page, l. 13, insert न after विना, or join विनास्त्रीयोपकारं.

whole grammar, however, was not published till 1808. In the mean time Forster had finished his grammar, and had actually delivered his MS. to the Council of the College of Fort William in 1804. But it was not published till 1810. The first part of Colebrooke's grammar was published in 1805, and therefore stands first in point of time of publication. Unfortunately it was not finished, because the grammars of Forster and Carey were then in course of publication, and would, as Colebrooke imagined, supply the deficient part of his own. Carey's grammar was published in 1806. Among these four publications, which as first attempts at making the ancient language of India accessible to European scholars, deserve the highest credit, Colebrooke's grammar is *facile princeps*. It is derived at first hand from the best native grammars, and evinces a familiarity with the most intricate problems of Hindu grammarians such as few scholars have acquired after him. No one can understand and appreciate the merits of this grammar who has not previously acquired a knowledge of the grammatical system of Pâṇini, and it is a great loss to Sanskrit scholarship that so valuable a work should have remained unfinished.

I owe most, indeed, to Colebrooke and Bopp, but I have derived many useful hints from other grammars also. There are some portions of Wilson's grammar which show that he consulted native grammarians, and the fact that he possessed the remaining portion of Colebrooke's * MS., gives to his list of verbs, with the exception of the Bhû class, which was published by Colebrooke, a peculiar interest. Professor Benfey in his large grammar performed a most useful task in working up independently the materials supplied by Pâṇini and Bhaṭṭojidîkshita ; and his smaller grammars too, published both in German and in English, have rendered good service to the cause of sound scholarship. There are besides, the grammars of Boller in German, of Oppert in French, of Westergaard in Danish, of Flecchia in Italian, each supplying something that could not be found elsewhere, and containing suggestions, many of which have proved useful to the writer of the present grammar.

But while thus rendering full justice to the honest labours of my predecessors, I am bound to say, at the same time, that with

---

* See Wilson's Sanscrit and English Dictionary, first edition, preface, p. xlv.

regard to doubtful or difficult forms, of which there are many in the grammar of the Sanskrit language, not one of them can be appealed to as an ultimate authority. Every grammar contains, as is well known, a number of forms which occur but rarely, if ever, in the literary language. It is necessary, however, for the sake of systematic completeness, to give these forms; and if they are to be given at all, they must be given on competent authority. Now it might be supposed that a mere reference to any of the numerous grammars already published would be sufficient for this purpose, and that the lists of irregular or unusual forms might safely be copied from their pages. But this is by no means the case. Even with regard to regular forms, whoever should trust implicitly in the correctness of any of the grammars, hitherto published, would never be certain of having the right form. I do not say this lightly, or without being able to produce proofs. When I began to revise my manuscript grammar which I had composed for my own use many years ago, and when on points on which I felt doubtful, I consulted other grammars, I soon discovered either that, with a strange kind of sequacity, they all repeated the same mistake, or that they varied widely from each other, without assigning any reason or authority. I need not say that the grammars which we possess differ very much in the degree of their trustworthiness; but with the exception of the first volume of Colebrooke and of Professor Benfey's larger Sanskrit grammar, it would be impossible to appeal to any of my predecessors as an authority on doubtful points. Forster and Carey, who evidently depend almost entirely. on materials supplied to them by native assistants, give frequently the most difficult forms with perfect accuracy, while they go wildly wrong immediately after, without, it would seem, any power of. controlling their authorities. The frequent inaccuracies in the grammars of Wilkins and Wilson have been pointed out by others; and however useful these works may have been for practical purposes, they were never intended as authorities on contested points of Sanskrit grammar.

Nothing remained in fact, in order to arrive at any satisfactory result, but to collate the whole of my grammar, with regard not only to the irregular but likewise to the regular forms, with Pâṇini and other native grammarians, and to supply for each doubtful case, and for rules that might seem to differ from those of any of my predecessors, a reference to Pâṇini or to other native authorities. This I have done, and in so doing I had to re-write nearly the whole of my grammar; but though the time and trouble expended on this work have been considerable, I believe that they have not been bestowed in vain. I only regret that I did not give these authoritative references throughout the whole of my work*, because, even where there cannot be any difference of opinion, some of my readers might thus have been saved the time and trouble of looking through Pâṇini to find the Sûtras that bear on every form of the Sanskrit language.

By this process which I have adopted, I believe that on many points a more settled and authoritative character has been imparted to the grammar of Sanskrit than it possessed before; but I do by no means pretend to have arrived on all points at a clear and definite view of the meaning of Pâṇini and his successors. The grammatical system of Hindu grammarians is so peculiar, that rules which we should group together, are scattered about in different parts of their manuals. We may have the general rule in the last, and the exceptions in the first book, and even then we are by no means certain that exceptions to these exceptions may not occur somewhere else. I shall give but one instance. There is a root जागृ *jâgri*, which forms its Aorist by adding इषं *isham*, ई: *îh*, ईत् *ît*. Here the simplest rule would be that final ऋ *ri* before इषं *isham* becomes र् *r* (Pâṇ. VI. 1, 77). This, however, is prevented by another rule which requires that final ऋ *ri* should take Guṇa before इषं *isham* (Pâṇ. VII. 3, 84). This would give us अजागरिषं *ajâgar-isham*. But now comes another general rule (Pâṇ. VII. 2, 1) which prescribes Vriddhi of final vowels before इषं *isham*, i.e. अजागारिषं *ajâgârisham*. Against this change, however, a new rule is cited (Pâṇ. VII. 3, 85), and this secures for जागृ *jâgri* a special exception from Vriddhi, and leaves its base again as जागर् *jâgar*. As soon as the base has been changed to जागर् *jâgar*, it falls under a new rule (Pâṇ. VII. 2, 3), and is forced to take Vriddhi, until this rule is again nullified by Pâṇ. VII. 2, 4, which does not allow Vriddhi in an Aorist that takes intermediate इ *i*, like अजागरिषं *ajâgarisham*. There is an exception, however,

---

* They have been given in the second edition.

to this rule also, for bases with short व *a*, beginning and ending with a consonant, may optionally take Vriddhi (Pâṇ. vii. 2, 7). This option is afterwards restricted, and roots with short व *a*, beginning with a consonant and ending in र *r*, like जागर् *jâgar*, have no option left, but are restricted afresh to Vriddhi (Pâṇ. vii. 2, 2). However, even this is not yet the final result. Our base जागर् *jâgar* is after all not to take Vriddhi, and hence a new special rule (Pâṇ. vii. 2, 5) settles the point by granting to जागृ *jâgri* a special exception from Vriddhi, and thereby establishing its Guṇa. No wonder that these manifold changes and chances in the formation of the First Aorist of जागृ *jâgri* should have inspired a grammarian, who celebrates them in the following couplet :

गुणो वृद्धिर्गुणो वृद्धिः प्रतिषेधो विकल्पनं ।
पुनर्वृद्धिर्निषेधोऽतो यणादूषी: प्राप्नयो नव ॥

" Guṇa, Vriddhi, Guṇa, Vriddhi, prohibition, option, again Vriddhi and then exception, these, with the change of *ṛi* into a semivowel in the first instance, are the nine results."

Another difficulty consists in the want of critical accuracy in the editions which we possess of Pâṇini, the Siddhânta-Kaumudî, the Laghu-Kaumudî, the Sârasvatî, and Vopadeva. Far be it from me to wish to detract from the merits of native editors, like Dharaṇîdhara, Kâśînâtha, Târânâtha, still less from those of Professor Boehtlingk, who published his text and notes nearly thirty years ago, when few of us were able to read a single line of Pâṇini. But during those thirty years considerable progress has been made in unravelling the mysteries of the grammatical literature of India. The commentary of Sâyaṇa to the Rig-veda has shown us how practically to apply the rules of Pâṇini ; and the translation of the Laghu-Kaumudî by the late Dr. Ballantyne has enabled even beginners to find their way through the labyrinth of native grammar. The time has come, I believe, for new and critical editions of Pâṇini and his commentators. A few instances may suffice to show the insecurity of our ordinary editions. The commentary to Pâṇ. vii. 2, 42, as well as the Sârasvatî ii. 25, 1, gives the Benedictive Âtmanepada वरिषीष्ट *varîshîshṭa* and स्तरिषीष्ट *starîshîshṭa* ; yet a reference to Pâṇ. vii. 2, 39 and 40, shows that these forms are impossible. Again, if Pâṇini (viii. 3, 92) is right—and how could the Infallible be wrong?—

in using अग्रगामिनि *agragâmini* with a dental *n* in the last syllable,
it is clear that he extends the prohibition given in VIII. 4, 34,
with regard to Upasargas, to other compounds. It is useless to
inquire whether in doing so he was right or wrong, for it is an article
of faith with every Hindu grammarian that whatever word is used
by Pâṇini in his Sûtras, is *eo ipso* correct. Otherwise, the rules
affecting compounds with Upasargas are by no means identical with
those that affect ordinary compounds; and though it may be right to
argue *a fortiori* from प्रगामिनि *pragâmini* to अग्रगामिनि *agragâmini*, it
would not be right to argue from अग्रयान *agrayâna* to प्रयान *prayâna*,
this being necessarily प्रयाण *prayâṇa*. But assuming अग्रगामिनि *agra-
gâmini* to be correct, it is quite clear that the compounds स्वर्गकामिणौ
svargakâmiṇau, वृषगामिणौ *vṛishagâmiṇau*, हरिकामाणि *harikâmâṇi*, and
हरिकामेण *harikâmeṇa*, given in the commentary to VIII. 4, 13, are all
wrong, though most of them occur not only in the printed editions
of Pâṇini and the Siddhânta-Kaumudî, but may be traced back to
the MSS. of the Prakriyâ-Kaumudî, the source, though by no means
the model, of the Siddhânta-Kaumudî. I was glad to learn from
my friend Professor Goldstücker, who is preparing an edition of the
Kâśikâ-Vṛitti, and whom I consulted on these forms, that the MSS.
of Vâmana which he possesses, carefully avoid these faulty examples
to Pâṇ. VIII. 4, 13.

After these explanations I need hardly add that I am not so san-
guine as to suppose that I could have escaped scot free where so many
men of superior knowledge and talent have failed to do so. All I can
say is, that I shall be truly thankful to any scholar who will take
the trouble to point out any mistakes into which I may have fallen;
and I hope that I shall never so far forget the regard due to truth
as to attempt to represent simple corrections, touching the declension
of nouns or the conjugation of verbs, as matters of opinion, or so far
lower the character of true scholarship as to appeal, on such matters,
from the verdict of the few to the opinion of the many.

Hearing from my friend Professor Bühler that he had finished
a Sanskrit Syntax, based on the works of Pâṇini and other native
grammarians, which will soon be published, I gladly omitted that
portion of my grammar. The rules on the derivation of nouns, by
means of Kṛit, Uṇâdi, and Taddhita suffixes, do not properly belong
to the sphere of an elementary grammar. If time and health permit,

I hope to publish hereafter, as a separate treatise, the chapter of the Prakriyâ-Kaumudî bearing on this subject.

In the list of verbs which I have given as an Appendix, pp. 244–285, I have chiefly followed the Prakriyâ-Kaumudî and the Sârasvatî. These grammars do not conjugate every verb that occurs in the Dhâtupâṭha, but those only that serve to illustrate certain grammatical rules. Nor do they adopt, like the Siddhânta-Kaumudî, the order of the verbs as given in Pâṇini's Dhâtupâṭha, but they group the verbs of each class according to their voices, treating together those that take the terminations of the Parasmaipada, those that take the terminations of the Âtmanepada, and, lastly, those that admit of both voices. In each of these subdivisions, again, the single verbs are so arranged as best to illustrate certain grammatical rules. In making a new selection among the verbs selected by Râmachandra and Anubhûtisvarûpâchârya, I have given a preference to those which occur more frequently in Sanskrit literature, and to those which illustrate some points of grammar of peculiar interest to the student. In this manner I hope that the Appendix will serve two purposes: it will not only help the student, when doubtful as to the exact forms of certain verbs, but it will likewise serve as a useful practical exercise to those who, taking each verb in turn, will try to account for the exact forms of its persons, moods, and tenses by a reference to the rules of this grammar. In some cases references have been added to guide the student, in others he has to find by himself the proper warranty for each particular form.

My kind friends Professor Cowell and Professor Kielhorn have revised some of the proof-sheets of my grammar, for which I beg to express to them my sincere thanks.

F. MAX MÜLLER.

PARIS,
5th April, 1866.

PREFACE

TO THE SECOND EDITION.

THE principal alterations in the new edition of my Sanskrit grammar consist in a number of additional references to Pâṇini, in all cases where an appeal to his authority seemed likely to be useful, and in the introduction of the marks of the accent. I have also been able to remove a number of mistakes and misprints which, in spite of all the care I had taken, had been overlooked in the first edition. Most of these I had corrected in the German translation of my grammar, published at Leipzig in 1868; some more have now been corrected. I feel most grateful to several of my reviewers for having pointed out these oversights, and most of all to Pandit Râjârâmaśâstrî, whose list of notes and queries to my grammar has been of the greatest value to me. It seems almost hopeless for a European scholar to acquire that familiarity with the intricate system of Pâṇini which the Pandits of the old school in India still possess; and although some of their refinements in the interpretation of Pâṇini's rules may seem too subtle, yet there can be no doubt that these living guides are invaluable to us in exploring the gigantic labyrinth of ancient Sanskrit grammar.

There is, however, one difficulty which we have to contend with, and which does not exist for them. They keep true throughout to one system, the system of Pâṇini; we have to transfer the facts of that system into our own system of grammar. What accidents are likely to happen during this process I shall try to illustrate by one instance. Râjârâmaśâstrî objects to the form पुंसु *punsu* as the locative plural of पुमान् *pumân*. From his point of view, he is perfectly right in his objection, for according to Pâṇini the locative plural has Anusvâra, पुंसु *puṁsu*. But in our own Sanskrit grammars we first have a general rule that स *s* is changed to ष *sh* after any vowel except अ and आ *â*, in spite of intervening Anusvâra (see § 100); and it has even been maintained that there is some kind of physiological reason for such a change. If then, after having laid down this rule, we yet write पुंसु *pumsu*, we simply commit a grammatical blunder; and I believe there is no Sanskrit grammar, except Colebrooke's, in which that blunder has not been committed. In order to avoid it, I wrote पुन्सु *punsu*, thus, by the retention of the dental न *n*, making it grammatically and physically possible for the स *s* to remain unchanged. It may be objected that on the same ground I ought to have written Instr. पुंसा *punsâ*, Gen. पुंसः *punsah*, &c.; but in these cases the स *s* is radical, and would therefore not be liable to be changed into ष *sh* after a vowel and Anusvâra (Pân. VIII. 3, 59). Professor Weber had evidently overlooked these simple rules, or he would have been less forward in blaming Dr. Keller for having followed my example in writing पुन्सु *punsu*, instead of पुंसु *pumsu*. In Pâṇini's grammar (as may be seen from my note appended to § 100) the rule on the change of स *s* into ष *sh* is so carefully worded that it just excludes the case of पुंसु *pumsu*, although the सु *su* of the loc. plur. is preceded by an Anusvâra. I have now, by making in my second edition the same reservation in the general rule, been able to conform to Pâṇini's authority, and have written पुंसु *pumsu*, instead of पुन्सु *punsu*, though even thus the fact remains that if the dot is really meant for Anusvâra, and if the सु *su* is the termination of the locative plural, the स *s* would be sounded as ष *sh*, according to the general tendency of the ancient Sanskrit pronunciation.

I have mentioned this one instance in order to show the peculiar difficulties which the writer of a Sanskrit grammar has to contend with in trying to combine the technical rules of Pâṇini with the more rational principles of European grammar; and I hope it may convince my readers, and perhaps even Professor Weber, that where I have deviated from the ordinary rules of our European grammars, or where I seem to have placed myself at variance with some of the native authorities, I have not done so without having carefully weighed the advantages of the one against those of the other system.

F. MAX MÜLLER.

PARKS END, OXFORD,
    August, 1870.

TABLE OF CONTENTS.

		PAGE
CHAPTER I.—THE ALPHABET.		
	The Devanâgarî letters . .	2
§ 1.	The Devanâgarî alphabet. .	3
2.	Direction of Sanskrit alphabet .	4
3.	How to write the letters . .	4
4.	Sounds represented by the Devanâgarî alphabet . .	4
5.	Number of letters . . .	5
6.	The letter *ḷi*	5
7.	Jihvâmûlîya and Upadhmânîya	5
8.	Signs of nasals and their substitute	5
9.	The three nasal semivowels .	6
10.	Consonants without corresponding nasals	6
11.	Anusvâra before *ś, sh, s, h* .	6
* 12.	Names of letters . . .	7
13.	Vowel signs, initial, medial, and final	7
14.	Consonants followed by vowels	7
15.	Virâma	7
16.	Combination of consonants .	7
17.	The sign for *r* . . .	8
18.	The Virâma used as a stop-gap	8
19.	The signs for a pause . .	8
20.	The Avagraha. List of compound consonants . .	8
21.	Numerical figures . . .	9
22.	Rules of pronunciation . .	10
CHAPTER II.—RULES OF SANDHI.		
§ 23.	Object and use of Sandhi. .	11
24.	Distinction between External and Internal Sandhi . .	11
25.	Classification of vowels, long, short, protracted . . .	12

		PAGE
§ 26.	Monophthongs and diphthongs .	12
27.	Nasalized vowels . . .	12
28.	Light and heavy vowels . .	13
29.	Acute, grave, and circumflexed vowels	13
30.	Guna and Vriddhi . . .	13
31.	Guna of *â, á*	13
32.	Combination of vowels at the end and beginning of words. No hiatus	13
33.	Vowels meeting the same vowels	13
34.	Vowels *â* and *á*, followed by different vowels . . .	14
35.	Vowels *â* and *á*, followed by diphthongs	14
36.	Vowels *î, û, ṛî*, followed by dissimilar vowels . . .	15
37.	Vowels *e* and *o*, followed by any vowel except *â* . . .	15
38.	Vowels *ai* and *au*, followed by any vowels	16
39.	Treatment of final *y* and *v* .	16
40.	The hiatus occasioned by Sandhi	17
41.	Vowels *e* and *o* before *â* . .	17
42.	Unchangeable or Pragrihya vowels	17
43.	Irregular Sandhi; prepositions ending in *â* or *á*, followed by *e* or *o*.	18
44.	Prepositions ending in *â* or *á*, followed by *ṛi* . . .	18
* 45.	The *o* of *oshṭhaḥ* and *otuḥ* .	18
* 46.	Irregular compounds . .	19
* 47.	The final *o* of indeclinable words	19
* 48.	Monosyllabic indeclinable words	19
* 49.	Sandhi of the particle *â* . .	19

	PAGE
* §50. Particles unaffected by Sandhi	19
* 51. Protracted vowels unaffected by Sandhi	19
52. Table showing the combination of final with initial vowels	20
53. Combination of final and initial consonants	21
54. The eleven final consonants	21
55. No word ends in two consonants	22
56. Classification of consonants, according to their place	22
57. Classification of consonants, according to their quality, i. e. contact, approach, opening	23
58. Surd and sonant consonants	23
59. Aspirated and unaspirated consonants	23
60. Changes of place, and changes of quality	24
61. Changes of place affect Dentals, Anusvâra, and Visarga	24
62. Final *t* before Palatals *ch, chh, j, jh, ñ, s*	24
63. Final *n* before *j, jh, ñ, s*	24
64. Final *t* before *t, th, d, dh, n* (not *sh*)	24
65. Final *n* before *d, dh, n* (not *sh*)	25
66. Changes of quality	25
67. Final *k, t, t, p* before nasals	26
* 68. Final *k, t, t, p* before *maya* or *mâtra*	27
* 69. Initial *h* after final *k, t, t, p*	27
70. Final *t* before *l*	27
71. Final *n* before *l*	27
72. Final *ñ, n, n* after a short vowel	27
73. Final *n* before the firsts and seconds	28
74. Final *ñ* and *n* before *s, sh, s*	28
75. Final *n* before *s* or *s* (not *sh*)	28
76. Final *t* before *s*	29
77. Anusvâra and final *m*	29
78. M *in pausâ*, and before consonants	30
79. Final *m* before *hn, hm, hy, hl, hv*	30
80. *Sam* before *kri, samskri*	30
81. *Sam* before *râj, samrâj*	31
82. Visarga and final *s* or *r*	31
§ 83. The only final sibilant *in pausâ*, Visarga, and its modifications	31
84. Visarga before a sonant letter changed to *r*, and exceptions	32
85. Final radical *r*	33
86. Final *r* before initial *r*	34
87. Pronouns *sah* and *eshah, syah*	34
88. *Bhoh*	34
89. Exceptions in compound words	34
90. Nouns ending in radical *r*	36
91. Initial *chh* and medial *chh*	36
92. Initial *s* changeable to *chh*	37
93. Final *h, gh, dh, dh, bh*, throwing their aspiration back on initial *g, d, d, b*	37
94. Table showing the combination of final with initial consonants	38
95. *Nati*, or change of *n* into *n*, and *s* into *sh*	41
96. Change of *n* into *n*	41
97. *Tripnoti* and *kshubhnâti* Table	42
98. Change of *n* into *n* in a compound	42
99. Optional changes of *n* into *n* in the preposition *ni*	46
100. Change of *s* into *sh*	47
101. Change of *s* into *sh* in the reduplicative syllable	48
102. Change of *s* into *sh* after prepositions	48
* 103. Extracts from Pâṇini on certain changes of *s* into *sh*	48
* 104. Change of *s* into *sh* in compounds	50
* 105. Change of *dh* into *dh*	50
106. RULES OF INTERNAL SANDHI	51
* 107. Final vowels. No hiatus	51
* 108. Final *â* and *â*, followed by vowels	52
* 109. Verbal bases in *â*	52
* 110. Final *i, i, u, û, ri* changed to *y, v, r;* final *i, i, u, û, ri, ri* changed to *iy, uv, ri, ir*	52
* 111. Final *ri*, before consonants, changed to *ir* or *ûr*	52

PAGE

*§112. Final *e, ai, o, au* changed to *ay, áy, av, áv;* roots ending in diphthongs . . . 53

113. Final consonants, only eleven 53

114. Two consonants at the end of a word impossible . . 54

115. Sonant and surd initials require sonant and surd finals . 54

116. Final aspirates lose their aspiration 55

* 117. Final *gh, ḍh, dh, bh,* followed by *t, th,* lose their aspiration and change *t, th* into *dh* . 55

* 118. Final *gh, ḍh, dh, bh,* followed by *dhv, bh,* and *s,* or final, lose their aspiration and throw it back on initial *g, ḍ, d, b* . 55

* 119. Final *ch, j, jh* changed to *k* or *g* 56

* 120. Final *sh* changed to *ṭ* . . 56

* 121. Final *sh* before *s* changed to *k* 56

* 122. Final *sh* before *t, th,* changes them to *ṭ, ṭh* . . . 56

* 123. Final *sh* changed to *ṭ* before other consonants . . 56

* 124. Final *j* in certain roots treated like *sh* 57

* 125. Final *ś, chh, ksh, śch* treated like *sh* 57

* 126. Final *ś* changed to *k* . . 57

* 127. Final *h* before *s* treated like *gh* 57

* 128. Final *h* treated like *gh* or *ḍh* . 57

* 129. Final *h* optionally treated like *gh* or *ḍh* 58

* 130. Final *h* of *nah* treated like *dh* 58

* 131. Final *s* changed into *t* in certain nominal bases . . 58

* 132. Final *s* before *s* changed into *t* in verbal bases ; *s* dropt before *dhi;* optionally changed into *t* 58

* 133. Final *n* or *m* before sibilants changed to Anusvâra . 59

* 134. *N* unchanged before semivowels 59

* 135. *M* unchanged before *y, r, l* . 59

* 136. *M* changed to *n* . . . 59

137. The five nasals abbreviated into the Anusvâra dot . 59

PAGE

§138. Anusvâra before *ś, sh, s, h* . 60

* 139. *N* after *ch* or *j* changed into *ñ* 60

140. *Chh* changed to *chchh* . . 60

* 141. *Chh* before *n* or *m* changed to *ś* 60

* 142. Final *y* and *v* dropt before consonants, except *y* . . 60

* 143. Final *iv, ir, ur* lengthened if followed by consonants . 60

* 144. Final *ir* and *ur* lengthened if ending a word . . . 60

* 145. Radical *is* or *us* at the end of nominal bases lengthened . 60

* 146, 147. Doubling of consonants . 61

148. Explanation of some grammatical terms used by native grammarians . . . 61

CHAPTER III.—DECLENSION.

§149. Gender, number, and case . 64

150. I. Bases ending in consonants; II. bases ending in vowels . 64

151. I. Bases ending in consonants; no bases in *ń, ñ, y* . . 64

152. Terminations . . . 64

153. I. 1. Unchangeable and I. 2. Changeable bases . . 65

154. I. 1. Unchangeable bases; *sugaṇ* 65

155. *Sarvaśak* 66

156. *Chitralikh* 66

* 157. *Harit, agnimath, suhṛid, budh, gup, kakubh* . . . 67

158. *Jalamuch* 67

* 159. Special bases in *ch; kruñch, prâñch, vṛiśch* . . 68

* 160. *Prâchh* 68

* 161. *Ruj, ûrj* 68

* 162. Bases in *j,* changeable to *ḍ; samrâj, vibhrâj, devej, viśva-sṛij, parivrâj, viśvarâj, bhṛijj* 68

* 163. Irregular nouns in *j; khañj, avayâj* 69

164. Bases in *r; gir, vâr, pur, dvâr, kir* 70

165. Bases in *s;* A. bases formed by *as, is, us; sumanas, sujyotis* 71

* 166. *Jaras* and *jarâ* . . . 72

* 167. *Nirjaras* and *nirjara* . . 73

PAGE

*§168. *Anehas, purudaṁśas* . . 74

* 169. *Uśanas* . . . 74

* 170. Bases in *s ;* B. bases ending in radical *s ; piṇḍagras, supis, sutus* 74

* 171. *Pipaṭhis* . . . 75

* 172. *Áśis, sajus ;* list of bases in *s* . 76

* 173. *Dhvas, sras* 77

* 174. Bases ending in *ś, sh, chh, ksh, h* 77

    1. *Diś, dṛiś, spṛiś* . . 77

    2. *Naś* 77

    3. *Viś* 77

    4. *Dhṛish* . . . 77

    5. *Dvish* . . . 77

    6. *Prâchh* . . . 77

    7. *Taksh* . . . 77

    8. *Lih, guh* . . . 78

    9. *Duh, ushṇih* . . 78

    10. *Druh, muh, snih, snuh* . 78

    11. *Nah* . . . 78

* 175. *Turâśâh* . . . 78

* 176. *Purodâś* . . . 78

* 177. *Ukthaśâs* . . . 79

* 178. *Praśâm* . . . 79

  179. I. 2. Nouns with changeable bases ; A. nouns with two bases, *adat* . . . 79

  180. *Prâch* 80

  181. B. Nouns with three bases, *pratyach* 81

  182. Bases in *at* and *ant ; adat* . 82

* 183. The nasal in the nom. and acc. dual of neuters, and in the feminine base . . . 83

* 184. The nasal in participles of reduplicated verbs . . 83

* 185. *Bṛihat, pṛishat* . . . 84

  186. *Mahat* 84

  187. Bases in *mat* and *vat* . . 84

* 188. *Bhavat,* Your Honour . . 85

* 189. *Arvat* and *arvan* . . . 86

* 190. *Kiyat* 86

  191. Bases in *an, man, van ; râjan, nâman* . . . 86

  192. *Brahman, dîvan* . . . 87

* 193. Feminines of bases of nouns in *an, van, man* . . . 88

PAGE

*§194. Optional feminine compounds 88

* 195. *Pathin, ṛibhukshin, mathin* . 89

  196. *Ahan* 89

* 197. *Ahan* at the end of compounds 90

* 198. *Ahan* at the end of compounds 90

  199. *Śvan, yuvan* . . . 90

* 200. *Maghavan* 90

* 201. *Pûshan, aryaman* . . 90

* 202. *Uan* 91

  203. Bases in *in, dhanin* . . 91

  204. Participles in *vas* . . . 92

  205. Participles in *ivas* . . 92

  206. Bases in *îyas, garîyas* . . 93

* 207. Miscellaneous nouns with changeable bases, *pâd* . 93

* 208. *Vâh* 94

* 209. *Śvetavâh* 94

* 210. *Anaḍuh* 94

  211. *Ap* 94

* 212. *Pums* 95

* 213. *Div, dyu* 95

* 214. *Asan* and other Metaplasta . 95

  215. II. Bases ending in vowels, subdivided . . . 96

  216. II. 1. Bases ending in any vowel except *â* 97

  217. Bases in *ai* and *au* . . . 97

  218. Bases in *o* 97

* 219. *Dyo* 98

* 220. Bases in *î* and *û* . . . 98

    1. Monosyllabic bases in *î* and *û,* being both masc. and fem. 98

    A. By themselves ; *dhî, krî, lû* 98

* 221. B. At the end of compounds . 98

* 222. 2. Polysyllabic bases in *î* and *û,* being both masc. and fem. . 100

* 223. The five fuller feminine terminations 103

  224. 1. Monosyllabic bases in *î* and *û,* being feminine only, *dhî, bhû* 103

  225. 2. Polysyllabic bases in *î* and *û,* being feminine only, *nadî, vadhû* 104

* 226. Compounds ending in monosyllabic feminine bases in *î* and *û, subhrû* . . . 105

PAGE

ı. Compounds ending in poly-
syllabic feminine bases in *î*
and *û, bahuśreyaśî* . . 107

ı. *Strî* 108

ı. *Atistrî* 108

ı. Bases in *i* and *u,* masc. fem. neut. 109

ı. *Kati* 111

ı. *Sakhi* 111

ı. *Pati* 112

ı. *Akshi, asthi, dadhi, sakthi* . 112

ı. Bases in *ṛi,* masc. fem. neut.,
naptṛi, pitṛi . . . 112

ı. *Kroshṭu* 113

ı. *Nṛi* 114

ı. II. 2. Bases ending in *a* and *â,
kântaḥ, tâ, tam* . . 114

ı. Bases in *â,* masc. and fem.,
viśvapâ . . . 115

ı. *Hâhâ* 116

CHAPTER IV.—ADJECTIVES.

. Declension of adjectives . 116

. Formation of feminine base . 117

. *Priyaḥ,* fem. *priyâ* . . 117

. *Pâchakaḥ, pâchikâ* . . 117

. Feminines formed by *î* . . 117

. Exceptional feminines in *î* . 117

. Irregular feminines . . 117

. Formation of feminine sub-
stantives 118

. Degrees of comparison . . 118

. *Tara* and *tama,* how added . 118

. *Îyas* and *ishṭha,* how added . 118

. Exceptional comparatives and
superlatives . . . 119

CHAPTER V.—NUMERALS.

. Cardinals and declension of
cardinals, *eka* . . . 120

. *Dvi* 124

. *Tri, tisṛi* 124

. *Chatur, chatasṛi* . . . 124

. *Pañchan, shash, ashṭan* . 124

. Construction of cardinals . 124

. Ordinals 125

. Numerical adverbs and other
derivatives . . . 126

PAGE

CHAPTER VI.—PRONOUNS.

§ 261. Personal pronouns . . 127

262. *Saḥ, sâ, tat* 128

✳ 263. *Syaḥ, syâ, tyat* . . . 128

264. Possessive pronouns . . 128

265. Reflexive pronouns, *svayam* . 129

266. *Âtman* 129

267. *Svaḥ, svâ, svam* . . . 129

268. Demonstrative pronouns, *eshaḥ,
eshâ, etat* 129

269. *Ayam, iyam, idam* . . 129

✳ 270. *Enam, enâm, enat* . . 130

271. *Asau, asau, adaḥ* . . . 130

272. *Yaḥ, yâ, yat* . . . 131

273. *Kaḥ, kâ, kim* . . . 131

✳ 274. Pronouns modified by *ak* . 131

275. Compound pronouns, *tâdṛiś* &c. 132

276. *Tâvat* &c. 132

277. *Kaśchit* &c. 132

278. Pronominal adjectives, *sarva,
viśva,* &c. . . . 133

279. *Anyaḥ, anyâ, anyat* . . 134

280. *Ubhau, ubhe, ubhe* . . 134

281. *Ubhayaḥ, yî, yam* . . 134

✳ 282. *Pûrva* and its optional forms . 134

✳ 283. *Prathama* and its optional
nominative plural . . 134

✳ 284. *Dvitîya* and its optional forms 135

✳ 285. Adverbial declension . . 135

CHAPTER VII.—CONJUGATION.

§ 286. Active and passive . . 137

287. Parasmaipada and Âtmanepada 137

288. Parasmaipada and Âtmanepada
in derivative verbs . . 138

289. Passive 138

290. The thirteen tenses and moods 138

291. Signification of tenses and
moods 139

292. Numbers and persons . . 140

CHAPTER VIII.—THE TEN CLASSES.

§ 293. Special and general tenses, in
the ten classes . . . 140

294. Special or modified, general or
unmodified tenses . . 140

295. Division of verbal bases . . 141

§296. I. First division; Bhû, Tud, Div, Chur classes . . 141
297. II. Second division, and subdivisions 142
298. II a. Su, Tan, Kri classes . 143
299. II b. Ad, Hu, Rudh classes . 143

CHAPTER IX.—Augment, Reduplication, and Terminations.

§300. Augment and reduplication . 145
301. Augment a 145
302. Reduplication in the perfect, and in the Hu verbs . . 145
303. General rules of reduplication 146
304. Aspirated initials . . . 146
305. Guttural initials . . . 146
306. Double initials . . . 146
307. Initial sibilant followed by a tenuis 146
308. The vowel of the reduplicative syllable is short . . . 146
309. Medial e and ai are reduplicated by i, o and au by u . 146
310. Final e, ai, o are reduplicated by a 146
311. Irregular reduplication by Samprasârana . . . 147
312. Short initial a . . . 147
313. Initial a followed by two consonants 148
314. Initial ri 148
315. Short initial i and u . . 148
316. Special rules of reduplication . 148
* 317. Nij, vij, vish . . . 148
* 318. Mâ, hâ 148
* 319. Han, hi, ji, chi . . . 148
320. Terminations . . . 149
321. Terminations of first and second divisions . . . 149
322. Regular conjugation . . 150

CHAPTER X.—General Tenses.

§323. General or unmodified tenses. 159
324. Reduplicated perfect . . 159
325. Verbs which may form the reduplicated perfect . . 159
326. The periphrastic perfect . 159

§327. Strong and weak terminations 160
328. Weakening of base . . 160
329. Bases ending in â and diphthongs, how changed . . 161
330. Bases ending in i, î, ri, u, û, rî, how changed . . . 161

CHAPTER XI.—Intermediate i.

§331. When it must be omitted, when it may be omitted, when it must be inserted . 162
* 332. List of verbs in which the intermediate i must be omitted . 163
* 333. Verbs in which the intermediate i must be omitted in certain tenses . . . 165
* 334. Special rules for the reduplicated perfect . . . 167
* 335. Special rules for the 2nd pers. sing. Par. of the red. perf. . 167
* 336. Table showing when intermediate i must be omitted . 168
* 337. Optional insertion of i . . 168
* 338. Necessary insertion of i . 170
339. The intermediate i never liable to Guna 171
340. Insertion of long î . . 171
* 341. Optional insertion of long î . 171
342. Periphrastic perfect . . 172
* 343. Periphrastic perfect of intensives and desideratives . 172
Paradigms of the reduplicated perfect 172

CHAPTER XII.—Strengthening and Weakening.

§344. Two classes of terminations, strengthening or weakening a verbal base . . . 175
* 345. Special forms of strengthening and weakening certain bases 177

CHAPTER XIII.—Aorist.

§346. First and second aorist . . 179
347. Four forms of the first aorist. 179
348. Rules for the first form . . 180

PAGE

9. Rules for desideratives, intensives, &c. . . . 181
0. Rules for the second form . 181
1. Terminations beginning with *st* or *sth* . . . 181
2. Roots in *â* and diphthongs . 181
3. *Mî, mi, dî, lî* . . . 181
4. *Han* 181
5. *Gam* 181
6. *Yam* 181
7. Rules for the third form . 182
8. *Mî, mi, lî* . . . 182
9. *Yam, ram, nam* . . 182
0. Rules for the fourth form . 182
1. *Slish* 182
2. *Duh, dih, lih, guh* . . 182
   Paradigms . . . 182
3. Second aorist . . 186
4. Roots ending in *â, e, i, ri; dri* 187
5. Roots with penultimate nasal . 187
6. Irregular forms . . 187
7. Verbs which take the second aorist . . . 187
8. Verbs which take the second aorist in the Par. only . 188
9. The Tan verbs . . 188
0. Reduplicated second aorist . 188
1. *Sri, dru, sru, kam; svi, dhe* . 189
2. Shortening of bases ending in *ay* 189
3. Bases that cannot be shortened 189
4. Compensation between base and reduplicative syllable . 189
5. Vowels of reduplicative syllable 190
6. Verbs beginning and ending with double consonants . 190
7. Verbs with penultimate *ri, rî* . 190
8. Verbs beginning with vowels . 191
9. Irregular reduplicated aorist . 191
   Paradigm . . . 191
0. When the different forms of the aorists are used . . 191

PTER XIV.—Future, Conditional, Periphrastic Future, and Benedictive.

1. Future . . . 192
2. Changes of the base . . 192

PAGE

§383. Conditional 193
384. Periphrastic future . . 194
385. Benedictive . . . 195
* 386. Bases ending in *ay* . . 195
387. Weakening in benedictive Parasmaipada, strengthening in benedictive Âtmanepada . 195
388. Intermediate *i* . . . 195
* 389. Weakening of base before *y* . 196
* 390. Verbs ending in *i, u, ri, rî* . 196
* 391. Verbs ending in *n* . . 196
* 392. Verbs ending in *â* . . 196
* 393. Verbs which take Samprasârana 197
* 394. Other verbs which take Samprasârana . . . 197
* 395. *Sâs* changed to *sish* . 197
396. Benedictive Âtmanepada . 198

CHAPTER XV.—Passive.

§397. Âtmanepada terminations . 198
398. Special tenses of passive . 198
* 399 Causative, denominative, intensive bases . . 198
400. Weakening of base. Paradigm 199
401. General tenses of passive . 199
402. The aorist passive . . 200
403. The 3rd pers. sing. aorist passive 200
* 404. Aorist of verbs ending in *â* . 200
* 405. Aorist of verbs ending in *ay* . 200
* 406. Aorist of intensive and desiderative bases . . 200
* 407. Irregular forms . . 201
* 408. Verbs ending in *am* . 201
409. Paradigm . . . 201
410. Future, conditional, and benedictive passive . . 201
411. Their optional forms . 201
* 412. Aorist passive of intransitive verbs . . . 203
* 413. Optional forms . . 203

CHAPTER XVI.—Participles, Gerunds, and Infinitive.

§414. Participle present Parasmaipada 203
415. Participle future Parasmaipada 204

PAGE

§416. Participle of reduplicated perfect Parasmaipada . . 204

* 417. Participle of reduplicated perfect with *i* 205

418. Participle of reduplicated perfect Âtmanepada . . 205

419. Participle present Âtmanepada 205

420. Participle future Âtmanepada 206

421. Participle present and future passive 206

422. Past participle passive and gerund 206

423. Gerund in *tvâ* . . . 206

* 424. I. The terminations *tah* and *tvâ*, with intermediate *i* . 207

* 425. Penultimate *u* with optional Guṇa 207

* 426. *Tvâ* with intermediate *i* and Guṇa 207

* 427. *Tvâ* with intermediate *i* and without Guṇa . . . 207

* 428. Nasal lost before *th, ph; vañch, luñch* 207

* 429. II. The terminations *tah* and *tvâ*, without intermediate *i*. 207

* 430. Final nasal dropt before *tah* and *tvâ* 207

* 431. Final *n* dropt and vowel lengthened; final *chh, v, rchh,* and *rv* 208

* 432. Roots changing *v* to *û* . . 208

* 433. Final *ai* changed to *â* or *î* . 208

* 434. *Do, so, mâ, sthâ, dhâ, hâ* change their final into *i* . . 208

* 435. *So* and *chho* take *i* or *â* . . 208

* 436. Exceptional forms . . 208

* 437. Verbs which take Samprasâraṇa 208

* 438. Verbs which lose penultimate nasal 209

439. Causal verbs . . . 209

440. Desiderative verbs . . 209

441. Intensive verbs . . . 209

442. Participles in *nah* . . 209

* 443. Adjectival participles . . 210

444. *Vat* added to participles . 210

445. Gerund in *ya* . . . 210

446. Gerund in *tya* . . . 210

PAGE

*§447. Gerund of causatives . . 211

* 448. *Ghu* verbs, *mâ, sthâ, gâ, pâ, hâ, so,* take final *â* . . 211

* 449. Verbs ending in nasals . . 211

* 450. Verbs ending in *ṛî* . . 211

* 451. *Ve, jyâ, vye* 211

* 452. *Mî, mi, dî, lî* . . . 211

CHAPTER XVII.—VERBAL ADJECTIVES.

§453. Verbal adjectives, *Kṛitya* . 211

454. Adjectives in *tavya* . . 212

455. Adjectives in *anîya* . . 212

456. Adjectives in *ya* . . . 213

* 457. Exceptional verbal adjectives in *ya* and *tya* . . . 214

* 458. Verbs changing final *ch* and *j* into *k* and *g* . . 214

459. Infinitive in *tum* . . . 214

460. Verbal adverbs in *am* . . 214

CHAPTER XVIII.—CAUSATIVE VERBS.

§461. Causal bases, how formed . 215

* 462. Guṇa or Vṛiddhi . . . 215

463. Exceptional causative bases, I. * II. 217

464. Conjugation of causative verbs 219

465. Passive of causative verbs . 219

466. General tenses of the passive . 219

CHAPTER XIX.—DESIDERATIVE VERBS.

§467. Desiderative bases, how formed 220

468. Desiderative bases, how conjugated 220

469. Desiderative bases, with or without intermediate *i* . 220

* 470. Strengthening of base . . 220

* 471. Exceptional strengthening or weakening 220

* 472. Desiderative bases, treated as Bhû verbs 221

473. Reduplication of desiderative bases 222

* 474. Bases in *av* and *âv* . . 222

* 475. *Sru, śru, dru, pru, plu, chyu* . 222

476. Internal reduplication . . 222

* 477. Exceptional forms . . . 222

CHAPTER XX.—INTENSIVE VERBS.

§478. Meaning of intensive or frequentative verbs . . 223
479. Verbs which may form intensive bases 223
480. Two kinds of intensive bases. Âtmanepada . . . 223
481. Intensive bases in *ya*, how formed and conjugated . 223
482. Parasmaipada bases, how formed and conjugated . . 224
483. Conjugation of Parasmaipada bases 224
484. Reduplication of intensive bases 224
∗ 485. Verbs which insert *nî* . . 225
∗ 486. Verbs ending in nasals . . 225
∗ 487. *Jap, jabh, dah, damś, bhañj, paś* 225
∗ 488. *Char, phal* 225
∗ 489. Verbs with penultimate *ṛi* . 225
∗ 490. Verbs ending in *ṛi* . . 226
∗ 491. Exceptional intensive bases . 226
492. Secondary and tertiary bases . 226

CHAPTER XXI.—DENOMINATIVE VERBS.

§493. Character of denominative verbs 227
494, 495. Denominatives in *ya*, Parasmaipada . . . 227
∗ 496. Changes of base . . . 227
497. Denominatives in *ya*, Âtmanepada 228
∗ 498. The Kaṇḍvâdi verbs . . 228
∗ 499. Denominatives in *sya* . . 229
∗ 500. Denominatives in *kâmya* . 229
501. Conjugation of denominatives 229
∗ 502. Denominatives in *aya* . . 229
∗ 503. Denominatives without affixes 230

CHAPTER XXII.—PREPOSITIONS AND PARTICLES.

§504. Prepositions, *Upasarga* . . 230
505. Prepositions, *Gati*. . . 230
506. Prepositions, *Karmapravachanîya*. 231
507. Adverbs 231

§508. Conjunctions . . . 233
509. Interjections . . . 233

CHAPTER XXIII.—COMPOUND WORDS.

§510. Manner of compounding nominal bases 233
∗ 511. Treatment of feminine bases . 234
512. Six classes of compounds . 234
　I. Tatpurusha, determinative compounds . . . 234
　　I *b.* Karmadhâraya, appositional determinative compounds . . · . 234
　　I *c.* Dvigu, numeral determinative compounds . 234
　II. Dvandva, collective comp. . 235
　III. Bahuvrîhi, possessive compounds . . . 235
　IV. Avyayîbhâva, adverbial compounds . . . 235
513. I. Determinative compounds . 235
∗ 514. Exceptional determinative compounds . . . 237
∗ 515. Inverted determinative compounds 237
∗ 516. Determinative compounds ending in verbal bases . . 237
517. I *b.* Appositional determinative compounds . . . 237
∗ 518. Inverted determinative compounds 238
519. I *c.* Numeral determinative compounds . . . 238
∗ 520. Modifications of the final letters of determinative compounds 238
521. II. Collective compounds, Itaretara and Samâhâra . . 240
∗ 522. Precedence of words . . 240
∗ 523. Nouns ending in *ṛi* . . 240
∗ 524. Names of deities &c. . . 240
∗ 525. Modifications of the final letters of collective compounds in the singular . . . 241
∗ 526. Idiomatic expressions . . 241
527. III. Possessive compounds . 241
∗ 528. Modifications of the final letters of possessive compounds . 241

§ 529. IV. Adverbial compounds . 242
* 530. Exceptional compounds . 243
* 531. Modifications of the final letters
  of adverbial compounds . 243

APPENDIX I.

LIST OF VERBS 244–285
 Bhû Class (Bhvâdi, I Class) . . 245
  I. Parasmaipada Verbs . . 245
  II. Âtmanepada Verbs . . 260
  III. Parasmaipada and Âtmanepada
   Verbs 263
 Tud Class (Tudâdi, VI Class) . . 265
  I. Parasmaipada and Âtmanepada
   Verbs 265
  II. Parasmaipada Verbs . . 266
  III. Âtmanepada Verbs . . 267
 Div Class (Divâdi, IV Class) . . 267
  I. Parasmaipada Verbs . . 267
  II. Âtmanepada Verbs . . 269
  III. Parasmaipada and Âtmanepada
   Verbs 269
 Chur Class (Churâdi, X Class). . 270
  Parasmaipada Verbs only . . 270
 Su Class (Svâdi, V Class) . . 270
  I. Parasmaipada and Âtmanepada
   Verbs 270
  II. Parasmaipada Verbs . . 271
  III. Âtmanepada Verbs . . 271

Tan Class (Tanvâdi, VIII Class) . 272
 Parasmaipada and Âtmanepada
  Verbs 272
Krî Class (Kryâdi, IX Class) . . 273
 I. Parasmaipada and Âtmanepada
  Verbs 273
 II. Parasmaipada Verbs . . 274
 III. Âtmanepada Verbs . . 274
Ad Class (Adâdi, II Class) . . 275
 I. Parasmaipada Verbs . . 275
 II. Âtmanepada Verbs . . 279
 III. Parasmaipada and Âtmanepada
  Verbs 280
Hu Class (Juhotyâdi, III Class) . 281
 I. Parasmaipada Verbs . . 281
 II. Âtmanepada Verbs . . 282
 III. Parasmaipada and Âtmanepada
  Verbs 283
Rudh Class (Rudhâdi, VII Class) . 284
 I. Parasmaipada and Âtmanepada
  Verbs 284
 II. Parasmaipada Verbs . . 284
 III. Âtmanepada Verbs . . 285

APPENDIX II.

ON THE ACCENT IN SANSKRIT . 286–292

INDEX OF NOUNS . . . 293–297

INDEX OF VERBS . . . 297–300

SANSKRIT GRAMMAR.

THE DEVANÂGARÎ LETTERS.

VOWELS.					CONSONANTS.					
Initial.	Medial.	Initial.	Medial.	Equivalent.						
अ	–	ख	–	a	क	क	k	प	प	p
आ	ा	आ	ा	â	ख	ख	kh	फ	फ	ph
इ	ि	इ	ि	i	ग	ग	g	ब	ब	b
ई	ी	ई	ी	î	घ	घ	gh	भ	भ	bh
उ	ु	उ	ु	u	ङ	ङ	ṅ	म	म	m
ऊ	ू	ऊ	ू	û	च	च	ch (or *k*)	य	य	y
ऋ	ृ	ऋ	ृ	ṛi (or *ri*)	छ	छ	chh (or *kh*)	र	र	r
ॠ	ॄ	ॠ	ॄ	ṛî (or *rî*)	ज	ज	j (or *g*)	ल	ळ	l
ऌ	ॢ	ऌ	ॢ	ḷi (or *li*)	झ	झ	jh (or *gh*)	व	व	v
ॡ	ॣ	ॡ	ॣ	ḷî (or *lî*)	ञ	ञ	ñ			
ए	े	ए	े	e	ट	ट	ṭ (or *t*)	श	श	ś (or *s*)
ऐ	ै	ऐ	ै	ai	ठ	ठ	ṭh (or *th*)	ष	ष	sh
ओ	ो	ओ	ो	o	ड¹	ड¹	ḍ (or *d*)	स	स	s
औ	ौ	औ	ौ	au	ढ²	ढ²	ḍh (or *dh*)	ह	ह	h
					ण	ण	ṇ (or *n*)			
					त	त	t	ं	ं	ṁ (or *m*)
					थ	थ	th	ँ	ँ	m̐ (or *m̐*)
					द	द	d	ः	ः	ḥ (or *h*)
					ध	ध	dh	✕	✕	(Jihvâmûlîya), χ
					न	न	n	✕	✕	(Upadhmânîya), φ

¹ Sometimes represented in the Veda by ळ, ऴ, ḷ (or *l*).

² Sometimes represented in the Veda by ळ्ह, ऴ्ह, ḷh (or *lh*).

CHAPTER I.

THE ALPHABET.

§ 1. SANSKRIT is properly written with the Devanâgarî alphabet; but the Bengali, Grantha, Telugu, and other modern Indian alphabets are commonly employed for writing Sanskrit in their respective provinces.

Note—*Devanâgarî* means the *Nâgarî* of the gods, or, possibly, of the Brâhmans. A more current style of writing, used by Hindus in all common transactions where Hindi is the language employed, is called simply *Nâgarî.* Why the alphabet should have been called *Nâgarî,* is unknown. If derived from *nagara,* city, it might mean the art of writing as first practised in cities. (Pâṇ. IV. 2, 128.) No authority has yet been adduced from any ancient author for the employment of the word *Devanâgarî.* In the *Lalita-vistara* (a life of Buddha, translated from Sanskrit into Chinese 76 A. D.), where a list of alphabets is given, the *Devanâgarî* is not mentioned, unless it be intended by the *Deva* alphabet. (See History of Ancient Sanskrit Literature, p. 518.) Albiruni, in the 11th century, speaks of the *Nagara* alphabet as current in Malva. (Reinaud, Mémoire sur l'Inde, p. 298.)

Beghrâm (*bhagdrâma,* abode of the gods) is the native name of one or more of the most important cities founded by the Greeks, such as Alexandria ad Caucasum or Nicæa. (See Mason's Memoirs in Prinsep's Antiquities, ed. Thomas, vol. I. pp. 344–350.) Could Devanâgarî have been meant as an equivalent of Beghrâmi?

No inscriptions have been met with in India anterior to the rise of Buddhism. The earliest authentic specimens of writing are the inscriptions of king *Priyadarśi* or *Aśoka,* about 250 B.C. These are written in two different alphabets. The alphabet which is found in the inscription of Kapurdigiri, and which in the main is the same as that of the Arianian coins, is written from right to left. It is clearly of Semitic origin, and most closely connected with the Aramaic branch of the old Semitic or Phenician alphabet. The Aramaic letters, however, which we know from Egyptian and Palmyrenian inscriptions, have experienced further changes since they served as the model for the alphabet of Kapurdigiri, and we must have recourse to the more primitive types of the ancient Hebrew coins and of the Phenician inscriptions in order to explain some of the letters of the Kapurdigiri alphabet.

But while the transition of the Semitic types into this ancient Indian alphabet can be proved with scientific precision, the second Indian alphabet, that which is found in the inscription of Girnar, and which is the real source of all other Indian alphabets, as well as of those of Tibet and Burmah, has not as yet been traced back in a satisfactory manner to any Semitic prototype. (Prinsep's Indian Antiquities by Thomas, vol. II. p. 42.) To admit, however, the independent invention of a native Indian alphabet is impossible. Alphabets were never invented, in the usual sense of that word. They were formed gradually, and purely phonetic alphabets always point back to earlier, syllabic or ideographic, stages. There are no such traces of the growth of an alphabet on Indian soil; and it is to be hoped that new discoveries may still bring to light the intermediate links by which the alphabet of Girnar, and through it the modern Devanâgarî, may be connected with one of the leading Semitic alphabets.

§ 2. Sanskrit is written from left to right.

Note—*Saṁskṛita* (संस्कृत) means what is rendered fit or perfect. But *Sanskrit* is not called so because the Brâhmans, or still less, because the first Europeans who became acquainted with it, considered it the most perfect of all languages. *Saṁskṛita* meant what is rendered fit for sacred purposes; hence purified, sacred. A vessel that is purified, a sacrificial victim that is properly dressed, a man who has passed through all the initiatory rites or *saṁskâras;* all these are called *saṁskṛita.* Hence the language which alone was fit for sacred acts, the ancient idiom of the Vedas, was called *Saṁskṛita*, or the sacred language. The local spoken dialects received the general name of *prâkṛita.* This did not mean originally vulgar, but derived, secondary, second-rate, literally 'what has a source or type,' this source or type (*prakṛiti*) being the Saṁskṛita or sacred language. (See Vararuchi's Prâkṛita-Prakâśa, ed. Cowell, p. xvii.)

The former explanation of *prâkṛita* in the sense of 'the natural, original continuations of the old language (*bhâshâ*),' is untenable, because it interpolates the idea of continuation. If *prâkṛita* had to be taken in the sense of 'original and natural,' a language so called would mean, as has been well shown by D'Alwis (An Introduction to Kachchâyana's Grammar, p. lxxxix), the original language, and *saṁskṛita* would then have to be taken in the sense of 'refined for literary purposes.' This view, however, of the meaning of these two names, is opposed to the view of those who framed the names, and is rendered impossible by the character of the Vedic language.

§ 3. In writing the Devanâgarî alphabet, the distinctive portion of each letter is written first, then the perpendicular, and lastly the horizontal line. Ex. ण, ल, क *k;* ल, भ, ख *kh;* 1, ॥, ग *g;* ६, घ, घ *gh;* ६, ङ *ṅ*, &c.

Beginners will find it useful to trace the letters on transparent paper, till they know them well, and can write them fluently and correctly.

§ 4. The following are the sounds which are represented in the Devanâgarî alphabet :

	Hard, (tenues.)	Hard and aspirated, (tenues aspiratæ.)	Soft, (mediæ.)	Soft and aspirated, (mediæ aspiratæ.)	Nasals.	Liquids.	Sibilants.	Vowels. Short, Long.	Diphthongs.
1. Gutturals,	क *k*	ख *kh*	ग *g*	घ *gh*	ङ *ṅ*	ह *h*[2]	×[4] (χ)	अ *a* आ *â*	ए *e* ऐ *ai*
2. Palatals,	च *ch*	छ *chh*	ज *j*	झ *jh*	ञ *ñ*	य *y*	श *ś*	इ *i* ई *î*	
3. Linguals,	ट *ṭ*	ठ *ṭh*	ड *ḍ*[1]	ढ *ḍh*[1]	ण *ṇ*	र *r*	ष *sh*	ऋ *ṛi* ॠ *ṛî*	ओ *o* औ *au*
4. Dentals,	त *t*	थ *th*	द *d*	ध *dh*	न *n*	ल *l*	स *s*	ऌ *ḷi* (ॡ *ḷî*)	
5. Labials,	प *p*	फ *ph*	ब *b*	भ *bh*	म *m*	व *v*[3]	×[4] (φ)	उ *u* ऊ *û*	

Unmodified Nasal or Anusvâra, ˙ *ṁ* or ꙶ *m̐*.

Unmodified Sibilant or Visarga, : *ḥ*.

---

[1] In the Veda ड *ḍ* and ढ *ḍh*, if between two vowels, are in certain schools written ळ *ḷ* and ळ्ह *ḷh*.

[2] ह *h* is not properly a liquid, but a soft breathing.

[3] व *v* is sometimes called Dento-labial.

[4] The signs for the guttural and labial sibilants have become obsolete, and are replaced by the two dots : *ḥ*.

Students should be cautioned against using the Roman letters instead of the Devanâgarî when beginning to learn Sanskrit. The paradigms should be impressed on the memory in their real and native form, otherwise their first impressions will become unsettled and indistinct. After some progress has been made in mastering the grammar and in reading Sanskrit, the Roman alphabet may be used safely and with advantage.

§ 5. There are fifty letters in the Devanâgarî alphabet, thirty-seven consonants and thirteen vowels, representing every sound of the Sanskrit language.

§ 6. One letter, the long ॡ *lî*, is merely a grammatical invention; it never occurs in the spoken language.

§ 7. Two sounds, the guttural and labial sibilants, are now without distinctive representatives in the Devanâgarî alphabet. They are called *Jihvâmûlîya*, the tongue-root sibilant, formed near the base of the tongue; and *Upadhmânîya*, i. e. afflandus, the labial sibilant. They are said to have been represented by the signs **X** (called *Vajrâkṛiti*, having the shape of the thunderbolt) and ꭗ (called *Gajakumbhâkṛiti*, having the shape of an elephant's two frontal bones). [See Vopadeva's Sanskrit Grammar, 1. 18; History of Ancient Sanskrit Literature, p. 508.] Sometimes the sign ꭗ, called *Ardha-visarga*, half-Visarga, is used for both. But in common writing these two signs are now replaced by the two dots, the *Dvivindu*, :, (*dvi*, two, *vindu*, dot,) properly the sign of the unmodified Visarga. The old sign of the Visarga is described in the Kâtantra as like the figure ४; in the Tantrâbhidhâna as like two ठ *ṭh*'s. (See Prinsep, Indian Antiquities, vol. 1. p. 75.)

§ 8. There are five distinct letters for the five nasals, ङ *ṅ*, ञ *ñ*, ण *ṇ*, न *n*, म *m*, as there were originally five distinct signs for the five sibilants. When, in the middle of words, these nasals are followed by consonants of their own class, (*ṅ* by *k*, *kh*, *g*, *gh*; *ñ* by *ch*, *chh*, *j*, *jh*; *ṇ* by *ṭ*, *ṭh*, *ḍ*, *ḍh*; *n* by *t*, *th*, *d*, *dh*; *m* by *p*, *ph*, *b*, *bh*,) they are often, for the sake of more expeditious writing, replaced by the dot, which is properly the sign of the unmodified nasal or Anusvâra. Thus we find

> संकिता instead of अङ्किता *aṅkitâ*.
> संचिता instead of अञ्चिता *añchitâ*.
> कुंडिता instead of कुण्डिता *kuṇḍitâ*.
> नंदिता instead of नन्दिता *nanditâ*.
> कंपिता instead of कम्पिता *kampitâ*.

The pronunciation remains unaffected by this style of writing. अंकिता must be pronounced as if it were written अङ्किता *aṅkitâ*, &c.

The same applies to final म *m* at the end of a sentence. This too, though frequently written and printed with the dot above the line, is to be pronounced as म् *m*. अहं, I, is to be pronounced अहम् *aham*. (See Preface to Hitopadeśa, in M. M.'s Handbooks for the Study of Sanskrit, p. viii.)

Note—According to the Kaumâras final म् m *in pausâ* may be pronounced as Anusvâra; cf. Sarasvatî-Prakriyâ, ed. Bombay, 1829*, pp. 12 and 13. कौमारास्त्ववसाने ऽप्यनुखारमिच्छंति । अवसाने वा । अवसाने मकारस्यानुखारो भवति २३ । देवं । देवम् ॥ The Kaumâras are the followers of Kumâra, the reputed author of the Kâtantra or Kalâpa grammar. (See Colebrooke, Sanskrit Grammar, Preface; and page 315, note.) Sarvavarman is quoted by mistake as the author of this grammar, and a distinction is sometimes made between the Kaumâras and the followers of the Kalâpa grammar.

§ 9. Besides the five nasal letters, expressing the nasal sound as modified by guttural, palatal, lingual, dental, and labial pronunciation, there are still three nasalized letters, the यँ, ल्ँ, वँ, or यं, ल्ं, वं, ẙ, l̃, ṽ, which are used to represent a final म् *m*, if followed by an initial य *y*, ल्र *l*, व *v*, and modified by the pronunciation of these three semivowels. (Pân. viii. 4, 59.)

Thus instead of तं याति *tam yâti* we may write तँयाति *taẙ yâti*;

        instead of तं लभते *tam labhate* we may write तँलभते *tal̃ labhate*;

        instead of तं वहति *tam vahati* we may write तँवहति *taṽ vahati*.

Or in composition,

        संयानं *samyânam* or सय्ँयानं *saẙyânam*;

        संलब्धं *samlabdham* or सल्ँलब्धं *sallabdham*;

        संवहति *samvahati* or सव्ँवहति *savvahati*.

But never if the म् *m* stands in the body of a word, such as काम्यः *kâmyaḥ*; nor if the semivowel represents an original vowel, e. g. Rig-veda x. 132, 3. सम् उ आरन् *sam u âran*, changed to सम्वारन् *sam vâran*.

§ 10. The only consonants which have no corresponding nasals are र *r*, श *ś*, ष *sh*, स *s*, ह *h*. A final म् *m*, therefore, before any of these letters at the beginning of words, can only be represented by the neutral or unmodified nasal, the Anusvâra.

तं रक्षति *tam rakshati*.	Or in composition, संरक्षति *samrakshati*.
तं शृणोति *tam śriṇoti*.	संस्कृणोति *samskriṇoti*.
तं शकारं *tam shakâram*.	संष्ठीवति *samshṭhîvati*.
तं सरति *tam sarati*.	संसरति *samsarati*.
तं हरति *tam harati*.	संहरति *samharati*.

§ 11. In the body of a word the only letters which can be preceded by

---

* This edition, which has lately been reprinted, contains the text—ascribed either to Vâṇî herself, i.e. Sarasvatî, the goddess of speech (MS. Bodl. 386), or to Anubhûti-svarûpa-âchârya, whoever that may be—and a commentary. The commentary printed in the Bombay editions is called महीपटी, or in MS. Bodl. 382. मेदासी, i.e. महीदासी. In MS. Bodl. 382. Mahîdhara or Mahîdâsabhaṭṭa is said to have written the Sârasvata in order that his children might read it, and to please Îśa, the Lord. The date given is 1634, the place Benares, (Sivarâjadhanî.)

Anusvâra are श *s,* ष *sh,* स *s,* ह *h.* Thus अंशः *amśah,* धनूंषि *dhanúmshi,* यशांसि *yaśámsi,* सिंहः *simhah.* Before the semivowels य *y,* र *r,* ल *l,* व *v,* the म *m,* in the body of a word, is never changed into Anusvâra. Thus गम्यते *gamyate,* नम्रः *namrah,* अम्लः *amlah.* In शंयोः *śamyoh* (Rv. I. 43, 4, &c.) the *m* stands 'padânte,' but not in शाम्यति *śámyati.* (See § 9.)

§ 12. With the exception of *Jihvâmûlîya* ⅹ χ (tongue-root letter), *Upadh-mânîya* ⅹ φ (to be breathed upon), *Anusvâra* ˙ *m* (after-sound), *Visarga* : *h* (emission, see Taitt.-Brâhm. III. p. 23 a), and *Repha r* (burring), all letters are named in Sanskrit by adding *kâra* (making) to their sounds. Thus अ *a* is called अकारः *akârah;* क *ka,* ककारः *kakârah,* &c.

§ 13. The vowels, if initial, are written,

         अ, आ, इ, ई, उ, ऊ, ऋ, (ॠ), ऌ, ए, ऐ, ओ, औ;

         a,   â,   i,   î,   ri,   rî,   li,   (lî),   u,   û,   e,   ai,   o,   au;

if they follow a consonant, they are written with the following signs—

         −, ा, ि, ी, ृ, ॄ, ॢ, (ॣ), ु, ू, े, ै, ो, ौ.

         a, â, i, î, ri, rî, li, (lî), u, û, e, ai, o, au.

There is one exception. If the vowel ऋ *ri* follows the consonant र *r,* it retains its initial form, and the *r* is written over it. Ex. निर्ऋतिः *nirritih.*

In certain words which tolerate an hiatus in the body of the word, the second vowel is written in its initial form. Ex. गोअग्र *goagra,* adj. preceded by cows, instead of गोऽग्र *go 'gra* or गवाग्र *gavâgra;* गोअश्वं *goaśvam,* cows and horses; प्रउग *praüga,* yoke; तितउ *titaü,* sieve.

§ 14. Every consonant, if written by itself, is supposed to be followed by a short *a.* Thus क is not pronounced *k,* but *ka;* य not *y,* but *ya.* But क *k* or any other consonant, if followed by any vowel except *a,* is pronounced without the inherent *a.* Thus

         का *kâ,* कि *ki,* की *kî,* कृ *kri,* कॄ *krî,* कॢ *kli,* (कॣ *klî*), कु *ku,* कू *kû,* के *ke,* कै *kai,* को *ko,* कौ *kau.*

The only peculiarity is that short कि *i* is apparently written before the con-sonant after which it is sounded. This arose from the fact that in the earliest forms of the Indian alphabet the long and short *i*'s were both written over the consonant, the short *i* inclining to the left, the long *i* inclining to the right. Afterwards these top-marks were, for the sake of distinctness, drawn across the top-line, so as to become कि and की, instead of कि and कि. (See Prinsep's Indian Antiquities, ed. Thomas, vol. II. p. 40.)

§ 15. If a consonant is to be pronounced without any vowel after it, the consonant is said to be followed by *Virâma,* i. e. stoppage, which is marked by ्. Thus *ak* must be written अक्; *kar,* कर्; *ik,* इक्.

§ 16. If a consonant is followed immediately by another consonant, the two or three or four or five or more consonants are written in one group (*saṁyoga*). Thus *atka* is written अत्क; *alpa* is written अल्प; *kârtsnya* is written कार्त्स्न्ये. These groups or compound consonants must be learnt by practice. It is easy, however, to discover some general laws in their formation. Thus the perpendicular and horizontal lines are generally dropt in one of the letters: क्+क=क्क *kka*; न्+द=न्द *nda*; त्+व=त्व *tva*; स्+ख =स्ख *skha*; च्+य=च्य *chya*; प्+त=प्त *pta*; क्+त=क्त *kta*; क्+त्+व= क्त्व *ktva*; क्+त्+य=क्त्य *ktya*.

§ 17. The र *r* following a consonant is written by a short transverse stroke at the foot of the letter; as क्+र=क्र or क्र *kra*; ग्+र=ग्र *gra*; त्+र=त्र or त्र *tra*; द्+र=द्र *dra*; ष्+त्+र=ष्ट्र *shṭra*.

The र *r* preceding a consonant is written by ˆ placed at the top of the consonant before which it is to be sounded. Thus अर्+क=अर्क *arka*; वर्+ ष्+म=वर्ष्म *varshma*. This sign for र *r* is placed to the right of any other marks at the top of the same letter. Ex. अर्कं *arkaṁ*; अर्केण *arkeṇa*; अर्केंदू *arkendû*.

क *k* followed by ष *sh* is written क्ष or क्ष *ksha*.

ज *j* followed by ञ *ñ* is written ज्ञ *jña*.

झ *jh* is sometimes written झ *jh*.

र *r* followed by उ *u* and ऊ *û* is written रु *ru*, रू *rû*.

द *d* followed by उ *u* and ऊ *û* is written दु *du*, दू *dû*.

श *ś*, particularly in combination with other letters, is frequently written श्. Ex. शु *śu*; शू *śû*; श्र *śra*.

§ 18. The sign of *Virâma* ‿ (stoppage), which if placed at the foot of a consonant, shows that its inherent short *a* is stopped, is sometimes, when it is difficult to write (or to print) two or three consonants in one group, placed after one of the consonants: thus युक्ते instead of युक्ते *yuṅkte*.

§ 19. The proper use of the Virâma, however, is at the end of a sentence, or portion of a sentence, the last word of which ends in a consonant.

At the end of a sentence, or of a half-verse, the sign । is used; at the end of a verse, or of a longer sentence, the sign ॥.

§ 20. The sign ऽ (*Avagraha* or *Arddhâkâra*) is used in most editions to mark the elision of an initial अ *a*, after a final ओ *o* or ए *e*. Ex. सोऽपि *so 'pi* for सो अपि *so api*, i. e. सस् अपि *sas api*; तेऽपि *te 'pi* for ते अपि *te api*.

List of Compound Consonants.

क्क *k-ka*, क्ख *k-kha*, क्च *k-cha*, क्त *k-ta*, क्त्य *k-t-ya*, क्त्र *k-t-ra*, क्त्र्य *k-t-r-ya*, क्त्व *k-t-va*, क्न *k-na*, क्न्य *k-n-ya*, क्म *k-ma*, क्य *k-ya*, क्र or क्र *k-ra*, क्र्य or क्र्य *k-r-ya*, क्ल *k-la*, क्व *k-va*, क्व्य *k-v-ya*, क्ष *k-sha*, क्ष्म *k-sh-ma*, क्ष्य *k-sh-ya*, क्ष्व *k-sh-va*;— ख्य *kh-ya*, ख्र *kh-ra*;—ग्य *g-ya*, ग्र *g-ra*, ग्र्य *g-r-ya*;—घ्न *gh-na*, घ्न्य *gh-n-ya*, घ्म *gh-ma*, घ्य *gh-ya*, घ्र *gh-ra*;—ङ्क *ṅ-ka*, ङ्क्त *ṅ-k-ta*, ङ्क्त्य *ṅ-k-t-ya*, ङ्क्य *ṅ-k-ya*, ṅ-k-sha, ṅ-k-sh-va, ṅ-kha, ṅ-kh-ya, ṅ-ga, ṅ-g-ya, ṅ-gha, ṅ-gh-ya, ṅ-gh-ra, ṅ-ṅa, ṅ-ma, ṅ-ya.

ch-cha, ch-chha, ch-chh-ra, ch-ña, ch-ma, ch-ya;—chh-ya, chh-ra;—j-ja, j-jha, j-ña, j-ñ-ya, j-ma, j-ya, j-ra, j-va;—ñ-cha, ñ-ch-ma, ñ-ch-ya, ñ-chha, ñ-ja, ñ-ña, ñ-ya.

ṭ-ṭa, ṭ-ya;—ṭh-ya, ṭh-ra;—ḍ-ga, ḍ-g-ya, ḍ-gha, ḍ-gh-ra, ḍ-ma, ḍ-ya;—ḍh-ya, ḍh-ra;—ṇ-ṭa, ṇ-ṭha, ṇ-ḍa, ṇ-ḍ-ya, ṇ-ḍ-ra, ṇ-ḍ-r-ya, ṇ-ḍha, ṇ-ṇa, ṇ-ma, ṇ-ya, ṇ-va.

t-ka, t-k-ra, t-ta, t-t-ya, t-t-ra, t-t-va, t-tha, t-na, t-n-ya, t-pa, t-p-ra, t-ma, t-m-ya, t-ya, or t-ra, t-r-ya, t-va, t-sa, t-s-na, t-s-n-ya, t-s-ya;—th-ya;—d-ga, d-gha, d-gh-ra, d-da, d-d-ya, d-dha, d-dh-ya, d-na, d-ba, d-bha, d-bh-ya, d-ma, d-ya, d-ra, d-r-ya, d-va, d-v-ya;—dh-na, dh-n-ya, dh-ma, dh-ya, dh-ra, dh-r-ya, dh-va;—n-ta, n-t-ya, n-t-ra, n-da, n-d-ra, n-dha, n-dh-ra, n-na, n-pa, n-p-ra, n-ma, n-ya, n-ra, n-sa.

p-ta, p-t-ya, p-na, p-pa, p-ma, p-ya, p-ra, p-la, p-va, p-sa, p-s-va;—b-gha, b-ja, b-da, b-dha, b-na, b-ba, b-bha, b-bh-ya, b-ya, b-ra, b-va;—bh-na, bh-ya, bh-ra, bh-va;—m-na, m-pa, m-p-ra, m-ba, m-bha, m-ma, m-ya, m-ra, m-la, m-va.

y-ya, y-va;—l-ka, l-pa, l-ma, l-ya, l-la, l-va;—v-na, v-ya, v-ra, v-va.

ś-cha, ś-ch-ya, ś-na, ś-ya, ś-ra, ś-r-ya, ś-la, ś-va, ś-v-ya, ś-śa;—sh-ṭa, sh-ṭ-ya, sh-ṭ-ra, sh-ṭ-r-ya, sh-ṭ-va, sh-ṭha, sh-ṇa, sh-ṇ-ya, sh-pa, sh-p-ra, sh-ma, sh-ya, sh-va;—s-ka, s-kha, s-ta, s-t-ya, s-t-ra, s-t-va, s-tha, s-na, s-n-ya, s-pa, s-pha, s-ma, s-m-ya, s-ya, s-ra, s-va, s-sa.

h-ṇa, h-na, h-ma, h-ya, h-ra, h-la, h-va.

Numerical Figures.

§ 21. The numerical figures in Sanskrit are

१	२	३	४	५	६	७	८	९	०
1	2	3	4	5	6	7	8	9	0

These figures were originally abbreviations of the initial letters of the Sanskrit numerals. The Arabs, who adopted them from the Hindus, called them Indian figures; in Europe, where they were introduced by the Arabs, they were called Arabic figures.

Thus ९ stands for ए *e* of एकः *ekaḥ*, one.

२ stands for द्व *dv* of द्वौ *dvau*, two.

३ stands for त्र *tr* of त्रयः *trayaḥ*, three.

४ stands for च *ch* of चत्वार *chatvdraḥ*, four.

५ stands for प *p* of पंच *pañcha*, five.

The similarity becomes more evident by comparing the letters and numerals as used in ancient inscriptions. See Woepcke, ' Mémoire sur la Propagation des Chiffres Indiens,' in Journal Asiatique, VI série, tome I ; Prinsep's Indian Antiquities by Thomas, vol. II. p. 70; Chips from a German Workshop, vol. II. p. 289.

Pronunciation.

§ 22. The Sanskrit letters should be pronounced in accordance with the transcription given page 4. The following rules, however, are to be observed :

1. The vowels should be pronounced like the vowels in Italian. The short अ *a*, however, has rather the sound of the English *a* in ' America.'

2. The aspiration of the consonants should be heard distinctly. Thus ख *kh* is said, by English scholars who have learnt Sanskrit in India, to sound almost like *kh* in ' inkhorn ;' थ *th* like *th* in ' pothouse ;' फ *ph* like *ph* in ' topheavy ;' घ *gh* like *gh* in ' loghouse ;' ध *dh* like *dh* in ' madhouse ;' भ *bh* like *bh* in ' Hobhouse.' This, no doubt, is a somewhat exaggerated description, but it is well in learning Sanskrit to distinguish from the first the aspirated from the unaspirated letters by pronouncing the former with an unmistakable emphasis.

3. The guttural ङ *ṅ* has the sound of *ng* in ' king.'

4. The palatal letters च *ch* and ज *j* have the sound of *ch* in ' church ' and of *j* in ' join.'

5. The lingual letters are said to be pronounced by bringing the lower surface of the tongue against the roof of the palate. As a matter of fact the ordinary pronunciation of *t, d, n* in English is what Hindus would call lingual, and it is essential to distinguish the Sanskrit dentals by bringing the tip of the tongue against the very edge of the upper front-teeth. In transcribing English words the natives naturally represent the English dentals by their linguals, not by their own dentals ; e. g. डिरेक्टर *Direkṭar*, गवर्नमेण्ट *Gavarṇmeṇṭ*, &c.*

6. The Visarga, *Jihvámúlíya* and *Upadhmáníya* are not now articulated audibly.

7. The dental स *s* sounds like *s* in ' sin,' the lingual ष *sh* like *sh* in ' shun,' the palatal श *ś* like *ss* in ' session.'

---

* Bühler, Madras Literary Journal, February, 1864. Rajendralal Mitra, ' On the Origin of the Hindví Language,' Journal of the Asiatic Society, Bengal, 1864, p. 509.

The real Anusvâra is sounded as a very slight nasal, like *n* in French ' bon.'
If the dot is used as a graphic sign in place of the other five nasals it
must, of course, be pronounced like the nasal which it represents *.

CHAPTER II.

RULES OF SANDHI OR THE COMBINATION OF LETTERS.

§ 23. In Sanskrit every sentence is considered as one unbroken chain
of syllables. Except where there is a stop, which we should mark by
interpunction, the final letters of each word are made to coalesce with the
initial letters of the following word. This coalescence of final and initial
letters, (of vowels with vowels, of consonants with consonants, and of
consonants with vowels,) is called *Sandhi*.

As certain letters in Sanskrit are incompatible with each other, i. e.
cannot be pronounced one immediately after the other, they have to be
modified or assimilated in order to facilitate their pronunciation. The rules,
according to which either one or both letters are thus modified, are called
the rules of Sandhi.

As according to a general rule the words in a sentence must thus be glued
together, the mere absence of Sandhi is in many cases sufficient to mark the
stops which in other languages have to be marked by stops. Ex. अस्त्वग्निमाहात्म्यं
इन्द्रस्तु देवानां महत्तमः *astvagnimâhâtmyam, indrastu devânâm mahattamaḥ*, Let
there be the greatness of Agni; nevertheless Indra is the greatest of the
gods.

Distinction between External and Internal Sandhi.

§ 24. It is essential, in order to avoid confusion, to distinguish between
the rules of Sandhi which determine the changes of final and initial letters
of words (*pada*), and between those other rules of Sandhi which apply to
the final letters of verbal roots (*dhâtu*) and nominal bases (*prâtipadika*) when
followed by certain terminations or suffixes. Though both are based on the
same phonetic principles and are sometimes identical, their application is
different. For shortness' sake it will be best to apply the name of *External*

---

* According to Sanskrit grammarians the real Anusvâra is pronounced in the nose only,
the five nasals by their respective organs and the nose. Siddh.-Kaum. to Pâṇ. I. I, 9.
मन्नव्यनानां नासिका च (चकारेण स्वस्वर्गोचारातानुकूलं तास्तादि समुचीयते) ॥ नासिकानुखारस्य ॥
The real Anusvâra is therefore *nâsikya*, nasal; the five nasals are *anunâsika*, nasalized,
i. e. pronounced by their own organ of speech, and uttered through the nose.

Sandhi or *Pada Sandhi* to the changes which take place at the meeting of final and initial letters of words, and that of *Internal Sandhi* to the changes produced by the meeting of radical and formative elements.

The rules which apply to final and initial letters of words (*pada*) apply, with few exceptions, to the final and initial letters of the component parts of compounds, and likewise to the final letters of nominal bases (*prâtipadika*) when followed by the so-called *Pada*-terminations (भ्यां *bhyâm*, भिः *bhih*, भ्यः *bhyah*, सु *su*), or by secondary (*taddhita*) suffixes beginning with any consonants except य *y*.

The changes produced by the contact of incompatible letters in the body of a word should properly be treated under the heads of declension, conjugation, and derivation. In many cases it is far easier to remember the words ready-made from the dictionary, or the grammatical paradigms from the grammar, than to acquire the complicated rules with their numerous exceptions which are generally detailed in Sanskrit grammars under the head of Sandhi. It is easier to learn that the participle passive of लिह् *lih*, to lick, is लीढः *lîdhah*, than to remember the rules according to which ह् + त *h* + *t* are changed into ढ् + त *dh* + *t*, ह् + ध *d* + *dh*, and ह् + ढ *d* + *dh*; ड् *d* is dropt and the vowel lengthened : while in परिवृह् + तः *parivrih* + *tah*, the vowel, under the same circumstances, remains short ; *parivrih* + *tah* = *parivridh* + *tah*, *parivrid* + *dhah* = *parivrid* + *dhah* = *parivridhah*. In Greek and Latin no rules are given with regard to changes of this kind. If they are to be given at all in Sanskrit grammars, they should, to avoid confusion, be kept perfectly distinct from the rules affecting the final and initial letters of words as brought together in one and the same sentence.

Classification of Vowels.

§ 25. Vowels are divided into short (*hrasva*), long (*dîrgha*), and protracted (*pluta*) vowels. Short vowels have one measure (*mâtrâ*), long vowels two, protracted vowels three. (Pâṇ. 1. 2, 27.) A consonant is said to last half the time of a short vowel.

1. Short vowels : अ *a*, इ *i*, उ *u*, ऋ *ri*, ऌ *li*.
2. Long vowels : आ *â*, ई *î*, ऊ *û*, ॠ *rî*, ए *e*, ऐ *ai*, ओ *o*, औ *au*.
3. Protracted vowels are indicated by the figure ३ *3* ; अ३ *a 3*, आ३ *â 3*, इ३ *i 3*, ई३ *î 3*, ए३ *e 3*, औ३ *au 3*. Sometimes we find अ३इ, *a 3 i*, instead of ए३, *e 3* ; or आ३उ, *â 3 u*, instead of औ३, *au 3*.

§ 26. Vowels are likewise divided into

1. Monophthongs (*samânâkshara*): अ *a*, आ *â*, इ *i*, ई *î*, उ *u*, ऊ *û*, ऋ *ri*, ॠ *rî*, ऌ *li*.
2. Diphthongs (*sandhyakshara*): ए *e*, ऐ *ai*, ओ *o*, औ *au*.

§ 27. All vowels are liable to be nasalized, or to become *anunâsika*: अँ *ă*, आँ *ấ*

§ 28. Vowels are again divided into light (*laghu*) and heavy (*guru*). This division is important for metrical purposes only.

1. Light vowels are वा *a*, इ *i*, उ *u*, ऋ *ṛi*, ऌ *ḷi*, if not followed by a double consonant.

2. Heavy vowels are आ *á*, ई *í*, ऊ *ú*, ॠ *ṛí*, ए *e*, ऐ *ai*, ओ *o*, औ *au*, and any short vowel, if followed by more than one consonant.

§ 29. Vowels are, lastly, divided according to accent, into *acute* (udâtta), *grave* (anudâtta), and *circumflexed* (svarita). The acute vowels are pronounced with a raised tone, the grave vowels with a low, the circumflexed with an even tone. (Pân. i. 2, 29–32.) Accents are marked in Vedic literature only.

Guṇa and Vṛiddhi.

§ 30. Guṇa is the strengthening of इ *ĭ*, ई *í*, उ *ŭ*, ऊ *ú*, ऋ *ṛi*, ॠ *ṛí*, ऌ *ḷi*, by means of a preceding वा *a*, which raises इ *i* and ई *í* to ए *e*, उ *u* and ऊ *ú* to ओ *o*, ऋ *ṛi* and ॠ *ṛí* to अर् *ar*, ऌ *ḷi* to अल् *al*. (Pân. i. i, 2.)

By a repetition of the same process the Vṛiddhi (increase) vowels are formed, viz. ऐ *ai* instead of ए *e*, औ *au* instead of ओ *o*, आर् *ár* instead of अर् *ar*, and आल् *ál* instead of अल् *al*. (Pân. i. i, i.)

Vowels are thus divided again into :

1. Simple vowels: वा *a*, आ *á*, इ *i*, ई *í*,   उ *u*, ऊ *ú*,   ऋ *ṛi*, ॠ *ṛí*,   ऌ *ḷi*.

2. Guṇa vowels: ———   ए *e* ($a + i$),   ओ *o* ($a + u$),   अर् *ar*, अल् *al*.

3. Vṛiddhi vowels: आ *á*   ऐ *ái*($a+a+i$),   औ *áu*($a+a+u$),   आर् *ár*, आल् *ál*.

§ 31. वा *a* and आ *á* do not take Guṇa, or, as other grammarians say, remain unchanged after taking Guṇa. Thus in the first person sing. of the reduplicated perfect, which requires Guṇa or Vṛiddhi, हन् *han* forms with Guṇa जघन *jaghana*, or with Vṛiddhi जघान *jaghâna*, I have killed.

Combination of Vowels at the end and beginning of words.

§ 32. As a general rule, Sanskrit allows of no hiatus (*vivṛitti*) in a sentence. If a word ends in a vowel, and the next word begins with a vowel, certain modifications take place in order to remove this hiatus.

§ 33. For the purpose of explaining the combination of vowels, they may be divided into two classes :

1. Those which are liable to be changed into semivowels, इ *i*, ई *í*, उ *u*, ऊ *ú*, ऋ *ṛi*, ॠ *ṛí*; also the diphthongs, ए *e*, ऐ *ai*, ओ *o*, औ *au*.

2. Those which are not, वा *a*, आ *á*.

Calling the former liquid *, the latter hard vowels, we may say : If the

---

* The Prâtisâkhya calls them *nâmin*, for a different reason ; see Rig-veda-prâtisâkhya, ed. M. M., p. xxiii.

same vowel (long or short) occurs at the end and beginning of words, the result is the long vowel. (Pân. VI. 1, 101.) Thus

अ or आ + अ or आ = आ *ă* + *ă* = *â*.
इ or ई + इ or ई = ई *ĭ* + *ĭ* = *î*.
उ or ऊ + उ or ऊ = ऊ *ŭ* + *ŭ* = *û*.
ऋ or ॠ + ऋ or ॠ = ॠ *rĭ* + *rĭ* = *rî* *.

Ex. उक्त्वा अपगच्छति = उक्त्वापगच्छति *uktvá + apagachchhati = uktvâpagachchhati*, having spoken he goes away.

नदी ईदृशी = नदीदृशी *nadî + îdriśî = nadîdriśî*, such a river.

कर्तृ ऋजु = कर्तॄजु *kartri + riju = kartrîju*, doing (neuter) right.

किंतु उदेति = किंतूदेति *kintu + udeti = kintûdeti*, but he rises.

Or in compounds, मही + ईशः = महीशः *mahî + îśah = mahîśah*, lord of the earth.

§ 34. If hard vowels (long or short) occur at the end of a word, and the next begins with a liquid vowel (except diphthongs), the result is Guṇa of the liquid vowel. (Pân. VI. 1, 87.) Thus

अ or आ + इ or ई = ए *ă* + *ĭ* = *e* (*ăi*).
अ or आ + उ or ऊ = ओ *ă* + *ŭ* = *o* (*ău*).
अ or आ + ऋ or ॠ = अर् *ă* + *rĭ* = *ar*. (Pân. I. 1, 51.)

Ex. तव इंद्रः = तवेंद्रः *tava + indrah = tavendrah*, thine is Indra.

सा उक्त्वा = सोक्त्वा *sá + uktvá = soktvá*, she having spoken.

† सा ऋद्धिः = सर्द्धिः *sá + riddhih = sarddhih*, this wealth.

तव ऌकारः = तवल्कारः *tava + ļikárah = tavalkârah*, thy letter *ļi*.

Or in compounds, काम्य + इष्टिः = काम्येष्टिः *kámya + ishţih = kámyeshţih*, an offering for a certain boon.

हित + उपदेशः = हितोपदेशः *hita + upadeśah = hitopadeśah*, good advice.

§ 35. If hard vowels (long or short) occur at the end of a word, and the next begins with a diphthong, the result is Vriddhi. (Pân. VI. 1, 88.) Thus

अ or आ + ए = ऐ *ă* + *e* = *âi*.
अ or आ + ऐ = ऐ *ă* + *âi* = *âi*.
अ or आ + ओ = औ *ă* + *o* = *âu*.
अ or आ + औ = औ *ă* + *âu* = *âu*.

Ex. तव एव = तवैव *tava + eva = tavaiva*, of thee only.

सा ऐक्षिष्ट = सैक्षिष्ट *sá + aikshishţa = saikshishţa*, she saw.

---

* The letter ऌ *ļi* is left out, because it is of no practical utility. It is treated like ऋ *ri*, only substituting ल् *l* for र *r* in Guṇa and Vriddhi. Thus ऌ + अनुबंधः *ļi + anubandhah* becomes ऌनुबंधः *lanubandhah*, i. e. having *ļi* as indicatory letter.

† Some grammarians consider the Sandhi of *ă* with *ri* optional, but they require the shortening of the long *â*. Ex. ब्रह्मा + ऋषिः *brahmá + rishih* = ब्रह्मर्षिः *brahmarshih* or ब्रह्म ऋषिः *brahma rishih*, Brahmâ, a Ṛishi.

तव ओष्ठ: = तवौष्ठ: *tava + oshṭhaḥ = tavaushṭhaḥ*, thy lip.

सा औत्सुक्यवती = सौत्सुक्यवती *sâ + autsukyavatî = sautsukyavatî*, she desirous.

Or in compounds, राम + ऐश्वर्यं = रामैश्वर्यं *ráma + aiśvaryam = rámaiśvaryam*, the lordship of Râma.

सीता + औपम्यं = सीतौपम्यं *sîtâ + aupamyam = sîtaupamyam*, similarity with Sîtâ, the wife of Râma.

§ 36. If a simple liquid vowel (long or short) occurs at the end of a word, and the next begins with any vowel or diphthong, the result is change of the liquid vowel into a semivowel. (Pâṇ. VI. 1, 77.) Thus

इ or ई
- अ or आ = य or या
- उ or ऋ = यृ or यॄ
- उ or ऊ = यु or यू
- ए or ऐ = ये or यै
- ओ or औ = यो or यौ

i
- *ă̂ = yă̂.*
- *r̥ĭ = yr̥ĭ.*
- *ŭ̂ = yŭ̂.*
- *e, ai = ye, yai.*
- *o, au = yo, yau.*

ऋ or ॠ
- अ or आ = र or रा
- इ or ई = रि or री
- उ or ऊ = रु or रू
- ए or ऐ = रे or रै
- ओ or औ = रो or रौ

r̥
- *ă̂ = ră̂.*
- *ĭ = rĭ.*
- *ŭ̂ = rŭ̂.*
- *e, ai = re, rai.*
- *o, au = ro, rau.*

उ or ऊ
- अ or आ = व or वा
- इ or ई = वि or वी
- उ or ऋ = वृ or वॄ
- ए or ऐ = वे or वै
- ओ or औ = वो or वौ

'ŭ̂
- *ă̂ = vă̂.*
- *ĭ = vĭ.*
- *r̥ĭ = vr̥ĭ.*
- *e, ai = ve, vai.*
- *o, au = vo, vau.*

Ex. दधि अत्र = दध्यत्र *dadhi + atra = dadhyatra*, milk here.

कर्तृ उत = कर्त्रुत *kartṛi + uta = kartruta*, doing moreover.

मधु इव = मध्विव *madhu + iva = madhviva*, like honey.

नदी ऐडस्य = नद्यैडस्य *nadî + aiḍasya = nadyaiḍasya*, the river of Aiḍa.

In compounds, नदी + अर्थं = नद्यर्थं *nadî + artham = nadyartham*, for the sake of a river.

Note—Some native grammarians allow, except in compounds, the omission of this Sandhi, but they require in that case that a long final vowel be shortened. Ex. चक्री अत्र *chakrî atra* may be चक्र्यत्र *chakryatra* or चक्रि अत्र *chakri atra*.

§ 37. If a Guṇa-vowel occurs at the end of a word, and the next begins with any vowel or diphthong (except ă), the last element of the Guṇa-vowel is changed into a semivowel. If ă follows, ă is elided, and no change takes place in the diphthong; see § 41. (Pâṇ. VI. 1, 78.) Thus

ए (*e*) + any vowel (except ă) = अय् (*ay*).

ओ (*o*) + any vowel (except ă) = अव् (*av*).

Ex. सखे आगच्छ = सखयागच्छ *sakhe ágachchha* = *sakhayágachchha*, Friend, come!

सखे इह = सखयिह *sakhe iha* = *sakhayiha*, Friend, here!

प्रभो एहि = प्रभवेहि *prabho ehi* = *prabhavehi*, Lord, come near!

प्रभो औषधं = प्रभवौषधं *prabho aushadham* = *prabhavaushadham*, Lord, medicine.

In compounds, गो + ईशः = गवीशः *go + íṣaḥ* = *gavíṣaḥ*. There are various exceptions in compounds where गो *go* is treated as गव *gava*. (§ 41.)

§ 38. If a Vṛiddhi-vowel occurs at the end of a word, and the next begins with any vowel or diphthong, the last element is changed into a semivowel. (Pâṇ. VI. 1, 78.) Thus

ऐ (*ai*) + any vowel = आय् (*áy*).

औ (*au*) + any vowel = आव् (*áv*).

Ex. श्रिये अर्थः = श्रियायर्थः *śriyai arthaḥ* = *śriyáyarthaḥ*.

श्रिये ऋते = श्रियायृते *śriyai ṛite* = *śriyáyṛite*.

रवौ अस्तमिते = रवावस्तमिते *ravau astamite* = *ravávastamite*, after sunset.

तौ इति = ताविति *tau iti* = *táviti*.

In composition, नौ + अर्थं = नावर्थं *nau + artham* = *návartham*, for the sake of ships.

§ 39. These two rules, however, are liable to certain modifications :

1. The final य् *y* and व् *v* of अय् *ay*, अव् *av*, which stand according to rule for ए *e*, ओ *o*, may be dropt before all vowels (except ă, § 41); not, however, in composition. Thus most MSS. and printed editions change

सखे आगच्छ *sakhe ágachchha*, not into सखयागच्छ *sakhayágachchha*, but into सख आगच्छ *sakha ágachchha*.

सखे इह *sakhe iha*, not into सखयिह *sakhayiha*, but into सख इह *sakha iha*.

प्रभो एहि *prabho ehi*, not into प्रभवेहि *prabhavehi*, but into प्रभ एहि *prabha ehi*.

प्रभो औषधं *prabho aushadham*, not into प्रभवौषधं *prabhavaushadham*, but into प्रभ औषधं *prabha aushadham*.

2. The final य् *y* of आय् *áy*, which stands for ऐ *ái*, may be dropt before all vowels, and it is usual to drop it in our editions. Thus

श्रिये अर्थः *śriyai arthaḥ* is more usually written श्रिया अर्थः *śriyá arthaḥ* instead of श्रियायर्थः *śriyáyarthaḥ*.

3. The final व् *v* of आव् *áv*, for औ *áu*, may be dropt before all vowels, but is more usually retained in our editions. Thus

तौ इति *tau iti* is more usually written ताविति *táviti*, and not ता इति *tá iti*.

Note—Before the particle उ *u* the dropping of the final य् *y* and व् *v* is obligatory.

It is without any reason that the final य् *y* of Guṇa and Vṛiddhi and the final व् *v* of Guṇa are generally dropt, while the final व् *v* of Vṛiddhi is generally retained. It would be more consistent either always to retain the final semivowels or always to drop them. See Rig-veda-prâtiśâkhya, ed. M. M., Sûtras 129, 132, 135 : Pâṇ. VI. 1, 78; VIII. 3, 19.

§ 40. In all these cases the hiatus, occasioned by the dropping of य् *y* and व् *v*, remains, and the rules of Sandhi are not to be applied again.

§ 41. ए *e* and ओ *o*, before short अ *a*, remain unchanged, and the initial अ *a* is elided. (Pâṇ. VI. 1, 109.)

Ex. शिवे अत्र = शिवेऽत्र *śive atra = śive'tra*, in Śiva there.

प्रभो अनुगृहाण = प्रभोऽनुगृहाण *prabho anugrihâṇa = prabho 'nugrihâṇa*, Lord, please.

In composition this elision is optional. (Pâṇ. VI. 1, 122.)

Ex. गो + अश्वाः = गोऽश्वाः or गोअश्वाः *go + aśvâḥ = go 'śvâḥ* or *go aśvâḥ*, cows and horses.

In some compounds गव *gava* must or may be substituted for गो *go*, if a vowel follows; गवाक्ष: *gavâkshaḥ*, a window, lit. a bull's eye; गवेंद्र: *gavendraḥ*, lord of kine, (a name of Kṛishṇa); गवाजिनं or गोऽजिनं *gavâjinam* or *go 'jinam*, a bull's hide.

Unchangeable Vowels (Pragṛihya).

§ 42. There are certain terminations the final vowels of which are not liable to any Sandhi rules. These vowels are called *pragṛihya* (Pâṇ. I. 1, 11) by Sanskrit grammarians. They are,

1. The terminations of the dual in ई *î*, ऊ *û*, and ए *e*, whether of nouns or verbs.

Ex. कवी इमौ *kavî imau*, these two poets.

गिरी एतौ *girî etau*, these two hills.

साधू इमौ *sâdhû imau*, these two merchants.

बंधू आनय *bandhû ânaya*, bring the two friends.

लते एते *late ete*, these two creepers.

विद्ये इमे *vidye ime*, these two sciences.

शयाते अर्भकौ *śayâte arbhakau*, the two children lie down.

शयावहे आवां *śayâvahe âvâm*, we two lie down.

याचेते अर्थं *yâchete artham*, they two ask for money.

Note—Exceptions occur, as मणीव *maṇîva*, i.e. मणी इव *maṇî iva*, like two jewels; दंपतीव *dampatîva*, i.e. दंपती इव *dampatî iva*, like husband and wife.

2. The terminations of अमी *amî* and अमू *amû*, the nom. plur. masc. and the nom. *dual* of the pronoun अदस् *adas*. (Pâṇ. I. 1, 12.)

Ex. अमी अश्वाः *amî aśvâḥ*, these horses.

अमी इषवः *amî ishavaḥ*, these arrows.

अमू अर्भकौ *amû arbhakau*, these two children. (This follows from rule 1.)

Irregular Sandhi.

§ 43. The following are a few cases of irregular Sandhi which require to be stated. When a preposition ending in अ or आ *á* is followed by a verb beginning with ए *e* or ओ *o*, the result of the coalescence of the vowels is ए *e* or ओ *o*, not ऐ *ai* or औ *au*. (Pân. VI. I, 94.)

Ex. प्र + एजते = प्रेजते *pra + ejate = prejate.*

उप + एषते = उपेषते *upa + eshate = upeshate.*

प्र + एषयति = प्रेषयति *pra + eshayati = preshayati* *.

परा + एखति = परेखति *pará + ekhati = parekhati.*

उप + ओषति = उपोषति *upa + oshati = uposhati.*

परा + ओहति = परोहति *pará + ohati = parohati.*

This is not the case before the two verbs एध् *edh*, to grow, and इ *i*, to go, if raised by Guṇa to ए *e*. (Pân. VI. I, 89.)

Ex. उप + एधते = उपैधते *upa + edhate = upaidhate.*

अव + एति = अवैति *ava + eti = avaiti.*

In verbs derived from nouns, and beginning with ए or ओ *e* or *o*, the elision of the final अ or आ *á* of the preposition is optional.

§ 44. If a root beginning with ऋ *ṛi* is preceded by a preposition ending in अ *a* or आ *á*, the two vowels coalesce into आर् *ár* instead of अर् *ar*. (Pân. VI. I, 91.)

Ex. अप + ऋच्छति = अपार्च्छति *apa + ṛichchhati = apárchchhati.*

अव + ऋणाति = अवार्णाति *ava + ṛiṇáti = avárṇáti.*

प्र + ऋजते = प्रार्जते *prà + ṛijate = prárjate.*

परा + ऋषति = परार्षति *pará + ṛishati = parárshati.*

In verbs derived from nouns and beginning with ऋ *ṛi*, this lengthening of the अ *a* of the preposition is optional. (Pân. VI. I, 92.)

In certain compounds ऋणं *ṛiṇam*, debt, and ऋत: *ṛitaḥ*, affected, take Vṛiddhi instead of Guṇa if preceded by अ *a*: प्र + ऋणं = प्रार्णं *pra + ṛiṇam = prárṇam*, principal debt; ऋण + ऋणं = ऋणार्णं *ṛiṇa + ṛiṇam = ṛiṇárṇam*, debt contracted to liquidate another debt; शोक + ऋत: = शोकार्त: *śoka + ṛitaḥ = śokártaḥ*, affected by sorrow. Likewise ऊह् *úh*, the substitute for वाह् *váh*, carrying, forms Vṛiddhi with a preceding अ *a* in a compound. Thus विश्व + ऊह: *viśva + úhaḥ*, the acc. plur. of विश्ववाह् *viśvaváh*, is विश्वौह: *viśvauhaḥ*. (Pân. VI. I, 89, vârt.)

§ 45. If the initial ओ *o* in ओष्ठ: *oshṭhaḥ*, lip, and ओतु: *otuḥ*, cat, is preceded in a compound by अ or आ *á*, the two vowels may coalesce into औ *au* or ओ *o*. (Pân. VI. I, 94, vârt.)

Ex. अधर + ओष्ठ: = अधरौष्ठ: or अधरोष्ठ: *adhara + oshṭhaḥ = adharaushṭhaḥ* or *adharoshṭhaḥ*, the lower lip.

स्थूल + ओतु: = स्थूलौतु: or स्थूलोतु: *sthúla + otuḥ = sthúlautuḥ* or *sthúlotuḥ*, a big cat.

---

* In nouns derived from प्रेष् *presh*, the rule is optional. Ex. प्रेष्य or प्रैष्य *preshya* or *praishya*, a messenger. प्रेष *presha*, a gleaner, is derived from प्र *pra* and ईष् *ísh*.

If ओष्ठ *oshṭha* and ओतु *otu* are preceded by अ or आ *a* in the middle of a sentence, they follow the general rule.

Ex. मम + ओष्ठः = ममौष्ठः *mama+oshṭhaḥ = mamaushṭhaḥ*, my lip.

§ 46. As irregular compounds the following are mentioned by native grammarians:

सैरं *svairam*, wilfulness, and सैरिन् *svairin*, self-willed, from स्व + ईर *sva+íra*.

अक्षौहिणी *akshauhiṇí*, a complete army, from अक्ष + अहिनी *aksha+íhiní*.

प्रौढः *praudhaḥ*, from प्र + अढः *pra+úḍhaḥ*, full-grown.

प्रौहः *prauhaḥ*, investigation, from प्र + अहः *pra+úhaḥ*.

प्रैषः *praishaḥ*, a certain prayer, from प्र + एषः *pra+eshaḥ*. (See § 43.)

प्रैष्यः *praishyaḥ*, a messenger.

§ 47. The final ओ *o* of indeclinable words is not liable to the rules of Sandhi. (Pâṇ. I. 1, 15.)

Ex. अहो अपेहि *aho apehi*, Halloo, go away!

§ 48. Indeclinables consisting of a single vowel, with the exception of आ *á* (§ 49), are not liable to the rules of Sandhi. (Pâṇ. I. 1, 14.)

Ex. इ इंद्र *i indra*, Oh Indra!　उ उमेश *u umeśa*, Oh lord of Umâ!

आ एवं *á evam*, Is it so indeed?

§ 49. If आ *á* (which is written by Indian grammarians आङ् *áṅ*) is used as a preposition before verbs, or before nouns in the sense of 'so far as' (inclusively or exclusively) or 'a little,' it is liable to the rules of Sandhi.

Ex. आ अभ्ययनात् = आभ्ययनात् *á adhyayanát = ádhyayanát*, until the reading begins.

आ एकदेशात् = ऐकदेशात् *á ekadeśát = aikadeśát*, to a certain place.

आ आलोचितं = आलोचितं *á álochitam = álochitam*, regarded a little.

आ उष्णं = ओष्णं *á ushṇam = oshṇam*, a little warm.

आ इहि = एहि *á ihi = ehi*, come here.

If आ *á* is used as an interjection, it is not liable to Sandhi, according to § 48.

Ex. आ एवं किल तत् *á, evam kila tat*, Ah,—now I recollect,—it is just so.

§ 50. Certain particles remain unaffected by Sandhi.

Ex. हे इंद्र *he indra*, Oh Indra.

§ 51. A protracted vowel remains unaffected by Sandhi, because it is always supposed to stand at the end of a sentence. (Pâṇ. VI. 1, 125; VIII. 2, 82.)

Ex. देवदत्ता ३ । एहि *devadattá 3 ehi*, Devadatta, come here!

§ 52. Table showing the Combination of Final with Initial Vowels.

FINAL	अ a	आ á	इ i	ई í	उ u	ऊ ú	ऋ ri	ॠ rí	ऌ li	ए e	ऐ ai	ओ o	औ au
अ a / आ á	आ á		ए e		ओ o		अर् ar		अल् al	ऐ ai		औ au	
इ i / ई í	य ya	या yá	ई í		यु yu	यू yú	यृ yri	यॄ yrí	यॢ yli	ये ye	यै yai	यो yo	यौ yau
उ u / ऊ ú	व va	वा vá	वि vi	वी ví	ऊ ú		वृ vri	वॄ vrí	वॢ vli	वे ve	वै vai	वो vo	वौ vau
ऋ ri / ॠ rí	र ra	रा rá	रि ri	री rí	रु ru	रू rú	रॄ rí[1]		र्ऌ rlí[2]	रे re	रै rai	रो ro	रौ rau
ऌ li	ल la	ळा lá	लि li	ळी lí	लु lu	लू lú	लृ lri	ळॄ lrí[3]	ऌ ll	ले le	लै lai	लो lo	लौ lau
ए e	एऽ e’	(अया ayá	अयि ayi	अयी ayí	अयु ayu	अयू ayú	अयृ ayri	अयॄ ayrí	अयॢ ayli	अये aye	अयै ayai	अयो ayo	अयौ ayau)
		अआ a â	अइ ai	अई aí	अउ au	अऊ aú	अऋ ari	अॠ arí	अऌ ali	अए ae	अरे a ai	अओ a o	अऔ a au
ऐ ai	(आय áya	आया áyá	आयि áyi	आयी áyí	आयु áyu	आयू áyú	आयृ áyri	आयॄ áyrí	आयॢ áyli	आये áye	आयै áyai	आयो áyo	आयौ áyau)
	आआ á a	आआ â á	आइ ái	आई áí	आउ áu	आऊ áú	आऋ ári	आॠ árí	आऌ áli	आए áe	आरे á ai	आओ á o	आौ á au
ओ o	ओऽ so’	अवा avá	अवि avi	अवी aví	अवु avu	अवू avú	अवृ avri	अवॄ avrí	अवॢ avli	अवे ave	अवै avai	अवो avo	अवौ avau
		(अआ a â	अइ ai	अई aí	अउ au	अऊ aú	अऋ ari	अॠ arí	अऌ ali	अए ae	अरे a ai	अओ a o	अऔ a au)
औ au	आव áva	आवा ává	आवि ávi	आवी áví	आवु ávu	आवू ávú	आवृ ávri	आवॄ ávrí	आवॢ ávli	आवे áve	आवै ávai	आवो ávo	आवौ ávau
	(आआ á a	आआ â á	आइ ái	आई áí	आउ áu	आऊ áú	आऋ ári	आॠ árí	आऌ áli	आए áe	आरे á ai	आओ á o	आौ á au)

[1] ऋ ॠ ábhyáṁ hrasva rikáre pare ri rí iti rúpadvayam ; dírghe tu rí ityeva. Rájá rámasástrí. [2] Rí or Ḹí, id. [3] Ḹí or rí, id.

Combination of Final and Initial Consonants.

§ 53. Here, as in the case of vowels, the rules which apply to the final consonants of words following each other in a sentence are equally applicable to the final consonants of words following each other in a compound. The final consonants of nominal bases too, before the so-called *Pada*-terminations (भ्यां *bhyâm*, भिः *bhiḥ*, भ्यः *bhyaḥ*, सु *su*) and before secondary (*taddhita*) suffixes beginning with any consonant but य *y*, are treated according to the same rules. But the derivatives formed by means of these and other suffixes are best learnt from the dictionary in their ready-made state ; while the changes of nominal and verbal bases ending in consonants, before the terminations of declension and conjugation and other suffixes, are regulated by different laws, and are best acquired in learning by heart the principal paradigms of nouns and verbs.

§ 54. In order to simplify the rules concerning the changes of final consonants, it is important to state at the outset that *eleven* only out of the thirty-five consonants can ever stand in Sanskrit at the end of a word; viz.

क् k, ङ् ṅ, ट् ṭ, ण् ṇ, त् t, न् n, प् p, म् m, ल् l, : ḥ, ˙ ṁ.

1. There are five classes of consonants, consisting of five letters each ; thus giving twenty-five. In every one of these five classes the aspirates, if final, are replaced by their corresponding unaspirated letters : ख् *kh* by क् *k;* घ् *gh* by ग् *g;* छ् *chh*, however, not by च् *ch*, but by ट् *ṭ*, &c. Ex. चित्रलिख् *chitralikh*, painter; voc. चित्रलिक् *chitralik*. This reduces the twenty-five letters to fifteen.

2. In every class the sonant (§ 58) letters, if final, are replaced by their corresponding surd letters ; ग् *g* by क् *k;* द् *d* by त् *t*, &c. Ex. हृद् *hṛid*, heart ; nom. हृत् *hṛit*. This reduces the fifteen to ten [*].

3. No palatal च् *ch* can ever be final; hence the only remaining palatal, the च् *ch*, is replaced by the corresponding guttural क् *k*[†]. Ex. वाच् *vâch*, speech ; voc. वाक् *vâk*. Final ञ् *ñ* does not occur. This reduces the ten to eight. In a few roots the final ज् *j* is replaced by a lingual instead of a guttural.

4. Of the semivowels, (य् *y*, र् *r*, ल् *l*, व् *v*,) ल् *l* is the only one that is found at the end of words. This raises the eight to nine letters.

5. ह् *h* cannot be final, but is changed into ट् *ṭ;* sometimes into क् *k* or त् *t*.

---

[*] Some grammarians allow the soft or sonant letters as final, but the MSS. and editions generally change them into the corresponding hard letters.

[†] The only exceptions are technical terms such as अच् *ach*, a vowel; अजन्तः *ajantaḥ*, ending in a vowel, instead of अगन्तः *agantaḥ*.

6. Of the sibilants, the only one that is found at the end of words is Visarga. For, radical ष *sh* cannot be final, but is replaced by ट् *t*. Thus द्विष् *dvish* becomes द्विट् *dvit*. In a few words final ष *sh* is changed into क् *k*.

Radical श *s* cannot be final, but is replaced by ट् *t*. Thus विश् *vis* becomes विट् *vit*. In some words final श *s* is changed into क् *k*. (§ 174.)

Final radical स *s* is treated as Visarga.

The Visarga, therefore, raises the nine to ten ; and the Anusvâra, to eleven letters, the only ones that can ever stand at the end of real words.

Hence the rules of Sandhi affecting final consonants are really reduced to *eleven* heads.

§ 55. It is important to observe that no word in Sanskrit ever ends in more than one consonant, the only exception being when an र् *r* precedes a final radical tenuis क् *k*, ट् *t*, त् *t*, प् *p*. Thus

अबिभर् + त् = अबिभर् *abibhar* + *t* = *abibhar*, 3. p. sing. impf. of भृ *bhri*, to carry.

अबिभर् + स् = अबिभर् *abibhar* + *s* = *abibhar*, 2. p. sing. impf. of भृ *bhri*, to carry.

सुवल्ग् + स् = सुवल् *suvalg* + *s* = *suval*, nom. sing. well jumping.

But ऊर्क् *úrk*, strength, nom. sing. of ऊर्ज् *úrj*.

अवरिवर्त् *avarivart*, 3. p. sing. impf. intens. of वृत् *vrit* or वृध् *vridh*.

अमार्ट् *amárt*, from मृज् *mrij*. (Pân. VIII. 2, 24.)

The nom. sing. of चिकीर्ष् *chikírsh* is चिकीः *chikíh*, because here the *r* is not followed by a tenuis.

Classification of Consonants.

§ 56. Before we can examine the changes of final and initial consonants, according to the rules of external Sandhi, we have to explain what is meant by the place and the quality of consonants.

1. The throat, the palate, the roof of the palate, the teeth, the lips, and the nose are called the places or organs of the letters. (See § 4.)

2. By contact between the tongue and the four places,—throat, palate, roof, teeth,—the guttural, palatal, lingual, and dental consonants are formed. Labial consonants are formed by contact between the lips.

3. In forming the nasals of the five classes the veil which separates the nose from the pharynx is withdrawn *. Hence these letters are called *Anunâsika*, i. e. co-nasal or nasalized.

4. The real Anusvâra is formed in the nose only, and is called *Nâsikya*, i. e. nasal.

5. The Visarga is said to be pronounced in the chest (*urasya*) ; the three or five sibilants in their respective places.

---

* Lectures on the Science of Language, Second Series, p. 145.

6. The semivowels, too, are referred to these five places, and three of them, य *y*, ल *l*, व *v*, can be nasalized, and are then called *Anunâsika*. (यँ, लँ, वँ, or य̇, ल̇, व̇, y̆, l̆, v̆.) र *r* cannot be nasalized in Sanskrit.

§ 57. According to their quality (*prayatna**, effort) letters arc divided into,

1. Letters formed by complete contact (*sprishṭa*) of the organs : क *k*, ख *kh*, ग *g*, घ *gh*, ङ *ṅ* ; च *ch*, छ *chh*, ज *j*, झ *jh*, ञ *ñ* ; ट *ṭ*, ठ *ṭh*, ड *ḍ*, ढ *ḍh*, ण *ṇ* ; त *t*, थ *th*, द *d*, ध *dh*, न *n* ; प *p*, फ *ph*, ब *b*, भ *bh*, म *m*. These are called *Sparśa* in Sanskrit, and, if they did not comprehend the nasals, would correspond to the classical *mutes*.

2. Letters formed by slight contact (*ishat sprishṭa*): य *y*, र *r*, ल *l*, व *v* (not ह *h*). These arc called *Antaḥsthâ* (fem.), i.e. intermediate between Sparśas and Ûshmans, which has been freely translated by *semivowel* or *liquid*.

3. Letters formed by slight opening (*ishad vivṛita*): ː χ, श *ś*, ष *sh*, स *s*, ꭓ φ, ह *h*. These are called *Ûshman* (flatus) in Sanskrit, which may be rendered by *sibilant* or *flatus*.

4. Vowels are said to be formed by complete opening (*vivṛita*)†.

§ 58. A second division, according to quality, is,

1. Surd letters : क *k*, ख *kh*, च *ch*, छ *chh*, ट *ṭ*, ठ *ṭh*, त *t*, थ *th*, प *p*, फ *ph*; ꭓ χ, श *ś*, ष *sh*, स *s*, ꭓ φ, and Visarga : *ḥ*. In their formation the glottis is open. They are called *Aghosha*, non-sonant.

2. Sonant letters : ग *g*, घ *gh*, ज *j*, झ *jh*, ड *ḍ*, ढ *ḍh*, द *d*, ध *dh*, ब *b*, भ *bh*, ङ *ṅ*, ञ *ñ*, ण *ṇ*, न *n*, म *m* ; ह *h*, य *y*, र *r*, ल *l*, व *v*, the Anusvâra ˙ *ṁ*, and all vowels. In their formation the glottis is closed. They are called *Ghoshavat*.

§ 59. Lastly, consonants are divided, according to quality, into,

1. Aspirated (*mahâprâṇa*): ख *kh*, घ *gh*, छ *chh*, झ *jh*, ठ *ṭh*, ढ *ḍh*, थ *th*, ध *dh*, फ *ph*, भ *bh*; ꭓ χ, श *ś*, ष *sh*, स *s*, ꭓ φ; ह *h*; the Visarga : *ḥ* and Anusvâra ˙ *ṁ*.

2. Unaspirated (*alpaprâṇa*): all the rest.

It will be seen, therefore, that the change of च *ch* into क *k* is a change of place, and that the change of च *ch* into ज *j* is a change of quality ; while in the

---

* Sanskrit grammarians call this आभ्यंतरः प्रयत्नः *âbhyantaraḥ prayatnaḥ*, mode of articulation preparatory to the utterance of the sound, and distinguish it from वाह्यः प्रयत्नः *vâhyaḥ prayatnaḥ*, mode of articulation at the close of the utterance of the sound, which produces the qualities of surd, sonant, aspirated, and unaspirated, as explained in § 58, 59.

† Some grammarians differ in their description of the degrees of closing or opening of the organs. Some ascribe to the semivowels *duḥsprishṭa*, imperfect contact, or *ishadasprishṭa*, slight non-contact, or *ishadvivṛita*, slight opening ; to the sibilants *nemasprishṭa*, half-contact, i.e. greater opening than is required for the semivowels, or *vivṛita*, complete opening ; while they require for the vowels either *vivṛita*, complete opening, or *asprishṭa*, non-contact. Siddh.-Kaum. vol. I. p. 10. Rig-veda-prâtiś. XIII. 3. In the Atharva-veda-prâtiśâkhya I. 33. we ought to read एके ऽस्पृष्टं *eke 'sprishṭam* instead of एके स्पृष्टं *eke sprishṭam*.

transition of च *ch* into ग्र *g*, or of त्‍ *t* into न्‍ *n*, we should have a change both of place and of quality.

§ 60. The changes which take place by the combination of the eleven final letters with initial vowels or consonants may be divided therefore into two classes.

Final letters are changed, 1. with regard to their places or organs, 2. with regard to their quality.

1. *Changes of Place.*

§ 61. The only final consonants which are liable to change of place are the Dentals, the Anusvâra, and Visarga. The Dentals, being incompatible with Palatals and Linguals, become palatal and lingual before these letters. Anusvâra and Visarga adapt themselves as much as possible to the place of the letter by which they are followed. All other changes of final consonants are merely changes of quality; these in the case of Dentals, Anusvâra, and Visarga, being superadded to the changes of place.

§ 62. Final त्‍ *t* before palatals (च *ch*, छ *chh*, ज *j*, झ *jh*, ञ *ñ*, श *ś*) is changed into a palatal. (Pâṇ. VIII. 4, 40.)

Ex. तत्‍ + च = तच्च *tat + cha = tachcha,* and this.

    तत्‍ + छिनत्ति = तच्छिनत्ति *tat + chhinatti = tachchhinatti,* he cuts this.

    तत्‍ + शृणोति = तच्छृणोति *tat + śriṇoti = tachśriṇoti,* he hears this *.

    तत्‍ + जायते = तज्जायते *tat + jâyate = tajjâyate,* this is born. The final त्‍ *t* is changed into च *ch* and then into ज *j* according to § 66.

In composition, जगत्‍ + नेता = जगन्नेता *jagat + jetâ = jagajjetâ,* conqueror of the world.

The same change would take place before an initial झ *jh;* and before an initial ञ *ñ*, त्‍ *t* might become either ज *j* or ञ *ñ*. (§ 68.)

§ 63. Final न्‍ *n* before ज *j*, झ *jh*, ञ *ñ*, and श *ś* is changed to palatal ञ *ñ.*

Ex. तान्‍ + जयति = ताञ्जयति *tân + jayati = tâñjayati,* he conquers them. (Pâṇ. VIII. 4, 40.)

Note—Rules on the changes of final न्‍ *n* before च *ch*, छ *chh*, and श *ś* will be given hereafter. See § 73, 74.

§ 64. Final त्‍ *t* before ट *ṭ*, ठ *ṭh*, ड *ḍ*, ढ *ḍh*, ण *ṇ* (not ष *sh*, Pâṇ. VIII. 4, 43) is changed into a lingual. (Pâṇ. VIII. 4, 41.)

Ex. तत्‍ + डयते = तड्डयते *tat + ḍayate = taḍḍayate.* The final त्‍ *t* is changed into ट *ṭ* and then into ड *ḍ* according to § 66.

In composition, तत्‍ + टीका = तट्टीका *tat + ṭîkâ = taṭṭîkâ,* a gloss on this.

    एतत्‍ + ठक्कुरः = एतट्ठक्कुरः *etat + ṭhakkuraḥ = etaṭṭhakkuraḥ,* the idol of him.

---

* श *ś*, according to § 92, is generally changed to छ *chh:* तच्छृणोति *tachchhriṇoti.*

The same change would take place before an initial ढ *dh;* and before an initial ण *ṇ,* न *t* might become either ड *ḍ* or ण *ṇ.* (§ 68.)

§ 65. Final न *n* before ड *ḍ,* ढ *ḍh,* ण *ṇ* (not ष *sh,* Pâṇ. VIII. 4, 43) is changed to ण *ṇ.*

Ex. महान् + डामरः = महाण्डामरः *mahán + ḍámaraḥ = mahâṇḍâmaraḥ,* a great uproar.

Note—Rules on the changes of न *n* before ट *t* and ठ *ṭh* (not ष *sh*) will be given hereafter (§ 74). The changes of place with regard to final Anusvâra (*ṁ*) and Visarga (*ḥ*) will be explained together with the changes of quality to which these letters are liable.

2. *Changes of Quality.*

§ 66. Sonant initials require sonant finals.

Surd initials require surd finals.

As all final letters (except nasals and ल् *l*) are surd, they remain surd before surds. They are changed into their corresponding sonant letters before sonants.

As the nasals have no corresponding surd letters, they remain unchanged in quality, though followed by surd letters, unless the contact can be avoided by inserting sibilants.

Examples :

1. क् *k* before sonants, changed into ग् *g:*

सम्यक् + उक्तं = सम्यगुक्तं *samyak + uktam = samyaguktam,* Well said !

धिक् + धनगर्वितं = धिग्धनगर्वितं *dhik + dhanagarvitam = dhigdhanagarvitam,* Fie on the purse-proud man !

In composition, दिक् + गजः = दिग्गजः *dik + gajaḥ = diggajaḥ,* an elephant supporting the globe at one of the eight points of the compass.

Before Pada-terminations: दिक् + भिः = दिग्भिः *dik + bhiḥ = digbhiḥ,* instrum. plur.

Before secondary suffixes beginning with consonants, except य *y:* वाक् + मिन् = वाग्मिन् *vák + min = vâgmin,* eloquent *.

2. ट *ṭ* before sonants, changed into ड *ḍ:*

परिव्राट् + अयं = परिव्राडयं *parivráṭ + ayam = parivrâḍayam,* he is a mendicant.

परिव्राट् + हसति = परिव्राड्हसति *parivráṭ + hasati = parivrâḍ hasati,* the mendicant laughs; (also परिव्राड् ढसति *parivrâḍ ḍhasati.* § 70.)

In composition, परिव्राट् + मित्रं = परिव्राड्मित्रं *parivráṭ + mitram = parivrâḍmitram,* a beggar's friend.

Before Pada-terminations : परिव्राट् + भिः = परिव्राड्भिः *parivráṭ + bhiḥ = parivrâḍbhiḥ.*

---

* Pâṇini is driven to admit a suffix *gmin* instead of *min,* in order to prevent the nasalization of the final consonant of *vâch;* cf. Pâṇ. VIII. 4, 45, vârt.

3. प् *p* before sonants, changed into ब् *b:*

कुकुप् + अत्र = ककुबत्र *kakup + atra = kakubatra,* a region there, (inflectional base ककुभ् *kakubh.*)

अप् + घटः = अब्घटः *ap + ghaṭaḥ = abghaṭaḥ,* a water-jar.

अप् + जयः = अब्जयः *ap + jayaḥ = abjayaḥ,* obtaining water.

अप् + मयः = अम्मयः *ap + mayaḥ = ammayaḥ,* watery. (§ 69.)

ककुप् + भिः = ककुब्भिः *kakup + bhiḥ = kakubbhiḥ,* instrum. plur.

4. त् *t* before sonants, changed into द् *d,* except before sonant palatals and linguals, when (according to § 62) it is changed into ज् *j* and ड् *ḍ:*

सरित् + अत्र = सरिदत्र *sarit + atra = saridatra,* the river there.

जगत् + ईशः = जगदीशः *jagat + īśaḥ = jagadīśaḥ,* lord of the world.

महत् + धनुः = महद्धनुः *mahat + dhanuḥ = mahaddhanuḥ,* a large bow.

महत् + भिः = महद्भिः *mahat + bhiḥ = mahadbhiḥ,* instrum. plur.

त् *t* before sonant palatals, changed into ज् *j:* see § 62 :

सरित् + जलं = सरिज्जलं *sarit + jalam = sarijjalam,* water of the river.

त् *t* before sonant linguals, changed into ड् *ḍ:* see § 62 :

एतत् + डामरः = एतड्डामरः *etat + ḍāmaraḥ = etaḍḍāmaraḥ,* the uproar of them.

Note—There are exceptions to this rule, but they are confined to Taddhita derivatives which are found in dictionaries. Thus final त् *t* before the possessive suffixes मत् *mat,* वत् *vat,* विन् *vin,* वल *vala* is not changed. Ex. विद्युत् + वत् = विद्युत्वत् *vidyut + vat = vidyutvat,* possessed of lightning. Final स् *s* too, which represents Visarga, remains unchanged before the same Taddhitas. Thus तेजस् + विन् = तेजस्विन् *tejas + vin = tejasvin,* instead of तेजोविन् *tejovin;* see § 84. 3. ज्योतिस् + मत् = ज्योतिष्मत् *jyotis + mat = jyotishmat,* instead of ज्योतिर्मत् *jyotirmat;* § 84. (Pân. I. 4, 19.)

§ 67. Additional changes take place if the final surds क् *k,* ट् *ṭ,* त् *t,* प् *p* are followed by initial nasals, chiefly न् *n* and म् *m.* The nasals being sonant, they require the change of क् *k,* ट् *ṭ,* त् *t,* and प् *p* into ग् *g,* ड् *ḍ,* द् *d,* and ब् *b;* but these final sonants may be further infected by the nasal character of the initial nasals, and may be written ङ् *ṅ,* ण् *ṇ,* न् *n,* म् *m.* (Pân. VIII. 4, 45.)

Ex. दिक् + नागः = दिग्नागः or दिङ्नागः *dik + nāgaḥ = dignāgaḥ* or *diṅnāgaḥ,* a world-elephant.

मधुलिट् + नर्दति = मधुलिड्नर्दति or मधुलिण्नर्दति *madhuliṭ + nardati = madhuliḍnardati* or *madhuliṇnardati,* the bee hums.

जगत् + नाथः = जगद्नाथः or जगन्नाथः *jagat + nāthaḥ = jagadnāthaḥ* or *jagannāthaḥ,* lord of the world.

अप् + नदी = अब्नदी or अम्नदी *ap + nadī = abnadī* or *amnadī,* water-river.

प्राक् + मुखः = प्राग्मुखः or प्राङ्मुखः *prāk + mukhaḥ = prāgmukhaḥ* or *prāṅmukhaḥ,* facing the east.

भवत् + मतं = भवद्मतं or भवन्मतं *bhavat + matam = bhavadmatam* or *bhavanmatam,* your opinion.

Note—If a word should begin with a guttural, palatal, or lingual *n* (ङ़ *ṅ*, ञ *ñ*, or ण *ṇ*) then a final त़ *t* would change its place or organ at the same time that it became a nasal. It would become ङ़ *ṅ*, ञ *ñ*, or ण *ṇ*. There are, however, no words in common use beginning with ङ़ *ṅ*, ञ *ñ*, or ण *ṇ*.

§ 68. Before the suffix मय *maya* and before मात्र *mátra* the change into the nasal is not optional, but obligatory. (Pâṇ. VIII. 4, 45, vârt.)

Ex. वाक़् + मयं = वाङ्मयं *vák + mayam = váṅmayam*, consisting of speech.

मधुलिट़् + मात्रं = मधुलिण्मात्रं *madhuliṭ + mátram = madhuliṇmátram*, merely a bee.

तत़् + मात्रं = तन्मात्रं *tat + mátram = tanmátram*, element.

Note—Ninety-six is always षण्णवति *shaṇṇavati*, never षड्णवति *shaḍṇavati*.

§ 69. The initial ह़ *h*, if brought into immediate contact with a final क़् *k* (ग़् *g*), ट़ *ṭ* (ड़ *ḍ*), त़ *t* (द़ *d*), प़ *p* (ब़ *b*), is commonly, not necessarily, changed into the sonant aspirate of the class of the final letter, viz. into घ *gh*, ढ *ḍh*, ध *dh*, भ *bh*. (Pâṇ. VIII. 4, 62.)

Ex. धिक़् + हस्तिन: = धिग्घस्तिन: or धिग्घस्तिन: *dhik + hastinaḥ = dhighastinaḥ* or *dhigghastinaḥ*, Fie on the elephants!

परिव्राट़् + हत: = परिव्राड्हत: or परिव्राड्ढत: *parivráṭ + hataḥ = parivráḍhataḥ* or *parivráḍḍhataḥ*, the mendicant is killed.

तत़् + हुतं = तद्हुतं or तद्धुतं *tat + hutam = tadhutam* or *taddhutam*, this is sacrificed.

अप़् + हरणं = अब्हरणं or अब्भरणं *ap + haraṇam = abharaṇam* or *abbharaṇam*, water-fetching.

§ 70. त़ *t* before ल *l* is not changed into द़ *d*, but into ल़ *l*. (Pâṇ. VIII. 4, 60.)

Ex. तत़् + लब्धं = तल्लब्धं *tat + labdham = tallabdham*, this is taken.

बृहत़् + ललाटं = बृहल्ललाटं *bṛihat + laláṭam = bṛihallaláṭam*, a large forehead.

§ 71. Final ऩ *n* before ल *l* is changed into ल *l*; but this ल *l* is pronounced through the nose, and is written with the Anusvâra dot over it. It is usual in this case to write the Anusvâra as a half-moon, called *Ardha-chandra*.

Ex. महाऩ् + लाभ: = महाँल्लाभ: *mahán + lábhaḥ = mahál̐ lábhaḥ*, large gain.

§ 72. Final ङ़ *ṅ*, ण *ṇ*, and ऩ *n*, preceded by a short vowel and followed by any vowel, are doubled. (Pâṇ. VIII. 3, 32.)

Ex. धावऩ् + अश्व: = धावन्नश्व: *dhávan + aśvaḥ = dhávannaśvaḥ*, a running horse.

प्रत्यङ़् + आस्ते = प्रत्यङ्ङास्ते *pratyaṅ + áste = pratyaṅṅáste*, he sits turned toward the west.

सुगण़् + आस्ते = सुगण्णास्ते *sugaṇ + áste = sugaṇṇáste*, he sits counting well*.

If ङ़ *ṅ*, ण *ṇ*, and ऩ *n* are preceded by a long vowel and followed by any vowel, no change takes place.

Ex. कवीऩ् + आह्वयस्व *kavín + áhvayasva*, call the poets.

---

* Technical terms like उणादि *uṇádi*, a list of suffixes beginning with *uṇ*, or तिङ्त *tiṅanta*, words ending in *tiṅ*, are exempt from this rule. See also Wilkins, Sanskrita Grammar, § 30.

§ 73. Final न् *n* before initial क *k*, ख *kh*, and प *p*, फ *ph*, remains unchanged.

Final न् *n* before च *ch*, छ *chh*, requires the intercession of श *s*.

Final न् *n* before ट *ṭ*, ठ *ṭh*, requires the intercession of ष *sh*.

Final न् *n* before त *t*, थ *th*, requires the intercession of स *s*. (Pâṇ. VIII. 3, 7.)

Before these inserted sibilants the original न् *n* is changed to Anusvâra.

Ex. हसन् + चकार = हसंश्चकार *hasan + chakâra = hasaṁśchakâra*, he did it laughing.

धावन् + छाग: = धावंश्छाग: *dhâvan + chhâgaḥ = dhâvaṁśchhâgaḥ*, a running goat.

चलन् + टिट्टिभ: = चलंष्टिट्टिभ: *chalan + ṭiṭṭibhaḥ = chalaṁshṭiṭṭibhaḥ*, a moving ṭiṭṭibha-bird.

महान् + ठक्कुर: = महांष्ठक्कुर: *mahân + ṭhakkuraḥ = mahâṁshṭhakkuraḥ*, a great idol.

पतन् + तरु: = पतंस्तरु: *patan + taruḥ = pataṁstaruḥ*, a falling tree.

Note—प्रशान् *prasân*, quiet, forms the nom. प्रशान् *prasân ;* but this final न् *n*, being the representation of an original म् *m*, is not allowed before च *ch*, छ *chh*, ट *ṭ*, ठ *ṭh*, त *t*, थ *th* to take a sibilant. Ex. प्रशान् + चिनोति = प्रशाचिनोति *prasân + chinoti = prasâñchinoti ;* not प्रशांचिनोति *prasâṁśchinoti*. (Pâṇ. VIII. 3, 7.)

§ 74. Final ङ् *ṅ* and ण् *ṇ* may be followed by initial श *ś*, ष *sh*, स *s* without causing any change; but it is optional to add a क *k* after the ङ् *ṅ* and a ट *ṭ* after the ण् *ṇ*. Thus ङ्श *ṅśa* becomes ङ्क्श *ṅkśa* (or ङ्क्छ *ṅkchha*, § 92); ङ्श *ṅsha* becomes ङ्क्ष *ṅksha*; ङ्स *ṅsa* becomes ङ्क्स *ṅksa*; ण्श *ṇśa* becomes ण्ट्श *ṇṭśa* (or ण्ट्छ *ṇṭchha*); ण्श *ṇsha* becomes ण्ट्ष *ṇṭsha*; ण्स *ṇsa* becomes ण्ट्स *ṇṭsa*. (Pâṇ. VIII. 3, 28.)

Ex. प्राङ् + शेते = प्राङ्क्शेते or प्राङ्क्शेते (or प्राङ्क्छेते) *prâṅ + śete = prâṅśete* or *prâṅkśete* (or *prâṅkchhete*).

सुगण् + सरति = सुगण्सरति or सुगण्ट्सरति *sugaṇ + sarati = sugaṇsarati* or *sugaṇṭsarati*.

§ 75. The same rule applies to final न् *n* before श *ś* and स *s*, but not before ष *sh*, where it remains unchanged. Before श *ś* it is first changed into palatal ञ *ñ** (§ 63); and ञ्श *ñś* may again be changed to ञ्च्श *ñchś*, ञ्च्छ *ñchchh* (§ 72, 92), or ञ्छ *ñchh*. Before स *s*, न *n* may remain unchanged, or न्स *ns* may be changed into न्त्स *nts*. (Pâṇ. VIII. 3, 30.)

Ex. तान् + षट् = तान्षट् *tân + shaṭ = tânshaṭ*, those six.

तान् + शार्दूलान् = ताञ्शार्दूलान् or ताञ्च्शार्दूलान् or ताञ्च्छार्दूलान् or ताञ्छार्दूलान् *tân + śârdûlân = tâñśârdûlân* or *tâñchśârdûlân* or *tâñchchhârdûlân* or *tâñchhârdûlân*, those tigers. (Pâṇ. VIII. 3, 31.)

---

* To allow न् *n* to remain unchanged before श *ś* was a mere misprint in Benfey's large grammar, and has long been corrected by that scholar.

तान् + सहते = तांसहते or तान्त्सहते *tân + sahate = tânsahate* or *tántsahate*,
he bears them.

हिन् (हिंस्) + सु = हिन्सु or हिन्त्सु *hin (hiṁs) + su = hinsu* or *hintsu*, among
enemies. (The base हिंस् *hiṁs*, before the सु *su* of the loc. plur., is
treated as a Pada.) See § 53, 55.

§ 76. A final ट् *ṭ* before स् *s* must remain unchanged, and त् *t* may be inserted.

Ex. षट् + सरिता: = षट्सरिता: or षट्त्सरिता: *shaṭ + saritah = shaṭsaritah* or *shaṭtsa-
ritah*, six rivers. (Pâṇ. VIII. 4, 42; 3, 29.)

Anusvâra and Final म *m*.

§ 77. म *m* at the end of words remains unchanged if followed by any
initial vowel.

Ex. किम् + अत्र *kim + atra* = किमत्र *kimatra*, What is there ?
Before consonants it may, without exception, be changed to Anusvâra. (Pâṇ.
VIII. 3, 23.)

This is the general rule. The exceptions are simply optional (Pâṇ. VIII.
4, 59), viz.

> Before क *k*, ख *kh*, ग *g*, घ *gh*, ङ *ṅ*, the final म *m* or Anusvâra may be
> changed into ङ *ṅ*.
> Before च *ch*, छ *chh*, ज *j*, झ *jh*, ञ *ñ*, to ञ *ñ*.
> Before ट *ṭ*, ठ *ṭh*, ड *ḍ*, ढ *ḍh*, ण *ṇ*, to ण *ṇ*.
> Before त *t*, थ *th*, द *d*, ध *dh*, न *n*, to न *n*.
> Before प *p*, फ *ph*, ब *b*, भ *bh*, म *m*, to म *m*.
> Before य *y*, ल *l*, व *v*, to य्ँ *ÿ*, ल्ँ *l̈*, व्ँ *v̈*. See § 56. 6.

Hence it follows that final म *m may* be changed into Anusvâra before all
consonants, and *must* be so changed only before श *ś*, ष *sh*, स *s*, ह *h*, and र *r*,
i. e. the five consonants which have no corresponding nasal class-letter.

It would be most desirable if scholars would never avail themselves of the optional
change of final Anusvâra into ङ *ṅ*, ञ *ñ*, ण *ṇ*, न *n*, म *m*. We should then be spared a number
of compound letters which are troublesome both in writing and printing; and we should
avoid the ambiguity as to the original nature of these class-nasals when followed by initial
sonant palatals, linguals, and dentals. Thus if तां जयति *tâṁ jayati*, he conquers her, is
written ताञ्जयति *tâñ jayati*, it may be taken for तान् जयति *tân jayati*, he conquers them,
which, according to § 63, must be changed into ताञ्जयति *tâñ jayati*. In the same manner
तान्दमयति *tân damayati* may be either तान् दमयति *tân damayati*, he tames them, or तां
दमयति *tâṁ damayati*, he tames her. All this uncertainty is at once removed if final म *m* is
always changed into Anusvâra, whatever be the initial consonant of the following word.

Ex. किम् + करोषि = किं करोषि (or किङ्करोषि) *kim + karoshi = kiṁ karoshi* (or
kiṅ karoshi), What doest thou ?
शत्रुम् + जहि = शत्रुं जहि (or शत्रुञ्जहि) *satrum + jahi = satruṁ jahi* (or *satruñ
jahi*), kill the enemy.

नदीम् + तरति = नदीं तरति (or नदीमारति) *nadîm* + *tarati* = *nadîm* *tarati* (or *nadín tarati*), he crosses the river.

गुरुम् + नमति = गुरुं नमति (or गुरुन्नमति) *gurum* + *namati* = *gurum* *namati* (or *gurun namati*), he salutes the teacher.

किम् + फलं = किं फलं (or किम्फलं) *kim* + *phalam* = *kim* *phalam* (or *kim phalam*), What is the use ?

शास्त्रम् + मीमांसते = शास्त्रं मीमांसते (or शास्त्रम्मीमांसते) *sâstram* + *mîmâmsate* = *sâstram* *mîmâmsate* (or *sâstram mîmâmsate*), he studies the book.

Before य *y*, ल *l*, व *v* :

सत्वरम् + याति = सत्वरं याति (or सत्वरय्याति) *satvaram* + *yâti* = *satvaram* *yâti* (or *satvaray̆ yâti*), he walks quickly.

विद्याम् + लभते = विद्यां लभते (or विद्याल्लभते) *vidyâm* + *labhate* = *vidyâm* *labhate* (or *vidyâl̆ labhate*), he acquires wisdom.

तम् + वेद = तं वेद (or तव्वेद) *tam* + *veda* = *tam* *veda* (or *tav̆ veda*), I know him.

Before र *r*, श *s*, ष *sh*, स *s*, ह *h* :

करुणम् + रोदिति = करुणं रोदिति *karunam* + *roditi* = *karunam roditi*, he cries piteously.

शय्यायाम् + शेते = शय्यायां शेते *sayyâyâm* + *sete* = *sayyâyâm* *sete*, he lies on the couch.

मोक्षम् + सेवेत = मोक्षं सेवेत *moksham* + *seveta* = *moksham* *seveta*, let a man cultivate spiritual freedom.

मधुरम् + हसति = मधुरं हसति *madhuram* + *hasati* = *madhuram* *hasati*, he laughs sweetly.

§ 78. म् *m* at the end of a word *in pausâ*, i. e. at the end of a sentence, is pronounced as *m*, not as Anusvâra. It may be written, however, for the sake of brevity, with the simple dot (§ 8, note), and it is so written throughout in this grammar. Ex. एवं *evam*, thus, (or एवम् *evam*.)

§ 79. Final म् *m* before ह *h*, if ह *h* be immediately followed by न *n*, म *m*, य *y*, ल *l*, व *v*, may be treated as if it were immediately followed by these letters (Pâṇ. VIII. 3, 26; 27). See, however, § 77.

Ex. किम् + ह्नुते = किं ह्नुते or किन्ह्नुते *kim* + *hnute* = *kim* *hnute* or *kin hnute*, What does he hide ?

किम् + ह्यः = किं ह्यः or किय्ह्यः *kim* + *hyah* = *kim* *hyah* or *kiy̆ hyah*, What about yesterday ?

किम् + ह्मलयति = किं ह्मलयति or किम्ह्मलयति *kim* + *hmalayati* = *kim* *hmalayati* or *kimhmalayati*, What does he move ?

§ 80. If कृ *kri* is preceded by the preposition सम् *sam*, an स *s* is inserted, and म् *m* changed to Anusvâra. (Pâṇ. VI. 1, 137; VIII. 3, 2—5.)

Ex. सम् + कृतः = संस्कृतः *sam* + *kritah* = *samskritah*, hallowed.

§ 81. In सम्राज् *samráj*, nom. सम्राट् *samráṭ*, king, म् *m* is never changed.
Pâṇ. viii. 3, 25.)

Visarga and Final स् *s and* र् *r.*

§ 82. The phonetic changes of final sibilants, which are considered the most difficult, may be reduced to a few very simple rules. It should only be borne in mind :

1. That there are really five sibilants, and not three ; that the signs for the guttural and labial sibilants became obsolete, and were replaced by the two dots (:) which properly belong to the Visarga only, i. e. to the unmodified sibilant.

2. That all sibilants and Visarga are surd, and that their proper corresponding sonant is the र् *r*.

§ 83. The only sibilant which can be final *in pausâ* is the Visarga. If Visarga is followed by a surd letter, it is changed into the sibilant of that class to which the following surd letter belongs, provided there is a sibilant.

It should be observed, however, that the· guttural and labial sibilants are now written by : *ḥ*, and that the same sign may also be used instead of any sibilant, if followed by a sibilant.

Ex. ततः + कामः = ततः कामः (originally तत ✕ कामः) *tataḥ + kámaḥ = tataḥ kámaḥ* (originally *tata χ kámaḥ*), hence love.

पूर्णः + चंद्रः = पूर्णश्चंद्रः *púrṇaḥ + chandrah = púrṇaś chandraḥ*, the full moon.

तरोः + छाया = तरोश्छाया *taroḥ + chhâyâ = taroś chhâyâ*, the shade of the tree.

भीतः + टलति = भीतष्टलति *bhítaḥ + ṭalati = bhítashṭalati*, the frightened man is disturbed.

भग्नः + ठक्कुरः = भग्नष्ठक्कुरः *bhagnaḥ + ṭhakkurah = bhagnashṭhakkuraḥ*, the broken idol.

नद्याः + तीरं = नद्यास्तीरं *nadyâḥ + tíram = nadyâstíram*, the border of the river.

नद्याः + पारं = नद्याः पारं (originally नद्या ✕ पारं) *nadyâḥ + páram = nadyâḥ páram* (originally *nadyâ φ páram*), the opposite shore of a river.

Visarga before sibilants (Pâṇ. viii. 3, 36):

सुप्तः + शिशुः = सुप्तश्शिशुः or सुप्तः शिशुः *suptaḥ + śiśuḥ = suptaś śiśuḥ* or *suptaḥ śiśuḥ*, the child sleeps.

भागः + षोडशः = भागष्षोडशः or भागः षोडशः *bhâgaḥ + shoḍaśaḥ = bhâgash shoḍaśaḥ* or *bhâgaḥ shoḍaśaḥ*, a sixteenth part.

प्रथमः + सर्गः = प्रथमस्सर्गः or प्रथमः सर्गः *prathamaḥ + sargaḥ = prathamas-sargaḥ* or *prathamaḥ sargaḥ*, the first section.

Note 1—If Visarga is followed by an initial त्स् *ts*, it is not changed into dental स् *s*, but remains Visarga, as if followed by स् *s*. (Pân. VIII. 3, 35.)

Ex. शठः + त्सरति = शठः त्सरति *śaṭhaḥ+tsarati = śaṭhaḥ tsarati*, a wicked man cheats.

कः + त्सरुः = कः त्सरुः *kaḥ+tsaruḥ = kaḥ tsaruḥ*, Which is the handle of the sword?

Note 2—If, on the contrary, Visarga is followed by a sibilant with a surd letter, the Visarga is frequently dropt in MSS. (Pân. VIII. 3, 36, vârt.)

Ex. देवाः + स्थ = देवाः स्थ or देवा स्थ *devâḥ+stha = devâḥ stha or devâ stha*, you are gods; (also देवास्थ *devâs stha*.)

हरिः + स्फुरति = हरिः स्फुरति or हरि स्फुरति *hariḥ+sphurati = hariḥ sphurati or hari sphurati*, Hari appears; (also हरिस्फुरति *haris sphurati*.)

Note 3—If nouns ending in इस् *is* or उस् *us*, like हविः *haviḥ* or धनुः *dhanuḥ*, are followed by words beginning with क् *k*, ख् *kh*, प् *p*, फ् *ph*, and are governed by these words, ष् *sh* may be substituted for final Visarga. सर्पिष्पिबति or सर्पिः पिबति *sarpishpibati or sarpiḥ pibati*, he drinks ghee; but तिष्ठतु सर्पिः पिब त्वमुदकं *tishṭhatu sarpiḥ, piba tvam udakam*, let the ghee stand, drink thou water. (Pân. VIII. 3, 44.)

§ 84. If final Visarga is followed by a sonant letter, consonant or vowel, the *general* rule is that it be changed into र् *r*. (See, however, § 86.) This rule admits, however, of the following exceptions :

1. If the Visarga is preceded by आ *â*, and followed by a sonant letter (vowel or consonant), the Visarga is dropt.

2. If the Visarga is preceded by अ *a*, and followed by any vowel except अ *a*, the Visarga is dropt.

3. If the Visarga is preceded by अ *a*, and followed by a sonant consonant, the Visarga is dropt, and the अ *a* changed to ओ *o*.

4. If the Visarga is preceded by अ *a*, and followed by अ *a*, the Visarga is dropt, अ *a* changed into ओ *o*, after which, according to § 41, the initial अ *a* must be elided. The sign of the elision is ऽ, called *Avagraha*.

Examples of the general rule :

कविः + अयं = कविरयं *kaviḥ + ayam = kavirayam*, this poet.

रविः + उदेति = रविरुदेति *raviḥ + udeti = ravir udeti*, the sun rises.

गौः + गच्छति = गौर्गच्छति *gauḥ + gachchhati = gaur gachchhati*, the ox walks.

विष्णुः + जयति = विष्णुर्जयति *vishṇuḥ + jayati = vishṇur jayati*, Vishṇu is victorious.

पशोः + बंधः = पशोर्बंधः *paśoḥ + bandhaḥ = paśorbandhaḥ*, the binding of the cattle.

मुहुः + मुहुः = मुहुर्मुहुः *muhuḥ + muhuḥ = muhurmuhuḥ*, gradually.

वायुः + वाति = वायुर्वाति *vâyuḥ + vâti = vâyur vâti*, the wind blows.

शिशुः + हसति = शिशुर्हसति *śiśuḥ + hasati = śiśur hasati*, the child laughs.

निः + धनः = निर्धनः *niḥ + dhanaḥ = nirdhanaḥ*, without wealth.

दुः + नीतिः = दुर्नीतिः *duḥ + nîtiḥ = durnîtiḥ*, of bad manners.

ज्योतिः + भिः = ज्योतिर्भिः *jyotiḥ + bhiḥ = jyotirbhiḥ*, instrum. plur.

Examples of the first exception:

अश्वाः + अमी = अश्वा अमी *aśváḥ + amí = aśvá amí*, these horses.

आगताः + ऋषयः = आगता ऋषयः *âgatâḥ + ṛishayaḥ = âgatá ṛishayaḥ*, the poets have arrived.

हताः + गजाः = हता गजाः *hatáḥ + gajâḥ = hatá gajâḥ*, the elephants are killed.

उन्नताः + नगाः = उन्नता नगाः *unnatâḥ + nagâḥ = unnatá nagâḥ*, the high mountains.

छात्राः + यतंते = छात्रा यतंते *chhâtráḥ + yatante = chhâtrá yatante*, the pupils strive.

माः + भिः = माभिः *mâḥ + bhiḥ = mâbhiḥ*, instrum. plur. of मास् *mâs*, moon.

Examples of the second exception:

कुतः + आगतः = कुत आगतः *kutaḥ + âgataḥ = kuta âgataḥ*, Whence come?

कः + एषः = क एषः *kaḥ + eshaḥ = ka eshaḥ*, Who is he?

कः + ऋषिः = क ऋषिः *kaḥ + ṛishiḥ = ka ṛishiḥ*, Who is the poet?

मनः + आदि = मन आदि *manaḥ + âdi = mana âdi*, beginning with mind.

Examples of the third exception:

शोभनः + गंधः = शोभनो गंधः *śobhanaḥ + gandhaḥ = śobhano gandhaḥ*, a sweet scent.

नूतनः + घटः = नूतनो घटः *nûtanaḥ + ghaṭaḥ = nûtano ghaṭaḥ*, a new jar.

मूर्धन्यः + णकारः = मूर्धन्यो णकारः *mûrdhanyaḥ + ṇakâraḥ = mûrdhanyo ṇakâraḥ*, the lingual *ṇ*.

निर्वाणः + दीपः = निर्वाणो दीपः *nirvâṇaḥ + dîpaḥ = nirvâṇo dîpaḥ*, the lamp is blown out.

अतीतः + मासः = अतीतो मासः *atîtaḥ + mâsaḥ = atîto mâsaḥ*, the past month.

कृतः + यत्नः = कृतो यत्नः *kṛitaḥ + yatnaḥ = kṛito yatnaḥ*, effort is made.

मनः + रमः = मनोरमः *manaḥ + ramaḥ = manoramaḥ*, (a compound), pleasing to the mind, delightful.

नः + भिः = नोभिः *naḥ + bhiḥ = nobhiḥ*, instrum. plur. with the noses.

Examples of the fourth exception:

नरः + अयं = नरोऽयं *naraḥ + ayam = naro 'yam*, this man.

वेदः + अधीतः = वेदोऽधीतः *vedaḥ + adhîtaḥ = vedo 'dhîtaḥ*, the Veda has been read.

अयः + अस्त्रं = अयोऽस्त्रं *ayaḥ + astram = ayo 'stram*, an iron-weapon.

§ 85. There are a few words in which the final letter is etymologically र *r*[*]. This र *r*, as a final, is changed into Visarga, according to § 82, and it

---

[*] It is called रजातो विसर्गः *rajâto visargaḥ*, the Visarga produced from *r*. It occurs, preceded by अ *a*, in पुनः *punaḥ*, again; प्रातः *prâtaḥ*, early; अंतः *antaḥ*, within; स्वः *svaḥ*, heaven; अहः *ahaḥ*, day (§ 196); in the voc. sing. of nouns in ऋ *ṛi*, ex. पितः *pitaḥ*, father, from पितृ *pitṛi*, &c.; and in verbal forms such as अजागर् *ajâgar*, 2.3. sing. impf. of जागृ *jâgṛi*.

follows all the rules affecting the Visarga except the exceptional rules § 84.
2, 3, 4; i. e. if preceded by व *a*, and followed by any sonant letter, vowel
or consonant, the र *r* is retained.

Ex. पुनः + अपि = पुनरपि *punaḥ + api = punarapi*, even again.

प्रातः + एव = प्रातरेव *prâtaḥ + eva = prâtareva*, very early.

भ्रातः + देहि = भ्रातर्देहि *bhrâtaḥ + dehi = bhrâtar dehi*, Brother, give !

§ 86. No र *r* can ever be followed by another र *r* (Pân. VIII. 3, 14). Hence
final Visarga, whether etymologically स *s* or र *r*, if followed by initial र *r*,
and therefore by § 84 changed to र *r*, is dropt, and its preceding vowel
lengthened. (Pân. VI. 3, 111.)

Ex. विधुः + राजते = विधू राजते *vidhuḥ + râjate = vidhú râjate*, the moon shines.

भ्रातः + रक्ष = भ्राता रक्ष *bhrâtaḥ + raksha = bhrâtá raksha*, Brother, protect!

पुनः + रोगी = पुना रोगी *punaḥ + rogí = punâ rogí*, ill again.

These are the general rules on the Sandhi of final Visarga, स *s* and र *r*.
The following rules refer to a few exceptional cases.

§ 87. The two pronouns सः *saḥ* and एषः *eshaḥ*, this, become स *sa* and
एष *esha* before consonants and vowels, except before short व *a* and at the
end of a sentence. (Pân. VI. 1, 132.)

Ex. सः + ददाति = स ददाति *saḥ + dadâti = sa dadâti*, he gives.

सः इंद्रः = स इंद्रः *saḥ indraḥ = sa indraḥ*, this Indra. The two vowels
are not liable to Sandhi.

But सः + अभवत् = सोऽभवत् *saḥ + abhavat = so 'bhavat*, he was.

मृतः सः *mritaḥ saḥ*, he is dead.

Sometimes Sandhi takes place, particularly for the sake of the metre.
Thus स एष *sa esha* becomes occasionally सैष *saisha*, he, this person. स इंद्रः
sa indraḥ appears as सेंद्रः *sendraḥ*. (Pân. VI. 1, 134.)

The pronoun स्यः *syaḥ*, he, follows the same rule optionally in poetry. (Pân.
VI. 1, 133.)

§ 88. भोः *bhoḥ*, an irregular vocative of भवत् *bhavat*, thou, drops its Visarga
before all vowels and all sonant consonants. (Pân. VIII. 3, 22.)

Ex. भोः + ईशान = भो ईशान *bhoḥ + îśâna = bho îśâna*, Oh lord !

भोः + देवाः = भो देवाः *bhoḥ + devâḥ = bho devâḥ*, Oh gods !

The same applies to the interjections भगोः *bhagoḥ* and अघोः *aghoḥ*, really
irregular vocatives of भगवत् *bhagavat*, God, and अघवत् *aghavat*, sinner.

§ 89. Numerous exceptions, which are best learnt from the dictionary,
occur in compound and derivative words. A few of the more important
may here be mentioned.

I. *Nouns in* अस् *as,* इस् *is,* उस् *us, forming the first part of a Compound.*

1. Before derivatives of कृ *kṛi,* to do (e. g. कर *kara,* कार *kára*), before derivatives of कम् *kam,* to desire (e. g. कांत *kánta,* काम *káma*), before कंस *kaṁsa,* goblet, कुंभ *kumbha,* jar, पात्र *pátra,* vessel, कुश *kuśá,* counter, board, कर्णी *karṇí,* ear, the final Visarga of bases in अस् *as* is changed to स् *s.* (Pâṇ. viii. 3, 46.)

Ex. श्रेय: + कर: = श्रेयस्कर: *śreyaḥ + karaḥ = śreyaskaraḥ,* making happy.

अह: + कर: = अहस्कर: *ahaḥ + karaḥ = ahaskaraḥ,* sun.

अय: + कुंभ: = अयस्कुंभ: *ayaḥ + kumbhaḥ = ayaskumbhaḥ,* iron-pot.

There are several words of the same kind—which are best learnt from the dictionary—in which the Visarga is changed into dental sibilant. (Pâṇ. viii. 3, 47.)

Ex. अध: + पदं = अधस्पदं *adhaḥ + padam = adhaspadam,* below the foot.

दिव: + पति: = दिवस्पति: *divaḥ + patiḥ = divaspatiḥ,* lord of heaven.

वाच: + पति: = वाचस्पति: *váchaḥ + patiḥ = váchaspatiḥ,* lord of speech.

भा: + कर: = भास्कर: *bháḥ + karaḥ = bháskaraḥ,* sun, &c.

2. Nouns in इस् *is* and उस् *us,* such as हवि: *haviḥ,* धनु: *dhanuḥ,* &c., before words beginning with क् *k,* ख् *kh,* प् *p,* and फ् *ph,* always take ष् *sh.* (Pâṇ. viii. 3, 45.)

Ex. सर्पि: + पानं = सर्पिष्पानं *sarpiḥ + pánam = sarpishpánam,* ghee-drinking.

आयु: + काम: = आयुष्काम: *áyuḥ + kámaḥ = áyushkámaḥ,* fond of life.

Note—भ्रातुष्पुत्र: *bhrátushputraḥ,* nephew, is used instead of भ्रातु: पुत्र: *bhrátuḥ putraḥ,* the son of the brother.

II. *Words in* अस् *as,* इस् *is,* उस् *us, treated as Prepositions.*

1. The words नम: *namaḥ,* पुर: *puraḥ,* तिर: *tiraḥ,* if compounded prepositionally with कृ *kṛi,* change Visarga into स् *s.* (Pâṇ. viii. 3, 40.)

Ex. नम: + कार: = नमस्कार: *namaḥ + káraḥ = namaskáraḥ,* adoration; (but नम: कृत्वा *namaḥ kṛitvá,* having performed adoration.)

पुर: + कृत्य = पुरस्कृत्य *puraḥ + kṛitya = puraskṛitya,* having preferred.

तिर: + कारी = तिरस्कारी *tiraḥ + kárí = tiraskárí,* despising. In तिर: *tiraḥ* the change is considered optional. (Pâṇ. viii. 3, 42.)

2. The words नि: *niḥ,* दु: *duḥ,* वहि: *vahiḥ,* आवि: *ávíḥ,* प्रादु: *práduḥ,* चतु: *chatuḥ,* if compounded with words beginning with क् *k,* ख् *kh,* प् *p* or फ् *ph,* take ष् *sh* instead of final Visarga. (Pâṇ. viii. 3, 41.)

Ex. नि: + काम: = निष्काम: *niḥ + kámaḥ = nishkámaḥ,* loveless.

नि: + फल: = निष्फल: *niḥ + phalaḥ = nishphalaḥ,* fruitless.

आवि: + कृतं = आविष्कृतं *ávíḥ + kṛitam = ávishkṛitam,* made manifest.

दु: + कृतं = दुष्कृतं *duḥ + kṛitam = dushkṛitam,* badly done, criminal.

चतु: + कोणं = चतुष्कोणं *chatuḥ + koṇam = chatushkoṇam,* square.

III. *Nouns in* अस् *as,* इस् *is,* उस् *us, before certain Taddhita Suffixes.*

1. Before the Taddhita suffixes मत् *mat,* वत् *vat,* विन् *vin,* and वल *vala,* the final स् *s* appears as स् *s* or ष् *sh* (§ 100).

Ex. तेज: + विन् = तेजस्विन् *tejaḥ + vin = tejasvin,* with splendour.

ज्योति: + मत् = ज्योतिष्मत् *jyotiḥ + mat = jyotishmat,* with light.

रज: + वल = रजस्वल *rajaḥ + vala = rajasvala,* a buffalo.

2. Before Taddhita suffixes beginning with त् *t*, the स् *s*, preceded by इ *i* or उ *u*, is changed into ष् *sh*, after which the त् *t* becomes ट् *ṭ*.

> Ex. अर्चिः + त्वं = अर्चिष्ट्वं *archiḥ+tvam = archishṭvam*, brightness.
>
> चतुः + तयं = चतुष्टयं *chatuḥ+tayam = chatushṭayam*, the aggregate of four.

3. Before the Taddhita suffixes पाश *páśa*, कल्प *kalpa*, क *ka*, and in composition with the verb काम्यति *kámyati*, nouns in अस् *as* retain their final स् *s*, while nouns in इस् *is* and उस् *us* change it into ष् *sh* (§ 100). (Pâṇ. VIII. 3, 39.)

> Ex. पयः + पाशं = पयस्पाशं *payaḥ+páśam = payaspáśam*, bad milk.
>
> पयः + कल्पं = पयस्कल्पं *payaḥ+kalpam = payaskalpam*, a little milk.
>
> यशः + कः = यशस्कः *yaśaḥ+kaḥ = yaśaskaḥ*, glorious.
>
> यशः + काम्यति = यशस्काम्यति *yaśaḥ+kámyati = yaśaskámyati*, he is ambitious.
>
> सर्पिः + पाशं = सर्पिष्पाशं *sarpiḥ+páśam = sarpishpáśam*, bad ghee.
>
> सर्पिः + कल्पं = सर्पिष्कल्पं *sarpiḥ+kalpam = sarpishkalpam*, a little ghee.
>
> धनुः + कः = धनुष्कः *dhanuḥ+kaḥ = dhanushkaḥ*, belonging to the bow.
>
> धनुः + काम्यति = धनुष्काम्यति *dhanuḥ+kámyati = dhanushkámyati*, he desires a bow.

§ 90. Nouns ending in radical र् *r* (§ 85) retain the र् *r* before the सु *su* of the loc. plur., and in composition before nouns even though beginning with surds.

> Ex. वार् + सु = वार्षु *vár + su = várshu*, in the waters.
>
> गिर् + पतिः = गीर्पतिः *gir + patiḥ = gírpatiḥ*, lord of speech.

In compounds, however, like गीर्पतिः *gírpatiḥ*, the optional use of Visarga is sanctioned (Pâṇ. VIII. 2, 70, vârt.), and we meet with गीःपतिः *gíḥpatiḥ*, धूःपतिः *dhúḥpatiḥ*, and धूर्पतिः *dhúrpatiḥ*; स्वःपतिः *svaḥpatiḥ* and स्वर्पतिः *svarpatiḥ*, lord of heaven; अहःपतिः *ahaḥpatiḥ* and अहर्पतिः *aharpatiḥ*, lord of the day.

अहर् *ahar*, the Pada base of अहन् *ahan*, day, is further irregular, because its final र् *r* is treated like स् *s* before the Pada-terminations, and in composition before words beginning with र् *r*: hence अहः + भिः = अहोभिः *ahaḥ+bhiḥ = ahobhiḥ*; अहः + सु = अहःसु *ahaḥ+su = ahaḥsu*; अहः + रात्रः = अहोरात्रः *ahaḥ+rátraḥ = ahorátraḥ*, day and night. (Pâṇ. VIII. 2, 68, vârt.)

§ 91. छ *chh* at the beginning of a word, after a final short vowel, and after the particles आ *á* and मा *má*, is changed to च्छ *chchh*.

> Ex. तव + छाया = तव च्छाया *tava + chháyá = tava chchháyá*, thy shade.
>
> मा + छिदत् = मा च्छिदत् *má + chhidat = má chchhidat*, let him not cut.
>
> आ + छादयति = आच्छादयति *á + chhádayati = áchchhádayati*, he covers.

After any other long vowels, this change is optional.

> बदरीछाया or बदरीच्छाया *badaríchháyá* or *badaríchchháyá*, shade of Badarís.

In the body of a word, the change of छ *chh* into च्छ *chchh* is necessary both after long and short vowels.

> Ex. इच्छति *ichchhati*, he wishes.   म्लेच्छः *mlechchhaḥ*, a barbarian. (Pâṇ. VI. 1, 73–76.)

§ 92. Initial श्र *s*, not followed by a hard consonant, may be changed into छ *chh*, if the final letter of the preceding word is a hard consonant or ङ *ñ* (for न *n*). (Pâṇ. VIII. 4, 63.)

Ex. वाक् + शतं = वाक्शतं or वाक्छतं *vâk + satam = vâksatam* or *vâkchhatam*, a hundred speeches.

परिव्राट् + शेते = परिव्राट् शेते or परिव्राट्छेते *parivrâṭ + sete = parivrâṭ sete* or *parivrâṭ chhete*, the beggar lies down.

महत् + शकटं = महत्शकटं or महच्छकटं *mahat + sakaṭam = mahach sakaṭam* or *mahach chhakaṭam*, a great car.

तत् + श्लोकेन = तच्छ्लोकेन *tat + slokena = tachchhlokena*, by that verse.

धावन् + शश: = धावन्शश: or धावञ्छश: *dhâvan + sasah = dhâvañ sasah* or *dhâvañ chhasah*, a running hare.

अप् + शब्द: = अप्शब्द: or अप्छब्द: *ap + sabdah = ap sabdah* or *apchhabdah*, the sound of water.

§ 93. If ह *h*, घ *gh*, ढ *ḍh*, ध *dh*, or भ *bh* stand at the end of a syllable which begins with ग *g*, ड *ḍ*, द *d*, or ब *b*, and lose their aspiration as final or otherwise, the initial consonants ग *g*, ड *ḍ*, द *d*, or ब *b* are changed into घ *gh*, ढ *ḍh*, ध *dh*, भ *bh*.

Ex. दुह् *duh*, a milker, becomes धुक् *dhuk*.

विश्वगुध् *visvagudh*, all attracting, becomes विश्वघुट् *visvaghut*.

बुध् *budh*, wise, becomes भुट् *bhut*.

§ 94. *Table showing the Combination of Final with Initial Consonants.*

FINAL	1 IN PAUSÂ	2 Â Á &c.	3 K	4 KH	5 G	6 GH	7 Ṅ	8 CH	9 CHH	10 J	11 JH	12 Ñ	13 Ṭ	14 ṬH	15 Ḍ	16 ḌH	17 Ṇ
I. K	k (g)	ga gâ	..	..	gg	ggh	gṅ ṅṅ	..	..	gj	gjh	gñ ññ	..	..	gḍ	gḍh	gṇ ṇṇ
II. Ṅ	..	ṅṅa ṅâ	..	..	..	..	..	..	..	..	..	..	..	..	..	..	..
III. Ṭ	ṭ (ḍ)	ḍa ḍâ	..	..	ḍg	ḍgh	ḍṅ ṅṅ	..	..	ḍj	ḍjh	ḍñ ññ	..	..	ḍḍ	ḍḍh	ḍṇ ṇṇ
IV. Ṇ	..	ṇṇa ṇâ	..	..	..	..	..	..	..	..	..	..	..	..	..	..	..
V. T	t (d)	da dâ	..	..	dg	dgh	dṅ ṅṅ	chch	chchh	jj	jjh	jñ ññ	ṭṭ	ṭṭh	ḍḍ	ḍḍh	dṇ ṇṇ
VI. N	..	nna nâ	..	..	..	..	..	ñśch	ñśchh	ñj	ñjh	ūñ	m̐ṣhṭ	m̐ṣhṭh	ṇḍ	ṇḍh	ṇṇ
VII. P	p (b)	ba bâ	..	..	bg	bgh	bṅ ṅṅ	..	..	bj	bjh	bñ mñ	..	..	bḍ	bḍh	bṇ mṇ
VIII. M	m (ṁ)	..	ṁk (ṅk)	ṁkh (ṅkh)	ṁg (ṅg)	ṁgh (ṅgh)	ṁṅ (ṅṅ)	ṁch (ūch)	ṁchh (ūchh)	ṁj (ūj)	ṁjh (ūjh)	ṁñ (ũñ)	ṁṭ (ṇṭ)	ṁṭh (ṇṭh)	ṁḍ (ṇḍ)	ṁḍh (ṇḍh)	ṁṇ (ṇṇ)
IXa. Ḥ and Ṛ exc. ÁḤ and ÂḤ	ḥ	ra râ	χk / ḥk	χkh / ḥkh	rg	rgh	rṅ	śch	śchh	rj	rjh	rñ	shṭ	shṭh	rḍ	rḍh	rṇ
IXb. ÁḤ	id.	âa ââ	id.	id.	âg	âgh	âṅ	id.	id.	âj	âjh	âñ	id.	id.	âḍ	âḍh	âṇ
ÁḤ (not ÂR)	id.	o' aâ	id.	id.	og	ogh	oṅ	id.	id.	oj	ojh	oñ	id.	id.	oḍ	oḍh	oṇ

FINAL	18 T	19 TH	20 D	21 DH	22 N	23 P	24 PH	25 B	26 BH	27 M	28 Y	29 R	30 L	31 V	32 Ś	33 SH	34 S	35 H
I. K	..	..	gd	gdh	gn nn	..	..	gb	gbh	gm ṅm	gy	gr	gl	gv	kś kchh	..	..	g-h ggh
II. Ṅ	..	..	..	..	..	..	..	..	..	..	..	..	..	..	ṅś ṅkś ṅkchh	ṅśh ṅkṣh	ṅs ṅks	..
III. Ṭ	..	..	ḍd	ḍdh	ḍn ṇn	..	..	ḍb	ḍbh	ḍm ṇm	ḍy	ḍr	ḍl	ḍv	ṭś ṭchh	..	ṭs ṭts	ḍ-h ḍḍh
IV. Ṇ	..	..	..	..	..	..	..	..	..	..	..	..	..	..	ṇś ṇṭś ṇṭchh	ṇṣh ṇṭṣh	ṇs ṇṭs	..
V. T	..	..	dd	ddh	dn nn	..	..	db	dbh	dm nm	dy	dr	ll	dv	(chś) chchh	..	..	d-h ddh
VI. N	m̐st	m̐sth	..	..	..	..	..	..	..	..	..	..	l̐l	..	ñś ñchś ñchchh ñchh	..	ns nts	..
VII. P	..	..	bd	bdh	bn mn	..	..	bb	bbh	bm mm	hy	br	bl	bv	pś pchh	..	..	b-h bbh
VIII. M	ṁt (nt)	ṁth (nth)	ṁd (nd)	ṁdh (ndh)	ṁn (nn)	ṁp (mp)	ṁph (mph)	ṁb (mb)	ṁbh (mbh)	ṁm (mm)	ṁy ẙy	ṁr	ṁl l̐l	ṁv r̐v	ṁś	ṁsh	ṁs	ṁh
IXa. Ḥ and Ṛ exc. ÁḤ and ÂḤ	st	sth	rd	rdh	rn	φp / ḥp	φph / ḥph	rb	rbh	rm	ry	ᵒr	rl	rv	śś / ḥś	shsh / ḥsh	ss / ḥs	rh
IXb. ÁḤ	id.	id.	âd	âdh	ân	id.	id.	âb	âbh	âm	ây	âr	âl	âv	id.	id.	id.	âh
ÁḤ (not ÂR)	id.	id.	od	odh	on	id.	id.	ob	obh	om	ov	or	ol	ov	id.	id.	id.	oh

Table showing the Combination of Final with Initial Consonants.

FINAL.	IN PAUSÂ.	1 अ आ &c.	2 क	3 ख	4 ग	5 घ	6 ङ	7 च	8 छ	9 ज	10 झ	11 ह	12 म	13 ट	14 ठ	15 ड	16 द	17 य
I. क्	क् (ग्)	ग	गा	…	…	ग्ग	ग्घ	ग्ङ्कु	…	…	ग्म	ग्ह	ग्म्कु	…	…	ग्ड	ग्ढ	ग्या कृष
II. ङ्	…	…	˘ङ्कु	ˆङ्खा	…	…	…	…	…	…	…	…	…	…	…	…	…	…
III. ट्	ट् (ड्)	ड	डा	…	…	झ्	य्	डु्यक	…	…	डु्म	डु्ह	डु्य्म	…	…	डु्	डु्	इय्य ब
IV. ण्	…	…	˘ण्य	ˆण्या	…	…	…	…	…	…	…	…	…	…	…	…	…	…
V. त्	त् (द्)	द	दा	…	…	ज	ब	द्कन्	ब	ज	ज	द्ह	न्स्म्	ड	ड	द्	द्	इय्य ब
VI. न्	…	…	˘ब	ˆना	…	…	…	…	˘ब	˘इछ	ज	म्ह	म्म्	˘ब	˘ब	ब	ब	ब
VII. प्	प् (ब्)	ब	बा	…	…	म्प	म	ड्कम्क	…	…	ज	ब्ह	ब्म्म	…	…	ब्ड	ब्ढ	म्या म्य
VIII. म्	म् (˙)	…	…	˙क(ङ्)	˙ख(ङ्ख)	˙ग(ङ्ग)	˙घ(ङ्घ)	˙च(ञ्च)	˙ज(ञ्ज)	˙न(ञ्)	˙ह(ह्ह)	˙म(म्म्)	˙ट(ण्ट)	˙ठ(ण्ठ)	˙ड(ण्ड)	˙ढ(ण्ढ)	˙य(य्य)
IX a. : and र् exc. ख: and आ:	:	र	य	+क :क	+ख :ख	गै	बे	कें	ब	ग्ह	मं	हिं	मैं	ड	ड	है	है	बो
IX b. आ:	id.	आब आभा	id.	id.	आग	आव	आक	id.	id.	आज	आह्र	आम	id.	id.	id.	आड	आढ	आय
ख: (not ख़र्)	id.	ओऽ बआ	id.	id.	ओग	ओव	ओक	id.	id.	ओज	ओह्र	ओम	id.	id.	id.	ओड	ओढ	ओय

Note—I. The sign … means that no change takes place in the initial or final letter. II. The sign ˘, before a letter, indicates that it is preceded by a short: the sign ˆ, that it is preceded by a long vowel: the sign o, that the letter is to be elided. III. In col. IX *b*, *id.* means that the form is the same as in col. IX *a*. IV. The sign ˙ is used to distinguish the real and necessary from the optional Anusvâra.

FINAL.	18 न	19 य	20 द	21 व	22 न	23 प	24 म	25 य	26 भ	27 म	28 य	29 र	30 ल	31 व	32 श	33 व	34 स	35 ह
I. क्	…	…	ग्द	ग्व	ग्न् / ग्ह्	…	…	ग्व	ग्भ	ग्म् / ग्ह्	ग्य	ग्र	ग्ल	ग्व	क्श / क्ष	…	…	ग्ह / ग्घ
II. ट्	…	…	…	…	…	…	…	…	…	…	…	…	…	…	ट्श / ड्श	ट्म / ड्म	ट्स / ड्स	…
III. द्	…	…	द्द	द्व	द्न् / द्ब्न	…	…	द्म	द्भ / ब्ल	द्म / द्ब्ल	द्य	ड्र	ड्	ड्	द्स / ह्द	…	द्स / द्ध	ह्द
IV. ष्	…	…	…	…	…	…	…	…	…	…	…	…	…	…	ष्श / ष्ट्श	ष्म / ष्ट्म	ष्स / ष्ट्स	…
V. म्	…	…	व	व	म्ब / म्व	…	…	व	व	म्न / म्म	व	द्र	व	व	(ष्) श / श	…	…	ह्ह
VI. न्	ँस	ँस्य	…	…	…	…	…	…	…	…	…	न्ल / ल्ल	…	न्व / म्व / म्म	म्य / ন্ম / म्म	…	न्स	…
VII. प्	…	…	ब्द	ब्व	ब्न् / ब्ब्न	…	…	ब्म	ब्भ	ब्म / ब्ब्म	ब्य	ब्र	ब्ल	ब्व	प्श / प्ष	…	…	ब्ह / ब्भ
VIII. र्	ँत (न)	ँय (न्य)	ँद (न्द)	ँथ (न्थ)	ँन (न)	ँय (न्य)	ँम (न्म)	ँव (न्न)	ँभ (न्भ)	ँम (न्म)	ँय / ँम	ँर	ँल / ँम	ँव / ँम	ँश	ँव / ँस	ँस	ँह
IXa. : and र् (exc. अः and आः)	स्त	स्य	दे	थे	नै	×प / :प	×म / :म	थे	भे	मे	ये	०र	ले	वे	श्श	म्य	स्स	हे
IXb. आः:	id.	id.	आद	आध	आन	id.	id.	आब	आभ	आम	आय	आर	आल	आव	id.	id.	id.	आह
IXb. अः (not अर्):	id.	id.	ओद	ओध	ओन	id.	id.	ओब	ओभ	ओम	ओय	ओर	ओल	ओव	id.	id.	id.	ओह

NATI, or Change of Dental न n *and* स s *into Lingual* ण ṇ *and* ष sh.

§ 95. In addition to the rules which require the modification of certain letters at the beginning and end of words, there are some other rules to be remembered which regulate the transition of dental न *n* and स *s* into lingual ण *ṇ* and ष *sh* in the body of words. Beginners should try to impress on their memory these rules as far as they concern the change of the dental nasal and sibilant into the lingual nasal and sibilant *in simple words :* with regard to compound nouns and verbs, the rules are very complicated and capricious, and can only be learnt by long practice.

Change of न n *into* ण ṇ.

§ 96. The dental न *n*, followed by a vowel, or by न *n*, म *m*, य *y*, and व *v*, is, in the middle of a word, changed into the lingual ण *ṇ* if it is preceded by the linguals ऋ *ṛi*, ॠ *ṛî*, र *r*, or ष *sh*. The influence of these letters on a following न *n* is not stopt by any vowel, by any guttural (क *k*, ख *kh*, ग *g*, घ *gh*, ङ *ṅ*, ह *h*, ˙ *ṁ*), or by any labial (प *p*, फ *ph*, ब *b*, भ *bh*, म *m*, व *v*), or by य *y*, intervening between the linguals and the न *n*. (Pâṇ. VIII. 4, 1; 2.)

Ex. नृ + नां = नृणां *nṛi + nâm = nṛiṇâm*, gen. plur. of नृ *nṛi*, man.

　कर्णः *karṇaḥ*, ear.

　दूषणं *dûshaṇam*, abuse.

　वृंहणं *vṛiṁhaṇam*, nourishing, (ह *h* is guttural and preceded by Anusvâra.)

　अर्केण *arkeṇa*, by the sun, (क *k* is guttural.)

　गृह्णाति *gṛihṇâti*, he takes, (ह *h* is guttural.)

　क्षिप्णुः *kshipṇuḥ*, throwing, (प *p* is labial.)

　प्रेम्णा *premṇâ*, by love, (म *m* is labial.)

　ब्रह्मण्यः *brahmaṇyaḥ*, kind to Brahmans, (ह *h* is guttural, म *m* is labial, and न *n* followed by य *y*.)

　निषण्णः *nishaṇṇaḥ*, rested, (न *n* is followed by न *n*, which is itself afterwards changed to ण *ṇ*.)

　अक्षण्वत् *akshaṇvat*, having eyes, (ण *ṇ* is followed by व *v*.)

　प्रायेण *prâyeṇa*, generally, (य *y* does not prevent the change.)

But　अर्चन *archana*, worship, (च *ch* is palatal.)

　अर्णवेन *arṇavena*, by the ocean, (ण *ṇ* is lingual.)

　दर्शनं *darśanam*, a system of philosophy, (श *ś* is palatal.)

　अर्धेन *ardhena*, by half, (ध *dh* is dental.)

　कुर्वन्ति *kurvanti*, they do, (न *n* is followed by त *t*.)

　रामान् *râmân*, the Râmas, (न *n* is final.)

Note—रुग्णः *rugṇaḥ*, like वृक्णः *vṛikṇaḥ* (Pâṇ. VI. 1, 16), should be written with ण ṇ. The ग *g* is no protection for the न *n*. Thus अग्नि *agni* has to be especially mentioned as an exception for not changing its न *n* into ण *ṇ* in compounds, such as शरदग्निः *śaradgniḥ*. (Pâṇ. *Gaṇa kshubhnâdi*.)

§ 97. The न n of नु nu, the sign of the Su conjugation, and the न n of
ना nâ, the sign of the Krî conjugation, are not changed into ण ṇ in the two
verbs तृप् trip and क्षुभ् kshubh (Pâṇ. VIII. 4, 39).   Hence

तृप्नोति tripnoti, he pleases *.   क्षुभ्नाति kshubhnâti, he shakes.
But   शृणोति śriṇoti, he hears.   पुष्णाति pushṇâti, he nourishes.
क्षुभाण kshubhâṇa, imper. shake.

Table showing the Changes of न n into ण ṇ.

ऋ ṛi,	in spite of intervening Vowels,	change	if there follow Vowels, or
ॠ ṛî,	Gutturals (including ह h and Anusvâra),	न n	न n,
र r,	Labials (including व v),	into	म m,
			य y,
ष sh,	and य y,	ण ṇ	व v.

§ 98. The changes here explained of न n in the middle of simple words,
(whether it belongs to a suffix or a termination,) are the most important to
remember.   But न n is likewise liable to be changed into ण ṇ when it
occurs in the second part of a compound the first part of which contains
one of the letters ऋ ṛi, ॠ ṛî, र r, or ष sh, and particularly after certain
prepositions.   Here, however, the rules are much more uncertain, and we
must depend on the dictionary rather than on the grammar for the right
employment of the dental or lingual nasals.   The following rules are the
most important :

1. The change of न n into ण ṇ does not take place unless the two members
of the compound are combined so as to express a single conception.
Hence वार्ध्री bârdhrî, a leathern thong, + नस nasa, nose, gives वार्ध्रीणसः
bârdhrîṇasaḥ, if it is the name of a certain animal ; according to Wilson,
of a goat with long ears ; according to others, of a rhinoceros, or a bird.
(Uṇâdi-Sûtras, ed. Aufrecht, s. v. Pâṇ. VIII. 4, 3.)   But चर्मन् charman,
leather, + नासिका nâsikâ, nose, gives चर्मनासिकः charmanâsikaḥ, if it means
having a leathern nose.   An important exception is सर्वनामन् sarvanâman,
a technical term for pronouns, (सर्व sarva being the first in their list,)
which Pâṇini himself employs with the dental न n only. (Pâṇ. I. I, 27.)
Other proper names not following the general rule, are त्रिनयनः trinayanaḥ†,

---

* In the Veda we find तृप्णुहि tripṇuhi, Rv. II. 16, 6 ; तृप्णवः tripṇavaḥ, Rv. III. 42, 2.

† The Sârasvatî says संज्ञायां वा, that the n is optionally changed when Trinayanaḥ is
a name.   Hence त्रिनयनः trinayanaḥ or त्रिणयनः triṇayanaḥ. ९. १६. २३.

three-eyed, name of S'iva; रघुनंदनः *raghunandanaḥ*, name of Râma; स्वर्भानुः *svarbhânuḥ*, name of Rahu, &c.

Words to be remembered:

अग्रणीः *agraṇîḥ*, first, principal, from अग्र *agra*, front, and नी *nî*, to lead.

ग्रामणीः *grâmaṇîḥ*, head borough, from ग्राम *grâma*, multitude, and नी *nî*, to lead.

वृत्रघ्नः *vritraghnaḥ*, Indra, killer of Vṛitra; but वृत्रहणं *vritrahaṇam*, acc. of वृत्रहन् *vritrahan*. (Pân. VIII. 4, 12; 22.)

गिरिनदी or गिरिणदी *girinadî* or *giriṇadî*, mountain-stream.

परात्ह्नं *parâhnam*, afternoon, from परा *parâ*, over, and अहन् *ahan*, day; but सर्वाह्नः *sarvâhṇaḥ*, the whole day, from सर्व *sarva*, all, and अहन् *ahan*, day; and the same whenever the first word ends in अ *a*. (Pân. VIII. 4, 7.)

There are minute distinctions, according to which, for instance, क्षीरपानं *kshîrapânam* if it means the drinking of milk, or a vessel for drinking milk, कंसः क्षीरपानः *kaṁsaḥ kshîrapânaḥ*, may be pronounced with dental or lingual *n* (न *n* or ण *ṇ*); but if it is the name of a tribe who live on milk, it must be pronounced क्षीरपाणः *kshîrapâṇaḥ*, milk-drinking. (Pân. VIII. 4, 9 and 10.) In the same manner दर्भवाह्णं *darbhavâhṇam*, a hay-cart, is spelt with lingual ण *ṇ*; while in ordinary compounds, such as इंद्रवाहनं *indravâhanam*, a vehicle belonging to Indra, the dental न *n* remains unchanged. (Pân. VIII. 4, 8.)

2. In a compound consisting of more than two words the न *n* of any one word can only be affected by the word immediately preceding. Hence माषवापेण *mâsha-vâpeṇa*, by sowing beans; but माषकुंभवापेन *mâsha-kumbha-vâpena*, by sowing from a bean-jar. (Pân. VIII. 4, 38.)

3. In a compound the change of न *n* into ण *ṇ* does not take place if the first word ends in ग *g*.

Ex. ऋक् + अयनं = ऋगयनं *ṛik* + *ayanam* = *ṛigayanam*.

Some grammarians restrict this to proper names. (Pân. VIII. 4, 3, 5.)

Or if it ends in ष *sh*, and the next is formed by a primary suffix with न *n*.

Ex. निः + पानं = निष्पानं *niḥ* + *pânam* = *nishpânam*.

यजुः + पावनं = यजुष्पावनं *yajuḥ* + *pâvanam* = *yajushpâvanam*. (Pân. VIII. 4, 35.)

4. In compounds the न *n* of nouns ending in न *n*, and the न *n* of case-terminations, if followed by a vowel, are always liable to change.

व्रीहिवापिन् *vrîhivâpin*, rice-sowing, may form the genitive व्रीहिवापिणः *vrîhivâpiṇaḥ*; but also व्रीहिवापिनः *vrîhivâpinaḥ*.

व्रीहिवापाणि or व्रीहिवापानि *vrîhivâpâṇi* or *vrîhivâpâni*, nom. plur. neut.

व्रीहिवापेण or व्रीहिवापेन *vrîhivâpeṇa* or *vrîhivâpena*, instrum. sing.

Likewise feminines such as व्रीहिवापिणी or व्रीहिवापिनी *vrîhivâpiṇî* or *vrîhivâpinî*.
(Kâs´.-Vṛitti VIII. 4, 11.)

Note—The न् n of secondary suffixes, attached to the end of compounds, is, under the general conditions, always changed to ण् ṇ. Thus खरप: *kharapaḥ* (i. e. donkey-keeper) becomes खारपायण: *khârapâyaṇaḥ*, the descendant of Kharapa. मातृभोगीण: *mâtṛibhogîṇaḥ*, fit to be possessed by a mother, from मातृ *mâtṛi*, mother, and भोग: *bhogaḥ*, enjoyment, with the adjectival suffix ईन *îna* (*samâsânta*), is always spelt with ण् ṇ. (See also § 98. 6.) Again, while गर्गभगिनी *gargabhaginî*, the sister of Garga, always retains its dental न् n, being an ordinary compound, गर्गभगिणी *gargabhagiṇî* would have the lingual ण् ṇ, if it was derived from गर्गभग: *gargabhagaḥ*, the share of Garga, with the adjectival suffix इन् *in*, fem. इनी *inî*, enjoying the share of Garga. Words which after they have been compounded take a new suffix are treated in fact like single words (*samânapada*), and therefore follow the general rule of § 96. (Pâṇ. VIII. 4, 3. Kâs´.-Vṛitti VIII. 4, 11, vârt.)

5. If the second part of the compound is monosyllabic, then the change of a final न् n followed by a terminational vowel, or of a terminational न् n, is obligatory. (Pâṇ. VIII. 4, 12.)

Ex. वृत्रहन् *vritrahan*, Vritra-killer; gen. वृत्रहण: *vritrahaṇaḥ*; but दीर्घाह्नी *dîrghâhnî*. (Pâṇ. VIII. 4, 7.)

सुरप: *surâpaḥ*, drinking surâ; nom. plur. neut. सुरापाणि *surâpâṇi*.

क्षीरप: *kshîrapaḥ*, drinking milk; instrum. sing. क्षीरपेण *kshîrapeṇa*.

6. If the second part of a compound contains a guttural, the change is obligatory, even though the second part be not monosyllabic. (Pâṇ. VIII. 4, 13.)

Ex. हरिकाम: *harikâmaḥ*, loving Hari; instrum. sing. हरिकामेण *harikâmeṇa*; but अग्रगामिनि *agragâmini*. (Pâṇ. VIII. 3, 92.)

शुष्कगोमयेण *śushkagomayeṇa*, instrum. sing. of शुष्कगोमय *śushkagomaya*; (शुष्क *śushka*, dry, गोमय *gomaya*, dung.)

7. Likewise after prepositions which contain an र् r, the न् n of primary affixes, such as अन *ana*, अनि *ani*, अनीय *anîya*, इन् *in*, न *na* (if preceded by a vowel), and मान *mâna*, is changed to ण् ṇ, but under certain restrictions. (Pâṇ. VIII. 4, 29.)

Ex. प्रवपणं *pravapaṇam*; प्रमाणं *pramâṇam*; प्राप्यमाणं *prâpyamâṇam*.

While in these cases the change is pronounced obligatory, it is said to be optional after causative verbs (Pâṇ. VIII. 4, 30), and after verbs beginning and ending in consonants with any vowel but अ *a* (Pâṇ. VIII. 4, 31); hence प्रयापणं and °नं *prayâpaṇam* and *prayâpanam*; प्रकोपणं or °नं *prakopaṇam* or *prakopanam*. Again, after verbs beginning in a vowel (not अ *a*) and strengthening their bases by nasalization, the change is necessary; it is forbidden in other verbs, not beginning with vowels, though they require nasalization: hence प्र + इंगनं = प्रेंगणं *pra + iṅganam = preṅgaṇam*; but प्र + कंपनं = प्रकंपनं *pra + kampanam = prakampanam*.

Lastly, there are several roots which defy all these rules, viz. भा *bhâ,* भू *bhû,* पू *pû,* कम् *kam,* गम् *gam,* प्याय् *pyây,* वेप् *vep :* hence प्रभानं *prabhânam* &c., never प्रभाणं *prabhâṇam ;* प्रवेपनं *pravepanam,* never प्रवेपणं *pravepaṇam.*

8. After prepositions containing an र *r,* such as अंतर् *antar,* निर् *nir,* परा *parâ,* परि *pari,* and प्र *pra,* and after दुर् *dur,* the change of न *n* into ण *ṇ* takes place :

1. In most roots beginning with न *n.* (Pâṇ. VIII. 4, 14.)

प्र + नमति = प्रणमति *pra + namati = praṇamati,* he bows.

परा + नुदति = पराणुदति *parâ + nudati = parâṇudati,* he pushes away.

अंतः + नयति = अंतर्णयति *antaḥ + nayati = antarṇayati,* he leads in.

प्र + नायकः = प्रणायकः *pra + nâyakaḥ = praṇâyakaḥ,* a leader.

The roots which are liable to this change of their initial न *n* are entered in the Dhâtupâṭha, the list of roots of native grammarians, as beginning with ण *ṇ.* Thus we should find the root नम् *nam* entered as णम् *ṇam,* simply in order thus to indicate its liability to change.

2. In a few roots this change is optional if they are followed by Kṛit affixes, viz. (Pâṇ. VIII. 4, 33.)

णिस् *nis,* to kiss; प्रणिंसितव्यं or प्रनिंसितव्यं *praṇiṁsitavyam* or *praniṁsitavyam.*

णिक्ष् *niksh,* to kiss; प्रणिक्षणं or प्रनिक्षणं *praṇikshaṇam* or *pranikshaṇam.*

णिद् *nid,* to blame; प्रणिंदनं or प्रनिंदनं *praṇindanam* or *pranindanam.*

3. In a few roots the initial न *n* resists all change, and these roots are entered in the Dhâtupâṭha as beginning with न *n,* viz. (Pâṇ. VI. 1, 65, vârt.)

नृत् *nṛit,* to dance.	नाट् *nâṭ,* to fall down, (Chur *.)
नंद् *nand,* to rejoice.	नाथ् *nâth,* to ask.
नर्द् *nard,* to howl.	नाध् *nâdh,* to beg.
नक्क् *nakk,* to destroy.	नी *nṛî,* to lead.

Ex. परिनर्तनं *parinartanam ;* परिनंदनं *parinandanam.*

4. The root नश् *naś,* to destroy, changes न *n* into ण *ṇ* only when its श *ś* is not changed to ष *sh.* प्र + नश्यते = प्रणश्यते *pra + naśyate = praṇaśyate ;* but प्र + नष्टः = प्रनष्टः *pra + nashṭaḥ = pranashṭaḥ,* destroyed. (Pâṇ. VIII. 4, 36.)

5. In the root अन् *an,* to breathe, the न *n* is changed to ण *ṇ* if the र *r* is not separated from the न *n* by more than one letter. Thus प्र + अनिति = प्राणिति *pra + aniti = prâṇiti,* he breathes; but परि + अनिति = पर्यनिति *pari + aniti = paryaniti* (Pâtañjali). The reduplicated aorist forms प्राणिणत् *prâṇiṇat ;* the desiderative with परा *parâ* is पराणिणिषति *parâṇiṇishati.* (Pâṇ. VIII. 4, 19, 21.)

---

* It is not नट् *naṭ,* to dance, but नट् *ṇaṭ* of the Chur class, and hence written with a long *â.* Siddh.-Kaum. vol. II. p. 41, note.

6. In the root हन् *han*, to kill, the न *n* is changed except where ह *h* has to be changed to घ *gh*. (Pâṇ. VIII. 4, 22.) Thus प्र + हन्यते = प्रहण्यते *pra* + *hanyate* = *prahaṇyate*, he is struck down; अंतर्हण्यते *antarhaṇyate* (Pâṇ. VIII. 4, 24); but प्र + घ्नंति = प्रघ्नंति *pra* + *ghnanti* = *praghnanti*, they kill. Also प्रहणनं *prahaṇanam*, killing.

The change is optional again where न *n* is followed by म *m* or व *v*. (Pâṇ. VIII. 4, 23.) Thus प्रहन्मि or प्रहण्मि *prahanmi* or *prahaṇmi*; प्रहन्वः or प्रहण्वः *prahanvaḥ* or *prahaṇvaḥ*.

7. The न *n* of नु *nu* of the Su and of ना *nâ* of the Krî conjugation is changed to ण *ṇ* in the verbs हि *hi*, to send, and मी *mî*, to destroy. (Pâṇ. VIII. 4, 15.)

Ex. प्रहिण्वंति *prahiṇvanti*; प्रमीण्वंति *pramîṇanti*.

8. The न *n* of the termination आनि *âni* in the imperative is changeable. (Pâṇ. VIII. 4, 16.) Thus प्र + भवानि = प्रभवाणि *pra* + *bhavâni* = *prabhavâṇi*.

9. The न *n* of the preposition नि *ni*, if preceded by प्र *pra*, परि *pari*, &c., is changed into ण *ṇ* before the verbs (Pâṇ. VIII. 4, 17) गद् *gad*, to speak, नद् *nad*, to shout, पत् *pat*, to fall, पद् *pad*, to go, the verbs called घु *ghu*, मांङ्* *mâ*, to measure, मेङ् *me*, to change, सो *so*, to destroy, हन् *han*, to kill, या *yâ*, to go, वा *vâ*, to blow, द्रा *drâ*, to flee or to sleep, प्सा *psâ*, to eat, वप् *vap*, to sow or to weave, वह् *vah*, to bear, शम् *śam*, to be tranquil (*div*), चि *chi*, to collect, दिह् *dih*, to anoint.

The same change takes place even when the augment intervenes. (Pâṇ. VIII. 4, 17, vârt.)

प्रण्यगदत् *praṇyagadat*; प्रण्यनदत् *praṇyanadat*.

§ 99. In all other verbs except those which follow गद् *gad*, the change of नि *ni* after प्र *pra*, परि *pari*, &c., is optional.

प्रनिपचति or प्रणिपचति *pranipachati* or *praṇipachati*.

Except again in verbs beginning with क *ka* or ख *kha*, or ending in ष *sh* (Pâṇ. VIII. 4, 18), in which the न *n* of नि *ni* remains unchanged.

प्रनिकरोति *pranikaroti*; प्रनिखादति *pranikhâdati*; प्रनिपिनष्टि *pranipinashṭi*.

---

* Where it seemed likely to be useful, the Sanskrit roots have been given with their diacritical letters (*anubandhas*), but only in their Devanâgarî form. Pâṇini in enumerating the roots which change नि *ni* after प्र *pra*, परि *pari*, &c., into णि *ṇi*, mentions मा *mâ*, but this, according to the commentaries, includes two roots, the root मांङ् *mâ*(*ṅ*), which forms मिमीते *mimîte*, he measures, and the root मेङ् *me*(*ṅ*), which forms मयते *mayate*, he changes. Where in this grammar the transcribed form of a root differs from its Devanâgarî original, the additional letters may always be looked upon as diacritical marks employed by native grammarians. Sometimes the class to which certain verbs belong has been indicated by adding the first verb of that class in brackets. Thus *śam* (*div*) means *śâmyati*, or *śam* conjugated like *div*, and not *śâmayate*.

Change of स् s into ष् sh.

§ 100. A dental स् *s* (chiefly of suffixes and terminations*), if preceded by any vowel except अ, आ *â*, or by क् *k*, र् *r*, ऌ *l*, is always changed into the lingual ष् *sh*, provided it be followed by a vowel, or by त् *t*, थ् *th*, न् *n*, म् *m*, य् *y*, or व् *v*; likewise by certain Taddhita suffixes, क *ka*, कल्प *kalpa*, पाश *pâsa*, &c.

If an inserted Anusvâra† or the Visarga or ष् *sh* intervenes between the vowel and the स् *s*, the change into ष् *sh* takes place nevertheless.

Ex. सर्पिस् *sarpis*, inflectional base; सर्पिः *sarpiḥ*, nom. sing. neut. clarified butter ; instrum. सर्पिषा *sarpishâ*; nom. plur. सर्पींषि *sarpîṁshi* (here the Anusvâra intervenes); loc. plur. सर्पिःषु *sarpiḥshu* (here the Visarga intervenes), or सर्पिष्षु *sarpishshu* (here the ष् *sh* intervenes).

वाक्षु *vâkshu*, loc. plur. of वाच् *vâch*, speech.

सर्वशक् + सु = सर्वशक्षु *sarvasak + su = sarvasakshu*, omnipotent.

चित्रलिख् (क्) + सु = चित्रलिक्षु *chitralikh (k) + su = chitralikshu*, painter.

गीर्षु *gîrshu*, loc. plur. of गिर् *gir*, speech.

कमल् + सु = कमल्षु *kamal + su = kamalshu*, naming the goddess Lakshmî.

ध्रोक्ष्यति *dhrokshyati*, fut. of द्रुह् *druh*, to hate; (here ह् *h* is changed to क् *k*, and the aspiration thrown on the initial द् *d*.)

पोक्ष्यति *pokshyati*, fut. of पुष् *push*, to nourish; (here ष् *sh* is changed into क् *k*.)

सर्पिः + कः = सर्पिष्कः *sarpiḥ + kaḥ = sarpishkaḥ* ; adj. formed by क *ka*, having clarified butter.

सर्पिः + तरः = सर्पिष्टरः *sarpiḥ + taraḥ = sarpishṭaraḥ*; (here the त् *t* of तरः *taraḥ* is changed into ट् *ṭ*, as in § 89, III. 2.) If the penultimate vowel be long, no change takes place ; गीस्तरा *gîstarâ*.   (Pân. VIII. 3, 101.)

सर्पिः + मत् = सर्पिष्मात् *sarpiḥ + mat = sarpishmat*, having clarified butter.

---

* The स् *s* must not be a radical स् *s*; hence सुपिसौ *supisau*, because the स् *s* belongs to the root पिस् *pis*. (Pân. VIII. 3, 59.) Yet आशिषः *âsishaḥ*, from root शास् *sâs*. The rules do not apply to final स् *s*; hence अग्निस्तत्र *agnis tatra*. (Pân. VIII. 3, 55.)

† The Anusvâra must be what Sanskrit grammarians call *num*, it must not represent a radical nasal; hence, even if we write पुंसु *puṁsu*, loc. plur. of पुंस् *puṁs*, man, Pada base पुम् *pum*, it does not become पुंषु *puṁshu*. (Pân. VIII. 3, 58.) According to Bopp and other European grammarians, who do not limit the Anusvâra to the inserted Anusvâra, we should have to write either पुंषु *puṁshu*, or, if we wish to preserve the स् *s*, पुंसु *puṁsu*. According to Pânini, however, पुंसु *puṁsu* is the right form. The Sârasvatî prescribes पुंक्षु *puṅkshu*.

Table showing the Changes of स s *into* ष sh.

Any Vowels except अ, आ *â,* (in spite of inserted Anusvâra, Visarga, or sibilant intervening,) also क *k,* र *r,* ल्ह *l* if immediately preceding,	change स *s* into ष *sh*	if there follow Vowels, or त *t,* थ *th,* न *n,* म *m,* य *y,* व *v.*

§ 101. The same rule produces the change of स *s* into ष *sh* in roots beginning with स *s,* if reduplicated, provided the vowel of the reduplicated syllable is not अ, आ *â:* Ex. स्वप् *svap,* to sleep ; Redupl. Perf. सुष्वाप *sushvâpa,* I have slept. सिध् *sidh,* Des. सिषित्सति *sishitsati.* This rule is liable to exceptions.

§ 102. Again, many roots beginning with स *s* change it into ष *sh* after prepositions requiring such a change, viz. अति *ati,* over, अनु *anu,* after, अपि *api,* upon, अभि *abhi,* towards, नि *ni,* in, निर् *nir,* out, परि *pari,* round, प्रति *prati,* towards, वि *vi,* away : Ex. अभि + स्तौति = अभिष्तौति *abhi + stauti =* *abhishṭauti,* he praises. The same change takes place even after the augment has been added, in which case the स *s* is really preceded by an अ *a :* Ex. अभ्यष्तौत् *abhyashṭaut,* he praised. Some verbs, after these prepositions, keep the ष *sh* in the reduplicated perfect : Ex. सिच् *sich,* to sprinkle ; अभिषिंचति *abhishiñchati,* he sprinkles ; अभिषिषेच *abhishishecha,* he has sprinkled. In the intensive सिच् *sich* does not follow this rule ; hence अभिसेसिच्यते *abhisesichyate* (Pâṇ. VIII. 3, 112) ; but in the desiderative स *s* is changed, अभिषिषिक्षति *abhishishikshati.* Many other cases must be learnt from the dictionary or from Pâṇini.

§ 103. In order to give an idea of the minuteness of the rules as collected by native grammarians, and of the complicated manner in which these rules are laid down, the following extracts from Pâṇini have been subjoined, though they by no means exhaust the subject according to the views of native grammarians. It need hardly be added that beginners should not attempt to burden their memory with these rules, though a glance at them may be useful by giving them an idea of the intricacies of Sanskrit grammar.

Native grammarians enumerate all monosyllabic verbs beginning with स *s,* and followed by a vowel or by a dental consonant, (likewise स्मि *smi,* to smile, स्विद् *svid,* to sweat, स्वद् *svad,* to taste, स्वञ्ज् *svañj,* to embrace, स्वप् *svap,* to sleep,) as if beginning with ष *sh.* Thus they write षिध् *shidh,* ष्ठा *shṭhâ,* ष्मि *shmi.* (Pâṇ. VI. 1, 64.)

This is not done with सृप् *srip,* to go, सृज् *srij,* to let off, स्तृ *stṛî,* to cover, स्तृ *stṛi,* to cover, स्त्यै *styai,* to sound, सेक् *sek,* to go, सृ *sṛi,* to go, in order to show that their initial स *s* is not liable to be changed into ष *sh* under any circumstances.

They then give the general rule that this initial ष *sh* is to be changed into स *s,* in all these verbs, except ष्ठिव् *shṭhiv,* to spit, and ष्वष्क् *shvashk,* to go, (and according to some in ष्त्यै *shṭyai,* Sâr.,) unless where ष *sh* is enjoined a second time.

Now ष् *sh* for स् *s* in these verbs is enjoined a second time:

1. When a preposition, or whatever else precedes it, requires such permutation, according to general rules. वि + स्तौति = विष्टौति *vi+stauti = vishṭauti*. सेव् *sev* forms सिषेव *sisheva* in the reduplicated perfect.

2. In desideratives, when the reduplicative syllable contains इ or उ *i* or *u*. सिध् *sidh*, Des. सिषित्सति *sishitsati*.

   But if the स् *s* of the desiderative element must itself be changed to ष् *sh*, the initial स् *s* remains unchanged. सिध् *sidh*, सिसेधिषति *sisedhishati*. (Pâṇ. VIII. 3, 61.)

   Except in स्तु *stu*, and in derivative verbs in अय *aya*, where स् *s* is changed to ष् *sh*. स्तु *stu*, Des. तुष्टूषति *tushṭūshati*. सिध् *sidh*, Caus. सेधयति *sedhayati*, Des. सिषेधयिषति *sishedhayishati*; but सुसूषति *susūshati*. (VIII. 3, 61.)

   Except again, in certain causatives, in अय *aya* (VIII. 3, 62), where स् *s* is not changed into ष् *sh*. स्विद् *svid*, सिस्वेदयिषति *sisvedayishati*. स्वद् *svad*, सिस्वादयिषति *sisvâdayishati*. सह् *sah*, सिसाहयिषति *sisâhayishati*.

3. In certain verbs, after prepositions which require such a change, even when they are separated from the verb by the augment, viz. सु *su* (*su*), सू *sû* (*tud*), सो *so* (*div*), स्तु *stu* (*ad*), स्तुभ् *stubh* (*bhû*); or even if separated by reduplication, in the verbs स्था *sthâ*, सेनय *senaya*, सिध् *sidh*, सिच् *sich*, संज् *sañj*, स्वंज् *svañj*, सद् *sad*, स्तंभ् *stambh*, स्वन् *svan*, सेव् *sev*, (the last only after परि *pari*, नि *ni*, वि *vi*: VIII. 3, 65.)

   After prepositions: अभिषुणोति *abhishuṇoti*. अभिषुवति *abhishuvati*. अभिष्यति *abhishyati*. परिष्टौति *parishṭauti*. परिष्टोभते *parishṭobhate*. अभिष्ठास्यति *abhishṭhâsyati*. अभिषेणयति *abhisheṇayati*. परिषेधति *parishedhati*. अभिषिंचति *abhishiñchati*. परिषजति *parishajati*. परिष्वजते *parishvajate* (VIII. 3, 65). निषीदति *nishîdati*, but प्रतिसीदति *pratisîdati* (VIII.3,66). अभिष्टभ्नाति *abhishṭabhnâti* (VIII.3,67 and 114). Also अवष्टभ्य *avashṭabhya* (VIII. 3, 68, in certain senses). वि and अवष्वणति *vi* and *avashvaṇati* (VIII. 3, 69, in the sense of eating). परिषेवते *parishevate*.

   After prepositions and augment: अभ्यषुणोत् *abhyashuṇot*. पर्यषुवत् *paryashuvat*. अभ्यष्यत् *abhyashyat*. पर्यष्टौत् *paryashṭaut*. अभ्यष्टोभत *abhyashṭobhata*. अभ्यष्ठात् *abhyashṭhât*. अभ्यषेणयत् *abhyasheṇayat*. पर्यषेधत् *paryashedhat*. अभ्यषिंचत् *abhyashiñchat*. पर्यषजत् *paryashajat*. अभ्यष्वजत *abhyashvajata*. अभ्यषीदत् *abhyashîdat*. अभ्यष्टभ्नात् *abhyashṭabhnât*. व्यष्वणत् *vyashvaṇat* and अवाष्वणत् *avâshvaṇat*. पर्यषेवत *paryashevata*.

   After prepositions and reduplication (VIII. 3, 64): अभितष्ठौ *abhitashṭhau*. अभिषिषेणयिषति *abhishisheṇayishati*. अभिषिषेधयिषति *abhishishedhayishati*. अभिषिषिक्षति *abhishishikshati*. अभिषिषंक्षति *abhishishankshati* and अभ्यषिषंक्षत् *abhyashishankshat*. परिषिष्वंक्षते *parishishvankshate*. निषिषत्सति *nishishatsati* (VIII. 3, 118). अभितष्टंभ *abhitashṭambha*. अवषष्व्वाण *avashashvâṇa*. परिषिषेव *parishisheva*, (the last only after परि *pari*, नि *ni*, वि *vi*.)

4. Only after the prepositions परि *pari*, नि *ni*, वि *vi*, the following words (VIII. 3, 70): the part. सितः *sitaḥ*, the subst. सयः *sayaḥ*, सिव् *siv*, सह् *sah*; कृ *kṛi* (if with initial स् *s*, स्कृ *skṛi*) and similar verbs; स्तु *stu*.

   The words mentioned in 4. and संज् *svañj* may optionally retain स् *s*, if the augment intervenes. (VIII. 3, 71.)

5. After the prepositions अनु *anu,* वि *vi,* परि *pari,* अभि *abhi,* नि *ni,* स्यंद् *syand* may take ष् *sh,* except when applied to living beings. (VIII. 3, 72.)

6. After the prep. वि *vi,* स्कंदिर् *skand* may take ष् *sh,* though not in the past participle in त *ta* (VIII. 3, 73), but after the prep. परि *pari,* throughout, even in the past participle (VIII. 3, 74). परिष्कन्नः or परिस्कन्नः *parishkannaḥ* or *pariskannaḥ.*

7. After the prep. निर् *nir,* नि *ni,* वि *vi,* the verbs स्फुर् *sphur* and स्फुल् *sphul* may take ष् *sh.* (VIII. 3, 76.)

8. After the prep. वि *vi,* स्कंभ् *skambh* must always take ष् *sh.* (VIII. 3, 77.)

9. The verb अस् *as,* after dropping its initial vowel, takes ष् *sh* after prepositions which cause such a change, and after प्रादुर् *prādur,* if the ष् *sh* is followed by य *y* or a vowel (VIII. 3, 87). अभिष्यात् *abhishyāt.* प्रादुःष्यात् *prāduḥshyāt.* प्रादुःषंति *prāduḥshanti.*

10. The verb स्वप् *svap,* when changed to सुप् *sup,* takes ष् *sh,* after सु *su,* वि *vi,* निर् *nir,* दुर् *dur* (VIII. 3, 88). सुषुप्तः *sushuptaḥ.* दुःषुप्तः *duḥshuptaḥ.*

Exceptional cases, where स् *s* is used, and not ष् *sh:*

11. The verb सिच् *sich,* followed by the intensive affix (VIII. 3, 112). अभिसेसिच्यते *abhisesichyate.*

12. The verb सिध् *sidh,* signifying to go (VIII. 3, 113). परिसेधति *parisedhati.*

13. The verb सह् *sah,* if changed to सोढ् *sodh* (VIII. 3, 115). परिसोढुं *parisodhum.*

14. The verbs स्तंभ् *stambh,* सिव् *siv,* सह् *sah,* in the reduplicated aorist (VIII. 3, 116). पर्यसीषहत् *paryasīshahat.*

15. The verb सु *su,* followed by the affixes of the 1st future, the conditional, or the desiderative (VIII. 3, 117). अभिसोष्यति *abhisoshyati.* अभिसुसूः *abhisusūḥ.*

16. The verbs सद् *sad,* स्वंज् *svañj,* in the reduplicated perfect (VIII. 3, 118). अभिषसाद *abhishasāda.* अभिषस्वजे *abhishasvaje.*

17. The verb सद् *sad,* optionally, if preceded by the augment (VIII. 3, 119). न्यषीदत् or न्यसीदत् *nyashīdat* or *nyasīdat.*

§ 104. There are many compounds in which the initial स् *s* of the second word is changed to ष् *sh,* if the first word ends in a vowel (except *ā*). Ex. युधिष्ठिर *yudhishṭhira,* from युधि *yudhi,* in battle, and स्थिर *sthira,* firm; सुष्ठु *sushṭhu,* well; दुष्ठु *dushṭhu,* ill; सुषमा *sushamā,* beautiful, विषमः *vishamaḥ,* difficult, from समः *samaḥ,* even; त्रिष्टुभ् *trishṭubh,* a metre; अग्नीषोमौ *agnīshomau,* Agni and Soma; मातृष्वसृ *mātṛishvasṛi,* mother's sister; पितृष्वसृ *pitṛishvasṛi,* father's sister; गोष्ठः *goshṭhaḥ,* cow-stable; अग्निष्टोमः *agnishṭomaḥ,* a sacrifice; ज्योतिष्टोमः *jyotishṭomaḥ,* a sacrifice, (here the final स् *s* of ज्योतिस् *jyotis* is dropt.) In तुरासाह् *turāsāh,* a name of Indra, and similar compounds, स् *s* is changed to ष् *sh* whenever ह् *h* becomes ट् *ṭ:* nom. तुरासाट् *turāshāṭ;* acc. तुरासाहं *turāsāham.* (Pân. VIII. 3, 56.)

Change of Dental ध dh into Lingual ढ ḍh.

§ 105. The ध *dh* of the second pers. plur. Âtm. is changed to ढ *ḍh* in the reduplicated perfect, the aorist, and in षीढ्वं *shīdhvam* of the benedictive, provided the ध *dh,* or the षी *sh* of षीढ्वं *shīdhvam,* follows immediately an inflective root ending in any vowel but अ, आ *ā.* (Pân. VIII. 3, 78.)

Ex. कृ *kṛi:* Perf. चकृढ्वे *chakṛiḍhve.*

  च्यु *chyu:* Aor. अच्योढ्वं *achyoḍhvam.*

  प्लु *plu:* Bened. प्लोषीढ्वं *ploshīḍhvam.*

But क्षिप् *kship;* Aor. अक्षिब्ध्वं *akshibdhvam.*

यज् *yaj;* Bened. यक्षीध्वं *yakshídhvam.*

If the same terminations are preceded by the intermediate इ *i,* and the इ *i* be preceded by य *y,* र *r,* ल *l,* व *v,* ह *h,* the change is optional.

Ex. लु *lu;* Perf. लुलुविध्वे *luluvidhve* or लुलुविढ्वे *luluviḍhve.*

लु *lu;* Aor. अलविध्वं *alavidhvam* or अलविढ्वं *alaviḍhvam.*

लु *lu;* Bened. लविषीध्वं *lavishídhvam* or लविषीढ्वं *lavishíḍhvam.*

But बुध् *budh;* Aor. अबोधिध्वं *abodhidhvam.*

Rules of Internal Sandhi.

§ 106. The phonetic rules contained in the preceding paragraphs (§ 32–94) apply, as has been stated, to the final and initial letters of words (*padas*), when brought into immediate contact with each other in a sentence, to the final and initial letters of words formed into compounds, and to the final letters of nominal bases before the Pada-terminations, and before certain secondary or Taddhita suffixes, beginning with any consonant except य *y.*

There is another class of phonetic rules applicable to the final letters of nominal (*prátipadika*) and verbal bases (*dhâtu*) before the other terminations of declension and conjugation, before primary or Krit suffixes, and before secondary or Taddhita suffixes, beginning with a vowel or य *y.* Some of these rules are general, and deserve to be remembered. But in many cases they either agree with the rules of External Sandhi, or are themselves liable to such numerous exceptions that it is far easier to learn the words or grammatical forms themselves, as we do in Greek and Latin, than to try to master the rules according to which they are formed or supposed to be formed.

The following are a few of the phonetic rules of what may be called *Internal Sandhi.* The student will find it useful to glance at them, without endeavouring, however, to impress them on his memory. After he has learnt that द्विष् *dvish,* to hate, forms द्वेष्मि *dveshmi,* I hate, द्वेक्षि *dvekshi,* thou hatest, द्वेष्टि *dveshṭi,* he hates, अद्वेट् *advet,* he hated, द्विद्धि *dviḍḍhi,* Hate! द्विट् *dvit,* a hater, द्विषः *dvishah,* of a hater, द्विट्सु *dvitsu,* among haters,—he will refer back with advantage to the rules, more or less general, which regulate the change of final ष *sh* into क *k,* ट *t,* ड *ḍ,* &c.; but he will never learn his declensions and conjugations properly, if, instead of acquiring first the paradigms as they are, he endeavours to construct each form by itself, according to the phonetic rules laid down in the following paragraphs.

1. *Final Vowels.*

§ 107. No hiatus is tolerated in the middle of Sanskrit words. Words such as प्रउग *praüga,* fore-yoke, तितउ *titaü,* sieve, are isolated exceptions. The hiatus in compounds, such as पुरएता *pura-étá,* going in front, नमउक्तिः *nama-uktih,* saying of praise, which is produced by the elision of a final स् *s* before certain vowels, has been treated of under the head of External Sandhi. (§ 84. 2.)

§ 108. Final अ *a* and आ *á* coalesce with following vowels according to the general rules of Sandhi.

तुद् + अमि *tuda*+*ami* = तुदामि *tudámi*, I beat.
तुद् + इ *tuda*+*i* = तुदे *tude*, I beat, Âtm.
दान + इ *dána*+*i* = दाने *dáne*, in the gift.
दान + ई *dána*+*í* = दाने *dáne*, the two gifts.

If we admit the same set of terminations after bases ending in consonants and in short अ *a*, it becomes necessary to lay down some rules requiring final अ *a* to be dropt before certain vowels. Thus if अम् *am* is put down as the general termination of the acc. sing., as in वाचं *vách-am*, it is necessary to enjoin the omission of final अ *a* of शिव *śiva* before the अं *am* of the acc. sing., in order to arrive at शिवं *śivam*. In the same manner, if अं *am* is put down as the termination of the 1. p. sing. impf. Par., and ए *e* as that of the 1. p. sing. pres. Âtm., we can form regularly अद्वेषं *advesh-am* and द्विषे *dvishe*; but we have to lay down a new rule, according to which the final अ *a* of तुद् *tuda* is dropt, in order to arrive at the correct forms अतुदं *atud(a)-am* and तुदे *tud(a)e*. By following the system adopted in this grammar of giving two sets of terminations, and thus enabling the student to arrive at the actual forms of declension and conjugation by a merely mechanical combination of base and termination, it is possible to dispense with a number of these phonetic rules.

Again, in the declension of bases ending in radical आ *á*, certain phonetic rules had to be laid down, according to which the final आ *á* had to be elided before certain terminations beginning with vowels. Thus the dative शंखध्मा + ए *śaṅkhadhmá*+*e* was said to form शंखध्मे *śaṅkhadhme*, (to the shell-blower,) by dropping the final आ *á*, and not शंखध्मै *śaṅkhadhmai*. Here, too, the same result is obtained by admitting two bases for this as for many other nouns, and assigning the weak base, in which the आ *á* is dropt, to all the so-called Bha cases; the cases which Bopp calls the weakest cases (Pân. VI. 4, 140). Each of these systems has its advantages and defects, and the most practical plan is, no doubt, to learn the paradigms by heart without asking any questions as to the manner in which the base and the terminations were originally combined or glued together.

§ 109. With regard to verbal bases ending in long आ *á*, many special rules have to be observed, according to which final आ *á* is either elided, or changed to ई *í* or to ए *e*. These rules will be given in the chapter on Conjugation. Thus

पुना + अंति *puná*+*anti* = पुनंति *punanti*, they cleanse.
पुना + मः *puná*+*mah* = पुनीमः *puními̇ah*, we cleanse.
दा + हि *dá*+*hi* = देहि *dehi*, Give!

§ 110. Final इ *i*, ई *í*, उ *u*, ऊ *ú*, ऋ *ṛi*, if followed by vowels or diphthongs, are generally changed to य् *y*, व् *v*, र् *r*.

Ex. मति + ऐ = मत्यै *mati*+*ai* = *matyai*, to the mind.
जिगि + उः = जिग्युः *jigi*+*uh* = *jigyuh*, they have conquered.
भानु + ओः = भान्वोः *bhánu*+*oh* = *bhánvoh*, of the two splendours.
पितृ + आ = पित्रा *pitṛi*+*á* = *pitrá*, by the father.
विभी + अति = विभ्यति *bibhí*+*ati* = *bibhyati*, they fear.

In some cases इ *i* and ई *í* are changed to इय् *iy;* उ *u* and ऊ *ú* to उव् *uv;* ऋ *ri* to रि् *ri;* ॠ *rí* to इर् *ir* and, after labials, to उर् *ur.*

Ex. शिश्रि + अथु: = शिश्रियथु: *sisri+athuh = sisriyathuh,* you (two) have gone.

भी + इ = भिय *bhí+i = bhiyi,* in fear.

यु + अंति = युवंति *yu+anti = yuvanti,* they join.

युयु + उ: = युयुयु: *yuyu+uh = yuyuvuh,* they have joined.

सुषु + ए = सुषुवे *sushu+e = sushuve,* I have brought forth.

भू + इ = भुवि *bhú+i = bhuvi,* on earth.

मृ + अते = म्रियते *mri+ate = mriyate,* he dies.

गृ + अति = गिरति *gri+ati = girati,* he swallows.

पपृ + इ = पपुरि *paprí+i = papuri,* liberal.

When either the one or the other takes place must be learnt from paradigms and from special rules given under the heads of Declension and Conjugation. See बिभ्यति *bibhyati* from भी *bhí,* but जिह्रियति *jihriyati* from ह्री *hrí.*

§ 111. Final ॠ *rí,* if followed by terminational consonants, is changed to इर् *ír;* and after labials to उर् *úr.*

गृ *grí,* to shout; Passive गीर्यते *gír-yate;* Part. गीर्ण: *gírnah.*

पृ *prí,* to fill; Passive पूर्यते *púr-yate;* Part पूर्ण: *púrnah.*

Before the य् *y* of the Passive, Intensive, and Benedictive, final इ *i* and उ *u* are lengthened, final ऋ *ri* changed to रि *ri,* final ॠ *rí* to इर् *ír* or उर् *úr.* (See § 390.)

§ 112. ए *e,* ऐ *ai,* ओ *o,* औ *au,* before vowels and diphthongs, are generally changed into अय् *ay,* आय् *áy,* अव् *av,* आव् *áv.*

दे + अते = दयते *de+ate = dayate,* he protects.

रै + ए = राये *rai+e = ráye,* to wealth.

गो + ए = गवे *go+e = gave,* to the cow.

नौ + अ: = नाव: *nau+ah = návah,* the ships.

Roots terminated by a radical diphthong (except व्ये *vye* in redupl. perf., Pâṇ. VI. 1, 46) change it into आ *á* before any affix except those of the so-called special tenses. (Pâṇ. VI. 1, 45.)

दे + ता = दाता *de+tá = dátá,* he will protect.

दे + सीय = दासीय *de+síya = dásíya,* May I protect !

म्लै + ता = म्लाता *mlai+tá = mlátá,* he will wither.

शो + ता = शाता *so+tá = sátá,* he will pare.

But in the Present ग्लै + अति = ग्लायति *glai+ati = gláyati,* he is weary.

2. *Final Consonants.*

§ 113. The rules according to which the consonants which can occur at the end of a word are restricted to क् *k,* ङ् *n,* ट् *t,* ण् *n,* त् *t,* न् *n,* प् *p,* म् *m,* ल् *l,* : *h,* ं *m,* must likewise be observed where the last letter of a nominal or verbal base becomes final, i. e. where it is not followed by any derivative letter or syllable.

Thus the nominal base युध् *yudh,* battle, would in the vocative singular be

युध् *yudh.* Here, however, the ध् *dh* must be changed into द् *d*, because no aspirate is tolerated as a final (§ 54. 1); and द् *d* is changed into त् *t*, because no word can end in a soft consonant (§ 54. 2). वाच् *vâch*, speech, in the voc. sing. would change its च् *ch* into क् *k*, because palatals can never be final (§ 54. 3).

In अधोक् *adhok*, instead of अदोह् *adoh*, the aspiration of the final is thrown back on the initial द् *d* (§ 118). The final ह् *h* or घ् *gh*, after losing its aspiration, becomes ग् *g*, which is further changed to क् *k*.

§ 114. Nominal or verbal bases ending in consonants and followed by terminations consisting of a single consonant, drop the termination altogether, two consonants not being tolerated at the end of a word (§ 55). The final consonants of the base are then treated like other final consonants.

वाच् + स् = वाक् *vâch + s = vâk*, speech ; nom. sing.

प्रांच् + स् = प्राङ् *prânch + s = prân*, eastern ; nom. sing. masc. Here प्राङ्क् *prânk*, which remains after the dropping of स् *s*, is, according to the same rule, reduced again to प्राङ् *prân*, the final nasal remaining guttural, because it would have been guttural if the final क् *k* had remained.

सुवल्ग् + स् = सुवल् *suvalg + s = suval*, well jumping. Here, after the dropping of स् *s*, there would remain सुवल्क् *suvalk*; but as no word can end in two consonants, this is reduced to सुवल् *suval*. Before the Pada-terminations सुवल्ग् *suvalg* assumes its Pada form सुवल् *suval* (§ 53); hence instrum. plur. सुवल्भिः *suvalbhih*.

अहन् + स् = अहन् *ahan + s = ahan*, thou killedst ; 2. p. sing. impf. Par.

अद्वेष् + त् = अद्वेट् *advesh + t = advet*, he hated ; 3. p. sing. impf. Par.

अदोह् + त् = अधोक् *adoh + t = adhok*, he milked ; 3. p. sing. impf. Par.

Exceptions will be seen under the heads of Declension and Conjugation.

§ 115. With regard to the changes of the final consonants of nominal and verbal bases, before terminations, the general rule is,

1. Terminations beginning with sonant letters, require a sonant letter at the end of the nominal or verbal base.

2. Terminations beginning with surd letters, require a surd letter at the end of the nominal or verbal base.

3. In this general rule the terminations beginning with *vowels, semivowels,* or *nasals* are excluded, i. e. they produce no change in the final consonant of the base.

1. वच् + धि = वग्धि *vach + dhi = vagdhi*, Speak ! 2. p. sing. imp. Par.

पृच् + ध्वे = पृग्ध्वे *prich + dhve = prigdhve*, you mix ; 2. p. plur. pres. Âtm.

2. अद् + सि = अत्सि *ad + si = atsi*, 2. p. sing. pres. thou eatest.

अद् + ति = अत्ति *ad + ti = atti*, 3. p. sing. pres. he eats.

3. मरुत् + इ = मरुति *marut + i = maruti*, loc. sing. in the wind.

वच् + मि = वच्मि *vach + mi = vachmi*, I speak.

ग्रथ् + यते = ग्रथ्यते *grath + yate = grathyate*, it is arranged.

Exceptions such as भिद् + नः = भिन्नः *bhid + nah = bhinnah*, divided, भज् + नः = भग्नः *bhaj + nah = bhagnah*, broken, must be learnt by practice rather than by rule.

§ 116. Aspirates, if followed by terminations beginning with any letter (except vowels and semivowels and nasals), lose their aspiration. (§ 54. 1.)

Ex. मामथ् + ति = मामत्ति *mâmath + ti = mâmatti*, 3. p. sing. pres. Par. of the intensive मामथ् *mâmath*, he shakes much.

रुन्ध् + ध्वे = रुन्द्ध्वे *rundh + dhve = runddhve*, 2. p. plur. pres. Âtm. of रुध् *rudh*, you impede.

लभ् + स्ये = लप्स्ये *labh + sye = lapsye*, I shall take.

But युध् + इ = युधि *yudh + i = yudhi*, loc. sing. in battle.

लोभ् + यः = लोभ्यः *lobh + yah = lobhyah*, to be desired.

क्षुभ् + नाति = क्षुभ्नाति *kshubh + nâti = kshubhnâti*, he agitates.

It is a general rule that two aspirates can never meet in ordinary Sanskrit.

§ 117. If final घ *gh*, ढ *dh*, ध *dh*, भ *bh* are followed by त *t* or थ *th*, they are changed to the corresponding soft letters, ग *g*, ड *d*, द *d*, ब *b*, but the त *t* and थ *th* are likewise softened, and the द *d* receives the aspiration. See also § 128.

Ex. रुणध् + ति = रुणद्धि *runadh + ti = runaddhi*, he obstructs.

लभ् + तः = लब्धः *labh + tah = labdhah*, taken.

रुन्ध् + थः = रुन्द्धः *rundh + thah = runddhah* (also spelt रुन्धः *rundhah*), you two obstruct.

रुन्ध् + तः = रुन्द्धः *rundh + tah = runddhah*, they two obstruct.

अबान्ध् + तं = अबान्द्धं *abândh + tam = abânddham*, 2. p. dual aor. 1. Par. you two bound.

अबंध् + थाः = अबंद्धाः *abandh + thâh = abanddhâh*, 2. p. sing. aor. 1. Âtm. thou boundest.

In अबान्द्धं *abânddham*, 2. p. dual aor. 1. Par., the aspiration of final ध *dh* is not thrown back upon the initial ब *b*, because it is supposed to be absorbed by the तं *tam* of the termination, changed into धं *dham*. The same applies to अबंद्धाः *abanddhâh*, though here the termination थाः *thâh* was aspirated in itself.

§ 118. If घ *gh*, ढ *dh*, ध *dh*, भ *bh*, ह *h*, at the end of a syllable, lose their aspiration either as final or as being followed by ध्व *dhv* (not by धि *dhi*), भ *bh*, स *s*, they throw their aspiration back upon the initial letters, provided these letters be no other than ग *g*, ड *d*, द *d*, ब *b*. See § 93.

Ex. Inflective base बुध् *budh*, to know; nom. sing. भुत् *bhut*, knowing.

Instrum. plur. भुद्भिः *bhudbhih*.

Loc. plur. भुत्सु *bhutsu*.

Second pers. plur. aor. Âtm. अभुद्ध्वं *abhuddhvam*.

Second pers. sing. pres. Intens. बोबोध् + सि = बोभोत्सि *bobodh + si = bobhotsi*.

Desiderative of दभ् *dabh*, धिप्सति *dhipsati*, he wishes to hurt.

First pers. sing. fut. of बंध् + स्यामि = भंत्स्यामि *bandh+syámi=bhantsyámi*, I shall bind.

दह् *dah*, to burn; धक् *dhak*, nom. sing. a burner.

दुह् *duh*, to milk; अधुग्ध्वं *adhugdhvam*, 2. p. plur. impf. Átm.: but 2. p. sing. imp. Par. दुग्धि *dugdhi*.

Note—दध् *dadh*, the reduplicated base of धा *dhá*, दधामि *dadhámi*, I place, throws the lost aspiration of the final ध *dh* back on the initial द *d*, not only before ध्व *dhv*, स *s*, but likewise before त *t* and थ *th*, where we might have expected the application of § 117. दध् + तः = धत्तः *dadh+tah=dhattah*; दध् + थः = धत्थः *dadh+thah=dhatthah*; दध् + से = धत्से *dadh+se=dhatse*; दध् + ध्वं = धद्ध्वं *dadh+dhvam=dhaddhvam*.

§ 119. If च *ch*, ज *j*, झ *jh* are final, or followed by a termination beginning with any letter, except vowels, semivowels, or nasals, they are changed to क *k* or ग *g*.

Ex. Nominal base वाच् *vách*; voc. वाक् *vák*, speech.

Verbal base वच् *vach*; 3. p. sing. pres. वच् + ति = वक्ति *vach+ti=vakti*.

युंज् + धि = युंग्धि *yuñj+dhi=yuṅgdhi*, 2. p. sing. imp. Join!

But loc. sing. वाच् + इ = वाचि *vách+i=váchi*.

वाच् + य = वाच्य *vách+ya=váchya*, to be spoken.

वच् + मः = वच्मः *vach+mah=vachmah*, we speak.

वच् + वः = वच्वः *vach+vah=vachvah*, we two speak. (See also § 124.)

§ 120. ष *sh* at the end of nominal and verbal bases, if it becomes the final of a word, is changed into ट *ṭ*.

Ex. Nominal base द्विष् *dvish*; nom. sing. द्विट् *dviṭ*, a hater.

Verbal base द्विष् *dvish*; 3. p. sing. impf. Par. अद्वेट् *advet*, he hated.

§ 121. Before verbal terminations beginning with स *s*, it is treated like क *k*.

Ex. द्वेष् + सि = द्वेक्षि *dvesh+si=dvekshi*, thou hatest; aor. अद्विक्षत् *advikshat*, he hated. पोक्ष्यति *pokshyati* (*posh+syati*), he will nourish.

§ 122. Before त *t* or थ *th* it remains unchanged itself, but changes त *t* and थ *th* into ट *ṭ* and ठ *ṭh*.

Ex. द्विष् + तः = द्विष्टः *dvish+tah=dvishṭah*, they (two) hate.

सर्पिष् + तमं = सर्पिष्टमं *sarpish+tamam=sarpishṭamam*, the best clarified butter.

This rule admits of a more general application, namely, that every dental त *t*, थ *th*, द *d*, ध *dh*, न *n*, and स *s*, is changed into the corresponding lingual, if preceded by ट *ṭ*, ठ *ṭh*, ड *ḍ*, ढ *ḍh*, ण *ṇ*, and ष *sh*. (Pâṇ. VIII. 4, 41.)

Ex. द्विड् + धि = द्विड्ढि *dviḍ+dhi=dviḍḍhi*, hate thou.

मृड् + नाति = मृड्णाति *mriḍ+náti=mriḍṇáti*.

ईड् + ते = ईट्टे *íḍ+te=íṭṭe*, he praises.

षड् + नां = षण्णां *shaṭ+nám=shaṇṇám*, of six.

षड् + नवतिः = षण्णवतिः *shaṭ+navatih=shaṇṇavatih*, ninety-six. (Pâṇ. VIII. 4, 42, vârt.)

§ 123. Before other consonantal terminations ष *sh* is treated like ट *ṭ*.

Ex. द्विष् + ध्वं = द्विड्ढ्वं *dvish+dhvam=dviḍḍhvam*, 2. p. plur. imp. Átm. Hate ye

द्विष् + सु = द्विट्सु *dvish+su=dviṭsu*, loc. plur. among haters.

Exceptions to this rule, such as धृष् *dhṛish*, nom. धृक् *dhṛik*, and to other rules will be seen under the heads of Declension and Conjugation.

§ 124. In the roots भ्राज् *bhrâj*, to shine, मृज् *mṛij*, to wipe, यज् *yaj*, to sacrifice, राज् *râj*, to shine, सृज् *sṛij*, to let forth, and भ्रज्ज् *bhrajj*, to roast (भ्रस्ज् *bhrasj*, Pân. VIII. 2, 36), the final ज् *j* is replaced by ष् *sh*, which, in the cases enumerated above, is liable to the same changes as an original ष् *sh*. Thus

मृज् + थ = मृष्ठ *mṛij+tha = mṛishṭha*, you wipe.

राज् + सु = राट्सु *râj+su = râṭsu*.　अयज् + ध्वं = अयद्ध्वं *ayaj+dhvam = ayaḍḍhvam*.

§ 125. Most verbal and nominal bases ending in श् *ś*, छ् *chh*, क्ष् *ksh*, श्च् *śch* (some in ज् *j*, § 124) are treated exactly like those ending in simple ष् *sh*.

Ex. Nominal base विश् *viś*; nom. विट् *viṭ*, a man of the third caste.

Fut. वेश् + स्यामि = वेक्ष्यामि *veś + syâmi = vekshyâmi*, I shall enter.

Fut. periphr. वेश् + ता = वेष्टा *veś + tâ = veshṭâ*, he will enter.

विश् + ध्वं = विड्ढ्वं *viś + dhvam = viḍḍhvam*, enter you.

Loc. plur. विश् + सु = विट्सु *viś + su = viṭsu*, among men.

Nominal base प्राछ् *prâchh*; nom. प्राट् *prâṭ*, an asker.

Verbal base प्रछ् *prachh*; प्रछ् + स्यामि = प्रक्ष्यामि *prachh + syâmi = prakshyâmi*, I shall ask.

प्रछ् + ता = प्रष्टा *prachh + tâ = prashṭâ*, he will ask.

प्राछ् + सु = प्राट्सु *prâchh + su = prâṭsu*, among askers.

Nominal base तक्ष् *taksh*; तक्ष् + सु = तट्सु *taksh + su = taṭsu*, among carpenters.

Nominal base रक्ष् *raksh*; गोरक्ष् + सु = गोरट्सु *goraksh + su = goraṭsu*, among cow-herds.

Verbal base चक्ष् *chaksh*; चक्ष् + से = चक्षे *chaksh + se = chakshe*, thou seest.

चक्ष् + ध्वे = चड्ढ्वे *chaksh + dhve = chaḍḍhve*, you see.

व्रश्च् *vraśch*, to cut; nom. sing. वृट् *vṛiṭ*.

व्रश्च् + स्यामि = व्रक्ष्यामि *vraśch + syâmi = vrakshyâmi*, I shall cut.

व्रश्च् + ता = व्रष्टा *vraśch + tâ = vrashṭâ*, he will cut.

§ 126. The श् *ś* of दिश् *diś*, to show, दृश् *dṛiś*, to see, स्पृश् *spṛiś*, to touch, if final, or followed by Pada-terminations, is changed into क् *k*.

Ex. Nominal base दिश् *diś*; nom. sing. दिक् *dik*; instrum. plur. दिग्भिः *digbhiḥ*; loc. plur. दिक्षु *dikshu*.

दृश् *dṛiś*; nom. sing. दृक् *dṛik*; instrum. plur. दृग्भिः *dṛigbhiḥ*.

In the root नश् *naś*, the change of श् *ś* into क् *k* or ट् *ṭ* is optional (Pân. VIII. 2, 63). For further particulars see Declension and Conjugation.

§ 127. ह् *h* at the end of verbal bases, if followed by a termination beginning with स् *s*, is treated like घ् *gh*, i. e. like a guttural with an inherent aspiration, which aspiration may be thrown forward on the initial letter.

Ex. लेह् + स्यामि = लेक्ष्यामि *leh + syâmi = lekshyâmi*, I shall lick.

दोह् + स्यामि = धोक्ष्यामि *doh + syâmi = dhokshyâmi*, I shall milk.

§ 128. In all other cases, whether at the end of a word or followed by terminations, ह् *h* is treated either (1) like घ् *gh* in most words beginning with द् *d* (Pân. VIII. 2, 32), and in उष्णिह् *ushṇih*; or (2) like ढ् *ḍh* in all other words.

I

Ex. (1) दुह् *duh;* nom. धुक् *dhuk;* instrum. plur. धुग्भिः *dhugbhiḥ;* loc. plur. धुक्षु *dhukshu;* part. pass. दुग्धः *dugdhaḥ.*

दृह् + तः = दृढः *dṛih+taḥ = dṛiḍhaḥ,* fast, is an exception.

Ex. (2) लिह् *lih;* nom. लिट् *liṭ;* instrum. plur. लिड्भिः *liḍbhiḥ;* loc. plur. लिट्सु *liṭsu* (वाड् *vḍh,* वाड्सु *vḍṭsu*).

लिह् + तः = लीढः *lih+taḥ = līḍhaḥ.*

रुह् + तः = रूढः *ruh+taḥ = rūḍhaḥ.*

In लीढः *līḍhaḥ* and रूढः *rūḍhaḥ,* द् + त् *dh+t* are changed to द् + द् *dh+dh,* or, more correctly, to ड् *d+*ड् *dh* (§ 117); then the first ड् *d* is dropt and the vowel lengthened. The only vowel which is not lengthened is ऋ *ṛi;* e. g. वृह् + त = वृढ *vṛih+ta = vṛiḍha.*

The vowel of सह् *sah* and वह् *vah* is changed into ओ *o* (Pâṇ. VI. 3, 112), unless Samprasâraṇa is required, as in the part. ऊढः *ūḍhaḥ.* (Pâṇ. VI. 1, 15.)

§ 129. The final ह् *h* of certain roots (दुह् *druh,* मुह् *muh,* स्नुह् *snuh,* स्निह् *snih*) is treated either as घ् *gh* or ड् *dh.* From दुह् *druh,* to hate, we have in compounds the nom. sing. ध्रुक् *dhruk* and ध्रुट् *dhruṭ* (Pâṇ. VIII. 2, 33); past participle दुग्धः *drugdhaḥ* or दूढः *drūḍhaḥ.*

§ 130. The final ह् *h* of नह् *nah,* to bind, is treated as ध् *dh.*

Ex. उपानह् *upânah,* slipper; nom. sing. उपानत् *upânat;* instrum. plur. उपानद्भिः *upâ-nadbhiḥ.*

Past part. pass. नह् + तः = नद्धः *nah+taḥ = naddhaḥ,* bound.

As to अनडुह् *anaḍuh,* ox, &c., see Declension.

§ 131. The स् *s* of the nominal bases ध्वस् *dhvas,* falling, and स्रस् *sras,* tearing, if final or followed by Pada-terminations, and the स् *s* of वस् *vas,* the termination of the part. perf. Par., before Pada-terminations only, is changed to त् *t* (Pâṇ. VIII. 2, 72). See, however, § 173, 204.

Ex. ध्वस् *dhvas,* to fall; nom. sing. ध्वत् *dhvat,* nom. plur. ध्वस: *dhvasaḥ,* instrum. plur. ध्वद्भिः *dhvadbhiḥ.*

§ 132. Verbal bases ending in स् *s,* change it to त् *t,* before terminations of the general tenses beginning with स् *s.* (Pâṇ. VII. 4, 49.)

Ex. वस् *vas,* to dwell; fut. वस् + स्यामि = वत्स्यामि *vas+syâmi = vatsyâmi.*

Before other terminations beginning with स् *s,* final स् *s* remains unchanged.

वस् + से = वस्से *vas+se = vasse,* thou dwellest.

सस् + सि = सस्सि *sas+si = sassi,* thou sleepest.

निंस् + से = निंस्से *niṁs+se = niṁsse,* thou kissest.

पेपेस् + सि = पेपेस्सि *pepes+si = pepeshshi,* thou hurtest. (§ 100.)

In certain verbs final स् *s* is dropt before धि *dhi* of the imperative.

शास् + धि = शाधि *śâs+dhi = śâdhi.* (Pâṇ. VI. 4, 35.)

चकास् + धि = चकाधि *chakâs+dhi = chakâdhi.*

In the same verbs final स् *s,* if immediately followed by the termination of the second person, स् *s,* may be changed to त् *t* or remain स् *s.*

अशास् + स् = अशात् or अशाः *aśâs+s = aśât or aśâḥ.*

Before the त् *t* of the third person, it always becomes त् *t.*

अशास् + त् = अशात् *aśâs+t = aśât.* (Pâṇ. VIII. 2, 73, 74.)

Final त् *t*, द् *d*, ध् *dh* before the स् *s* of the 2nd pers. sing. Imperf. Par. may be regularly represented by त् *t* or by स् *s*; अवेत् *avet* or अवे: *aveh*, thou knewest; अरुणत् *aruṇat* or अरुण: *aruṇah*, thou preventedst. (Pâṇ. VIII. 2, 75.)

§ 133. न् *n* and म् *m* at the end of a nominal or verbal base, before sibilants (but not before the सु *su* of the loc. plur.), are changed to Anusvâra.

Ex. जिघांसति *jighâṁsati*, he wishes to kill, from हन् *han*.

क्रंस्यते *kraṁsyate*, he will step, from क्रम् *kram*.

But सुहिन्सु *suhinsu*, among good strikers, from सुहिन् *suhin*, Pada base of सुहिंस् *suhiṁs*. If न् *n* were changed to Anusvâra, we should have to write सुहिंषु *suhiṁshu*.

§ 134. न् *n* remains unchanged before semivowels.

Ex. हन्यते *hanyate*, he is killed, from हन् *han*.   तन्वन् *tanvan*, extending, from तन् *tan*. .

प्रेन्वनं *prenvanam**, propelling, from इन्व *inv*.

§ 135. म् *m* remains unchanged before the semivowels य् *y*, र् *r*, ल् *l*.

Ex. काम्य: *kâm-yah*, to be loved, from कम् *kam*.

ताम्रं *tâmram*, copper, from तम् *tam* and suffix र *ra*.

अम्ल: *amlah*, sour, from अम् *am* and suffix ल *la*.

§ 136. म् *m* at the end of a nominal or verbal base, if no suffix follows, or if followed by a Pada-termination, or by personal terminations beginning with म् *m* or व् *v*, is changed into न् *n*. (Pâṇ. VIII. 2, 65.)

Ex. प्रशान् *praśân*, nom. sing., and प्रशान्भि: *praśânbhih*, instrum. plur., प्रशान्सु *praśânsu*, loc. plur., from प्रशाम् *praśâm*, quieting. (Pâṇ. VIII. 2, 64.)

अगन्म *aganma*, we went, and अगन्व *aganva*, we two went, from गम् + म *gam+ma*, गम् + व *gam+va*.

But nom. plur. प्रशाम: *praśâmah*.

§ 137. With regard to nasals, the general rule is that in the body of a word the firsts, the seconds, the thirds, and the fourths of each class can only be preceded by their own fifths, though in writing the dot may be used as a general substitute. (§ 8.)

Ex. आशङ्कते or आशंकते *âśaṅkate* or *âśaṁkate*, he fears.

आलिङ्गति or आलिंगति *âliṅgati* or *âliṁgati*, he embraces.

वञ्चयति or वंचयति *vañchayati* or *vaṁchayati*, he cheats.

उत्कण्ठते or उत्कंठते *utkaṇṭhate* or *utkaṁṭhate*, he longs.

गन्तुं or गंतुं *gantum* or *gaṁtum*, to go.

कम्पते or कंपते *kampate* or *kaṁpate*, he trembles.

In compounds, such as सम् + कल्प: *sam + kalpah*, it is optional to change final म् *m*, standing at the end of a Pada, into the fifth or into real Anusvâra; hence संकल्प: or सङ्कल्प: *saṁkalpah* or *saṅkalpah*. (See § 77.)

---

* If the न् *n* before व् *v* were treated as Anusvâra, the second न् *n* would have to be changed into a lingual (§ 96). Pâṇ. VIII. 4, 2, vârt.

§ 138. In the body of a word, Anusvâra is the only nasal that can stand before the sibilants श *ś*, ष *sh*, स *s*, and ह *h*.

Ex. दंशनं *damśanam*, biting.. यजूंषि *yajûmshi*, the prayers. हंस: *hamsah*, goose. रंहते *ramhate*, he goes.

§ 139. न *n* following immediately after च *ch* or ज *j* is changed to ञ *ñ*.
Ex. याञ्जा *yâchñâ*, prayer. राज्ञी *rájñî*, queen. जज्ञे *jajñe*, he was born.

§ 140. छ *chh* in the middle of a word between vowels or diphthongs must be changed to च्छ *chchh*. (See § 91.)
Ex. ऋछ *richh*, to go; ऋच्छति *richchhati*, he goes. म्लेच्छ: *mlechchhah*, a barbarian.

§ 141. छ *chh* before a suffix beginning with न *n* or म *m* is changed to श *ś*.
Ex. प्रछ + न = प्रश्न: *prachh+na = praśnah*, question. पाप्रछ + मि = पाप्रश्मि *pâprachh+mi = pâpraśmi*, I ask frequently.
Before व *v* this change is optional.

§ 142. Roots ending in य *y* and व *v* throw off their final letters before terminations beginning with consonants, except य *y*.
Ex. पूय + त: = पूत: *pûy+tah = pûtah*, decaying. तुर्व + न: = तूर्ण: *turv+nah = túrnah*, killed. दिदिव + वान् = दिदिवान् *didiv+vân = didivân*, having played.

§ 143. Roots ending in व *v* and र *r*, if preceded by इ *i* or उ *u*, lengthen their इ *i* and उ *u*, if व *v* or र *r* is followed immediately by a terminational consonant. (Pâṇ. VIII. 2, 77.) See No. 92, त्वर् *tvar*.
Ex. दिव् *div*, to play, दीव्यति *dívyati*, he plays. Bened. दीव्यासं *dív-yâsam*. गुर् *gur*, to exert, गूर्ण: *gúrnah*. जॄ *jrî* (i. e. जिर् *jir*), to grow old, जीर्यति *jîryati*. गिर् *gir*, voice; instrum. plur. गीर्भि: *gírbhih*, loc. plur. गीर्षु *gírshu*.
There are exceptions. (Pâṇ. VIII. 2, 79.)
कुर् *kur*, to sound. Bened. कुर्यासं *kuryâsam*.
On a similar principle उ *u* is lengthened in तुर्व + आव: = तूर्वाव: *turv+âvah = túrvâvah*. (Pâṇ. VIII. 2, 78.)

§ 144. Nominal and verbal bases ending in इर् *ir* and उर् *ur* lengthen इ *i* and उ *u*, when र *r* becomes final after the loss of another final consonant. (Pâṇ. VIII. 2, 76.)
Ex. गिर् + स् = गीर् or गी: *gir+s = gîr* or *gîh*, nom. sing. voice.

§ 145. Nominal bases ending in इस् *is* or उस् *us* (the इस् *is* or उस् *us* being radical) lengthen इ *i* and उ *u* when final, and before terminations beginning with भ *bh* or स् *s*.
Loc. plur. सुपिस् + सु = सुपी:षु *supis+su = supîshu*; nom. sing. masc. and neut. सुपी: *supîh*.
Nom. sing. masc. सजुस् + स् = सजू: *sajus+s = sajûh*; nom. sing. neut. सजू: *sajûh*.

Doubling of Consonants.

§ 146. According to some grammarians any consonant except ₹ *r* and ₹ *h*, followed by another consonant and preceded by a vowel, may be doubled; likewise any consonant preceded by ₹ *r* or ₹ *h*, these letters being themselves preceded by a vowel. As no practical object is obtained by this practice, it is best, with S'âkalya, to discontinue it throughout.

In our editions doubling takes place most frequently where any consonant, except the sibilants and ₹ *h*, is preceded by ₹ *r* or ₹ *h*, these being again preceded by a vowel. Thus

अर्क *arka*, sun, is frequently written अर्क्क *arkka*.

ब्रह्मन् *brahman* may be written ब्रह्म्मन् *brahmman*.

If an aspirated consonant has to be doubled, the first loses its aspiration. Thus वर्धन or वर्द्धन *vardhana* or *varddhana*, increase.

§ 147. A sibilant after ₹ *r* must not be doubled, unless it is followed by a consonant. Thus it is always, वर्षाः *varshâḥ*, rainy season; आदर्शः *âdarśaḥ* (Prât. 387), mirror. But we may write either दर्श्यते or दर्श्श्यते *darśyate* or *darśśyate*, it is shown.

Explanation of some Grammatical Terms used by Native Grammarians.

§ 148. Some of the technical terms used by native grammarians have proved so useful that they have found ready admittance into our own grammatical terminology. *Guna* and *Vriddhi* are terms adopted by comparative grammarians in the absence of any classical words to mark the exact changes of vowels comprehended under these words by Pâṇini and others. Most Sanskrit grammars have besides sanctioned the use of such terms as *Parasmaipada, Âtmanepada, Tatpurusha, Bahuvrîhi, Karmadhâraya, Kṛit, Taddhita, Uṇâdi*, and many more. Nothing can be more perfect than the grammatical terminology of Pâṇini; but as it was contrived for his own peculiar system of grammar, it is difficult to adopt part of it without at the same time adopting the whole of his system. A few remarks, however, on some of Pâṇini's grammatical terms may be useful.

All words without exception, or according to some grammarians with very few exceptions, are derived from roots or *dhâtus*. These roots have been collected in what are called *Dhâtupâṭhas*, root-recitals, the most important of which is ascribed by tradition to Pâṇini*.

From these *dhâtus* or roots are derived by means of *pratyayas* or suffixes, not only all kinds of verbs, but all substantives and adjectives, and according to some, even all pronouns and particles. Thus from the root मन् *man*, to think, we have not only मनुते *man-u-te*, he thinks, but likewise मनस् *man-as*, mind, मानस *mânas-a*, mental, &c. Words thus formed, but without as yet any case-terminations attached to them, are called *Prâtipadika*, nominal bases. Thus from the root जन् *jan*, to beget, we have the *prâtipadika* or

---

* Siddhânta-Kaumudî, ed. Târânâtha, vol. II. p. I.

nominal base जन *jan-a*, man, and this by the addition of the sign of the nom. sing. becomes जनः *jan-a-ḥ*, a man.

Suffixes for the formation of nouns are of two kinds :

1. Those by which nouns are derived direct from roots ; Primary Suffixes.

2. Those by which nouns are derived from other nouns ; Secondary Suffixes. The former are called *Kṛit*, the latter *Taddhita*. Thus जन *jana*, man, is derived from the root जन् *jan* by the Kṛit suffix अ *a;* but जनीन *janína*, appropriate for man, is derived from जन *jana* by the Taddhita suffix ईन *ína*. The name *prátipadika* would apply both to जन *jana* and जनीन *janína*, as nominal bases, ready to receive the terminations of declension.

The Kṛit suffixes are subdivided into three classes:

1. *Kṛit*, properly so called, i. e. suffixes by which nouns can be regularly formed from roots with certain more or less definite meanings.   Thus by means of the suffix अथु *athu*, Sanskrit grammarians form

   वेपथु *vepathu*, trembling, from वेप् *vep*, to tremble.

   श्वयथु *śvayathu*, swelling, from श्वि *śvi*, to swell.

   क्षवथु *kshavathu*, sneezing, from क्षु *kshu*, to sneeze.

   दवथु *davathu*, vexation, from दु *du*, to vex, to burn.

2. *Kṛitya*, certain suffixes, such as तव्य *tavya*, अनीय *aníya*, य *ya*, एलिम *elima*, which may be treated as declinable verbal terminations.   Thus from कृ *kar*, to do, is formed कर्तव्य *kartavya*, करणीय *karaníya*, कार्य *kárya*, what is to be done, *faciendum*.

3. *Uṇádi*, suffixes used in the formation of nouns which to native grammarians seemed more or less irregular, either in form or meaning.   Thus from वस् *vas*, to dwell, both वस्तु *vastu*, a thing, and वास्तु *vástu*, a house.

The *Taddhita* suffixes are no further subdivided, but the feminine suffixes (*strípratyaya*) are sometimes treated as a separate class.

A root, followed by a suffix (*pratyaya*), whether *Kṛit* or *Taddhita*, is raised to the dignity of a base (*prátipadika*), and finally becomes a real word (*pada*) when it is finished by receiving a case-termination (*vibhakti*).

Every base, with regard to the suffix which is attached to it, is called *Aṅga*, body.   For technical purposes, however, new distinctions have been introduced by Sanskrit grammarians, according to which, in certain declensions, a base is only called *Aṅga* before the terminations of the nom. and acc. sing., nom. and acc. dual, and nom. plur. of masc. and fem. nouns; besides the nom. and acc. plur. of neuters.   The vocative generally follows the nominative.   These *Aṅga* cases together are called the *Sarvanámasthána*. Bopp calls them the *Strong Cases*.

Before terminations beginning with consonants (likewise before *Taddhitas* beginning with any consonant except य *y*) the base is called *Pada*, the same term which, as we saw before, was used to signify a noun, with a case-termination attached to it. The rules of Sandhi before these terminations are in the main the same as at the end of words.

Before the remaining terminations which begin with vowels (likewise before *Taddhitas* beginning with vowels and य *y*) the base is called *Bha*. Bopp calls the Pada and Bha cases together the *Weak Cases*; and when it is necessary to distinguish, he calls the Pada the *Middle* and the Bha the *Weakest Cases*.

Nouns, whether substantives, adjectives, or pronouns, are declined through three numbers with seven or, if we include the vocative, eight cases. A case-termination is called सुप् *sup* or विभक्ति *vibhakti*, lit. division.

Verbs are conjugated through the active and passive voices, and some through a middle voice also, in ten moods and tenses, with three persons and three numbers. A personal termination is called तिङ् *tiṅ* or विभक्ति *vibhakti*.

A declined noun as well as a conjugated verb, ending in a *vibhakti*, is called *Pada*.

Particles are comprehended under the name of *Nipâta*, literally what falls into a sentence, what takes its place before or after other words.

All particles are indeclinable (*avyaya*).

Particles are,

1. Those beginning with च *cha*, and, i. e. a list of words consisting of conjunctions, adverbs, interjections, collected by native grammarians.

2. Those beginning with प्र *pra*, before, i. e. a list of prepositions collected in the same manner by native grammarians.

When the prepositions beginning with प्र *pra* govern a substantive, they are called *Karmapravachanîya*. When they are joined to a root, they are called *Upasarga* or *Gati*. The name of *Gati* is also given to a class of adverbs which enter into close combination with verbs. Ex. अरी *ûrî* in अरीकृत्य *ûrîkritya*, assenting; खाट् *khât* in खाट्कृत्य *khâtkritya*, having made *khât*, i. e. the sound produced by clearing the throat.

CHAPTER III.

DECLENSION.

§ 149. Sanskrit nouns have three genders, Masculine, Feminine, and Neuter; three numbers, Singular, Dual, and Plural; and eight cases, Nominative, Accusative, Instrumental, Dative, Ablative, Genitive, Locative, and Vocative.

Note—There are a few nouns which are indeclinable in Sanskrit: खर् *svar*, heaven; अयास् *ayás*, fire; संवत् *samvat*, year, (of Vikramâditya's era); स्वयं *svayam*, self; साधि *sámi*, half; भूर् *bhúr*, atmosphere; सुदि *sudi*, the light fortnight, and बदि *badi*, the dark fortnight, the usual abbreviations for शुक्रपष्ठ: *suklapakshaḥ* and कृष्णपष्ठ: *krishṇapakshaḥ*, or बहुलपष्ठ: *bahulapakshaḥ*, (Warren, Kâlasankalita, p. 361.) According to Râdhakânta, सुदि *sudi* is used in the West only.

Some nouns are *pluralia tantum*, used in the plural only; दारा: *dárâḥ*, plur. masc. wife; आप: *ápaḥ*, plur. fem. water; वर्षा: *varshâḥ*, plur. fem. the rainy season, i. e. the rains; सिकता: *sikatâḥ*, plur. fem. sand; बहुला: *bahulâḥ*, the Pleiades.

§ 150. Sanskrit nouns may be divided into two classes:

1. Those that have bases ending in consonants.
2. Those that have bases ending in vowels.

1. *Bases ending in Consonants.*

§ 151. Nominal bases may end in all consonants except ङ *ṅ*, ञ *ñ*, य *y*. The final letters of the inflective bases of nouns, being either final or brought in contact with the initial letters of the terminations, are subject to some of the phonetic rules explained above.

§ 152. Bases ending in consonants receive the following terminations:

Terminations for Masculines and Feminines.

	SINGULAR.	DUAL.	PLURAL.
Nom.	स् *s* (which is always dropt)	औ *au*	अ: *aḥ*
Acc.	अं *am*	औ *au*	अ: *aḥ*
Instr.	आ *á*	भ्यां *bhyâm*	भि: *bhiḥ*
Dat.	ए *e*	भ्यां *bhyâm*	भ्य: *bhyaḥ*
Abl.	अ: *aḥ*	भ्यां *bhyâm*	भ्य: *bhyaḥ*
Gen.	अ: *aḥ*	ओ: *oḥ*	आं *ám*
Loc.	इ *i*	ओ: *oḥ*	सु *su*
Voc.	like Nom., except bases in न *n* and स् *s*	औ *au*	अ: *aḥ* .

Neuters have no termination in the Nom., Acc., and Voc. singular (Pada cases).

They take ई *í* in the Nom., Acc., and Voc. dual (Bha cases).

They take इ *i* in the Nom., Acc., and Voc. plural, and insert a nasal before the final consonant of the inflective base (Aṅga cases). This nasal is

determined by the consonant which follows it; hence ङ् *ṅ* before gutturals, ञ् *ñ*
before palatals, ण् *ṇ* before linguals, न् *n* before dentals, म् *m* before labials, Anu-
svâra before sibilants and ह् *h*.   Neuters ending in a nasal or a semivowel do
not insert the nasal in the plural. (See Sârasv. i. 8, 5; Colebrooke, p. 83.)

§ 153. Bases ending in consonants are divided again into two classes:

1. Unchangeable bases.

2. Changeable bases.

Nouns of the first class have the same base before all terminations, this base
being liable to such changes only as are required by the rules of Sandhi.
Nouns of the second class have two or three bases, according as they are
followed by certain terminations.

Thus from प्रत्यच् *pratyach*, Nom. Dual प्रत्यंची *pratyañch-au*; base प्रत्यंच् *pra-
tyañch*. (Aṅga.)

Instrum. Plur. प्रत्यग्भिः *pratyag-bhiḥ*; base प्रत्यच् *pratyach*. (Pada.)

Gen. Dual प्रतीचोः *pratîch-oḥ*; base प्रतीच् *pratîch*. (Bha.)

I. Unchangeable Bases.

Paradigm of a regular Noun with unchangeable Base.

§ 154. Bases ending in ण् *ṇ* and ल् *l* are not liable to any phonetic changes
before the terminations, except that in the Nom. Sing. the स् *s* of the termi-
nation is dropt (see § 114; 55); and that in the Loc. Plur. a ट् *ṭ* may be
inserted after the final ण् *ṇ*.

Base सुगण् *sugáṇ*, a ready reckoner, masc. fem. neut. (from सु *su*, well, and
root गण् *gaṇ*, to count.) (Accent, Pâṇ. vi. 1, 169.)

	SINGULAR. MASC. FEM.	DUAL. MASC. FEM.	PLURAL. MASC. FEM.
N.	सुगण् *sugáṇ*	सुगणौ *sugáṇ-au*	सुगणः *sugáṇ-aḥ*
A.	सुगणं *sugáṇ-am*		
I.	सुगणा *sugáṇ-á*	सुगणभ्यां *sugáṇ-bhyâm*	सुगणिभः *sugáṇ-bhiḥ*
D.	सुगणे *sugáṇ-e*		सुगणभ्यः *sugáṇ-bhyaḥ*
Ab.	सुगणः *sugáṇ-aḥ*	सुगणोः *sugáṇ-oḥ*	सुगणां *sugáṇ-ám*
G.			सुगणसु *sugáṇ-su* *
L.	सुगणि *sugáṇ-i*		
V.	सुगण् *súgaṇ*	सुगणौ *súgaṇ-au*	सुगणः *súgaṇ-aḥ*

	NEUTER.		
	SINGULAR.	DUAL.	PLURAL.
N. A. V.	सुगण् *sugáṇ* †	सुगणी *sugáṇ-î*	सुगणि *sugáṇ-i*.

* Or सुगंट्सु *sugáṇṭ-su*, § 74.

† As the accent in the vocative is always on the first syllable, it should be remembered,
once for all, that wherever the nom. acc. and voc. are given together, the vocative is under-
stood to have its proper accent on the first syllable. The vocative of the neuter *sugaṇ*
would therefore be, not *sugáṇ*, but *súgaṇ*.

§ 155. Bases ending in gutturals, क *k*, ख *kh*, ग *g*, घ *gh*.

These bases require no special rules.

Base सर्वशक् *sarvaśák*, omnipotent, masc. fem. neut. (from सर्व *sarva*, all, and root शक् *śak*, to be able.)

	SINGULAR. MASC. FEM.	DUAL. MASC. FEM.	PLURAL. MASC. FEM.
N.V.	सर्वशक् *sarvaśák*	सर्वशकौ *sarvaśákau*	सर्वशकः *sarvaśákaḥ*
A.	सर्वशकं *sarvaśákam*		
I.	सर्वशका *sarvaśákd*		सर्वशग्भिः *sarvaśágbhiḥ*
D.	सर्वशके *sarvaśáke*	सर्वशग्भ्यां *sarvaśágbhyám*	सर्वशग्भ्यः *sarvaśágbhyaḥ*
Ab. G.	सर्वशकः *sarvaśákaḥ*	सर्वशकोः *sarvaśákoḥ*	सर्वशकां *sarvaśákdm*
L.	सर्वशकि *sarvaśáki*		सर्वशक्षु *sarvaśákshu* *

NEUTER.

	SINGULAR.	DUAL.	PLURAL.
N.A.V.	सर्वशक् *sarvaśák*	सर्वशकी *sarvaśákí*	सर्वशंकि *sarvaśánki*

All regular nouns ending in क *k*, ख *kh*, ग *g*, घ *gh*, ट *ṭ*, ठ *ṭh*, ड *ḍ*, ढ *ḍh*, त *t*, थ *th*, द *d*, ध *dh*, प *p*, फ *ph*, ब *b*, भ *bh*, may be declined after the model of सर्वशक् *sarvaśák*.

§ 156. Base ending in ख *kh*. चित्रलिख् *chitralikh*, painter, (from चित्र *chitra*, picture, and root लिख् *likh*, to paint.)

	SINGULAR. MASC. FEM.	DUAL. MASC. FEM.	PLURAL. MASC. FEM.
N.V.	चित्रलिक् *chitralik†*	चित्रलिखौ *chitralikhau*	चित्रलिखः *chitralikhaḥ*
A.	चित्रलिखं *chitralikham*		
I.	चित्रलिखा *chitralikhd*		चित्रलिग्भिः *chitraligbhiḥ*
D.	चित्रलिखे *chitralikhe*	चित्रलिग्भ्यां *chitraligbhydm*	चित्रलिग्भ्यः *chitraligbhyaḥ*
Ab. G.	चित्रलिखः *chitralikhaḥ*	चित्रलिखोः *chitralikhoḥ*	चित्रलिखां *chitralikhdm*
L.	चित्रलिखि *chitralikhi*		चित्रलिक्षु *chitralikshu* *

NEUTER.

	SINGULAR.	DUAL.	PLURAL.
N.A.V.	चित्रलिक् *chitralik†*	चित्रलिखी *chitralikhí*	चित्रलिंखि *chitralinkhi*

Note—In the paradigms of regular nouns with unchangeable consonantal bases it will be sufficient to remember the Nom. Sing., Nom. Plur., Instr. Plur., Loc. Plur., and Nom.

---

* On the change of सु *su* after क *k*, see § 100.

† क *k* instead of ख *kh*, see § 113; 54. 1.

Plur. Neut. The Acc. Instr. Dat. Abl. Gen. Loc. Sing., Nom. Acc. Voc. Gen. Loc. Dual, Acc. Gen. Plur., follow the Nom. Plur. The Instr. Dat. Abl. Dual, Dat. Abl. Plur., follow the Instr. Plur. The Vocative is the same as the Nominative.

§ 157. Regular nouns to be declined like सर्वेशक् *sarvaśak*.

BASE.	NOM. S.	NOM. PL. M. F.	INSTR. PL.	LOC. PL.	NOM. PL. NEUT.
हरित् *harit*, green m. f. n.	हरित् *harit*	हरितः *haritah*	हरिद्भिः *haridbhih*	हरित्सु *haritsu*	हरिंति *harinti*
अग्निमथ् *agnimath*, fire-kindling m. f. n.	अग्निमात् *agnimat* *	अग्निमथः *agnimathah*	अग्निमद्भिः *agnimadbhih* †	अग्निमात्सु *agnimatsu* ‡	अग्निमंथि *agnimanthi*
सुहृद् *suhrid*, friendly m. f. n.	सुहृत् *suhrit*	सुहृदः *suhridah*	सुहृद्भिः *suhridbhih*	सुहृत्सु *suhritsu*	सुहृंदि *suhrindi*
बुध् *budh*, knowing m. f. n.	भुत् *bhut* ‖	बुधः *budhah*	भुद्भिः *bhudbhih*	भुत्सु *bhutsu*	बुंधि *bundhi*
गुप् *gup*, guardian m. f. n.	गुप् *gup*	गुपः *gupah*	गुब्भिः *gubbhih*	गुप्सु *gupsu*	गुंपि *gumpi*
ककुभ् *kakubh*, region f.	ककुप् *kakup*	ककुभः *kakubhah*	ककुब्भिः *kakubbhih*	ककुप्सु *kakupsu*	ºककुंभि *-kakumbhi*

§ 158. Bases ending in palatals, च *ch*, छ *chh*, ज *j*, झ *jh*.

Bases ending in च *ch* change च *ch* into क *k*, or ग *g*, except when followed by a termination beginning with a vowel.

Base जलमुच् *jalamuch*, masc. cloud (water-dropping).

	SINGULAR. MASC. FEM.	DUAL. MASC. FEM.	PLURAL. MASC. FEM.
N.V.	जलमुक् *jalamuk*	जलमुचौ *jalamuchau*	जलमुचः *jalamuchah*
A.	जलमुचं *jalamucham*	जलमुचौ *jalamuchau*	जलमुचः *jalamuchah*
I.	जलमुचा *jalamuchá*	जलमुग्भ्यां *jalamugbhyám*	जलमुग्भिः *jalamugbhih*
D.	जलमुचे *jalamuche*	जलमुग्भ्यां *jalamugbhyám*	जलमुग्भ्यः *jalamugbhyah*
Ab.	जलमुचः *jalamuchah*	जलमुग्भ्यां *jalamugbhyám*	जलमुग्भ्यः *jalamugbhyah*
G.	जलमुचः *jalamuchah*	जलमुचोः *jalamuchoh*	जलमुचां *jalamuchám*
L.	जलमुचि *jalamuchi*	जलमुचोः *jalamuchoh*	जलमुक्षु *jalamukshu*

NEUTER.		
SINGULAR.	DUAL.	PLURAL.
N. A. V. जलमुक् *jalamuk*	जलमुची *jalamuchí*	जलमुंचि *jalamuñchi*

Decline like जलमुच् *jalamuch*,—वाच् *vách*, fem. speech; त्वच् *tvach*, fem. skin; रुच् *ruch*, fem. light; सुच् *sruch*, fem. ladle.

---

* थ् *th* final changed into त् *t*. See § 113; 54. 1.   Final स् *s* dropt, § 55.
† See § 66.   ‡ See § 54. 1.   ‖ See § 118.

§ 159. Special bases in च ch.

BASE.	NOM. S.	INSTR. PL.	LOC. PL.	NOM. PL.
कुंच् *kruñch* *, moving crookedly, a curlew	कुंङ् *krúṅ*	कुंग्भिः *krúṅbhiḥ*	कुंक्षु *krúṅkshu*	कुंचः *krúñchaḥ* (Accent, Pâṇ. vi. 1, 182)
प्रांच् *prâñch*, if it means worshipping	प्रांङ् *prâṅ*	प्रांग्भिः *prâṅbhiḥ*	प्रांक्षु *prâṅkshu*	प्रांचः *prâñchaḥ* (Accent, Pâṇ. vi. 1, 182) (Acc. the same)
वृश्च् *vriśch* †, cutting	वृट् *vríṭ* ‡	वृड्भिः *vriḍbhíḥ*	वृट्सु *vriṭsú*	वृश्चः *vríśchaḥ* (Accent, Pâṇ. vi. 1, 168)

§ 160. Bases ending in छ *chh* change छ *chh* into श *ś*, which becomes ट *ṭ*, when final, and before consonants. (See § 125; 174. 6: Pâṇ. vi. 4, 19.)

BASE.	NOM. SING.	NOM. PL.	INSTR. PL.	LOC. PL.	NOM. PL. NEUT.
प्राछ् *prâchh*, an asker	प्राट् *prâṭ*	प्राशः *prâśaḥ*	प्राड्भिः *prâḍbhíḥ*	प्राट्सु *prâṭsú*	प्रांषि *prâṃśi*

§ 161. Bases ending in ज *j*, if regular, follow the example of nouns in च *ch*, except that they preserve ज *j* before vowels.

BASE.	NOM. SING.	NOM. PL.	INSTR. PL.	LOC. PL.	NOM. PL. NEUT.
रुज् *ruj*, disease	रुक् *rúk*	रुजः *rújaḥ*	रुग्भिः *rugbhíḥ*	रुक्षु *rukshú*	रुंजि *rúñji*
ऊर्ज् *úrj*, strength	ऊर्क् *úrk* ‖	ऊर्जः *úrjaḥ*	ऊर्ग्भिः *úrgbhiḥ*	ऊर्क्षु *úrkshu*	ऊर्जि *úrji*

Other regular nouns in ज *j*,—वणिज् *vaṇij*, m. merchant; भिषज् *bhishaj*, m. physician; ऋत्विज् *ritvij*, m. priest; स्रज् *sraj*, f. garland; असृज् *asrij*, n. blood. (On the optional forms of असृज् *asrij*, see § 214.) मज्ज् *majj*, Nom. Sing. मक् *mak*, diving.

§ 162. Bases ending in ज *j* changeable to ड *ḍ*.

Some bases ending in ज *j* change ज *j* into ट *ṭ* or ड *ḍ* when final, and before terminations beginning with consonants.

---

* Derived from the root कुंच् *kruñch*. The Nom. Sing. would have been कुंङ् + स् *kruṅk* + *s*; स् *s* and क् *k* are dropt, see § 114.

† Derived from the root व्रश्च् *vraśch*, (in the Dhâtupâṭha, ओव्रश्चू), to cut. According to Sanskrit grammarians, the penultimate स् *s* or श् *ś* is dropt, and च *ch* before consonants or if final changed into ट *ṭ*. (See § 114.)

‡ The form वृट् *vriṭ* (not व्रट् *vraṭ*) is confirmed by Siddhânta-Kaumudî (1863), vol. i. p. 182.

‖ On the two final consonants, see § 55. The Nom. Plur. Neut. would be ऊर्जि *úrji* or ऊंर्जि *úṃrji*. At the end of compounds the optional forms are ऊर्जि *úrji* or ऊर्ञि *úrñji*. The latter form is confirmed by Colebrooke, the Siddhânta-Kaumudî, vol. i. p. 194, and the Prakriyâ-Kaumudî. The Prakriyâ-Kaumudî (p. 44 a) says: ऊर्जि । झो नुधेति केषिात् । बहूर्जि नुम्प्रतिषेधः । बहूर्जि कुलानि । अंत्यात्पूर्वे नुमिज्ंत्येके । बहूर्ञि । (Pâṇ. vii. 1, 72, vârt.)

Base सम्राज् *samráj*, masc. sovereign.

	SINGULAR. MASC. FEM.	DUAL. MASC. FEM.	PLURAL. MASC. FEM.
N.V.	सम्राट् *samrát*	सम्राजौ *samrájau*	सम्राजः *samrájaḥ*
A.	सम्राजं *samrájam*		
I.	सम्राजा *samrájá*	सम्राड्भ्यां *samráḍbhyám*	सम्राड्भिः *samráḍbhiḥ*
D.	सम्राजे *samráje*		सम्राड्भ्यः *samráḍbhyaḥ*
Ab.	सम्राजः *samrájaḥ*		
G.		सम्राजोः *samrájoḥ*	सम्राजां *samrájám*
L.	सम्राजि *samráji*		सम्राट्सु *samrátsu* or सम्राट्त्सु *samráttsu* *

The words which follow this declension are mostly nouns derived, without any suffix, from the roots भ्राज् *bhráj* (दुभ्राज्, not भ्राज्), to shine; मृज् *mṛij*, to clean; यज् *yaj* (except ऋत्विज् *ṛitvij*), to sacrifice; राज् *ráj*, to shine, to rule; सृज् *sṛij*, to dismiss, to create, (स्रज् *sraj*, wreath, and असृज् *asṛij*, blood, are not derived from सृज् *sṛij*); भ्रज्ज् *bhrajj*, to roast (भ्रस्ज्). Also परिव्राज् *parivráj*, a mendicant.

BASE.	NOM. SING.	NOM. PLUR.	INSTR. PLUR.	LOC. PLUR.
विभ्राज् *vibhráj*, resplendent	विभ्राट् *vibhrát*†	विभ्राजः *vibhrájah*	विभ्राड्भिः *vibhráḍbhiḥ*	विभ्राट्सु *vibhrátsu*
देवेज् *devej*‡, worshipper of the gods	देवेट् *devet*	देवेजः *devejah*	देवेड्भिः *deveḍbhiḥ*	देवेट्सु *devetsu*
विश्वसृज् *viśvasṛij*, creator of the universe	विश्वसृट् *viśvasṛit*	विश्वसृजः *viśvasṛijah*	विश्वसृड्भिः *viśvasṛiḍbhiḥ*	विश्वसृट्सु *viśvasṛitsu*
परिव्राज् *parivráj*, a mendicant	परिव्राट् *parivrát*	परिव्राजः *parivrájah*	परिव्राड्भिः *parivráḍbhiḥ*	परिव्राट्सु *parivrátsu*
विश्वराज् *viśvaráj*‖, an universal monarch	विश्वाराट् *viśvárát*	विश्वराजः *viśvarájah*	विश्वाराड्भिः *viśváráḍbhiḥ*	विश्वाराट्सु *viśvárátsu*
भ्रज्ज् *bhṛijj*, roasting	भृट् *bhṛit*	भृज्जः *bhṛijjah*	भृड्भिः *bhṛiḍbhiḥ*	भृट्सु *bhṛitsú*

§ 163. Irregular bases in ज् *j*.

BASE.	NOM. SING.	NOM. PLUR.	INSTR. PLUR.	LOC. PLUR.
1. खञ्ज् *kháñj*¶, lame	खन् *khán*	खञ्जः *kháñjah*	खन्भिः *khanbhíḥ*	खन्सु *khansú*

---

* Cf. § 76.

† From another root, विभ्राक् *vibhrák*, विभ्राग्भिः *vibhrágbhiḥ* &c. may be formed. (Siddh.-Kaum. vol. I. p. 165.)

‡ From देव *deva*, god, and यज् *yaj*, to sacrifice, contracted into इज् *ij*.

‖ The lengthening of the अ *a* in विश्व *viśva* takes place whenever ज् *j* is changed into a lingual. (Pâṇ. VI. 3, 128.)

¶ See Siddh.-Kaum. ed. Târânâtha, vol. I. p. 165.

2. अवयाज् *avayáj*, name of a Vedic priest, has two bases. The Nom. Sing. is अवया: *avayáḥ*, and all the cases beginning with consonants (Pada cases) are formed from the same base, अवयस् *avayas*. The Voc. Sing., too, is irregular, being, against the rule of these bases, identical with the Nom. Sing. Some grammarians, however, allow हे अवय: *he avayaḥ*.

Base अवयस् *avayas* and अवयाज् *avayáj*.

	SINGULAR. MASC. FEM.	DUAL. MASC. FEM.	PLURAL. MASC. FEM.
N.	अवया: *avayáḥ*	अवयाजौ *avayájau*	अवयाज: *avayájaḥ*
A.	अवयाजं *avayájam*		
I.	अवयाजा *avayájá*		अवयोभि: *avayobhíḥ*
D.	अवयाजे *avayáje*	अवयोभ्यां *avayobhyám*	अवयोभ्य: *avayobhyaḥ*
Ab.	अवयाज: *avayájaḥ*		अवयाजां *avayájám*
G.		अवयाजो: *avayájoḥ*	
L.	अवयाजि *avayáji*		अवयःसु *avayaḥsu*
V.	अवया: *avayáḥ* or अवय: *avayaḥ*	like Nom.	like Nom.

§ 164. Bases ending in र *r*.

Bases ending in र *r* are regular, only इ *i* and उ *u*, preceding the र *r*, are lengthened, if the र *r* is final or followed by a consonant (§ 144). In the Loc. Plur. the final र *r* remains unchanged though followed by ष *sh*. (§ 90.)

Base गिर् *gir*, fem. voice.

	SINGULAR. MASC. FEM.	DUAL. MASC. FEM.	PLURAL. MASC. FEM.
N.V.	गी: *gíḥ*	गिरौ *gírau*	गिर: *gíraḥ*
A.	गिरं *gíram*		गीर्भि: *gírbhíḥ*
I.	गिरा *girá*	गीर्भ्यां *gírbhyám*	गीर्भ्य: *gírbhyáḥ*
D.	गिरे *giré*		
Ab.	गिर: *giráḥ*	गिरो: *giróḥ*	गिरां *girám*
G.			
L.	गिरि *girí*		गीर्षु *gírshu*

Base वार् *vár*, neut. water.

	SINGULAR.	NEUTER. DUAL.	PLURAL.
N.A.V.	वा: *váḥ*	वारी *várí**	वारि *vári*
I.	वारा *várá*	वार्भ्यां *várbhyám*	वार्भि: *várbhíḥ*, &c.

BASE.	NOM. SING.	NOM. PLUR.	INSTR. PLUR.	LOC. PLUR.
पुर् *pur*, f. town	पू: *púḥ*	पुर: *púraḥ*	पूर्भि: *púrbhíḥ*	पूर्षु *púrshu*
द्वार् *dvár*, f. door	द्वा: *dváḥ*	द्वार: *dváraḥ*	द्वार्भि: *dvárbhíḥ*	द्वार्षु *dvárshu*
किर् *kir*, m. f. n. scattering	की: *kíḥ*	किर: *kíraḥ*	कीर्भि: *kírbhíḥ*	कीर्षु *kírshu*†

---

* According to Pâṇ. VI. 1, 168, *várí* would have the accent on the first, while *hridí*, according to Pâṇ. VI. 1, 171, would have it on the second syllable, because the Nom. and Acc. Dual in the neuter are not Tritîyâdi, but are Asarvanâmasthâna.

† Siddh.-Kaum. vol. I. p. 125.

§ 165. Bases in स् s.

(A.) Bases formed by the suffixes अस् as, इस् is, उस् us.

Bases ending in स् s change the स् s according to the general euphonic rules explained above.　Thus

अस् as, if final, becomes अः aḥ.　(§ 83.)

अस् as followed by terminations beginning with vowels remains unchanged.

इस् and उस् is and us followed by terminations beginning with vowels are changed to इष् and उष् ish and ush.　(See § 100.)

अस् as before भ् bh becomes ओ o (§ 84. 3); इस् is and उस् us before भ् bh become इर् ir and उर् ur.　(§ 82.)

अस् as before सु su becomes अस् as or अः aḥ; इस् is and उस् us before सु su become इष् ish or इः iḥ, उष् ush or उः uḥ.

Besides these general rules, the following special rules should be observed:

1. Nouns formed by the suffix अस् as lengthen their अ a in the Nom. Sing. masc. and fem., but not in the Vocative.　Thus Nom. Sing. m. f. सुमनाः sumanâḥ, well-minded (εὐμενής); Voc. सुमनः sumanaḥ.

2. Nouns formed by the suffixes इस् or उस् is or us do not lengthen their vowel in the Nom. Sing. masc. and fem.　Hence Nom. Sing. m. f. सुज्योतिः sujyotiḥ, having good light, from सु su, good, and ज्योतिः jyotiḥ, n. light; सुचक्षुः suchakshuḥ, having good eyes, from सु su, good, and चक्षुः chakshuḥ, n. eye.　(Pân. v. 4, 133, com.)

3. Neuter nouns in अस् as, इस् is, उस् us, lengthen their vowel and nasalize it in the Nom. Acc. Voc. Plur.　From मनः manaḥ, मनांसि manâṁsi; from ज्योतिः jyotiḥ, ज्योतींषि jyotîṁshi; from चक्षुः chakshuḥ, चक्षूंषि chakshûṁshi.

Base सुमनस् sumânas, well-minded, masc. fem. neut. (from सु su and मनस् mánas, neut. mind.)

	SINGULAR. MASC. FEM.	DUAL. MASC. FEM.	PLURAL. MASC. FEM.
N.	सुमनाः sumânâḥ	सुमनसौ sumânasau	सुमनसः sumânasaḥ
A.	सुमनसं sumânasam	सुमनसौ sumânasau	सुमनसः sumânasaḥ
I.	सुमनसा sumânasâ	सुमनोभ्यां sumânobhyâm	सुमनोभिः sumânobhiḥ
D.	सुमनसे sumânase	सुमनोभ्यां sumânobhyâm	सुमनोभ्यः sumânobhyaḥ
Ab.	सुमनसः sumânasaḥ	सुमनसोः sumânasoḥ	सुमनोभ्यः sumânobhyaḥ
G.	सुमनसः sumânasaḥ	सुमनसोः sumânasoḥ	सुमनसां sumânasâm
L.	सुमनसि sumânasi	सुमनसोः sumânasoḥ	सुमनःसु sumânaḥsu
V.	सुमनः súmanaḥ	सुमनसौ súmanasau	सुमनसः súmanasaḥ

NEUTER.

	SINGULAR.	DUAL.	PLURAL.
N. A.V.	सुमनः sumânaḥ	सुमनसी sumânasî	सुमनांसि sumânâṁsi

The rest like the masc. and fem.

Base सुज्योतिस् *sujyotis*, well-lighted, masc. fem. neut. (from सु *su* and ज्योतिस् *jyotis*, neut. light.)

	SINGULAR.	DUAL.	PLURAL.
	MASC. FEM.	MASC. FEM.	MASC. FEM.
N.V.	सुज्योति: *sujyótiḥ*	सुज्योतिषौ *sujyótishau*	सुज्योतिष: *sujyótishaḥ*
A.	सुज्योतिषं *sujyótisham*		
I.	सुज्योतिषा *sujyótishá*	सुज्योतिर्भ्यां *sujyótirbhyám*	सुज्योतिर्भि: *sujyótirbhiḥ*
D.	सुज्योतिषे *sujyótishe*		सुज्योतिर्भ्य: *sujyótirbhyaḥ*
Ab.	सुज्योतिष: *sujyótishaḥ*		
G.		सुज्योतिषो: *sujyótishoḥ*	सुज्योतिषां *sujyótishám*
L.	सुज्योतिषि *sujyótishi*		सुज्योति:षु *sujyótiḥshu*

NEUTER.

	SINGULAR.	DUAL.	PLURAL.
N. A.V.	सुज्योति: *sujyótiḥ*	सुज्योतिषी *sujyótishí*	सुज्योतींषि *sujyótímshi*

The rest like the masc. and fem.

Decline after the model of सुमनस् *sumanas* and सुज्योतिस् *sujyotis* the following bases:

वेधस् *vedhas*, Nom. sing. वेधा: *vedháḥ*, m. wise. चंद्रमस् *chandramas*, N. s. चंद्रमा: *chandramáḥ*, m. moon. प्रचेतस् *prachetas*, N. s. प्रचेता: *prachetáḥ*, m., Nom. prop. of a lawgiver. दिवौकस् *divaukas*, N. s. दिवौका: *divaukáḥ*, m. a deity. विहायस् *viháyas*, N. s. विहाया: *viháyáḥ*, m. bird. अप्सरस् *apsaras*, N. s. अप्सरा: *apsaráḥ*, f. a nymph. महौजस् *mahaujas*, N. s. महौजा: *mahaujáḥ*, m. f. n. very mighty. पयस् *payas*, N. s. पय: *payaḥ*, n. milk. अयस् *ayas*, N. s. अय: *ayaḥ*, n. iron. यशस् *yaśas*, N. s. यश: *yaśaḥ*, n. praise. हविस् *havis*, N. s. हवि: *haviḥ*, n. oblation. अर्चिस् *archis*, N. s. अर्चि: *archiḥ*, n. splendour. आयुस् *áyus*, N. s. आयु: *áyuḥ*, n. life, age. वपुस् *vapus*, N. s. वपु: *vapuḥ*, n. body*.

§ 166. जरा *jará*, old age, may be declined throughout regularly as a feminine. (See § 238.) There is, however, another base जरस् *jaras*, equally feminine†, and equally regular, except that it is defective in all cases the terminations of which begin with consonants.

---

* Any of these neuter nouns may assume masc. and fem. terminations at the end of a compound; नष्टहवि: *nashṭahaviḥ*, Nom. sing. masc. one whose oblation is destroyed.

† Boehtlingk (Declination im Sanskrit, p. 125) gave जरस् *jaras*, rightly as feminine; in the dictionary, though oxytone, it is by mistake put down as neuter.

	Base जरा *jará.*		Base जरस् *jaras,*
	SINGULAR.		**SINGULAR.**
N.	जरा *jará**		deest; term. स् *s*
A.	जरां *jarám*		जरसं *jarás-am*
I.	जरया *jaráyá*		जरसा *jarás-á*
D.	जरायै *jaráyai*		जरसे *jarás-e*
Ab.	जराया: *jaráyáh*		जरस: *jarás-ah*
G.	जराया: *jaráyáh*		जरस: *jarás-ah*
L.	जरायां *jaráyám*		जरसि *jarás-i*
V.	जरे *járe*		deest
	DUAL.		**DUAL.**
N.A.V.	जरे *jaré*		जरसौ *jarás-au*
I.D.Ab.	जराभ्यां *jarábhyám*		deest; term. भ्यां *bhyám*
G.L.	जरयो: *jaráyoh*		जरसो: *jarás-oh*
	PLURAL.		**PLURAL.**
N.V.	जरा: *jaráh*		जरस: *jarás-ah*
A.	जरा: *jaráh*		जरस: *jarás-ah*
I.	जराभि: *jarábhih*		deest; term. भि: *bhih*
D.Ab.	जराभ्य: *jarábhyah*		deest; term. भ्य: *bhyah*
G.	जरायां *jaráṇám*		जरसां *jarás-ám*
L.	जरासु *jarásu*		deest; term. सु *su*

§ 167. In compositions, besides the regular forms from जरा *jará,* viz. निर्जर: *nirjarah,* निर्जरा *nirjará,* निर्जरं *nirjaram,* (ageless,) grammarians allow the base in स् *s* to be used before all terminations beginning with vowels†.

	SINGULAR.	**SINGULAR.**
	MASC.	**MASC. FEM.**
N.	निर्जर: *nirjarah* ‡	deest
A.	निर्जरं *nirjaram* or	निर्जरसं *nirjarasam*
I.	निर्जरेण *nirjareṇa* or	निर्जरसा *nirjarasá* (निर्जरसिन *nirjarasina,* masc.)
D.	निर्जराय *nirjaráya* or	निर्जरसे *nirjarase*
Ab.	निर्जरात् *nirjarát* or	निर्जरस: *nirjarasah* (निर्जरसात् *nirjarasát,* masc.)
G.	निर्जरस्य *nirjarasya* or	निर्जरस: *nirjarasuh* (निर्जरसस्य *nirjarasasya,* masc.)
L.	निर्जरे *nirjare* or	निर्जरसि *nirjarasi*
V.	निर्जर *nirjara*	deest

---

* The declension of जरा *jará,* as a regular fem. in आ *á,* is given here by anticipation for the sake of comparison with the defective जरस् *jarás.*

† By a pedantic adherence to the Sûtras of Pâṇini some monstrous forms (included in brackets) have been deduced by certain native grammarians, but deservedly reprobated by others.   (Siddh.-Kaum. vol. I. pp. 103, 141.)

‡ The declension of निर्जर: *nirjarah,* as a regular masc. in अ *a,* is given by anticipation for the sake of comparison with the defective निर्जरस् *nirjaras.*

	DUAL.	DUAL.
N. A. V.	निर्जरौ *nirjarau* or	निर्जरसौ *nirjarasau*
I. D. Ab.	निर्जराभ्यां *nirjarábhyám*	deest
G. L.	निर्जरयो: *nirjarayoh* or	निर्जरसो: *nirjarasoh*

	PLURAL.	PLURAL.
N. V.	निर्जरा: *nirjaráh* or	निर्जरस: *nirjarasah*
A.	निर्जरान् *nirjarán* or	निर्जरस: *nirjarasah*
I.	निर्जरै: *nirjaraih*	deest (निर्जरसै: *nirjarasaih*, masc.)
D. Ab.	निर्जरेभ्य: *nirjarebhyah*	deest
G.	निर्जराणां *nirjaránám* or	निर्जरसां *nirjarasám*
L.	निर्जरेषु *nirjareshu*	deest

Fem. निर्जरा *nirjará*, like कांता *kántá*. Neut. निर्जरं *nirjaram*, like कांतं *kántam*.	Neut. Sing. deest (निर्जरसं *nirjarasam*); Dual निर्जरसी *nirjarasí*; Plur. निर्जरांसि *nirjarámsi*.

§ 168. अनेहस् *anehas*, m. time, पुरुदंशस् *purudamśas*, m. name of Indra, form the Nom. Sing. अनेहा *anehá*, पुरुदंशा *purudamśá*, without final Visarga. The other cases are regular, like सुमनस् *sumanas*, m.   Voc. हे अनेह: *he anehah*.

§ 169. उशनस् *uśanas*, m. proper name, forms the Nom. Sing. उशना *uśaná* and the Voc. Sing. उशनस् *uśanas* or उशन: *uśanah* or उशन *uśana*. (Sâr. 1. 9, 73.)

§ 170. (B.) Bases ending in radical स् *s*.

1. From पिंड *pinda*, a lump, and ग्रस् *gras*, to swallow, a compound is formed, पिंडग्रस् *pindagras*, a lump-eater.

   From पिस् *pis*, to walk, and सु *su*, well, a compound is formed, सुपिस् *supis*, well-walking.

   From तुस् *tus*, to sound, and सु *su*, well, a compound is formed, सुतुस् *sutus*, well-sounding.

2. In forming the Nom. Sing. m. f. (and neuter), the rules laid down before with regard to nouns in which अस् *as*, इस् *is*, उस् *us*, belong to a suffix, are simply inverted. Nouns in इस् *is* and उस् *us* lengthen the vowel, nouns in अस् *as* leave it short.

   Ex. Nom. Sing. m. f. n. पिंडग्रा: *pindagrah*, सुपी: *supíh*, सुतू: *sutúh*.

3. In the Nom. Acc. Voc. Plur. of neuters, nouns in अस् *as*, इस् *is*, उस् *us*, nasalize their vowels, but do not lengthen them.

   Ex. Nom. Acc. Voc. Plur. neut. पिंडग्रांसि *pindagramsi*, सुपिंसि *supimsi*, सुतुंसि *sutumsi*.

4. Nouns in इस् *is* and उस् *us* lengthen their vowels before all terminations beginning with consonants.

   Ex. Instr. Plur. सुपीर्भि: *supírbhih*, सुतूर्भि: *sutúrbhih*, सुतूषु *sutúshu*.

5. The radical स् *s* of nouns ending in इस् *is* and उस् *us*, though followed by vowels, is not liable to be changed into ष *sh*. (See § 100, note.)

Base पिंडग्रस् *piṇḍagras*, eating a mouthful, masc. fem. neut.

SINGULAR. MASC. FEM.	DUAL. MASC. FEM.	PLURAL. MASC. FEM.
N.V. पिंडग्रः *piṇḍagraḥ*	पिंडग्रसौ *piṇḍagrasau*	पिंडग्रसः *piṇḍagrasaḥ*
A. पिंडग्रसं *piṇḍagrasam*		
I. पिंडग्रसा *piṇḍagrasá*		पिंडग्रोभिः *piṇḍagrobhiḥ*
D. पिंडग्रसे *piṇḍagrase*	पिंडग्रोभ्यां *piṇḍagrobhyám*	पिंडग्रोभ्यः *piṇḍagrobhyaḥ*
Ab. } पिंडग्रसः *piṇḍagrasaḥ*		
G.		पिंडग्रसां *piṇḍagrasám*
L. पिंडग्रसि *piṇḍagrasi*	पिंडग्रसोः *piṇḍagrasoḥ*	पिंडग्रःसु *piṇḍagraḥsu*

SINGULAR.	DUAL.	PLURAL.
N.A.V. पिंडग्रः *piṇḍagraḥ*	पिंडग्रसी *piṇḍagrasí*	पिंडग्रंसि *piṇḍagraṃsi*

Base सुतुस् *sutus*, well-sounding, masc. fem. neut.

SINGULAR. MASC. FEM.	DUAL. MASC. FEM.	PLURAL. MASC. FEM.
N.V. सुतूः *sutúḥ*	सुतुसौ *sutusau*	सुतुसः *sutusaḥ*
A. सुतुसं *sutusam*		
I. सुतुसा *sutusá*		सुतूर्भिः *sutúrbhiḥ*
D. सुतुसे *sutuse*	सुतूर्भ्यां *sutúrbhyám*	सुतूर्भ्यः *sutúrbhyaḥ*
Ab. } सुतुसः *sutusaḥ*		
G.		सुतुसां *sutusám*
L. सुतुसि *sutusi*	सुतुसोः *sutusoḥ*	सुतूःषु *sutúḥshu* or सुतूष्षु *sutúshshu**

SINGULAR.	DUAL.	PLURAL.
N.A.V. सुतूः *sutúḥ*	सुतुसी *sutusí*	सुतुंसि *sutuṃsi*

§ 171. Nouns derived from desiderative verbs change स् *s* into ष् *sh* when necessary.

Base पिपठिस् *pipaṭhis*, wishing to read, masc. fem. neut.

SINGULAR. MASC. FEM.	DUAL. MASC. FEM.	PLURAL. MASC. FEM.
N. पिपठीः *pipaṭhíḥ*	पिपठिषौ *pipaṭhishau*	पिपठिषः *pipaṭhishaḥ*
A. पिपठिषं *pipaṭhisham*		
I. पिपठिषा *pipaṭhishá*		पिपठीर्भिः *pipaṭhírbhiḥ*
D. पिपठिषे *pipaṭhishe*	पिपठीर्भ्यां *pipaṭhírbhyám*	पिपठीर्भ्यः *pipaṭhírbhyaḥ*
Ab. } पिपठिषः *pipaṭhishaḥ*		
G.		पिपठिषां *pipaṭhishám*
L. पिपठिषि *pipaṭhishi*	पिपठिषोः *pipaṭhishoḥ*	पिपठीःषु *pipaṭhíḥshu*

SINGULAR.	DUAL.	PLURAL.
N.A.V. पिपठीः *pipaṭhíḥ*	पिपठिषी *pipaṭhishí*	पिपठिषि *pipaṭhishi* (see § 172)

---

* Siddh.-Kaum. vol. I. p. 187. § 83.

§ 172. The nouns आशिस् *âsis*, fem. blessing, and सजुस् *sajush*, masc. a companion, are declined like पिपठिस् *pipathis*, except in the Nom. Acc. and Voc. Plur., if they should be used as neuters at the end of compounds*.

List of different Bases in स् *s.*

Base.	Nom. Sing. Masc. Fem.	Nom. Sing. Neut.	Nom. Pl. Masc. Fem.	Nom. Pl. Neut.	Instr. Pl.	Loc. Pl.
सुमनस् *sumanas*, kind, m.f.n.	सुमना: *sumanâḥ*[1]	°न: -*naḥ*	सुमनस: *sumanasah*	सुमनांसि *sumanâṁsi*	सुमनोभि: *sumanobhiḥ*	सुमनस्सु or °न:सु *sumanassu* or -*naḥsu*
सुज्योतिस् *sujyotis*, well-lighted, m.f.n.	सुज्योति: *sujyotiḥ*	id.	सुज्योतिष: *sujyotishaḥ*	सुज्योतींषि *sujyotîṁshi*	सुज्योतिभि: *sujyotirbhiḥ*	सुज्योतिष्षु or °ति:षु *sujyotishshu* or -*tiḥshu*
पिंड्ग्रस् *pindagras*, lump-eating, m.f.n.	पिंड्ग्र: *pindagraḥ*	id.	पिंड्ग्रस: *pindagrasah*	पिंड्ग्रांसि *pindagramsi*	पिंड्ग्रोभि: *pindagrobhiḥ*	पिंड्ग्रस्सु or °ग्र:सु *pindagrassu* or -*graḥsu*
चकास् *chakâs*, splendid, m.f.n.	चका: *chakâḥ*	id.	चकास: *chakâsah*	चकांसि *chakâṁsi*	चकाभि: *chakâbhiḥ*	चकास्सु or चका:सु *chakâssu* or *chakâḥsu*
दोस् *dos*[2], arm, m.(n.) (Accent, P.vi.1,171)	दो: *doḥ*	id.	दोष: *dóshaḥ*	दोंषि *dóṁshi*	दोर्भि: *dórbhiḥ*	दोष्षु or दो:षु *dóshshu* or *dóḥshu*
सुपिस् *supis*, well-going, m.f.n.	सुपी: *supîḥ*	id.[3]	सुपिस: *supisah*[4]	सुपिंसि *supiṁsi*	सुपीर्भि: *supîrbhiḥ*	सुपीष्षु or सुपी:षु *supîshshu* or *supîḥshu*
सुतुस् *sutus*, well-sounding, m.f.n.	सुतू: *sutûḥ*	id.	सुतुस: *sutusah*	सुतूंसि *sutûṁsi*	सुतूर्भि: *sutûrbhiḥ*	सुतूष्षु or सुतू:षु *sutûshshu* or *sutûḥshu*
पिपठिस् *pipathis*, desirous of reading, m.f.n.	पिपठी: *pipathîḥ*	id.[3]	पिपठिष: *pipathishah*	पिपठिंषि *pipathishi*[3]	पिपठीर्भि: *pipathîrbhiḥ*	पिपठीष्षु or °ठी:षु *pipathîshshu* or -*thîḥshu*
चिकीर्स् *chikîrs*, desirous of acting, m.f.n.	चिकी: *chikîḥ*	id.	चिकीर्ष: *chikîrshaḥ*	चिकीर्षि *chikîrshi*[5]	चिकीर्भि: *chikîrbhiḥ*	चिकीर्षु *chikîrshu*
आशिस् *âsis*, blessing, f.	आशी: *âsîḥ* (Voc. id.)	id.	आशिष: *âsishaḥ*	आशींषि *âsîṁshi*	आशीर्भि: *âsîrbhiḥ*	आशीष्षु or आशी:षु *âsîshshu* or *âsîḥshu*
सजुस् *sajus*, companion, m.	सजू: *sajûḥ* (Voc. id.)	id.	सजुष: *sajushaḥ*	सजूंषि *sajûṁshi*	सजूर्भि: *sajûrbhiḥ*	सजूष्षु or सजू:षु *sajûshshu* or *sajûḥshu*
सुहिंस् *suhiṁs*, one who strikes well, m.f.n.	सुहिन् *suhin*	id.	सुहिंस: *suhiṁsah*	सुहिंसि *suhiṁsi*	सुहिन्भि: *suhinbhiḥ*	सुहिन्सु *suhinsu*[6]

---

* Some grammarians do not allow the lengthening of the vowels in आशींषि *âsîṁshi* and सजूंषि *sajûṁshi*. (सांतेति सूत्रे । पा॰ ६. ४. १०. । महच्छन्दसाहचर्येण प्रातिपदिकावयवसांतसंयोगस्यैव ग्रहणेनात्र दीर्घाप्राप्ते: ॥ सजुष: षांतत्वेन सांतसंयोगस्याभावात् ॥) This may be right according to the strict interpretation of Pânini, but the Prâtisâkhya (xiii. 7) gives the rule in a more general form, stating that every neuter ending in an Ûshman has a long vowel before the Anusvâra, the Anusvâra being followed by *si* or *shi*.

[1] The Vocative is सुमन: *sumanaḥ*. In the other paradigms it is the same as the Nominative.

[2] दोस् *dos* may be declined regularly throughout as a masculine. But it is likewise declined as a neuter. On its irregular or optional forms, see § 214.

[3] Siddh.-Kaum. vol. 1. p. 197.   [4] स् *s* not changed into ष् *sh*; see § 100, note.

[5] Siddh.-Kaum. vol. 1. p. 194.   [6] See § 75.

§ 173. ध्वस् *dhvas* (from ध्वंस् *dhvaṁs*, to fall) and स्रस् *sras* (from संस् *sraṁs*, to fall), when used at the end of compounds, change their स् *s* into त् *t*, in the Nom. and Voc. Sing., and before terminations beginning with consonants.

N.V. पर्णध्वत् *parṇadhvat* N.A.V. पर्णध्वसौ *parṇadhvasau* N.A. पर्णध्वस: *parṇadhvasaḥ*

A. पर्णध्वसं *parṇadhvasam* I.D.Ab. पर्णध्वद्भ्यां *parṇadhvadbhyám* I. पर्णध्वद्भि: *parṇadhvadbhiḥ*

I. पर्णध्वसा *parṇadhvasá* G.L. पर्णध्वसो: *parṇadhvasoḥ* L. पर्णध्वत्सु *parṇadhvatsu*

§ 174. Bases ending in श *ś*, ष *sh*, छ *chh*, क्ष *ksh*, ह *h*.

Bases ending in these consonants retain them unchanged before all terminations beginning with vowels. Before all other terminations and when final, their final consonants are treated either like त् *t* or like क् *k*.

1. Bases derived from दिश *diś*, to show, दृश *driś*, to see, स्पृश *spriś*, to touch, change श *ś* into क *k*. (§ 126.)

BASE.	NOM. SING.	NOM. PLUR.	NOM.PLUR. NEUT.	INSTR. PLUR.	LOC. PLUR.
दिश *diś*, f. country	दिक् *dík*	दिश: *díśaḥ*	दिंशि *díṁśi*	दिग्भि: *digbhíḥ*	दिक्षु *dikshú*

2. Bases derived from नश *naś*, to destroy, change श *ś* into त् *t* or क *k*.

BASE.	NOM. SING.	N. PL.	N.PL.NEUT.	INSTR. PL.	LOC. PL.
जीवनश *jívanaś*, m.f.n. life-destroying	°नद् or °नक् *jívanat* or *-nak*	°नश: *-naśaḥ*	°नंशि *-naṁśi*	°नद्भि: or °नग्भि: *-nadbhiḥ* or *-nagbhiḥ*	°नत्सु or °नक्षु *-natsu* or *-nakshu*

3. All other bases in श *ś* change their final into त् *t*.

BASE.	NOM. SING.	NOM. PL.	NOM.PL.NEUT.	INSTR. PL.	LOC. PL.
विश *viś*, m.f.n. one who enters	विट् *vít*	विश: *víśaḥ*	विंशि *víṁśi*	विड्भि: *vidbhíḥ*	विट्सु *vitsú*

4. Bases derived from धृष *dhrish*, to dare, change ष *sh* into क *k*.

BASE.	NOM. SING.	NOM. PL.	NOM. PL. NEUT.	INSTR. PL.	LOC. PL.
दधृष *dadhrish*, m.f.n. bold	दधृक् *dadhrik*	दधृष: *dadhrishaḥ*	दधृंषि *dadhriṁshi*	दधृग्भि: *dadhrigbhiḥ*	दधृक्षु *dadhrikshu*

5. All other bases derived from verbs with final ष *sh* change ष *sh* into त् *t*.

BASE.	NOM. SING.	NOM. PL.	NOM. PL. NEUT.	INSTR. PL.	LOC. PL.
द्विष *dvish*, m.f.n. hating	द्विट् *dvít*	द्विष: *dvíshaḥ*	द्विंषि *dvíṁshi*	द्विड्भि: *dvidbhíḥ*	द्विट्सु *dvitsú*

6. Bases ending in छ *chh* change छ *chh* into त् *t*.

BASE.	NOM. SING.	NOM. PL.	NOM.PL.NEUT.	INSTR. PL.	LOC. PL.
प्राछ *práchh*, m.f.n. asking	प्राट् *prát*	प्राश: *práśaḥ*	प्रांषि *práṁśi*	प्राड्भि: *prádbhíḥ*	प्राट्सु *prátsú*

7. Bases ending in क्ष *ksh* change क्ष *ksh* into त् *t*.

BASE.	NOM. SING.	NOM. PL.	NOM. PL. NEUT.	INSTR. PL.	LOC. PL.
तक्ष *taksh*, m.f.n. paring	तट् *tát* *	तक्ष: *tákshaḥ*	तंक्षि *táṁkshi*	तड्भि: *tadbhíḥ*	तट्सु *tatsú*

---

* If differently derived तक्ष *taksh* may form its Nom. Sing. तक् *tak*. गोरक्ष *goraksh*, cow-herd, which regularly forms its Nom. Sing. गोरट् *gorat*, may, according to a different derivation, form गोरक् *gorak*. (See Colebrooke, p. 90, note; Siddh.-Kaum. vol. 1. p. 187.) So पिपक्ष *pipak*, Nom. Dual पिपक्षौ *pipakshau*, desirous of maturing; विवक्ष *vivak*, Nom. Dual विवक्षौ *vivakshau*, desirous of saying; दिधक्ष *didhak*, Nom. Dual दिधक्षौ *didhakshau*, desirous of burning.

8. Most bases ending in इ *h* change इ *h* into द *ṭ*.

BASE.	NOM. SING.	NOM. PL.	NOM. PL. NEUT.	INSTR. PL.	LOC. PL.
लिह् *lih*, m.f.n. licking	लिट् *líṭ*	लिहः *líhaḥ*	लिंहि *líṁhi*	लिड्भिः *liḍbhíḥ*	लिट्सु *liṭsú*
गुह् *guh*, m.f.n. covering	घुट् *ghúṭ*	गुहः *gúhaḥ*	गुंहि *gúṁhi*	घुड्भिः *ghuḍbhíḥ*	घुट्सु *ghuṭsú*

On the change of initial ग *g* into घ *gh*, see § 93.

9. Bases derived from roots ending in इ *h*, and beginning with द *d*, change इ *h* into क *k*. Likewise उष्णिह् *ushṇih*, a metre.

BASE.	NOM. SING.	NOM. PL.	NOM. PL. NEUT.	INSTR. PL.	LOC. PL.
दुह् *duh*, m.f.n. milking	धुक् *dhúk*	दुहः *dúhaḥ*	दुंहि *dúṁhi*	धुग्भिः *dhugbhíḥ*	धुक्षु *dhukshú*

10. Bases derived from the roots द्रुह् *druh*, to hate, मुह् *muh*, to confound, स्निह् *snih*, to love, स्नुह् *snuh*, to spue, may change the final इ *h* into द *ṭ* or क *k*.

BASE.	NOM. SING.	NOM. PL.	N. PL. NEUT.	INSTR. PL.	LOC. PL.
द्रुह् *druh*, m.f.n. hating	धुट् or धुक् *dhrúṭ* or *dhrúk*	द्रुहः *drúhaḥ*	द्रुंहि *drúṁhi*	धुड्भिः: or धुग्भिः: *dhruḍbhíḥ* or *dhrugbhíḥ*	धुट्सु or धुक्षु *dhruṭsú* or *dhrukshú*

11. Bases derived from नह् *nah*, to bind, change इ *h* into त *t*.

BASE.	NOM. SING.	NOM. PL.	INSTR. PL.	LOC. PL.
उपानह् *upánah*, f. a shoe	उपानत् *upánat*	उपानहः *upánahaḥ*	उपानद्भिः *upánadbhiḥ*	उपानत्सु *upánatsu*

Decline विपाश् *vipáś*, f. the Beyah river in the Punjab. विष् *vish*, f. ordure. रुष् *rush*, f. anger. विप्रुष् *viprush*, f. drop of water. विविक्ष् *viviksh*, wishing to enter. स्निह् *snih*, loving. गोदुह् *goduh*, cow-milker. मधुलिह् *madhulih*, bee. त्विष् *tvish*, f. splendour. बहुत्विष् *bahutvish*, m. f. n. very splendid. रत्नमुष् *ratnamush*, a stealer of gems. ईदृश् *ídṛiś*, m. f. n. such. कीदृश् *kídṛiś*, m. f. n. Which? मर्मस्पृश् *marmaspṛiś*, giving pain.

§ 175. तुरासाह् *turásáh*, m. name of Indra, changes स *s* into ष *sh* whenever इ *h* is changed into ड *ḍ* or द *ṭ*.

Nom. Sing. तुरासाट् *turásháṭ*. Nom. Dual तुरासाहौ *turásáhau*. Instr. Plur. तुरासाड्भिः *turásháḍbhiḥ*.

§ 176. पुरोडाश् *purodáś*, m. an offering, or a priest, is irregular. The Nom. Sing. is पुरोडाः *purodáḥ*, and all the cases beginning with consonants (Pada cases) are formed from a base पुरोडस् *purodas*. The Voc. Singular, too, is irregular, being identical with the Nom. Sing. (§ 152), though some grammarians allow हे पुरोडः *he purodaḥ*.

	SINGULAR.	DUAL.	PLURAL.
N.	पुरोडाः *purodáḥ*	पुरोडाशौ *purodáśau*	पुरोडाशः *purodáśaḥ*
A.	पुरोडाशं *purodáśam*	पुरोडाशौ *purodáśau*	पुरोडाशः *purodáśaḥ*
I.	पुरोडाशा *purodáśá*	पुरोडोभ्यां *purodobhyám*	पुरोडोभिः *purodobhiḥ*
D.	पुरोडाशे *purodáśe*	पुरोडोभ्यां *purodobhyám*	पुरोडोभ्यः *purodobhyaḥ*
Ab.	पुरोडाशः *purodáśaḥ*	पुरोडोभ्यां *purodobhyám*	पुरोडोभ्यः *purodobhyaḥ*
G.	पुरोडाशः *purodáśaḥ*	पुरोडाशोः *purodáśoḥ*	पुरोडाशां *purodáśám*
L.	पुरोडाशि *purodáśi*	पुरोडाशोः *purodáśoḥ*	पुरोडःसु *purodaḥsu*
V.	पुरोडाः or °डः *purodáḥ* or -*daḥ*	पुरोडाशौ *purodáśau*	पुरोडाशः *purodáśaḥ*

§ 177. Another word, उक्थशास् *ukthaśás*, a reciter of hymns, is declined like पुरोडाश् *puroḍáś*.

Nom. उक्थशाः *ukthaśáḥ*. Acc. Sing. उक्थशासं *ukthaśásam*. Instr. Plur. उक्थशोभिः *ukthaśobhiḥ*. Voc. Sing. उक्थशाः or उक्थशः *ukthaśáḥ* or *ukthaśaḥ*.

§ 178. Bases in म् *m*.

Bases ending in म् *m* retain म् *m* before all terminations beginning with vowels. Before all other terminations and when final, the म् *m* is changed into न् *n*.

Base प्रशाम् *praśám*, mild.

	SINGULAR. MASC. FEM.	DUAL. MASC. FEM.	PLURAL. MASC. FEM.
Nom. Voc.	प्रशान् *praśán*	प्रशामौ *praśámau*	प्रशामः *praśámaḥ*
Acc.	प्रशामं *praśámam*	प्रशामौ *praśámau*	प्रशामः *praśámaḥ*
Instr.	प्रशामा *praśámá*	प्रशाम्भ्यां *praśánbhyám*	प्रशान्भिः *praśánbhiḥ*
Loc.	प्रशामि *praśámi*	प्रशामोः *praśámoḥ*	प्रशान्सु *praśánsu*

2. Nouns with changeable Bases.

A. *Nouns with two Bases.*

§ 179. Many nouns in Sanskrit have more than one base, or rather they modify their base according to rule before certain terminations.

Nouns with two bases, have one base for the

Nom. Voc. and Acc. Sing.
Nom. Voc. and Acc. Dual } of masc. nouns*;
Nom. Voc (not Acc.) Plural
Nom. Voc. and Acc. Plural of neuter nouns;

and a second base for all other cases.

The former base will be called the *Aṅga* base. Bopp calls it the strong base, and the terminations the weak terminations.

The second base will be called the *Pada and Bha* base. Bopp calls it the weak base, and the terminations the strong terminations.

The general rule is that the simple base, which appears in the Pada and Bha cases, is strengthened in the Aṅga cases. Thus the Pada and Bha base प्राच् *prách* becomes in the Aṅga cases प्रांच् *práñch*. The Pada base of the present participle अदत् *adat*, eating, becomes अदंत् *adant* in the Aṅga

---

* Most nouns with changeable bases form their feminines in ई *í*. A few, however, such as दामन् *dáman*, are said to be feminine without taking the ई *í*, and some of them occur as feminine at the end of compounds.

cases. This gives us the following system of terminations for words with two bases :

	SINGULAR. MASC.	DUAL. MASC.	PLURAL. MASC.	
Nom.Voc.	स् *s* (which is always dropt)	औ *au*	अः *aḥ*	*
Acc.	ं *am*	औ *au*	अः *aḥ*	
Instr.	आ *á*	भ्यां *bhyám*	भिः *bhiḥ*	
Dat.	ए *e*	भ्यां *bhyám*	भ्यः *bhyaḥ*	
Abl.	अः *aḥ*	भ्यां *bhyám*	भ्यः *bhyaḥ*	
Gen.	अः *aḥ*	ओः *oḥ*	आं *ám*	
Loc.	इ *i*	ओः *oḥ*	सु *su*	

NEUTER.

	SINGULAR.	DUAL.	PLURAL.	
Nom. Acc.	——	ई *í*	इ *i*	*

§ 180. Certain words derived from अन्च् *añch*, to move, have two, others three bases.

प्राच् *prách*, forward, eastern, has two bases, प्रान्च् *práñch* for its Anga, प्राच् *prách* for its Pada and Bha base, and is declined accordingly†.

	SINGULAR. MASC.	DUAL. MASC.	PLURAL. MASC.	
N. V.	प्राङ् *prán* ‡	प्रान्चौ *práñchau*	प्रान्चः *práñchaḥ*	
A.	प्रान्चं *práñcham*	प्रान्चौ *práñchau*	प्राचः *práchaḥ* ‖
I.	प्राचा *práchá*	प्राग्भ्यां *prágbhyám*	प्राग्भिः *prágbhiḥ*	
D.	प्राचे *práche*	प्राग्भ्यां *prágbhyám*	प्राग्भ्यः *prágbhyaḥ*	
Ab.	प्राचः *práchaḥ*			
G.	प्राचः *práchaḥ*	प्राचोः *práchoḥ*	प्राचां *práchám*	
L.	प्राचि *práchi*	प्राचोः *práchoḥ*	प्राक्षु *prákshu*	

---

* Anga base, or, according to Bopp, strong base with weak terminations. The terminations are called in Sanskrit the *Sarvanámasthána* terminations.

† Compounds ending in अच् *ach* retain the accent on the preposition, except after prepositions ending in इ *i* or उ *u*. This rule does not apply to नि *ní* and अधि *ádhi* (Pâṇ. VI. 2, 52–53). Hence पराच् *párách*, अवाच् *ávách*, प्राच् *prách*, उदच् *údach*: also न्यच् *nyách*, अध्यच् *ádhyach*: सध्र्यच् *sadhryách*, विश्वच् *víshvach*: but प्रत्यच् *pratyách*, सम्यच् *samyách*, अन्वच् *anvách*.

‡ प्राङ् *prán* stands for प्राङ्क् *práṅk*; this for प्रान्च्+स् *práñch*+*s*.

‖ In the declension of words ending in अच् *ach*, the rule is that if अच् *ach* has the Udâtta, as in प्रत्यच् *pratyách*, सम्यच् *samyách*, अन्वच् *anvách* (§ 180, note), all terminations, except the Sarvanámasthânas, take the Udâtta (Pâṇ. VI. 1, 169–170). The rule Pâṇ. VI. 1, 182, refers to अन्च् *añch*, not to अच् *ach*. The rule Pâṇ. VI. 1, 222, is restricted in the Veda by VI. 1, 170. प्राच् *prách* is treated as if the accent were on the preposition.

NEUTER.

	SINGULAR.	DUAL.	PLURAL.
N. A. V.	प्राक् *prák*	प्राची *práchí*	प्राञ्चि *práñchi*
I.	प्राचा *práchá*	same as masc.	

The feminine of प्राच् *prách* is प्राची *práchí*, declined like fem. in ई *í*.
Decline अवाच् *ávách*, downward, south.   Strong base अवाञ्च् *ávánch*.

B. *Nouns with three Bases.*

§ 181. Nouns with three bases have their *Anga* or strong base in the same cases as the nouns with two bases. In the other cases, however, they have one base, the Pada base, before all terminations beginning with consonants ; and another base, the Bha base, before all terminations beginning with vowels.

In these nouns with three cases, Bopp calls Anga base the strong base ;
the Pada base the middle base ;
the Bha base the weakest base.

This gives us the following system of terminations for words with three bases :

	SINGULAR. MASC.	DUAL. MASC.	PLURAL. MASC.
Nom. Voc.	स् *s* (always dropt)	औ *au*	अः *aḥ*
Acc.	अं *am*	औ *au*	अः *aḥ*
Instr.	आ *á*	भ्यां *bhyám*	भिः *bhiḥ*
Dat.	ए *e*	भ्यां *bhyám*	भ्यः *bhyaḥ*
Abl.	अः *aḥ*	भ्यां *bhyám*	भ्यः *bhyaḥ*
Gen.	अः *aḥ*	ओः *oḥ*	आं *ám*
Loc.	इ *i*	ओः *oḥ*	सु *su*

NEUTER.

	SINGULAR.	DUAL.	PLURAL.
Nom. Acc.	——	ई *í*	इ *i*

Terminations included in two lines require Anga or strong base.
Terminations included in one line require Pada or middle base.
Terminations not included in lines require Bha or weakest base.

Words derived from अंच् *ańch*, to move, with three bases.

प्रत्यच् *pratyach*, behind, has for its Anga or strongest base प्रत्यंच् *pratyańch* ; for its Bha or weakest प्रतीच् *pratích*. The Pada or middle base is प्रत्यच् *pratyach*. Hence प्रत्यङ् *pratyań*, Nom. Sing. masc. ; प्रत्यक् *pratyak*, Nom. Sing. neut. ; प्रतीची *pratíchí*, Nom. Sing. fem.

M

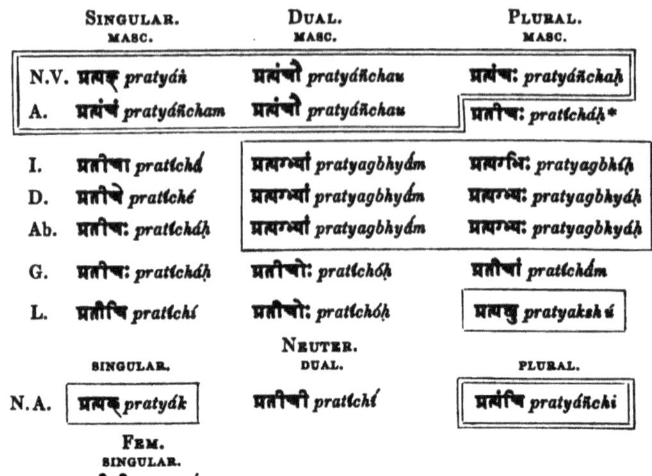

	SINGULAR. MASC.	DUAL. MASC.	PLURAL. MASC.
N.V.	प्रत्यङ् *pratyáṅ*	प्रत्यञ्चौ *pratyáñchau*	प्रत्यञ्च: *pratyáñchaḥ*
A.	प्रत्यञ्चं *pratyáñcham*	प्रत्यञ्चौ *pratyáñchau*	प्रतीच: *pratícháḥ**
I.	प्रतीचा *pratíchá*	प्रत्यग्भ्यां *pratyagbhyám*	प्रत्यग्भि: *pratyagbhíḥ*
D.	प्रतीचे *pratíché*	प्रत्यग्भ्यां *pratyagbhyám*	प्रत्यग्भ्य: *pratyagbhyáḥ*
Ab.	प्रतीच: *pratícháḥ*	प्रत्यग्भ्यां *pratyagbhyám*	प्रत्यग्भ्य: *pratyagbhyáḥ*
G.	प्रतीच: *pratícháḥ*	प्रतीचो: *pratíchóḥ*	प्रतीचां *pratíchám*
L.	प्रतीचि *pratíchí*	प्रतीचो: *pratíchóḥ*	प्रत्यक्षु *pratyaksh ú*

NEUTER.

	SINGULAR.	DUAL.	PLURAL.
N.A.	प्रत्यक् *pratyák*	प्रतीची *pratíchí*	प्रत्यञ्चि *pratyáñchi*

FEM. SINGULAR.

N.   प्रतीची *pratíchí.*

The following words, derived from अञ्च् *añch*, to move, have three bases:

Aṅga or Strong Base.	Pada or Middle Base.	Bha or Weak Base.
प्रत्यञ्च् *pratyáñch*, behind (Pâṇ. vi. 2, 52)	प्रत्यच् *pratyach*	प्रतीच् *pratích*
सम्यञ्च् *samyáñch*, right (vi. 2, 52)	सम्यच् *samyach*	समीच् *samích*
न्यञ्च् *nyáñch*, low (vi. 2, 53)	न्यच् *nyach*	नीच् *ních*
सध्र्यञ्च् *sadhryáñch*, accompanying (vi. 3, 95)	सध्र्यच् *sadhryach*	सध्रीच् *sadhrích*
अन्वञ्च् *anváñch*, following (vi. 2, 52)	अन्वच् *anvach*	अनूच् *anúch*
विश्वञ्च् *víshvañch*, all-pervading	विश्वच् *víshvach*	विषूच् *víshúch*
उदञ्च् *údañch*, upward (vi. 2, 52)	उदच् *údach*	उदीच् *údích*
तिर्यञ्च् *tiryáñch*, tortuous	तिर्यच् *tiryach*	तिरश्च् *tiraśch*

Bases in अत् *at* and अन्त् *ant.*

1. *Participles Present.*

§ 182. Participles of the present have two bases, the Pada and Bha base in अत् *at*, the Aṅga base in अन्त् *ant*. (Accent, Pâṇ. vi. 1, 173.)

	SINGULAR. MASC.	DUAL. MASC.	PLURAL. MASC.
N.V.	अदन् *adán*	अदंतौ *adántau*	अदंत: *adántaḥ*
A.	अदंतं *adántam*	अदंतौ *adántau*	अदत: *adatáḥ*
I.	अदता *adatá*	अदद्भ्यां *adádbhyám*	अदद्भि: *adádbhiḥ*
D.	अदते *adaté*	अदद्भ्यां *adádbhyám*	अदद्भ्य: *adádbhyaḥ*
Ab.	अदत: *adatáḥ*	अदद्भ्यां *adádbhyám*	अदद्भ्य: *adádbhyaḥ*
G.	अदत: *adatáḥ*	अदतो: *adatóḥ*	अदतां *adatám*
L.	अदति *adatí*	अदतो: *adatóḥ*	अदत्सु *adátsu*

* Rv. i. 173, 5.

NEUTER.

SINGULAR.	DUAL.	PLURAL.
N. A. अदत् *adát*	अदती *adatí*	अदंति *adánti*

FEM.

SINGULAR.

N.   अदती *adatí*, &c., like नदी *nadí*.

§ 183. There is a very difficult rule according to which certain participles keep the न् *n* in the Nom. and Acc. Dual of neuters, and before the ई *í* of the feminine. This rule can only be fully understood by those who are acquainted with the ten classes of conjugations. It is this,

I. Participles of verbs following the Bhû, Div, and Chur classes *must* preserve the न् *n*.

II. Participles of verbs following the Tud class *may* or *may not* preserve the न् *n*. The same applies to all participles of the future in स्यत् *syat*, and to the participles of verbs of the Ad class in आ *á*.

III. Participles of all other verbs *must* reject the न् *n*.

I. भवत् *bhávat.*	Nom. and Acc. Dual Neut. भवंती *bhávantí.*
दीव्यत् *dívyat.*	दीव्यंती *dívyantí.*
चोरयत् *choráyat.*	चोरयंती *choráyantí.*
II. तुदत् *tudát.*	तुदंती *tudántí* or तुदती *tudatí.*
भविष्यत् *bhavishyát* (fut.).	भविष्यंती *bhavishyántí* or भविष्यती *bhavishyatí.*
यात् *yát.*	यांती *yántí* or याती *yátí.*
III. अदत् *adát.*	Nom. and Acc. Dual Neut. अदती *adatí.*
जुह्वत् *júhvat.*	जुह्वती *júhvatí.*
सुन्वत् *sunvát.*	सुन्वती *sunvatí.*
रुंधत् *rundhát.*	रुंधती *rundhatí.*
तन्वत् *tanvát.*	तन्वती *tanvatí.*
क्रीणत् *kríṇát.*	क्रीणती *kríṇatí.*

The feminine base is throughout identical in form with the Nom. Dual Neut. Hence भवंती *bhávantí*, being, fem.; तुदंती *tudántí* or तुदती *tudatí*, striking, fem.; अदती *adatí*, eating, fem. The feminine base is declined regularly as a base in ई *í*.

§ 184. Another rule, which ought not to be mixed up with the preceding rule, prohibits the strengthening of the Aṅga base throughout in the participles present of reduplicated verbs, except in the Nom. Acc. Voc. Plur. Neut., where the insertion of न् *n* is optional. With this exception, these participles are therefore really declined like nouns in त् *t* with unchangeable bases.

Base ददत् *dádat*, giving, from दा *dá*, to give, ददामि *dádámi*, I give.

	SINGULAR.		DUAL.		PLURAL.	
	MASC.	NEUT.	MASC.	NEUT.	MASC.	NEUT.
N.V.	ददत् *dádat*	ददत् *dádat*	ददतौ *dádatau*	ददती *dádatí*	ददतः *dádataḥ*	ददति *dádati* *
A.	ददतं *dádatam*	ददत् *dádat*				
I.	ददता *dádatá*				ददद्भिः *dádadbhiḥ*	
D.	ददते *dádate*		ददद्भ्यां *dádadbhyám*		ददद्भ्यः *dádadbhyaḥ*	
Ab.	ददतः *dádataḥ*					
G.			ददतोः *dádatoḥ*		ददतां *dádatám*	
L.	ददति *dádati*				ददत्सु *dádatsu*	

* Or ददंति *dádanti.*

The same rule applies to the participles जक्षत् *jakshat*, eating; जाग्रत् *jágrat*, waking; दरिद्रत् *daridrat*, being poor; शासत् *śásat*, commanding; चकासत् *chakásat*, shining. But जगत् *jágat*, neut. the world, forms Nom. Plur. जगंति *jáganti*, only.

§ 185. वृहत् *brihát*, great, पृषत् *príshat*, m. a deer, n. a drop of water, are declined like participles of verbs of the Ad class.

	SINGULAR. MASC.	DUAL. MASC.	PLURAL. MASC.
N.V.	वृहन् *brihán*	वृहंतौ *brihántau*	वृहंत: *brihántah*
A.	वृहंतं *brihántam*	वृहंतौ *brihántau*	वृहत: *brihatáh*

	NEUTER. SINGULAR.	DUAL.	PLURAL.
N.A.	वृहत् *brihát*	वृहती *brihatí*	वृहंति *brihánti*

FEM.
SINGULAR.

N.	वृहती *brihatí*

§ 186. महत् *mahat*, great, likewise originally a participle of the Ad class, forms its Aṅga or strong base in आंत् *ánt*.

	SINGULAR. MASC.	DUAL. MASC.	PLURAL. MASC.
N.	महान् *mahán*	महांतौ *mahántau*	महांत: *mahántah*
A.	महांतं *mahántam*	महांतौ *mahántau*	महत: *mahatáh*
I.	महता *mahatá*	महद्भ्यां *mahádbhyám*	महद्भि: *mahádbhih*
D.	महते *mahaté*	महद्भ्यां *mahádbhyám*	महद्भ्य: *mahádbhyah*
Ab.	महत: *mahatáh*	महतो: *mahatóh*	महतां *mahatám*
G.	महत: *mahatáh*	महतो: *mahatóh*	महत्सु *mahátsu*
L.	महति *mahatí*		महतां *mahatám*
V.	महन् *máhan*		महत्सु *mahátsu*

	NEUTER. SINGULAR.	DUAL.	PLURAL.
N.A.V.	महत् *mahát*	महती *mahatí*	महांति *mahánti*

The rest like the masculine.

FEM.
SINGULAR.

N.	महती *mahatí*

Bases ending in the Suffixes मत् *mat and* वत् *vat, forming their Aṅga Bases in* मंत् *mant and* वंत् *vant.*

§ 187. The possessive suffixes मत् *mat* and वत् *vat* form their Aṅga or strong base in मंत् *mant* and वंत् *vant*. They lengthen their vowel in the Nom. Sing. Masc. These suffixes are of very frequent occurrence.

अग्निमत् *agnimat*, having fire.

	SINGULAR. MASC.	DUAL. MASC.	PLURAL. MASC.
N.	अग्निमान् *agnimán*	अग्निमंतौ *agnimantau*	अग्निमंत: *agnimantaḥ*
A.	अग्निमंतं *agnimantam*	अग्निमंतौ *agnimantau*	अग्निमात: *agnimataḥ*
V.	अग्निमन् *agniman*		

	NEUTER.		
	SINGULAR.	DUAL.	PLURAL.
N. V.	अग्निमत् *agnimat*	अग्निमती *agnimatí*	अग्निमंति *agnimanti*

	FEM. SINGULAR.
N.	अग्निमती *agnimatí*

वत् *vat* is used 1. after bases in अ *a* and आ *á*.

Ex. ज्ञानवत् *jñánavat*, having knowledge. विद्यावत् *vidyávat*, having knowledge.

But अग्निमत् *agnimat*, having fire. हनुमत् *hanumat*, having jaws.

2. After bases ending in nasals, semivowels, or sibilants, if preceded by अ *a* or आ *á*. (Pân. VIII. 2, 10.)

Ex. पयस्वत् *payasvat*, having milk. उदन्वत् *udanvat*, having water.

But ज्योतिष्मत् *jyotishmat*, having light. गीर्वत् *gírvat*, having a voice.

3. After bases ending in any other consonants, by whatever vowel they may be preceded.

Ex. विद्युत्वत् *vidyutvat*, having lightning.

There are exceptions to these rules. (Pân. VIII. 2, 9–16.)

§ 188. भवत् *bhavat*, Your Honour, which is frequently used in place of the pronoun of the second person, followed by the third person of the verb, is declined like a noun derived by वत् *vat*. Native grammarians derive it from भा *bhá*, with the suffix वत् *vat*, and keep it distinct from भवत् *bhavat*, being, the participle present of भू *bhú*, to be.

भवत् *bhavat*, Your Honour.

	SINGULAR. MASC.	DUAL. MASC.	PLURAL. MASC.
N.	भवान् *bhaván*	भवंतौ *bhavantau*	भवंत: *bhavantaḥ*
A.	भवंतं *bhavantam*	भवंतौ *bhavantau*	भवत: *bhavataḥ*
V.	भवन् *bhavan* or भो: *bhoḥ*		

	NEUTER.		
	SINGULAR.	DUAL.	PLURAL.
N. A. V.	भवत् *bhavat*	भवती *bhavatí*	भवंति *bhavanti*

	FEM. SINGULAR.
N.	भवती *bhavatí*

भवत् *bhavat*, being, part. present.

SINGULAR.	DUAL.	PLURAL.
MASC.	MASC.	MASC.
N. भवन् *bhavan*	भवंतौ *bhavantau*	भवंतः *bhavantaḥ*
A. भवंतं *bhavantam*	भवंतौ *bhavantau*	भवतः *bhavataḥ*
V. भवन् *bhavan*		

	NEUTER.	
SINGULAR.	DUAL.	PLURAL.
N. A. V. भवत् *bhavat*	भवंती *bhavantí*	भवंति *bhavanti*

FEM.

SINGULAR.

N. भवंती *bhavantí*

§ 189. अर्वत् *arvat*, masc. horse, is declined regularly like nouns in वत् *vat*, except in the Nom. Sing., where it has अर्वा *arvā*. अर्वन् *arvan* in अनर्वन् *anarvan*, without a foe, is a totally different word, and declined like a noun in अन् *an*; Nom. Sing. अनर्वा *anarvā*; Nom. Dual अनर्वाणौ *anarvāṇau*; Acc. Sing. अनर्वाणं *anarvāṇam*; Instr. Sing. अनर्वणा *anarvaṇā*; Instr. Plur. अनर्वभिः *anarvabhiḥ*. The feminine of अर्वत् *arvat* is अर्वती *arvatí*.

§ 190. कियत् *kiyat*, How much? इयत् *iyat*, so much, are declined like bases in मत् *mat*. Their feminines are कियती *kiyatí*, इयती *iyatí*.

SINGULAR.	DUAL.	PLURAL.
MASC.	MASC.	MASC.
N. कियान् *kíyán*	कियंतौ *kíyantau*	कियंतः *kíyantaḥ*
A. कियंतं *kíyantam*	कियंतौ *kíyantau*	कियतः *kíyataḥ*
I. कियता *kíyatá*	कियद्भ्यां *kíyadbhyám*	कियद्भिः *kíyadbhiḥ*
V. कियन् *kíyan*		

	NEUTER.	
SINGULAR.	DUAL.	PLURAL.
N. A. V. कियत् *kiyat*	कियती *kiyatí*	कियंति *kíyanti*

Bases in अन् an (अन् an, मन् man, वन् van.)

§ 191. Words in अन् *an* have three bases: their Aṅga or strong base is आन् *án*; their Bha or weakest base न् *n*; and their Pada or middle base अ *a*.

Mark besides,

1. That the Nom. Sing. masc. has आ *á*, not आन् *án*(*s*).

2. That the Nom. Sing. neut. has अ *a*, not अन् *an*.

3. That the Voc. Sing. neut. may be either identical with the Nominative, or take न् *n*.

4. That words ending in मन् *man* and वन् *van* keep मन् *man* and वन् *van* as their Bha bases, without dropping the अ *a*, when there is a consonant immediately before the मन् *man* and वन् *van*. This is to avoid the concurrence of three consonants, such as पर्व्न् *parvn* from पर्वन् *parvan*,

or आत्म्न् *âtmn* from आत्मन् *âtman*. This rule applies only to words ending in मन् *man* and वन् *van*, not to words ending in simple अन् *an*. Thus तक्षन् *takshan* forms तक्ष्णा *takshnâ*; मूर्धन् *mûrdhan*, मूर्ध्ना *mûrdhnâ*, &c.

5. That in all other words the loss of the अ *a* is optional in the Loc. Sing., and in the Nom. Acc. Voc. Dual of neuters. The feminine, however, drops the अ *a*; thus राज्ञी *râjñî*.

राजन् *râjan*, m. king. Anga, राजान् *râjân*; Pada, राज *râja*; Bha, राज्ञ् *râjñ*.

MASCULINE.

	SINGULAR.	DUAL.	PLURAL.
N.	राजा *râjâ*	राजानौ *râjânau*	राजानः *râjânah*
A.	राजानं *râjânam*	राजानौ *râjânau*	राज्ञः *râjñah*
V.	राजन् *râjan*		
I.	राज्ञा *râjñâ*	राजभ्यां *râjabhyâm*	राजभिः *râjabhih*
D.	राज्ञे *râjñe*	राजभ्यां *râjabhyâm*	राजभ्यः *râjabhyah*
Ab.	राज्ञः *râjñah*	राजभ्यां *râjabhyâm*	राजभ्यः *râjabhyah*
G.	राज्ञः *râjñah*	राज्ञोः *râjñoh*	राज्ञां *râjñâm*
L.	राज्ञि *râjñi* or राजनि *râjani*	राज्ञोः *râjñoh*	राजसु *râjasu*

नामन् *nâman*, n. name. Anga, नामान् *nâmân*; Pada, नाम *nâma*; Bha, नाम्न् *nâmn*.

NEUTER.

	SINGULAR.	DUAL.	PLURAL.
N.A.	नाम *nâma*	नाम्नी *nâmnî* or नामनी *nâmanî*	नामानि *nâmâni*
V.	नाम *nâma* or नामन् *nâman*		
I.	नाम्ना *nâmnâ*	नामभ्यां *nâmabhyâm*	नामभिः *nâmabhih*
D.	नाम्ने *nâmne*	नामभ्यां *nâmabhyâm*	नामभ्यः *nâmabhyah*
Ab.	नाम्नः *nâmnah*	नामभ्यां *nâmabhyâm*	नामभ्यः *nâmabhyah*
G.	नाम्नः *nâmnah*	नाम्नोः *nâmnoh*	नाम्नां *nâmnâm*
L.	नाम्नि *nâmni* or नामनि *nâmani*	नाम्नोः *nâmnoh*	नामसु *nâmasu*

§ 192. Nouns in which the suffixes मन् *man* and वन् *van* are preceded by a consonant, such as ब्रह्मन् *brahman*, m. n. the creator, यज्वन् *yajvan*, m. sacrificer, पर्वन् *parvan*, n. joint, form their Bha base in मन् *man* and वन् *van*.

ब्रह्मन् *brahmán*, m. creator. Anga, ब्रह्मान् *brahmân*; Pada, ब्रह्म *brahmá*; Bha, ब्रह्मन् *brahmán*.

MASCULINE.

	SINGULAR.	DUAL.	PLURAL.
N.	ब्रह्मा *brahmá*	ब्रह्माणौ *brahmáṇau*	ब्रह्माणः *brahmáṇaḥ*
A.	ब्रह्माणं *brahmáṇam*	ब्रह्माणौ *brahmáṇau*	ब्रह्मणः *brahmáṇaḥ*
V.	ब्रह्मन् *bráhman*		
I.	ब्रह्मणा *brahmáṇá*	ब्रह्मभ्यां *brahmábhyám*	ब्रह्मभिः *brahmábhiḥ*
D.	ब्रह्मणे *brahmáṇe*	ब्रह्मभ्यां *brahmábhyám*	ब्रह्मभ्यः *brahmábhyaḥ*
Ab.	ब्रह्मणः *brahmáṇaḥ*	ब्रह्मभ्यां *brahmábhyám*	ब्रह्मभ्यः *brahmábhyaḥ*
G.	ब्रह्मणः *brahmáṇaḥ*	ब्रह्मणोः *brahmáṇoḥ*	ब्रह्मणां *brahmáṇám*
L.	ब्रह्मणि *brahmáṇi*	ब्रह्मणोः *brahmáṇoḥ*	ब्रह्मसु *brahmásu*

NEUTER.

	SINGULAR.	DUAL.	PLURAL.
N. A.	ब्रह्म *bráhma*	ब्रह्मणी *bráhmaṇí*	ब्रह्माणि *bráhmáṇi*
V.	ब्रह्म *bráhma* or ब्रह्मन् *bráhman*		

Decline यज्वन् *yajvan*, sacrificer; आत्मन् *átman*, self; सुधर्मन् *sudharman*, virtuous.

प्रतिदिवन् *pratidivan*, one who sports, from दिव् दीव्यति *div dívyati*, lengthens the दि *di* to दी *dí*, whenever the व् *v* is immediately followed by न् *n*. Nom. Sing. प्रतिदिवा *pratidivá*; Nom. Plur. प्रतिदिवानः *pratidivánaḥ*; Acc. Plur. प्रतिदीव्नः *pratidívnaḥ* (§ 143).

§ 193. Words in अन् *an*, like राजन् *rájan*, king, form their feminine in ई *í*, dropping the अ *a* before the न् *n*; राज्ञी *rájñí*, queen.

Words in वन् *van*, like धीवन् *dhívan*, fisherman, form their feminine in वरी *varí*; धीवरी *dhívarí*, wife of a fisherman. (See, however, Pâṇ. IV. 1, 7, vârt.)

Words in मन् *man*, if feminine, are declined like masculines. दामन् *dáman*, fem. rope; Nom. Sing. दामा *dámá*, Acc. दामानं *dámánam*; but there is an optional base दामा *dámá*, Acc. Sing. दामां *dámám*. (Pâṇ. IV. 1, 11; 13.)

§ 194. Nouns in अन् *an*, मन् *man*, वन् *van*, at the end of adjectival compounds, may either use their masculine forms as feminines, or form feminines in आ *á*. Those in अन् *an*, if in the Bha base they can drop the अ *a* before the न् *n*, may also take ई *í* (Pâṇ. IV. 1, 28). Thus, Nom. Sing. masc. and fem. सुचर्मा *sucharmá*, having good leather, Nom. Dual सुचर्माणौ *sucharmáṇau*; सुपर्वा *suparvá*, सुपर्वाणौ *suparváṇau*: or, Nom. Sing. fem. सुचर्मा *sucharmá*, Nom. Dual सुचर्मे *sucharme*, Plur. सुचर्माः *sucharmáḥ*; सुपर्वा *suparvá*, सुपर्वे *suparve*, सुपर्वाः *suparváḥ*. Of बहुराजन् *bahurájan*, having many kings, the feminine may be,

1. बहुराजा *bahurájá*, Dual बहुराजानौ *bahurájánau*.
2. बहुराजा *bahurájá*, Dual बहुराजे *bahuráje*.
3. बहुराज्ञी *bahurájñí*, Dual बहुराज्ञ्यौ *bahurájñyau*.

द्विदाम्नी *dvidámní* (Pâṇ. IV. 1, 27), having two ropes, is an exception.

Adjectives in वन् *van*, which form their fem. in वरी *varí*, धीवन् *dhívan*, a fisherman, धीवरी *dhívarí*, पीवन् *pívan*, पीवरी *pívarí*, fat, may do the same at the end of compounds, or take वा *vá. बहुधीवरी *bahudhívarí* or बहुधीवा *bahudhívá*, Nom. Dual बहुधीवे *bahudhíve*, having many fishermen. (Siddh.-Kaum. vol. i. p. 209.)

§ 195. पथिन् *pathin*, m. path, has

> for its Anga base पंथान् *pánthán* (like राजान् *ráján*);
> for its Bha base पथ् *path*;
> for its Pada base पथि *pathí*.

It is irregular in the Nom. and Voc. Sing., where it is पंथा: *pántháh*.

SINGULAR.		DUAL.		PLURAL.	
N.V.	पंथा: *pántháh*	पंथानौ *pánthánau*		N. पंथान: *pánthánah*	
A.	पंथानं *pánthánam*	पंथानौ *pánthánau*		A. पथ: *patháh*	
I.	पथा *pathá*	पथिभ्यां *pathíbhyám*		I. पथिभि: *pathíbhih*	

The terminations after पथ् *path* have the Udâtta, because they replace a lost Udâtta. (Pân. VI. 1, 199.)

ऋभुक्षिन् *ribhukshín*, m. a name of Indra, and मथिन् *mathín*, m. a churning-stick, are declined in the same manner. The three bases are,

> ऋभुक्षान् *ribhukshán*
> मंथान् *mánthán* } Anga;
>
> ऋभुक्ष् *ribhuksh*
> मथ् *math* } Bha;
>
> ऋभुक्षि *ribhukshí*
> मथि *mathí* } Pada.

The Nom. and Voc. Sing. are ऋभुक्षा: *ríbhuksháh* and मंथा: *mántháh*.

पथिन् *pathin*, ऋभुक्षिन् *ribhukshin*, and मथिन् *mathin* form their feminines पथी *pathí*, ऋभुक्षी *ribhukshí*, मथी *mathí*.

§ 196. A word of very frequent occurrence is अहन् *áhan*, n. day, which takes अहस् *áhas* as its Pada base. Otherwise it is declined like नामन् *náman*.

	SINGULAR.			DUAL.			PLURAL.	
P.	N.A.V. अह: *áhah*	Bh.	N.A.V. अह्नी *áhní**	An.	N.A.V. अहानि *áháni*			
Bh.	I. अह्ना *áhná*	P.	I.D.Ab. अहोभ्यां *áhobhyám*	P.	I. अहोभि: *áhobhih*			
Bh.	D. अह्ने *áhne*	Bh.	G.L. अह्नो: *áhnoh*	P.	D.Ab. अहोभ्य: *áhobhyah*			
Bh.	Ab.G. अह्न: *áhnah*			Bh.	G. अह्नां *áhnám*			
Bh.	L. अह्नि *áhni†*			P.	L. अहस्सु *áhassu‡*			

The Visarga in the Nominative Singular is treated like an original र *r* (§ 85). Hence अहरह: *ahar-ahah*, day by day. In composition, too, the same rule applies ; अहर्गण: *ahargaṇah*, a month (Pân. VIII. 2, 69): though not always, अहोरात्र: *ahorátrah*, day and night. (See § 90.)

---

* Or अह्नी *áhní*.　　† Or अह्नि *áhani*.　　‡ Or अह:सु *áhahsu*.

§ 197. At the end of a compound, too, अहन् *ahan* is irregular. Thus दीर्घाहन् *dírghâhan*, having long days, is declined:

SINGULAR.	DUAL.	PLURAL.
N. दीर्घाहाः *dírghâhâḥ* *	N.A.V. दीर्घाहायौ *dírghâhâṇau*	N.V. दीर्घाहाः *dírghâhâṇaḥ*
V. दीर्घाह: *dírghâhaḥ*		A. दीर्घाहूः *dírghâhnaḥ*
A. दीर्घाहायं *dírghâhâṇam*		I. दीर्घाहोभि:*dírghâhobhiḥ*, &c.

Feminine, दीर्घाह्नी *dírghâhní* (Pâṇ. viii. 4, 7).

§ 198. In derivative compounds with numerals, and with वि *vi* and साय *sâya*, अह्न *ahna* is substituted for अहन् *ahan*: but in the Loc. Sing. both forms are admitted; e. g. द्यह्न: *dvyahnaḥ*, produced in two days; Loc. Sing. द्यह्ने *dvyahne* or द्यह्नि *dvyahni* or द्यहनि *dvyahani*. (Pâṇ. vi. 3, 110.)

§ 199. श्वन् *śvan*, m. dog, युवन् *yuvan*, m. young, take शुन् *śun*, यून् *yûn* as their Bha bases. For the rest, they are declined regularly, like ब्रह्मन् *brahman*, m. (Accent, Pâṇ. vi. 1, 182.)

SINGULAR.	DUAL.	PLURAL.
N. श्वा *śvá*	N.A.V. श्वानौ *śvánau*	N. श्वान: *śvánaḥ*
A. श्वानं *śvánam*		A. शुन: *śúnaḥ*
V. श्वन् *śván*		I. श्वभि: *śvábhiḥ*

The feminine of श्वन् *śvan* is शुनी *śuní*; of युवन् *yúvan*, युवति: *yuvatíḥ*; according to some grammarians, यूनी *yûní*.

§ 200. मघवन् *maghavan*, the Mighty, a name of Indra, takes मघोन् *maghon* as its Bha base.

SINGULAR.	DUAL.	PLURAL.
N. मघवा *maghává*	N.A.V. मघवानौ *maghávánau*	N. मघवान: *maghávnaḥ*
A. मघवानं *maghávánam*		A. मघोन: *maghónaḥ*
V. मघवन् *mághavan*		I. मघवभि: *maghávabhiḥ* †

The same word may likewise be declined like a masculine with the suffix वत् *vat* or मत् *mat*; (see अग्निमत् *agnimat*.)

SINGULAR.	DUAL.	PLURAL.
N. मघवान् *magháván*	N.A.V. मघवंतौ *maghávantau*	N. मघवंत: *maghávantaḥ*
A. मघवंतं *maghávantam*		A. मघवत: *maghávataḥ*
V. मघवन् *mághavan*		I. मघवद्भि: *maghávadbhiḥ*

The feminine is accordingly either मघोनी *maghóní* or मघवती *maghavatí*.

§ 201. पूषन् *pûshán* and अर्यमन् *aryamán*, two names of Vedic deities, do not lengthen their vowel except in the Nom. Sing. and the Nom. Acc. Voc. Plur. neut.; (in this they follow the bases in इन् *in*; § 203.) For the rest, they are declined like nouns in अन् *an*; (see राजन् *rájan*.)

---

* Pâṇ. viii. 2, 69, vârt. 1; Siddh.-Kaum. vol. i. p. 194; but Colebrooke, p. 83, has दीर्घाहा *dírghâhá* as Nom. Sing.

† Colebrooke, Sanskrit Grammar, p. 81.

BASE.	NOM. SING.	NOM. PL.	ACC. PL.	INSTR. PL.	NOM. PL. NEUT.
पूषन्, पूष, पूष्ण्	पूषा	पूषणः	पूष्णः	पूषभिः	पूषाणि
púshan, púsha, púshṇ	*púshá*	*púsháṇaḥ*	*púshṇáḥ*	*púsháḍbhiḥ*	*púsháṇi*
अर्यमन्, अर्यम, अर्यम्ण्	अर्यमा	अर्यमणः	अर्यम्णः	अर्यमभिः	अर्यमाणि
aryaman, aryama, aryamṇ	*aryamá*	*aryamáṇaḥ*	*aryamṇáḥ*	*aryamáḍbhiḥ*	*aryamáṇi*

Loc. Sing. पूष्णि *púshṇi* or पूषणि *púsháṇi;* or, according to some, पूषि *púshi.* (Sâr. I. 9, 31.)

§ 202. The root हन् *han,* to kill, if used as a noun, follows the same rule; only that when the vowel between ह *h* and न् *n* is dropt, ह *h* becomes घ् *gh.*

BASE.	NOM. SING.	NOM. PL.	ACC. PL.	INSTR. PL.	NOM. PL. NEUT.
हन् *han*, ह *ha*, घ् *ghn*	हा *há*	हनः *hanaḥ*	घ्नः *ghnaḥ*	हभिः *habhiḥ*	हानि *háni*
ब्रह्महन्, ह, घ्	ब्रह्महा	ब्रह्महणः	ब्रह्मघ्नः	ब्रह्महभिः	ब्रह्महाणि
brahmahan, ha, ghn	*brahmahá*	*brahmaháṇaḥ*	*brahmaghnáḥ*	*brahmaháḍbhiḥ*	*brahmaháṇi*

Loc. Sing. ब्रह्मघ्नि *brahmaghni* or ब्रह्महाणि *brahmaháṇi.*

Bases in इन् in.

§ 203. Words in इन् *in* are almost regular; it is to be observed that

1. They drop the न् *n* at the end of the Pada base.
2. They form the Nom. Sing. masc. in ई *í;* the Nom. Acc. Sing. neut. in इ *i;* and the Nom. Acc. Plur. neut. in ईनि *íni.*

MASCULINE.

SINGULAR.	DUAL.	PLURAL.
N. धनी *dhaní*	धनिनौ *dhanínau*	धनिनः *dhanínaḥ*
A. धनिनं *dhanínam*	धनिनौ *dhanínau*	धनिनः *dhanínaḥ*
I. धनिना *dhanínd*	धनिभ्यां *dhaníbhyám*	धनिभिः *dhaníbhiḥ*
D. धनिने *dhaníne*	धनिभ्यां *dhaníbhyám*	धनिभ्यः *dhaníbhyaḥ*
Ab. धनिनः *dhanínaḥ*	धनिभ्यां *dhaníbhyám*	धनिभ्यः *dhaníbhyaḥ*
G. धनिनः *dhanínaḥ*	धनिनोः *dhanínoḥ*	धनिनां *dhanínám*
L. धनिनि *dhaníni*	धनिनोः *dhanínoḥ*	धनिषु *dhaníshu*
V. धनिन् *dhánin*	धनिनौ *dháninau*	धनिनः *dháninaḥ*

NEUTER.

SINGULAR.	DUAL.	PLURAL.
N.A. धनि *dhaní*	धनिनी *dhaníní*	धनीनि *dhaníni*
V. धनि *dháni* or धनिन् *dhánin*		

FEM.

SINGULAR.
N. धनिनी *dhaniní*

Decline मेधाविन् *medhávin,* wise; यशस्विन् *yaśasvin,* glorious; वाग्मिन् *vágmin,* loquacious; कारिन् *kárin,* doing.

Note—These nouns in इन् *in,* (etymologically a shortened form of अन् *an,*) follow the analogy of nouns in अन् *an* (like राजन् *rájan,* नामन् *náman*) in the Nom. Sing. masc. and neut., and in the Voc. Sing. and in the Nom. Acc. Plur. neut. They might be ranged, in fact, with the nouns having unchangeable bases; for the lengthening of the vowel in the Nom. and Acc. Plur. neut. is but a compensation for the absence of the nasal which is inserted in these cases in all bases except those ending in nasals and semivowels.

Participles in वस् *vas.*

§ 204. Participles of the reduplicated perfect in वस् *vas* have three bases; वांस् *vâṁs* as the Anga, उष् *ush* as the Bha, and वस् *vas* as the Pada base. According to Sanskrit grammarians, they change the स् *s* of वस् *vas* into त् *t*, if the स् *s* is final, or if it is followed by terminations beginning with भ् *bh* and स् *s*; (see § 173, 131.) But the fact is, that the Pada base is really वत् *vat*, not वस् *vas*.

Anga, रुरुद्वांस् *rurudvâṁs*; Pada, रुरुद्वस् *rurudvas*; Bha, रुरुदुष् *rurudush*.

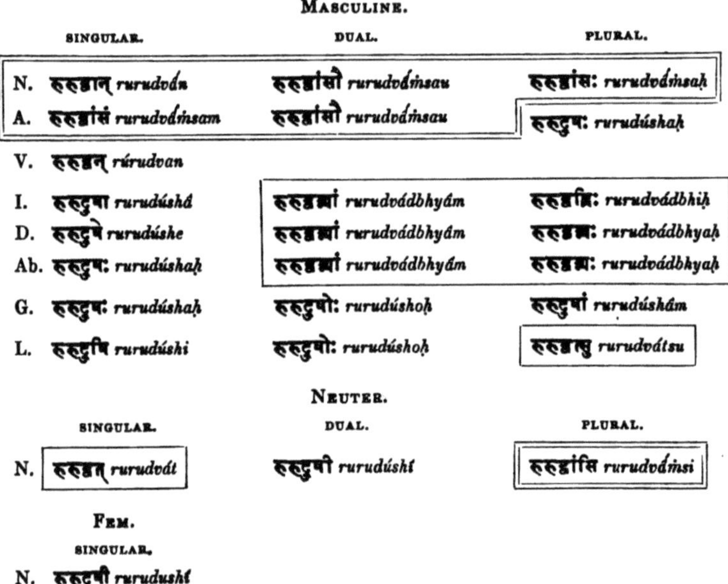

MASCULINE.

	SINGULAR.	DUAL.	PLURAL.
N.	रुरुद्वान् *rurudvân*	रुरुद्वांसौ *rurudvâṁsau*	रुरुद्वांसः *rurudvâṁsaḥ*
A.	रुरुद्वांसं *rurudvâṁsam*	रुरुद्वांसौ *rurudvâṁsau*	रुरुदुषः *rurudúshaḥ*
V.	रुरुद्वन् *rúrudvan*		
I.	रुरुदुषा *rurudúshâ*	रुरुद्वद्भ्यां *rurudvádbhyâm*	रुरुद्वद्भिः *rurudvádbhiḥ*
D.	रुरुदुषे *rurudúshe*	रुरुद्वद्भ्यां *rurudvádbhyâm*	रुरुद्वद्भ्यः *rurudvádbhyaḥ*
Ab.	रुरुदुषः *rurudúshaḥ*	रुरुद्वद्भ्यां *rurudvádbhyâm*	रुरुद्वद्भ्यः *rurudvádbhyaḥ*
G.	रुरुदुषः *rurudúshaḥ*	रुरुदुषोः *rurudúshoḥ*	रुरुदुषां *rurudúshâm*
L.	रुरुदुषि *rurudúshi*	रुरुदुषोः *rurudúshoḥ*	रुरुद्वत्सु *rurudvátsu*

NEUTER.

	SINGULAR.	DUAL.	PLURAL.
N.	रुरुद्वत् *rurudvát*	रुरुदुषी *rurudúshî*	रुरुद्वांसि *rurudvâṁsi*

FEM.

SINGULAR.

N.	रुरुदुषी *rurudushî*

§ 205. Participles in वस् *vas* which insert an इ *i* between the reduplicated root and the termination, drop the इ *i* whenever the termination वस् *vas* is changed into उष् *ush*. Thus

तस्थिवान् *tasthivân*, from स्था *sthâ*, to stand, forms the fem. तस्थुषी *tasthushî*. पेचिवान् *pechivân*, from पच् *pach*, to cook, forms the fem. पेचुषी *pechushî*.

A very common word following this declension is विद्वान् *vidvân*, wise, (for विविद्वान् *vividvân*); fem. विदुषी *vidúshî*.

If the root ends in इ *i* or ई *î*, this radical vowel is never dropt before उष् *ush*, the contracted form of वस् *vas*. Hence from नी *nî*, निनीवान् *ninîvân*; Instr. निन्युषा *ninyushâ*; fem. निन्युषी *ninyushî*.

Decline the following participles:

PADA BASE.	NOM. SING.	NOM. PLUR.	ACC. PLUR.	INSTR. PLUR.
शुश्रुवस् *śuśruvas*	शुश्रुवान् *śuśruván*	शुश्रुवांसः *śuśruvámsah*	शुश्रुवुषः *śuśruvushah*	शुश्रुवद्भिः *śuśruvadbhih*
पेचिवस् *pechivas*	पेचिवान् *pechiván*	पेचिवांसः *pechivámsah*	पेचुषः *pechushah*	पेचिवद्भिः *pechivadbhih*
जग्मिवस् *jagmivas*	जग्मिवान् *jagmiván*	जग्मिवांसः *jagmivámsah*	जग्मुषः *jagmushah*	जग्मिवद्भिः *jagmivadbhih*
जगन्वस् * *jaganvas*	जगन्वान् *jaganván*	जगन्वांसः *jaganvámsah*	जग्मुषः *jagmushah*	जगन्वद्भिः *jaganvadbhih*
जघ्निवस् *jaghnivas*	जघ्निवान् *jaghniván*	जघ्निवांसः *jaghnivámsah*	जघ्नुषः *jaghnushah*	जघ्निवद्भिः *jaghnivadbhih*
जघन्वस् *jaghanvas*	जघन्वान् *jaghanván*	जघन्वांसः *jaghanvámsah*	जघ्नुषः *jaghnushah*	जघन्वद्भिः *jaghanvadbhih*

Bases in ईयस् *îyas.*

§ 206. Bases in ईयस् *íyas* (termination of the comparative) form their Anga base in ईयांस् *íyáms*.

Pada and Bha base गरीयस् *garíyas*, heavier; Anga base गरीयांस् *garíyáms*.

MASCULINE.

SINGULAR.	DUAL.	PLURAL.
N. गरीयान् *garíyán*	गरीयांसौ *garíyámsau*	गरीयांसः *garíyámsah*
A. गरीयांसं *garíyámsam*	गरीयांसौ *garíyámsau*	गरीयसः *garíyasah*
V. गरीयन् *garíyan*		
I. गरीयसा *garíyasá*	गरीयोभ्यां *garíyobhyám*	गरीयोभिः *garíyobhih*, &c.

NEUTER.

SINGULAR.	DUAL.	PLURAL.
N. गरीयः *garíyah*	गरीयसी *garíyasí*	गरीयांसि *garíyámsi*

FEM.

SINGULAR.
N. गरीयसी *garíyasí*

Miscellaneous Nouns with changeable Consonantal Bases.

§ 207. Words ending in पाद् *pád*, foot, retain पाद् *pád* as Anga and Pada base, but shorten it to पद् *pad* as Bha base.

SINGULAR.	DUAL.	PLURAL.	
N.V. सुपाद् *supád*	सुपादौ *supádau*	सुपादः *supádah*	(Anga)
A. सुपादं *supádam*	सुपादौ *supádau*	सुपदः *supadah*	(Bha)
		I. सुपाद्भिः *supádbhih*	(Pada)

---

* म् *m* changed into न् *n* according to § 136.

The feminine is either सुपाद् *supád* or सुपदी *supadí* (Pân. IV. 1, 8); but a metre consisting of two feet is called द्विपदा *dvipadá*.

§ 208. Words ending in वाह् *váh*, carrying, retain वाह् *váh* as Anga and Pada base, but shorten it to ऊह् *úh* as Bha base. The fem. is ऊही *úhí*.

Final ह् *h* is interchangeable with ध् *dh*, ड् *d*, ढ् *ḍ*. (See § 128; 174, 8.)

The ऊ *ú* of ऊह् *úh* forms Vriddhi with a preceding अ *a* or आ *á* (§ 46). Thus विश्ववाह् *viśvaváh*, upholder of the universe. (Accent, Pân. VI. 1, 171.)

SINGULAR.	DUAL.	PLURAL.
N.V. विश्ववाद् *viśvavát*	विश्ववाहौ *viśvavdhau*	विश्ववाह: *viśvavdhaḥ*
A. विश्ववाहं *viśvavdham*	विश्ववाहौ *viśvavdhau*	विश्वौह: *viśvauháḥ*
		I. विश्ववाहभि: *viśvavádbhíḥ*

§ 209. श्वेतवाह् *śvetaváh* is further irregular, forming its Pada base in वस् *vas*, and retaining it in the Nom. and Voc. Sing.; e.g. Nom.Voc. श्वेतवा: *śvetaváḥ*; Acc. श्वेतवाहं *śvetavdham*; Instr. श्वेतौहा *śvetauhá*; Instr. Plur. श्वेतवोभि: *śvetavobhíḥ*, &c.; Loc. Plur. श्वेतव:सु *śvetavaḥsú*.

Some grammarians allow श्वेतवाह् *śvetaváh*, instead of श्वेतौह् *śvetauh*, in all the Bha cases (Sâr. 1. 9, 14), and likewise श्वेतव: *śvétavaḥ* in Voc. Sing.

§ 210. A more important compound with वाह् *váh* is अनड्वाह् *anaḍváh*, an ox, (i.e. a cart-drawer.) It has three bases: 1. The Anga base अनड्वाह् *anaḍváh*; 2. The Pada base अनड्वद् *anaḍud*; 3. The Bha base अनड्वह् *anaḍuh*.

It is irregular besides in the Nom. and Voc. Sing.

SINGULAR.		DUAL.		PLURAL.	
N. अनड्वान् *anaḍván*	N. A.V. अनड्वाहौ *anaḍvdhau*		N. अनड्वाह: *anaḍvdhaḥ*		
V. अनड्वन् *anaḍvan*	I. D. Ab. अनड्वभ्यां *anaḍudbhyám*		A. अनड्वह: *anaḍuhaḥ*		
A. अनड्वाहं *anaḍváham*	G. L. अनड्वहो: *anaḍuhoḥ*		I. अनड्वभि: *anaḍudbhiḥ*		
I. अनड्वहा *anaḍuhá*			L. अनड्वत्सु *anaḍutsu*		

If used as a neuter, at the end of a compound, it forms

SINGULAR.	DUAL.	PLURAL.
N.A.V. अनड्वद् *anaḍud*	अनड्वही *anaḍuhí*	अनड्वांहि *anaḍvámhi*

The rest like the masculine.

The feminine is अनड्वही *anaḍuhí* or अनड्वाही *anaḍvdhí* (Pân. VII. 1, 98, vârt.).

§ 211. अप् *ap*, water, is invariably plural, and makes its अ *a* long in the Anga base, and substitutes त् *t* for प् *p* before an affix beginning with भ् *bh*.

Plural: Nom. आप: *ápaḥ*, Acc. अप: *apáḥ*, Instr. अभि: *adbhíḥ*, Loc. अप्सु *apsú*. (Accent, Pân. VI. 1, 171.)

In composition अप् *ap* is said to form स्वाप् *sváp*, Nom. Sing. masc. and fem., having good water; Acc. स्वापं *svápam*; Instr. स्वपा *svapá*, &c. Nom. Plur. स्वाप: *svápaḥ*; Acc. स्वप: *svapaḥ*; Instr. स्वभि: *svadbhíḥ*, &c. The neuter forms the Nom. Sing. स्वप् *svap*; Nom. Plur. स्वंपि *svampi* or स्वांपि *svámpi*, according to different interpretations of Pânini. (Colebrooke, p. 101, note.) The Sârasvatî (1. 9, 62) gives स्वांपि तडागानि *svámpi taḍágáni*, tanks with good water.

§ 212. पुंस् *puṁs*, man, has three bases: 1. The Aṅga base पुमांस् *pumáṁs;* 2. The Pada base पुम् *pum;* 3. The Bha base पुंस् *puṁs.* (Accent, Pâṇ. VI. 1, 171.)

	SINGULAR.		DUAL.		PLURAL.
N.	पुमान् *pumán*	N.A.V.	पुमांसौ *pumáṁsau*	N.	पुमांस: *pumáṁsaḥ*
V.	पुमन् *púman*	I.D.Ab.	पुंभ्यां *pumbhyám*	A.	पुंस: *puṁsáḥ*
A.	पुमांसं *pumáṁsam*	G.L.	पुंसो: *puṁsóḥ*	I.	पुंभि: *pumbhíḥ*
I.	पुंसा *puṁsá*			L.	पुंसु *puṁsú*

The Loc. Plur. is written पुंसु *puṁsú*, not पुंषु *pumshú* or पुन्सु *punsú* (§ 100, note). The Sârasvatí gives पुंक्षु *puṅkshú* (1. 9, 70). Pâṇini (VIII. 3, 58) says that नुं *num* only, not Anusvâra in general, does not prevent the change of स् *s* into ष् *sh;* and therefore that change does not take place in सुहिंसु *suhinsu* and पुंसु *pumsu.* In the first, न् *n* is radical, not inserted; in the second, the Anusvâra represents an original म् *m.* Cf. Siddh.-Kaum. vol. I. p. 186: सुहिन्सु पुंखिमादावनुखारसत्त्वे ऽपि तस्य नुमस्थानिकत्वाभावात् षत्वमिति भाव: ।

In composition it is declined in the same manner if used in the masc. or fem. gender. As a neuter it is, Nom. Sing. सुपुम् *supum*, Nom. Dual सुपुंसी *supuṁsí*, Nom. Plur. सुपुमांसि *supumáṁsi*.

§ 213. दिव् *div* or द्यु *dyu*, f. sky, is declined as follows, (Accent, Pâṇ. VI. 1, 171; 183):
Base दिव् *div*, द्यु *dyu*. (See § 219.)

	SINGULAR.		DUAL.		PLURAL.
N.	द्यौ: *dyaúḥ*	N.A.V.	दिवौ *dívau*	N.	दिव: *dívaḥ*
A.	दिवं *dívam*	I.D.Ab.	द्युभ्यां *dyúbhyám*	A.	दिव: *diváḥ*
I.	दिवा *divá*	G.L.	दिवो: *divóḥ*	I.	द्युभि: *dyúbhiḥ*
D.	दिवे *divé*			D.Ab.	द्युभ्य: *dyúbhyaḥ*
Ab.G.	दिव: *diváḥ*			G.	दिवां *divám*
L.	दिवि *diví*			L.	द्युषु *dyúshu*
V.	द्यौ: *dyaúḥ*				

Another base द्यो *dyo* is declined as a base ending in a vowel, and follows the paradigm of गो *go*, § 219. (See Siddh.-Kaum. vol. I. p. 138.)

Compounds like सुदिव् *sudiv*, having a good sky, are declined in the masc. and fem. like दिव् *div.* Hence सुद्यौ: *sudyauḥ*, सुदिवं *sudivam*, &c.

In the neuter they form Nom. Acc. Voc. Sing. सुद्यु *sudyu*, having a good sky; Dual सुदिवी *sudiví;* Plur. सुदिवि *sudivi.*

§ 214. A number of words in Sanskrit are what Greek grammarians would call *Metaplasta,* i. e. they exist under two forms, each following a different declension, but one being deficient in the Sarvanâmasthâna cases, i. e. Nom. Voc. Acc. Sing. and Dual, Nom. Voc. Plur., and Nom. Voc. Acc. Plur. of neuters. (Pâṇ. VI. 1, 63.) Thus

DEFECTIVE BASE:	BASE DECLINED THROUGHOUT:
*1. असन् *asan*, n. blood ;	असृज् *asṛij*, n.
*2. आसन् *ásan*, n. face ;	आस्य *ásya*, n.
*3. उदन् *udan*, n. water ;	उदक *udaka*, n.
4. दत् *dat*, m. tooth; Acc. Pl. दत: *datáḥ;*	दंत *danta*, m.

---

*5. दोषन् *doshan*, (m.) n. arm ;	दोस् *dos*, m. n.
6. नस् *nas*, f. nose ; Acc. Pl. नस: *nasáh;*	नासिका *násiká*, f.
7. निश् *niś*, f. night ; Acc. Pl. निश: *niśáh ;*	निशा *niśá*, f.
8. पद् *pad*, m. foot ; Acc. Pl. पद: *padáh ;*	पाद *páda*, m.
9. पृत् *prit*, f. army † ; Loc. Pl. पृत्सु *pritsú ;*	पृतना *pritaná*, f.
10. मांस् *máms*, n. meat‡ ;	मांस *mámsa*, n.
11. मास् *más*, m. month ‖ ; मास: *másáh ;*	मास *mása*, m.
*12. यकन् *yakan*, n. liver¶ ;	यकृत् *yakrit*, n.
*13. यूषन् *yúshan*, m. pea-soup ;	यूष *yúsha*, m.
*14. शकन् *śakan*, n. ordure ;	शकृत् *śakrit*, n.
15. स्नु *snu*, n. ridge ;	सानु *sánu*, n.
16. हृद् *hrid*, n. (m.); Gen. Sing. हृद: *hridáh;*	हृदय *hridaya*, n.

Hence in

No. 1. N.V.A. Sing. is असृक् *asrik* only ;
        N.V.A. Dual is असृजी *asrijí* only ; but { A. Plur. असृंजि *asriñji* or असानि *asáni.*
        N.V. Plur. is असृंजि *asriñji* only ;   { I. Sing. असृजा *asrijá* or अस्ना *asná.*
                                                    { I. Du. असृग्भ्यां *asrigbhyám* or असभ्यां *asabhyám.*

No. 4. N.A.V. Sing. is दंत:, °तं, °त *dantah, am, a,* only;
        N.V.A. Dual is दंतौ *dantau* only ; but { A. Plur. दंतान् *dantán* or दत: *datah.*
        N.V. Plur. is दंता: *dantáh* only ;   { I. Sing. दंतेन *dantena* or दता *datá.*
                                                   { I. Dual दंताभ्यां *dantábhyám* or दद्भ्यां *dadbhyám.*

No. 11. N.A.V. Sing. is मास:, °सं, °स *másah, am, a,* only;
        N.V.A. Dual is मासौ *másau* only ; but { A. Plur. मासान् *másán* or मास: *másah.*
        N.V. Plur. is मासा: *másáh* only ;   { I. Sing. मासेन *másena* or मासा *másá.*
                                                  { I. Dual मासाभ्यां *másábhyám* or माभ्यां *mábhyám.*

No. 13. N.A.V. Sing. is यूष:, °षं, °ष *yúshah, am, a,* only;
        N.A.V. Dual is यूषौ *yúshau* only ; but { A. Plur. यूषान् *yúshán* or यूष्ण: *yúshnah.*
        N.V. Plur. is यूषा: *yúsháh* only ;   { I. Sing. यूषेण *yúshena* or यूष्णा *yúshná.*
                                                  { I. Du. यूषाभ्यां *yúshábhyám* or °ष्ण्यां *-shnabhyám.*
                                                  { L. Sing. यूषे *yúshe* or °षणि *-shani* or °ष्णि *-shni.*

Grammarians differ on the exact meaning of Pánini's rule ; and forms such as दोषणी *doshaní*, Nom. Dual Neut., would seem to show that in the Nom. Acc. Voc. Dual the base दोषन् *doshan* may be used. (See Siddh.-Kaum. vol. i. pp. 107, 131, 141, 144.) By some the rule is restricted to the Veda.

2. *Bases ending in Vowels.*

§ 215. Bases ending in vowels may be subdivided into two classes :

1. Bases ending in any vowels, except derivative अ *a* and आ *á.*

2. Bases ending in derivative अ *a* and आ *á.*

---

* No accent on Vibhakti. (Pán. VI. 1, 171.)   † Siddh.-Kaum. vol. i. p. 131.
‡ Siddh.-Kaum. vol. i. p. 141.   ‖ The Sárasvatí gives all cases of मास् *más* (1. 6, 35).
¶ Pán. VI. 1, 63.

1. *Bases ending in any Vowels, except derivative* व a *and* आ â.

§ 216. Instead of attempting to learn, either according to the system followed by native grammarians, or according to the more correct views of comparative philologists, how the terminations appended to consonantal bases are changed when appended to bases ending in vowels, it will be far easier to learn by heart the paradigms such as they are, without entering at all into the question whether there was originally but one set of terminations for all nouns, or whether, from the beginning, different terminations were used after bases ending in consonants and after bases ending in vowels.

Bases in ऐ ai *and* औ au.

§ 217. These bases are, with few exceptions, declined like bases ending in consonants. The principal rules to be observed are that before consonants ऐ *ai* becomes आ *â*, while औ *au* remains unchanged; and that before vowels both ऐ *ai* and औ *au* become आय् *áy* and आव् *áv*.

Base रै *rai*, राय् *ráy*, m. wealth; (Accent, Pân. vi. 1, 171.) नौ *nau*, नाव् *náv*, f. ship; (Accent, Pân. vi. 1, 168.)

	SINGULAR.		DUAL.		PLURAL.	
N.V.	रा: *rá-ḥ*	नौ: *naú-ḥ*	रायौ *ráy-au*	नावौ *náv-au*	राय: *ráy-aḥ*	नाव: *náv-aḥ*
A.	रायं *ráy-am*	नावं *náv-am*			राय: *ráy-áḥ* *	नाव: *náv-aḥ*
I.	राया *ráy-á*	नावा *náv-á*	राभ्यां *rá-bhyám*	नौभ्यां *nau-bhyám*	राभि: *rá-bhíḥ*	नौभि: *nau-bhíḥ*
D.	राये *ráy-é*	नावे *náv-é*			राभ्य: *rá-bhyáḥ*	नौभ्य: *nau-bhyáḥ*
Ab.	राय: *ráy-áḥ*	नाव: *náv-áḥ*	रायो: *ráy-óḥ*	नावो: *náv-óḥ*	रायां *ráy-ám*	नावां *náv-ám*
G.						
L.	रायि *ráy-í*	नावि *náv-í*			रासु *rá-sú*	नौषु *nau-shú*

Decline ग्लौ: *glauḥ*, m. the moon.

Bases in ओ o.

§ 218. The only noun of importance is गो *go*, a bull or cow. It is slightly irregular in Nom. Acc. Abl. and Gen. Sing. and in the Acc. Plur. (Accent, Pân. vi. 1, 182.)

	SINGULAR.	DUAL.	PLURAL.
N.V.	गौ: *gaú-ḥ*	गावौ *gáv-au*	गाव: *gáv-aḥ*
A.	गां *gá-m*		गा: *gá-ḥ*
I.	गवा *gáv-á*	गोभ्यां *gó-bhyám*	गोभि: *gó-bhiḥ*
D.	गवे *gáv-e*		गोभ्य: *gó-bhyaḥ*
Ab.	गो: *gó-ḥ*	गवो: *gáv-oḥ*	गवां *gáv-ám*
G.			
L.	गवि *gáv-i*		गोषु *gó-shu*

---

* In the Veda the Acc. Plur. of रै *rai* occurs both as *ráyaḥ* (Rv. i. 68, 5; 98, 3; vii. 34, 22; viii. 52, 10; x. 140, 4) and *ráyáḥ* (Rv. i. 113, 4; iii. 2, 15).

If bases in ऐ *ai*, ओ *o*, औ *au* are to be declined as neuters at the end of compounds, they shorten ऐ *ai* to इ *i*, and ओ *o* and औ *au* to उ *u*, and are then declined like neuters in इ *i* and उ *u*. The masculine forms, however, are equally allowed (if the base is masculine) in all cases except the Nom. Acc. Voc. Sing. Dual and Plural. Hence Instr. Sing. neut. सुरिणा *suriṇá* or सुराया *suráyá*; but only सुनुना *sununá*.

§ 219. द्यो *dyo*, fem. heaven, is declined like गो *go*. It coincides in the Nom. and Voc. Sing. with दिव् *div*, sky, but differs from it in all other cases. (§ 213.)

	SINGULAR.	DUAL.	PLURAL.
N.	द्यौः *dyaúḥ*	द्यावौ *dyávau*	द्यावः *dyávaḥ*
A.	द्याम् *dyám* *		द्याः *dyáḥ* *
I.	द्यवा *dyává*	द्योभ्याम् *dyóbhyám*	द्योभिः *dyóbhiḥ*
D.	द्यवे *dyáve*		द्योभ्यः *dyóbhyaḥ*
Ab.	द्योः *dyóḥ*		द्यावाम् *dyávám*
G.		द्यवोः *dyávoḥ* .	
L.	द्यवि *dyávi*		द्योषु *dyóshu*
V.	द्यौः *dyaúḥ*		

Forms of *dyu* which occur in the Rig-veda :

Sing. N. *dyaús*; A. *dívam, dyám*; I. *divá* (*dívá*, by day); D. *divé*; G. *diváḥ, dyóḥ*; L. *diví, dyávi*; V. *dyaús* (Rv. vi. 51, 5). Plur. N. *dyávaḥ*; A. *dyán*; I. *dyúbhiḥ*. Dual N. *dyává*.

Being used at the end of a compound द्यो *dyo* forms its neuter base as द्यु *dyu*; e.g. प्रद्यु *pradyu*, eminently celestial, Dual प्रद्युनी *pradyuní*, Plur. प्रद्यूनि *pradyúni* (Siddh.-Kaum. vol. I. pp. 144, 145); while from दिव् *div* the neuter adjective was, as we saw, सुद्यु *sudyu*, having a good sky, Dual सुदिवी *sudiví*, Plur. सुदीवि *sudívi* (Colebr. pp. 67, 73). प्रद्यु *pradyu*, as a neuter, cannot take the optional masculine cases (Siddh.-Kaum. vol. I. p. 145).

Note—There are no real nouns ending in ए *e*, though grammarians imagine such words as ए: *eḥ*, the sun, उद्यदे: *udyadeḥ*, the rising sun ; Nom. Dual उद्यदयौ *udyadayau*, Nom. Plur. उद्यदय: *udyadayaḥ*.

Bases in ई *í* and ऊ *ú*.

1. *Monosyllabic Bases in* ई *í and* ऊ *ú, being both Masculine and Feminine.*

(A.) By themselves.

§ 220. Monosyllabic bases, derived from verbs without any suffix, like धी *dhí*, thinking, क्री *krí*, buying, लू *lú*, cutting, take the same terminations as consonantal bases. They remain unchanged before terminations beginning with consonants, but change final ई *í* and ऊ *ú* into इय् *iy* and उव् *uv*, before vowels. (Pâṇ. vi. 4, 82, 83.) Their Vocative is the same as their Nominative.

(B.) At the end of compounds.

§ 221. These monosyllabic bases rarely occur except at the end of compounds. Here

---

ey may either change ई *i* and ऊ *û* into इय् *iy* and उव् *uv*, or into य् *y* and व् *v*. They
ange it

1. Into इय् *iy* and उव् *uv*:

a. If the first member of the compound forms the predicate of the second, and the
second maintains its nominal character. Thus परमनी: *paramanîh*, the best leader,
Acc. Sing. परमनियं *paramaniyam*. Here नी: *nîh* is treated as a noun, and seems
to have lost its verbal character. शुद्धधी: *śuddhadhîh*, a pure thinker, a man of pure
thought, Acc. Sing. शुद्धधियं *śuddhadhiyam;* कुधी: *kudhîh*, a man of bad thought,
Acc. Sing. कुधियं *kudhiyam*. (Sâr.)

b. If ई *i* and ऊ *û* are preceded by two radical initial consonants. जलक्री: *jalakrîh*, a buyer
of water, makes Acc. Sing. जलक्रियं *jalakriyam*. सुश्री: *suśrîh*, well faring, Acc. Sing.
सुश्रियं *suśriyam*. (Siddh.-Kaum. vol. 1. p. 119.) This is a merely phonetic change,
intended to facilitate pronunciation. (Pâṇ. vi. 4, 82.)

2. Into य् *y* and व् *v*, under all other circumstances, i. e. wherever the monosyllabic bases
retain their verbal character. ग्रामणी: *grâmaṇîh*, leader of a village, Acc. Sing. ग्रामण्यं
grâmaṇyam; here ग्राम *grâma* is not the predicate of नी: *nîh*, but is governed by नी: *nîh*,
which retains so far its verbal character. प्रधी: *pradhîh*, thinking in a high degree, Acc.
Sing. प्रध्यं *pradhyam;* here प्र *pra* is a preposition belonging to धी *dhî*, which retains
its verbal nature. उन्नी: *unnîh*, leading out, Acc. Sing. उन्न्यं *unnyam;* here उद् *ud* is
a preposition belonging to नी *nî*. Though ई *i* is preceded by two consonants, one
only belongs to the root. शुद्धधी: *śuddhadhîh* (if a Tatpurusha compound), thinking
pure things, would form the Acc. Sing. शुद्धध्यं *śuddhadhyam*, and thus be distinguished
from शुद्धधी: *śuddhadhîh* (as a Karmadhâraya compound), a pure thinker, or as a
Bahuvrîhi compound, a man possessed of pure thoughts (Siddh.-Kaum. vol. 1. p. 119),
which both have शुद्धधियं *śuddhadhiyam* for their accusative. The general idea which
suggested the distinction between bases changing their final ई *i* and ऊ *û* either into
इय् *iy* and उव् *uv*, or into य् *y* and व् *v*, seems to have been that the former were treated
as real monosyllabic nouns that might be used by themselves (धी: *dhîh*, a thinker), or
in such compounds as a noun admits of (सुधी: *sudhîh**, a good thinker; शुद्धधी:
śuddhadhîh, a pure thinker or pure thoughted); while the latter always retained
somewhat of their verbal character, and could therefore not be used by themselves,
but only at the end of compounds, preceded either by a preposition (प्रधी: *pradhîh*,
providens) or by a noun which was governed by them. The nouns in which ई *i* and
ऊ *û* stand after two radical consonants form an exception to this general rule, which
exception admits, however, of a phonetic explanation (§ 330), so that the only real
exception would be in the case of certain compounds ending in भू *bhû*. Thus भू *bhû*
becomes भुव् *bhuv* before vowels, whether it be verbal or nominal. (Pâṇ. vi. 4, 85.)
Ex. स्वयंभू: *svayambhûh*, self-existing, Acc. Sing. स्वयंभुवं *svayambhuvam*. (Sâr. 1. 6, 61.
Siddh.-Kaum. vol. 1. p. 119.) Not, however, in वर्षाभू: *varshâbhûh*, frog, Acc. Sing.
वर्षाभ्वं *varshâbhvam* (Pâṇ. vi. 4, 84), and in some other compounds, such as करभू:
karabhûh or कारभू: *kârabhûh*, nail, पुनर्भू: *punarbhûh*, re-born, दृन्भू: *dṛinbhûh*, thunder-
bolt. (Pâṇ. vi. 4, 84, vârt.)

---

* सुधी: *sudhîh* is never to be treated as a verbal compound, but always forms Acc. Sing.
सुधियं *sudhiyam*, &c., as if it were a Karmadhâraya compound. (Pâṇ. vi. 4, 85.)

2. Polysyllabic Bases in ई *î and* ऊ *û.*

§ 222. Polysyllabic bases in ई *î* and ऊ *û* being both masculine and feminine, such as
पपी: *papîh*, protector, the sun, ययी: *yayîh*, road, and नृतू: *nritûh*, dancer, are declined like
the verbal compounds प्रधी: *pradhîh* and वृक्षलू: *vrikshalûh*, except that

1. they form the Acc. Sing. in ई *îm* and ऊ *ûm;*
2. they form the Acc. Plur. in ईन् *în* and ऊन् *ûn*.

Remember also, that those in ई *î* form the Loc. Sing. in ई *î*, not in यि *yi*.

वातप्रमी: *vâtapramîh*, antelope, may be declined like पपी: *papîh;* but if derived by क्विप्
kvip, it may entirely follow the verbal प्रधी: *pradhîh* (Siddh.-Kaum. vol. 1. p. 116). The same
applies to nouns like सुती: *sutîh*, wishing for a son; सुखी: *sukhîh*, wishing for pleasure.
They follow the verbal प्रधी: *pradhîh* throughout, but they have their Gen. and Abl. Sing.
in उ: *uh;* सुत्यु: *sutyuh* (Siddh.-Kaum. vol. 1. p. 120). If the final long ई *î* is preceded by
two consonants, it is changed before vowels into इय् *iy*. Ex. शुष्की: *śushkîh*, शुष्कियौ
śushkiyau, &c.

	Monosyllabic, masc. and fem.	The same, at the end of compounds, used as a noun, masc. and fem.	The same, at the end of compounds, with initial double consonants, masc. and fem.	The same, in composition with prepositions, masc. and fem.	The same, in composition with a governed noun, masc. and fem.	Polysyllabic, masc. and fem.
	thinking.	a pure thinker.	water-buyer.	high-thinking.	village-leader.	sun.
	SINGULAR.	SINGULAR.	SINGULAR.	SINGULAR.	SINGULAR.	SINGULAR.
N.	धी: dhîḥ	शुद्धधी: śuddhadhîḥ	जलक्री: jalakrîḥ	प्रधी: pradhîḥ	ग्रामणी: grâmaṇîḥ	पपी: papîḥ
A.	धियं dhiyam	शुद्धधियं śuddhadhiyam	जलक्रियं jalakriyam	प्रध्यं pradhyam	ग्रामण्यं grâmaṇyam	पपीं papîm
I.	धिया dhiyâ	शुद्धधिया śuddhadhiyâ	जलक्रिया jalakriyâ	प्रध्या pradhyâ	ग्रामण्या grâmaṇyâ	पप्या papyâ
D.	धिये dhiye	शुद्धधिये śuddhadhiye	जलक्रिये jalakriye	प्रध्ये pradhye	ग्रामण्ये grâmaṇye	पप्ये papye
Ab. G.	धिय: dhiyaḥ	शुद्धधिय: śuddhadhiyaḥ	जलक्रिय: jalakriyaḥ	प्रध्य: pradhyaḥ	ग्रामण्य: grâmaṇyaḥ	पप्य: papyaḥ
L.	धियि dhiyi	शुद्धधियि śuddhadhiyi	जलक्रियि jalakriyi	प्रध्यि pradhyi	ग्रामण्यां grâmaṇyâm *	पपी papî
V.	धी: dhîḥ	शुद्धधी: śuddhadhîḥ	जलक्री: jalakrîḥ	प्रधी: pradhîḥ	ग्रामणी: grâmaṇîḥ	पपी: papîḥ
	DUAL.	DUAL.	DUAL.	DUAL.	DUAL.	DUAL.
N. A. V.	धियौ dhiyau	शुद्धधियौ śuddhadhiyau	जलक्रियौ jalakriyau	प्रध्यौ pradhyau	ग्रामण्यौ grâmaṇyau	पप्यौ papyau
I. D. Ab.	धीभ्यां dhîbhyâm	शुद्धधीभ्यां śuddhadhîbhyâm	जलक्रीभ्यां jalakrîbhyâm	प्रधीभ्यां pradhîbhyâm	ग्रामणीभ्यां grâmaṇîbhyâm	पपीभ्यां papîbhyâm
G. L.	धियो: dhiyoḥ	शुद्धधियो: śuddhadhiyoḥ	जलक्रियो: jalakriyoḥ	प्रध्यो: pradhyoḥ	ग्रामण्यो: grâmaṇyoḥ	पप्यो: papyoḥ
	PLURAL.	PLURAL.	PLURAL.	PLURAL.	PLURAL.	PLURAL.
N.	धिय: dhiyaḥ	शुद्धधिय: śuddhadhiyaḥ	जलक्रिय: jalakriyaḥ	प्रध्य: pradhyaḥ	ग्रामण्य: grâmaṇyaḥ	पप्य: papyaḥ
A.	धिय: dhiyaḥ	शुद्धधिय: śuddhadhiyaḥ	जलक्रिय: jalakriyaḥ	प्रध्य: pradhyaḥ	ग्रामण्य: grâmaṇyaḥ	पपीन् papîn ‡
I.	धीभि: dhîbhiḥ	शुद्धधीभि: śuddhadhîbhiḥ	जलक्रीभि: jalakrîbhiḥ	प्रधीभि: pradhîbhiḥ	ग्रामणीभि: grâmaṇîbhiḥ	पपीभि: papîbhiḥ
D. Ab.	धीभ्य: dhîbhyaḥ	शुद्धधीभ्य: śuddhadhîbhyaḥ	जलक्रीभ्य: jalakrîbhyaḥ	प्रधीभ्य: pradhîbhyaḥ	ग्रामणीभ्य: grâmaṇîbhyaḥ	पपीभ्य: papîbhyaḥ
G.	धियां dhiyâm	शुद्धधियां śuddhadhiyâm	जलक्रियां jalakriyâm	प्रध्यां pradhyâm	ग्रामण्यां grâmaṇyâm †	पप्यां papyâm ‖
L.	धीषु dhîshu	शुद्धधीषु śuddhadhîshu	जलक्रीषु jalakrîshu	प्रधीषु pradhîshu	ग्रामणीषु grâmaṇîshu	पपीषु papîshu

* Words ending in नी nî, leader, form their Loc. Sing. in आं âm. (Sâr.) or नां nâm. (Sâr. 1. 6, 62.)

† Or ग्रामणीनां grâmaṇînâm. Words of the Senânî class take आं âm ‖ It does not take नां nâm. (Siddh.-Kaum. vol. 1. p. 116.)

‡ पपी: papîḥ, at the end of a fem. comp.; Rûpâvali, p. 9 b.

	Monosyllabic, masc. and fem.	The same, at the end of compounds, used as a noun, masc. and fem.	The same, at the end of compounds, with initial double consonants, masc. and fem.	The same, in composition with prepositions, masc. and fem.	The same, in composition with a governed noun, masc. and fem.	Polysyllabic, masc. and fem.
	cutter.	best cutter.	dice-player.	cutting asunder.	corn-cutter.	dancer.
	SINGULAR.	SINGULAR.	SINGULAR.	SINGULAR.	SINGULAR.	SINGULAR.
N.	लूः *lūḥ*	परमलूः *paramalūḥ*	कटमूः *kaṭaprūḥ*	विलूः *vilūḥ*	यवलूः *yavalūḥ*	नृतूः *nṛitūḥ*
A.	लुवं *luvam*	परमलुवं *paramaluvam*	कटमुवं *kaṭapruvam*	विल्वं *vilvam*	यवल्वं *yavalvam*	नृतूं *nṛitūm*
I.	लुवा *luvā*	परमलुवा *paramaluvā*	कटमुवा *kaṭapruvā*	विल्वा *vilvā*	यवल्वा *yavalvā*	नृत्वा *nṛitvā*
D.	लुवे *luve*	परमलुवे *paramaluve*	कटमुवे *kaṭapruve*	विल्वे *vilve*	यवल्वे *yavalve*	नृत्वे *nṛitve*
Ab.G.	लुवः *luvaḥ*	परमलुवः *paramaluvaḥ*	कटमुवः *kaṭapruvaḥ*	विल्वः *vilvaḥ*	यवल्वः *yavalvaḥ*	नृत्वः *nṛitvaḥ*
L.	लुवि *luvi*	परमलुवि *paramaluvi*	कटमुवि *kaṭapruvi*	विल्वि *vilvi*	यवल्वि *yavalvi*	नृत्वि *nṛitvi*
V.	लूः *lūḥ*	परमलूः *paramalūḥ*	कटमूः *kaṭaprūḥ*	विलूः *vilūḥ*	यवलूः *yavalūḥ*	नृतूः *nṛitūḥ*
	DUAL.	DUAL.	DUAL.	DUAL.	DUAL.	DUAL.
N. A. V.	लुवौ *luvau*	परमलुवौ *paramaluvau*	कटमुवौ *kaṭapruvau*	विल्वौ *vilvau*	यवल्वौ *yavalvau*	नृत्वौ *nṛitvau*
I. D. Ab.	लूभ्यां *lūbhyām*	परमलूभ्यां *paramalūbhyām*	कटमूभ्यां *kaṭaprūbhyām*	विलूभ्यां *vilūbhyām*	यवलूभ्यां *yavalūbhyām*	नृतूभ्यां *nṛitūbhyām*
G. L.	लुवोः *luvoḥ*	परमलुवोः *paramaluvoḥ*	कटमुवोः *kaṭapruvoḥ*	विल्वोः *vilvoḥ*	यवल्वोः *yavalvoḥ*	नृत्वोः *nṛitvoḥ*
	PLURAL.	PLURAL.	PLURAL.	PLURAL.	PLURAL.	PLURAL.
N.	लुवः *luvaḥ*	परमलुवः *paramaluvaḥ*	कटमुवः *kaṭapruvaḥ*	विल्वः *vilvaḥ*	यवल्वः *yavalvaḥ*	नृत्वः *nṛitvaḥ*
A.	लुवः *luvaḥ*	परमलुवः *paramaluvaḥ*	कटमुवः *kaṭapruvaḥ*	विल्वः *vilvaḥ*	यवल्वः *yavalvaḥ*	नृतून *nṛitūn* †
I.	लूभिः *lūbhiḥ*	परमलूभिः *paramalūbhiḥ*	कटमूभिः *kaṭaprūbhiḥ*	विलूभिः *vilūbhiḥ*	यवलूभिः *yavalūbhiḥ*	नृतूभिः *nṛitūbhiḥ*
D. Ab.	लूभ्यः *lūbhyaḥ*	परमलूभ्यः *paramalūbhyaḥ*	कटमूभ्यः *kaṭaprūbhyaḥ*	विलूभ्यः *vilūbhyaḥ*	यवलूभ्यः *yavalūbhyaḥ*	नृतूभ्यः *nṛitūbhyaḥ*
G.	लुवां *luvām*	परमलुवां *paramaluvām*	कटमुवां *kaṭapruvām*	विल्वां *vilvām*	यवल्वां *yavalvām* *	नृत्वां *nṛitvām*
L.	लूषु *lūshu*	परमलूषु *paramalūshu*	कटमूषु *kaṭaprūshu*	विलूषु *vilūshu*	यवलूषु *yavalūshu*	नृतूषु *nṛitūshu*

* The Sâr. gives also यवलूनां *yavalūnām*.

† नृतूः *nṛitūḥ*, at the end of a fem. comp.

§ 223. All these compounds may be used without any change, whether they refer to nouns in the masculine or in the feminine gender. If the head-borough or the sweeper should be of the female sex, the Dat. Sing. would still be ग्रामण्ये स्त्रियै *grâmaṇye striyai*, खलप्वे स्त्रियै *khalapve striyai* (Kâsikâ I. 4, 3). Sometimes, however, if the meaning of a compound is such that it may by itself be applied to a woman as well as to a man, e. g. प्रधी: *pradhîḥ*, thinking, some grammarians allow such compounds to be declined in the feminine, like लक्ष्मी: *lakshmîḥ*, except in the Acc. Sing. and Plur., where they takeं *am* and ा: *aḥ;* प्रध्यं *pradhyam*, प्रध्य: *pradhyaḥ*, not प्रधीं *pradhîm* or प्रधी: *pradhîḥ* (Siddh.-Kaum. vol. I. p. 136). A similar argument is applied to पुनर्भू: *punarbhûḥ*, if it means a woman married a second time. It may then form its Vocative हे पुनर्भु *he punarbhu* (Siddh.-Kaum. vol. I. p. 138), and take the *five fuller feminine terminations* (§ 224).

	MASC. AND FEM.	FEM. ONLY.
	SINGULAR.	SINGULAR.
N.	प्रधी: *pradhîḥ*	प्रधी: *pradhîḥ*
A.	प्रध्यं *pradhyam*	प्रध्यं *pradhyam*
I.	प्रध्या *pradhyâ*	प्रध्या *pradhyâ*
D.	प्रध्ये *pradhye*	or प्रध्यै *pradhyai*
Ab.	प्रध्य: *pradhyaḥ*	or प्रध्या: *pradhyâḥ*
G.	प्रध्य: *pradhyaḥ*	or प्रध्या: *pradhyâḥ*
L.	प्रध्यि *pradhyi*	or प्रध्यां *pradhyâm*
V.	प्रधी: *pradhîḥ*	or प्रधि *pradhi*
	DUAL.	DUAL.
N. A. V.	प्रध्यौ *pradhyau*	प्रध्यौ *pradhyau*
I. D. Ab.	प्रधीभ्यां *pradhîbhyâm*	प्रधीभ्यां *pradhîbhyâm*
G. L.	प्रध्यो: *pradhyoḥ*	प्रध्यो: *pradhyoḥ*
	PLURAL.	PLURAL.
N.	प्रध्य: *pradhyaḥ*	प्रध्य: *pradhyaḥ*
A.	प्रध्य: *pradhyaḥ*	प्रध्य: *pradhyaḥ*
I.	प्रधीभि: *pradhîbhiḥ*	प्रधीभि: *pradhîbhiḥ*
D. Ab.	प्रधीभ्य: *pradhîbhyaḥ*	प्रधीभ्य: *pradhîbhyaḥ*
G.	प्रध्यां *pradhyâm*	or प्रधीनां *pradhînâm*
L.	प्रधीषु *pradhîshu*	प्रधीषु *pradhîshu*

I. *Monosyllabic Bases in* ई *î and* ऊ *û, being Feminine only.*

§ 224. Bases like धी *dhî*, intellect, श्री *srî*, happiness, ह्री *hrî*, shame, भी *bhî*, fear, and भ्रू *bhrû*, brow, may be declined throughout exactly like the monosyllabic bases in इ *i* and उ *u*, such as लू *lû*, a cutter. Their only peculiarity consists in their admitting a number of optional forms in the Dat. Abl. Gen. and Loc. Sing. and Gen. Plur. These may be called the *five fuller feminine terminations* in ऐ *ai*, आ: *âḥ*, आ: *âḥ*, आं *âm*, and नां *nâm*.

Monosyllabic, fem. only.	Optional fuller forms.	Monosyllabic, fem. only.	Optional fuller forms.
thought.		*earth.*	
SINGULAR.		SINGULAR.	
N. धी: *dhíḥ*		भू: *bhúḥ*	
A. धियं *dhíyam*		भुवं *bhúvam*	
I. धिया *dhiyá*		भुवा *bhuvá*	
D. धिये *dhiyé*	धियै *dhiyaí*	भुवे *bhuvé*	भुवै *bhuvaí*
Ab. धिय: *dhiyáḥ*	धिया: *dhiyáḥ*	भुव: *bhuváḥ*	भुवा: *bhuváḥ*
G. धिय: *dhiyáḥ*	धिया: *dhiyáḥ*	भुव: *bhuváḥ*	भुवा: *bhuváḥ*
L. धिषि *dhiyí*	धियां *dhiyám*	भुवि *bhuví*	भुवां *bhuvám*
V. धी: *dhíḥ*		भू: *bhúḥ*	
DUAL.		DUAL.	
N.A.V. धियौ *dhíyau*		भुवौ *bhúvau*	
I.D.Ab. धीभ्यां *dhíbhyám*		भूभ्यां *bhúbhyám*	
G.L. धियो: *dhiyóḥ*		भुवो: *bhuvóḥ*	
PLURAL.		PLURAL.	
N. धिय: *dhíyaḥ*		भुव: *bhúvaḥ*	
A. धिय: *dhíyaḥ*		भुव: *bhúvaḥ*	
I. धीभि: *dhíbhíḥ*		भूभि: *bhúbhíḥ*	
D.Ab. धीभ्य: *dhíbhyáḥ*		भूभ्य: *bhúbhyáḥ*	
G. धियां *dhiyám*	धीनां *dhínám*	भुवां *bhuvám*	भूनां *bhúnám*
L. धीषु *dhíshú*		भूषु *bhúshú*	

2. *Polysyllabic Bases in* इ *î and* उ *û, being Feminine only.*

§ 225. (1) These bases always take the full feminine terminations.

(2) They change their final इ *í* and उ *ú* into य् *y* and व् *v* before terminations beginning with vowels.

(3) They take म् *m* and स् *s* as the terminations of the Acc. Sing. and Plural.

(4) They shorten their final ई *í* and ऊ *ú* in the Vocative Singular.

(5) Remember that most nouns in ई *í* have no स् *s* in the Nom. Sing., while those in ऊ *ú* have it.

Note—Some nouns in ई *í* take स् *s* in the Nom. Sing.: अवी: *avíḥ*, not desiring (applied to women); लक्ष्मी: *lakshmíḥ*, goddess of prosperity; तरी: *taríḥ*, boat; तंत्री: *tantríḥ*, lute.

Versus memorialis: अवीलक्ष्मीतरीतंत्रीधीहीश्रीयामुदात्तः समानामेव शब्दानां खिलोपो न कदाचन ॥ (Sâr. p. 18 a.)

Base नदी *nadí* and नद्य् *nady.*	Base वधू *vadhú* and वध्व् *vadhv.*
SINGULAR.	SINGULAR.
FEM.	FEM.
N. नदी *nadí*	N. वधू: *vadhú-ḥ*
A. नदीं *nadí-m*	A. वधूं *vadhú-m*
I. नद्या *nady-á*	I. वध्वा *vadhv-á*

<table>
<tr><td>

D. नद्यै *nady-aí*
Ab. नद्याः *nady-áḥ*
G. नद्याः *nady-áḥ*
L. नद्यां *nady-ám*
V. नदि *nádi*

</td><td>

D. वध्वै *vadhv-aí*
Ab. वध्वाः *vadhv-áḥ*
G. वध्वाः *vadhv-áḥ*
L. वध्वां *vadhv-ám*
V. वधु *vádhu*

</td></tr>
<tr><td align="center">

DUAL.

</td><td align="center">

DUAL.

</td></tr>
<tr><td>

N. A. V. नद्यौ *nady-aũ*
I. D. Ab. नदीभ्यां *nadí-bhyám*
G. L. नद्योः *nady-óḥ*

</td><td>

N. A. V. वध्वौ *vadhv-aũ*
I. D. Ab. वधूभ्यां *vadhú-bhyám*
G. L. वध्वोः *vadhv-óḥ*

</td></tr>
<tr><td align="center">

PLURAL.

</td><td align="center">

PLURAL.

</td></tr>
<tr><td>

N. V. नद्यः *nady-ãḥ*
A. नदीः *nadí-ḥ*
I. नदीभिः *nadí-bhiḥ*
D. नदीभ्यः *nadí-bhyaḥ*
Ab. नदीभ्यः *nadí-bhyaḥ*
G. नदीनां *nadí-nám*
L. नदीषु *nadí-shu*

</td><td>

N. V. वध्वः *vadhv-ãḥ*
A. वधूः *vadhú-ḥ*
I. वधूभिः *vadhú-bhiḥ*
D. वधूभ्यः *vadhú-bhyaḥ*
Ab. वधूभ्यः *vadhú-bhyaḥ*
G. वधूनां *vadhú-nám*
L. वधूषु *vadhú-shu*

</td></tr>
</table>

Compounds ending in Monosyllabic Feminine Bases in ई *í and* ऊ *ú.*

§ 226. Compounds the last member of which is a monosyllabic feminine base in ई *í* or ऊ *ú*, are declined alike in the masculine and feminine. Thus सुधीः *sudhíḥ*, masc. and fem.[*] if it means a good mind, or having a good mind, is declined exactly like धीः *dhíḥ*. सुभ्रूः *subhrúḥ*, masc. and fem. having a good brow, is declined exactly like भ्रूः *bhrúḥ*[†], without

---

[*] The following rule is taken from the Siddh.-Kaum. vol. i. p. 136. If धीः *dhíḥ*, intellect, stands at the end of the Karmadháraya compound like प्रधीः *pradhíḥ*, eminent intellect, or if it is used as a Bahuvrîhi compound in the feminine, such as प्रधीः *pradhíḥ*, possessed of eminent intellect, it is in both cases declined like लक्ष्मीः *lakshmíḥ*. It would thus become identical with प्रधीः *pradhíḥ*, thinking eminently, when it takes exceptionally the feminine terminations (§ 223). The Acc. Sing. and Plur., however, take ईं *am* and ईः *aḥ*. The difference, therefore, would be the substitution of य् *y* for इय् *iy* before vowels, the obligation of using the fuller fem. terminations only, and the Vocative in इ *í*, these being the only points of difference between the declension of लक्ष्मीः *lakshmíḥ* and धीः *dhíḥ*, fem. The Siddhânta-Kaumudî, while giving these rules for प्रधीः *pradhíḥ*, agrees with the rules given above with regard to सुधीः *sudhíḥ*, &c.

[†] The Voc. Sing. सुभ्रु *subhru* is used by Bhaṭṭi, in a passage where Ráma in great grief exclaims, हा पितः क्वासि हे सुभ्रु *há pitaḥ kvási he subhru*, Oh father, where art thou, Oh thou fine-browed (wife)! Some grammarians admit this Vocative as correct; others call it a mistake of Bhaṭṭi; others, again, while admitting that it is a mistake, consider that Bhaṭṭi made Ráma intentionally commit it as a token of his distracted mind. (Siddh.-Kaum. vol. i. p. 137.)

106   DECLENSION.   § 226–

excluding the fuller terminations (ए *ai*, आः *áḥ*, आं *ám*, नां *nám*)[*] for the masculine, or the simple terminations (ए *e*, अः *aḥ*, अः *aḥ*, इ *i*, आं *ám*) for the feminine. The same applies to the compound सुधीः *sudhíḥ*, when used as a substantive, good intellect.

If the same compounds are used as neuters, they shorten the final ई *í* or ऊ *ú* of their base, and are declined like वारि *vári* and मृदु *mṛidu*, with this difference, however, that in the Inst. Dat. Abl. Gen. Loc. Sing. Dual and Plural they may optionally take the masculine forms.

Masc. and Fem.	Optional fuller forms.	Optional forms for neuters, except Nom. Acc. Voc.
good-thoughted.		
SINGULAR.	**SINGULAR.**	**SINGULAR.**
N. सुधीः *sudhíḥ*		सुधि *sudhi*
A. सुधियं *sudhiyam*		सुधि *sudhi*
I. सुधिया *sudhiyá*		or सुधिना *sudhiná*
D. सुधिये *sudhiye*	सुधियै *sudhiyai*	or सुधिने *sudhine*
Ab. सुधियः *sudhiyaḥ*	सुधियाः *sudhiyáḥ*	or सुधिनः *sudhinaḥ*
G. सुधियः *sudhiyaḥ*	सुधियाः *sudhiyáḥ*	or सुधिनः *sudhinaḥ*
L. सुधियि *sudhiyi*	सुधियां *sudhiyám*	or सुधिनि *sudhini*
V. सुधीः *sudhíḥ*		सुधि *sudhi* or सुधे *sudhe*
DUAL.	**DUAL.**	**DUAL.**
N. A. V. सुधियौ *sudhiyau*		सुधिनी *sudhiní*
I. D. Ab. सुधीभ्यां *sudhíbhyám*		or सुधिभ्यां *sudhibhyám*
G. L. सुधियोः *sudhiyoḥ*		or सुधिनोः *sudhinoḥ*
PLURAL.	**PLURAL.**	**PLURAL.**
N. V. सुधियः *sudhiyaḥ*		सुधीनि *sudhíni*
A. सुधियः *sudhiyaḥ*		सुधीनि *sudhíni*
I. सुधीभिः *sudhíbhiḥ*		or सुधिभिः *sudhibhiḥ*
D. सुधीभ्यः *sudhíbhyaḥ*		or सुधिभ्यः *sudhibhyaḥ*
Ab. सुधीभ्यः *sudhíbhyaḥ*		or सुधिभ्यः *sudhibhyaḥ*
G. सुधियां *sudhiyám*	सुधीनां *sudhínám*	or सुधीनां *sudhínám*
L. सुधीषु *sudhíshu*		or सुधिषु *sudhishu*

[*] I can find no authority by which these fuller terminations are excluded. In बहुश्रेयसी *bahuśreyasí*, the feminine श्रेयसी *śreyasí* retains its feminine character (*sadítva*) throughout (Siddh.-Kaum. vol. I. p. 116); and the same is distinctly maintained for the compound प्रधीः *pradhíḥ*, possessed of distinguished intellect, if used as a masculine (Siddh.-Kaum. vol. I. p. 119).

	Masc. and Fem.	Optional fuller forms.	Optional forms for neuters, except Nom. Acc. Voc.
	with beautiful brows. SINGULAR.	SINGULAR.	SINGULAR.
N.	सुभ्रू: *subhrûḥ*		सुभ्रु *subhru*
A.	सुभ्रुवं *subhruvam*		सुभ्रु *subhru*
I.	सुभ्रुवा *subhruvá*		or सुभ्रुणा *subhruṇá*
D.	सुभ्रुवे *subhruve*	सुभ्रुवै *subhruvai*	or सुभ्रुणे *subhruṇe*
Ab.	सुभ्रुव: *subhruvaḥ*	सुभ्रुवा: *subhruvâḥ*	or सुभ्रुण: *subhruṇaḥ*
G.	सुभ्रुव: *subhruvaḥ*	सुभ्रुवा: *subhruvâḥ*	or सुभ्रुण: *subhruṇaḥ*
L.	सुभ्रुवि *subhruvi*	सुभ्रुवां *subhruvâm*	or सुभ्रुणि *subhruṇi*
V.	सुभ्रू: *subhrûḥ*		सुभ्रु *subhru* or °भ्रो *-bhro*
	DUAL.	DUAL.	DUAL.
N. A. V.	सुभ्रुवौ *subhruvau*		सुभ्रुणी *subhruṇî*
I. D. Ab.	सुभ्रूभ्यां *subhrûbhyâm*		or सुभ्रुभ्यां *subhrubhyâm*
G. L.	सुभ्रुवो: *subhruvoḥ*		or सुभ्रुणो: *subhruṇoḥ*
	PLURAL.	PLURAL.	PLURAL.
N. V.	सुभ्रुव: *subhruvaḥ*		सुभ्रूणि *subhrûṇi*
A.	सुभ्रुव: *subhruvaḥ*		सुभ्रूणि *subhrûṇi*
I.	सुभ्रूभि: *subhrûbhiḥ*		or सुभ्रुभि: *subhrubhiḥ*
D.	सुभ्रूभ्य: *subhrûbhyaḥ*		or सुभ्रुभ्य: *subhrubhyaḥ*
Ab.	सुभ्रूभ्य: *subhrûbhyaḥ*		or सुभ्रुभ्य: *subhrubhyaḥ*
G.	सुभ्रुवां *subhruvâm*	सुभ्रूणां *subhrûṇâm*	or सुभ्रूणां *subhrûṇâm*
L.	सुभ्रूषु *subhrûshu*		or सुभ्रुषु *subhrushu*

Compounds ending in Polysyllabic Feminine Bases in ई *î and* ऊ *û.*

§ 227. Feminine nouns like नदी *nadî* and चमू *chamú* may form the last portion of compounds which are used in the masculine gender. Thus बहुश्रेयसी *bahuśreyasî*, a man who has many auspicious qualities (Siddh.-Kaum. vol. I. pp. 116, 117), and अतिचमू *atichamú*, one who is better than an army (Siddh.-Kaum. vol. I. p. 123), are declined in the masculine and feminine :

	SINGULAR.	DUAL.	PLURAL.
N.	बहुश्रेयसी *bahuśreyasî* *	बहुश्रेयस्यौ *bahuśreyasyau*	बहुश्रेयस्य: *bahuśreyasyaḥ*
A.	बहुश्रेयसीं *bahuśreyasîm*	बहुश्रेयस्यौ *bahuśreyasyau*	बहुश्रेयसीन् *bahuśreyasîn*
I.	बहुश्रेयस्या *bahuśreyasyá*	बहुश्रेयसीभ्यां *bahuśreyasîbhyâm*	बहुश्रेयसीभि: *bahuśreyasîbhiḥ*
D.	बहुश्रेयस्यै *bahuśreyasyai*	बहुश्रेयसीभ्यां *bahuśreyasîbhyâm*	बहुश्रेयसीभ्य: *bahuśreyasîbhyaḥ*
Ab.	बहुश्रेयस्या: *bahuśreyasyâḥ*	बहुश्रेयसीभ्यां *bahuśreyasîbhyâm*	बहुश्रेयसीभ्य: *bahuśreyasîbhyaḥ*
G.	बहुश्रेयस्या: *bahuśreyasyâḥ*	बहुश्रेयस्यो: *bahuśreyasyoḥ*	बहुश्रेयसीनां *bahuśreyasînâm*
L.	बहुश्रेयस्यां *bahuśreyasyâm*	बहुश्रेयस्यो: *bahuśreyasyoḥ*	बहुश्रेयसीषु *bahuśreyasîshu*
V.	बहुश्रेयसि *bahuśreyasi*	बहुश्रेयस्यौ *bahuśreyasyau*	बहुश्रेयस्य: *bahuśreyasyaḥ*

* From लक्ष्मी: *lakshmîḥ*, the Nom. Sing. would be अतिलक्ष्मी: *atilakshmîḥ*.

SINGULAR.	DUAL.	PLURAL.
N. अतिचमूः *atichamûḥ*	अतिचम्वौ *atichamvau*	अतिचम्व्यः *atichamvaḥ*
A. अतिचमूं *atichamûm*	अतिचम्वौ *atichamvau*	अतिचमून् *atichamûn*
I. अतिचम्वा *atichamvâ*	अतिचमूभ्यां *atichamûbhyâm*	अतिचमूभिः *atichamûbhiḥ*
D. अतिचम्वै *atichamvai*	अतिचमूभ्यां *atichamûbhyâm*	अतिचमूभ्यः *atichamûbhyaḥ*
Ab. अतिचम्वाः *atichamvâḥ*	अतिचमूभ्यां *atichamûbhyâm*	अतिचमूभ्यः *atichamûbhyaḥ*
G. अतिचम्वाः *atichamvâḥ*	अतिचम्वोः *atichamvoḥ*	अतिचमूनां *atichamûnâm*
L. अतिचम्वां *atichamvâm*	अतिचम्वोः *atichamvoḥ*	अतिचमूषु *atichamûshu*
V. अतिचमु *atichamu*	अतिचम्वौ *atichamvau*	अतिचम्व्यः *atichamvaḥ**

Nouns like कुमारी *kumârî*, a man who behaves like a girl, are declined like बहुश्रेयसी *bahuśreyasî*, except in the Acc. Sing. and Plur., where they form कुमार्यं *kumâryam* and कुमार्यः *kumâryaḥ*. (Siddh.-Kaum. vol. I. pp. 118, 119.)

§ 228. स्त्री *strî*, woman, is declined like नदी *nadî*, only that the accumulation of four consonants is avoided by the regular insertion of an इ *i*, e.g. स्त्रिया *striyâ*, and not स्त्या *stryâ*. Remember also two optional forms in the Acc. Sing. and Plur.

Base स्त्री *strî* and स्त्रिय् *striy*. (Accent, Pân. VI. 1, 168.)

SINGULAR.	DUAL.	PLURAL.
N. स्त्री *strî*	N.A.V. स्त्रियौ *stríyau*	N. स्त्रियः *stríyaḥ*
A. स्त्रीं *strîm* or स्त्रियं *stríyam*	I.D.Ab. स्त्रीभ्यां *strîbhyâm*	A. स्त्रीः *strîḥ* or स्त्रियः *stríyaḥ*
I. स्त्रिया *striyâ*	G.L. स्त्रियोः *striyóḥ*	I. स्त्रीभिः *strîbhíḥ*
D. स्त्रियै *striyaí*		D.Ab. स्त्रीभ्यः *strîbhyáḥ*
Ab.G. स्त्रियाः *striyâḥ*		G. स्त्रीणां *strîṇâm* (Pân. I. 4, 5)
L. स्त्रियां *striyâm*		L. स्त्रीषु *strîshú*
V. स्त्रि *strí* (Pân. I. 4, 4)		

§ 229. When स्त्री *strî* forms the last portion of a compound, and has to be treated as a masculine, feminine, and neuter, the following forms occur:

<table>
<tr><td></td><td colspan="3" align="center">SINGULAR.</td></tr>
<tr><td></td><td align="center">MASC.</td><td align="center">FEM.</td><td align="center">NEUT.</td></tr>
<tr><td>N.</td><td>अतिस्त्रिः atistriḥ</td><td>अतिस्त्रिः atistriḥ</td><td>अतिस्त्रि atistri</td></tr>
<tr><td>A.</td><td>अतिस्त्रिं atistrim or
अतिस्त्रियं atistriyam</td><td>अतिस्त्रिं atistrim or
अतिस्त्रियं atistriyam</td><td>अतिस्त्रि atistri</td></tr>
<tr><td>I.</td><td>अतिस्त्रिणा atistriṇâ</td><td>अतिस्त्रिया atistriyâ</td><td>अतिस्त्रिणा atistriṇâ</td></tr>
<tr><td>D.</td><td>अतिस्त्रये atistraye</td><td>अतिस्त्रियै atistriyai or
अतिस्त्रये atistraye</td><td>अतिस्त्रिणे atistriṇe or
अतिस्त्रये atistraye</td></tr>
<tr><td>Ab.G.</td><td>अतिस्त्रेः atistreḥ</td><td>अतिस्त्रियाः atistriyâḥ or
अतिस्त्रेः atistreḥ</td><td>अतिस्त्रिणः atistriṇaḥ or
अतिस्त्रेः atistreḥ</td></tr>
<tr><td>L.</td><td>अतिस्त्रौ atistrau</td><td>अतिस्त्रियां atistriyâm or
अतिस्त्रौ atistrau</td><td>अतिस्त्रिणि atistriṇi or
अतिस्त्रौ atistrau</td></tr>
<tr><td>V.</td><td>अतिस्त्रे atistre</td><td>अतिस्त्रे atistre</td><td>अतिस्त्रे atistre</td></tr>
</table>

* The neuter is said to be N.A.V. Sing. बहुश्रेयसी *bahuśreyasî*, N.A.V. Dual बहुश्रेयसीनी *bahuśreyasînî*, N.A.V. Plur. बहुश्रेयसीनि *bahuśreyasîni*, Dat. Sing. बहुश्रेयस्यै (°स्ये?) or °सीने *bahuśreyasyai* (-*sye*?) or -*sîne*, &c.

DUAL.

	MASC.	FEM.	NEUT.
N.A.V.	अतिस्त्रियौ *atistriyau*	अतिस्त्रियौ *atistriyau*	अतिस्त्रिणी *atistriṇí*
I.D.Ab.	अतिस्त्रिभ्यां *atistribhyâm*	अतिस्त्रिभ्यां *atistribhyâm*	अतिस्त्रिभ्यां *atistribhyâm*
G.L.	अतिस्त्रियोः *atistriyoh*	अतिस्त्रियोः *atistriyoh*	अतिस्त्रिणोः *atistriṇoh*

PLURAL.

	MASC.	FEM.	NEUT.
N.V.	अतिस्त्रय: *atistrayah*	अतिस्त्रय: *atistrayah*	अतिस्त्रीणि *atistríṇi*
A.	अतिस्त्रीन् *atistrín* or अतिस्त्रिय: *atistriyah*	अतिस्त्री: *atistríh* or अतिस्त्रिय: *atistriyah*	अतिस्त्रीणि *atistríṇi*
I.	अतिस्त्रिभि: *atistribhih*	अतिस्त्रिभि: *atistribhih*	अतिस्त्रिभि: *atistribhih*
D.Ab.	अतिस्त्रिभ्य: *atistribhyah*	अतिस्त्रिभ्य: *atistribhyah*	अतिस्त्रिभ्य: *atistribhyah*
G.	अतिस्त्रीणां *atistríṇâm*	अतिस्त्रीणां *atistríṇâm*	अतिस्त्रीणां *atistríṇâm*
L.	अतिस्त्रिषु *atistrishu*	अतिस्त्रिषु *atistrishu*	अतिस्त्रिषु *atistrishu*

In the masculine final ई *î* is shortened to इ *i*, and the compound declined like कवि: *kavih*, except in the Nom. Acc. Voc. and Gen. Loc. Dual. In the Acc. Sing. and Plur. optional forms are admitted. (Siddh.-Kaum. vol. I. p. 134.)

The feminine may be the same as the masculine, except in the Instr. Sing. and Acc. Plur., but it may likewise be declined like स्त्री *strî* in the Dat. Abl. Gen. Loc. Sing.

The neuter has the usual optional forms.

Bases in इ i and उ u, Masculine, Feminine, Neuter.

§ 230. There are masculine, feminine, and neuter bases in इ *i* and उ *u*. They are of frequent occurrence, and should be carefully committed to memory.

Adjectives in इ *i* are declined like substantives, only that the masculine may optionally be substituted for the neuter in all cases except the Nom. and Acc. Sing.; Nom. Acc. and Voc. Dual and Plur. Ex. शुचि: *śuchih*, masc. bright; शुचि: *śuchih*, fem.; शुचि *śuchi*, neut.

The same applies to adjectives in उ *u*, except that they may form their feminine either without any change, or by adding ई *î*. Thus लघु: *laghuh*, light, is in the fem. either लघु: *laghuh*, to be declined as a feminine, or लघ्वी *laghvî*, to be declined like नदी *nadî*.

If the final उ *u* is preceded by more than one consonant, the fem. does not take ई *î*. Thus पांडु *pâṇḍu*, pale; fem. पांडु: *pâṇḍuh*.

Some adjectives in उ *u* lengthen their vowel in the fem., and are then declined like वधू: *vadhûh*. Thus पंगु: *paṅguh*, lame; fem. पंगू: *paṅgûh*. Likewise कुरु: *kuruh*, a Kuru; fem. कुरू: *kurûh*: some compounds ending in ऊरु: *ûruh*, thigh, such as वामोरु: *vâmoruh*, with handsome thighs, fem. वामोरू: *vâmorûh*.

Bases in इ i.   Bases in उ u.

SINGULAR.

	MASC.	FEM.	NEUT.	MASC.	FEM.	NEUT.
Base	कवि kaví, poet	मति matí, thought	वारि vári, water	मृदु mridú, soft	मृदु mridú, soft	मृदु mridú, soft
N.	कवि: kaví-ḥ	मति: matí-ḥ	वारि vári	मृदु: mridú-ḥ	मृदु: mridú-ḥ	मृदु mridú
A.	कविं kaví-m	मतिं matí-m	वारि vári	मृदुं mridú-m	मृदुं mridú-m	मृदु mridú
I.	कविना kaví-ná	मत्या maty-á	वारिणा vári-ṇá	मृदुना mridú-ná	मृद्वा mridv-á	मृदुना mridú-ná
D.	कवये kaváy-e	मतये matáy-e or मत्यै maty-aí	वारिणे vári-ṇe	मृदवे mridáv-e	मृद्वे mridáv-e or मृद्वै mridv-aí	मृदुने mridú-ne or मृदवे mridáv-e
Ab.G.	कवे: kavé-ḥ	मते: maté-ḥ or मत्या: maty-áḥ	वारिण: vári-ṇaḥ	मृदो: mridó-ḥ	मृदो: mridó-ḥ or मृद्वा: mridv-áḥ	मृदुन: mridú-naḥ or मृदो: mridó-ḥ
L.	कवौ kavaú	मतौ mataú or मत्यां maty-ám	वारिणि vári-ṇi	मृदौ mridaú	मृदौ mridaú or मृद्वां mridv-ám	मृदुनि mridú-ni or मृदौ mridaú
V.	कवे káve	मते máte	वारि vári or वारे váre*	मृदो mrído	मृदो mrído	मृदु mrídu or मृदो mrído*

DUAL.

	MASC.	FEM.	NEUT.	MASC.	FEM.	NEUT.
N.A.V.	कवी kaví	मती matí	वारिणी vári-ṇí	मृदू mridú	मृदू mridú	मृदुनी mridú-ní
I.D.Ab.	कविभ्यां kaví-bhyám	मतिभ्यां matí-bhyám	वारिभ्यां vári-bhyám	मृदुभ्यां mridú-bhyám	मृदुभ्यां mridú-bhyám	मृदुभ्यां mridú-bhyám
G.L.	कव्यो: kavy-óḥ	मत्यो: maty-óḥ	वारिणो: vári-ṇoḥ	मृद्वो: mridv-óḥ	मृद्वो: mridv-óḥ	मृदुनो: mridú-no or मृद्वो: mridv-óḥ

PLURAL.

	MASC.	FEM.	NEUT.	MASC.	FEM.	NEUT.
N.V.	कवय: kaváy-aḥ	मतय: matáy-aḥ	वारीणि várí-ṇi	मृदव: mridáv-aḥ	मृदव: mridáv-aḥ	मृदूनि mridú-ni
A.	कवीन् kaví-n	मती: matí-ḥ	वारीणि várí-ṇi	मृदून् mridú-n	मृदू: mridú-ḥ	मृदूनि mridú-ni
I.	कविभि: kaví-bhiḥ	मतिभि: matí-bhiḥ	वारिभि: vári-bhiḥ	मृदुभि: mridú-bhiḥ	मृदुभि: mridú-bhiḥ	मृदुभि: mridú-bhiḥ
D.Ab.	कविभ्य: kaví-bhyaḥ	मतिभ्य: matí-bhyaḥ	वारिभ्य: vári-bhyaḥ	मृदुभ्य: mridú-bhyaḥ	मृदुभ्य: mridú-bhyaḥ	मृदुभ्य: mridú-bhyaḥ
G.	कवीनां kaví-nám †	मतीनां matí-nám	वारीणां várí-ṇám	मृदूनां mridú-nám	मृदूनां mridú-nám	मृदूनां mridú-nám
L.	कविषु kaví-shu	मतिषु matí-shu	वारिषु vári-shu	मृदुषु mridú-shu	मृदुषु mridú-shu	मृदुषु mridú-shu ‡

* The Guṇa in the Voc. Sing. of neuters in इ i, उ u, ऋ ri, is approved by Mâdhyandini Vyâghrapâd, as may be seen from the following verse: संबोधने गूशनसक्तिरूपं सांतं तथा नांतमधाप्यदंतं । माध्यंदिनिर्वैष्टि गुणं त्रिगंते नपुंसके व्याघ्रपदां वरिष्ठ: ॥

† Nouns ending in short इ i, उ u, ऋ ri, and अ a, and having the accent on these vowels, may throw the accent on नां nám in the Gen. Plur. (Pâṇ. VI. I, 177). Hence matínám, or, more usually, matínám.

‡ The lines of separation placed in the transcribed paradigms are not intended to divide

§ 231. कति *kati*, how many, यति *yati*, as many (relat.), and तति *tati*, so many, are used in the Plural only, and take no terminations in the Nom. and Acc. Plural. For the rest, they are declined like कवि *kavi*, and without distinction of gender.

Nom. Voc.	कति *káti*
Acc.	कति *káti*
Instr.	कतिभिः *kátibhih*
Dat.	कतिभ्यः *kátibhyah*
Abl.	कतिभ्यः *kátibhyah*
Gen.	कतीनां *kátínám*
Loc.	कतिषु *kátishu*

§ 232. सखि *sákhi*, friend, has two bases :

सखाय् *sákháy* for the Anga, i. e. the strong base.

सखि *sákhi* for the Pada and Bha base.

It is irregular in some of its cases.

	SINGULAR.	DUAL.	PLURAL.
N.	सखा *sákhá*	सखायौ *sákháyau*	सखायः *sákháyah*
A.	सखायं *sákháyam*	सखायौ *sákháyau*	सखीन् *sákhín*
I.	सख्या *sákhyá*	सखिभ्यां *sákhibhyám*	सखिभिः *sákhibhih*
D.	सख्ये *sákhye*	सखिभ्यां *sákhibhyám*	सखिभ्यः *sákhibhyah*
Ab.	सख्युः *sákhyuh*	सखिभ्यां *sákhibhyám*	सखिभ्यः *sákhibhyah*
G.	सख्युः *sákhyuh*	सख्योः *sákhyoh*	सखीनां *sákhínám*
L.	सख्यौ *sákhyau*	सख्योः *sákhyoh*	सखिषु *sákhishu*
V.	सखे *sákhe*	like Nom.	like Nom.

The feminine सखी *sakhí* is regular, like नदी *nadí*.

At the end of compounds, we find सखि *sakhi*, masc. declined as follows :

Base सुसखि *susakhi*, a good friend, masc.

	SINGULAR.	DUAL.	PLURAL.
N.	सुसखा *susakhá*	सुसखायौ *susakháyau*	सुसखायः *susakháyah* *
A.	सुसखायं *susakháyam*	सुसखायौ *susakháyau*	सुसखीन् *susakhín*
I.	सुसखिना *susakhiná*	सुसखिभ्यां *susakhibhyám*	सुसखिभिः *susakhibhih*
D.	सुसखये *susakhaye*	सुसखिभ्यां *susakhibhyám*	सुसखिभ्यः *susakhibhyah*
Ab.	सुसखेः *susakheh*	सुसखिभ्यां *susakhibhyám*	सुसखिभ्यः *susakhibhyah*
G.	सुसखेः *susakheh*	सुसख्योः *susakhyoh*	सुसखीनां *susakhínám*
L.	सुसखौ *susakhau*	सुसख्योः *susakhyoh*	सुसखिषु *susakhishu*
V.	सुसखे *susakhe*	सुसखायौ *susakháyau*	सुसखायः *susakháyah*

At the end of a neuter compound सखि *sakhi* is declined like वारि *vári* (§ 230).

---

the real terminations from the real base, but only to facilitate the learning by heart of these nouns. Masculine nouns in short उ *u* are भानु *bhánu*, sun, वायु *váyu*, wind, विष्णु *vishnu*, nom. prop. पीलु *pílu*, as masc., is the name of a tree; as neuter, the name of its fruit (Sâr. I. 8, 17). Feminine nouns in short उ *u* are धेनुः *dhenuh*, cow, रज्जुः *rajjuh*, rope, तनुः *tanuh*, body.

* Siddh.-Kaum. vol. I. p. 112.

§ 233. पति *pati*, lord, is irregular :

SINGULAR.	DUAL.	PLURAL.
N. पतिः *pátiḥ*	N. A. V. पती *pátí*	N. पतयः *pátayaḥ*
A. पतिं *pátim*	I. D. Ab. पतिभ्यां *pátibhyám*	A. पतीन् *pátín*
I. पत्या *pátyá*	G. L. पत्योः *pátyoḥ*	I. पतिभिः *pátibhiḥ*
D. पत्ये *pátye*		D. Ab. पतिभ्यः *pátibhyaḥ*
Ab. G. पत्युः *pátyuḥ*		G. पतीनां *pátínám*
L. पत्यौ *pátyau*		L. पतिषु *pátishu*
V. पते *páte*		V. पतयः *pátayaḥ*

पति *pati* at the end of compounds, e. g. भूपति *bhúpati*, lord of the earth, प्रजापति *prajápati*, lord of creatures, is regular, like कवि *kavi*. The feminine of पति *pati* is पत्नी *patní*, wife, i. e. legitimate wife, she who takes part in the sacrifices of her husband. (Pâṇ. IV. 1, 33.)

§ 234. The neuter bases अक्षि *akshi*, eye, अस्थि *asthi*, bone, दधि *dadhi*, curds, सक्थि *sakthi*, thigh, are declined regularly like वारि *vári;* but in the Bha cases they substitute the bases अक्ष्ण् *akshṇ*, अस्थ्न् *asthn*, दध्न् *dadhn*, सक्थ्न् *sakthn*. In these cases they are declined, in fact, like neuters in अन् *an*, such as नामन् *náman*. (See note to § 203.)

Aṅga and Pada base अक्षि *akshi*, Bha base अक्ष्ण् *akshṇ*.

SINGULAR.	DUAL.	PLURAL.
N. A. अक्षि *ákshi*	N. A. V. अक्षिणी *ákshiṇí*	N. A. V. अक्षीणि *ákshíṇi*
I. अक्ष्णा *akshṇá*	I. D. Ab. अक्षिभ्यां *ákshibhyám*	I. अक्षिभिः *ákshibhiḥ*
D. अक्ष्णे *akshṇé*	G. L. अक्ष्णोः *akshṇóḥ*	D. Ab. अक्षिभ्यः *ákshibhyaḥ*
Ab. G. अक्ष्णः *akshṇáḥ*		G. अक्ष्णां *akshṇám*
L. अक्ष्णि *akshṇí* and अक्षाणि *aksháṇi*		L. अक्षिषु *ákshishu*
V. अक्षे *ákshe* (or अक्षि *ákshi*)		

Bases in ऋ *ṛi*, Masculine, Feminine, Neuter.

§ 235. These bases are declined after two models :

SINGULAR.

I.	MASC.	FEM.	NEUT.
Base	नप्तृ *náptṛi*, grandson	स्वसृ *svásṛi*, sister	धातृ *dhátṛí*, providence
N.	नप्ता *náptá*	स्वसा *svásá*	धातृ *dhátṛí*
A.	नप्तारं *náptár-am*	स्वसारं *svásár-am*	धातृ *dhátṛí*
I.	नप्त्रा *náptr-á*	स्वस्रा *svásr-á*	धातृणा *dhátṛí-ṇá* or धात्रा *dhátrá**
D.	नप्त्रे *náptr-e*	स्वस्रे *svásr-e*	धातृणे *dhátṛí-ṇe* or धात्रे *dhátré*
Ab. G.	नप्तुः *náptuḥ*	स्वसुः *svásuḥ*	धातृणः *dhátṛí-ṇaḥ* or धातुः *dhátúḥ*
L.	नप्तरि *náptar-i*	स्वसरि *svásar-i*	धातृणि *dhátṛí-ṇi* or धातरि *dhátári*
V.	नप्तः *náptaḥ* (r)	स्वसः *svásaḥ* (r)	धातृ *dhátṛi* or धातः *dhátaḥ* (r)

* If ऋ *ṛi* has Udâtta and becomes र् *r* and is preceded by a consonant, the feminine and the Ajâdi Asarvanâmasthâna cases have the Udâtta.

PLURAL.

N.	नप्तार: *náptár-aḥ*	खसार: *svásár-aḥ*	भातृंषि *dhátṛí-ṇi*
A.	नप्तून् *náptṛí-n*	खसृ: *svásṛí-ḥ*	भातृंषि *dhátṛí-ṇi*
I.	नप्तृभि: *náptṛí-bhiḥ*	खसृभि: *svásṛí-bhiḥ*	भातृभि: *dhátṛí-bhiḥ*
D.	नप्तृभ्य: *náptṛí-bhyaḥ*	खसृभ्य: *svásṛí-bhyaḥ*	भातृभ्य: *dhátṛí-bhyaḥ*
Ab.	नप्तृभ्य: *náptṛí-bhyaḥ*	खसृभ्य: *svásṛí-bhyaḥ*	भातृभ्य: *dhátṛí-bhyaḥ*
G.	नप्तॄणां *náptṛí-ṇ́ám*	खसॄणां *svásṛí-ṇám* (Ved. *svásrám*)	भातॄणां *dhátṛí-ṇ́ám*
L.	नप्तृषु *náptṛí-shu*	खसृषु *svásṛí-shu*	भातृषु *dhátṛí-shu*

DUAL.

N.A.V.	नप्तारौ *náptár-au*	खसारौ *svásár-au*	भातृणी *dhátṛí-ṇí*
I.D.Ab.	नप्तृभ्यां *náptṛí-bhyám*	खसृभ्यां *svásṛí-bhyám*	भातृभ्यां *dhátṛí-bhyám*
G.L.	नप्त्रो: *náptṛ-oḥ*	खस्रो: *svásr-oḥ*	भातृणो: *dhátṛí-ṇoḥ*

2. The second model differs from the first in the Acc. Sing., Nom. Acc. Voc.
Dual, and Nom. Plur., by not lengthening the च *a* before the ऋ *r*.

Base पितृ *pitṛí*, मातृ *mátṛí*.

	SINGULAR.		DUAL.		PLURAL.	
	MASC.	FEM.	MASC.	FEM.	MASC.	FEM.
N.	पिता *pitá*	माता *mátá*	पितरौ *pitár-au*	मातरौ *mátár-au*	पितर: *pitár-aḥ*	मातर: *mátár-aḥ*
A.	पितरं *pitár-am*	मातरं *mátár-am*			पितृन् *pitṛí-n*	मातृ: *mátṛí-ḥ*
I.	पित्रा *pitr-á*	मात्रा *mátr-á*			पितृभि: *pitṛí-bhiḥ*	मातृभि: *mátṛí-bhiḥ*
D.	पित्रे *pitr-é*	मात्रे *mátr-é*	पितृभ्यां *pitṛí-bhyám*	मातृभ्यां *mátṛí-bhyám*	पितृभ्य: *pitṛí-bhyaḥ*	मातृभ्य: *mátṛí-bhyaḥ*
Ab.	पितु: *pitúḥ*	मातु: *mátúḥ*				
G.	पितु: *pitúḥ*	मातु: *mátúḥ*	पित्रो: *pitr-óḥ*	मात्रो: *mátr-óḥ*	पितॄणां *pitṛí-ṇ́ám*	मातॄणां *mátṛí-ṇ́ám*
L.	पितरि *pitár-i*	मातरि *mátár-i*			पितृषु *pitṛí-shu*	मातृषु *mátṛí-shu*
V.	पित: *pítaḥ(r)*	मात: *mátaḥ(r)*	पितरौ *pítarau*	मातरौ *mátarau*	पितर: *pítaraḥ*	मातर: *mátaraḥ*

After the first model are declined most *nomina actoris* derived from verbs
by the suffix तृ *tṛí* : दातृ *dátṛí*, giver; कर्तृ *kartṛí*, doer; त्वष्टृ *tváshṭṛí*, carpenter;
होतृ *hótṛí*, sacrificer; भर्तृ *bhartṛí*, husband.

After the second model are declined masculines, such as भातृ *bhrátṛí*,
brother; जामातृ *jámátṛí*, son-in-law; देवृ *devṛí*, husband's brother; सव्येष्टृ
savyeshṭhṛí, a charioteer : and feminines, such as दुहितृ *duhitṛí*, daughter;
ननंदृ *nánandṛí* or नानंदृ *nánandṛí*, husband's sister; यातृ *yátṛí*, husband's
brother's wife. Most terms of relationship in ऋ *ṛí* (except खसृ *svásṛí*, sister,
and नप्तृ *náptṛí*, grandson) do not lengthen their अर् *ar*.

Note—If words in ऋ *ṛí* are used as adjectives, the masculine forms may be used for the
neuter also, except in the Nom. and Acc. Sing. and Nom. Acc. Voc. Dual and Plural. The
feminine is formed by ई *í*; कर्तृ *kartṛí*, fem. कर्त्री *kartṛí*, like नदी *nadí*.

§ 236. क्रोष्टु *króshṭu*, a jackal, is irregular ; but most of its irregularities
may be explained by admitting two bases, क्रोष्टु *króshṭu* (like मृदु *mṛídu*) and
क्रोष्टृ *kroshṭṛí* (like नप्तृ *naptṛí*).

	SINGULAR.		DUAL.		PLURAL.
N.	क्रोष्टा *kroshṭá*	N.A.V.	क्रोष्टारौ *kroshṭárau*	N.	क्रोष्टारः *kroshṭáraḥ*
A.	क्रोष्टारं *kroshṭáram*			A.	क्रोष्टून् *kroshṭún*
I.	क्रोष्टुना *kroshṭuná* / क्रोष्ट्रा *kroshṭrá*	I.D.Ab.	क्रोष्टुभ्यां *kroshṭubhyám*	I.	क्रोष्टुभिः *kroshṭubhiḥ*
D.	क्रोष्टवे *kroshṭave* / क्रोष्ट्रे *kroshṭre*			D.Ab.	क्रोष्टुभ्यः *kroshṭubhyaḥ*
Ab.G.	क्रोष्टोः *kroshṭoḥ* / क्रोष्टुः *kroshṭuḥ*	G.L.	क्रोष्ट्वोः *kroshṭvoḥ* / क्रोष्ट्रोः *kroshṭroḥ*	G.	क्रोष्टूनां *kroshṭúnám*
L.	क्रोष्टौ *kroshṭau* / क्रोष्टरि *kroshṭari*			L.	क्रोष्टुषु *kroshṭushu*
V.	क्रोष्टो *kroshṭo*				

The base क्रोष्टृ *kroshṭri* is the only one admissible as Aṅga, i. e. in the strong cases, excepting the Vocative. (हे क्रोष्टः *he kroshṭaḥ* is, I believe, wrongly admitted by Wilson.)

The base क्रोष्टु *kroshṭu* is the only one admissible as Pada, i. e. before terminations beginning with consonants.

The other cases may be formed from both bases, but the Acc. Plur. is क्रोष्टून् *kroshṭún* only. (Pân. VII. 1, 95–97.)

Those who admit क्रोष्टॄन् *kroshṭrín* as Acc. Plur. likewise admit क्रोष्टुं *kroshṭum* as Acc. Sing. (Sâr. 1. 6, 70.)

The feminine is क्रोष्ट्री *kroshṭrí*, declined like नदी *nadí*.

§ 237. नृ *nṛi*, man, a word of frequent occurrence, though, for convenience sake, often replaced by नर *nara*, is declined regularly like पितृ *pitṛi*, except in the Gen. Plural, where it may be either नॄणां *nṛíṇám* or नृणां *nṛiṇám*.   (Pân. VI. 4, 6.)

	SINGULAR.	DUAL.	PLURAL.
N.	ना *ná*	नरौ *nárau*	नरः *náraḥ*
A.	नरं *náram*	नरौ *nárau*	नॄन् *nṛín*
I.	ना *nrá*	नृभ्यां *nṛíbhyám* *	नृभिः *nṛíbhíḥ*
D.	ने *nré* (Ved. *náre*)	नृभ्यां *nṛíbhyám*	नृभ्यः *nṛíbhyáḥ*
Ab.	नुः *núḥ*	नृभ्यां *nṛíbhyám*	नृभ्यः *nṛíbhyáḥ*
G.	नुः *núḥ* (Ved. *náraḥ*)	नोः *nróḥ*	नृणाम् *nṛiṇám* or नॄणां *nṛíṇám* (Ved. *nardm*)
L.	नरि *nári*	नोः *nróḥ*	नृषु *nṛíshú*
V.	नः *náḥ*	नरौ *nárau*	नरः *náraḥ*

The feminine is नारी *nárí*.

2. *Bases ending in* अ *a and* आ *â.*

§ 238. This class is the most numerous and most important in Sanskrit, like the corresponding classes of nouns and adjectives in *us, a, um* in Latin,

---

* The accent may be on the first or on the second syllables in the Pada cases beginning with भ *bh* and स *s*. (Pân. VI. 1, 184.)

and *os, η, ov* in Greek.   The case-terminations are peculiar, and it is best to learn कांतः *kántaḥ*, कांता *kántá*, कांतं *kántam* by heart in the same manner as we learn *bonus, bona, bonum*, without asking any questions as to the origin of the case-terminations, or their relation to the terminations appended to bases ending in consonants.

SINGULAR.

	MASC.	FEM.	NEUT.
Base	कांत *kántá*	कांता *kántá*	कांत *kántá*
N.	कांतः *kántáḥ*	कांता *kántá*	कांतं *kántám*
A.	कांतं *kántám*	कांतां *kántám*	कांतं *kántám*
I.	कांतेन *kánténa*	कांतया *kántáyá*	कांतेन *kánténa*
D.	कांताय *kántáya*	कांतायै *kántáyai*	कांताय *kántáya*
Ab.	कांतात् *kántát*	कांतायाः *kántáyáḥ*	कांतात् *kántát*
G.	कांतस्य *kántásya*	कांतायाः *kántáyáḥ*	कांतस्य *kántásya*
L.	कांते *kánté*	कांतायां *kántáyám*	कांते *kánté*
V.	कांत *kánta*	कांते *kánte* *	कांत *kánta*

DUAL.

	MASC.	FEM.	NEUT.
N. A. V.	कांतौ *kántaú*	कांते *kánté*	कांते *kánté*
I. D. Ab.	कांताभ्यां *kántábhyám*	कांताभ्यां *kántábhyám*	कांताभ्यां *kántábhyám*
G. L.	कांतयोः *kántáyoḥ*	कांतयोः *kántáyoḥ*	कांतयोः *kántáyoḥ*

PLURAL.

	MASC.	FEM.	NEUT.
N. V.	कांताः *kántáḥ*	कांताः *kántáḥ*	कांतानि *kántáni*
A.	कांतान् *kántán*	कांताः *kántáḥ*	कांतानि *kántáni*
I.	कांतैः *kántaiḥ*	कांताभिः *kántábhiḥ*	कांतैः *kántaiḥ*
D. Ab.	कांतेभ्यः *kántébhyaḥ*	कांताभ्यः *kántábhyaḥ*	कांतेभ्यः *kántébhyaḥ*
G.	कांतानां *kántánám*	कांतानां *kántánám*	कांतानां *kántánám*
L.	कांतेषु *kántéshu*	कांतासु *kántásu*	कांतेषु *kántéshu*

Note — Certain adjectives in अः *aḥ*, आ *á*, अं *am*, which follow the ancient pronominal declension, will be explained in the chapter on Pronouns (§ 278).

Bases in आ á, Masculine and Feminine.

§ 239. These bases are derived immediately from verbs ending in आ *á*, such as पा *pá*, ध्मा *dhmá*.   They are declined in the same way in the masculine and feminine gender.   In the neuter the final आ *á* is shortened, and the word declined like कांतं *kántam*.

Aṅga and Pada base विश्वपा *viśvapá*, Bha base विश्वप् *viśvap*, all-preserving, (masc. and fem.)   The neuter is declined like कांतं *kántam* (§ 238).

---

* Bases in आ *á*, meaning mother, form their Vocative in अ *a*; e. g. अक्क *akka*, अंब *amba*, अल्ल *alla!* But अंबाडा *ambáḍá*, अंबाला *ambálá*, and अंबिका *ambiká* form the regular Vocatives अंबाडे *ambáḍe*, अंबाले *ambále*, अंबिके *ambike*.

Q 2

MASCULINE AND FEMININE.

	SINGULAR.	DUAL.	PLURAL.
N. V.	विश्वपा: *viśvapá-ḥ*	विश्वपौ *viśvapau*	विश्वपा: *viśvapá-ḥ*
A.	विश्वपां *viśvapá-m*	विश्वपौ *viśvapau*	विश्वप: *viśvap-aḥ*
I.	विश्वपा *viśvap-á*	विश्वपाभ्यां *viśvapá-bhyám*	विश्वपाभि: *viśvapá-bhiḥ*
D.	विश्वपे *viśvap-e*	विश्वपाभ्यां *viśvapá-bhyám*	विश्वपाभ्य: *viśvapá-bhyaḥ*
Ab.	विश्वप: *viśvap-aḥ*	विश्वपाभ्यां *viśvapá-bhyám*	विश्वपाभ्य: *viśvapá-bhyaḥ*
G.	विश्वप: *viśvap-aḥ*	विश्वपो: *viśvap-oḥ*	विश्वपां *viśvap-ám*
L.	विश्वपि *viśvap-i*	विश्वपो: *viśvap-oḥ*	विश्वपासु *viśvapá-su*

NEUTER.

N.	विश्वपं *viśvapam*	विश्वपे *viśvape*	विश्वपानि *viśvapáni*, &c.

Decline सोमपा: *somapáḥ*, Soma drinker; शंखध्मा: *śaṅkhadhmáḥ*, shell-blower; धनदा: *dhanadáḥ*, wealth giver.

§ 240. Masculines in आ *á*, not being derived by a Kṛit suffix from verbal roots, are declined as follows:

Base हाहा *háhá*.

	SINGULAR.	DUAL.	PLURAL.
N.V.	हाहा: *háháḥ*	हाहौ *háhau*	हाहा: *háháḥ*
A.	हाहां *hahám*	हाहौ *háhau*	हाहान् *háhán* *
I.	हाहा *háhá*	हाहाभ्यां *háhábhyám*	हाहाभि: *háhábhiḥ*
D.	हाहै *háhai*	हाहाभ्यां *háhábhyám*	हाहाभ्य: *háhábhyaḥ*
Ab.	हाहा: *háháḥ*	हाहाभ्यां *háhábhyám*	हाहाभ्य: *háhábhyaḥ*
G.	हाहा: *háháḥ*	हाहौ: *háhauḥ*	हाहां *háhám*
L.	हाहै *háhe*	हाहौ: *háhauḥ*	हाहासु *háhásu*

CHAPTER IV.

DECLENSION OF ADJECTIVES.

§ 241. As every noun in Sanskrit may, at the end of a compound, form the final portion of an adjective, all the essential rules for the declension of such compound adjectives had to be given in the preceding chapter. Thus in the declension of neuter nouns in अस् *as*, like मनस् *mánas*, mind, the declension of सुमनस् *sumánas*, as an adjective masc. fem. and neut., was exhibited at the same time (§ 165). In the declension of nouns ending in consonants, and admitting of no distinction between masculine and feminine terminations, (this applies to

---

* The Sâr. 1. 6, 38, gives the optional form हाहा: *háháḥ* in the masculine. At the end of a feminine compound the same form is sanctioned in the Rûpâvali, p. 9 b.

all nouns with unchangeable bases,) the special forms of the neuter in Nom. Acc. Voc. Sing. Dual and Plur. had to be exhibited. See § 158, जलमुक् *jalamuk*, जलमुची *jalamuchí*, जलमुंचि *jalamuñchi*. In the declension of nouns with changeable bases, the more important feminine and neuter forms were separately mentioned ; and in the declension of nouns ending in vowels, all necessary rules with regard to the same subject were fully stated.

§ 242. The chief difficulty which remains with regard to the declension of adjectives is the exact formation of the feminine base, and the rules on this subject are often so complicated that they have to be learnt by practice rather than by rule. The feminine bases, however, once given, there can be no doubt as to their declension, as they follow exactly the declension of the corresponding feminine nouns. A few observations on this point must suffice.

§ 243. Adjectives * in व *a* form their feminines in आ *á*. Ex. प्रिय *priya*, dear, masc. प्रिय: *priyah*, fem. प्रिया *priyá*, neut. प्रियं *priyam*, to be declined like कांत *kánta* (§ 238).

§ 244. Certain adjectives derived by अक *aka* form their feminines in इका *iká*. Ex. पाचक *páchaka*, cooking, masc. पाचक: *páchakah*, fem. पाचिका *páchiká*, neut. पाचकं *páchakam*. Likewise masc. सर्वक: *sarvakah*, fem. सर्विका *sarviká*, every ; कारक: *kárakah*, doing, कारिका *káriká* ; इहत्यक: *ihatyakah*, present here, इहत्यिका *ihatyiká*. But क्षिपका *kshipaká*, fem. one who sends ; कन्यका *kanyaká*, fem. maiden ; चटका *chataká*, fem. sparrow ; तारका *táraká*, fem. star. Sometimes both forms occur ; अजका *ajaká* and अजिका *ajiká*, a she-goat.

§ 245. Bases in ऋ *ri* and in न् *n* take ई *í* as the sign of the feminine : कर्तृ *kartri*, doer, कर्त्री *kartrí* (§ 235) ; दंडिन् *dandin*, a mendicant, दंडिनी *dandiní* (§ 203). Likewise most bases ending in consonants, if they admit of a separate feminine base : प्राच् *prách*, प्राची *práchí* (§ 181) ; श्वन् *svan*, dog, शुनी *suní* (§ 199) ; भवत् *bhavat*, भवती *bhavatí* (§ 188). Some adjectives in वन् *van* form their feminine base in वरी *varí* : पीवन् *pívan*, fat, पीवरी *pívarí* (§ 193).

§ 246. Many adjectives in व *a* form their feminine base in ई *í* (§ 225), instead of आ *á* : तृणमय: *trinamayah*, made of grass, तृणमयी *trinamayí* ; देव: *devah*, god, divine, देवी *deví* ; तरुण: *tarunah* or तलुन: *talunah*, a youth, तरुणी *taruní* ; कुमार: *kumárah*, a boy, कुमारी *kumárí* ; गोप: *gopah*, cowherd, गोपी *gopí*, his wife, but गोपा *gopá*, a female shepherd ; नर्तक: *nartakah*, actor, नर्तकी *nartakí* ; मृग: *mrigah*, a deer, मृगी *mrigí*, a doe ; सूकर: *súkarah*, boar, सूकरी *súkarí* ; कुंभकार: *kumbhakárah*, a potter, कुंभकारी *kumbhakárí*. It will be observed, however, that many of these words are substantives rather than adjectives. Thus मत्स्य: *matsyah*, fish, forms मत्सी *matsí* (य *ya* being expunged before ई *í*) ; मनुष्य: *manushyah*, man, मनुषी *manushí*.

§ 247. Certain adjectives in त: *tah*, expressive of colour, form their feminine either in ता *tá* or in नी *ní* : श्येत: *syetah*, white, श्येता *syetá*, श्येनी *syení* ; एत: *etah*, variegated, एता *etá* or एनी *ení* ; रोहित: *rohitah*, red, रोहिता *rohitá* or रोहिणी *rohiní*, but श्वेत: *svetah*, white, श्वेता *svetá* ; असिता *asitá*, white ; पलिता *palitá*, grey-haired.

---

* गुणवचन *gunavachana*, the name for adjective, occurs in Pân. v. 3, 58.

§ 248. The formation of feminine substantives must be learnt from the dictionary. Thus अज: *ajaḥ*, goat, forms अजा *ajá*. अश्व: *aśvaḥ*, horse, forms अश्वा *aśvá*.

बाल: *bálaḥ*, boy, forms बाला *bálá*.

शूद्र: *śúdraḥ*, a S'údra, forms { शूद्रा *śúdrá*, a woman of the S'údra caste.
शूद्री *śúdrí*, the wife of a S'údra. }

मातुल: *mátulaḥ*, maternal uncle, forms मातुली *mátulí* or मातुलानी *mátulání*, an uncle's wife.

आचार्य: *ácháryaḥ*, teacher, forms आचार्यानी *ácháryání**, wife of the teacher; but आचार्या *ácháryá*, a female teacher.

पति: *patiḥ*, lord, forms पत्नी *patní*, wife, &c.

Degrees of Comparison.

§ 249. The Comparative is formed by तर *tara*, or ईयस् *íyas* (§ 206); the Superlative by तम *tama*, or इष्ठ *ishṭha*†. These terminations तर *tara* and तम *tama* are not restricted in Sanskrit to adjectives. Substantives such as नृ *nṛi*, man, form नृतम: *nṛitamaḥ*, a thorough man; स्त्री *strí*, woman, स्त्रीतरा *strítará*‡, more of a woman. Even after case-terminations or personal terminations, तर *tara* and तम *tama* may be used. Thus from पूर्वाह्ण *púrváhṇe*, in the forenoon, पूर्वाह्णेतरे *púrváhṇetare*, earlier in the forenoon (Pâṇ. VI. 3, 17). From पचति *pachati*, he cooks, पचतितराम् *pachatitarám*, he cooks better (Pâṇ. V. 3, 57), पचतितमाम् *pachatitamám*, he cooks best (Pâṇ. V. 3, 56).

§ 250. तर *tara* and तम *tama*, if added to changeable bases, require the Pada base. Thus from प्राच् *prách* (§ 180), प्राक्तर *práktara*; from धनिन् *dhanin* (§ 203), धनितर *dhanitara*; from धनवत् *dhanavat* (§ 187), धनवत्तर *dhanavattara*; from विद्वस् *vidvas* (§ 204), विद्वत्तम *vidvattama*; from प्रत्यच् *pratyach* (§ 181), प्रत्यक्तर *pratyaktara*. There are, however, a few exceptions, such as दस्युहन्तम: *dasyuhantamaḥ*, from दस्युहन् *dasyuhan*, demon-killer; सुपथिन्तर: *supathintaraḥ*, from सुपथिन् *supathin*, with good roads.

§ 251. ईयस् *íyas* and इष्ठ *ishṭha* are never added to the secondary suffixes तृ *tṛi*, मत् *mat*, वत् *vat*, वल *vala*, विन् *vin*, इन् *in*. If adjectives ending in these suffixes require ईय: *íyaḥ* and इष्ठ *ishṭha*, the suffixes are dropt, and the ईय: *íyaḥ* and इष्ठ *ishṭha* added to the last consonant of the original base. बलवान् *balaván*, strong, बलीयस् *bal-íyas*, बलिष्ठ *bal-ishṭha*. दोग्धृ *dogdhṛi*, milking, दोहीयस् *doh-íyas*, दोहिष्ठ *doh-ishṭha*. स्रग्विन् *sragvin*, garlanded, स्रजीयस् *sraj-íyas*, more profusely garlanded. मतिमान् *matimán*, wise, मतीयस् *mat-íyas*, मतिष्ठ *mat-ishṭha*.

---

* On the dental न *n*, see Gaṇa Kshubhnâdi in the Kâś.-Vṛitti.

† Before तर *tara* and तम *tama* adjectives retain their accent; before ईयस् *íyas* and इष्ठ *ishṭha* they throw it on their first syllable (Pâṇ. III. 1, 4; VI. 1, 197). There are a few exceptions.

‡ Feminines in ई *í*, derived from masculines, must shorten the ई *í* before तर *tara* and तम *tama*; ब्राह्मणी *bráhmaṇí* forms ब्राह्मणितरा *bráhmaṇitará*. Other feminines in ई *í* or ऊ *ú* may or may not shorten their vowels; स्त्री *strí* forms स्त्रीतरा *strítará* or स्त्रितरा *stritará*. Also श्रेयसीतरा *śreyasítará* or श्रेयसितरा *śreyasitará*; विदुषीतरा *vidushítará* or विदुषितरा *vidushitará* (Pâṇ. VI. 3, 43–45).

§ 252. Other adjectives, too, lose their derivative elements before ईयस् *íyas* and इष्ठ *ishṭha*, or are otherwise irregular by substituting new bases for the Comparative and Superlative.　पापः *pâpaḥ*, bad ; पापीयस् *pâp-íyas*, worse ; पापिष्ठ *pâp-ishṭha*, worst.

	SECOND BASE.	COMPARATIVE.	SUPERLATIVE.
1. अंतिक *antika*, near	नेद् *ned*	नेदीयस् *nedíyas*	नेदिष्ठ *nedishṭha*
2. अल्प *alpa*, small	कन् *kan*	कनीयस् *kaníyas*	कनिष्ठ *kanishṭha*
		or अल्पीयस् *alpíyas*	अल्पिष्ठ *alpishṭha*
3. उरु *uru*, wide	वर् *var*	वरीयस् *varíyas*	वरिष्ठ *varishṭha*
4. ऋजु *riju*, straight	ऋज् *rij*	ऋजीयस् *rijíyas*	ऋजिष्ठ *rijishṭha*
		Vedic रजीयस् *rajíyas*	रजिष्ठ *rajishṭha* *
5. कृश *kriśa*, lean	क्रश् *kraś*	क्रशीयस् *kraśíyas*	क्रशिष्ठ *kraśishṭha*
6. क्षिप्र *kshipra*, quick	क्षेप् *kshep*	क्षेपीयस् *kshepíyas*	क्षेपिष्ठ *kshepishṭha*
7. क्षुद्र *kshudra*, mean	क्षोद् *kshod*	क्षोदीयस् *kshodíyas*	क्षोदिष्ठ *kshodishṭha*
8. गुरु *guru*, heavy	गर् *gar*	गरीयस् *garíyas*	गरिष्ठ *garishṭha*
9. तृप्र *tripra*, satisfied	त्रप् *trap*	त्रपीयस् *trapíyas*	त्रपिष्ठ *trapishṭha*
10. दीर्घ *dírgha*, long	द्राघ् *drâgh*	द्राघीयस् *drâghíyas*	द्राघिष्ठ *drâghishṭha*
11. दूर *dúra*, far	दव् *dav*	दवीयस् *davíyas*	दविष्ठ *davishṭha*
12. दृढ *dridha*, firm	द्रढ् *dradh*	द्रढीयस् *dradhíyas*	द्रढिष्ठ *dradhishṭha*
13. परिवृढ *parivridha*, exalted	परिव्रढ् *parivradh*	परिव्रढीयस् *parivradhíyas*	परिव्रढिष्ठ *parivradhishṭha*
14. पृथु *prithu*, broad	प्रथ् *prath*	प्रथीयस् *prathíyas*	प्रथिष्ठ *prathishṭha*
15. प्रशस्य *praśasya*, praiseworthy	श्र *śra*	श्रेयस् *śreyas*	श्रेष्ठ *śreshṭha*
	or ज्य *jya*	ज्यायस् *jyâyas*	ज्येष्ठ *jyeshṭha* †
16. प्रिय *priya*, dear	प्र *pra*	प्रेयस् *preyas*	प्रेष्ठ *preshṭha*
17. बहु *bahu*, many	भू *bhú*	भूयस् *bhúyas*	भूयिष्ठ *bhúyishṭha*
18. बहुल *bahula*, frequent	बंह् *bamh*	बंहीयस् *bamhíyas*	बंहिष्ठ *bamhishṭha* †
19. भृश *bhriśa*, excessive	भ्रश् *bhraś*	भ्रशीयस् *bhraśíyas*	भ्रशिष्ठ *bhraśishṭha*
20. मृदु *mridu*, soft	म्रद् *mrad*	म्रदीयस् *mradíyas*	म्रदिष्ठ *mradishṭha*
21. युवन् *yuvan*, young	यव् *yav*	यवीयस् *yavíyas*	यविष्ठ *yavishṭha*
	or कन् *kan*	कनीयस् *kaníyas*	कनिष्ठ *kanishṭha* †
22. वाढ *vâdha*, firm	साध् *sâdh*	साधीयस् *sâdhíyas*	साधिष्ठ *sâdhishṭha* ‡
23. वृद्ध *vriddha*, old	वर्ष् *varsh*	वर्षीयस् *varshíyas*	वर्षिष्ठ *varshishṭha*
	or ज्य *jya*	ज्यायस् *jyâyas*	ज्येष्ठ *jyeshṭha*
24. वृंदारक *vrindâraka*, beautiful	वृंद् *vrind*	वृंदीयस् *vrindíyas*	वृंदिष्ठ *vrindishṭha*
25. स्थिर *sthira*, firm	स्थ *stha*	स्थेयस् *stheyas*	स्थेष्ठ *stheshṭha*
26. स्थूल *sthúla*, strong	स्थव् *sthav*	स्थवीयस् *sthavíyas*	स्थविष्ठ *sthavishṭha*
27. स्फिर *sphira*, thick	स्फ *spha*	स्फेयस् *spheyas*	स्फेष्ठ *spheshṭha*
28. ह्रस्व *hrasva*, short	ह्रस् *hras*	ह्रसीयस् *hrasíyas*	ह्रसिष्ठ *hrasishṭha*

---

* Pân. VI. 4, 162.　　　† See Phiṭsûtra, ed. Kielhorn, I. 7; 23 (20).　　　‡ Pân. v. 3, 63.

CHAPTER V.

NUMERALS.

 Cardinals.

1 ९ एकः, एका, एकं, *ékaḥ, ékâ, ékam,* one.   (Base एक *eka.*)

2 २ द्वौ, द्वे, द्वे, *dvaú, dvé, dvé,* two.   (Base द्व *dva;* in comp. द्वि *dvi.*)

3 ३ त्रयः, तिस्रः, त्रीणि, *tráyaḥ, tisráḥ, tríṇi,* three.   (Base त्रि *tri.*)

4 ४ चत्वारः, चतस्रः, चत्वारि, *chatvâraḥ, chátasraḥ, chatvâri,* four.   (Base चतुर् *chatur.*)

5 ५ पंच *páñcha,* m. f. n. five.   (Base पंचन् *pañchan.*)

6 ६ षट् *sháṭ,* m. f. n. six.   (Base षष् *shash.*)

7 ७ सप्त *saptá,* m. f. n. seven.   (Base सप्तन् *saptan.*)

8 ८ अष्टौ *ashṭaú,* m. f. n. eight.   (Base अष्टन् *ashṭan.*)

9 ९ नव *náva,* m. f. n. nine.   (Base नवन् *navan.*)

10 ९० दश *dáśa,* m. f. n. ten.   (Base दशन् *daśan.*)

11 ११ एकादश *ékâdaśa,* eleven.   (Base as in दशन् *daśan.*)

12 १२ द्वादश *dvâdaśa.*

13 १३ त्रयोदश *tráyodaśa.*

14 १४ चतुर्दश *cháturdaśa.*

15 १५ पंचदश *páñchadaśa.*

16 १६ षोडश *shódaśa.*

17 १७ सप्तदश *saptádaśa.*

18 १८ अष्टादश *ashṭâdaśa.*

19 १९ नवदश *návadaśa* or अनविंशतिः *únaviṁśatiḥ.*

20 २० विंशतिः *viṁśátiḥ,* fem.

21 २१ एकविंशतिः *ekaviṁśatiḥ.*

22 २२ द्वाविंशतिः *dvâviṁśatiḥ.*

23 २३ त्रयोविंशतिः *trayoviṁśatiḥ.*

24 २४ चतुर्विंशतिः *chaturviṁśatiḥ.*

25 २५ पंचविंशतिः *pañchaviṁśatiḥ.*

26 २६ षड्विंशतिः *shaḍviṁśatiḥ.*

27 २७ सप्तविंशतिः *saptaviṁśatiḥ.*

28 २८ अष्टाविंशतिः *ashṭâviṁśatiḥ.*

29 २९ नवविंशतिः *navaviṁśatiḥ.*

30 ३० त्रिंशत् *triṁśát,* fem.

31 ३१ एकत्रिंशत् *ekatriṁśat.*

32 ३२ द्वात्रिंशत् *dvâtriṁśat.*

33 ३३ त्रयस्त्रिंशत् *trayastriṁśat.*

34 ३४ चतुस्त्रिंशत् *chatustriṁśat.*

35 ३५ पंचत्रिंशत् *pañchatriṁśat.*

36 ३६ षट्त्रिंशत् *shaṭtriṁśat.*

37 ३७ सप्तत्रिंशत् *saptatriṁśat.*

38 ३८ अष्टात्रिंशत् *ashṭâtriṁśat.*

39 ३९ नवत्रिंशत् *navatriṁśat.*

40 ४० चत्वारिंशत् *chatvâriṁśát,* fem.

41 ४१ एकचत्वारिंशत् *ekachatvâriṁśat.*

42 ४२ द्वाचत्वारिंशत् *dvâchatvâriṁśat* or द्विचत्वारिंशत् *dvichatvâriṁśat.*

43 ४३ त्रयश्चत्वारिंशत् *trayaśchatvâriṁśat* or त्रिचत्वारिंशत् *trichatvâriṁśat.*

44 ४४ चतुश्चत्वारिंशत् *chatuśchatvâriṁśat.*

45 ४५ पंचचत्वारिंशत् *pañchachatvâriṁśat.*

46 ४६ षट्चत्वारिंशत् *shaṭchatvâriṁśat.*

47 ४७ सप्तचत्वारिंशत् *saptachatvâriṁśat.*

48 ४८ अष्टाचत्वारिंशत् *ashṭâchatvâriṁśat* or अष्टचत्वारिंशत् *ashṭachatvâriṁśat.*

49 ४९ नवचत्वारिंशत् *navachatvâriṁśat.*

50 ५० पंचाशत् *pañchâśát,* fem.

51 ५१ एकपंचाशत् *ekapañchâśat.*

52 ५२ द्वापंचाशत् *dvâpañchâśat* or द्विपंचाशत् *dvipañchâśat.*

53 ५३ त्रयःपंचाशत् *trayaḥpañchâśat* or त्रिपंचाशत् *tripañchâśat.*

54 ५४ चतुःपंचाशत् *chatuḥpañchāśat.*	77 ७७ सप्तसप्ततिः *saptasaptatiḥ.*
55 ५५ पंचपंचाशत् *pañchapañchāśat.*	78 ७८ अष्टासप्ततिः *ashṭāsaptatiḥ* or
56 ५६ षट्पंचाशत् *shaṭpañchāśat.*	अष्टसप्ततिः *ashṭasaptatiḥ.*
57 ५७ सप्तपंचाशत् *saptapañchāśat.*	79 ७९ नवसप्ततिः *navasaptatiḥ.*
58 ५८ अष्टापंचाशत् *ashṭāpañchāśat* or	80 ८० अशीतिः *aśītiḥ.*
अष्टपंचाशत् *ashṭapañchāśat.*	81 ८१ एकाशीतिः *ekāśītiḥ.*
59 ५९ नवपंचाशत् *navapañchāśat.*	82 ८२ द्व्यशीतिः *dvyaśītiḥ.*
60 ६० षष्टिः *shashṭiḥ,* fem.	83 ८३ त्र्यशीतिः *tryaśītiḥ.*
61 ६१ एकषष्टिः *ekashashṭiḥ.*	84 ८४ चतुरशीतिः *chaturaśītiḥ.*
62 ६२ द्वाषष्टिः *dvāshashṭiḥ* or	85 ८५ पंचाशीतिः *pañchāśītiḥ.*
द्विषष्टिः *dvishashṭiḥ.*	86 ८६ षडशीतिः *shaḍaśītiḥ.*
63 ६३ त्रयःषष्टिः *trayahshashṭiḥ* or	87 ८७ सप्ताशीतिः *saptāśītiḥ.*
त्रिषष्टिः *trishashṭiḥ.*	88 ८८ अष्टाशीतिः *ashṭāśītiḥ.*
64 ६४ चतुःषष्टिः *chatushshashṭiḥ.*	89 ८९ नवाशीतिः *navāśītiḥ.*
65 ६५ पंचषष्टिः *pañchashashṭiḥ.*	90 ९० नवतिः *navatiḥ.*
66 ६६ षट्षष्टिः *shaṭshashṭiḥ.*	91 ९१ एकनवतिः *ekanavatiḥ.*
67 ६७ सप्तषष्टिः *saptashashṭiḥ.*	92 ९२ द्वानवतिः *dvānavatiḥ* or
68 ६८ अष्टाषष्टिः *ashṭāshashṭiḥ* or	द्विनवतिः *dvinavatiḥ.*
अष्टषष्टिः *ashṭashashṭiḥ.*	93 ९३ त्रयोनवतिः *trayonavatiḥ* or
69 ६९ नवषष्टिः *navashashṭiḥ.*	त्रिनवतिः *trinavatiḥ* (not या ॰).
70 ७० सप्ततिः *saptatiḥ,* fem.	94 ९४ चतुर्नवतिः *chaturnavatiḥ.*
71 ७१ एकसप्ततिः *ekasaptatiḥ.*	95 ९५ पंचनवतिः *pañchanavatiḥ.*
72 ७२ द्वासप्ततिः *dvāsaptatiḥ* or	96 ९६ षण्णवतिः *shaṇṇavatiḥ.*
द्विसप्ततिः *dvisaptatiḥ.*	97 ९७ सप्तनवतिः *saptanavatiḥ.*
73 ७३ त्रयःसप्ततिः *trayahsaptatiḥ* or	98 ९८ अष्टानवतिः *ashṭānavatiḥ* or
त्रिसप्ततिः *trisaptatiḥ.*	अष्टनवतिः *ashṭanavatiḥ.*
74 ७४ चतुःसप्ततिः *chatuḥsaptatiḥ.*	99 ९९ नवनवतिः *navanavatiḥ* or
75 ७५ पंचसप्ततिः *pañchasaptatiḥ.*	ऊनशतं *ūnaśatam.*
76 ७६ षट्सप्ततिः *shaṭsaptatiḥ.*	

100 १०० शतं *śatám,* neut. and masc. (Siddh.-Kaum. vol. ii. p. 635.)

101 १०१ एकाधिकं शतं *ekādhikam śatam,* hundred exceeded by one; or as a compound, एकाधिकशतं *ekādhika-śatam,* or एकशतं *ekaśatam,* as before.

102 १०२ द्व्यधिकं शतं *dvyadhikam śatam* or द्विशतं *dviśatam.* (Pâṇ. vi. 3, 49.)

103 १०३ त्र्यधिकं शतं *tryadhikam śatam* or त्रिशतं *triśatam.*

104 १०४ चतुरधिकं शतं *chaturadhikam śatam* or चतुःशतं *chatuḥśatam.*

105 १०५ पंचाधिकं शतं *pañchādhikam śatam* or पंचशतं *pañchaśatam.*

106 १०६ षडधिकं शतं *shaḍadhikam śatam* or षट्शतं *shaṭśatam.*

107 १०७ सप्ताधिकं शतं *saptādhikam śatam* or सप्तशतं *saptaśatam.*

108 १०८ अष्टाधिकं शतं *ashṭādhikam śatam* or अष्टशतं *ashṭaśatam.* (Pâṇ. vi. 3, 49.)

109 १०९ नवाधिकं शतं *navādhikam śatam* or नवशतं *navaśatam.*

110 ११० दशाधिकं शतं *daśddhikam śatam* or दशशतं *daśaśatam.*

111 १११ एकादशाधिकं शतं *ekddaśddhikam śatam* or एकादशशतं *ekddaśaśatam* &c.
or एकादशं शतं *ekddaśam śatam,* i. e. a hundred having eleven (in
excess). Pân. v. 2, 45.

112 ११२ द्वादशाधिकं शतं *dvddaśddhikam śatam* or द्वादशं शतं *dvddaśam śatam.*

113 ११३ त्रयोदशाधिकं शतं *trayodaśddhikam śatam* or त्रयोदशं शतं *trayodaśam śatam.*

114 ११४ चतुर्दशाधिकं शतं *chaturdaśddhikam śatam* or चतुर्दशं शतं *chaturdaśam śatam.*

115 ११५ पंचदशाधिकं शतं *pañchadaśddhikam śatam* or पंचदशं शतं *pañchadaśam śatam.*

116 ११६ षोडशाधिकं शतं *shoḍaśddhikam śatam* or षोडशं शतं *shoḍaśam śatam.*

117 ११७ सप्तदशाधिकं शतं *saptadaśddhikam śatam* or सप्तदशं शतं *saptadaśam śatam.*

118 ११८ अष्टादशाधिकं शतं *ashṭddaśddhikam śatam* or अष्टादशं शतं *ashṭddaśam śatam.*

119 ११९ नवदशाधिकं शतं *navadaśddhikam śatam* or नवदशं शतं *navadaśam śatam.*

120 १२० विंशत्यधिकं शतं *vimśatyadhikam śatam* or विंशं शतं *vimśam śatam* *.

121 १२१ एकविंशत्यधिकं शतं *ekavimśatyadhikam śatam* or एकविंशं शतं *ekavimśam
śatam* *, &c.

130 १३० त्रिंशदधिकं शतं *trimśadadhikam śatam* or त्रिंशं शतं *trimśam śatam* *.

140 १४० चत्वारिंशदधिकं शतं *chatvdrimśadadhikam śatam* or चत्वारिंशं शतं *chatvd-
rimśam śatam* *.

150 १५० पंचाशदधिकं शतं *pañchdśadadhikam śatam* or पंचाशं शतं *pañchdśam śatam* *
or सार्धशतं *sdrdhaśatam,* 100 + $\frac{1}{2}$ (hundred).

160 १६० षष्ट्यधिकं शतं *shashṭyadhikam śatam* or षष्टिशतं *shashṭiśatam.*

170 १७० सप्तत्यधिकं शतं *saptatyadhikam śatam* or सप्ततिशतं *saptatiśatam.*

180 १८० अशीत्यधिकं शतं *aśītyadhikam śatam* or अशीतिशतं *aśītiśatam.*

190 १९० नवत्यधिकं शतं *navatyadhikam śatam* or नवतिशतं *navatiśatam.*

200 २०० द्वे शते *dve śate* or द्विशतं *dviśatam* or द्विशती *dviśatî.*

300 ३०० त्रीणि शतानि *trîṇi śatâni* or त्रिशतं *triśatam.*

400 ४०० चत्वारि शतानि *chatvdri śatâni* or चतुःशतं *chatuḥśatam.*

500 ५०० पंच शतानि *pañcha śatâni* or पंचशतं *pañchaśatam.*

600 ६०० षट् शतानि *shaṭ śatâni* or षट्शतं *shaṭśatam.*

700 ७०० सप्त शतानि *sapta śatâni* or सप्तशतं *saptaśatam.*

800 ८०० अष्ट शतानि *ashṭa śatâni* or अष्टशतं *ashṭaśatam.*

900 ९०० नव शतानि *nava śatâni* or नवशतं *navaśatam.*

1000 १००० दश शतानि *daśa śatâni* or दशशती *daśaśatî,* fem., or सहस्रं *sahásram,*
neut. and masc.†

2000 २००० द्वे सहस्रे *dve sahasre.*

3000 ३००० त्रीणि सहस्राणि *trîṇi sahasrâṇi.*

10,000 १०,००० अयुतं *ayutam,* neut. and masc.†

---

* Pân. v. 2, 46. The same rules apply to सहस्रं *sahasram,* 1000, so that 1011 might be
rendered by एकादशं सहस्रं *ekddaśam sahasram,* 1041 by एकचत्वारिंशं सहस्रं *ekachatvdrimśam
sahasram,* &c.   † Siddh.-Kaum. vol. II. p. 635.

100,000 १००,००० लषं *laksham,* neut. or fem.*, or निथुतं *niyutam,* neut. and masc.†

One million, प्रयुतं *prayutam,* neut. or masc.*

Ten millions, कोटि *koṭi,* fem.‡

A hundred millions, अर्बुद *arbuda,* masc. and neut.

A thousand millions, महार्बुद *mahárbuda,* masc. and neut., or पम *padma,* neut., i. e. lotus.

Ten thousand millions, खर्व *kharva,* neut., i. e. minute.

A hundred thousand millions, निखर्व *nikharva,* neut.

A billion, महापम *mahápadma,* neut.

Ten billions, शंकु *śaṅku,* masc., i. e. an ant-hill.

A hundred billions, शंख *śaṅkha,* masc. neut., i. e. a conch-shell, or समुद्र *samudra,* masc., i. e. sea.

A thousand billions, महाशंख *maháśaṅkha,* or अंत्य *antya,* ultimate.

Ten thousand billions, हाहा *háhá,* masc., or मध्य *madhya,* middle.

A hundred thousand billions, महाहाहा *maháháhá,* or परार्ध *parárdha,* i. e. other half.

One million billions, धुन *dhuna,* neut.

Ten million billions, महाधुन *mahádhuna.*

A hundred million billions, अक्षौहिणी *akshauhiṇí,* fem., i. e. a host.

A thousand million billions, महाक्षौहिणी *mahákshauhiṇí.*

In the same manner as अधिक *adhika,* exceeding, ऊन *úna,* diminished, may be used to form numerical compounds. पंचोनं शतं *pañchonam śatam* or पंचोनशतं *pañchonaśatam,* 100 − 5, i. e. 95. If one is to be deducted, ऊन *úna,* without एक *eka,* suffices. ऊनविंशतिः *únavimśatiḥ* or एकोनविंशतिः *ekonavimśatiḥ,* 20 − 1, i. e. 19. Another way of expressing nineteen and similar numbers is by prefixing एकान्न *ekánna,* i. e. by one not ; एकान्नविंशतिः *ekánnavimśatiḥ,* by one not twenty, i. e. 19. (Pâṇ. VI. 3, 76.)

Declension of Cardinals.
एक *eka,* one.

	SINGULAR.			PLURAL.		
	MASC.	FEM.	NEUT.	MASC.	FEM.	NEUT.
N.	एकः *ékaḥ*	एका *éká*	एकं *ékam*	एके *eke*	एकाः *ékáḥ*	एकानि *ékáni*
A.	एकं *ékam*	एकां *ékám*	एकं *ékam*	एकान् *ékán*	एकाः *ékáḥ*	एकानि *ékáni*
I.	एकेन *ékena*	एकया *ékayá*	एकेन *ékena*	एकैः *ékaiḥ*	एकाभिः *ékábhiḥ*	एकैः *ékaiḥ*
D.	एकस्मै *ékasmai*	एकस्यै *ékasyai*	एकस्मै *ékasmai*	एकेभ्यः *ékebhyaḥ*	एकाभ्यः *ékábhyaḥ*	एकेभ्यः *ékebhyaḥ*
Ab.	एकस्मात् *ékasmát*	एकस्याः *ékasyáḥ*	एकस्मात् *ékasmát*	एकेभ्यः *ékebhyaḥ*	एकाभ्यः *ékábhyaḥ*	एकेभ्यः *ékebhyaḥ*
G.	एकस्य *ékasya*	एकस्याः *ékasyáḥ*	एकस्य *ékasya*	एकेषां *ékeshám*	एकासां *ékásám*	एकेषां *ékeshám*
L.	एकस्मिन् *ékasmin*	एकस्यां *ékasyám*	एकस्मिन् *ékasmin*	एकेषु *ékeshu*	एकासु *ékásu*	एकेषु *ekeshu*
V.	एक *éka*	एके *éke*	एक *éka*	एके *éke*	एकाः *ékáḥ*	एकानि *ékáni*

---

* Siddh.-Kaum. vol. II. p. 635.   † Amara-Kosha III. 6, 3, 24.

‡ A different string of names is given in the Vâjasan.-Sanhitâ XVII. 2. See also Woepcke, Mémoire sur la propagation des chiffres indiens (1863), p. 70; Lalita-vistara, ed. Calcutt. p. 168.

§ 254. द्वि *dvi*, two, base द्व *dva*, like कान्त *kánta* (§ 238).

DUAL.

	MASC.	FEM.	NEUT.
N. A. V.	द्वौ *dvaú*	द्वे *dvé*	द्वे *dvé*
I. D. Ab.	द्वाभ्यां *dvábhyám*	द्वाभ्यां *dvábhyám*	द्वाभ्यां *dvábhyám*
G. L.	द्वयोः *dváyoh*	द्वयोः *dváyoh*	द्वयोः *dváyoh*

§ 255. त्रि *tri*, three, fem. तिसृ *tisṛi*.

	MASC.	FEM.	NEUT.
N. V.	त्रयः *tráyah*	तिस्रः *tisráh* (Pâṇ. VI. 1, 166)	त्रीणि *tríṇi*
A.	त्रीन् *trín*	तिस्रः *tisráh* *	त्रीणि *tríṇi*
I.	त्रिभिः *tribhíh*	तिसृभिः *tisṛíbhih*	त्रिभिः *tribhíh*
D. Ab.	त्रिभ्यः *tribhyáh*	तिसृभ्यः *tisṛíbhyah*	त्रिभ्यः *tribhyáh*
G.	त्रयाणां *trayáṇám* (Ved. *tríṇám*)	तिसृणां *tisṛiṇám* †	त्रयाणां *trayáṇám*
L.	त्रिषु *trishú*	तिसृषु *tisṛíshu*	त्रिषु *trishú*

§ 256. चतुर् *chatur*, four, fem. चतसृ *chatasṛi*.

	MASC.	FEM.	NEUT.
N. V.	चत्वारः *chatvárah* (Pâṇ. VII. 1, 98)	चतस्रः *chátasrah*	चत्वारि *chatvári*
A.	चतुरः *chatúrah* (Pâṇ. VI. 1, 167)	चतस्रः *chátasrah* *	चत्वारि *chatvári*
I.	चतुर्भिः *chatúrbhih*	चतसृभिः *chatasṛíbhih*	चतुर्भिः *chatúrbhih*
D. Ab.	चतुर्भ्यः *chatúrbhyah*	चतसृभ्यः *chatasṛíbhyah*	चतुर्भ्यः *chatúrbhyah*
G.	चतुर्णां *chaturṇám*	चतसृणां *chatasṛiṇám* †	चतुर्णां *chaturṇám*
L.	चतुर्षु *chatúrshu*	चतसृषु *chatasṛíshu*	चतुर्षु *chatúrshu*

§ 257. पंचन् *pañchan*, five. षष् *shash*, six. अष्टन् *ashṭan*, eight.

N. A. V.	पंच *páñcha*	षट् *sháṭ*	अष्टौ *ashṭaú* or अष्ट *ashṭá*
I.	पंचभिः *pañchábhih* ‡	षड्भिः *shaḍbhíh*	अष्टाभिः *ashṭábhíh* or अष्टभिः *ashṭábhih* ∥
D. Ab.	पंचभ्यः *pañchábhyah*	षड्भ्यः *shaḍbhyáh*	अष्टाभ्यः *ashṭábhyáh* or अष्टभ्यः *ashṭábhyah*
G.	पंचानां *pañchánám* ¶	षण्णां *shaṇṇám* ¶	अष्टानां *ashṭánám* ¶
L.	पंचसु *pañchásu*	षट्सु *shaṭsú*	अष्टासु *ashṭású* or अष्टसु *ashṭásu*

Cardinals with bases ending in न् *n*, such as सप्तन् *saptan*, नवन् *navan*, दशन् *dasan*, एकादशन् *ekádasan*, &c., follow the declension of पंचन् *pañchan*. विंशतिः *vimsatih* is declined like a feminine in इ *i*; those in त् *t* like feminines in त् *t*; शतं *satam* like a neut. or masc. in अ *a*.

§ 258. The construction of the cardinals from 1 to 19 requires a few remarks. एक *eka* is naturally used in the singular only, except when it means some; एके वदंति *eke vadanti*,

---

* Not तिसृः *tisṛíh*, nor चतसृः *chatasṛíh*. (Accent, Pâṇ. VI. 1, 167, vârt.; VII. 2, 99, vârt.)

† Not तिसृणां *tisṛíṇám*, nor चतसृणां *chatasṛíṇám* (Pâṇ. VI. 4, 4), though these forms occur in the Veda and Epic poetry.

‡ Accent, Pâṇ. VI. 1, 180; 181. ∥ Pâṇ. VI. 1, 172. ¶ Pâṇ. VII. 1, 55.

some people say. द्वि *dvi* is always used as a dual, all the rest from 3 to 19 as plurals.
Ex. त्रिभिः पुरुषैः *tribhih purushaih*, with three men ; एकादश पुरुषान् *ekádasa purushán*, eleven
men, acc. The cardinals after four do not distinguish the gender ; एकादश नारी: *ekádasa
náríh*, eleven women, acc.

While the numerals from 1 to 19 are treated as adjectives, agreeing with their substantives in gender, if possible, and in number and case, विंशति: *vimsatih* and the rest may be treated both as adjectives and as substantives. Hence विंशति: शत्रूणां *vimsatih satrúnám*, twenty enemies, or विंशति: शत्रव: *vimsatih satravah ;* षष्टि: शिशव: *shashtih sisavah*, sixty boys ; शतं फलानि *satam phaláni*, a hundred fruits ; त्रिंशता वृद्धे: *trimsatá vriddhaih*, by thirty elders ; शतं दासीनां *satam dásínám* or शतं दास्य: *satam dásyah*, a hundred slaves ; सहस्रं पितर: *sahasram pitarah*, a thousand ancestors.

Exceptionally these cardinals may take the plural number : पंचाशद्भिर्हयैः *panchásadbhir hayaih*, with fifty horses.

§ 259.   *Ordinals.*

प्रथम:, °मा, °मं, *prathamáh, á, am,*
अग्रिम:, °मा, °मं, *agrimáh, á, am,* ⎫ the first.
आदिम:, °मा, °मं, *ádimáh, á, am,* ⎭

द्वितीय:, °या, °यं, *dvitíyah, á, am*, the second.

तृतीय:, °या, °यं, *tritíyah, á, am*, the third.

चतुर्थ:, °र्थी, °र्थं, *chaturtháh, í, am,* ⎫
तुरीय:, °या, °यं, *turíyah, á, am,* ⎬ the fourth.
तुर्य:, °र्या, °र्यं, *túryah, á, am,* ⎭

पंचम:, °मी, °मं, *panchamáh, í, am*, the fifth.

षष्ठ:, °ष्ठी, °ष्ठं, *shashtháh, í, am*, the sixth.

सप्तम:, °मी, °मं, *saptamáh, í, am*, the seventh.

अष्टम:, °मी, °मं, *ashtamáh, í, am*, the eighth.

नवम:, °मी, °मं, *navamáh, í, am*, the ninth.

दशम:, °मी, °मं, *dasamáh, í, am*, the tenth.

एकादश:, °शी, °शं, *ekádasáh, í, am*, the eleventh.

नवदश:, °शी, °शं, *navadasáh, í, am,* ⎫
अनविंश:, °शी, °शं, *únavimsáh, í, am,* ⎬ the nineteenth.
अनविंशतितम:, °मी, °मं, *únavimsatitamáh, í, am,* ⎭

विंश:, °शी, °शं, *vimsáh, í, am* (Pân. v. 2, 56), ⎫ the twentieth.
विंशतितम:, °मी, °मं, *vimsatitamáh, í, am,* ⎭

त्रिंश:, °शी, °शं, *trimsáh, í, am,* ⎫ the thirtieth.
त्रिंशत्तम:, °मी, °मं, *trimsattamáh, í, am,* ⎭

चत्वारिंश:, °शी, °शं, *chatvárimsáh, í, am,* ⎫ the fortieth.
चत्वारिंशत्तम:, °मी, °मं, *chatvárimsattamáh, í, am,* ⎭

पंचाश:, °शी, °शं, *panchásáh, í, am,* ⎫ the fiftieth.
पंचाशत्तम:, °मी, °मं, *panchásattamáh, í, am,* ⎭

षष्टितम: *shashṭitamáḥ*, the sixtieth *.

एकषष्टितम: *ekashashṭitamáḥ,*
एकषष्ट: *ekashashṭáḥ,* } the sixty-first.

सप्ततितम: *saptatitamáḥ*, the seventieth.

एकसप्ततितम: *ekasaptatitamáḥ,*
एकसप्तत: *ekasaptatáḥ,* } the seventy-first.

अशीतितम: *aśítitamáḥ*, the eightieth.

एकाशीतितम: *ekáśítitamáḥ,*
एकाशीत: *ekáśítáḥ,* } the eighty-first.

नवतितम:, °मी, °मं, *navatitamáḥ, í, am*, the ninetieth.

एकनवतितम: *ekanavatitamáḥ,*
एकनवत: *ekanavatáḥ,* } the ninety-first.

शततम:, °मी, °मं, *śatatamáḥ, í, am*, the hundredth. (Pâṇ. v. 2, 57.)

एकशततम: *ekaśatatamáḥ*, the hundred and first.

सहस्रतम: *sahasratamáḥ*, the thousandth.

§ 260. *Numerical Adverbs and other Derivatives.*

सकृत् *sakṛit*, once.
द्वि: *dviḥ*, twice.
त्रि: *triḥ*, thrice.
चतु: *chatuḥ*, four times.
पंचकृत्व: *pañchakṛitvaḥ*, five times.
षट्कृत्व: *shaṭkṛitvaḥ*, six times, &c.

एकधा *ekadhá*, in one way.
द्विधा *dvidhá* or द्वेधा *dvedhá*, in two ways.
त्रिधा *tridhá* or त्रेधा *tredhá*, in three ways.
चतुर्धा *chaturdhá*, in four ways.
पंचधा *pañchadhá*, in five ways.
षोढा *shoḍhá*, in six ways, &c. (or षड्धा?)

एकश: *ekaśaḥ*, one-fold.
द्विश: *dviśaḥ*, two-fold.
त्रिश: *triśaḥ*, three-fold, &c. (Pâṇ. v. 4, 43.)

द्वयं *dvayam* or द्वितयं *dvitayam*, a pair. (Pâṇ. v. 2, 42.)
त्रयं *trayam* or त्रितयं *tritayam* or त्रयी *trayí*, a triad.
चतुष्टयं *chatushṭayam*, a tetrad.
पंचतयं *pañchatayam*, a pentad, &c.

These are also used as adjectives, in the sense of five-fold &c., and may then form their plural as पंचतया: *pañchatayáḥ* or पंचतये *pañchataye* (§ 283).

पंचत् *pañchat*, a pentad, दशत् *daśat*, a decad (Pâṇ. v. 1, 60), are generally used as feminine; but both words occur likewise as masculine in the commentary to Pâṇ. v. 1, 59, and in the Kâśikâ-Vṛitti.

---

* The ordinals from sixty admit of one form only, that is तम: *tamaḥ;* but if preceded by another numeral, both forms are allowed (Pâṇ. v. 2, 58). शतं *śatam* forms its ordinal as शततम: *śatatamaḥ* only (Pâṇ. v. 2, 57).

CHAPTER VI.

PRONOUNS AND PRONOMINAL ADJECTIVES.

§ 261.   *Personal Pronouns.*

Base (in composition) मद् *mad* and   Base (in composition) त्वद् *tvad* and
    अस्मद् *asmad.*   युष्मद् *yushmad.*

SINGULAR.

N.	अहं *ahám*, I	त्वं *tvám*, thou
A.	मां *mám*, मा *má*, me	त्वां *tvám*, त्वा *tvá*, thee
I.	मया *máyá*, by me	त्वया *tváyá*, by thee
D.	मह्यं *máhyam*, मे *me*, to me	तुभ्यं *túbhyam*, ते *te*, to thee
Ab.	मात् *mát*, from me	त्वत् *tvát*, from thee
G.	मम *máma*, मे *me*, of me	तव *táva*, ते *te*, of thee
L.	मयि *máyi*, in me	त्वयि *tváyi*, in thee

DUAL.

N.	आवां *ávám*, we two	युवां *yuvám*, you two
A.	आवां *ávám*, नौ *nau*, us two	युवां *yuvám*, वां *vám*, you two
I.	आवाभ्यां *ávábhyám*, by us two	युवाभ्यां *yuvábhyám*, by you two
D.	आवाभ्यां *ávábhyám*, नौ *nau*, to us two	युवाभ्यां *yuvábhyám*, वां *vám*, to you two
Ab.	आवाभ्यां *ávábhyám*, from us two	युवाभ्यां *yuvábhyám*, from you two
G.	आवयो: *ávávoh*, नौ *nau*, of us two	युवयो: *yuvávoh*, वां *vám*, of you two
L.	आवयो: *ávávoh*, in us two	युवयो: *yuvávoh*, in you two

PLURAL.

N.	वयं *vayám*, we	यूयं *yúyám*, you
A.	अस्मान् *asmán*, न: *nah*, us	युष्मान् *yushmán*, व: *vah*, you
I.	अस्माभि: *asmábhih*, by us	युष्माभि: *yushmábhih*, by you
D.	अस्मभ्यं *asmábhyam*, न: *nah*, to us	युष्मभ्यं *yushmábhyam*, व: *vah*, to you
Ab.	अस्मात् *asmát*, from us	युष्मात् *yushmát*, from you
G.	अस्माकं *asmákam*, न: *nah*, of us	युष्माकं *yushmákam*, व: *vah*, of you
L.	अस्मासु *asmásu*, in us	युष्मासु *yushmásu*, in you

The substitutes in the even cases, मा *má*, मे *me*, नौ *nau*, न: *nah*, त्वा *tvá*,
ते *te*, वां *vám*, व: *vah*, have no accent and are never used at the beginning of
a sentence, nor can they be followed by such particles as च *cha*, and, वा *vá*,
or, एव *eva*, indeed, ह *ha*, अह *aha*.

§ 262. Base (in composition) तद् *tad*, he, she, it. (Accent, Pâṇ. VI. 1, 182.)

	SINGULAR.			PLURAL.		
	MASC.	FEM.	NEUT.	MASC.	FEM.	NEUT.
N.	स: *sáḥ*	सा *sá*	तत् *tát*	ते *té*	ता: *táḥ*	तानि *táni*
A.	तं *tám*	तां *tám*	तत् *tát*	तान् *tán*	ता: *táḥ*	तानि *táni*
I.	तेन *téna*	तया *táyá*	तेन *téna*	तै: *taíḥ*	ताभि: *tábhiḥ*	तै: *taíḥ*
D.	तस्मै *tásmai*	तस्यै *tásyai*	तस्मै *tásmai*	तेभ्य: *tébhyaḥ*	ताभ्य: *tábhyaḥ*	तेभ्य: *tébhyaḥ*
Ab.	तस्मात् *tásmát*	तस्या: *tásyáḥ*	तस्मात् *tásmát*	तेभ्य: *tébhyaḥ*	ताभ्य: *tábhyaḥ*	तेभ्य: *tébhyaḥ*
G.	तस्य *tásya*	तस्या: *tásyáḥ*	तस्य *tásya*	तेषां *téshám*	तासां *tásám*	तेषां *téshám*
L.	तस्मिन् *tásmin*	तस्यां *tásyám*	तस्मिन् *tásmin*	तेषु *téshu*	तासु *tásu*	तेषु *téshu*

	DUAL.		
	MASC.	FEM.	NEUT.
N. A.	तौ *taú*	ते *té*	ते *té*
I. D. Ab.	ताभ्यां *tábhyám*	ताभ्यां *tábhyám*	ताभ्यां *tábhyám*
G. L.	तयो: *táyoḥ*	तयो: *táyoḥ*	तयो: *táyoḥ*

§ 263. Base (in composition) त्यद् *tyad*.

	SINGULAR.			PLURAL.		
	MASC.	FEM.	NEUT.	MASC.	FEM.	NEUT.
N.	स्य: *syáḥ*	स्या *syá*	त्यत् *tyát*	त्ये *tyé*	त्या: *tyáḥ*	त्यानि *tyáni*
A.	त्यं *tyám*	त्यां *tyám*	त्यत् *tyát*	त्यान् *tyán*	त्या: *tyáḥ*	त्यानि *tyáni*
I.	त्येन *tyéna*	त्यया *tyáyá*	त्येन *tyéna*	त्यै: *tyaíḥ*	त्याभि: *tyábhiḥ*	त्यै: *tyaíḥ*
D.	त्यस्मै *tyásmai*	त्यस्यै *tyásyai*	त्यस्मै *tyásmai*	त्येभ्य: *tyébhyaḥ*	त्याभ्य: *tyábhyaḥ*	त्येभ्य: *tyébhyaḥ*
Ab.	त्यस्मात् *tyásmát*	त्यस्या: *tyásyáḥ*	त्यस्मात् *tyásmát*	त्येभ्य: *tyébhyaḥ*	त्याभ्य: *tyábhyaḥ*	त्येभ्य: *tyébhyaḥ*
G.	त्यस्य *tyásya*	त्यस्या: *tyásyáḥ*	त्यस्य *tyásya*	त्येषां *tyéshám*	त्यासां *tyásám*	त्येषां *tyéshám*
L.	त्यस्मिन् *tyásmin*	त्यस्यां *tyásyám*	त्यस्मिन् *tyásmin*	त्येषु *tyéshu*	त्यासु *tyásu*	त्येषु *tyéshu*

	DUAL.		
	MASC.	FEM.	NEUT.
N. A.	त्यौ *tyaú*	त्ये *tyé*	त्ये *tyé*
I. D. Ab.	त्याभ्यां *tyábhyám*	त्याभ्यां *tyábhyám*	त्याभ्यां *tyábhyám*
G. L.	त्ययो: *tyáyoḥ*	त्ययो: *tyáyoḥ*	त्ययो: *tyáyoḥ*

Possessive Pronouns.

§ 264. From the bases of the three personal pronouns, possessive adjectives are formed by means of ईय *íya*.

मदीय:, °या, °यं, *madíyaḥ, yá, yam*, mine.

त्वदीय:, °या, °यं, *tvadíyaḥ, yá, yam*, thine.

तदीय:, °या, °यं, *tadíyaḥ, yá, yam*, his, her, its.

अस्मदीय:, °या, °यं, *asmadíyaḥ, yá, yam*, our.

युष्मदीय:, °या, °यं, *yushmadíyaḥ, yá, yam*, your.

तदीय:, °या, °यं, *tadíyaḥ, yá, yam*, their.

Other derivative possessive pronouns are मामक:* *mámákaḥ*, mine; तावक *távákaḥ*, thine; आस्माक: *ásmákaḥ*, our; यौष्माक: *yaushmákaḥ*, your.   Likewise

---

* Pâṇ. IV. 3, 1–3; IV. 1, 30; VII. 3, 44.

मामकीन: *mâmakînaḥ*, mine ; तावकीन: *tâvakînaḥ*, thine ; आस्माकीन: *âsmâkînaḥ*, our ; यौष्माकीण: *yaushmâkîṇaḥ*, your.

Reflexive Pronouns.

§ 265. स्वयं *svayám*, self, is indeclinable. स्वयं वृतवान् *svayam vṛitavân*, I chose it myself, thou chosest it thyself, he chose it himself ; स्वयं वृतवती *svayam vṛitavatî*, she chose it herself ; स्वयं वृतवंत: *svayam vṛitavantaḥ*, we, you, they chose it by our, your, themselves.

§ 266. आत्मन् *âtmán*, self, is declined like ब्रह्मन् *brahman* (§ 192). Ex. आत्मानमात्मना पश्य *âtmánam âtmánâ paśya*, see thyself by thyself, *gnosce te ipsum* ; आत्मनो दोषं ज्ञात्वा *âtmano dosham jñâtvâ*, having known his own fault. It is used in the singular even when referring to two or three persons : आत्मनो देशमागम्य मृता: *âtmano deśam âgamya mṛitâḥ*, having returned to their country, they died.

§ 267. स्व:, स्वा, स्वं, *sváḥ*, *svá*, *svám*, is a reflexive adjective, corresponding to Latin *suus, sua, suum*. स्वं पुत्रं दृष्ट्वा *svam putram dṛishṭvâ*, having seen his own son. On the declension of स्व *sva*, see § 278.

Demonstrative Pronouns.

§ 268. Base (in composition) एतद् *etad*, this (very near).

	SINGULAR.			PLURAL.		
	MASC.	FEM.	NEUT.	MASC.	FEM.	NEUT.
N.	एष: *eshâḥ*	एषा *eshâ*	एतत् *etát*	एते *eté*	एता: *etâḥ*	एतानि *etâni*
A.	एतं *etám*	एतां *etâm*	एतत् *etát*	एतान् *etân*	एता: *etâḥ*	एतानि *etâni*
I.	एतेन *eténa*	एतया *etáyâ*	एतेन *eténa*	एतै: *etaiḥ*	एताभि: *etâbhiḥ*	एतै: *etaiḥ*
D.	एतस्मै *etásmai*	एतस्यै *etásyai*	एतस्मै *etásmai*	एतेभ्य: *etébhyaḥ*	एताभ्य: *etâbhyaḥ*	एतेभ्य: *etébhyaḥ*
Ab.	एतस्मात् *etásmât*	एतस्या: *etásyâḥ*	एतस्मात् *etásmât*	एतेभ्य: *etébhyaḥ*	एताभ्य: *etâbhyaḥ*	एतेभ्य: *etébhyaḥ*
G.	एतस्य *etásya*	एतस्या: *etásyâḥ*	एतस्य *etásya*	एतेषां *etéshâm*	एतासां *etâsâm*	एतेषां *etéshâm*
L.	एतस्मिन् *etásmin*	एतस्यां *etásyâm*	एतस्मिन् *etásmin*	एतेषु *etéshu*	एतासु *etâsu*	एतेषु *etéshu*

	DUAL.		
	MASC.	FEM.	NEUT.
N. A.	एतौ *etaú*	एते *eté*	एते *eté*
I. D. Ab.	एताभ्यां *etâbhyám*	एताभ्यां *etâbhyám*	एताभ्यां *etâbhyám*
G. L.	एतयो: *etáyoḥ*	एतयो: *etáyoḥ*	एतयो: *etáyoḥ*

§ 269. Base (in composition) इदं *idam*, this (indefinitely). (Accent, Pâṇ. VI. I, 171.)

	SINGULAR.			PLURAL.		
	MASC.	FEM.	NEUT.	MASC.	FEM.	NEUT.
N.	अयं *ayám*	इयं *iyám*	इदं *idám*	इमे *imé*	इमा: *imâḥ*	इमानि *imâni*
A.	इमं *imám*	इमां *imâm*	इदं *idám*	इमान् *imân*	इमा: *imâḥ*	इमानि *imâni*
I.	अनेन *anéna*	अनया *anáyâ*	अनेन *anéna*	एभि: *ebhíḥ*	आभि: *âbhíḥ*	एभि: *ebhíḥ*
D.	अस्मै *asmaí*	अस्यै *asyaí*	अस्मै *asmaí*	एभ्य: *ebhyáḥ*	आभ्य: *âbhyáḥ*	एभ्य: *ebhyáḥ*
Ab.	अस्मात् *asmât*	अस्या: *asyâḥ*	अस्मात् *asmât*	एभ्य: *ebhyáḥ*	आभ्य: *âbhyáḥ*	एभ्य: *ebhyáḥ*
G.	अस्य *asyá*	अस्या: *asyâḥ*	अस्य *asyá*	एषां *eshâm*	आसां *âsâm*	एषां *eshâm*
L.	अस्मिन् *asmín*	अस्यां *asyâm*	अस्मिन् *asmín*	एषु *eshú*	आसु *âsú*	एषु *eshú*

DUAL.

	MASC.	FEM.	NEUT.
N.A.V.	इमौ *imaú*	इमे *imé*	इमे *imé*
I.D.Ab.	आभ्यां *ábhyám*	आभ्यां *ábhyám*	आभ्यां *ábhyám*
G.L.	अनयो: *anáyoh*	अनयो: *anáyoh*	अनयो: *anáyoh*

§ 270. एतद् *etád* and इदं *idám*, when repeated in a second sentence with reference to a preceding एतद् *etad* and इदं *idam*, vary in the following cases, by substituting एन *ena*, which has no accent.

SINGULAR.   PLURAL.

	MASC.	FEM.	NEUT.		MASC.	FEM.	NEUT.
A.	एनं *enam*	एनां *enám*	एनत् *enat*	A.	एनान् *enán*	एना: *enáh*	एनानि *enáni*
I.	एनेन *enena*	एनया *enayá*	एनेन *enena*				

DUAL.

	MASC.	FEM.	NEUT.
A.	एनौ *enau*	एने *ene*	एने *ene*
G.L.	एनयो: *enayoh*	एनयो: *enayoh*	एनयो: *enayoh*

Ex. अनेन व्याकरणमधीतं एनं छंदोऽध्यापय *anena vyákaranam adhítam, enam chhando 'dhyápaya*, the grammar has been studied by this person, teach him prosody.

अनयो: पवित्रं कुलं एनयो: प्रभूतं स्वं *anayoh pavitram kulam, enayoh prabhútam svam*, the family of these two persons is decent, and their wealth vast.

§ 271. Base (in composition) अदस् *adas*, that (mediate).

SINGULAR.

	MASC.	FEM.	NEUT.
N.	असौ *asaú*	असौ *asaú*	अद: *adáh*
A.	अमुं *amúm*	अमूं *amúm*	अद: *adáh*
I.	अमुना *amúná*	अमुया *amuyá* (Rv. I. 29, 5)	अमुना *amúná*
D.	अमुष्मै *amúshmai*	अमुष्यै *amúshyai*	अमुष्मै *amúshmai*
Ab.	अमुष्मात् *amúshmát*	अमुष्या: *amúshyáh*	अमुष्मात् *amúshmát*
G.	अमुष्य *amúshya*	अमुष्या: *amúshyáh*	अमुष्य *amúshya*
L.	अमुष्मिन् *amúshmin*	अमुष्यां *amúshyám*	अमुष्मिन् *amúshmin*

PLURAL.

	MASC.	FEM.	NEUT.
N.	अमी *amí*	अमू: *amúh*	अमूनि *amúni*
A.	अमून् *amún*	अमू: *amúh*	अमूनि *amúni*
I.	अमीभि: *amíbhih*	अमूभि: *amúbhih*	अमीभि: *amíbhih*
D.Ab.	अमीभ्य: *amíbhyah*	अमूभ्य: *amúbhyah*	अमीभ्य: *amíbhyah*
G.	अमीषां *amíshám*	अमूषां *amúshám*	अमीषां *amíshám*
L.	अमीषु *amíshu*	अमूषु *amúshu*	अमीषु *amíshu*

DUAL.

MASC. FEM. NEUT.

N.A.V. अमू *amú*	I.D.Ab. अमूभ्यां *amúbhyám*	G.L. अमुयो: *amáyoh*

Relative Pronoun.

§ 272. Base (in composition) यद् *yád*, who or which.

	SINGULAR.			**PLURAL.**		
	MASC.	FEM.	NEUT.	MASC.	FEM.	NEUT.
N.	य: *yáḥ*	या *yá*	यत् *yát*	ये *yé*	या: *yáḥ*	यानि *yáni*
A.	यं *yám*	यां *yám*	यत् *yát*	यान् *yán*	या: *yáḥ*	यानि *yáni*
I.	येन *yéna*	यया *yáyá*	येन *yéna*	यै: *yaíḥ*	याभि: *yábhiḥ*	यै: *yaíḥ*
D.	यस्मै *yásmai*	यस्यै *yásyai*	यस्मै *yásmai*	येभ्य: *yébhyaḥ*	याभ्य: *yábhyaḥ*	येभ्य: *yébhyaḥ*
Ab.	यस्मात् *yásmát*	यस्या: *yásyáḥ*	यस्मात् *yásmát*	येभ्य: *yébhyaḥ*	याभ्य: *yábhyaḥ*	येभ्य: *yébhyaḥ*
G.	यस्य *yásya*	यस्या: *yásyáḥ*	यस्य *yásya*	येषां *yéshám*	यासां *yásám*	येषां *yéshám*
L.	यस्मिन् *yásmin*	यस्यां *yásyám*	यस्मिन् *yásmin*	येषु *yéshu*	यासु *yásu*	येषु *yéshu*

	DUAL.		
	MASC.	FEM.	NEUT.
N.A.V.	यौ *yaú*	ये *yé*	ये *yé*
I.D.Ab.	याभ्यां *yábhyám*	याभ्यां *yábhyám*	याभ्यां *yábhyám*
G.L.	ययो: *yáyoḥ*	ययो: *yáyoḥ*	ययो: *yáyoḥ*

Interrogative Pronouns.

§ 273. Base (in composition) किं *kím*, Who or which?

	SINGULAR.			**PLURAL.**		
	MASC.	FEM.	NEUT.	MASC.	FEM.	NEUT.
N.	क: *káḥ*	का *ká*	किं *kím*	के *ké*	का: *káḥ*	कानि *káni*
A.	कं *kám*	कां *kám*	किं *kím*	कान् *kán*	का: *káḥ*	कानि *káni*
I.	केन *kéna*	कया *káyá*	केन *kéna*	कै: *kaíḥ*	काभि: *kábhiḥ*	कै: *kaíḥ*
D.	कस्मै *kásmai*	कस्यै *kásyai*	कस्मै *kásmai*	केभ्य: *kébhyaḥ*	काभ्य: *kábhyaḥ*	केभ्य: *kébhyaḥ*
Ab.	कस्मात् *kásmát*	कस्या: *kásyáḥ*	कस्मात् *kásmát*	केभ्य: *kébhyaḥ*	काभ्य: *kábhyaḥ*	केभ्य: *kébhyaḥ*
G.	कस्य *kásya*	कस्या: *kásyáḥ*	कस्य *kásya*	केषां *késhám*	कासां *kásám*	केषां *késhám*
L.	कस्मिन् *kásmin*	कस्यां *kásyám*	कस्मिन् *kásmin*	केषु *késhu*	कासु *kásu*	केषु *késhu*

	DUAL.		
	MASC.	FEM.	NEUT.
N.A.	कौ *kaú*	के *ké*	के *ké*
I.D.Ab.	काभ्यां *kábhyám*	काभ्यां *kábhyám*	काभ्यां *kábhyám*
G.L.	कयो: *káyoḥ*	कयो: *káyoḥ*	कयो: *káyoḥ*

§ 274. Pronouns admit the interposition of अक् *ak* before their last vowel or syllable, to denote contempt or dubious relation (Páṇ. v. 3, 71). त्वयका *tvayaká*, By thee! instead of त्वया *tvayá*. युवकयो: *yuvakayoḥ*, Of you two! अस्मकाभि: *asmakábhiḥ*, With us! अयकं *ayakam*. असकौ *asakau*, &c. (See Siddh.-Kaum. vol. i. p. 706.)

Compound Pronouns.

§ 275. By adding दृश् *dṛiś*, दृश *dṛiśa*, or दृक्ष *dṛiksha*, to certain pronominal bases, the following compound pronouns have been formed:

तादृश् *tâdṛiś*, तादृश *tâdṛiśa*, तादृक्ष *tâdṛiksha*, such like.

एतादृश् *etâdṛiś*, एतादृश *etâdṛiśa*, एतादृक्ष *etâdṛiksha*, this like.

यादृश् *yâdṛiś*, यादृश *yâdṛiśa*, यादृक्ष *yâdṛiksha*, what like.

ईदृश् *îdṛiś*, ईदृश *îdṛiśa*, ईदृक्ष *îdṛiksha*, this like.

कीदृश् *kîdṛiś*, कीदृश *kîdṛiśa*, कीदृक्ष *kîdṛiksha*, What like?

These are declined in three genders, forming the feminine in ई *î*. तादृक् *tâdṛik*, m. n.; तादृशी *tâdṛiśî*, f.; or तादृश:, °शी, °शं, *tâdṛiśaḥ*, *î*, *am*. Similarly formed are मादृश *mâdṛiśa*, त्वादृश *tvâdṛiśa*, like me, like thee, &c.

§ 276. By adding वत् *vat* and यत् *yat* to certain pronominal bases, the following compound pronouns, implying quantity, have been formed:

तावत् *tâvat*, so much,
एतावत् *etâvat*, so much, } declined like nouns in वत् *vat* (§ 187).
यावत् *yâvat*, as much,

इयत् *iyat*, so much,
कियत् *kiyat*, How much? } इयान् *iyân*, इयती *iyatî*, इयत् *iyat*.

Note—On the declension of कति *kâti*, How many? तति *tâti*, so many, and यति *yâti*, as many, see § 231.

§ 277. By adding चित् *chit*, चन *chana*, or अपि *api*, to the interrogative pronoun किं *kim*, it is changed into an indefinite pronoun.

कश्चित् *kaśchit*, काचित् *kâchit*, किंचित् *kimchit*, some one; also कचित् *kachchit*, anything.

कश्चन *kaśchana*, काचन *kâchana*, किंचन *kimchana*, some one.

कोऽपि *ko 'pi*, कापि *kâpi*, किमपि *kimapi*, some one.

In the same manner indefinite adverbs are formed: कदा *kadâ*, When? कदाचित् *kadâchit*, कदाचन *kadâchana*, once; क्व *kva*, Where? न क्वापि *na kvâpi*, not anywhere.

Sometimes the relative pronoun is prefixed to the interrogative, to render it indefinite: य: क: *yaḥ kaḥ*, whosoever; यस्य कस्य *yasya kasya*, whosesoever. Likewise य: कश्चित् *yaḥ kaśchit*, whosoever, or य: कश्च *yaḥ kaścha*, or य: कश्चन *yaḥ kaśchana*.

The relative pronoun, if doubled, assumes an indefinite or rather distributive meaning: यो य:, या या, यद्यद्, *yo yaḥ, yâ yâ, yad yad,* whosoever. Occasionally the relative and demonstrative pronouns are combined for the same purpose: यत्तद् *yattad*, whatsoever.

Pronominal Adjectives.

§ 278. Under the name of *Sarvanâman*, which has been freely translated by Pronoun, but which really means a class of words beginning with *sarva*, native grammarians have included, besides the real pronouns mentioned before, the following words which share in common with the real pronouns certain peculiarities of declension. They may be called Pronominal Adjectives, and it is to be remembered that they are affected by these peculiarities of declension only if they are used in certain senses.

1. सर्व *sarva*, all; 2. विश्व *viśva*, all; 3. उभ *ubha*, two; 4. उभय *ubhaya*, both; 5. अन्य *anya*, other; 6. अन्यतर *anyatara*, either; 7. इतर *itara*, other; 8. त्व *tva*, other (some add त्वत् *tvat*, other); 9. words formed by the suffixes तर *tara* and तम *tama*, such as 9. कतर *katara*, Which of two? 10. कतम *katama*, Which of many? 10. सम *sama*, all; 11. सिम *sima*, whole; 12. नेम *nema*, half; 13. एक *eka*, one; 14. पूर्व *pûrva*, east or prior; 15. पर *para*, subsequent; 16. अवर *avara*, west or posterior; 17. दक्षिण *dakshiṇa*, south or right; 18. उत्तर *uttara*, north or subsequent; 19. अपर *apara*, other or inferior; 20. अधर *adhara*, west or inferior; 21. स्व *sva*, own; 22. अंतर *antara*, outer, (except अंतरा पू: *antarâ pûḥ*, suburb,) or lower (scil. garment).

If सम *sama* means equal or even, it is not a pronominal adjective; nor दक्षिण *dakshiṇa*, if it means clever; nor स्व *sva*, if it means kinsman or wealth; nor अंतर *antara*, if it means interval, &c.; nor any of the seven from पूर्व *pûrva* to अधर *adhara*, unless they imply a relation in time or space. Hence दक्षिणा गाथका: *dakshiṇâ gâthakâḥ*, clever minstrels; उत्तरा: कुरव: *uttarâḥ kuravaḥ*, the northern Kurus, (a proper name); प्रभूता: स्वा: *prabhûtâḥ svâḥ*, great treasures (Kâś. 1.1,35); ग्रामयोरंतरे वसति *grâmayor antare vasati*, he lives between the two villages.

MASCULINE.

	SINGULAR.	DUAL.	PLURAL.
N.	सर्व: *sárvaḥ* *	सर्वौ *sárvau*	सर्वे *sárve*
A.	सर्वं *sárvam*	सर्वौ *sárvau*	सर्वान् *sárvân*
I.	सर्वेण *sárveṇa*	सर्वाभ्यां *sárvâbhyâm*	सर्वै: *sárvaiḥ*
D.	सर्वस्मै *sárvasmai*	सर्वाभ्यां *sárvâbhyâm*	सर्वेभ्य: *sárvebhyaḥ*
Ab.	सर्वस्मात् *sárvasmât*	सर्वाभ्यां *sárvâbhyâm*	सर्वेभ्य: *sárvebhyaḥ*
G.	सर्वस्य *sárvasya*	सर्वयो: *sárvayoḥ*	सर्वेषां *sárveshâm*
L.	सर्वस्मिन् *sárvasmin*	सर्वयो: *sárvayoḥ*	सर्वेषु *sárveshu*
V.	सर्व *sárva*	सर्वौ *sárvau*	सर्वे *sárve*

FEMININE.

	SINGULAR.	DUAL.	PLURAL.
N.	सर्वा *sárvâ*	सर्वे *sárve*	सर्वा: *sárvâḥ*
A.	सर्वां *sárvâm*	सर्वे *sárve*	सर्वा: *sárvâḥ*

---

* Accent, Pâṇ. vi. 1, 191.

I.	सर्वया *sárvayá*	सर्वाभ्यां *sárvábhyám*	सर्वाभिः *sárvábhiḥ*
D.	सर्वस्यै *sárvasyai*	सर्वाभ्यां *sárvábhyám*	सर्वाभ्यः *sárvábhyaḥ*
Ab.	सर्वस्याः *sárvasyáḥ*	सर्वाभ्यां *sárvábhyám*	सर्वाभ्यः *sárvábhyaḥ*
G.	सर्वस्याः *sárvasyáḥ*	सर्वयोः *sárvayoḥ*	सर्वासां *sárvásám*
L.	सर्वस्यां *sárvasyám*	सर्वयोः *sárvayoḥ*	सर्वासु *sárvásu*

NEUTER.

	SINGULAR.	DUAL.	PLURAL.
N.A.V.	सर्वं *sárvam*	सर्वे *sárve*	सर्वाणि *sárváṇi*

The rest like the masculine.

§ 279. अन्य *anya*, अन्यतर *anyatara*, इतर *itara*, कतर *katara*, कतम *katama*, take न् *t* in the Nom. Acc.Voc. Sing. of the neuter:

Nom. Sing. अन्यः *anyaḥ*, masc.; अन्या *anyá*, fem.; अन्यत् *anyat*, neut.

§ 280. उभ *ubha* is used in the Dual only:

Masc. N. A. V. उभौ *ubhau*, I. D. Ab. उभाभ्यां *ubhábhyám*, G. L. उभयोः *ubhayoḥ*; उभे *ubhe*, N. A. V. fem. and neut.

§ 281. उभयः *ubhayaḥ*, °यी *-yí*, °यं *-yam*, is never used in the Dual, but only in the Sing. and Plur.   Haradatta admits the Dual.

MASCULINE.

	SINGULAR.		PLURAL.
N.	उभयः *ubhayaḥ*	———	उभये *ubhaye*
A.	उभयं *ubhayam*		उभयान् *ubhayán*
I.	उभयेन *ubhayena*		उभयैः *ubhayaiḥ*
D.	उभयस्मै *ubhayasmai*, &c.		उभयेभ्यः *ubhayebhyaḥ*, &c.

§ 282. The nine words from पूर्व *púrva* to अंतर *antara* (14 to 22), though used in their pronominal senses, may take in the Nom. Plur. इ *i* or अः *aḥ*; in the Abl. Sing. स्मात् *smát* or अत् *at*; in the Loc. Sing. स्मिन् *smin* or इ *i*.

	SINGULAR.	DUAL.	PLURAL.
N.	पूर्वः *púrvaḥ*	पूर्वौ *púrvau*	पूर्वे *púrve* or पूर्वाः *púrváḥ*
A.	पूर्वं *púrvam*	पूर्वौ *púrvau*	पूर्वान् *púrván*
I.	पूर्वेण *púrveṇa*	पूर्वाभ्यां *púrvábhyám*	पूर्वैः *púrvaiḥ*
D.	पूर्वस्मै *púrvasmai*	पूर्वाभ्यां *púrvábhyám*	पूर्वेभ्यः *púrvebhyaḥ*
Ab.	पूर्वस्मात् *púrvasmát* or पूर्वात् *púrvát*	पूर्वाभ्यां *púrvábhyám*	पूर्वेभ्यः *púrvebhyaḥ*
G.	पूर्वस्य *púrvasya*	पूर्वयोः *púrvayoḥ*	पूर्वेषां *púrveshám*
L.	पूर्वस्मिन् *púrvasmin* or पूर्वे *púrve*	पूर्वयोः *púrvayoḥ*	पूर्वेषु *púrveshu*

§ 283. The following words may likewise take अः *aḥ* or इ *i* in the Nom. Plur. masc. (Páṇ. I. 1, 33.)

प्रथमः *prathamaḥ*, first, प्रथमौ *prathamau* प्रथमे *prathame* or प्रथमाः *prathamáḥ*; fem. प्रथमा *prathamá*.

चरमः *charamaḥ*, last, चरमौ *charamau* चरमे *charame* or चरमाः *charamáḥ*.

द्वितयः *dvitayaḥ*, two-fold, fem. द्वितयी *dvitayí*, and similar words in तय *taya*; त्रितयः *tritayaḥ*, three-fold; त्रितये *tritaye* or त्रितयाः *tritayáḥ*.

द्वय: *dvayaḥ*, two-fold, fem. द्वयी *dvayî*, and similar words in य *ya*; त्रय: *trayaḥ*.

अल्प: *alpaḥ*, few, अल्पे *alpe* or अल्पा: *alpâḥ*.

अर्ध: *ardhaḥ*, half, अर्धे *ardhe* or अर्धा: *ardhâḥ*.

कतिपय: *katipayaḥ*, some, कतिपये *katipaye* or कतिपया: *katipayâḥ*.

नेम: *nemaḥ*, half, नेमे *neme* or नेमा: *nemâḥ*.

In all other cases these words are regular, like कांत: *kântaḥ*.

§ 284. द्वितीय: *dvitîyaḥ* and other words in तीय *tîya* are declined like कांत *kânta*, but in the Dat. Abl. and Loc. Sing. they may follow सर्व *sarva*.

MASCULINE.

SINGULAR.	DUAL.	PLURAL.
N. द्वितीय: *dvitîyaḥ*	द्वितीयौ *dvitîyau*	द्वितीया: *dvitîyâḥ*
A. द्वितीयं *dvitîyam*	द्वितीयौ *dvitîyau*	द्वितीयान् *dvitîyân*
I. द्वितीयेन *dvitîyena*	द्वितीयाभ्यां *dvitîyâbhyâm*	द्वितीयै: *dvitîyaiḥ*
D. द्वितीयाय *dvitîyâya* or द्वितीयस्मै *dvitîyasmai*	द्वितीयाभ्यां *dvitîyâbhyâm*	द्वितीयेभ्य: *dvitîyebhyaḥ*
Ab. द्वितीयात् *dvitîyât* or द्वितीयस्मात् *dvitîyasmât*	द्वितीयाभ्यां *dvitîyâbhyâm*	द्वितीयेभ्य: *dvitîyebhyaḥ*
G. द्वितीयस्य *dvitîyasya*	द्वितीययो: *dvitîyayoḥ*	द्वितीयानां *dvitîyânâm*
L. द्वितीये *dvitîye* or द्वितीयस्मिन् *dvitîyasmin*	द्वितीययो: *dvitîyayoḥ*	द्वितीयेषु *dvitîyeshu*

At the end of Bahuvrîhi compounds the Sarvanâmans are treated like ordinary words: Dat. Sing. प्रियोभयाय *priyobhayâya*, to him to whom both are dear (Pân. 1. 1, 29). The same at the end of compounds such as मासपूर्व: *mâsapûrvaḥ*, a month earlier; Dat. मासपूर्वाय *mâsapûrvâya* (Pân. 1. 1, 30). Likewise in Dvandvas; पूर्वापराणां *pûrvâparâṇâm*, of former and later persons (Pân. 1. 1, 31), though in the Nom. Plur. these Dvandvas may take इ *i*; पूर्वापरे *pûrvâpare* or पूर्वापरा: *pûrvâparâḥ*. Only in compounds expressive of points of the compass, such as उत्तरपूर्व *uttara-pûrva*, north-east, the last element may throughout take the pronominal terminations (Pân. 1. 1, 28).

Adverbial Declension.

§ 285. In addition to the regular case-terminations by which the declension of nouns is effected, the Sanskrit language possesses other suffixes which differ from the ordinary terminations chiefly by being restricted in their use to certain words, and particularly to pronominal bases. The ordinary case-terminations, too, are frequently used in an adverbial sense. Thus

Acc. चिरं *chiram*, a long time.

Instr. चिरेण *chireṇa*, in a long time.

Dat. चिराय *chirâya*, for a long time.

Abl. चिरात् *chirât*, long ago.

Gen. चिरस्य *chirasya*, a long time.

Loc. चिरे *chire*, long.

Other adverbial terminations are,

1. त: *taḥ*, with an ablative meaning, becoming generally local.

2. त्र *tra*, with a locative meaning.

3. दा *dâ*, with a temporal meaning; also raised to दानीं *dânîm*.

4. तात् *tât*, with a locative meaning.

5. या *thá*, with a meaning of modality; likewise थं *tham* and थ *tha*.

6. सात् *sát*, expressive of effect.

7. आ *á* and आहि *dhi*, local.

8. र्हि *rhi*, temporal and causal.

9. तर् *tar*, local.

10. ह *ha*, local.

See also the terminations for forming numeral adverbs (§ 260).

1. तः *taḥ*, with an ablative meaning.

ततः *tataḥ*, thence.   यतः *yataḥ*, whence.   इतः *itaḥ*, hence; (cf. इति *iti*, thus, इव *iva*, as.) अतः *ataḥ*, hence.   कुतः *kutaḥ*, Whence?   अमुतः *amutaḥ*, thence.   मत्तः *mattaḥ*, from me. अस्मत्तः *asmattaḥ*, from us.   भवतः *bhavattaḥ*, from your Honour.   पूर्वतः *párvataḥ*, before (in a general local or temporal sense).   सर्वतः *sarvataḥ*, always.   अग्रतः *agrataḥ*, before, like अग्रे *agre*.   अभितः *abhitaḥ*, around, near.   उभयतः *ubhayataḥ*, on both sides. परितः *paritaḥ*, all round.   ग्रामतः *grámataḥ*, from the village.   अज्ञानतः *ajñánataḥ*, from ignorance.

2. त्र *tra*, locative; originally त्रा *trá*, as in पुरुषत्रा *purushatrá*, amongst men.

तत्र *tatra*, there.   यत्र *yatra*, where.   कुत्र *kutra*, Where?   अत्र *atra*, here.   अमुत्र *amutra*, there, in the next world.   एकत्र *ekatra*, at one place, together.   सत्रा *satrá*, with, and सत्रं *satram*, with (see सह *saha*).

3. दा *dá*, temporal.

तदा *tadá*, then, and तदानीं *tadánīm*.   यदा *yadá*, when.   कदा *kadá*, When?   अन्यदा *anyadá*, another time.   सर्वदा *sarvadá*, always, at all times.   एकदा *ekadá*, at one time. सदा *sadá*, always.   इदा *idá*, in the Veda, later इदानीं *idánīm*, now.

4. तात् *tát*, local.

प्राक्तात् *práktát*, in front.

Frequently after a base in स् *s*:

पुरस्तात् *purastát*, before.   अधरस्तात् *adharastát*, below.   परस्तात् *parastát*, afterwards. अधस्तात् *adhastát*, below.   उपरिष्टात् *uparishtát*, above.

5. था *thá*, modal.

तथा *tathá*, thus.   यथा *yathá*, as.   सर्वथा *sarvathá*, in every way.   उभयथा *ubhayathá*, in both ways.   अन्यथा *anyathá*, in another way.   अन्यतरथा *anyatarathá*, in one of two ways.   इतरथा *itarathá*, in the other way.   वृथा *vṛithá*, vainly(?).   Or थं *tham*, in कथं *katham*, How?   इत्थं *ittham*, thus.   Or थ *tha*, in अथ *atha*, thus.

6. सात् *sát*, effective.

राजसात् *rájasát*, (राज्ञोऽधीनं *rájño 'dhínam*, dependent on the king.)   भस्मसात् *bhasmasát*, reduced to ashes.   अग्निसात् *agnisát*, reduced to fire.

7. आ *á* and आहि *dhi*, local.

दक्षिणाहि *dakshiṇáhi*, in the South, or दक्षिणा *dakshiṇá*.   उत्तराहि *uttaráhi*, in the North, or उत्तरा *uttará*.   अंतरा *antará* (or °रं *-ram*, or °रे *-re*, or °रेण *-reṇa*), between.   पुरा *purá*, in the East, in front, formerly, (or पुरः *puraḥ* and पुरस्तात् *purastát*, before.) पश्चा *paśchá*, behind, (or पश्चात् *paśchát*.)

Adverbs such as मुधा *mudhá*, in vain, मृषा *mṛishá*, falsely, are instrumental cases of obsolete nouns ending in consonants.

8. हिं *rhi*, temporal and causal.

   एतहिं *etarhi*, at this time, (Wilson.)   कहिं *karhi*, At what time?   यहिं *yarhi*, wherefore.   तहिं *tarhi*, therefore, at that time, (Wilson.)

9. तर् *tar*, local.

   प्रातर् *prátar*, early, in the morning.   सनुतर् *sanutar*, in concealment.

10. ह *ha*, locative.

   कुह *kuha*, Where?   इह *iha*, here.   सह *saha*, with.

CHAPTER VII.

CONJUGATION.

§ 286. Sanskrit verbs are conjugated in the Active and the Passive. Ex. बोधति *bódhati*, he knows; बुध्यते *budhyáte*, he is known.

§ 287. The Active has two forms:

1. The *Parasmai-pada*, i. e. transitive, (from परस्मै *parasmai*, Dat. Sing. of पर *para*, another, i. e. a verb the action of which refers to another.) Ex. ददाति *dadáti*, he gives.

2. The *Átmane-pada*, i. e. intransitive, (from आत्मने *átmane*, Dat. Sing. of आत्मन् *átman*, self, i. e. a verb the action of which refers to the agent.) Ex. आदत्ते *ádatte*, he takes.

Note—The distinction between the Parasmaipada and Âtmanepada is fixed by usage rather than by rule. Certain verbs in Sanskrit are used in the Parasmaipada only, others in the Âtmanepada only; others in both voices. Those which are used in the Parasmaipada only, are verbs the action of which was originally conceived as transitive; e. g. भूमिं मंथति *bhúmim manthati*, he shakes the earth; मांसं खादति *mánsam khádati*, he eats meat; ग्रामम् अतति *grámam atati*, he goes to or approaches the village. Those which are used in the Âtmanepada only, were originally verbs expressive of states rather than of actions; e. g. एधते *edhate*, he grows; स्पंदते *spandate*, he trembles; मोदते *modate*, he rejoices; शेते *śete*, he lies down. Such roots are marked in the Dhâtupâṭha as *n-it* or *anudátta-it* (Pâṇ. I. 3, 12).

In the language of the best authors, however, many verbs which we should consider intransitive, are conjugated in the Parasmaipada, while others which govern an accusative, are always conjugated in the Âtmanepada. हसति *hasati*, he laughs, is always Parasmaipadin, whether used as transitive or neuter (Colebr. p. 297): it is so even when reciprocity of action is indicated, in which case verbs in Sanskrit mostly take the Âtmanepada; e. g. व्यतिहसंते *vyatihasanti*, they laugh at each other (Pâṇ. I. 3, 15, vârt. 1, 2). But स्मयते *smayate*, he smiles, is restricted by grammarians to the Âtmanepada; and verbs like त्रायते *tráyate*, he protects, are Âtmanepadin (i. e. used in the Âtmanepada), though they govern an accusative; e. g. त्रायस्व मां *tráyasva mám*, Protect me! These correspond to the Latin deponents.

Verbs which are used both in the Parasmaipada and Âtmanepada, take the one or the other form according as the action of the verb is conceived to be either transitive or reflective;

e.g. पचति *pachati*, he cooks; पचते *pachate*, he cooks for himself; यजति *yajati*, he sacrifices; यजते *yajate*, he sacrifices for himself. The same applies to Causals (Pâṇ. 1. 3, 74).

These distinctions, however, rest in many cases, in Sanskrit as well as in Greek, on peculiar conceptions which it is difficult to analyse or to realize; and in Sanskrit as well as in Greek, the right use of the active and middle voices is best learnt by practice. Thus नी *nî*, to lead, is used as Parasmaipada in such expressions as गंडं विनयति *gaṇḍam vinayati**, he carries off a swelling; but as Âtmanepada, in क्रोधं विनयते *krodham vinayate*, he turns away or dismisses wrath; a subtle distinction which it is possible to appreciate when stated, but difficult to bring under any general rules.

Again, in Sanskrit as well as in Greek, some verbs are middle in certain tenses only, but active or middle in others; e. g. Âtm. वर्धते *vardhate*, he grows, never वर्धति *vardhati*; but Aor. अवृधत् *avṛidhat*, Par., or अवर्धिष्ट *avardhishṭa*, Âtm. he grew. (Pâṇ. 1. 3, 91.)

Others take the Parasmaipada or Âtmanepada according as they are compounded with certain prepositions; e. g. विशति *viśati*, he enters; but निविशते *ni-viśate*, he enters in. (Pâṇ. 1. 3, 17.)

§ 288. Causal verbs are conjugated both in the Parasmaipada and Âtmanepada. Desideratives generally follow the Pada of the simple root (Pâṇ. 1. 3, 62). Denominatives ending in आय *áya* have both forms (Pâṇ. 1. 3, 90). The intensives have two forms: one in य *ya*, which is always Âtmanepada; the other without य *ya*, which is always Parasmaipada.

§ 289. The passive takes the terminations of the Âtmanepada, and prefixes य *yá* to them in the four special or modified tenses. In the other tenses the forms of the passive are, with a few exceptions, the same as those of the Âtmanepada.

§ 290. There are in Sanskrit thirteen different forms, corresponding to the tenses and moods of Greek and Latin.

I. *Formed from the Special or Modified Base.*

	PARASMAIPADA.	ÂTMANEPADA.
1. The Present (Laṭ)	भवामि *bhávâmi*	भवे *bháve*
2. The Imperfect (Laṅ)	अभवं *ábhavam*	अभवे *ábhave*
3. The Optative (Liṅ)	भवेयं *bháveyam*	भवेय *bháveya*
4. The Imperative (Loṭ)	भवानि *bhávâni*	भवै *bhávai*

II. *Formed from the General or Unmodified Base.*

	PARASMAIPADA.	ÂTMANEPADA.
5. The Reduplicated Perfect (Liṭ)	बभूव *babhúva*	बभूवे *babhúvé*
6. The Periphrastic Perfect (Liṭ)	चोरयां बभूव *choraydm babhúva*	चोरयां चक्रे *choraydm chak*
7. The First Aorist (Luṅ)	अबोधिषं *ábodhisham*	अभविषि *ábhavishi*
8. The Second Aorist (Luṅ)	अभूवं *ábhúvam*	असिचे *ásiche*
9. The Future (Lṛiṭ)	भविष्यामि *bhavishyámi*	भविष्ये *bhavishyé*

---

* Cf. Siddhânta-Kaumudî, ed. Târânâtha, vol. ii. p. 250. Colebrooke, Grammar, p. 337.

10. The Conditional (Lṛiṅ)   अभविष्यं *ábhavishyam*   अभविषे *ábhavishye*
11. The Periphrastic Future (Luṭ)   भवितास्मि *bhavitásmi*   भविताहे *bhavitáhe*
12. The Benedictive (Âśir liṅ)   भूयासं *bhúyásam*   भविषीय *bhavishíyá*
13. The Subjunctive (Leṭ) occurs in the Veda only.

Signification of the Tenses and Moods.

§ 291. 1. 2. The Present and Imperfect require no explanation. The Imperfect takes the Augment (§ 300), which has always the accent.

3. The principal senses of the Optative are,

a. Command; e.g. तं ग्रामं गच्छे: *tvam grâmam gachchheḥ*, thou mayest go, i.e. go thou to the village.

b. Wish; e.g. भवानिहासीत *bhavân ihâsíta*, Let your honour sit here!

c. Inquiring; e.g. वेदमधीयीय उत तर्कमधीयीय *vedam adhíyíya, uta tarkam adhíyíya*, Shall I study the Veda or shall I study logic?

d. Supposition (*sambhâvana*); e.g. भवेदसौ वेदपारगो ब्राह्मणत्वात् *bhaved asau vedapârago bráhmanatvát*, he probably is a student of the Veda, because he is a Brâhman.

e. Condition; e.g. दंडश्चेन्न भवेल्लोके विनश्येयुरिमा: प्रजा: *dandaś chen na bhavel loke vinaśyeyur imâḥ prajâḥ*, if there were not punishment in the world, the people would perish.   य: पठेत् स आप्नुयात् *yaḥ paṭhet sa âpnuyát*, he who studies, will obtain.   यद्यद्रोचेत विप्रेभ्यस्तत्तद्दद्यादमत्सर: *yad yad rocheta viprebhyas tat tad dadyâd amatsarah*, whatever pleases the Brâhmans let one give that to them not niggardly.

f. It is used in relative dependent sentences; e.g. यच्च त्वमेवं कुर्या न श्रद्दधे *yach cha tvam evam kuryá na śraddadhe*, I believed not that thou couldst act thus.   यत्तादृशा: कृष्णं निंदेरन्नाश्चर्यं *yat tádriśáḥ krishnam ninderann áścharyam*, that such persons should revile Krishṇa, is wonderful.

4. The Imperative requires no explanation, as far as the second person is concerned; e.g. तुद *tuda*, Strike! The first and third persons are used in many cases in place of the Optative; e.g. इच्छामि भवान्भुङ्क्तां *ichchhâmi bhavân bhuṅktâm*, I wish your honour may eat.

5. The Reduplicated Perfect denotes something absolutely past.

6. Certain verbs which are not allowed to form the reduplicated perfect, form their perfect periphrastically, i.e. by means of an auxiliary verb.

7. 8. The First and Second Aorists refer generally to time past, and are the common historical tenses in narration. They take the Augment (§ 300).

9. The Future, also called the Indefinite Future; e.g. देवश्चेद्वर्षिष्यति धान्यं वप्स्याम: *devaś ched varshishyati dhânyam vapsyâmah*, if it rain, we shall sow rice.   यावज्जीवमन्नं दास्यति *yávaj-jívam annam dâsyati*, as long as life

lasts, he will give food. Under certain circumstances this Future may be used optionally with the Periphrastic Future; e. g. कदा भोक्ता *kadâ bhoktá* or भोक्ष्यते *bhokshyate*, When will he eat?

10. The Conditional is used, instead of the Optative, if things are spoken of that might have, but have not happened (Pâṇ. III. 3, 139); e. g. सुवृष्टिश्चेदभविष्यत्तदा सुभिक्षमभविष्यत् *suvrishṭiś ched abhavishyat tadâ subhiksham abhavishyat*, if there had been abundant rain, there would have been plenty. The Conditional takes the Augment (§ 300).

11. The Periphrastic or Definite Future; e. g. अयोध्यां श्वः प्रयातासि *ayodhyâm śvaḥ prayâtâsi*, thou wilt to-morrow proceed to Ayodhyâ.

12. The Benedictive is used for expressing not only a blessing, but also a wish in general; e. g. श्रीमान्भूयात् *śrîmân bhúyât*, May he be happy! चिरं जीव्यात् *chiram jívyât*, May he live long!

13. The Subjunctive occurs in the Veda only.

§ 292. The Sanskrit verb has in each tense and mood three numbers, Singular, Dual, and Plural, with three persons in each.

CHAPTER VIII.

SPECIAL AND GENERAL TENSES AND THE TEN CLASSES OF VERBS.

§ 293. Sanskrit grammarians have divided all verbs into ten classes, according to certain modifications which their roots undergo before the terminations of the Present, the Imperfect, the Optative, and Imperative. This division is very useful, and will be retained with some slight alterations. One and the same root may belong to different classes. Thus भ्राश् *bhrâś*, भ्लाश् *bhlâś*, भ्रम् *bhram*, क्रम् *kram*, क्लम् *klam*, त्रस् *tras*, त्रुट् *truṭ*, लश् *lash* belong to the Bhû and Div classes; भ्राशते *bhrâśate* or भ्राश्यते *bhrâśyate*, &c. (Pâṇ. III. 1, 70). Again, सु *sku*, स्तम्भ् *stambh*, स्तुम्भ् *stumbh*, स्कम्भ् *skambh*, स्कुम्भ् *skumbh* belong to the Su and Krî classes; स्कुनोति *skunoti* or स्कुनाति *skunâti* (Pâṇ. III. 1, 82).

§ 294. The four tenses and moods which require this modification of the root will be called the *Special or Modified Tenses*; the rest the *General or Unmodified Tenses*. Thus the root चि *chi* is changed in the Present, Imperfect, Optative, and Imperative into चिनु *chi-nu*. Hence चिनुमः *chi-nu-máh*, we search; अचिनुम *áchi-nu-ma*, we searched. But the Past Participle चितः *chitáh*, searched, or the Reduplicated Perfect चिच्युः *chichy-úh*, they have searched, without the नु *nu*. We call चि *chi*, the root, चिनु *chinu*, the base of the special tenses.

§ 295. Verbal bases are first divided into two divisions:

I. Bases which in the modified tenses end in ब *a*.

II. Bases which in the modified tenses end in any letter but ब *a*.

This second division is subdivided into,

II *a*. Bases which insert नु *nu*, उ *u*, or नी *nî*, between the root and the terminations.

II *b*. Bases which take the terminations without any intermediate element.

I. *First Division.*

§ 296. The first division comprises four classes:

1. The Bhû class (the first with native grammarians, and called by them भ्वादि *bhvâdi*, because the first verb in their lists is भू *bhû*, to be).

  a. ब *a* is added to the last letter of the root.

  b. The vowel of the root takes Guṇa, where possible (i. e. long or short *i*, *u*, *ri*, if final; short *i*, *u*, *ri*, *li*, if followed by *one* consonant).

  Ex. बुध् *budh*, to know; बोधति *bódh-a-ti*, he knows. भू *bhû*, to be; भवति *bháv-a-ti*, he is.

Note—The accent in verbs of the Bhû class (as we know from the ancient Vedic language) rests on the radical vowel, except where it is drawn on the augment.

Many derivative verbs,—such as causatives, भावयति *bhâváyati*, he causes to be; desideratives, बुभूषति *búbhûshati*, he wishes to be, from भू *bhû*: intensives in the Âtmanepada, बेभिद्यते *bebhidyáte*, he cuts much; and denominatives, नमस्यति *namasyáti*, he worships, लोहितायति *lohitâyáti*, he grows red,—follow this class.

2. The Tud class (the sixth with native grammarians, and called by them तुदादि *tudâdi*, because the first root in their lists is तुद् *tud*, to strike).

  a. ब *a* is added to the last letter of the root.

  b. Before this ब *a*, final इ *i* and ई *î* are changed to इय् *iy*.

उ *u* and ऊ *û*　　　　　to उव् *uv*.

ऋ *ri*　　　　　　　　to रिय् *riy*.

ॠ *rî*　　　　　　　　to इर् *ir* (§ 110).

  Ex. तुद् *tud*, to strike; तुदति *tud-á-ti*. रि *ri*, to go; रियति *riy-á-ti*. नू *nû*, to praise; नुवति *nuv-á-ti*. मृ *mri*, to die; म्रियते *mriy-á-te*. कॄ *krî*, to scatter; किरति *kir-á-ti*.

Note—The accent in verbs of the Tud class rests on the intermediate ब *a*: hence never Guṇa of the radical vowel.

3. The Div class (the fourth with native grammarians, and called by them दिवादि *divâdi*, because the first root in their lists is दिव् *div*, to play).

  a. य *ya* is added to the last letter of the root.

  Ex. नह् *nah*, to bind; नह्यति *náh-ya-ti*. बुध् *budh*, to awake; बुध्यते *búdh-ya-te*.

Note—The accent in verbs of the Div class rests on the radical vowel; though there are traces to show that some verbs of this class had the accent originally on य *ya*.

4. The Chur class (the tenth with native grammarians, and called by them चुरादि *churádi*, because the first root in their lists is चुर् *chur*, to steal).

a. अय *aya* is added to the last letter of the root.

b. If the root ends in a simple consonant, preceded by अ *a*, अ *a* is lengthened to आ *á*.

Ex. दल् *dal*, to cut; दालयति *dál-áya-ti*, (many exceptions.)

c. If the root ends in a simple consonant, preceded by इ *i*, उ *u*, ऋ *ri*, ऌ *li*, these vowels take Guṇa, while ऋ *ri* becomes ईर् *ír*.

Ex. श्लिष् *slish*, to embrace; श्लेषयति *slesh-áya-ti*. चुर् *chur*, to steal; चोरयति *chor-áya-ti*. मृष् *mrish*, to endure; मर्षयते *marsh-áya-te*. कृत् *krit*, to praise; कीर्तयति *kírt-áya-ti*.

d. Final इ *i*, ई *í*, उ *u*, ऊ *ú*, ऋ *ri*, and ऌ *ri*, take Vriddhi.

Ex. जि *jri*, to grow old; जारयति *jráy-áya-ti*. मी *mí*, to walk; माययति *máy-áya-ti*. धृ *dhri*, to hold; धारयति *dhár-áya-ti*. पृ *pri*, to fill; पारयति *pár-áya-ti*.

Note—Many, if not all roots arranged under this class by native grammarians, are secondary roots, and identical in form with causatives, denominatives, &c. This class differs from other classes, inasmuch as verbs belonging to it, keep their modificatory syllable अय *aya* throughout, in the unmodified as well as in the modified tenses, except in the Benedictive Par. and the Reduplicated Aorist. The accent rests on the first अ *a* of अय *áya*.

II. *Second Division.*

§ 297. The second division comprises all verbs which do not, in the special tenses, end in अ *a* before the terminations.

It is a distinguishing feature of this second division that, before certain terminations, all verbs belonging to it require strengthening of their radical vowel, or if they take नु *nu*, उ *u*, नी *ní*, strengthening of the vowels of these syllables. This strengthening generally takes place by means of Guṇa, but नी *ní* is raised to ना *ná* in the Krî, and न *n* to न *na* in the Rudh class.

We shall call the terminations which require strengthening of the inflective base, the weak terminations, and the base before them, the strong base; and *vice versá*, the terminations which do not require strengthening of the base, the strong terminations, and the base before them, the weak base.

As a rule, the accent falls on the first vowel of strong terminations, or, if the terminations are weak, on the strong base, thus establishing throughout an equilibrium between base and termination.

II *a*. Bases which take नु *nu*, उ *u*, नी *ní*.

§ 298. This first subdivision comprises three classes :

1. The Su class (the fifth class with native grammarians, and called by them स्वादि *svádi*, because the first root in their lists is सु *su*).

नु *nu* is added to the last letter of the root, before strong terminations, नो *no* before weak terminations.

Ex. सु *su*, to squeeze out; सुनुम: *su-nu-máh*, 1st pers. plur. Pres.
सुनोमि *su-nó-mi*, 1st pers. sing. Pres.

2. The Tan class (the eighth class with native grammarians, and called by them तनादि *tanádi*, because the first root in their lists is तन् *tan*).

उ *u* is added to the last letter of the root, before strong terminations, ओ *o* before weak terminations.

Ex. तन् *tan*, to stretch ; तनुम: *tan-u-máh*, 1st pers. plur. Pres.
तनोमि *tan-ó-mi*, 1st pers. sing. Pres.

Note—All verbs belonging to this class end in न् *n*, except one, कृ *kri*, करोमि *karomi*, I do.

3. The Krí class (the ninth with native grammarians, and called by them क्र्यादि *kryádi*, because the first root in their lists is क्री *krí*).

नी *ní* is added to the last letter of the root, before strong terminations, ना *ná* before weak terminations, न् *n* before strong terminations beginning with vowels.

Ex. क्री *krí*, to buy ; क्रीणीम: *krí-ní-máh*, 1st pers. plur. Pres.
क्रीणामि *krí-ṇd-mi*, 1st pers. sing. Pres.
क्रीणंति *krí-ṇ-ánti*, 3rd pers. plur. Pres.

II *b*. Bases to which the terminations are joined immediately.

§ 299. The second division comprises three classes :

1. The Ad class (the second class with native grammarians, and called by them अदादि *adádi*, because the first root in their lists is अद् *ad*, to eat).

a. The terminations are added immediately to the last letter of the base; and in the contact of vowels with vowels, vowels with consonants, consonants with vowels, and consonants with consonants, the phonetic rules explained above (§ 107–145) must be carefully observed.

b. The strong base before the weak terminations takes Guṇa where possible (§ 296, 1. *b*).

Ex. लिह् *lih*, to lick : लिह्म: *lih-máh*, we lick ; लेह्मि *léh-mi*, I lick ; लेक्षि *lék-shi*, thou lickest (§ 127); लीढ *líḍhá*, you lick (§ 128); अलेट् *álet*, thou lickedst (§ 128).

The accent is on the first vowel of the terminations, except in case of weak terminations, when the accent falls on the radical vowel.

2. The Hu class (the third class with native grammarians, and called by them नुहोत्यादि *juhotyádi*, because the first root in their lists is हु *hu*, नुहोति *juhóti*).

a. The terminations are added as in the Ad class.

b. The strong base before the weak terminations takes Guṇa, where possible.

c. The root takes reduplication.   (Rules of Reduplication, § 302.)

Ex. हु *hu*, to sacrifice : नुहुमः *ju-hu-máḥ*, we sacrifice ; नुहोमि *ju-hó-mi*, I sacrifice. (Pâṇ. VI. 1, 192.)

The intensive verbs, conjugated in the Parasmaipada, follow this class.

The accent is on the first syllable of the verb, if the terminations are weak, likewise if the terminations are strong, but begin with a vowel. Ex. दधाति *dádhâti ;* दधति *dádhati* (Pâṇ. VI. 1, 189–190).   Whether this rule extends to the Optative Âtmanepada is doubtful. We find in the Rig-veda both *dádhîta* and *dadhîtá*. Prof. Benfey, who at first accentuated *dadhîtá*, now places the accent on the first syllable, like Boehtlingk and Bopp.   The Âgama sîyuṭ is, no doubt, avidyamânavat svaravidhau (Pâṇ. III. 1, 3, vârt. 2); but the question is whether *îta* is to be treated as ajâdi, beginning with a vowel, or whether the termination is *ta* with Âgama *î*.   I adopt the former view, and see it confirmed by the Pratyudâharaṇa given in VI. 1, 189.   For if *yât* of *dad-yât* is no longer ajâdi, then *îta* in *dád-îta* must be ajâdi on the same ground.   The reduplicated verbs *bhî, hrî, bhṛi, hu, mad, jan, dhan, daridrâ, jâgṛi* have the Udâtta on the syllable preceding the terminations, if the terminations are weak.   Ex. विभर्ति *bibhárti*, but विभ्रति *bíbhrati* (Pâṇ. VI. 1, 192).

3. The Rudh class (the seventh class with native grammarians, and called by them रुधादि *rudhâdi*, because the first root in their lists is रुध् *rudh*, रुणद्धि *ruṇáddhi*, to obstruct).

a. The terminations are added as in the Ad class.

b. Between the radical vowel and the final consonant न *n* is inserted, which in the strong base before weak terminations is raised to न *na*.

Ex. युज् *yuj*, to join : युञ्जः *yu-ñ-j-máḥ*, we join ; युनज्मि *yu-ná-j-mi*, I join.

The accent falls on न *na*, wherever it appears, unless it is attracted by the augment.

First Division.

Bhû class, with native grammarians, Bhvâdi, I class.

Tud class,	—	—	Tudâdi, VI class.
Div class,	—	—	Divâdi, IV class.
Chur class,	—	—	Churâdi, X class.

Second Division.

Su class, with native grammarians, Svâdi, V class.

Tan class,	—	—	Tanâdi, VIII class.
Krî class,	—	—	Kryâdi, IX class.
Ad class,	—	—	Adâdi, II class.
Hu class,	—	—	Juhotyâdi, III class.
Rudh class,	—	—	Rudhâdi, VII class.

CHAPTER IX.

AUGMENT, REDUPLICATION, AND TERMINATIONS.

§ 300. Before we can leave the subject which occupies us at present, viz. the preparation of the root previous to its assuming the terminations, we have to consider two processes, the Augment and the Reduplication, modifications of the root with which we are familiar in Greek, and which in Sanskrit as well as in Greek form the distinguishing features of certain tenses (Imperfect, Aorist, Conditional, and Perfect) in every verb.

§ 301. Roots beginning with consonants take short अ *a* as their initial augment. This अ *a* has the accent. Thus from बुध् *budh*, Present बोधामि *bódhâmi*; Imperfect अबोधं *ábodham.*

Roots beginning with vowels always take Vṛiddhi, the irregular result of the combination of the augment with the initial vowels. (Pâṇ. vi. 1, 90.)

अ *a* with अ *a*, or आ *â*, = आ *â.*
अ *a* with इ *i*, ई *î*, ए *e*, or ऐ *ai*, = ऐ *ai.*
अ *a* with उ *u*, ऊ *û*, ओ *o*, or औ *au*, = औ *au.*
अ *a* with ऋ *ṛi*, or ॠ *ṛî*, = आर् *âr.*

From अर्च् *arch*, अर्चति *archati*, he praises, आर्चत् *árchat*, he praised.
From ईक्ष् *îksh*, ईक्षते *îkshate*, he sees, ऐक्षत *aíkshata*, he saw.
From उन्द् *und*, उनत्ति *unatti*, he wets, औनत् *aúnat*, he wetted.
From ऋ *ṛi*, ऋच्छति *ṛichchhati*, he goes, आर्च्छत् *árchchhat*, he went.

In the more ancient Sanskrit, as in the more ancient Greek, the augment is frequently absent. In the later Sanskrit, too, it has to be dropt after the negative particle मा *mâ* (Pâṇ. vi. 4, 74). मा भवान् कार्षीत् *mâ bhavân kârshît*, Let not your Honour do this! or मा स्म करोत् *mâ sma karot*, May he not do it!

Reduplication.

§ 302. Reduplication takes place in Sanskrit not only in the reduplicated perfect, but likewise in all verbs of the Hu class. Most of the rules of reduplication are the same in forming the base of the perfect of all verbs, and in forming the special base of the verbs of the Hu class. These will be stated first; afterwards those that are peculiar either to the reduplication of the perfect or to that of the verbs of the Hu class.

The reduplication in intensive and desiderative verbs and in one form of the aorist will have to be treated separately.

General Rules of Reduplication.

§ 303. The first syllable of a root (i. e. that portion of it which ends with a vowel) is repeated.

बुध् *budh* = बुबुध् *bubudh*. भू *bhû* is exceptional in forming बभू *babhû*. (Pân. VII. 4, 73.)

§ 304. Aspirated letters are represented in reduplication by their corresponding unaspirated letters.

भिद् *bhid*, to cut, = बिभिद् *bibhid*.
धू *dhû*, to shake, = दुधू *dudhû*.

§ 305. Gutturals are represented in reduplication by their corresponding palatals; ह *h* by ज *j*. (Pân. VII. 4, 62.)

कुट् *kuṭ*, to sever, = चुकुट् *chukuṭ*.
खन् *khan*, to dig, = चखन् *chakhan*.
गम् *gam*, to go, = जगम् *jagam*.
हस् *has*, to laugh, = जहस् *jahas*.

§ 306. If a root begins with more than one consonant, the first only is reduplicated.

कुश् *kruś*, to shout, = चुकुश् *chukruś*.
क्षिप् *kship*, to throw, = चिक्षिप् *chikship*.

§ 307. If a root begins with a sibilant followed by a tenuis or aspirated tenuis, the tenuis only is reduplicated.

स्तु *stu*, to praise, = तुष्टु *tushṭu* (§ 103, 1).
स्तन् *stan*, to sound, = तस्तन् *tastan*.
स्पर्ध् *spardh*, to strive, = पस्पर्ध् *paspardh*.
स्था *sthâ*, to stand, = तस्था *tasthâ*.
श्च्युत् *śchyut*, to drop, = चुश्च्युत् *chuśchyut*.
But स्मृ *smṛi*, to pine, = सस्मृ *sasmṛi*.

§ 308. If the radical vowel, whether final or medial, is long, it is shortened in the reduplicative syllable.

गाह् *gâh*, to enter, = जगाह् *jagâh*.
क्री *krî*, to buy, = चिक्री *chikrî*.
सूद् *sûd*, to strike, = सुसूद् *sushûd*.

§ 309. If the radical (not final) vowel is ए *e* or ऐ *ai*, it becomes इ *i*; if it is ओ *o* or औ *au*, it becomes उ *u*.

सेव् *sev*, to worship, = सिषेव् *sishev*.
ढौक् *ḍhauk*, to approach, = दुढौक् *ḍuḍhauk*.

§ 310. Roots with final ए *e*, ऐ *ai*, ओ *o*, are treated like roots ending in आ *â*, taking अ *a* in the reduplicative syllable.

धे *dhe*, to feed, = दधौ *dadhau*.
गै *gai*, to sing, = जगौ *jagau*.
शो *śo*, to sharpen, = शशौ *śaśau*.

§ 311. The following roots are slightly irregular on account of the semivowels which they contain, and which are liable to be changed into vowels. (This change is called *Samprasárana*.) Pân. VI. 1, 17.

Root.	First Pers. Sing. Redupl. Perf.	Weak Form *.	Weakest Form †.
यज् *yaj* = इयाज *iydja*, to sacrifice, (for ययाज *yayája*.)	ईज् *íj.*	(इज् *ij.*)
वच् *vach* = उवाच *uvácha*, to speak.	ऊच् *úch.*	(उच् *uch.*)
वद् *vad* = उवाद *uvádda*, to say.	ऊद् *úd.*	(उद् *ud.*)
वप् *vap* = उवाप *uvápa*, to sow.	ऊप् *úp.*	(उप् *up.*)
वश् *vaś* = उवाश *uváśa*, to wish.	ऊश् *úś.*	(उश् *uś.*)
वस् *vas* = उवास *uvása*, to dwell.	ऊस् *ús.*	(उस् *us.*)
वह् *vah* = उवाह *uvádha*, to carry.	ऊह् *úh.*	(उह् *uh.*)
वय् ‡ *vay* = उवाय *uváya*, to weave.	ऊय् *úy* or ऊव् *úv* ‖.	(उ *u.*)
व्यच् *vyach* = विव्याच *vivyácha*, to surround.	विविच् *vivich.*	(विच् *vich.*)
व्यध् *vyadh* = विव्याध *vivyádha*, to strike.	विविध् *vividh.*	(विध् *vidh.*)
व्यथ् *vyath* = विव्ये *vivyathé* (Pân. VII. 4, 68).	विव्यथ् *vivyath.*	(व्यथ् *vyath.*)
स्वप् *svap* = सुष्वाप *sushvápa*, to sleep.	सुषुप् *sushup.*	(सुप् *sup.*)
श्वि *śvi* = शुशाव *suśáva*, to swell ¶.	शुशू *śuśú.*	(शू *śú.*)
व्ये *vye* = विव्याय *vivyáya*, to cover.	विवी *viví.*	(वी *ví.*)
ज्या *jyá* = जिज्यौ *jijyaú*, to grow old.	जिजी *jijí.*	(जी *jí.*)
ह्वे *hve* = जुहाव *juháva*, to call (Pân. VI. 1, 33).	जुहू *juhú.*	(हू *hú.*)
प्याय् *pyáy* = पिप्ये *pipyé*, to grow fat (Pân. VI. 1, 29).	पिपी *pipí.*	(पी *pí.*)
ग्रह् *grah* = जग्राह *jagráha*, to take.	जगृह् *jagrih.*	(गृह् *grih.*)
व्रश्च् *vraśch* = वव्राश्च *vavráścha*, to cut (Pân. VI. 1, 17).	वव्रश्च् *vavriśch.*	(वृश्च् *vriśch.*)
प्रछ् *prachh* = पप्रच्छ *papráchchha*, to ask.	पप्रच्छ् *paprachchh.*	(पृच्छ् *prichchh.*)
भ्रज्ज् *bhrajj* = बभ्रज्ज *babhrájja*, to fry.	बभ्रज्ज् *babhrajj.*	(भृज्ज् *bhrijj.*)

In the last three verbs the weak form in the reduplicated perfect is protected against Samprasârana by the final double consonant. (Pân. I. 2, 5.)

Roots beginning with व *va*, but ending in double consonants, do not change व *va* to उ *u*. Ex. ववृते *vavrité;* ववृधे *vavridhé.*

§ 312. Roots beginning with short अ *a*, and ending in a single consonant, contract अ *a* + अ *a* into आ *á.*

अद् *ad*, to eat, = आद् *ád.*

---

* The weak forms appear in all persons of the reduplicated perfect where neither Vriddhi nor Guna is required.

† The weakest forms of these verbs do not belong to the reduplicated perfect, but have been added as useful hereafter for the formation of the past participle, the benedictive, the passive, &c.

‡ वय् *vay* is a substitute for वे *ve*, in the reduplicated perfect (Pân. II. 4, 41). If that substitution does not take place, then वे *ve* forms ववौ *vavau*, ववुः *vavuh* (Pân. VI. 1, 40).

‖ Pân. VI. 1, 38, 39.   ¶ Or शिश्वाय *śiśváya* (Pân. VI. 1, 30).

§ 313. Roots beginning with short ज *a*, and ending with more than one consonant, prefix आन् *án*. (Pâṇ. VII. 4, 71.)

अर्च् *arch* = आनर्च् *ánárch*. (Also अश् *aś* (Su), आनशे *ánaśe*.) Pâṇ. VII. 4, 72.

§ 314. The root ऋ *ṛi* forms the base of the reduplicated perfect as आर् *ár*. Other roots beginning with ऋ *ṛi* prefix आन् *án*. (Pâṇ. VII. 4, 71.)

ऋज् *ṛij*, to obtain, = आनृज् *án-ṛij*. ऋध् *ṛidh*, to thrive, = आनृध् *ánṛidh*. These roots are treated in fact as if they were अर्च् *arch*, अर्ध् *ardh*, &c.

§ 315. Roots beginning with इ *i* or उ *u* (not prosodially long), contract इ + इ *i + i* and उ + उ *u + u* into ई *í* and ऊ *ú*; but if the radical इ *i* or उ *u* take Guṇa or Vṛiddhi, य् *y* and व् *v* are inserted between the reduplicative syllable and the base. (Pâṇ. VI. 4, 78.)

इष् *ish* = ईषतु: *ísh-átuḥ*, they two have gone.

= इयेष *iy-ésh-a* (Guṇa), I have gone.

उख् *ukh* = ऊखतु: *úkh-átuḥ*, they two have withered.

= उवोख *uv-ókh-a* (Guṇa), I have withered.

As to roots which cannot be reduplicated or are otherwise irregular, see the rules given for the formation of the Reduplicated and Periphrastic Perfect.

Special Rules of Reduplication.

§ 316. So far the process of reduplication would be the same, whether applied to the bases of the Reduplicated Perfect or to those of the Hu class. But there are some points on which these two classes of reduplicated bases differ; viz.

1. In the Reduplicated Perfect, radical ऋ *ṛi*, ॠ *ṛí*, whether final or medial, are represented in reduplication by अ *a*.

2. In the bases of the Hu class, final ऋ *ṛi* and ॠ *ṛí* (they do not occur as medial) are represented in reduplication by इ *i*.

REDUPLICATED PERFECT.	HU CLASS. PRESENT, &c.
भृ *bhṛi*, to bear, = बभार *babhára*.	भृ *bhṛi* = बिभर्ति *bibhárti*.
सृ *sṛi*, to go, = ससार *sasára*.	सृ *sṛi* = सिसर्ति *sísarti*.
हृ *hṛi*, to take, = जहार *jahára*.	हृ *hṛi* = जिहर्ति *jíharti*.

The root ऋ *ṛi*, to go, forms इयर्ति *iy-arti*; पृ *pṛí*, to fill, पिपर्ति *píparti*.

§ 317. The three verbs निज् *nij*, विज् *vij*, and विष् *vish* of the Hu class take Guṇa in the reduplicated syllable. (Pâṇ. VII. 4, 75.)

निज् *nij*, to wash, नेनेक्ति *nénekti*, नेनिक्ते *nenikte*; विज् *vij*, to separate, वेवेक्ति *vévekti*; विष् *vish*, to pervade, वेवेष्टि *véveshṭi*.

§ 318. The two verbs मा *má*, to measure, and हा *há*, to go, of the Hu class take इ *i* in the reduplicative syllable. (Pâṇ. VII. 4, 76.)

मा *má*, मिमीते *mimíté*; हा *há*, जिहीते *jihíté*.

§ 319. Certain roots change their initial consonant if they are reduplicated.

हन् *han*, to kill, जघान *jaghána*. Likewise in the desiderative जिघांसति *jigháṁsati*, and the intensive जंघन्यते *jaṅghanyáte*. (Pâṇ. VII. 3, 55.)

हि *hi*, to send (Su), जिघाय *jigháya*. Likewise in the desiderative जिघीषति *jighíshati*, and the intensive जेघीयते *jeghíyáte*. (Pâṇ. VII. 3, 56.)

फ़ि *ji*, to conquer, जिगाय *jigáya*. Likewise in the desiderative जिगीषति *jigíshati;* but not in the intensive, which is always जेजीयते *jejíyáte*. (Pâṇ. VII. 3, 57.)

चि *chi*, to gather, has optionally चिचाय *chicháya* or चिकाय *chikáya*. The same option applies to the desiderative, but in the intensive we have चेचीयते *chechíyáte* only. (Pâṇ. VII. 3, 58.)

Terminations.

§ 320. After having explained how the verbal roots are modified in ten different ways before they receive the terminations of the four special tenses, the Present, Imperfect, Optative, and Imperative, we give a table of the terminations for these so-called special or modified tenses and moods.

§ 321. The terminations for the modified tenses, though on the whole the same for all verbs, are subject to certain variations, according as the verbal bases take ब *a* (First Division), or नु *nu*, उ *u*, नी *ní* (Second Division, A.), or nothing (Second Division, B.) between themselves and the terminations. Instead of giving the table of terminations according to the system of native grammarians, or according to that of comparative philologists, and explaining the real or fanciful changes which they are supposed to have undergone in the different classes of verbs, it will be more useful to give them in that form in which they may mechanically be attached to each verbal base. The beginner should commit to memory the actual paradigms rather than the different sets of terminations. Instead of taking आथे *áthe* as the termination of the 2nd pers. dual Âtm., and learning that the आ *á* of आथे *áthe* is changed to इ *i* after bases in ब *a* (Pâṇ. VII. 2, 81), it is simpler to take इथे *ithe* as the termination in the First Division; but still simpler to commit to memory such forms as बोधेथे *bodhethe*, द्विषाथे *dvisháthe*, मिमाथे *mimáthe*, without asking at first any questions as to how they came to be what they are.

FIRST DIVISION.

Bhú, Tud, Div, and Chur Classes.

	PARASMAIPADA.			ÂTMANEPADA.			
Present.	Imperf.	Optative.	Imperat.	Present.	Imperfect.	Optative.	Imperative.
1. अमि *ami*	म् *m*	इयं *iyam*	आनि *ani*	ए *i*	ए *i*	इय *iya*	ए *e*
2. सि *si*	: *ḥ*	ई: *iḥ*	— *	से *se*	था: *tháḥ*	इथा: *itháḥ*	स्व *sva*
3. ति *ti*	त् *t*	इत् *it*	तु *tu* *	ते *te*	त *ta*	इत *ita*	तां *tám*
1. अवः *avaḥ*	अव *ava*	इव *iva*	अव *ava*	अवहे *avahe*	अवहि *avahi*	इवहि *ivahi*	अवहै *avahai*
2. थः *thaḥ*	तं *tam*	इतं *itam*	तं *tam*	इथे *ithe*	इथां *ithám*	इयाथां *iyáthám*	इथां *ithám*
3. तः *taḥ*	तां *tám*	इतां *itám*	तां *tám*	इते *ite*	इतां *itám*	इयातां *iyátám*	इतां *itám*
1. अमः *amaḥ*	अम *ama*	इम *ima*	अम *ama*	अमहे *amahe*	अमहि *amahi*	इमहि *imahi*	अमहै *amahai*
2. थ *tha*	त *ta*	इत *ita*	त *ta*	ध्वे *dhve*	ध्वं *dhvam*	इध्वं *idhvam*	ध्वं *dhvam*
3. नि *nti*	न् *n*	इयु: *iyuḥ*	नु *ntu*	ते *nte*	न्त *nta*	इरन् *iran*	नां *ntám*

* In the second and third persons तात् *tát* may be used as termination after all verbs, if the sense is benedictive.

SECOND DIVISION.
Su, Tan, Kri, Ad, Hu, and Rudh Classes.

	PARASMAIPADA.				ÂTMANEPADA.		
	Present.	Imperfect.	Optative.	Imperative.	Present.	Imperfect.	Optative.	Imperative.
1.	*mi*	*am*	*yâm*	*âni*	*e*	*i*	*îya*	*ai*
2.	*si*	*ḥ*	*yâḥ*	*hi*[1]	*se*	*thâḥ*	*îthâḥ*	*sva*
3.	*ti*	*t*	*yât*	*tu*	*te*	*ta*	*îta*	*tâm*
1.	*vaḥ*	*va*	*yâva*	*âva*	*vahe*	*vahi*	*îvahi*	*âvahai*
2.	*thaḥ*	*tam*	*yâtam*	*tam*	*âthe*	*âthâm*	*îyâthâm*	*âthâm*
3.	*taḥ*	*tâm*	*yâtâm*	*tâm*	*âte*	*âtâm*	*îyâtâm*	*âtâm*
1.	*maḥ*	*ma*	*yâma*	*âma*	*mahe*	*mahi*	*îmahi*	*âmahai*
2.	*tha*	*ta*	*yâta*	*ta*	*dhve*	*dhvam*	*îdhvam*	*dhvam*
3.	*anti*[2]	*an*[3]	*yuḥ*	*antu*[2]	*ate*	*ata*	*îran*	*atâm*

The terminations enclosed in squares are the weak, i. e. unaccented terminations which require strengthening of the base.

Note 1—When फ़ि *hi* is added immediately to the final consonant of a root (in the Ad, Rudh, or Hu classes), it is changed to धि *dhi* (Pâṇ. vi. 4, 101. See No. 162). The verb हु *hu*, though ending in a vowel, takes धि *dhi* instead of फ़ि *hi*, for the sake of euphony. (Pâṇ. vi. 4, 101.)

Kri verbs ending in consonants form the 2nd pers. sing. imp. in आन *âna*. (See No. 155. Pâṇ. iii. 1, 83.)

In the 2nd pers. sing. imp. Parasm. verbs of the Su and Tan classes take no termination, except when उ *u* is preceded by a conjunct consonant. (See No. 177.)

Note 2—In the 3rd pers. plur. pres. and imper. Parasm. verbs of the Hu class and अभ्यस्त *abhyasta*, i. e. reduplicated bases, take अति *ati* and अतु *atu*.

Note 3—In the 3rd pers. plur. imp. Parasm. verbs of the Hu class, reduplicated bases, and विद् *vid*, to know, take उः *uḥ*, before which, verbs ending in a vowel, require Guṇa. उः *uḥ* is used optionally after verbs in आ *â*, and after द्विष् *dviṣh*, to hate. (Pâṇ. iii. 4, 109–112.)

§ 322. By means of these terminations the student is able to form the Present, Imperfect, Optative, and Imperative in the Parasmaipada and Âtmanepade of all regular verbs in Sanskrit; and any one who has clearly understood how the verbal bases are prepared in ten different ways for receiving their terminations, and who will attach to these verbal bases the terminations as given above, according to the rules of Sandhi, will have no difficulty in writing out for himself the paradigms of any Sanskrit verb in four of the most important tenses and moods, both in the Parasmaipada and Âtmanepada. Some verbs, however, are irregular in the formation of their base; these must be learnt from the Dhâtupâṭha.

Present.

Root.	Verbal Base.	मि ami	सि si	ति ti	वः avaḥ	थः thaḥ	तः taḥ	मः amaḥ	थ tha	न्ति nti
	First Division.	मि ami	सि si	ति ti	वः avaḥ	थः thaḥ	तः taḥ	मः amaḥ	थ tha	न्ति nti
भू bhū	भव bhava	भवामि bhávâmi	भवसि bhávasi	भवति bhávati	भवावः bhávâvaḥ	भवथः bhávathaḥ	भवतः bhávataḥ	भवामः bhávâmaḥ	भवथ bhávatha	भवन्ति bhávanti
तुद् tud	तुद tuda	तुदामि tudâmi	तुदसि tudási	तुदति tudáti	तुदावः tudâvaḥ	तुदथः tudáthaḥ	तुदतः tudátaḥ	तुदामः tudâmaḥ	तुदथ tudátha	तुदन्ति tudánti
दिव् div	दीव्य dívya	दीव्यामि dívyâmi	दीव्यसि dívyasi	दीव्यति dívyati	दीव्यावः dívyâvaḥ	दीव्यथः dívyathaḥ	दीव्यतः dívyataḥ	दीव्यामः dívyâmaḥ	दीव्यथ dívyatha	दीव्यन्ति dívyanti
चुर् chur	चोरय choraya	चोरयामि choráyâmi	चोरयसि choráyasi	चोरयति choráyati	चोरयावः choráyâvaḥ	चोरयथः choráyathaḥ	चोरयतः choráyataḥ	चोरयामः choráyâmaḥ	चोरयथ choráyatha	चोरयन्ति choráyanti
	Second Division.	मि mi	सि si	ति ti	वः vaḥ	थः thaḥ	तः taḥ	मः maḥ	थ tha	अन्ति anti
सु su	सुनु सुनो sunu suno	सुनोमि sunómi	सुनोषि sunóshi	सुनोति sunóti	सुनुवः[1] sunuváḥ	सुनुथः sunutháḥ	सुनुतः sunutáḥ	सुनुमः[2] sunumáḥ	सुनुथ sunuthá	सुन्वन्ति sunvánti
तन् tan	तनु तनो tanu tano	तनोमि tanómi	तनोषि tanóshi	तनोति tanóti	तनुवः[3] tanuváḥ	तनुथः tanutháḥ	तनुतः tanutáḥ	तनुमः[4] tanumáḥ	तनुथ tanuthá	तन्वन्ति tanvánti
क्री krī	क्रीणि क्रीणा क्रीण् krīṇi krīṇā krīṇ	क्रीणामि krīṇámi	क्रीणासि krīṇási	क्रीणाति krīṇáti	क्रीणीवः krīṇíváḥ	क्रीणीथः krīṇítháḥ	क्रीणीतः krīṇítáḥ	क्रीणीमः krīṇímáḥ	क्रीणीथ krīṇíthá	क्रीणन्ति krīṇánti
अद् ad	अद् अद् ad ad	अद्मि ádmi	अत्सि átsi	अत्ति átti	अद्वः adváḥ	अत्थः attháḥ	अत्तः attáḥ	अद्मः admáḥ	अत्थ atthá	अदन्ति adánti
हु hu	जुहु जुहो juhu juho	जुहोमि juhómi	जुहोषि juhóshi	जुहोति juhóti	जुहुवः juhuváḥ	जुहुथः juhutháḥ	जुहुतः juhutáḥ	जुहुमः juhumáḥ	जुहुथ juhuthá	जुह्वति[5] júhvati
रुध् rudh	रुन्ध रुणध् rundh ruṇadh	रुणध्मि ruṇádhmi	रुणत्सि ruṇátsi	रुणद्धि ruṇáddhi	रुन्ध्वः rundhváḥ	रुन्द्धः runddháḥ	रुन्द्धः runddháḥ	रुन्ध्मः rundhmáḥ	रुन्द्ध runddhá	रुन्धन्ति rundhánti

[1] Or सुन्वः sunváḥ. See No. 139.   [2] Or सुम्मः summáḥ.   [3] Or तन्वः tanváḥ.   [4] Or तन्मः tanmáḥ.   [5] See § 321, note 2.

PARASMAIPADA.
Imperfect.

Root.	Verbal Base.									
	First Division.	म् *m*	: *ḥ*	त् *t*	अव *ava*	तं *tam*	तां *tām*	अम *ama*	त *ta*	न् *n*
भू *bhú*	भव *bhava*	अभवं *ábhavam*	अभव: *ábhavaḥ*	अभवत् *ábhavat*	अभवाव *ábhavâva*	अभवतं *ábhavatam*	अभवतां *ábhavatām*	अभवाम *ábhavāma*	अभवत *ábhavata*	अभवन् *ábhavan*
तुद् *tud*	तुद *tuda*	अतुदं *átudam*	अतुद: *átudaḥ*	अतुदत् *átudat*	अतुदाव *átudāva*	अतुदतं *átudatam*	अतुदतां *átudatām*	अतुदाम *átudāma*	अतुदत *átudata*	अतुदन् *átudan*
दिव् *div*	दीव्य *dívya*	अदीव्यं *ádívyam*	अदीव्य: *ádívyaḥ*	अदीव्यत् *ádívyat*	अदीव्याव *ádívyâva*	अदीव्यतं *ádívyatam*	अदीव्यतां *ádívyatām*	अदीव्याम *ádívyāma*	अदीव्यत *ádívyata*	अदीव्यन् *ádívyan*
चुर् *chur*	चोरय *choraya*	अचोरयं *áchorayam*	अचोरय: *áchorayaḥ*	अचोरयत् *áchorayat*	अचोरयाव *áchorayâva*	अचोरयतं *áchorayatam*	अचोरयतां *áchorayatām*	अचोरयाम *áchorayāma*	अचोरयत *áchorayata*	अचोरयन् *áchorayan*
	Second Division.	अं *am*	: *ḥ*	त् *t*	व *va*	तं *tam*	तां *tām*	म *ma*	त *ta*	अन् *an*
सु *su*	सुनु सुनो *sunu suno*	असुनवं *ásunavam*	असुनो: *ásunoḥ*	असुनोत् *ásunot*	असुनुव[1] *ásunuva*	असुनुतं *ásunutam*	असुनुतां *ásunutām*	असुनुम[2] *ásunuma*	असुनुत *ásunuta*	असुन्वन् *ásunvan*
तन् *tan*	तनु तनो *tanu tano*	अतनवं *átanavam*	अतनो: *átanoḥ*	अतनोत् *átanot*	अतनुव[3] *átanuva*	अतनुतं *átanutam*	अतनुतां *átanutām*	अतनुम[4] *átanuma*	अतनुत *átanuta*	अतान्वन् *átanvan*
क्री *krí*	क्रीणी क्रीणा क्रीण् *kríṇí kríṇâ kríṇ*	अक्रीणां *ákríṇâm*	अक्रीणा: *ákríṇâḥ*	अक्रीणात् *ákríṇât*	अक्रीणीव *ákríṇíva*	अक्रीणीतं *ákríṇítam*	अक्रीणीतां *ákríṇítām*	अक्रीणीम *ákríṇíma*	अक्रीणीत *ákríṇíta*	अक्रीणन् *ákríṇan*
अद् *ad*	अद् अद् *ad ad*	आदं[5] *ádam*	आद: *ádaḥ*	आदत् *ádat*	आद्व *ádva*	आत्तं *áttam*	आत्तां *áttām*	आद्म *ádma*	आत्त *átta*	आदन् *ádan*
हु *hu*	जुहु जुहो *juhu juho*	अजुहवं *ájuhavam*	अजुहो: *ájuhoḥ*	अजुहोत् *ájuhot*	अजुहुव *ájuhuva*	अजुहुतं *ájuhutam*	अजुहुतां *ájuhutām*	अजुहुम *ájuhuma*	अजुहुत *ájuhuta*	अजुहवु:[6] *ájuhavuḥ*
रुध् *rudh*	रुन्ध् रुणध् *rundh ruṇadh*	अरुणधं *áruṇadham*	अरुणत्[7] *áruṇat*	अरुणत् *áruṇat*	अरुन्ध्व *árundhva*	अरुन्द्धं *árunddham*	अरुन्द्धां *árunddhām*	अरुन्ध्म *árundhma*	अरुन्द्ध *árunddha*	अरुन्धन् *árundhan*

1 Or असुन्व *ásunva*.　2 Or असुन्म *ásunma*.　3 Or अतन्व *átanva*.　4 Or अतन्म *átanma*.　5 See § 301.　6 See § 321, note 3.　7 Or अरुणः *áruṇaḥ*, § 114, 132.

Optative.

Root.	Verbal Base.								
	First Division.	इयं iyam	इः iḥ	इत् it	इव iva	इतं itam	इतां itám	इम ima	इत ita	इयुः iyuḥ
भू bhú	भव bhava	भवेयं bháveyam	भवेः bháveḥ	भवेत् bhávet	भवेव bháveva	भवेतं bhávetam	भवेतां bhávetám	भवेम bhávema	भवेत bháveta	भवेयुः bháveyuḥ
तुद् tud	तुद tuda	तुदेयं tudéyam	तुदेः tudéḥ	तुदेत् tudét	तुदेव tudéva	तुदेतं tudétam	तुदेतां tudétám	तुदेम tudéma	तुदेत tudéta	तुदेयुः tudéyuḥ
दिव् div	दीव्य dívya	दीव्येयं dívyeyam	दीव्येः dívyeḥ	दीव्येत् dívyet	दीव्येव dívyeva	दीव्येतं dívyetam	दीव्येतां dívyetám	दीव्येम dívyema	दीव्येत dívyeta	दीव्येयुः dívyeyuḥ
चुर् chur	चोरय choraya	चोरयेयं choráyeyam	चोरयेः choráyeḥ	चोरयेत् choráyet	चोरयेव choráyeva	चोरयेतं choráyetam	चोरयेतां choráyetám	चोरयेम choráyema	चोरयेत choráyeta	चोरयेयुः choráyeyuḥ
	Second Division.	यां yám	याः yáḥ	यात् yát	याव yáva	यातं yátam	यातां yátám	याम yáma	यात yáta	युः yuḥ
सु su	सुनु sunu	सुनुयां sunuyám	सुनुयाः sunuyáḥ	सुनुयात् sunuyát	सुनुयाव sunuyáva	सुनुयातं sunuyátam	सुनुयातां sunuyátám	सुनुयाम sunuyáma	सुनुयात sunuyáta	सुनुयुः sunuyúḥ
तन् tan	तनु tanu	तनुयां tanuyám	तनुयाः tanuyáḥ	तनुयात् tanuyát	तनुयाव tanuyáva	तनुयातं tanuyátam	तनुयातां tanuyátám	तनुयाम tanuyáma	तनुयात tanuyáta	तनुयुः tanuyúḥ
क्री krí	क्रीणी kríṇí	क्रीणीयां kríṇíyám	क्रीणीयाः kríṇíyáḥ	क्रीणीयात् kríṇíyát	क्रीणीयाव kríṇíyáva	क्रीणीयातं kríṇíyátam	क्रीणीयातां kríṇíyátám	क्रीणीयाम kríṇíyáma	क्रीणीयात kríṇíyáta	क्रीणीयुः kríṇíyúḥ
अद् ad	अद् ad	अद्यां adyám	अद्याः adyáḥ	अद्यात् adyát	अद्याव adyáva	अद्यातं adyátam	अद्यातां adyátám	अद्याम adyáma	अद्यात adyáta	अद्युः adyúḥ
हु hu	जुहु juhu	जुहुयां juhuyám	जुहुयाः juhuyáḥ	जुहुयात् juhuyát	जुहुयाव juhuyáva	जुहुयातं juhuyátam	जुहुयातां juhuyátám	जुहुयाम juhuyáma	जुहुयात juhuyáta	जुहुयुः juhuyúḥ
रुध् rudh	रुंध rundh	रुंध्यां rundhyám	रुंध्याः rundhyáḥ	रुंध्यात् rundhyát	रुंध्याव rundhyáva	रुंध्यातं rundhyátam	रुंध्यातां rundhyátám	रुंध्याम rundhyáma	रुंध्यात rundhyáta	रुंध्युः rundhyúḥ

PARASMAIPADA.
Imperative.

Root.	Verbal Base.	आनि *áni*	—	तु *tu*	अव *ava*	तं *tam*	तां *tám*	अम *ama*	त *ta*	नु *ntu*
	First Division.									
भू *bhú*	भव *bhava*	भवानि *bhávái*	भव *bháva*	भवतु *bhávatu*	भवाव *bháváva*	भवतं *bhávatam*	भवतां *bhávatám*	भवाम *bháváma*	भवत *bhávata*	भवंतु *bhávantu*
तुद् *tud*	तुद *tuda*	तुदानि *tuddni*	तुद *tudá*	तुदतु *tudátu*	तुदाव *tudáva*	तुदतं *tudátam*	तुदतां *tudátám*	तुदाम *tudáma*	तुदत *tudáta*	तुदंतु *tudántu*
दिव् *div*	दीव्य *dívya*	दीव्यानि *dívyáni*	दीव्य *dívya*	दीव्यतु *dívyatu*	दीव्याव *dívyáva*	दीव्यतं *dívyatam*	दीव्यतां *dívyatám*	दीव्याम *dívyáma*	दीव्यत *dívyata*	दीव्यंतु *dívyantu*
चुर् *chur*	चोरय *choraya*	चोरयानि *choráyáni*	चोरय *choráya*	चोरयतु *choráyatu*	चोरयाव *choráyáva*	चोरयतं *choráyatam*	चोरयतां *choráyatám*	चोरयाम *choráyáma*	चोरयत *choráyata*	चोरयंतु *choráyantu*
	Second Division.	आनि *áni*	हि *hi*	तु *tu*	आव *áva*	तं *tam*	तां *tám*	आम *áma*	त *ta*	अंतु *antu*
सु *su*	सुनु सुनो *sunu suno*	सुनवानि *sunávdni*	सुनु[1] *sunú*	सुनोतु *sunótu*	सुनवाव *sunávava*	सुनुतं *sunutám*	सुनुतां *sunutám*	सुनवाम *sunávama*	सुनुत *sunutá*	सुन्वंतु *sunvántu*
तन् *tan*	तनु तनो *tanu tano*	तनवानि *tanávdni*	तनु *tanú*	तनोतु *tanótu*	तनवाव *tanávava*	तनुतं *tanutám*	तनुतां *tanutám*	तनवाम *tanávama*	तनुत *tanutá*	तन्वंतु *tanvántu*
क्री *krí*	क्रीणी क्रीणा क्रीण *kríní kríná krín*	क्रीणानि *kríndni*	क्रीणीहि[2] *kríníhí*	क्रीणातु *kríndtu*	क्रीणाव *kríndva*	क्रीणीतं *kríníttám*	क्रीणीतां *kríníttám*	क्रीणाम *kríndma*	क्रीणीत *kríníttá*	क्रीणंतु *kríndntu*
अद् *ad*	अद् अद् *ad ad*	अदानि *ádáni*	अद्धि[3] *addhí*	अत्तु *áttu*	अदाव *ádáva*	अत्तं *attám*	अत्तां *attám*	अदाम *ádáma*	अत्ता *attá*	अदंतु *adántu*
हु *hu*	जुहु जुहो *juhu juho*	जुहवानि *juhávdni*	जुहुधि[4] *juhudhí*	जुहोतु *juhótu*	जुहवाव *juhávava*	जुहुतं *juhutám*	जुहुतां *juhutám*	जुहवाम *juhávama*	जुहुत *juhutá*	जुह्वतु[5] *júhvatu*
रुध् *rudh*	रुन्ध् रुणध् *rundh ruṇadh*	रुणध्यानि *ruṇádháni*	रुंद्धि[3] *runddhí*	रुणद्धु *ruṇáddhu*	रुणध्याव *ruṇádháva*	रुंद्धं *runddhám*	रुंद्धां *runddhám*	रुणध्याम *ruṇádháma*	रुंद्धा *runddhá*	रुंधंतु *rundhántu*

ÂTMANEPADA.
Present.

First Division.

Root.	Verbal Base.	इ i	से se	ते te	अवहे avahe	इथे ithe	इते ite	अमहे amahe	ध्वे dhve	न्ते nte
भू bhû	भव bhava	भवे bhâve	भवसे bhâvase	भवते bhâvate	भवावहे bhâvâvahe	भवेथे bhâvethe	भवेते bhâvete	भवामहे bhâvâmahe	भवध्वे bhâvadhve	भवन्ते bhâvante
तुद् tud	तुद tuda	तुदे tudé	तुदसे tudáse	तुदते tudáte	तुदावहे tudávahe	तुदेथे tudéthe	तुदेते tudéte	तुदामहे tudámahe	तुदध्वे tudádhve	तुदन्ते tudánte
दिव् div	दीव्य dívya	दीव्ये dívye	दीव्यसे dívyase	दीव्यते dívyate	दीव्यावहे dívyávahe	दीव्येथे dívyethe	दीव्येते dívyete	दीव्यामहे dívyámahe	दीव्यध्वे dívyadhve	दीव्यन्ते dívyante
चुर् chur	चोरय choraya	चोरये choráye	चोरयसे choráyase	चोरयते choráyate	चोरयावहे choráyávahe	चोरयेथे choráyethe	चोरयेते choráyete	चोरयामहे choráyámahe	चोरयध्वे choráyadhve	चोरयन्ते choráyante

Second Division.

Root.	Verbal Base.	ए e	से se	ते te	वहे vahe	आथे áthe	आते áte	महे mahe	ध्वे dhve	अते ate
सु su	सुनु sunu	सुन्वे sunvé	सुनुषे sunushé	सुनुते sunuté	सुनुवहे[1] sunuváhe	सुन्वाथे sunváthe	सुन्वाते sunváte	सुनुमहे[2] sunumáhe	सुनुध्वे sunudhvé	सुन्वाते sunváte
तन् tan	तनु tanu	तन्वे tanvé	तनुषे tanushé	तनुते tanuté	तनुवहे[3] tanuváhe	तन्वाथे tanváthe	तन्वाते tanváte	तनुमहे[4] tanumáhe	तनुध्वे tanudhvé	तन्वाते tanváte
क्री krî	क्रीणी क्रीण् krîní krîn	क्रीणे krîné	क्रीणिषे krînishé	क्रीणिते krînité	क्रीणिवहे krînìváhe	क्रीणाथे krînáthe	क्रीणाते krînáte	क्रीणिमहे krînìmáhe	क्रीणीध्वे krînìdhvé	क्रीणाते krînáte
अद् ad	अद् ad	अदे adé	आत्से atsé	आत्ते atté	अद्वहे advâhe	अदाथे adáthe	अदाते adáte	अद्महे admâhe	अद्ध्वे addhvé	अदाते adáte
हु hu	जुहु juhu	जुह्वे juhvé	जुहुषे juhushé	जुहुते juhuté	जुहुवहे juhuváhe	जुह्वाथे juhváthe	जुह्वाते juhváte	जुहुमहे juhumáhe	जुहुध्वे juhudhvé	जुह्वाते juhváte
रुध् rudh	रुन्ध् rundh	रुन्धे rundhé	रुन्त्से runtsé	रुन्द्धे runddhé	रुन्ध्वहे rundhváhe	रुन्धाथे rundháthe	रुन्धाते rundháte	रुन्ध्महे rundhmáhe	रुन्द्ध्वे runddhvé	रुन्धाते rundháte

[1] Or सुन्वहे sunváhe. [2] Or सुन्महे sunmáhe. [3] Or तन्वहे tanváhe. [4] Or तन्महे tanmáhe.

X 2

ÂTMANEPADA.
Imperfect.

अ.	VERBAL BASE	इ i	याः thâḥ	त ta	अवहि avahi	इथां ithâm	इतां itâm	अमहि amahi	ध्वं dhvam	न nta
	First Division.									
भू bhû	भव bhava	अभवे ábhave	अभवथाः ábhavathâḥ	अभवत ábhavata	अभवावहि ábhavávahi	अभवेथां ábhavethâm	अभवेतां ábhavetâm	अभवामहि ábhavâmahi	अभवध्वं ábhavadhvam	अभवंत ábhavanta
तुद् tud	तुद tuda	अतुदे átude	अतुदथाः átudathâḥ	अतुदत átudata	अतुदावहि átudávahi	अतुदेथां átudethâm	अतुदेतां átudetâm	अतुदामहि átudámahi	अतुदध्वं átudadhvam	अतुदंत átudanta
दिव् div	दीव्य divya	अदीव्ये ádívye	अदीव्यथाः ádívyathâḥ	अदीव्यत ádívyata	अदीव्यावहि ádívyávahi	अदीव्येथां ádívyethâm	अदीव्येतां ádívyetâm	अदीव्यामहि ádívyámahi	अदीव्यध्वं ádívyadhvam	अदीव्यंत ádívyanta
चुर् chur	चोरय choraya	अचोरये áchoraye	अचोरयथाः áchorayathâḥ	अचोरयत áchorayata	अचोरयावहि áchorayávahi	अचोरयेथां áchorayethâm	अचोरयेतां áchorayetâm	अचोरयामहि áchorayámahi	अचोरयध्वं áchorayadhvam	अचोरयंत áchorayanta

अ.	VERBAL BASE	इ i	याः thâḥ	त ta	वहि vahi	आथां âthâm	आतां âtâm	महि mahi	ध्वं dhvam	अत ata
	Second Division.									
सु su	सुनु sunu	असुन्वि ásunvi	असुनुथाः ásunuthâḥ	असुनुत ásunuta	असुनुवहि[1] ásunuvahi	असुन्वाथां ásunváthâm	असुन्वातां ásunvâtâm	असुनुमहि[2] ásunumahi	असुनुध्वं ásunudhvam	असुन्वत ásunvata
तन् tan	तनु tanu	अतन्वि átanvi	अतनुथाः átanuthâḥ	अतनुत átanuta	अतनुवहि[3] átanuvahi	अतन्वाथां átanváthâm	अतन्वातां átanvâtâm	अतनुमहि[4] átanumahi	अतनुध्वं átanudhvam	अतन्वत átanvata
क्री krî	क्रीणी क्रीण् krîṇî krîṇ	अक्रीणि ákrîṇi	अक्रीणीथाः ákrîṇithâḥ	अक्रीणीत ákrîṇita	अक्रीणीवहि ákrîṇivahi	अक्रीणाथां ákrîṇáthâm	अक्रीणातां ákrîṇâtâm	अक्रीणीमहि ákrîṇimahi	अक्रीणीध्वं ákrîṇidhvam	अक्रीणत ákrîṇata
अद् ad	अद ad	आदि ádi	आत्थाः átthâḥ	आत्त átta	आद्वहि ádvahi	आदाथां ádáthâm	आदातां ádâtâm	आद्महि ádmahi	आद्ध्वं áddhvam	आदत ádata
हु hu	जुहु juhu	अजुह्वि ájuhvi	अजुहुथाः ájuhuthâḥ	अजुहुत ájuhuta	अजुहुवहि ájuhuvahi	अजुह्वाथां ájuhvâthâm	अजुह्वातां ájuhvâtâm	अजुहुमहि ájuhumahi	अजुहुध्वं ájuhudhvam	अजुह्वत ájuhvata
रुध् rudh	रुन्ध rundh	अरुन्धि árundhi	अरुन्द्धाः árunddhâḥ	अरुन्द्ध árunddha	अरुन्ध्वहि árundhvahi	अरुन्धाथां árundhâthâm	अरुन्धातां árundhâtâm	अरुन्ध्महि árundhmahi	अरुन्द्ध्वं árunddhvam	अरुन्धत árundhata

1 Or असुन्वहि ásunvahi. 2 Or असुन्महि ásunmahi. 3 Or अतन्वहि átanvahi. 4 Or अतन्महि átanmahi.

ÂTMANEPADA.
Optative.

Root.	Verbal Base.	इय *iya*	इथाः *ithâḥ*	इत *ita*	इवहि *ivahi*	इयाथां *iyâthâm*	इयातां *iyâtâm*	इमहि *imahi*	इध्वं *idhvam*	इरन् *iran*
	First Division.									
भू *bhû*	भव *bhava*	भवेय *bháveya*	भवेथाः *bhávethâḥ*	भवेत *bháveta*	भवेवहि *bhávevahi*	भवेयाथां *bháveyâthâm*	भवेयातां *bháveyâtâm*	भवेमहि *bhávemahi*	भवेध्वं *bhávedhvam*	भवेरन् *bháveran*
तुद् *tud*	तुद *tuda*	तुदेय *tudéya*	तुदेथाः *tudéthâḥ*	तुदेत *tudéta*	तुदेवहि *tudévahi*	तुदेयाथां *tudéyâthâm*	तुदेयातां *tudéyâtâm*	तुदेमहि *tudémahi*	तुदेध्वं *tudédhvam*	तुदेरन् *tudéran*
दिव् *div*	दीव्य *dívya*	दीव्येय *dívyeya*	दीव्येथाः *dívyethâḥ*	दीव्येत *dívyeta*	दीव्येवहि *dívyevahi*	दीव्येयाथां *dívyeyâthâm*	दीव्येयातां *dívyeyâtâm*	दीव्येमहि *dívyemahi*	दीव्येध्वं *dívyedhvam*	दीव्येरन् *dívyeran*
चुर् *chur*	चोरय *choraya*	चोरयेय *choráyeya*	चोरयेथाः *choráyethâḥ*	चोरयेत *choráyeta*	चोरयेवहि *choráyevahi*	चोरयेयाथां *choráyeyâthâm*	चोरयेयातां *choráyeyâtâm*	चोरयेमहि *choráyemahi*	चोरयेध्वं *choráyedhvam*	चोरयेरन् *choráyeran*
	Second Division.	ईय *íya*	ईथाः *íthâḥ*	ईत *íta*	ईवहि *ívahi*	ईयाथां *íyâthâm*	ईयातां *íyâtâm*	ईमहि *ímahi*	ईध्वं *ídhvam*	ईरन् *íran*
सु *su*	सुनु *sunu*	सुन्वीय *sunvíyá*	सुन्वीथाः *sunvíthâḥ*	सुन्वीत *sunvíta*	सुन्वीवहि *sunvíváhi*	सुन्वीयाथां *sunvíyâthâm*	सुन्वीयातां *sunvíyâtâm*	सुन्वीमहि *sunvímáhi*	सुन्वीध्वं *sunvídhvám*	सुन्वीरन् *sunvírán*
तन् *tan*	तनु *tanu*	तन्वीय *tanvíyá*	तन्वीथाः *tanvíthâḥ*	तन्वीत *tanvíta*	तन्वीवहि *tanvíváhi*	तन्वीयाथां *tanvíyâthâm*	तन्वीयातां *tanvíyâtâm*	तन्वीमहि *tanvímáhi*	तन्वीध्वं *tanvídhvám*	तन्वीरन् *tanvírán*
क्री *krî*	क्रीणी क्रीण् *krîṇî krîṇ*	क्रीणीय *krîṇíyá*	क्रीणीथाः *krîṇíthâḥ*	क्रीणीत *krîṇíta*	क्रीणीवहि *krîṇíváhi*	क्रीणीयाथां *krîṇíyâthâm*	क्रीणीयातां *krîṇíyâtâm*	क्रीणीमहि *krîṇímáhi*	क्रीणीध्वं *krîṇídhvám*	क्रीणीरन् *krîṇírán*
अद् *ad*	अद *ad*	अदीय *adíyá*	अदीथाः *adíthâḥ*	अदीत *adíta*	अदीवहि *adíváhi*	अदीयाथां *adíyâthâm*	अदीयातां *adíyâtâm*	अदीमहि *adímáhi*	अदीध्वं *adídhvám*	अदीरन् *adírán*
हु *hu*	जुहु *juhu*	जुह्वीय *júhvíya*	जुह्वीथाः *júhvíthâḥ*	जुह्वीत *júhvíta*	जुह्वीवहि *júhvívahi*	जुह्वीयाथां *júhvíyâthâm*	जुह्वीयातां *júhvíyâtâm*	जुह्वीमहि *júhvímahi*	जुह्वीध्वं *júhvídhvam*	जुह्वीरन् *júhvíran*
रुध् *rudh*	रुंध *rundh*	रुंधीय *rundhíyá*	रुंधीथाः *rundhíthâḥ*	रुंधीत *rundhíta*	रुंधीवहि *rundhíváhi*	रुंधीयाथां *rundhíyâthâm*	रुंधीयातां *rundhíyâtâm*	रुंधीमहि *rundhímáhi*	रुंधीध्वं *rundhídhvám*	रुंधीरन् *rundhírán*

ÂTMANEPADA.
Imperative.

Root.	Verbal Base.	ए e	स्व sva	तां tâm	अवहै avahai	इथां ithâm	इतां itâm	आमहै amahai	ध्वं dhvam	न्तां ntâm
	First Division.									
भू bhû	भव bhava	भवै bhávai	भवस्व bhávasva	भवतां bhávatâm	भवावहै bhávávahai	भवेथां bhávethâm	भवेतां bhávetâm	भवामहै bhávámahai	भवध्वं bhávadhvam	भवंतां bhávantâm
तुद् tud	तुद tuda	तुदै tudai	तुदस्व tudásva	तुदतां tudátâm	तुदावहै tuddávahai	तुदेथां tudéthâm	तुदेतां tudétâm	तुदामहै tuddámahai	तुदध्वं tudádhvam	तुदंतां tudántâm
दिव् div	दीव्य dívya	दीव्यै dívyai	दीव्यस्व dívyasva	दीव्यतां dívyatâm	दीव्यावहै dívyávahai	दीव्येथां dívyethâm	दीव्येतां dívyetâm	दीव्यामहै dívyámahai	दीव्यध्वं dívyadhvam	दीव्यंतां dívyantâm
चुर् chur	चोरय choraya	चोरयै choráyai	चोरयस्व choráyasva	चोरयतां choráyatâm	चोरयावहै choráyávahai	चोरयेथां choráyethâm	चोरयेतां choráyetâm	चोरयामहै choráyámahai	चोरयध्वं choráyadhvam	चोरयंतां choráyantâm
	Second Division.	ऐ ai	स्व sva	तां tâm	आवहै ávahai	आथां âthâm	आतां âtâm	आमहै ámahai	ध्वं dhvam	अतां atâm
सु su	सुनु सुनो sunu suno	सुनवै sunávai	सुनुष्व sunushvá	सुनुतां sunutâm	सुनवावहै sunávávahai	सुन्वाथां sunvâthâm	सुन्वातां sunvâtâm	सुनवामहै sunávámahai	सुनुध्वं sunudhvám	सुन्वातां sunvâtâm
तन् tan	तनु तनो tanu tano	तनवै tanávai	तनुष्व tanushvá	तनुतां tanutâm	तनवावहै tanávávahai	तन्वाथां tanvâthâm	तन्वातां tanvâtâm	तनवामहै tanávámahai	तनुध्वं tanudhvám	तन्वातां tanvâtâm
क्री krî	क्रीणी क्रीणा क्रीण krîṇî krîṇâ krîṇ	क्रीणै krîṇai	क्रीणीष्व krîṇîshvá	क्रीणीतां krîṇîtâm	क्रीणावहै krîṇávahai	क्रीणाथां krîṇâthâm	क्रीणातां krîṇâtâm	क्रीणामहै krîṇámahai	क्रीणीध्वं krîṇîdhvám	क्रीणातां krîṇâtâm
अद् ad	अद् अद ad ad	अदै ádai	अत्स्व atsvá	अत्तां attâm	अदावहै ádávahai	अदाथां addâthâm	अदातां addâtâm	अदामहै ádámahai	अद्ध्वं addhvám	अदातां adâtâm
हु hu	जुहु जुहो juhu juho	जुहवै júhavai	जुहुष्व juhushvá	जुहुतां juhutâm	जुहवावहै júhavávahai	जुह्वाथां júhvâthâm	जुह्वातां júhvâtâm	जुहवामहै júhavámahai	जुहुध्वं juhudhvám	जुह्वातां júhvatâm
रुध् rudh	रुन्ध रुणध् rundh ruṇadh	रुणध्है ruṇádhai	रुन्त्स्व runtsvá	रुन्द्धां runddhâm	रुणध्वावहै ruṇádhávahai	रुन्धाथां rundhâthâm	रुन्धातां rundhâtâm	रुन्द्धामहै runddhámahai	रुन्द्ध्वं runddhvám	रुन्धातां rundhâtâm

CHAPTER X.

GENERAL OR UNMODIFIED TENSES.

§ 323. In the tenses which remain, the Reduplicated Perfect, the Periphrastic Perfect, the First and Second Aorist, the Future, the Conditional, the Periphrastic Future, and Benedictive, the distinction of the ten classes vanishes. All verbs are treated alike, to whatever class they belong in the modified tenses; and the distinguishing features, the inserted नु *nu*, उ *u*, नी *nî*, &c., are removed again from the roots to which they had been attached in the Present, the Imperfect, the Optative, and Imperative. Only the verbs of the Chur class preserve their अय *áya* throughout, except in the Aorist and Benedictive.

Reduplicated Perfect.

§ 324. The root in its primitive state is reduplicated. The rules of reduplication have been given above. (§ 302–319.)

§ 325. The Reduplicated Perfect can be formed of all verbs, except

1. Monosyllabic roots which begin with any vowel prosodially long but अ *a* or आ *á:* such as ईड् *íḍ*, to praise; एध् *edh*, to grow; इन्ध् *indh*, to light; उंद् *und*, to wet.

2. Polysyllabic roots, such as चकास् *chakás*, to be bright.

3. Verbs of the Chur class and derivative verbs, such as Causatives, Desideratives, Intensives, Denominatives.

§ 326. Verbs which cannot form the Perfect by reduplication, form the Periphrastic Perfect by means of composition. (§ 340.)

So do likewise दय् *day*, to pity, &c., अय् *ay*, to go, आस् *ás*, to sit down (Pân. iii. 1, 37), कास् *kás*, to cough (Pân. iii. 1, 35); also कास् *kás*, to shine (Sâr.); optionally उष् *ush*, to burn, (ओषां *oshám*), विद् *vid*, to know, (विदां *vidám*), जागृ *jágri*, to wake, (जागरां *jágarám*, Pân. iii. 1, 38); and, after taking reduplication, भी *bhî* (बिभयां *bibhayám*), ह्री *hrî* (जिह्रयां *jihrayám*), भृ *bhṛi* (बिभरां *bibharám*), and हु *hu* (जुहवां *juhavám*, Pân. iii. 1, 39).

The verb ऊर्णु *úrṇu*, to cover, although polysyllabic, allows only of ऊर्णुनाव *úrṇunáva* as its Perfect.

ऋछ् *richh*, to fail, although its base in the Perfect ends in two consonants, forms only आनर्च्छ *ánarchchha*. It is treated, in fact, as if अर्छ् *archchh*. (§ 313.)

Terminations of the Reduplicated Perfect.

SINGULAR.

1.	अ *a*		ए *e*
2.	इथ *itha*		इषे *ishe*
3.	अ *a*		ए *e*

DUAL.

1. इव *iva*		इवहे *ivahe*
2. अयु: *athuḥ*		आथे *âthe*
3. अतु: *atuḥ*		आते *âte*

PLURAL.

1. इम *ima*		इमहे *imahe*
2. अ *a*		इध्वे *idhve* or इढ्वे *iḍhve*
3. उ: *uḥ*		इरे *ire*

These terminations are here given, without any regard to the systems of native or comparative grammarians, in that form in which they may be mechanically added to the reduplicated roots. The rules on the omission of the initial इ *i* of certain terminations will be given below.

§ 327. The accent falls on the terminations in the Parasmaipada and Âtmanepada, except in the *three persons singular Parasmaipada*. In these the accent falls on the root, which therefore is strengthened according to the following rules :

1. Vowels capable of Guṇa, take Guṇa throughout the singular, if followed by one consonant.

भिद् *bhid*, बिभेद *bibhéd-a*, बिभेदिथ *bibhéd-itha*, बिभेद *bibhéd-a*.

बुध् *budh*, बुबोध *bubódh-a*, बुबोधिथ *bubódh-itha*, बुबोध *bubódh-a*.

But जीव् *jîv*, a long medial vowel not being liable to Guṇa, forms जिजीव *jijîv-a*, जिजीविथ *jijîv-itha*, जिजीव *jijîv-a*.

2. Final vowels take Vṛiddhi or Guṇa in the first, Guṇa in the second, Vṛiddhi only in the third person singular.

नी *nî*, निनाय *nináy-a* or निनय *nináy-a*, निनेथ *ninétha* or निनयिथ *nináy-itha*, निनाय *nináy-a*.

3. अ *a* if followed by a single consonant, takes Vṛiddhi or Guṇa in the first, Guṇa in the second, Vṛiddhi only in the third person singular.

हन् *han*, जघान *jaghán-a* or जघन *jaghán-a*, जघनिथ *jaghán-itha*, जघान *jaghán-a*.

Note—If the second person singular Parasmaipada is formed by थ *tha*, the accent falls on the root; if with इथ *itha*, the accent may fall on any syllable, but generally it is on the termination. In this case the radical vowel may, in certain verbs, be without Guṇa, विज् *vij*, विवेज *vivéja*, but विविजिथ *vivijitha*. (Pân. I. 2, 2; 3.)

§ 328. As there is a tendency to strengthen the base in the three persons singular Parasmaipada, so there is a tendency to weaken the base, under certain circumstances, before the other terminations of the Perfect, Parasmai and Âtmanepada. Here the following rules must be observed :

1. Roots like पत् *pat*, i. e. roots in which अ *a* is preceded and followed by a single consonant, and which in their reduplicated syllable repeat the initial consonant without any change (this excludes roots beginning with aspirates and with gutturals; roots beginning with व *v*, and

श्रस् *śas* * and दद् *dad* are likewise excepted), contract such forms as पपत् *papat* into पेत् *pet*, before the accented terminations, (including इथ *itha*, Pân. VI. 4, 120, 121.)

पच् *pach*, पपक्थ *papáktha*, but पेचिथ *pechithá*, पेचिम *pechimá*, पेचु: *pechúḥ*. तन् *tan*, तेनिथ *tenithá*, तेनिम *tenimá*, तेनु: *tenúḥ*.

2. Roots mentioned in § 311 take their weak form.

वह् *vah*, उवाह *uváha*, ऊहिम *úhimá*.　वच् *vach*, उवाच *uvácha*, ऊचु: *úchúḥ*.

Note—The roots तृ *tṛí*, फल् *phal*, भज् *bhaj*, त्रप् *trap*, श्रथ् *śrath* (Pân. VI. 4, 122), and राध् *rádh*, in the sense of 'killing' (123), form their Reduplicated Perfect like पत् *pat*. The roots जृ *jṛí*, भ्रम् *bhram*, and त्रस् *tras* (124) may do so optionally; and likewise फण् *phaṇ*, राज् *ráj*, भ्रज् *bhráj*, भ्राश् *bhráś*, भ्लाश् *bhláś*, स्यम् *syam*, स्वन् *svan*.

3. The roots गम् *gam*, हन् *han*, जन् *jan*, खन् *khan*, घस् *ghas* drop their radical vowel.　(Pân. VI. 4, 98.)

गम् *gam*, जग्मतु: *jagmátuḥ*.　हन् *han*, जघ्नतु: *jaghnátuḥ*.　खन् *khan*, चख्नतु: *chakhnátuḥ*.　घस् *ghas*, जक्षतु: *jakshátuḥ*.

4. Roots ending in more than one consonant, particularly in consonants preceded by a nasal (Pân. I. 2, 5), such as मन्थ् *manth*, स्रंस् *sraṁs*, &c., do not drop their nasal in the weakening forms.　Ex. 3rd pers. dual: बभ्रज्जतु: *babhrajjátuḥ*; ममन्थतु: *mamanthátuḥ*; सस्रंसे *sasraṁsé*.

5. The verbs श्रन्थ् *śranth*, ग्रन्थ् *granth*, दम्भ् *dambh*, and स्वञ्ज् *svañj*, however, may be weakened, and form श्रेथतु: *śrethátuḥ*, ग्रेथतु: *grethátuḥ*, देभतु: *debhátuḥ*, सस्वजे *sasvajé* (loss of nasal and e, cf. Pân. I. 2, 6, vârt.).　But according to some grammarians the forms सश्रन्थतु: *saśranthátuḥ* &c. are more correct.

§ 329. Roots ending in आ *á*, and many roots ending in diphthongs, drop their final vowel before all terminations beginning with a vowel (Pân. VI. 4, 64). In the general tenses, verbs ending in diphthongs are treated like verbs ending in आ *á*.

The same roots take औ *au* for the termination of the first and third persons singular Parasmaipada.

दा *dá*, ददौ *dad-aú*, ददिव *dad-ivá*, ददतु: *dad-áthuḥ*, ददिरे *dad-iré*.

म्लै *mlai*, मम्लौ *maml-aú*, मम्लिव *maml-ivá*, मम्लतु: *maml-áthuḥ*, मम्लिरे *maml-iré*. Except व्ये *vye*, ह्वे *hve*, &c.; see § 311.

§ 330. Roots ending in इ *i*, ई *í*, ऋ *ṛi*, if preceded by one consonant, change their vowels, before terminations beginning with vowels, into य् *y*, र् *r*.

If preceded by more than one consonant, they change their vowels into इय् *iy*, अर् *ar* †. (§ 221.)

---

* श्रसु हिंसायामिति केचित् केचिच्च शश मुतगतात्विति । Prasâda, p. 13 a.　In a later passage the Prasâda (p. 17 b) decides for both, श्रस् *śas* and श्रश् *śaś*.

† ऋ *ṛi* forms the perf. आर *ára*, 3rd pers. dual आरतु: *árátuḥ*.　ऋछ् *ṛichh* forms आनर्छ *ánárchchha*, 3rd pers. dual आनर्छतु: *ánarchchhátuḥ*.　(Pân. VII. 4, 11.)

Roots ending in उ *u,* ऊ *û,* change these vowels always into उव् *uv.*

Most roots ending in ऋ *ṛi,* change the vowel to अर् *ar* (Pâṇ. VII. 4, 11). गृ *gṛi,* जगरतुः *jagarâtuḥ* *.

नी *nî,* निन्यिव *niny-ivá,* we two have led.   श्रि *śri,* शिश्रियिव *śiśriy-ivá,* we two have gone.   कृ *kṛi,* चक्रथुः *chakr-áthuḥ,* you two have done.   स्तृ *stṛi,* तस्तरथुः *tastar-áthuḥ,* you two have spread.   यु *yu,* युयुवथुः *yuyuv-áthuḥ,* you two have joined.   स्तु *stu,* तुष्टुवथुः *tushṭuv-áthuḥ,* you two have praised.   कॄ *kṝi,* चकरथुः *chakar-áthuḥ,* you two have scattered.

<hr>

CHAPTER XI.

THE INTERMEDIATE इ *i.*

§ 331. Before we can proceed to form the paradigms of the Reduplicated Perfect by means of joining the terminations with the root, it is necessary to consider the intermediate इ *i,* which in the Reduplicated Perfect and in the other unmodified tenses has to be inserted between the verbal base and the terminations, originally beginning with consonants.   The rules which *require, allow,* or *prohibit* the insertion of this इ *i* form one of the most difficult chapters of Sanskrit grammar, and it is the object of the following paragraphs to simplify these rules as much as possible.

The general tendency, and, so far, the general rule, is that the terminations of the unmodified or general tenses, originally beginning with consonants, insert the vowel इ *i* between base and termination; and from an historical point of view it would no doubt be more correct to speak of the rules which require the addition of an intermediate इ *i* than (as has been done in § 326) to represent the इ *i* as an integral part of the terminations, and to give the rules which require its omission.   But as the intermediate इ *i* has prevailed in the vast majority of verbs, it will be easier, for practical purposes, to state the exceptions, i. e. the cases in which the इ *i* is not employed, instead of defining the cases in which it *must* or *may* be inserted.

One termination only, that of the 3rd pers. plur. Perf. Âtm., इरे *ire,* keeps the intermediate इ *i* under all circumstances.   In the Veda, however, this इ *i,* too, has not yet become fixed, and is occasionally omitted; e. g. दुदुह्रे *duduh-ré.*

<hr>

* In कॄ *kṝi,* दॄ *dṛi,* and पॄ *pṝi* a further shortening may take place; शशरतुः *śaśarátuḥ* being shortened to शश्रतुः *śaśrátuḥ,* &c.   (Pâṇ. VII. 4, 12.)

Let it be remembered then, that there are three points to be considered:

1. When is it *necessary* to omit the इ *i* ?
2. When is it *optional* to insert or to omit the इ *i* ?
3. When is it *necessary* to insert the इ *i* ?

For the purposes of reading Sanskrit, all that a student is obliged to know is, When it is *necessary* to omit the इ *i*. Even for writing Sanskrit this knowledge would be sufficient, for in all cases except those in which the omission is necessary, the इ *i* may safely be inserted, although, according to views of native grammarians, it may be equally right to omit it. A student therefore, and particularly a beginner, is safe if he only knows the cases in which इ *i* is necessarily omitted, nor will anything but extensive reading enable him to know the verbs in which the insertion is either optional or necessary. Native grammarians have indeed laid down a number of rules, but both before and after Pâṇini the language of India has changed, and even native grammarians are obliged to admit that on the optional insertion of इ *i* authorities differ; that is to say, that the literary language of India differed so much in different parts of that enormous country, and at different periods of its long history, that no rules, however minute, would suffice to register all its freaks and fancies.

§ 332. Taking as the starting-point the general axiom (Pâṇ. VII. 2, 35) that every termination beginning originally with a consonant (except य् *y*) takes the इ *i*, which we represent as a portion of the termination, we proceed to state the exceptions, i. e. the cases in which the इ *i* must on no account be inserted, or, as we should say, must be cut off from the beginning of the termination.

The following verbs, which have been carefully collected by native grammarians (Pâṇ. VII. 2, 10), are not allowed to take the intermediate इ *i* in the so-called general or unmodified tenses, before terminations or affixes beginning originally with a consonant (except य् *y*). (Note—The reduplicated perfect and its participle in वस् *vas* are not affected by these rules; see § 334.)

1. All monosyllabic roots ending in आ *â*.
2. All monosyllabic roots ending in इ *i*, except श्रि *śri*, to attend (21, 31)[*]; श्वि *śvi*, to grow (23, 41). (Note—स्मि *smi*, to laugh, must take इ *i* in the Desiderative. Pâṇ. VII. 2, 74.)
3. All monosyllabic roots ending in ई *î*, except डी *ḍî*, to fly (22, 72; 26, 26. *anudâtta*), and श्री *śî*, to rest (24, 22).
4. All monosyllabic roots ending in उ *u*, except यु *yu*, to mix (24, 23; not 31, 9); रु *ru*, to sound (24, 24); नु *nu*, to praise (24, 26; 28, 104?); क्षु *kshu*, to sound (24, 27); क्ष्णु *kshṇu*, to sharpen (24, 28). स्नु *snu*, to flow (24, 29), takes इ *i* in Parasmaipada (Pâṇ. VII. 2, 36). (Note—स्तु *stu*, to praise, and सु *su*, to pour, take इ *i* in the First Aorist Parasmaipada. Pâṇ. VII. 2, 72.)

---

[*] These figures refer to the Dhâtupâṭha in Westergaard's Radices Linguæ Sanscritæ, 1841.

5. All monosyllabic roots ending in ऋ *ṛi*, except वृ *vṛi*, to choose (31, 38).

Important exception : in the Fut. and Cond. in स्य *sya*, all verbs in ऋ *ṛi* take इ *i* (Pâṇ. VII. 2, 70).

स्वृ *svṛi*, to sound, *may* take इ *i* (Pâṇ. VII. 2, 44). भृ *bhṛi*, to carry, *may* take इ *i* in the Desider. (Pâṇ. VII. 2, 49). दृ *dṛi*, to regard, धृ *dhṛi*, to hold, and ऋ *ṛi*, to go, take इ *i* in the Desider. (Pâṇ. VII. 2, 74, 75).

In the Benedictive and First Aorist Âtmanepada verbs ending in ऋ *ṛi* and beginning with a conjunct consonant may take इ *i* (Pâṇ. VII. 2, 43).

6. All monosyllabic roots ending in ए *e*, ऐ *ai*, ओ *o*.

Therefore, with few exceptions, as mentioned above, all monosyllabic roots ending in vowels, except the vowels आ *â* and ऋ *ṛi*, must not take इ *i*.

7. Of roots ending in क् *k*, शक् *śak*, to be able (26, 78; 27, 15).

8. Of roots ending in च् *ch*, पच् *pach*, to cook (23, 27); वच् *vach*, to speak (24, 55); मुच् *much*, to loose (28, 136); सिच् *sich*, to sprinkle (28, 140); रिच् *rich*, to leave (29, 4); विच् *vich*, to separate (29, 5).

9. Of roots ending in छ् *chh*, प्रछ् *prachh*, to ask (28, 120). It must take इ *i* in the Desider. (Pâṇ. VII. 2, 75).

10. Of roots ending in ज् *j*, स्वञ्ज् *svañj*, to embrace (23, 7); त्यज् *tyaj*, to leave (23, 17); सञ्ज् *sañj*, to adhere (23, 18); भज् *bhaj*, to worship (23, 29); रञ्ज् *rañj*, to colour (23, 30; 26, 58); यज् *yaj*, to sacrifice (23, 33); निज् *nij*, to clean (25, 11); विज् *vij*, to separate (25, 12; not 28, 9, or 29, 23); [Kâś. मृज् *mṛij*]; युज् *yuj*, to meditate (26, 68), to join (29, 7); सृज् *sṛij*, to let off (26, 69; 28, 121); भ्रज्ज् *bhrajj*, to bake (28, 4, except Desider.); मज्ज् *majj*, to dip (28, 122); रुज् *ruj*, to break (28, 123); भुज् *bhuj*, to bend (28, 124), to protect (29, 17); भञ्ज् *bhañj*, to break (29, 16).

11. Of roots ending in द् *d*, हद् *had*, to evacuate (23, 8); स्कन्द् *skand*, to step (23, 10); अद् *ad*, to eat (24, 1); पद् *pad*, to go (26, 60); खिद् *khid*, to be distressed, &c. (26, 61; 28, 142; 29, 12); विद् *vid*, to be (26, 62); स्विद् *svid*, to sweat (26, 79); तुद् *tud*, to strike (28, 1); नुद् *nud*, to push (28, 2; 28, 132); सद् *sad*, to droop (28, 133); शद् *śad*, to perish (28, 134); विद् *vid*, to find (28, 138? 29, 13; not 24, 56); भिद् *bhid*, to cut (29, 2); छिद् *chhid*, to divide (29, 3); क्षुद् *kshud*, to pound (29, 6).

12. Of roots ending in ध् *dh*, बुध् *budh*, to know (26, 63); युध् *yudh*, to fight (26, 64); रुध् *rudh*, with अनु *anu*, to love (26, 65), to keep off (29, 1); राध् *râdh*, to grow (26, 71; 27, 16); व्यध् *vyadh*, to strike (26, 72); क्रुध् *krudh*, to be angry (26, 80); क्षुध् *kshudh*, to be hungry (26, 81), except Part. क्षुधित *kshudhita* and Ger. क्षुधित्वा *kshudhitvâ* (Pâṇ. VII. 2, 52); शुध् *śudh*, to clean (26, 82); सिध् *sidh*, to succeed (26, 83); साध् *sâdh*, to achieve (27, 16); बन्ध् *bandh*, to bind (31, 37).

13. Of roots ending in न् *n*, हन् *han*, to kill (24, 2), except the Fut. and Cond. (Pâṇ. VII. 2, 70); likewise its substitute वध् *badh*; मन् *man*, to think (26, 67).

14. Of roots ending in प् *p*, तिप् *tip*, to pour (10, 1?); सृप् *sṛip*, to go (23, 14); तप् *tap*, to heat (23, 16; 26, 50); शप् *śap*, to swear (23, 31; 26, 59); वप् *vap*, to sow (23, 34); स्वप् *svap*, to sleep (24, 60); आप् *âp*, to reach (27, 14); क्षिप् *kship*, to throw (28, 5); लुप् *lup*, to cut (28, 137); लिप् *lip*, to anoint (28, 139); छुप् *chhup*, to touch (28, 125). (Note— तृप् *tṛip* and दृप् *dṛip*, which are generally included, may take इ *i*, according to Pâṇ. VII. 2, 45.)

15. Of roots ending in भ् *bh*, रभ् *rabh*, to desire (23, 5); लभ् *labh*, to take (23, 6); यभ् *yabh*, coire (23, 11).

16. Of roots ending in म *m*, रम *ram*, to play (20, 23); नम *nam*, to incline (23, 12); यम *yam*, to cease (23, 15).   But these three take इ *i* in Aor. Par. (Pâṇ. VII. 2, 73).   गम *gam*, to go (23, 13), but it takes इ *i* before स *s* of Fut., Cond., and Desider. Par. (Pâṇ. VII. 2, 58).   Also क्रम *kram*, to step (13, 31), in Âtm. (Pâṇ. VII. 2, 36).

17. Of roots ending in श *ś*, क्रुश *kruś*, to shout (20, 26); दृश *driś*, to see (23, 19); दंश *daṁś*, to bite (23, 20); लिश *liś*, to be small (26, 70; 28, 127); दिश *diś*, to show (28, 3); रुश *ruś*, to hurt (28, 126); रिश *riś*, to hurt (28, 126); स्पृश *spriś*, to touch (28, 128); विश *viś*, to enter (28, 130); मृश *mriś*, to rub (28, 131).

18. Of roots ending in ष *sh*, कृष *krish*, to draw (23, 21; 28, 6); त्विष *tvish*, to shine (23, 32); द्विष *dvish*, to hate (24, 3); विष *vish*, to pervade (25, 13), to separate (31, 54; not 17, 47); पुष *push*, to nourish (26, 73; not 17, 50); शुष *śush*, to dry (26, 74); तुष *tush*, to please (26, 75); दुष *dush*, to spoil (26, 76); श्लिष *ślish*, to embrace (26, 77); शिष *śish*, to distinguish (29, 14); पिष *pish*, to pound (29, 15).

19. Of roots ending in स *s*, वस *vas*, to dwell (23, 36), except Part. उषित: *ushitaḥ* and Ger. उषित्वा *ushitvâ* (Pâṇ. VII. 2, 52); घस *ghas*, to eat (17, 65, as substitute for अद *ad*).

20. Of roots ending in ह *h*, रुह *ruh*, to grow (20, 29); दह *dah*, to burn (23, 22); मिह *mih*, to sprinkle (23, 23); वह *vah*, to carry (23, 35); दुह *duh*, to milk (24, 4; not 17, 87); दिह *dih*, to smear (24, 5); लिह *lih*, to lick (24, 6); नह *nah*, to bind (26, 57).

§ 333. Other roots there are, which must not take इ *i* in certain only of the general tenses.

A. In the future (formed by ता *tâ*), the future and conditional (formed by स्य *sya*), the desiderative, and the participle in त *ta* (Pâṇ. VII. 2, 15; 44), the verb क्लृप *klṛp* must not take इ *i*, if used in the Parasmaipada. (Pâṇ. VII. 2, 60.)

क्लृप *klṛp*, to shape, Fut. कल्प्ता *kalptâ*, Fut. कल्प्स्यति *kalpsyati*, Cond. अकल्प्स्यत *akalpsyat*; Desid. चिक्लृप्सति *chiklṛpsati*; Part. क्लृप्त: *klṛptaḥ*.

B. In the future and conditional (formed by स्य *sya*), the desiderative base, and the participle in त *ta*, the following four verbs must not take इ *i*, if used in the Parasmaipada. (Pâṇ. VII. 2, 59.)

वृत *vrit*, to exist, Fut. वर्त्स्यति *vartsyati*, Cond. अवर्त्स्यत *avartsyat*; Desid. विवृत्सति *vivritsati*; Part. वृत्त: *vrittaḥ*. (Pâṇ. VII. 2, 15; 56.)

वृध *vridh*, to grow, Fut. वर्त्स्यति *vartsyati*, Cond. अवर्त्स्यत *avartsyat*; Desid. विवृत्सति *vivritsati*; Part. वृद्ध: *vriddhaḥ*.

स्यंद *syand*, to drop, Fut. स्यंत्स्यति *syantsyati*, Cond. अस्यंत्स्यत *asyantsyat*; Desid. सिस्यंत्सति *sisyantsati*; Part. स्यन्न: *syannaḥ*.

सृध *śridh*, to hurt, Fut. शर्त्स्यति *śartsyati*, Cond. अशर्त्स्यत *aśartsyat*; Desid. शिशृत्सति *śiśritsati*; Part. सृद्ध: *śriddhaḥ*.

C. In the desiderative bases, and in the participle in त *ta*, monosyllabic roots ending in उ *u*, ऊ *û*, ऋ *ri*, ॠ *rî*, and ग्रह *grah*, to take, and गुह *guh*, to hide, do not take इ *i*. (Pâṇ. VII. 2, 12.)

भू *bhû*, to be, बुभूषति *bubhûshati*; Part. भूत: *bhûtaḥ*.

ग्रह *grah*, जिघृक्षति *jighrikshati*; Part. गृहीत: *grihîtaḥ* (long î by special rule, cf. Pâṇ. VII. 2, 37).

गुह *guh*, जुघुक्षति *jughukshati*; Part. गूढ: *gûḍhaḥ* (cf. Pâṇ. VII. 2, 44).

(Verbs ending in ऋ *ri* and वृ *vri* are liable to exceptions. See § 337. Pâṇ. VII. 2, 38-41.)

D. Participial formations.

1. Roots which *may* be without the इ *i* in any one of the general tenses, *must* be without it in the participle in त *ta*.

(Remark that the participle in त *ta* is most opposed, as the reduplicated perfect is most disposed to the admission of इ *i.*)

Monosyllabic roots ending in उ *u*, ऋ *ri*, ॠ *rí*, do not take इ *i* before the participle in त *ta*, nor before other terminations which tend to weaken a verbal base. (Pâṇ. VII. 2, 11.)

यु *yu*, to join, युतः *yu-taḥ*, युतवान् *yu-taván*, युत्वा *yu-tvá.* (Pâṇ. VII. 2, 11.)

लू *lú*, to cut, लूनः *lú-naḥ*, लूनवान् *lú-naván*, लूत्वा *lú-tvá.* (Except पू *pú*, § 335, II. 6.)

वृ *vṛi*, to cover, वृतः *vṛi-taḥ*, वृतवान् *vṛi-taván*, वृत्वा *vṛi-tvá.*

गाह् *gáh*, to enter, may form (Pâṇ. VII. 2, 44) the future as गाहिता *gáh-i-tá* or गाढा *gáḍhá;* hence its participle गाढः *gáḍhaḥ* only.

गुप् *gup*, to protect, may form (Pâṇ. VII. 2, 44) the future गोपिता *gop-i-tá* or गोप्ता *gop-tá;* hence its participle गुप्तः *guptaḥ* only.

2. Roots which by native grammarians are marked with technical आ *á* or ई *í* do not take इ *i* in the participle in त *ta.* (Pâṇ. VII. 2, 14, 16.) *

स्विद् *svid*, to sweat (marked as मिश्विदा *ñishvidá*); स्विन्नः *svinnaḥ.*

लज् *laj*, to be ashamed (marked as ओलजी *olají*); लग्नः *lagnaḥ.*

List of Participles in त *ta or* न *na which for special reasons and in special senses do not take* इ i.

श्रि *śri*, to go; श्रितः *śritaḥ*, श्रित्वा *śritvá.* (Pâṇ. VII. 2, 11.) See § 332, 2.

श्वि *śvi*, to swell; शूनः *śúnaḥ.* (Pâṇ. VII. 2, 14.) See § 332, 2.

क्षुभ् *kshubh*, to shake; क्षुब्धः *kshubdhaḥ*, if it means the churning-stick. (Pâṇ. VII. 2, 18.) See § 332, 15.

स्वन् *svan*, to sound; स्वान्तः *svántaḥ*, if it means the mind.

ध्वन् *dhvan*, to sound; ध्वान्तः *dhvántaḥ*, if it means darkness.

लग् *lag*, to be near; लग्नः *lagnaḥ*, if it means attached.

म्लेच्छ् *mlechchh*, to speak indistinctly; म्लिष्टः *mlishṭaḥ*, if it means indistinct.

विरेभ् *virebh*, to sound; विरिब्धः *viribdhaḥ*, if it refers to a note.

फण् *phaṇ*, to prepare; फाण्टः *pháṇṭaḥ*, if it means without an effort.

वाह् *váh*, to labour; वाढः *váḍhaḥ*, if it means excessive.

धृष् *dhṛish*, to be confident; धृष्टः *dhṛishṭaḥ*, if it means bold. (Pâṇ. VII. 2, 19.)

विशस् *viśas*, to praise; विशस्तः *viśastaḥ*, if it means arrogant.

दृह् *dṛih*, to grow; दृढः *dṛiḍhaḥ*, if it means strong. (Pâṇ. VII. 2, 20.)

परिवृह् *parivṛih*, to grow; परिवृढः *parivṛiḍhaḥ*, if it means lord. (Pâṇ. VII. 2, 21.)

कष् *kash*, to try; कष्टः *kashṭaḥ*, if it means difficult or impervious. (Pâṇ. VII. 2, 22.)

घुष् *ghush*, to manifest; घुष्टः *ghushṭaḥ*, if it does not mean proclaimed. (Pâṇ. VII. 2, 23.)

अर्द् *ard*, with the prepos. सं *sam*, नि *ni*, वि *vi*, अर्णः *arṇṇaḥ;* समर्णः *samarṇṇaḥ*, plagued. (Pâṇ. VII. 2, 24.)

अर्द् *ard*, with the prepos. अभि *abhi;* अभ्यर्णः *abhyarṇṇaḥ*, if it means near. (Pâṇ. VII. 2, 25.)

वृत् *vṛit* (as causative), वृत्तः *vṛittaḥ*, if it means read.

---

* मिद् *mid*, to be soft, though having a technical आ *á*, may, in certain senses, form its participle as मेदितः *meditaḥ* or मिन्नः *minnaḥ* (Pâṇ. VII. 2, 17). The same applies to all verbs marked by technical आ *á.*

Intermediate इ i *in the Reduplicated Perfect.*

§ 334. The preceding rules, prohibiting in a number of roots the इ *i* for all or most general tenses, do not affect the reduplicated perfect. Most of the verbs just enumerated which must omit इ *i* in all other general tenses, do not omit it in the perfect. So general, in fact, has the use of the इ *i* become in the perfect, that eight roots only are absolutely prohibited from taking it. These are (Pâṇ. VII. 2, 13),

1. कृ *kṛi*, to do, (unless it is changed to स्कृ *skṛi*), 1st pers. dual चकृव *chakṛi-va;* but संचस्करिव *saṁchaskariva;* 2nd pers. sing. संचस्करिथ *saṁchaskaritha.*

2. सृ *sṛi*, to go, ससृव *sasṛi-va.*

3. भृ *bhṛi*, to bear, बभृव *babhṛi-va.*

4. वृ *vṛi* (वृम् *vṛiṅ* and वृङ् *vṛiṅ**), to choose, Par. ववृव *vavṛi-va †*, Âtm. ववृवहे *vavṛi-vahe,* ववृषे *vavṛi-she.*

5. स्तु *stu*, to praise, तुष्टुव *tushṭu-va.* तुष्टोथ *tushṭo-tha.*

6. द्रु *dru*, to run, दुद्रुव *dudru-va.* दुद्रोथ *dudro-tha.*

7. स्रु *sru*, to flow, सुस्रुव *susru-va.* सुस्रोथ *susro-tha.*

8. श्रु *śru*, to hear, शुश्रुव *śuśru-va.* शुश्रोथ *śuśro-tha.*

§ 335. In the second person singular of the reduplicated perfect Par. the इ *i* before थ *tha* must necessarily be left out,

1. In the eight roots, enumerated before. (The form ववर्थ *vavar-tha*, however, being restricted to the Veda, ववरिथ *vavaritha* is considered the right form. See No. 142, in the Dhâtupâṭha.)

2. In roots ending in vowels, which are necessarily without इ *i* in the future (ता *tá*), Pâṇ. VII. 2, 61. See § 332, where these roots are given.

　　　या *yá*, to go; Fut. याता *yátá;* ययाथ *yayá-tha.*
　　　चि *chi*, to gather; Fut. चेता *chetá;* चिचेथ *chiche-tha.*

3. In roots ending in consonants and having an अ *ă* for their radical vowel, which are necessarily without इ *i* in the future (ता *tá*), Pâṇ. VII. 2, 62. See § 332, where these roots are given.

　　　पच् *pach*, to cook; Fut. पक्ता *paktá;* पपक्थ *papak-tha.*

But कृषति *kṛishati*, he drags; Fut. कर्ष्टा *karshṭá;* चकर्षिथ *chakarsh-i-tha.*

(Bharadvâja requires the omission of इ *i* after roots with ऋ *ṛi* only, which are necessarily without इ *i* in the periphrastic future (Pâṇ. VII. 2, 63), except root ऋ *ṛi* itself. Hence he allows पेचिथ *pechitha*, besides पपक्थ *papaktha;* इयजिथ *iyajitha*, besides इयष्ठ *iyashṭha:* also ययिथ *yayitha*, चिचयिथ *chichayitha*, &c.)

4. All other verbs ending in consonants with any other radical vowel but अ *a*, require इ *i*, and so do all verbs with which इ *i* is either optional or indispensable in the future (ता *tá*).

---

* वृम् *vṛiṅ*, (27, 8) वरणे *varaṇe*, Su. वृम् *vṛiṅ*, (34, 8) आवरणे *ávaraṇe*, Chur. वृङ् *vṛiṅ*, (31, 38) संभक्तौ *sambhaktau*, Kṛi.

† The form ववरिव *vavariva*, which Westergaard mentions, may be derived from another root वृ *vṛi*, the rule of Pâṇini being restricted by the commentator to वृम् *vṛiṅ* and वृङ् *vṛiṅ*.

Exceptions:

1. In सृज् *srij* and दृश् *dṛiś*, the omission is optional.

    सृज् *srij*, सस्रष्ट *sasrashṭha*, or ससृजिथ *sasrijitha*.

2. The verbs अत्ति *atti*, अर्ति *arti*, व्ययति *vyayati* must take इ *i.* § 338, 7.

    अद् *ad*, आदिथ *ād-i-tha*, (exception to No. 3.)

    ऋ *ṛi*, आरिथ *ār-i-tha*, (exception to No. 2.)

    व्ये *vye*, विव्ययिथ *vivyay-i-tha*, (exception to No. 2.)

Tables showing the cases in which the intermediate इ i *must* be omitted between the Unmodified *Root and the Terminations of the so-called General Tenses, originally beginning with a* *Consonant, except* य् y.

§ 336. In these tables त *ta* stands for the Past Participle; सन् *san* stands for the Desiderative; स्य *sya* for the Future and Conditional; ता *tá* for the Periphrastic Future; सिच् *sich* for the First Aorist; लिङ् *liṅ* for the Benedictive.

I. For all General Tenses, except the Reduplicated Perfect,

Omit इ *i,*

1. Before त *ta*, सन् *san*, स्य *sya*, ता *tá*, सिच् *sich*, लिङ् *liṅ* :

    In the verbs enumerated § 332.

2. Before त *ta*, सन् *san*, स्य *sya*, ता *tá* :

    In क्लृप् *kḷip*, if Parasmaipada. § 333, A.

3. Before त *ta*, सन् *san*, स्य *sya* :

    In वृत् *vṛit*, वृध् *vṛidh*, स्यन्द् *syand*, सृध् *sṛidh*, if Parasmaipada. § 333, B.

4. Before त *ta*, सन् *san* :

    In monosyllabic verbs ending in उ, ऊ, ऋ, ॠ *ṛí*, ग्रह् *grah*, and गुह् *guh*. § 333, C.

5. Before त *ta* :

    a. All verbs which by native grammarians are marked with ओ *d*, इ *i*, or अ *d* *.

    b. The verb श्रि *śri* and others enumerated in a general list, § 333, D.

II. For the Reduplicated Perfect,

Omit इ i,

1. Before all terminations, except इरे *ire* :

    In eight verbs, mentioned § 334.

2. Before थ *tha*, 2nd pers. sing.:

<table>
<tr><td>All verbs of § 332 ending in vowels</td><td rowspan="2">if without इ i in the periphrastic future.</td></tr>
<tr><td>All verbs of § 332 ending in consonants with अ a as radical vowel</td></tr>
</table>

Optional insertion of इ i.

§ 337. For practical purposes, as was stated before, it is sufficient to know when it would be wrong to use the intermediate इ *i;* for in all other cases, whatever the views of different grammarians, or the usage of different writers, it is safe to insert the इ *i.*

As native grammarians, however, have been at much pains to collect the cases in which इ *i* must or may be inserted, a short abstract of their rules may here follow, which the early student may safely pass by.

---

* The technical अ *d* shows that in the other general tenses the इ *i* is optional. § 337, I. 2.

इ i *may or may not* be inserted:

I. Before any *árdhadhátuka* (i. e. an affix of the general tenses not requiring the modified verbal base) beginning with consonants, except य् *y.*

1. In the verbs स्वृ *svṛi;* Per. Fut. स्वरिता *svar-i-tá,* or स्वर्ता *svartá,* &c. (Pâṇ. VII. 2, 44.) (Except future in स्य *sya,* स्वरिष्यति *svarishyati* only. Pâṇ. VII. 2, 70.)

सू *sú* (as Ad and Div, not as Tud), सविता *sav-i-tá,* or सोता *sotá,* &c.

धू *dhú* (not as Tud), धविता *dhav-i-tá,* or धोता *dhotá,* &c. (Except aorist Parasmaipada, which must take इ *i.* Pâṇ. VII. 2, 72.)

2. In all verbs having a technical ऊ *ú* (Pâṇ. VII. 2, 44). गाह् *gáh,* Per. Fut. गाहिता *gáh-i-tá,* or गाढा *gáḍhá.* (See § 333, D. 1.)

But अन्ज् *añj* (though marked अन्जू *añjú*) *must* take इ *i* in the first aorist. (Pâṇ. VII. 2, 71.) आञ्जिषुः *áñjishuḥ.*

3. In the eight verbs beginning with रध् *radh.* (Pâṇ. VII. 2, 45.)

(26, 84) रध् *radh,* to perish, रधिता *radh-i-tá,* or रद्धा *raddhá.*

(26, 85) नश् *naś,* to vanish, नशिता *naś-i-tá,* or नंष्टा *naṁshṭá.*

(26, 86) तृप् *tṛip,* to delight, तर्पिता *tarp-i-tá,* or तर्प्ता *tarptá,* or त्राप्ता *traptá.*

(26, 87) दृप् *dṛip,* to be proud, दर्पिता *darp-i-tá,* or दर्प्ता *darptá,* or द्राप्ता *draptá.*

(26, 88) द्रुह् *druh,* to hate, द्रोहिता *droh-i-tá,* or द्रोग्धा *drogdhá,* or द्रोढा *droḍhá.*

(26, 89) मुह् *muh,* to be bewildered, मोहिता *moh-i-tá,* or मोग्धा *mogdhá,* or मोढा *moḍhá.*

(26, 90) स्नुह् *snuh,* to vomit, स्नोहिता *snoh-i-tá,* or स्नोग्धा *snogdhá,* or स्नोढा *snoḍhá.*

(26, 91) स्निह् *snih,* to love, स्नेहिता *sneh-i-tá,* or स्नेग्धा *snegdhá,* or स्नेढा *sneḍhá.*

According to some this option extends to the reduplicated perfect; but this is properly denied by others.

4. In the verb कुष् *kush* (Chur class), preceded by निर् *nir;* but here इ *i* is necessary in the participle with त *ta.* (Pâṇ. VII. 2, 46; 47.)

इ i *may or may not* be inserted:

II. Before certain *árdhadhátukas* only:

1. Before *árdhadhátukas* beginning with त *t:*

In the verbs इष् *ish* (Tud only), सह् *sah,* लुभ् *lubh,* रुष् *rush,* रिष् *rish.* (Pâṇ. VII. 2, 48.) The participles in त *ta* or न *na* are treated separately under No. 7. Hence इष्टः *ishṭaḥ* only, but either इष्ट्वा *ishṭvá* or इषित्वा *ishitvá.*

2. Before *árdhadhátukas* beginning with स *s,* but not in the aorist:

In the verbs कृत् *kṛit,* to cut; चृत् *chṛit,* to kill; छृद् *chhṛid,* to play; तृद् *tṛid,* to strike; नृत् *nṛit,* to dance. (Pâṇ. VII. 2, 57.)

3. Before the termination of the desiderative base (सन् *san*):

In the verb वृ *vṛi,* and all verbs ending in ऋ *ṛí.* (Pâṇ. VII. 2, 41.)

In the verbs ending in इव् *iv,* and in रिध् *ridh,* भ्रस्ज् *bhrasj,* दम्भ् *dambh,* श्रि *śri,* स्वृ *svṛi,* यु *yu,* ऊर्णु *úrṇu,* भृ *bhṛi* (Bhû class), ज्ञप् *jñap,* सन् *san;* also तन् *tan,* पत् *pat,* दरिद्रा *daridrá.* (Pâṇ. VII. 2, 49.)

4. Before the terminations of the benedictive (लिङ् *liṅ*) and first aorist (सिच् *sich*) in the Âtmanepada:

In the verb वृ *vṛi,* and all verbs ending in ऋ *ṛí* (Pâṇ. VII. 2, 42). The ऋ *ṛí* is changed into ईर् *ír* or अर् *ár.*

In verbs ending in ऋ *ṛi* and beginning with a conjunct consonant. (Pâṇ. VII. 2, 43.)

5. Before the gerundial termination त्वा *tvá :*

In verbs having a technical उ *u.*   (Pân. VII. 2, 56.)

शम् *śam* (शमु *śamu*), शमित्वा *śamitvá* or शान्त्वा *śántvá.*

6. Before the gerundial termination त्वा *tvá* and the participle in त *ta :*

In the verb क्लिश् *kliś.*   (Pân. VII. 2, 50.)

क्लिशित्वा *kliśitvá* or क्लिष्ट्वा *klishtvá,* क्लिशित: *kliśitaḥ* or क्लिष्ट: *klishṭaḥ.*

In the verb पू *pú.*   (Pân. VII. 2, 51.)

पवित्वा *pavitvá* or पूत्वा *pútvá,* पवित: *pavitaḥ* or पूत: *pútaḥ.*   It must take इ *i* in the desiderative (Pân. VII. 2, 74).

7. Before the participial terminations त *ta* or न *na;* (see also § 333, D. 2, note):

In the verbs दम् *dam,* to tame, दान्त: *dántaḥ* or दमित: *damitaḥ.*   (Pân. VII. 2, 27.)

शम् *śam,* to quiet, शान्त: *śántaḥ* or शमित: *śamitaḥ.*

पूर् *púr,* to fill, पूर्ण: *púrṇaḥ* or पूरित: *púritaḥ.*

दस् *das,* to perish, दस्त: *dastaḥ* or दासित: *dásitaḥ.*

स्पश् *spaś,* to touch, स्पष्ट: *spashṭaḥ* or स्पाशित: *spáśitaḥ.*

छद् *chhad,* to cover, छन्न: *chhannaḥ* or छादित: *chháditaḥ.*

ज्ञप् *jñap,* to inform, ज्ञप्त: *jñaptaḥ* or ज्ञपित: *jñapitaḥ.*

रुष् *rush,* to hurt, रुष्ट: *rushṭaḥ* or रुषित: *rushitaḥ.* (Pân. VII. 2, 28.)

अम् *am,* to go, आन्त: *ántaḥ* or अमित: *amitaḥ.*

त्वर् *tvar,* to hasten, तूर्ण: *túrṇaḥ* or त्वरित: *tvaritaḥ.*

संघुष् *saṅ-ghush,* to shout, संघुष्ट: *saṅghushṭaḥ* or संघुषित: *saṅghushitaḥ.* (See § 333, D. 2.)

आस्वन् *ásvan,* to sound, आस्वान्त: *ásvántaḥ* or आस्वनित: *ásvanitaḥ.* (See § 333, D. 2.)

हृष् *hṛish,* to rejoice, हृष्ट: *hṛishṭaḥ* or हृषित: *hṛishitaḥ,* if applied to horripilation. (Pân. VII. 2, 29.)

अपचि *apa-chi,* to honour, अपचित: *apachitaḥ* or अपचायित: *apacháyitaḥ* *.

8. Before the participle of the reduplicated perfect in वस् *vas :*

In the verbs गम् *gam,* to go, जग्मिवान् *jagmiván* or जगन्वान् *jaganván* †.

हन् *han,* to kill, जघ्निवान् *jaghniván* or जघन्वान् *jaghanván.*

विद् *vid,* to know, विविदिवान् *vividiván* or विविद्वान् *vividván.*

विश् *viś,* to enter, विविशिवान् *viviśiván* or विविश्वान् *viviśván.*

दृश् *dṛiś,* to see, ददृशिवान् *dadṛiśiván* or ददृश्वान् *dadṛiśván.*

Necessary insertion of इ i.

§ 338. इ *i* must be inserted in all verbs in which, as stated before, it is neither prohibited, nor only optionally allowed (Pân. VII. 2, 35). Besides these, the following special cases may be mentioned:

1. Before वस् *vas,* participle of reduplicated perfect:

In the verbs ending in आ *á* (Pân. VII. 2, 67). पा *pá,* पपिवान् *papiván.*

In the verbs reduced to a single syllable in the reduplicated perfect (Pân. VII. 2, 67).

अश् *aś,* to eat, आशिवान् *áśiván.*

In the verb घस् *ghas,* to eat, जक्षिवान् *jakshiván.*

Other verbs reject it.

---

* Pân. VII. 2, 30.   † Pân. VII. 2, 68.

2. Before स्य *sya* of the future and conditional :

> In all verbs ending in ऋ *ṛi*, and in हन् *han* (Pâṇ. VII. 2, 70). In गम् *gam*, if used in the Parasmaipada (Pâṇ. VII. 2, 58).

3. Before the terminations of the first aorist (सिच् *sich*) :

> In the verbs स्तु *stu,* सु *su,* धू *dhû* in the Parasmaipada (Pâṇ. VII. 2, 72). Thus from स्तु *stu,* to praise, First Aorist (First Form), अस्ताविषं *astâvisham;* but in the Âtmanepada, अस्तोषि *astoshi.*

4. Before the terminations of the desiderative (सन् *san*) :

> In the verbs कृ *kṛi,* गृ *gṛi,* दृ *dṛi,* धृ *dhṛi,* and प्रछ् *prachh* (Pâṇ. VII. 2, 75); and in गम् *gam,* if used in the Parasmaipada (Pâṇ. VII. 2, 58).
>
> In the verbs स्मि *smi,* पू *pû,* ऋ *ṛi,* अंज् *añj,* and अश् *aś.* (Pâṇ. VII. 2, 74.)

5. Before the gerundial त्वा *tvâ* and the participial termination त *ta.* (Pâṇ. VII. 2, 52–54.)

> In the verbs वस् *vas,* to dwell; क्षुध् *kshudh,* to hunger; अंच् *añch,* to worship; लुभ् *lubh,* to confound (Dhâtupâṭha 28, 22).

6. Before त्वा *tvâ* only :

> In जॄ *jṛî,* to grow old; व्रश्च् *vraśch,* to cut. (Pâṇ. VII. 2, 55.)

7. Before थ *tha,* 2nd pers. sing. reduplicated perfect :

> In अद् *ad,* to eat; ऋ *ṛi,* to go; व्ये *vye,* to cover. आदिथ *âditha,* against § 335, 3; आरिथ *âritha,* § 335, 3, note; विव्ययिथ *vivyayitha.*

§ 339. The vowel इ *i* thus inserted is never liable to Guṇa or Vṛiddhi.

Insertion of the long ई î.

§ 340. Long ई *î* may be substituted for the short when subjoined to a verb ending in ऋ *ṛi,* also to वृ *vṛi,* except in the reduplicated perfect, the aorist Parasmaipada, and the benedictive. (Pâṇ. VII. 2, 38–40.)

ऋ *tṛî;* Per. Fut. तरीता *tarîtâ* or तरिता *taritâ,* &c.; but Perf. 2nd pers. sing. तेरिथ *teritha;* I. Aor. Par. 3rd pers. plur. अतारिषुः *atârishuḥ;* Bened. 3rd pers. sing. तरिषीष्ट *tarishîshṭa* *.

वृ *vṛi;* Per. Fut. वरीता *varîtâ* or वरिता *varitâ;* but Perf. ववरिथ *vavaritha;* Aor. Par. अवारिषुः *avârishuḥ;* Bened. वरिषीष्ट *varishîshṭa.*

§ 341. In the desiderative and in the aorist Âtm. and benedictive Âtm. these verbs may or may not have इ *i* (Pâṇ. VII. 2, 41–42), which, if used, is liable to be changed to ई *î;* not, however, as far as I can judge, in the benedictive Âtmanepada.

ऋ *tṛî;* Des. तितरिषति *titarishati;* तितरीषति *titarîshati;* तितीर्षति *titîrshati;* Aor. Âtm. अतरिष्ट *atarishṭa,* अतरीष्ट *atarîshṭa,* and अतीर्ष्ट *atîrshṭa;* Bened. तरिषीष्ट *tarishîshṭa,* तीर्षीष्ट *tîrshîshṭa.*

वृ *vṛi;* Des. विवरिषते *vivarishate;* विवरीषते *vivarîshate;* वुवूर्षते *vuvûrshate;* Aor. Âtm. अवरिष्ट *avarishṭa,* अवरीष्ट *avarîshṭa,* and अवृष्ट *avṛita;* Bened. वरिषीष्ट *varishîshṭa,* वृषीष्ट *vṛishîshṭa.*

The verb ग्रह् *grah,* too, takes the long ई *î,* except in the reduplicated perfect, the desiderative, and certain tenses of the passive. (Pâṇ. VII. 2, 37.)

ग्रह् *grah;* Per. Fut. ग्रहीता *grahîtâ;* Inf. ग्रहीतुं *grahîtum;* but Perf. जगृहिम *jagṛihima.*

---

* The forms given in the Calcutta edition of Pâṇini VII. 2, 42, वरीषीष्ट *varîshîshṭa,* स्तरीषीष्ट *starîshîshṭa,* are wrong. (See Pâṇ. VII. 2, 39.)

Periphrastic Perfect.

§ 342. Verbs which, according to § 325, cannot form a reduplicated perfect, form their perfect by affixing आं *ám* (an accusative termination of a feminine abstract noun in आ *á*) to the verbal base, and adding to this the reduplicated perfect of कृ *kṛi*, to do, भू *bhú*, to be, or अस् *as*, to be.

उंद् *und*, to wet, उंदांचकार, बभूव, आस, *undáṁchakára, babhúva, ása.*

चकास् *chakás*, to shine, चकासांचकार, बभूव, आस, *chakásáṁchakára, babhúva, ása.*

बोधय *bodhaya*, to make known, बोधयांचकार, बभूव, आस, *bodhayáṁchakára, babhúva, ása.*

After verbs which are used in the Âtmanepada, the auxiliary verb कृ *kṛi* is conjugated as Âtmanepada, but अस् *as* and भू *bhú* in the Parasmaipada. Hence from एधते *edhate*, he grows,

एधांचक्रे *edh-áṁchakre;* but बभूव *babhúva* and आस *ása.*

In the passive all three auxiliary verbs follow the Âtmanepada.

§ 343. Intensive bases which can take Guṇa, take it before आं *áṁ;* desiderative bases never admit of Guṇa. (§ 339.)

बोभू *bobhú*, frequentative base of भू *bhú*, बोभवांचकार *bobhaváṁchakára.*

But बुबोधिष् *bubodhish*, desiderative base of बुध् *budh*, बुबोधिषांचकार &c. *bubodhisháṁchakára* &c.

Paradigms of the Reduplicated Perfect.

1. Verbal bases in आ *á*, requiring intermediate इ *i*.

धा *dhá*, to place.

PARASMAIPADA.			ÂTMANEPADA.		
SINGULAR.	DUAL.	PLURAL.	SINGULAR.	DUAL.	PLURAL.
1. दधौ *dadhaú*	दधिव *dadhivá*	दधिम *dadhimá*	दधे *dadhé*	दधिवहे *dadhiváhe*	दधिमहे *dadhimáhe*
2. दधाथ *dadháṭha* or दधिथ *dadhitha* *	दधथुः *dadháthuḥ*	दध *dadhá*	दधिषे *dadhishé*	दधाथे *dadháṭhe*	दधिध्वे *dadhidhvé*
3. दधौ *dadhaú*	दधतुः *dadhátuḥ*	दधुः *dadhúḥ*	दधे *dadhé*	दधाते *dadháte*	दधिरे *dadhiré*

2. Verbal bases in इ *i* and ई *í*, preceded by *one* consonant, and requiring intermediate इ *i*.

नी *ní*, to lead.

PARASMAIPADA.			ÂTMANEPADA.		
SINGULAR.	DUAL.	PLURAL.	SINGULAR.	DUAL.	PLURAL.
1. निनाय *nindya* or निनय *nindya*	निनियिव *ninyivá*	निनियिम *ninyimá*	निन्ये *ninyé*	निनियिवहे *ninyiváhe*	निनियिमहे *ninyimáhe*
2. निनेथ *ninétha* or निनयिथ *ninayitha* *	निन्ययुः *ninyáthuḥ*	निन्य *ninyá*	निन्यिषे *ninyishé*	निन्याथे *ninyáthe*	निन्यिध्वे *ninyidhvé* or °ढ्वे (§ 105) *ninyidhvé* or -ḍhvé
3. निनाय *nindya*	निन्यतुः *ninyátuḥ*	निन्युः *ninyúḥ*	निन्ये *ninyé*	निन्याते *ninyáte*	निन्यिरे *ninyiré*

---

* § 335, 2, and § 335, 3.

3. Verbal bases in ऋ *ri*, preceded by *one* consonant, and requiring intermediate इ *i*.

धृ *dhṛi*, to hold.

	Sing.	Du.	Pl.			
1.	दधार *dadhára* or दधर *dadhára*	दध्रिव *dadhrivá*	दध्रिम *dadhrimá*	दध्रे *dadhré*	दध्रिवहे *dadhrivdhe*	दध्रिमहे *dadhrimdhe*
2.	दधर्थ *dadhártha* *	दभ्रथुः *dadhráthuḥ*	दध्र *dadhrá*	दध्रिषे *dadhrishé*	दध्राथे *dadhráthe*	दध्रिध्वे *dadhridhvé* or -*dhvé*
3.	दधार *dadhára*	दध्रतुः *dadhrátuḥ*	दध्रुः *dadhrúḥ*	दध्रे *dadhré*	दध्राते *dadhráte*	दध्रिरे *dadhriré*

4. Verbal bases in ऋ *ri*, preceded by *one* consonant, not admitting intermediate इ *i*.

कृ *kṛi*, to do.

	Sing.	Du.	Pl.			
1.	चकार *chakára* or चकर *chakára*	चक्रिव *chakrivá*	चक्रिम *chakrimá*	चक्रे *chakré*	चक्रिवहे *chakrivdhe*	चक्रिमहे *chakrimdhe*
2.	चकर्थ *chakártha*	चक्रथुः *chakráthuḥ*	चक्र *chakrá*	चक्रिषे *chakrishé*	चक्राथे *chakráthe*	चक्रिध्वे *chakridhvé*
3.	चकार *chakára*	चक्रतुः *chakrátuḥ*	चक्रुः *chakrúḥ*	चक्रे *chakré*	चक्राते *chakráte*	चक्रिरे *chakriré*

5. Verbal bases in इ *i* or ई *í*, preceded by *two* consonants, and requiring intermediate इ *i*.

क्री *krí*, to buy.

	Sing.	Du.	Pl.			
1.	चिक्राय *chikráya* or चिक्रय *chikráya*	चिक्रियिव *chikriyivá*	चिक्रियिम *chikriyimá*	चिक्रिये *chikriyé*	चिक्रियिवहे *chikriyivdhe*	चिक्रियिमहे *chikriyimdhe*
2.	चिक्रेथ *chikrétha* or चिक्रयिथ *chikrayitha*	चिक्रियथुः *chikriyáthuḥ*	चिक्रिय *chikriyá*	चिक्रियिषे *chikriyishé*	चिक्रियाथे *chikriyáthe*	चिक्रियिध्वे *chikriyidhvé* or -*dhvé*
3.	चिक्राय *chikráya*	चिक्रियतुः *chikriyátuḥ*	चिक्रियुः *chikriyúḥ*	चिक्रिये *chikriyé*	चिक्रियाते *chikriyáte*	चिक्रियिरे *chikriyiré*

6. Verbal bases in उ *u* or ऊ *ú*, preceded by *one or two* consonants, and requiring intermediate इ *i*.

यु *yu*, to join.

	Sing.	Du.	Pl.			
1.	युयाव *yuyáva* or युयव *yuyáva*	युयुविव *yuyuvivá*	युयुविम *yuyuvimá*	युयुवे *yuyuvé*	युयुविवहे *yuyuvivdhe*	युयुविमहे *yuyuvimdhe*
2.	युयविथ *yuyavitha* †	युयुवथुः *yuyuváthuḥ*	युयुव *yuyuvá*	युयुविषे *yuyuvishé*	युयुवाथे *yuyuváthe*	युयुविध्वे *yuyuvidhvé* or -*dhvé*
3.	युयाव *yuyáva*	युयुवतुः *yuyuvátuḥ*	युयुवुः *yuyuvúḥ*	युयुवे *yuyuvé*	युयुवाते *yuyuváte*	युयुविरे *yuyuviré*

7. Verbal bases in उ *u*, preceded by *one or two* consonants, and not admitting the intermediate इ *i*.

स्तु *stu*, to praise.

	Sing.	Du.	Pl.			
1.	तुष्टाव *tushtáva* or तुष्टव *tushtáva*	तुष्टुव *tushtuvá*	तुष्टुम *tushtumá*	तुष्टुवे *tushtuvé*	तुष्टुवहे *tushtuvdhe*	तुष्टुमहे *tushtumdhe*
2.	तुष्टोथ *tushtótha* ‡	तुष्टुवथुः *tushtuváthuḥ*	तुष्टुव *tushtuvá*	तुष्टुषे *tushtushé*	तुष्टुवाथे *tushtuvdthe*	तुष्टुध्वे *tushtudhvé*
3.	तुष्टाव *tushtáva*	तुष्टुवतुः *tushtuvátuḥ*	तुष्टुवुः *tushtuvúḥ*	तुष्टुवे *tushtuvé*	तुष्टुवाते *tushtuvdte*	तुष्टुविरे *tushtuviré*

---

* § 335, 2, and § 335, 3.

† If यु *yu* is taken from Dhâtupâtha 31, 9, it may form युयोथ *yuyótha*. (See § 335, 2, and Westergaard, Radices, p. 46, note.)

‡ Bharadvâja might allow तुष्टविथ *tushtavitha* even against Pân. vii. 2, 13.

8. Verbal bases in ऋ *ṛi*, preceded by *two* consonants, and requiring intermediate इ *i*.

स्तृ *stṛi*, to spread.

1. { तस्तार *tastára* or तस्तर *tastára*	तस्तरिव *tastarivá*	तस्तरिम *tastarimá*	तस्तरे *tastaré*	तस्तरिवहे *tastariváhe*	तस्तरिमहे *tastarimáhe*
2. तस्तर्थ *tastártha*	तस्तरपु: *tastardthuḥ*	तस्तर *tastará*	तस्तरिषे *tastarishé*	तस्तराथे *tastardthe*	तस्तरिध्वे *tastaridhvé* or -ध्वे
3. तस्तार *tastára*	तस्तरतु: *tastarátuḥ*	तस्तरु: *tastarúḥ*	तस्तरे *tastaré*	तस्तराते *tastardte*	तस्तरिरे *tastariré*

9. Verbal bases in ऋ *ṛi*, requiring intermediate इ *i*.

कृ *kṛi*, to scatter.

1. { चकार *chakára* or चकर *chakára*	चकरिव *chakarivá*	चकरिम *chakarimá*	चकरे *chakaré*	चकरिवहे *chakariváhe*	चकरिमहे *chakarimáhe*
2. चकरिथ *chakaritha*	चकरपु: *chakaráthuḥ*	चकर *chakará*	चकरिषे *chakarishé*	चकराथे *chakardthe*	चकरिध्वे *chakaridhvé* or -ध्वे
3. चकार *chakára*	चकरतु: *chakarátuḥ*	चकरु: *chakarúḥ*	चकरे *chakaré*	चकराते *chakardte*	चकरिरे *chakariré*

10. Verbal bases in consonants, requiring intermediate इ *i*.

तुद् *tud*, to strike.

1. तुतोद *tutóda*	तुतुदिव *tutudivá*	तुतुदिम *tutudimá*	तुतुदे *tutudé*	तुतुदिवहे *tutudiváhe*	तुतुदिमहे *tutudimáhe*
2. तुतोदिथ *tutoditha*	तुतुदपु: *tutudáthuḥ*	तुतुद *tutudá*	तुतुदिषे *tutudishé*	तुतुदाथे *tutuddthe*	तुतुदिध्वे *tutudidhvé*
3. तुतोद *tutóda*	तुतुदतु: *tutudátuḥ*	तुतुदु: *tutudúḥ*	तुतुदे *tutude*	तुतुदाते *tutuddte*	तुतुदिरे *tutudiré*

11. Verbal bases in consonants, having ए *e*, and requiring intermediate इ *i*.

तन् *tan*, to stretch.

1. { ततान *tatána* or ततान *tatána*	तेनिव *tenivá*	तेनिम *tenimá*	तेने *tené*	तेनिवहे *teniváhe*	तेनिमहे *tenimáhe*
2. तेनिथ *tenitha*	तेनपु: *tendthuḥ*	तेन *tená*	तेनिषे *tenishé*	तेनाथे *tendthe*	तेनिध्वे *tenidhve*
3. ततान *tatána*	तेनतु: *tendtuḥ*	तेनु: *tenúḥ*	तेने *tené*	तेनाते *tendte*	तेनिरे *tenire*

12. Verbal bases in consonants, having Samprasâraṇa, and requiring इ *i*.

यज् *yaj*, to sacrifice.

1. { इयाज *iyája* or इयज *iyája*	ईजिव *íjivá*	ईजिम *íjimá*	ईजे *íjé*	ईजिवहे *íjiváhe*	ईजिमहे *íjimáhe*
2. { इयष्ठ *iyáshṭha* or इयजिथ *iyajitha*	ईजपु: *íjáthuḥ*	ईज *íjá*	ईजिषे *íjishé*	ईजाथे *íjdthe*	ईजिध्वे *íjidhvé*
3. इयाज *iyája*	ईजतु: *íjátuḥ*	ईजु: *íjúḥ*	ईजे *íjé*	ईजाते *íjdte*	ईजिरे *íjiré*

13. Verbal bases in consonants, requiring contraction, and intermediate इ *i*.

हन् han, to kill.

1. { जघान *jaghána* or	जघ्निव	जघ्निम	जघ्ने	जघ्निवहे	जघ्निमहे
जघन *jaghána*	*jaghnivá*	*jaghnimá*	*jaghné*	*jaghniváhe*	*jaghnimáhe*
2. { जघंथ *jaghántha* or	जघ्नुः	जघ्न	जघ्निषे	जघ्नाथे	जघ्निध्वे
जघनिथ *jaghanitha*	*jaghnáthuḥ*	*jaghná*	*jaghnishé*	*jaghnáthe*	*jaghnidhvé*
3. जघान *jaghána*	जघ्नतुः	जघ्नुः	जघ्ने	जघ्नाते	जघ्निरे
	jaghnátuḥ	*jaghnúḥ*	*jaghné*	*jaghnáte*	*jaghniré*

14. Verbal base भू bhú (irregular).

1. बभूव *babhúva*	बभूविव	बभूविम	बभूवे	बभूविवहे	बभूविमहे
	babhúvivá	*babhúvimá*	*babhúvé*	*babhúvivádhe*	*babhúvimáhe*
2. बभूविथ *babhúvitha*	बभूवथुः	बभूव	बभूविषे	बभूवाथे	बभूविध्वे or °ढ्वे
	babhúváthuḥ	*babhúvá*	*babhúvishé*	*babhúvádthe*	*babhúvidhvé* or -*ḍhvé*
3. बभूव *babhúva*	बभूवतुः	बभूवुः	बभूवे	बभूवाते	बभूविरे
	babhúvátuḥ	*babhúvúḥ*	*babhúvé*	*babhúvádte*	*babhúviré* ·

CHAPTER XII.

STRENGTHENING AND WEAKENING OF THE VERBAL BASES IN THE SIX REMAINING GENERAL TENSES.

§ 344. It may be useful, without entering into minute details, to distinguish between two sets of general tenses, moods, and verbal derivatives, which differ from each other by a tendency either to strengthen or to weaken their base. The strengthening takes place chiefly by Guṇa, but, under special circumstances, likewise by Vṛiddhi, by lengthening of the vowel, or by nasalization. The weakening takes place by shortening, by changing ऋ *ṛí* to इर् *ir*, or, before consonants, to ईर् *ír*, by Samprasâraṇa, or by dropping of a nasal. There are many roots, however, which either cannot be strengthened or cannot be weakened, and which therefore are liable to change in one only of these sets. Some resist both strengthening and weakening, as, for instance, all derivative bases, causatives, desideratives, and intensives (in the Âtm.), which generally have been strengthened, as far as their bases will allow, previously to their taking the conjugational terminations.

The base is, if possible, strengthened in :	The base is not strengthened, and, if possible, weakened in :
1. The Future.	1. The Participle in त *ta* (unless it takes intermediate इ *i*).
2. The Conditional.	2. The Gerund in त्वा *tvâ* (unless it takes intermediate इ *i*).
3. The Periphrastic Future.	3. The Passive.
4. The Benedictive Âtmanepada. (Except bases ending in conson. or ऋ *ri*, and not taking interm. इ *i*. Pân. I. 2, 11; 12. VII. 2, 42.)	4. The Benedictive Parasmaipada.
5. The First Aorist, I. II. (Except First Aor. II. Âtm. of verbs ending in conson., ऋ *ri*, or आ *â*. § 350–352.)	5. The First Aorist, IV.
	6. The Second Aorist. (Except verbs in ऋ *ri*, &c. § 364.)

I. Root.	Base strengthened.	Future.	Conditional.	Per. Fut.	Ben. Âtm. (Except bases ending in cons. not taking interm. इ *i*.)	First Aor. I. II.
भू *bhû*	भो *bho*	भविष्यति *bhavishyáti*	अभविष्यत् *ábhavishyat*	भविता *bhavitá*	भविषीष्ट *bhavishîshtá*	अभविष्ट *ábhavishta* Âtm.
तुद् *tud*	तोद् *tod*	तोत्स्यति *totsyáti*	अतोत्स्यत् *átotsyat*	तोत्ता *tottá*	(तुत्सीष्ट) *(tutsîshtá)*	अतौत्सीत् *átautsît*
दिव् *div*	देव् *dev*	देविष्यति *devishyáti*	अदेविष्यत् *ádevishyat*	देविता *devitá*	देविषीष्ट *devishîshtá*	अदेवीत् *ádevît*
चुर् *chur*	चोरय् *choray*	चोरयिष्यति *chorayishyáti*	अचोरयिष्यत् *áchorayishyat*	चोरयिता *chorayitá*	चोरयिषीष्ट *chorayishîshtá*	
कृ *kri*	कार् *kar*	करिष्यति *karíshyáti*	अकरिष्यत् *ákaríshyat*	करिता *karîtá*	करिषीष्ट *karishîshtá*	अकारीत् *ákárît*
सु *su*	सो *so*	सोष्यति *soshyáti*	असोष्यत् *ásoshyat*	सोता *sotá*	सोषीष्ट *soshîshtá*	असावीत् *ásávît*
तन् *tan*	तन् *tan*	तनिष्यति *tanishyáti*	अतनिष्यत् *átanishyat*	तनिता *tanitá*	तनिषीष्ट *tanishîshtá*	अतनीत् *átanît* or अतानी *átánî*
श्री *krî*	श्रे *kre*	श्रेष्यति *kreshyáti*	अश्रेष्यत् *ákreshyat*	श्रेता *kretá*	श्रेषीष्ट *kreshîshtá*	अश्रैषीत् *ákraishît*
द्विष् *dvish*	द्वेष् *dvesh*	द्वेक्ष्यति *dvekshyáti*	अद्वेक्ष्यत् *ádvekshyat*	द्वेष्टा *dveshtá*	(द्विक्षीष्ट) *(dvikshîshtá)*	
हु *hu*	हो *ho*	होष्यति *hoshyáti*	अहोष्यत् *áhoshyat*	होता *hotá*	होषीष्ट *hoshîshtá*	अहौषीत् *áhaushît*
रुध् *rudh*	रोध् *rodh*	रोत्स्यति *rotsyáti*	अरोत्स्यत् *árotsyat*	रोद्धा *roddhá*	(रुत्सीष्ट) *(rutsîshtá)*	अरौत्सीत् *árautsît*
कृ *kri* Caus.	कारय् *kâray*	कारयिष्यति *kârayishyáti*	अकारयिष्यत् *ákârayishyat*	कारयिता *kârayitá*	कारयिषीष्ट *kârayishîshtá*	
कृ *kri* Des.	चिकीर्ष् *chikîrsh*	चिकीर्षिष्यति *chikîrshishyáti*	अचिकीर्षिष्यत् *áchikîrshishyat*	चिकीर्षिता *chikîrshitá*	चिकीर्षिषीष्ट *chikîrshishîshtá*	अचिकीर्षीत् *áchikîrshît*
कृ *kri* Int.	चेक्रीय् *chekrîy*	चेक्रीयिष्यते *chekrîyishyáte*	अचेक्रीयिष्यत *áchekrîyishyata*	चेक्रीयिता *chekrîyitá*	चेक्रीयिषीष्ट *chekrîyishîshtá*	अचेक्रीयिष्ट *áchekrîyishta*

I. Root.	Base not strengthened.	Part. न ta, without इ i.	Ger. त्वा tvá, without इ i.	Passive.	Ben. Par.	Second Aor.	First Aor. IV. and Sec. Aor.
भू bhú	भू bhú	भूतः bhútáh	भूत्वा bhútvá	भूयते bhúyáte	भूयात् bhúyát	अभूत् ábhút	
तुद् tud	तुद् tud	तुन्नः tunnáh	तुत्वा tuttvá	तुद्यते tudyáte	तुद्यात् tudyát		अतुत्त átutta
कृ krí	कीर् kír	कीर्णः kírnáh	कीर्त्वा kírtvá	कीर्यते kíryáte	कीर्यात् kíryát		अकीर्ष्ट ákírshta
⌈ दिव् div	दिव् div	द्यूतः dyútáh	द्यूत्वा dyútvá	दीव्यते dívyáte [1]	दीव्यात् dívyát		
⌊ पुष् push	पुष् push	पुष्टः pushtáh	पुष्ट्वा pushtvá	पुष्यते pushyáte	पुष्यात् pushyát		अपुषत् ápushat
चुर् chur	(चोरय्) (choray)	(चोरितः) (choritáh)	(चोरयित्वा) (chorayitvá)	(चोर्यते) (choryáte)	(चोर्यात्) (choryát)	अचूचुरत् áchúchurat	
सु su	सु su	सुतः sutáh	सुत्वा sutvá	सूयते súyáte	सूयात् súyát		
तन् tan	तन् & त tan & ta	ततः tatáh	तत्वा [2] tatvá	तन्यते [3] tanyáte	तन्यात् tanyát		अतत átata
क्री krí	क्री krí	क्रीतः krítáh	क्रीत्वा krítvá	क्रीयते kríyáte	क्रीयात् kríyát		
द्विष् dvish	द्विष् dvish	द्विष्टः dvishtáh	द्विष्ट्वा dvishtvá	द्विष्यते dvishyáte	द्विष्यात् dvishyát		अद्विक्षत् ádvikshat
हु hu	हु hu	हुतः hutáh	हुत्वा hutvá	हूयते húyáte	हूयात् húyát		
रुध् rudh	रुध् rudh	रुद्धः ruddháh	रुद्ध्वा ruddhvá	रुध्यते rudhyáte	रुध्यात् rudhyát	अरुधत् árudhat	अरुद्ध áruddha
कृ Caus. kri	कारय् káray	कारितः káritáh	कारयित्वा kárayitvá	कार्यते káryáte	कार्यात् káryát	अचीकरत् áchíkarat	
कृ Des. kri	चिकीर्ष chikírsh	चिकीर्षितः chikírshitáh	चिकीर्षित्वा chikírshitvá	चिकीर्ष्यते chikírshyáte	चिकीर्ष्यात् chikírshyát		
कृ Int. kri	चेक्रीय chekríy	चेक्रीयितः chekríyitáh	चेक्रीयित्वा chekríyitvá				

§ 345. Certain roots which strengthen their base in a peculiar manner, by Vriddhi, like मृज् mrij, by lengthening, like गुह् guh, by transposition, like सृज् srij, by changing इ i into आ á, like मि mi, by nasalization, like नश् nas, drop all these marks of strengthening, in the weak forms.

I. Root.	Base strengthened.	Future.	Conditional.	Per. Fut.	Ben. Âtm.	First Aorist.
मृज् mrij	मार्ज् [4] márj	मार्क्ष्यति márkshyáti	अमार्क्ष्यत् ámárkshyat	मार्ष्टा márshtá	मार्जिषीष्ट márjishíshtá	अमार्क्षीत् ámárkshít
	or मार्जिष्यति márjishyáti		अमार्जिष्यत् ámárjishyat	मार्जिता márjitá	(मृक्षीष्ट) (mrikshíshtá)	अमार्जीत् ámárjít

---

[1] § 143. [2] Or तनित्वा tanitvá. [3] Or तायते táyáte (§ 391).

[4] Pâṇ. VII. 2, 114.

A a

गुह् *guh*	गूह्[1] *gúh*	घोक्ष्यति *ghokshyáti*	अघोक्ष्यत् *dghokshyat*	गोढा *godhá*	(घुक्षीष्ट) *(ghukshíshtá)*	
		or गूहिष्यति *gúhishyáti*	अगूहिष्यत् *dgúhishyat*	गूहिता *gúhitá*	गूहिषीष्ट *gúhishíshtá*	अगूहीत् *dgúhít*
सृज् *srij*	स्रज्[2] *sraj*	स्रक्ष्यति *srakshyáti*	अस्रक्ष्यत् *dsrakshyat*	स्रष्टा *srashtá*		अस्राक्षीत् *dsrákshít*
मि *mi*	मा[3] *má*	मास्यति *másyáti*	अमास्यत् *ámásyat*	माता *mátá*	मासीष्ट *másíshtá*	अमासीत् *ámásít*
नश् *naś*	नंश्[4] *namś*	नंक्ष्यति *nankshyáti*	अनंक्ष्यत् *dnankshyat*	नंष्टा *namshtá*		
संस् *srams*	संस्[5] *srams*	संसिष्यते *sramsiskyáte*	असंसिष्यत *dsramsiskyata*	संसिता *sramsitá*	संसिषीष्ट *sramsishíshtá*	असंसिष्ट *dsramsishta*
बंध् *bandh*	बंध् *bandh*	भंत्स्यति *bhantsyáti*	अभंत्स्यत् *dbhantsyat*	बंद्धा *banddhá*		अभांत्सीत् *dbhántsít*

II. Root.	Base not strengthened.	Part. न *ta*, without इ *i*.	Ger. त्वा *tvá*, without इ *i*.	Passive.	Ben. Par.	Sec. Aor.	First Aor. IV. and II. Âtm.
मृज् *mrij*	मृज् *mrij*	मृष्टः *mrishtáh*	मृष्ट्वा[6] *mrishtvá*	मृज्यते *mrijyáte*	मृज्यात् *mrijyát*		
गुह् *guh*	गुह् *guh*	गूढः[7] *gúdháh*	गूढ्वा[8] *gúdhvá*	गुह्यते *guhyáte*	गुह्यात् *guhyát*		अघुक्षत् *dghukshat*
सृज् *srij*	सृज् *srij*	सृष्टः *srishtáh*	सृष्ट्वा *srishtvá*	सृज्यते *srijyáte*	सृज्यात् *srijyát*		
मि *mi*	मि *mi*	मितः *mitáh*	मित्वा *mitvá*	मीयते *míyáte*	मेयात् *meyát*	.	
नश् *naś*	नश् *naś*	नष्टः *nashtáh*	नष्ट्वा[9] *nashtvá*	नश्यते *naśyáte*	नश्यात् *naśyát*	अनशत् *dnaśat*	
संस् *srams*	स्रस् *sras*	स्रस्तः[10] *srastáh*	स्रस्त्वा[11] *srastvá*	स्रस्यते *srasyáte*	स्रस्यात् *srasyát*	अस्रसत् *dsrasat*	
बंध् *bandh*	बध् *badh*	बद्धः *baddháh*	बद्ध्वा *baddhvá*	बध्यते *badhyáte*	बध्यात् *badhyát*		

---

[1] Pân. VI. 4, 89.   [2] Pân. VI. 1, 58.   [3] Pân. VI. 1, 50.   [4] Pân. VII. 1, 60.

[5] Pân. VI. 4, 24.   [6] But with इ *i*, मार्जित्वा *márjitvá*, not मर्जित्वा *marjitvá*.

[7] As to the long ऊ *ú*, see § 128.   [8] Or गूहित्वा *gúhitvá*, § 337, I. 2.   [9] Or नंष्ट्वा *namshtvá*.

[10] Roots which may thus drop their nasal, are written in the Dhâtupâtha with their nasal, संस् or स्रस् *srams*: while others which retain their nasal throughout, are written without the nasal, but with an indicatory इ *i*: नदि *nad*, &c. (Pân. VI. 4, 24; VII. 1, 58). Two verbs thus marked by इ *i*, लगि *lag* and कपि *kap*, may, however, drop their nasal, the general rule notwithstanding, if used in certain meanings, विलगितं *vilagitam*, burnt; विकपितं *vikapitam*, deformed (Pân. VI. 4, 24, vârt. 1, 2). वृहि *vrih*, वृंहति *vrimhati*, drops its nasal before terminations beginning with a vowel, but not before the intermediate इ *i*: वर्हयति *varhayati*, but वृंहिता *vrimhitá*. रंज् *ranj*, to tinge, may drop its nasal, even in the causative (i.e. before a vowel), if it means to sport; रजयति *rajayati* (Pân. VI. 4, 24, vârt. 3, 4). The same root, like some others, drops its nasal before *sárvadhátuka* affixes; रजति *rajati*, &c. (Pân. VI. 4, 26). अंच् *anch*, if it means to worship, must retain its nasal (Pân. VI. 4, 30) and take the intermediate इ *i* (Pân. VII. 2, 53): अंचितः *anchitah*, worshipped; otherwise अक्तः *aktah* or अंचितः *anchitah*, bent.

[11] Or संसित्वा *sramsitvá*.

Note—The verbs beginning with कुट् *kuṭ* (Dhâtupâṭha 28, 73–108) do not strengthen their base, except before terminations which are marked by म् *ñ* or ण् *ṇ;* कुट् *kuṭ,* to be bent, Fut. कुटिष्यति *kuṭishyáti,* Per. Fut. कुटिता *kuṭitá,* First Aor. अकुटीत् *ákuṭít* (Pâṇ. 1. 2, 1). विज् *vij,* to fear, never takes Guṇa before intermediate इ *i;* Per. Fut. विजिता *vijitá* (Pâṇ. 1. 2, 2). ऊर्णु *úrṇu,* to cover, may do so optionally; अर्णुविता *úrṇuvitá* or अर्णविता *úrṇavitá* (Pâṇ. 1. 2, 3).

CHAPTER XIII.

AORIST.

§ 346. We can distinguish in Sanskrit, as in Greek, between two kinds of Aorists, one formed by means of a sibilant inserted between root and termination,—this we call the First,—another, formed by adding the terminations to the base, this we call the Second Aorist.

Both Aorists take the Augment, which always has the Udâtta, and, with some modifications, the terminations of the Imperfect.

§ 347. The First Aorist is formed in four different ways.

Terminations of the First Aorist.

I.　　　　　　　　　First Form.

PARASMAIPADA.				ÂTMANEPADA.		
इषं *isham*	इष्व *ishva*	इष्म *ishma*	इषि *ishi*	इष्वहि *ishvahi*	इष्महि *ishmahi*
ईः *íḥ*	इष्टं *ishṭam*	इष्ट *ishṭa*	इष्ठाः *ishṭháḥ*	इषाथां *isháthám*	इध्वं or इढुं *idhvam* or *iḍhvam*
ईत् *ít*	इष्टां *ishṭám*	इषुः *ishuḥ*	इष्ट *ishṭa*	इषातां *ishátám*	इषत *ishata*

In this first set of terminations the intermediate इ *i* stands as part of the terminations, because all the verbs that take this form are verbs liable to take the intermediate इ *i.* The first and second forms of the First Aorist differ, in fact, by this only, that the former is peculiar to verbs which take, the latter to verbs which reject intermediate इ *i.* (See § 332, 4, note.)

2.　　　　　　　　　Second Form.

PARASMAIPADA.				ÂTMANEPADA.		
सं *sam*	स्व *sva*	स्म *sma*	सि *si*	स्वहि *svahi*	स्महि *smahi*
सीः *síḥ*	स्तं *stam* or तं *tam*	स्त *sta* or त *ta*	स्याः *stháḥ* or याः *tháḥ*	साथां *sáthám*	ध्वं *dhvam* or ढुं *ḍhvam*
सीत् *sít*	स्तां *stám* or तां *tám*	सुः *suḥ*	स्त *sta* or त *ta*	सातां *sátám*	सत *sata*

3.   Third Form.

There are some verbs which add स् *s* to the end of the root before taking the terminations of the Aorist, and which after this स् *s*, employ the usual terminations with इ *i*, viz. इषं *isham*, &c. They are conjugated in the Parasmaipada only.

PARASMAIPADA.

सिषं *s-i-sham*	सिष्व *s-ishva*	सिष्म *s-ishma*
सी: *s-îh* (for सिष: *sish(a)ḥ*)	सिष्टं *s-ishṭam*	सिष्ट *s-ishṭa*
सीत् *s-ît* (for सिषत् *sish(a)t*)	सिष्टां *s-ishṭâm*	सिषु: *s-ishuḥ*

4.   Fourth Form.

Lastly, there are some few verbs, ending in श *ś*, ष *sh*, ह *h*, preceded by इ *i*, उ *u*, ऋ *ri*, which take the following terminations, without an intermediate इ *i* (*ksa*).

PARASMAIPADA.   ÂTMANEPADA.

सं *sam*	साव *sâva*	साम *sâma*	सि *si*	सावहि *sâvahi* or वहि *vahi*		सामहि *sâmahi*
स: *saḥ*	सतं *satam*	सत *sata*	सथा: *sathâḥ* or था: *thâḥ*	साथां *sâthâm*	सध्वं *sadhvam* or ध्वं *dhvam*	
सत् *sat*	सतां *satâm*	सन् *san*	सत *sata* or त *ta*	सातां *sâtâm*		संत *santa*

Special Rules for the First Form of the First Aorist.

§ 348. For final vowel, Vriddhi in Parasmaipada*. लू *lû*, to cut, अलाविषं *álâvisham* (Pân. VII. 2, 1).

For final vowel, Guṇa in Âtmanepada. लू *lû*, अलविषि *álavishi*.

For medial or initial vowel, Guṇa (if possible) both in Par. and Âtm. बुध् *budh*, to know; Par. अबोधिषं *ábodhisham*; Âtm. अबोधिषि *ábodhishi*.

The vowel अ *a*, followed by a single final consonant, may or may not take Vriddhi in Par. if the verb begins with a consonant†. कण् *kaṇ*, to sound, अकाणिषं *ákâṇisham* or अकणिषं *ákaṇisham* (Pân. VII. 2, 7); Âtm. अकणिषि *ákaṇishi*.

---

* Except श्वि *śvi*, to swell, अश्वयीत् *áśvayît*; जागृ *jâgṛi*, to wake, अजागरीत् *ajâgarît* (Pân. VII. 2, 5). ऊर्णु *ûrṇu*, to cover, may or may not take Vriddhi; और्णुवीत् *aurṇuvît*, or और्णावीत् *aurṇâvît*, or और्णवीत् *aurṇavît* (Pân. VII. 2, 6).

† Roots ending in अल् *al* or अर् *ar* always take Vriddhi in the Parasmaipada; ज्वल् *jval*, to burn, अज्वालीत् *ájvâlît* (Pân. VII. 2, 2). Likewise वद् *vad*, to speak, and व्रज् *vraj*, to go (Pân. VII. 2, 3). Roots ending in ह *h*, म *m*, य *y*, the roots क्षण् *kshaṇ*, to hurt, श्वस् *śvas*, to breathe, and verbs of the Chur class, roots with technical ए *e*, do not take Vriddhi (Pân. VII. 2, 5). ग्रह् *grah*, to take, अग्रहीत् *ágrahît*; स्यम् *syam*, to sound, अस्यमीत् *ásyamît*; व्यय् *vyay*, to throw, अव्ययीत् *ávyayît*; क्षण् *kshaṇ*, to hurt, अक्षणीत् *ákshaṇît*; श्वस् *śvas*, to breathe, अश्वसीत् *áśvasît*; ऊनय् *ûnay*, to minish, औनयीत् *aûnayît*; रग् *rag*, to suspect, अरगीत् *áragît*. दीधी *dîdhî*, to shine, वेवी *vevî*, to desire, and दरिद्रा *daridrâ*, to be poor, drop their final vowels, according to the rules on intermediate इ *i*; दरिद्रा *daridrâ*, अदरिद्रीत् *ádaridrît*.

§ 349. No Guṇa takes place in desiderative bases. बुध् *budh;* Desid. बुबोधिष् *bubodhish;* Aor. अबुबोधिषिषं *ábubodhishisham.*

Intensives in य् *y,* if preceded by a consonant, *must,* certain denominatives in य् *y may,* drop their final य् *y.* If the intensive य् *y* is preceded by a vowel, य् *y* is left between the final vowel and the intermediate इ *i.* भिद् *bhid,* to cut; Int. base बेभिद्य् *bebhidy;* Aor. Âtm. अबेभिदिषि *ábebhidishi.* भू *bhú,* to be; Int. base बोभूय् *bobhúy;* Aor. Âtm. अबोभूयिषि *ábo-bhúyishi.* Denom. base नमस्य् *namasy,* to worship; Aor. अनमस्यिषं *ánamasy-isham* or अनमसिषं *ánamas-isham.*

Special Rules for the Second Form of the First Aorist.

§ 350. Vṛiddhi in Parasmaipada. क्षिप् *kship,* अक्षैप्सं *ákshaipsam;* शि *śi,* अशैषं *áśaisham* (Pâṇ. VII. 2, 1); पच् *pach,* अपाक्षीत् *ápâkshít* (Pâṇ. VII. 2, 3).

Guṇa in Âtmanepada, if the verb ends in इ, ई *i,* उ, ऊ *u* (not in ऋ *ṛi,* Pâṇ. I. 2, 12); otherwise no change of vowel. शि *śi,* अशेषि *áśeshi;* but क्षिप् *kship,* अक्षिप्सि *ákshipsi;* कृ *kṛi,* अकृषि *ákṛishi.* Final ऋ *ṛí* becomes ईर् *ír.*

§ 351. Terminations beginning with स्त् *st* or स्थ् *sth* drop their स् *s* if the base ends in a short vowel or in a consonant, except nasals. Ex. 2. p. dual अक्षैप्तं *ákshaip-tam,* 3. p. dual अक्षैप्तां *ákshaip-tâm,* 2. p. plur. अक्षैप्त *ákshaip-ta,* of क्षिप् *kship;* 2. p. sing. Âtm. अकृथाः *ákṛithâḥ,* 3. p. sing. अकृत *ákṛita,* of कृ *kṛi,* Âtm. But from मन्यते *mányate,* अमंस्त *ámaṁsta.*

§ 352. The roots स्था *sthá,* to stand, दा *dá,* to give, धा *dhá,* to place, दे *de,* to pity, धे *dhe,* to feed, दो *do,* to cut, change their final vowels into इ *i* before the terminations of the Âtmanepada (Pâṇ. I. 2, 17). स्था *sthá,* उपास्थित *úpâsthi-ta;* उपास्थिषातां *úpâsthi-shâtâm.* In the Parasmaipada they take the Second Aorist. (§ 368.)

§ 353. The roots मी *mí* (*mínáti*), to hurt, मि *mi* (*minoti*), to throw, and दी *dí,* Âtm., to decay, instead of taking Guṇa, change their final vowels into आ *á* in the Âtmanepada; and ली *lí,* to stick, does so optionally (Pâṇ. VI. 1, 50–51)*. Thus from मी *mí* and मि *mi,* अमास्त *amásta;* from दी *dí,* अदास्त *adásta;* from ली *lí,* अलास्त *alásta* or अलेष्ट *aleshṭa.* In the Parasmaipada these verbs take the Third Form.

§ 354. हन् *han,* to kill, drops its nasal in the Âtmanepada (Pâṇ. I. 2, 14); अहत *ahata,* अहसातां *ahasátâm,* &c.

§ 355. गम् *gam,* to go, drops its nasal in the Âtmanepada optionally (Pâṇ. I. 2, 13); अगत *agata* or अगंस्त *agaṁsta.* The same rule applies to the benedictive Âtmanepada; गसीष्ट *gasíshṭa* or गंसीष्ट *gaṁsíshṭa.*

§ 356. यम् *yam* drops its nasal, necessarily or optionally, according to its various meanings; उदयत *udayata,* he divulged (Pâṇ. I. 2, 15); उपायत *upáyata,* he espoused, or उपायंस्त *upáyaṁsta* (Pâṇ. I. 2, 16).

---

* Prof. Weber (Kuhn's Beiträge, vol. VI. p. 102) blames Dr. Kellner for having admitted अमासिषम् *amásisham* and similar forms, and denies that these forms are authorised by Pâṇini. Dr. Kellner, however, was right, as will be seen from the commentary to Pâṇ. VI. 1, 50. The substitution of आ *á* takes place wherever there would otherwise have been एच् *ech,* excepting in Śit forms.

Special Rules for the Third Form of the First Aorist.

§ 357. Most verbs taking this form of the Aorist end in आ *á*, or in diphthongs which take आ *á* as their substitute. This आ *á* remains unchanged. In the Âtmanepada these verbs take the Second Form.

§ 358. The verbs मी *mî*, to hurt, मि *mi*, to throw, and ली *lî*, to stick, in taking this form, change likewise their final vowels into आ *á*. Ex. अमासिषं *amásisham*, I threw, and I hurt; अलासिषं *alásisham* (or अलैषं *alaisham*). § 353.

§ 359. Three roots ending in म् *m* take this form; यम् *yam*, to hold, रम् *ram*, to rejoice, नम् *nam*, to bend, Aor. अयंसिषं *ayamsisham*, &c. (Pâṇ. vii. 2, 73.)

Special Rules for the Fourth Form of the First Aorist.

§ 360. The roots which take this form must end in श् *s* (as to दृश् *dṛís*, to see, cf. Pâṇ. iii. 1, 47), ष् *sh*, स् *s*, ह् *h*, preceded by any vowel but अ, आ *á*. They must be verbs which reject the intermediate इ *i*; § 332, 17–20; (Pâṇ. iii. 1, 45.) Their radical vowel remains unchanged.

§ 361. The root श्लिष् *ślish* takes this form only if it means to embrace (Pâṇ. iii. 1, 46); अश्लिक्षत् *aślikshat*. Other verbs, such as पुष् *push* and शुष् *śush*, are specially excepted. (§ 366.)

§ 362. The roots दुह् *duh*, to milk, दिह् *dih*, to anoint, लिह् *lih*, to lick, गुह् *guh*, to hide (Pâṇ. vii. 3, 73), may take in the Âtmanepada

था: *tháḥ*	instead of	सथा: *satháḥ*.	वहि *vahi* instead of सावहि *sávahi*.
त *ta*	—	सत *sata*.	ध्वं *dhvam* — सध्वं *sadhvam*.

They thus approach to the Second Form of the first aorist in most, but not in all persons.

Ex. दुह् *duh*; 2. p. sing. Âtm. अदुग्धा: *adugdháḥ* or अधुक्षथा: *adhukshatháḥ*.

3. p. sing. Âtm. अदुग्ध *adugdha* or अधुक्षत *adhukshata*.

1. p. dual Âtm. अदुह्वहि *aduhvahi* or अधुक्षावहि *adhukshávahi*.

2. p. plur. Âtm. अधुग्ध्वं *adhugdhvam* or अधुक्षध्वं *adhukshadhvam*.

First Aorist.

First Form,

with intermediate इ *i*.

a. Verbs ending in a vowel; लू *lû*, to cut.

Vṛiddhi in Parasmaipada, Guṇa in Âtmanepada.

PARASMAIPADA.

1. अलाविषं *áláv-isham*	अलाविष्व *áláv-ishva*	अलाविष्म *áláv-ishma*
2. अलावी: *áláv-îḥ*	अलाविष्ट्ं *áláv-ishṭam*	अलाविष्ट *álávi-shṭa*
3. अलावीत् *áláv-ît*	अलाविष्टां *áláv-ishṭám*	अलाविषु: *álávi-shuḥ*

ÂTMANEPADA.

1. अलविषि *álav-ishi*	अलविष्वहि *álav-ishvahi*	अलविष्महि *álav-ishmahi*
2. अलविष्ठा: *álav-ishṭháḥ*	अलविषाथां *álav-isháthám*	अलविध्वं *álav-idhvam* or °ढुं -ḍhvam
3. अलविष्ट *álav-ishṭa*	अलविषातां *álav-ishátám*	अलविषत *álav-ishata*

b. Verbs ending in consonants; बुध् *budh,* to know.

Guṇa in Parasmaipada and Âtmanepada.

PARASMAIPADA.

1. अबोधिषं *abodh-isham*	अबोधिष्व *abodh-ishva*	अबोधिष्म *abodh-ishma*
2. अबोधी: *abodh-îh*	अबोधिष्टं *abodh-ishtam*	अबोधिष्ट *abodh-ishta*
3. अबोधीत् *abodh-ît*	अबोधिष्टां *abodh-ishtâm*	अबोधिषु: *abodh-ishuh*

ÂTMANEPADA.

1. अबोधिषि *abodh-ishi*	अबोधिष्वहि *abodh-ishvahi*	अबोधिष्महि *abodh-ishmahi*
2. अबोधिष्ठा: *abodh-ishthâh*	अबोधिषाथां *abodh-ishâthâm*	अबोधिध्वं *abodh-idhvam*
3. अबोधिष्ट *abodh-ishta*	अबोधिषातां *abodh-ishâtâm*	अबोधिषत *abodh-ishata*

Second Form,

without intermediate इ *i.*

a. Verbs ending in consonants; क्षिप् *kship,* to throw.

Vṛiddhi in Parasmaipada, no change in Âtmanepada.

PARASMAIPADA.

1. अक्षैप्सं *akshaip-sam*	अक्षैप्स्व *akshaip-sva*	अक्षैप्स्म *akshaip-sma*
2. अक्षैप्सी: *akshaip-sîh*	अक्षैप्तं *akshaip-tam* (§ 351)	अक्षैप्त *akshaip-ta*
3. अक्षैप्सीत् *akshaip-sît*	अक्षैप्तां *akshaip-tâm*	अक्षैप्सु: *akshaip-suh*

ÂTMANEPADA.

1. अक्षिप्सि *akship-si*	अक्षिप्स्वहि *akship-svahi*	अक्षिप्स्महि *akship-smahi*
2. अक्षिप्था: *akship-thâh*	अक्षिप्साथां *akship-sâthâm*	अक्षिब्ध्वं *akshib-dhvam*
3. अक्षिप्त *akship-ta*	अक्षिप्सातां *akship-sâtâm*	अक्षिप्सत *akship-sata*

b. Verbs ending in vowels (इ, ई î, उ, ऊ û); नी *nî,* to lead.

Vṛiddhi in Parasmaipada, Guṇa in Âtmanepada.

PARASMAIPADA.

1. अनैषं *anaisham*	अनैष्व *anaishva*	अनैष्म *anaishma*
2. अनैषी: *anaishîh*	अनैष्टं *anaishtam*	अनैष्ट *anaishta*
3. अनैषीत् *anaishît*	अनैष्टां *anaishtâm*	अनैषु: *anaishuh*

ÂTMANEPADA.

1. अनेषि *aneshi*	अनेष्वहि *aneshvahi*	अनेष्महि *aneshmahi*
2. अनेष्ठा: *aneshthâh*	अनेषाथां *aneshâthâm*	अनेड्ढुं *anedhvam*
3. अनेष्ट *aneshta*	अनेषातां *aneshâtâm*	अनेषत *aneshata*

c. Verbs ending in ऋ *ṛi;* कृ *kṛi,* to do.

Vṛiddhi in Parasmaipada, no change in Âtmanepada.

PARASMAIPADA.

1. अकार्षं *akârsham*	अकार्ष्व *akârshva*	अकार्ष्म *akârshma*
2. अकार्षी: *akârshîh*	अकार्ष्टं *akârshtam*	अकार्ष्ट *akârshta*
3. अकार्षीत् *akârshît*	अकार्ष्टां *akârshtâm*	अकार्षु: *akârshuh*

ÂTMANEPADA.

1. अकृषि *akṛishi*	अकृष्वहि *akṛishvahi*	अकृष्महि *akṛishmahi*
2. अकृथाः *akṛithâḥ*	अकृषाथां *akṛishâthâm*	अकृढुं *akṛiḍhvam*
3. अकृत *akṛita*	अकृषातां *akṛishâtâm*	अकृषत *akṛishata*

d. Verbs ending in आ *â;* दा *dâ,* to give.
Âtmanepada only; आ *â* changed into इ *i.*

ÂTMANEPADA.

1. अदिषि *adishi*	अदिष्वहि *adishvahi*	अदिष्महि *adishmahi*
2. अदिथाः *adithâḥ*	अदिषाथां *adishâthâm*	अदिढुं *adiḍhvam*
3. अदित *adita*	अदिषातां *adishâtâm*	अदिषत *adishata*

e. Verbs ending in ॄ *ṛî;* स्तॄ *stṛî,* to stretch.
Vṛiddhi in Parasmaipada, with intermediate इ *i.*

In Âtmanepada the insertion of इ *i* is optional. (See § 337, II. 4. Pâṇ. VII. 2, 42.)

If इ *i* is inserted, then Guṇa (§ 348) and optionally lengthening of इ *i.* (§ 341.)

If इ *i* is not inserted, then ॄ *ṛî* changed to ईर् *îr.* (§ 350.)

PARASMAIPADA.

अस्तारिषं *astârisham,* &c., like *First Form.*

First Form, with इ *i.*	ÂTMANEPADA. SINGULAR.	*Second Form,* without इ *i.*
1. अस्तरिषि or अस्तरीषि *astarishi* or *astarîshi*		अस्तीर्षि *astîrshi*
2. अस्तरिष्ठाः or अस्तरीष्ठाः *astarishṭhâḥ* or *astarîshṭhâḥ*		अस्तीर्ष्टाः *astîrshṭhâḥ*
3. अस्तरिष्ट or अस्तरीष्ट *astarishṭa* or *astarîshṭa*		अस्तीर्ष्ट *astîrshṭa*

DUAL.

1. अस्तरिष्वहि or अस्तरीष्वहि *astarishvahi* or *astarîshvahi*		अस्तीर्ष्वहि *astîrshvahi*
2. अस्तरिषाथां or अस्तरीषाथां *astarishâthâm* or *astarîshâthâm*		अस्तीर्षाथां *astîrshâthâm*
3. अस्तरिषातां or अस्तरीषातां *astarishâtâm* or *astarîshâtâm*		अस्तीर्षातां *astîrshâtâm*

PLURAL.

1. अस्तरिष्महि or अस्तरीष्महि *astarishmahi* or *astarîshmahi*		अस्तीर्ष्महि *astîrshmahi*
2. अस्तरिध्वं °ढुं or अस्तरीध्वं °ढुं *astaridhvam -ḍhvam* or *astarîdhvam -ḍhvam*		अस्तीर्ढुं *astîrḍhvam*
3. अस्तरिषत or अस्तरीषत *astarishata* or *astarîshata*		अस्तीर्षत *astîrshata*

f. Verbs with penultimate ऋ *ṛi;* सृज् *sṛij,* to let off.
Peculiar Vṛiddhi in Parasmaipada, no change in Âtmanepada.

PARASMAIPADA.

1. अस्राक्षं *asrâksham*	अस्राक्ष्व *asrâkshva*	अस्राक्ष्म *asrâkshma*
2. अस्राक्षीः *asrâkshîḥ*	अस्राष्टं *asrâshṭam*	अस्राष्ट *asrâshṭa*
3. अस्राक्षीत् *asrâkshît*	अस्राष्टां *asrâshṭâm*	अस्राक्षुः *asrâkshuḥ*

ÂTMANEPADA.

1. असृक्षि *asṛikshi*	असृक्ष्वहि *asṛikshvahi*	असृक्ष्महि *asṛikshmahi*
2. असृष्ठाः *asṛishṭhâḥ*	असृक्षाथां *asṛikshâthâm*	असृद्ढुं *asṛiddhvam*
3. असृष्ट *asṛishṭa*	असृक्षातां *asṛikshâtâm*	असृक्षत *asṛikshata*

g. Verbs ending in इ *h*; दह *dah*, to burn.

PARASMAIPADA.

1. अधाक्षं *adhâksham* अधाक्ष्व *adhâkshva* अधाक्ष्म *adhâkshma*
2. अधाक्षी: *adhâkshîḥ* अदाग्धं *adâgdham* अदाग्ध *adâgdha*
3. अधाक्षीत् *adhâkshît* अदाग्धां *adâgdhâm* अधाक्षु: *adhâkshuḥ*

ÂTMANEPADA.

1. अधक्षि *adhakshi* अधक्ष्वहि *adhakshvahi* अधक्ष्महि *adhakshmahi*
2. अदग्धा: *adagdhâḥ* अधक्षाथां *adhakshâthâm* अधग्ध्वं *adhagdhvam*
3. अदग्ध *adagdha* अधक्षातां *adhakshâtâm* अधक्षत *adhakshata*

FIRST AORIST.

Third Form.

PARASMAIPADA ONLY.

या *yâ*, to go.

1. अयासिषं *ayâsisham* अयासिष्व *ayâsishva* अयासिष्म *ayâsishma*
2. अयासी: *ayâsîḥ* अयासिष्टं *ayâsishṭam* अयासिष्ट *ayâsishṭa*
3. अयासीत् *ayâsît* अयासिष्टां *ayâsishṭâm* अयासिषु: *ayâsishuḥ*

नम् *nam*, to bend.

1. अनंसिषं *anaṁsisham* अनंसिष्व *anaṁsishva* अनंसिष्म *anaṁsishma*
2. अनंसी: *anaṁsîḥ* अनंसिष्टं *anaṁsishṭam* अनंसिष्ट *anaṁsishṭa*
3. अनंसीत् *anaṁsît* अनंसिष्टां *anaṁsishṭâm* अनंसिषु: *anaṁsishuḥ*

FIRST AORIST.

Fourth Form.

दिश् *diś*, to show.

PARASMAIPADA.

1. अदिक्षं *adiksham* अदिक्षाव *adikshâva* अदिक्षाम *adikshâma*
2. अदिक्ष: *adikshaḥ* अदिक्षतं *adikshatam* अदिक्षत *adikshata*
3. अदिक्षत् *adikshat* अदिक्षतां *adikshatâm* अदिक्षन् *adikshan*

ÂTMANEPADA.

1. अदिक्षि *adikshi* अदिक्षावहि *adikshâvahi* अदिक्षामहि *adikshâmahi*
2. अदिक्षथा: *adikshathâḥ* अदिक्षाथां *adikshâthâm* अदिक्षध्वं *adikshadhvam*
3. अदिक्षत *adikshata* अदिक्षातां *adikshâtâm* अदिक्षंत *adikshanta*

गुह् *guh*, to hide.

PARASMAIPADA.

1. अघुक्षं *aghuksham* अघुक्षाव *aghukshâva* अघुक्षाम *aghukshâma*
2. अघुक्ष: *aghukshaḥ* अघुक्षतं *aghukshatam* अघुक्षत *aghukshata*
3. अघुक्षत् *aghukshat* अघुक्षतां *aghukshatâm* अघुक्षन् *aghukshan*

ÂTMANEPADA.

1. अघुक्षि *aghukshi*   अघुक्षावहि *aghukshávahi* or अगुह्वहि *aguhvahi*   अघुक्षामहि *aghukshámahi*
2. अघुक्षथाः *aghukshatháh* or अगूढाः *agúdháh*   अघुक्षाथां *aghuksháthám*   अघुग्ध्वं or अघूढुं [1]
3. अघुक्षत *aghukshata* or अगूढ *agúdha*   अघुक्षातां *aghukshátám*   अघुक्षंत *aghukshanta*

It may also follow the First Form, अगूहिषं *agúhisham* and अगूहिषि *agúhishi*. (§ 337, I. 1.)

लिह् lih, to smear.

PARASMAIPADA.

1. अलिक्षं *aliksham*   अलिक्षाव *aliksháva*   अलिक्षाम *aliksháma*
2. अलिक्षः *alikshah*   अलिक्षतं *alikshatam*   अलिक्षत *alikshata*
3. अलिक्षत् *alikshat*   अलिक्षातां *alikshatám*   अलिक्षन् *alikshan*

ÂTMANEPADA.

1. अलिक्षि *alikshi*   अलिक्षावहि *alikshávahi* or अलिह्वहि *alikvahi*   अलिक्षामहि *alikshámahi*
2. अलिक्षथाः *alikshatháh* or अलीढाः *alídháh*   अलिक्षाथां *aliksháthám*   अलिग्ध्वं or अलीढुं [2]
3. अलिक्षत *alikshata* or अलीढ *alídha*   अलिक्षातां *alikshátám*   अलिक्षंत *alikshanta*

दुह् duh, to milk.

PARASMAIPADA.

अधुक्षं *adhuksham*, &c.

ÂTMANEPADA.

1. अधुक्षि *adhukshi*   अधुक्षावहि *adhukshávahi* or अदुह्वहि *aduhvahi*   अधुक्षामहि *adhukshámahi*
2. अधुक्षथाः *adhukshatháh* or अदुग्धाः *adugdháh*   अधुक्षाथां *adhuksháthám*   अधुग्ध्वं or अधुग्ध्वं [3]
3. अधुक्षत *adhukshata* or अदुग्ध *adugdha*   अधुक्षातां *adhukshátám*   अधुक्षंत *adhukshanta*

दिह् dih, to anoint.

PARASMAIPADA.

अधिक्षं *adhiksham*, &c.

ÂTMANEPADA.

1. अधिक्षि *adhikshi*   अधिक्षावहि or अदिह्वहि [4]   अधिक्षामहि *adhikshámahi*
2. अधिक्षथाः or अदिग्धाः [5]   अधिक्षाथां *adhiksháthám*   अधिग्ध्वं or अधिग्ध्वं [6]
3. अधिक्षत or अदिग्ध [7]   अधिक्षातां *adhikshátám*   अधिक्षंत *adhikshanta*

SECOND AORIST.

First Form.

§ 363. Verbs adopting this form take the augment, and attach the terminations (First Division) of the imperfect to a verbal base ending in व *a*, like those of the Tud form.

---

[1] *aghukshadhvam* or *aghúdhvam.*   [2] *alikshadhvam* or *alídhvam.*
[3] *adhukshadhvam* or *adhugdhvam.*   [4] *adhikshávahi* or *adihvahi.*
[5] *adhikshatháh* or *adigdháh.*   [6] *adhikshadhvam* or *adhigdhvam.*
[7] *adhikshata* or *adigdha.*

सिच् *sich*, to sprinkle. Pres. सिंचामि *siñchámi*; Impf. असिंचं *asiñcham*.

PARASMAIPADA.

1. असिचं *asicham*	असिचाव *asicháva*	असिचाम *asicháma*
2. असिच: *asichah*	असिचतं *asichatam*	असिचत *asichata*
3. असिचत् *asichat*	असिचतां *asichatám*	असिचन् *asichan*

ÂTMANEPADA.

1. असिचे *asiche*	असिचावहि *asichávahi*	असिचामहि *asichámahi*
2. असिचथा: *asichatháh*	असिचेथां *asichethám*	असिचध्वं *asichadhvam*
3. असिचत *asichata*	असिचेतां *asichetám*	असिचन्त *asichanta*

ह्वे *hve*, to call. Pres. ह्वयामि *hvayámi*; Impf. अह्वयं *ahvayam*; General base हू *hú.*

PARASMAIPADA.

1. अह्वं *ahvam*	अह्वाव *ahváva*	अह्वाम *ahváma*
2. अह्व: *ahvah*	अह्वतं *ahvatam*	अह्वत *ahvata*
3. अह्वत् *ahvat*	अह्वतां *ahvatám*	अह्वन् *ahvan*

ÂTMANEPADA.

1. अह्वे *ahve*	अह्वावहि *ahvávahi*	अह्वामहि *ahvámahi*
2. अह्वथा: *ahvatháh*	अह्वेथां *ahvethám*	अह्वध्वं *ahvadhvam*
3. अह्वत *ahvata*	अह्वेतां *ahvetám*	अह्वन्त *ahvanta*

§ 364. Roots ending in आ *á*, ए *e*, इ *i*, drop these vowels, and substitute a base ending in अ *a:* ह्वे *hve* substitutes ह्व *hva*, Aor. अह्वं *ahvam*; ष्वि *śvi* substitutes श्व *śva*, Aor. अश्वं *aśvam*. Roots ending in ऋ *ri*, and the root दृश् *driś*, to see, take Guṇa (Pâṇ. VII. 4, 16), and then form a base ending in short अ *a:* सृ *sri*, to go, असरत् *asarat*; दृश् *driś*, to see, अदर्शत् *adarśat*.

§ 365. Roots with penultimate nasal, drop it: स्कंद् *skand*, to step, अस्कदं *askadam*.

§ 366. Irregular forms are, अवोचं *avocham*, I spoke, from वच् *vach* (according to Bopp a contracted reduplicated aorist, § 370, for अववचं *avavacham*); अपप्तं *apaptam*, I flew, from पत् *pat* (possibly a contracted reduplicated aorist for अपपतं *apapatam*); अनेशं *anesam*, I perished, Kâs. on Pâṇ. VI. 4, 120 (possibly for अननशं *ananasam*); अशिशं *aśisham*, I ordered, from शास् *śás;* आस्थं *ástham*, I threw, from अस् *as*. (Pâṇ. VII. 4, 17.)

§ 367. Roots which take this form are,

अस् *as*, to throw (आस्थं *ástham*), वच् *vach*, to speak (अवोचं *avocham*), ख्या *khyá*, to speak (अख्यं *akhyam*), if the agent is implied. (Pâṇ. III. 1, 52.)

लिप् *lip*, to paint, सिच् *sich*, to sprinkle, ह्वे *hve*, to call (irregularly अह्वं *ahvam*), in Par., and optionally in Âtm. (Pâṇ. III. 1, 53, 54). Par. अलिपत् *alipat*, Âtm. अलिपत *alipata* or अलिप्त *alipta*.

The verbs classed as पुषादि *pushádi*, beginning with पुष् *push* (Dh. P. 26, 73–136), द्युतादि *dyutádi*, beginning with द्युत् *dyut* (Dh. P. 18), and those marked by a technical ऌ *li*, in the Parasmaipada. (Pâṇ. III. 1, 55.)

B b 2

The verbs सृ *sri*, to go, शास् *śás*, to order, and ऋ *ri*, to go (आर्द *áram*), in Par. and Âtm. (Pân. iii. 1, 56.)

Optionally, verbs technically marked by इर् *ir*, but in the Parasmaipada only (Pân. iii. 1, 57). अभिदत् *abhidat* or अभैत्सीत् *abhaitsít*.

Optionally, जॄ *jrí*, to fail, स्तम्भ् *stambh*, to stiffen (अस्तभत् *astabhat* or अस्तम्भीत् *astambhít*), म्रुच् *mruch*, to go (अमुचत् *amruchat* or अमोचीत् *amrochít*), म्लुच् *mluch*, to go, ग्रुच् *gruch*, to steal, ग्लुच् *gluch*, to steal, ग्लुञ्च् *gluñch*, to go (अग्लुचत् *agluchat* or अग्लुञ्चीत् *agluñchít*), श्वि *śvi*, to grow (irregularly अश्वत् *aśvat*), but in the Parasmaipada only. (Pân. iii. 1, 58.)

§ 368. There are a few verbs, ending in आ *á*, ए *e*, ओ *o*, which take this form of the second aorist in the Parasmaipada; also भू *bhú*, to be. They retain throughout the long final vowel, except before the उः *uḥ* of the 3rd pers. plur., before which the final आ *á* is rejected. In the Âtmanepada these verbs in आ *á* take the Second Form of the first aorist, and change आ *á* to इ *i*.

दा *dá*, to give. Pres. ददामि *dadámi*; Impf. अददां *adadám*.

PARASMAIPADA.

1. अदां *adám*	अदाव *adáva*	अदाम *adáma*
2. अदाः *adáḥ*	अदातं *adátam*	अदात *adáta*
3. अदात् *adát*	अदातां *adátám*	अदुः *aduḥ*

भू *bhú*, to be. Pres. भवामि *bhavámi*; Impf. अभवं *abhavam*.

PARASMAIPADA.

1. अभूवं *abhúvam* *	अभूव *abhúva*	अभूम *abhúma*
2. अभूः *abhúḥ*	अभूतं *abhútam*	अभूत *abhúta*
3. अभूत् *abhút*	अभूतां *abhútám*	अभूवन् *abhúvan*

Verbs which take this form are,

गा *gá*, to go; दा *dá*, to give; धा *dhá*, to place; पा *pá*, to drink; स्था *sthá*, to stand; दे *de*, to guard; दो *do*, to cut; भू *bhú*, to be. (Pân. ii. 4, 77.)

Optionally, घ्रा *ghrá*, to smell; धे *dhe*, to drink; शो *śo*, to sharpen; छो *chho*, to cut; सो *so*, to destroy. (Pân. ii. 4, 78.)

§ 369. The nine roots of the Tan class ending in न *n* or ण *ṇ* may form the 2nd and 3rd pers. sing. Âtm. in थाः *tháḥ* and त *ta*, before which the final nasal is rejected. तन् *tan*, to stretch; Aor. अतनिष्ट *atanishṭa* or अतत *atata*; अतनिष्ठाः *atanishṭháḥ* or अतथाः *atatháḥ* (Pân. ii. 4, 79). These forms might be considered as irregular Âtmanepada forms of the second aorist, or of the first aorist II, with loss of initial स् *s*.

Second or Reduplicated Form of the Second Aorist.

§ 370. A few primitive verbs, and the very numerous class of the Chur roots, the denominatives and causatives in अय् *ay*, reduplicate their base in the second aorist, taking the augment as before, and the usual terminations of the imperfect.

---

* Irregular in the 1st pers. sing., dual, and plur., and in the 3rd pers. plur.

§ 371. The primitive verbs which take this form are,

श्रि *śri*, to go, द्रु *dru*, to run, सु *sru*, to flow, कम् *kam*, to love (Pân. iii. 1, 48), if expressing the agent. Ex. अशिश्रियत् *aśiśriyat*.

Optionally, श्वि *śvi*, to grow, धे *dhe*, to suck (Pân. iii. 1, 49), if expressing the agent. Ex. अदधत् *adadhat*, § 364, (or अधात् *adhât* or अधासीत् *adhâsît*.)

Their reduplicative syllable, as far as consonants are concerned, is formed like that of the reduplicated perfect.

अशिश्रियत् *aśiśriyat*, he went. अदुद्रुवत् *adudruvat*, he ran. असुस्रुवत् *asusruvat*, he flowed. अचकमत् *achakamat*, he loved. अदधत् *adadhat*, he sucked. अशिश्वियत् *aśiśviyat*, he grew; also Sec. Aor. अश्वत् *aśvat* and First Aor. अश्वयीत् *aśvayît* (Pân. iii. 1, 49). ह्वे *hve*, to call, forms its Aor. Caus. अजूहवत् *ajûhavat* (Pân. vi. 1, 32).

§ 372. The verbs in अय् *ay* drop अय् *ay*, and (with certain exceptions*) reduce their Guṇa and Vṛiddhi vowels to the simple base vowels: आ *â* to अ *ă* ; ए *e* to इ *i* ; ओ *o* to उ *u* ; अर्, आर् *ăr*, to ऋ *ṛi* ; ईर् *îr* to ऋ *ṛi*. (Pân. vii. 4, 7.)

Thus मादयति *mâdayati* would become मद् *mad*, (Aor. अमीमदं *amîmadam*.)

    भेदयति *bhedayati* — — भिद् *bhid*, (Aor. अबीभिदं *abîbhidam*.)

    मोदयति *modayati* — — मुद् *mud*, (Aor. अमूमुदं *amûmudam*.)

§ 373. In the exceptional roots, which do not admit this shortening process, आ *â*, ई *î*, ए *e*, ऐ *ai*, ऊ *û*, ओ *o*, औ *au* are represented in the reduplicative syllable by अ *ă*, इ *ĭ*, इ *ĭ*, इ *ĭ*, उ *ŭ*, उ *ŭ*, उ *ŭ*†.

मालयति *mâlayati*, अममालं *amamâlam*. टीकयति *tîkayati*, अटिटीकं *aṭiṭîkam*. लोकयति *lokayati*, अलुलोकं *alulokam*.

§ 374. In the vast majority of roots, however, the shortening takes place, thus leaving bases with short अ *a*, इ *i*, उ *u*, ऋ *ṛi*. Here the tendency is to make the reduplicated base, with the augment, either ∪ — ∪ or ∪ ∪ —. Hence all roots in which the shortened vowel is not long by position, lengthen the vowel of the reduplicative syllable (*amûmudat*). Those in which the vowel is long by position, leave the vowel of the reduplicative syllable short (*ararakshat*).

Where, as in roots beginning with double consonants, the vowel of the reduplicative syllable is necessarily long by position, it is not changed into the

---

* These exceptional verbs are (Pân. vii. 4, 2, 3),

Certain denominatives: From माला *mâlâ*, a garland, is formed the denominative मालयति *mâlayati*, Red. Aor. अममालत् *amamâlat* ; शास् *śâs*, Caus. शासयति *śâsayati*, he punishes, Red. Aor. अशशासत् *aśaśâsat*.

Those with technical ऋ *ṛi*: बाध् *bâdh*, to hurt; Caus. बाधयति *bâdhayati* ; Aor. अबबाधत् *ababâdhat*.

भ्राज् *bhrâj*, to shine, भास् *bhâs*, to shine, भाष् *bhâsh*, to speak, दीप् *dîp*, to lighten, जीव् *jîv*, to live, मील् *mîl*, to meet, पीड् *pîḍ*, to vex, shorten their vowel optionally. Ex. भ्राज् *bhrâj*: अबभ्राजत् *ababhrâjat* or अबिभ्रजत् *abibhrajat* (§ 374).

† वेष्टय् *veshṭay*, to surround, चेष्टय् *cheshṭay*, to move, take either इ *i* or अ *a* in the reduplicative syllable; अववेष्टत् *avaveshṭat* or अविवेष्टत् *aviveshṭat*. द्योतय् *dyotay*, to lighten, takes इ *i*: अदिद्युतत् *adidyutat*.

long vowel (*achuchyutat*, not *achúchyutat*).   In roots beginning and ending in
two consonants, this metrical rhythm is necessarily broken (*achaskandat*).

§ 375. In the roots which do not resist the shortening process,
चा *a*,   इ *i*, उ *u*, ऋ *ri* are represented in the reduplicative syllable by
चा *a* or इ *i*, इ *i*, उ *u*, इ *i*; and all lengthened, where necessary.

Second or Reduplicated Form of the Second Aorist.

I. ∪ – ∪.

पच् *pach*, to cook, पाचयति *páchayati*; अपीपचत् *ápipachat**.
भिद् *bhid*, to cut, भेदयति *bhedáyati*; अबीभिदत् *ábibhidat*.
मुद् *mud*, to rejoice, मोदयति *modáyati*; अमूमुदत् *ámúmudat*.
वृत् *vrit*, to exist, वर्तयति *vartáyati*; अवीवृतत् *ávivritat*.
मृज् *mrij*, to cleanse, मार्जयति *márjáyati*; अमीमृजत् *ámímrijat*.
कृत् *krit*, to praise, कीर्तयति *kírtáyati*; अचीकृतत् *áchíkritat*†.

The lengthening becomes superfluous before roots beginning with two conso-
nants, because the two consonants make the short vowel heavy (*guru*).

त्यज् *tyaj*, to leave, त्याजयति *tyájáyati*; अतित्यजत् *átityajat*.
भ्राज् *bhráj*, to shine, भ्राजयति *bhrájáyati*; अबिभ्रजत् *ábibhrajat*.
क्षिप् *kship*, to throw, क्षेपयति *kshepáyati*; अचिक्षिपत् *áchikshipat*.
च्युत् *chyut*, to fall, च्योतयति *chyotáyati*; अचुच्युतत् *áchuchyutat*.
स्वृ *svri*, to sound, स्वारयति *svdráyati*; असिस्वरत् *ásisvarat*.

2. ∪ ∪ –.

रक्ष् *raksh*, to protect, रक्षयति *raksháyati*; अररक्षत् *árarakshat*‡.
भिक्ष् *bhiksh*, to beg, भिक्षयति *bhiksháyati*; अबिभिक्षत् *ábibhikshat*.

§ 376. If the root begins and ends with double consonants, this rhythmical law is
broken.

प्रच्छ् *prachh*, to ask, प्रच्छयति *prachchháyati*; अपप्रच्छत् *ápaprachchhat*.
स्कन्द् *skand*, to step, स्कन्दयति *skandáyati*; अचस्कन्दत् *áchaskandat*.

§ 377. Roots with radical ऋ *ri* or ॠ *rí*, followed by a consonant, may optionally take
the ∪ – ∪ or ∪ ∪ – forms.

---

* गण्य् *gaṇáy* and कथय् *katháy* take ई *í* or च *a* optionally; अजीगणत् *ájígaṇat* or
अजगणत् *ájagaṇat*.

† The following verbs take च *a* instead of इ *i* or ई *í* in the reduplicative syllable of the
aorist in the causative:

स्मृ *smri*, दृ *dri*, त्वर् *tvar*, प्रथ् *prath*, म्रद् *mrad*, स्तृ *stri*, स्पश् *spaś*.

स्मृ *smri*; Caus. स्मारयति *smáráyati*; Aor. असस्मरत् *ásasmarat*.

The same verbs which, as will be shown hereafter (§ 474), reduplicate अव् *av*, (the Guṇa of
उ, ऊ *ú*,) in the desiderative by उ *u*, take उ *u* instead of इ *i* in the reduplicated aorist:

नु *nu*; Caus. नावयति *návdyati*; Des. नुनावयिषति *núnávayishati*; Aor. of Caus. अनूनवं *ánúnavam*.

‡ Radical च *a* is reduplicated by च *a* if the root ends in a double consonant.

वृत् *vrit*, to be, वर्तयति *vartáyati;* अवीवृतत् *ávivritat* or अववर्तत् *ávavartat*. (Pâṇ. VII. 4, 7.)

मृज् *mrij*, to cleanse, मार्जयति *márjáyati;* अमीमृजत् *ámimrijat* or अममार्जत् *ámamárjat*.

कृत् *krit*, to praise, कीर्तयति *kirtáyati;* अचीकृतत् *áchikritat* or अचिकीर्तत् *áchikirtat*.

§ 378. Roots beginning with a vowel have the same internal reduplication, which will be described hereafter in the desiderative bases.

Thus अश् *aś* forms the Caus. आशय् *áśáy*. This after throwing off अय् *ay*, and shortening the vowel, becomes अश् *aś*; this reduplicated, अशिश् *aś-iś*; and lastly, with augment and termination, आशिशं *áś-iś-am*.

In the same manner, आर्चिचं *árchicham*, औब्जिजं *aúbjijam*, &c. (§ 476.)

§ 379. Are slightly irregular :

पा *pá*, to drink, which forms its causal aorist as अपीप्यत् *ápipyat* (instead of अपीपयत् *ápipayat*). Pâṇ. VII. 4, 4.

स्था *sthá*, to stand, which forms its causal aorist as अतिष्ठिपत् *átishṭhipat* (instead of अतिष्ठपत् *átishṭhapat*).

घ्रा *ghrá*, to smell, which forms its causal aorist as अजिघ्रिपत् *ájighripat* or अजिघ्रपत् *ájighrapat*.

REDUPLICATED AORIST.

PARASMAIPADA.

1. अशिश्रयं *áśiśrayam*	अशिश्रयाव *aśiśrayáva*	अशिश्रयाम *aśiśrayáma*
2. अशिश्रय: *aśiśrayaḥ*	अशिश्रयतं *aśiśrayatam*	अशिश्रयत *aśiśrayata*
3. अशिश्रयत् *aśiśrayat*	अशिश्रयतां *aśiśrayatám*	अशिश्रयन् *aśiśrayan*

ÂTMANEPADA.

1. अशिश्रये *aśiśraye*	अशिश्रयावहि *aśiśrayávahi*	अशिश्रयामहि *aśiśrayámahi*
2. अशिश्रयथा: *aśiśrayatháḥ*	अशिश्रयेथां *aśiśrayethám*	अशिश्रयध्वं *aśiśrayadhvam*
3. अशिश्रयत *aśiśrayata*	अशिश्रयेतां *aśiśrayetám*	अशिश्रयंत *aśiśrayanta*

§ 380. In the preceding §§ occasional rules have been given as to the particular forms of the aorist which certain verbs or classes of verbs adopt. As in Greek, so in Sanskrit, too, practice only can effectually teach which forms do actually occur of each verb; and the rules of grammarians, however minute and complicated, are not unfrequently contradicted by the usage of Sanskrit authors.

However, the general rule is that verbs follow the first aorist, unless this is specially prohibited, and that they take the first form of the first aorist, unless they are barred by general rules from the employment of the intermediate इ *i*. Verbs, thus barred, take the second form of the first aorist.

The number of verbs which take the third form of the first aorist is very limited, three roots ending in म् *m*, and roots ending in आ *á*.

The fourth form of the first aorist is likewise of very limited use; see § 360.

As to the second aorist, the roots which must or may follow it are indicated in § 367, and so are the roots which take the reduplicated form of the second aorist in § 371.

Roots which follow the second aorist optionally, or in the Parasmaipada only, are allowed to be conjugated in the first aorist, subject to the general rules.

CHAPTER XIV.

FUTURE, CONDITIONAL, PERIPHRASTIC FUTURE, AND BENEDICTIVE.

Future.

§ 381. Terminations.

PARASMAIPADA.

SINGULAR.	DUAL.	PLURAL.
1. इष्यामि *ishyámi*	इष्यावः *ishyávah*	इष्यामः *ishyámah*
2. इष्यसि *ishyási*	इष्यथः *ishyáthah*	इष्यथ *ishyátha*
3. इष्यति *ishyáti*	इष्यातः *ishyátah*	इष्यंति *ishyánti*

ÁTMANEPADA.

1. इष्ये *ishyé*	इष्यावहे *ishyávahe*	इष्यामहे *ishyámahe*
2. इष्यसे *ishyáse*	इष्येथे *ishyéthe*	इष्यध्वे *ishyádhve*
3. इष्यते *ishyáte*	इष्येते *ishyéte*	इष्यंते *ishyánte*

The cases in which the इ *i* of इष्यामि *ishyámi* &c. must be or may be omitted have been stated in chapter XI, § 331 seq. For the cases in which इ *i* is changed to ई *í*, see § 340. On the change of ष *sha* and स *sa*, see § 100 seq. On the strengthening of the radical vowel, see chapter XII, § 344 seq.

§ 382. The changes which the base undergoes before the terminations of the strengthening tenses, the two futures, the conditional, and the benedictive Átm. are regulated by one general principle, that of giving weight to the base, though their application varies according to the peculiarities of certain verbs. See illustrations in § 344 (*bhavishyámi*) and § 345 (*márkshyámi*). These peculiarities must be learnt by practice, but a few general rules may here be repeated :

1. Final ए *e*, ऐ *ai*, ओ *o* are changed to आ *á*; गै *gai*, to sing, गास्यामि *gásyámi*, &c.

2. Final इ *i* and ई *í*, उ *u*, ऊ *ú*, ऋ *ri* and ॠ *rí*, take Guṇa; जि *ji*, to conquer, जेष्यामि *jeshyámi*; भू *bhú*, भविष्यामि *bhavishyámi*; कृ *kri*, करिष्यामि *karishyámi*; दृ *drí*, to tear, दरिष्यामि *darishyámi* or दरीष्यामि *daríshyámi*. There are the usual exceptions, कू *kú*, to sound, कुविष्यामि *kuvishyámi*. (§ 345, note.)

3. Penultimate इ *i*, उ *u*, ऋ *ri*, prosodially short, take Guṇa; ॠ *rí* becomes इर् *ir*; बुध् *budh*, बोधिष्यामि *bodhishyámi*; भिद् *bhid*, भेत्स्यति *bhetsyáti*.

बुध् *budh*, to know,
with intermediate इ *i.*

PARASMAIPADA.

SINGULAR.	DUAL.	PLURAL.
1. बोधिष्यामि *bodhishyámi*	बोधिष्याव: *bodhishyávah*	बोधिष्याम: *bodhishyámah*
2. बोधिष्यसि *bodhishyási*	बोधिष्यथ: *bodhishyáthah*	बोधिष्यथ *bodhishyátha*
3. बोधिष्यति *bodhishyáti*	बोधिष्यत: *bodhishyátah*	बोधिष्यंति *bodhishyánti*

ÂTMANEPADA.

1. बोधिष्ये *bodhishyé*	बोधिष्यावहे *bodhishyávahe*	बोधिष्यामहे *bodhishyámahe*
2. बोधिष्यसे *bodhishyáse*	बोधिष्येथे *bodhishyéthe*	बोधिष्यध्वे *bodhishyáddhve*
3. बोधिष्यते *bodhishyáte*	बोधिष्येते *bodhishyéte*	बोधिष्यंते *bodhishyánte*

इ *i*, to go,
without intermediate इ *i.*

PARASMAIPADA.

1. एष्यामि *eshyámi*	एष्याव: *eshyávah*	एष्याम: *eshyámah*
2. एष्यसि *eshyási*	एष्यथ: *eshyáthah*	एष्यथ *eshyátha*
3. एष्यति *eshyáti*	एष्यत: *eshyátah*	एष्यंति *eshyánti*

ÂTMANEPADA.

1. एष्ये *eshyé*	एष्यावहे *eshyávahe*	एष्यामहे *eshyámahe*
2. एष्यसे *eshyáse*	एष्येथे *eshyéthe*	एष्यध्वे *eshyáddhve*
3. एष्यते *eshyáte*	एष्येते *eshyéte*	एष्यंते *eshyánte*

Conditional.

§ 383. The future is changed into the conditional by the same process
by which a present of the Tud class is changed into an imperfect.

बुध् *budh*, to know,
with intermediate इ *i.*

PARASMAIPADA.

SINGULAR.	DUAL.	PLURAL.
1. अबोधिष्यं *ábodhishyam*	अबोधिष्याव *abodhishyáva*	अबोधिष्याम *abodhishyáma*
2. अबोधिष्य: *abodhishyah*	अबोधिष्यतं *abodhishyatam*	अबोधिष्यत *abodhishyata*
3. अबोधिष्यत् *abodhishyat*	अबोधिष्यतां *abodhishyatám*	अबोधिष्यन् *abodhishyan*

ÂTMANEPADA.

1. अबोधिष्ये *ábodhishye*	अबोधिष्यावहि *abodhishyávahi*	अबोधिष्यामहि *abodhishyámahi*
2. अबोधिष्यथा: *abodhishyatháh*	अबोधिष्येथां *abodhishyethám*	अबोधिष्यध्वं *abodhishyadhvam*
3. अबोधिष्यत *abodhishyata*	अबोधिष्येतां *abodhishyetám*	अबोधिष्यंत *abodhishyanta*

इ *i*,
without intermediate इ *i.*

PARASMAIPADA.

1. ऐष्यं *aishyam*	ऐष्याव *aishyáva*	ऐष्याम *aishyáma*
2. ऐष्य: *aishyah*	ऐष्यतं *aishyatam*	ऐष्यत *aishyata*
3. ऐष्यत् *aishyat*	ऐष्यतां *aishyatám*	ऐष्यन् *aishyan*

ÂTMANEPADA.

1. रेप्ये *aishye*	रेप्यावहि *aishyâvahi*	रेप्यामहि *aishyâmahi*
2. रेप्यथा: *aishyathâh*	रेप्येथां *aishyethâm*	रेप्यध्वं *aishyadhvam*
3. रेप्यत *aishyata*	रेप्येतां *aishyetâm*	रेप्यंत *aishyanta*

Periphrastic Future.

§ 384. The terminations are,

PARASMAIPADA.

1. इतास्मि *itâsmi*	इतास्व: *itâsvah*	इतास्म: *itâsmah*
2. इतासि *itâsi*	इतास्य: *itâsthah*	इतास्थ *itâstha*
3. इता *itâ*	इतारौ *itârau*	इतार: *itârah*

ÂTMANEPADA.

1. इताहे *itâhe*	इतास्वहे *itâsvahe*	इतास्महे *itâsmahe*
2. इतासे *itâse*	इतासाथे *itâsâthe*	इताध्वे *itâddhve*
3. इता *itâ*	इतारौ *itârau*	इतार: *itârah*

These terminations are clearly compounded of ता *tâ* (base तृ *tṛi*), the common suffix for forming *nomina agentis*, and the auxiliary verb अस् *as*, to be. There is, however, with regard to ता *tâ*, no distinction of number and gender in the 1st and 2nd persons, and no distinction of gender in the 3rd person.

On the retention or omission of intermediate इ *i* or ई *î*, see § 331 seq. On the strengthening of the radical vowel, see § 382.

बुध् *budh*, to know,
with intermediate इ *i*.

PARASMAIPADA.

SINGULAR.	DUAL.	PLURAL.
1. बोधितास्मि *bodhitâsmi*	बोधितास्व: *bodhitâsvah*	बोधितास्म: *bodhitâsmah*
2. बोधितासि *bodhitâsi*	बोधितास्य: *bodhitâsthah*	बोधितास्थ *bodhitâstha*
3. बोधिता *bodhitâ*	बोधितारौ *bodhitârau*	बोधितार: *bodhitârah*

ÂTMANEPADA.

1. बोधिताहे *bodhitâhe*	बोधितास्वहे *bodhitâsvahe*	बोधितास्महे *bodhitâsmahe*
2. बोधितासे *bodhitâse*	बोधितासाथे *bodhitâsâthe*	बोधिताध्वे *bodhitâddhve*
3. बोधिता *bodhitâ*	बोधितारौ *bodhitârau*	बोधितार: *bodhitârah*

इ *i*,
without intermediate इ *i*.

PARASMAIPADA.

1. एतास्मि *etâsmi*	एतास्व: *etâsvah*	एतास्म: *etâsmah*
2. एतासि *etâsi*	एतास्य: *etâsthah*	एतास्थ *etâstha*
3. एता *etâ*	एतारौ *etârau*	एतार: *etârah*

ÂTMANEPADA.

1. इतासे *etáhe*	इतास्वहे *etásvahe*	इतास्महे *etásmahe*
2. इतासे *etáse*	इतासाथे *etásáthe*	इताध्वे *etáddhve*
3. इता *etá*	इतारौ *etárau*	इतार: *etáraḥ*

Benedictive.

§ 385. The so-called benedictive is formed in close analogy to the optative. It differs from the optative by not admitting the full modified verbal base, and, secondly, by the insertion of an स् *s* before the personal terminations. In the Parasmaipada this स् *s* stands between the या *yá* of the optative and the actual signs of the persons, being lost, however, in the 2nd and 3rd pers. sing. Thus, instead of

Opt. या:, या:, यात्, याव, यातं, यातां, याम, यात, यु:,
yám, yáḥ, yát, yáva, yátam, yátám, yáma, yáta, yúḥ, we have

Ben. यासं, या:, यात्, यास्व, यास्तं, यास्तां, यास्म, यास्त, यासु:.
yásam, yáḥ, yát, yásva, yástam, yástám, yásma, yásta, yásuḥ.

As the optative is a verbal compound of the modified base with an ancient second aorist of the root या *yá*, the benedictive seems a similar compound of the unmodified base with an ancient first aorist of या *yá*. In या: *yáḥ* and यात् *yát* we have contractions of यास्स् *yáss* and यास्त् *yást*. In the Veda the 3rd pers. sing. is या: *yáḥ*. (See Bollensen, Zeitschrift der D. M. G., vol. xxii. p. 594; and Pâṇ. viii. 2, 73–74.)

In the Âtmanepada the स् *s* stands *before* the terminations of the optative, e. g. सीय *síya* instead of ईय *íya*. Besides this, the personal terminations originally beginning with त *t* or थ *th* take an additional स् *s*. Cf. § 351. Thus, instead of

Opt. ईय, ईया:, ईत, ईवहि, ईयाथां, ईयातां, ईमहि, ईध्वं, ईरन्,
íya, ítháḥ, ítá, íváhi, íyáthám, íyátám, ímáhi, ídhvám, írán, we have

Ben. सीय, सीष्ठा:, सीष्ट, सीवहि, सीयास्थां, सीयास्तां, सीमहि, सीध्वं, सीरन्.
síyá, síshṭháḥ, síshṭá, sívábi, síyásthám, síyástám, símáhi, sídhvám, sírán.

The benedictive in the Âtmanepada is really an optative of the first aorist. Thus from भू *bhú*, Aor. अभविषि *abhavishi*, Ben. भविषीय *bhavishíya*; from स्तु *stu*, Opt. Âtm. स्तुवीत *stuvíta*, Aor. अस्तोष्ट *astoshṭa*, Ben. स्तोषीष्ट *stoshíshṭa*; from कृ *kṛ*, Opt. Âtm. कृषीरन् *kṛshíran*, Aor. अकृषत *akṛshata*, Ben. कृषीरन् *kṛshíran*.

§ 386. Verbal bases ending in अय *ay* (Chur, Caus. Denom. &c.) drop अय *ay* before the terminations of the benedictive Par.: चोरय *choray*, Ben. चोर्यासं *choryásam*; but in Âtm. चोरयिषीय *chorayishíyá*. Denominative bases in य *y* drop य *y* in the Ben. Par.: पुत्रीय *putríy*, Ben. पुत्रीयासं *putríyásam*; but in Âtm. पुत्रीयिषीय *putríyishíyá*.

§ 387. The benedictive Parasmaipada belongs to the weakening, the benedictive Âtmanepada to the strengthening forms (§ 344). Hence from चित् *chit*, Par. चित्यासं *chityásam*, Âtm. चेतिषीय *chetishíyá*.

§ 388. The benedictive Parasmaipada never takes intermediate इ *i*. The benedictive Âtmanepada generally takes intermediate इ *i*. Exceptions are provided for by the rules § 331 seq.

C C 2

Weakening of the Base before Terminations beginning with य *y.*

§ 389. Some of the rules regulating the weakening of the base, which is required in the benedictive Parasmaipada, may here be stated together with the rules that apply to the weakening of the base in the passive and intensive.

§ 390. While, generally speaking, the terminations of the benedictive, passive, and intensive exercise a weakening influence on the verbal base, there is one important, though only apparent, exception to this rule with regard to verbs ending in इ *i,* उ *u,* ऋ *ri.* Final इ *i* and उ *u,* before the य *y* of the terminations of benedictive, passive, and intensive, are lengthened (Pâṇ. VII. 4, 25), but not strengthened by Guṇa.

चि *chi,* to gather; Ben. चीयात् *chiyât;* Pass. चीयते *chiyâte;* Int. चेचीयते *chechiyâte.*

Final ऋ *ri* is changed to रि *ri.* (Pâṇ. VII. 4, 28.)

कृ *kri,* to do; Ben. क्रियात् *kriyât;* Pass. क्रियते *kriyâte.* (The Intensive has चेक्रीयते *chekriyâte,* Pâṇ. VII. 4, 27.)

In roots, however, beginning with conjunct consonants, final ऋ *ri* is actually strengthened by Guṇa, and appears as अर् *ar.* (Pâṇ. VII. 4, 29.)

स्मृ *smri,* to remember; Ben. स्मर्यात् *smaryât;* Pass. स्मर्यते *smaryâte;* Int. सास्मर्यते *sâsmaryâte.*
Also in ऋ *ri,* to go; Ben. अर्यात् *aryât;* Pass. अर्यते *aryâte;* Int. अरार्यते *arâryâte.*

Final ऋ *ri* is changed to ईर् *îr,* and, after labials, to ऊर् *ûr.*

स्तृ *stri,* to stretch; Ben. स्तीर्यात् *stîryât;* Pass. स्तीर्यते *stîryâte;* Int. तेस्तीर्यते *testîryâte.*
पृ *pri,* to fill; Ben. पूर्यात् *pûryât;* Pass. पूर्यते *pûryâte;* Int. पोपूर्यते *popûryâte.*

Exceptions: शी *sî* is changed to शय् *say.*

शी *sî,* to lie down; (Ben. शय्यात् *sayyât* does not occur, because the verb is Âtmanepadin); Pass. शय्यते *sayyâte;* Int. शाशय्यते *sâsayyâte.* (Pâṇ. VII. 4, 22.)

इ *i,* after prepositions, does not lengthen the final इ *i* in the benedictive.

इ *i,* to go; Ben. ईयात् *iyât;* but समियात् *samiyât.* (Pâṇ. VII. 4, 24.)

ऊह् *ûh,* to understand, after prepositions, is shortened to उह् *uh.* (Pâṇ. VII. 4, 23.)

Ben. ऊह्यात् *ûhyât;* Pass. ऊह्यते *ûhyâte.*
Ben. समुह्यात् *samuhyât;* Pass. समुह्यते *samuhyâte.*

§ 391. The following roots may or may not drop their final न् *n,* and then lengthen the preceding vowel. (Pâṇ. VI. 4, 43.)

जन् *jan,* to beget; Ben. जायात् *jâyât* or जन्यात् *janyât;* Pass. जायते *jâyâte* or जन्यते *janyâte;* Int. जाजायते *jâjâyâte* or जंजन्यते *jañjanyâte.*

सन् *san,* to obtain; Ben. सायात् *sâyât* or सन्यात् *sanyât;* Pass. सायते *sâyâte* or सन्यते *sanyâte;* Int. सासायते *sâsâyâte* or संसन्यते *samsanyâte.*

खन् *khan,* to dig; Ben. खायात् *khâyât* or खन्यात् *khanyât;* Pass. खायते *khâyâte* or खन्यते *khanyâte;* Int. चाखायते *châkhâyâte* or चंखन्यते *chankhanyâte.*

In the passive only, तन् *tan,* to stretch; Ben. तन्यात् *tanyât;* Pass. तायते *tâyâte* or तन्यते *tanyâte;* Int. तंतन्यते *tantanyâte.*

§ 392. According to a general rule, roots ending in ऐ *ai* and ओ *o* change their final diphthong in the general tenses into आ *â:* ध्यै *dhyai,* ध्यायते *dhyâyâte.* Roots ending in आ *â* retain it: पा *pâ,* पायते *pâyâte,* he is protected. But the following roots change their final vowel into ई *î* in the passive and intensive; into ए *e* in the benedictive Par.; and keep it unchanged before gerundial य *ya.* (Pâṇ. VI. 4, 66, 67, 69.)

The six verbs called चु *ghu* *, and the following verbs:

	PASSIVE.	INTENSIVE.	BENEDICTIVE †.	GERUND.
दा *dá*, to give	दीयते *díyáte*	देदीयते *dedíyáte*	देयात् *deydt*	प्रदाय *praddya*
मा *má*, to measure	मीयते *míyáte*	मेमीयते *memíyáte*	मेयात् *meydt*	प्रमाय *pramdya*
स्था *sthá*, to stand	स्थीयते *sthíyáte*	तेष्ठीयते *teshthíyáte*	स्थेयात् *stheydt*	प्रस्थाय *prasthdya*
गै *gai*, to sing	गीयते *gíyáte*	जेगीयते *jegíyáte*	गेयात् *geydt*	प्रगाय *pragdya*
पा *pá*, to drink	पीयते *píyáte*	पेपीयते *pepíyáte*	पेयात् *peydt*	प्रपाय *prapdya*
हा *há*, to leave	हीयते *híyáte*	जेहीयते *jehíyáte*	हेयात् *heydt*	प्रहाय *prahdya*
सो *so*, to finish	सीयते *síyáte*	सेषीयते *seshíyáte*	सेयात् *seydt*	प्रसाय *prasdya*

§ 393. The following verbs take Samprasârana in the benedictive (Pân. III. 4, 104), passive, participle, and gerund. (Pân. VI. 1, 15.)

वच् *vach*, to speak; स्वप् *svap* ‡ ||, to sleep; वश् *vaś* (Pân. VI. 1, 20), to wish; and the यजादि *yajddi*, i. e. those following यज् *yaj*.

Ben. उच्यात् *uchyát*; Pass. उच्यते *uchyáte*; Part. उक्त: *uktáh*; Ger. उक्त्वा *uktvá*.

The यजादि are, (23, 33–41) यज् *yaj*, to sacrifice; वप् *vap*, to sow; वह् *vah*, to carry; वस् *vas*, to dwell; वे *ve*, to weave; व्ये *vye* ||, to cover; ह्वे *hve* ||, to call; वद् *vad*, to speak; श्वि *śvi* ||, to grow.

§ 394. The following verbs take Samprasârana in the benedictive, passive, participle, gerund, and intensive. (Pân. VI. 1, 16.)

ग्रह् *grah*, to take; ज्या *jyá*, to fail; व्यध् *vyadh*, to pierce; व्यच् *vyach*, to surround; व्रश्च् *vraśch*, to cut; प्रच्छ् *prachh*, to ask; भ्रज्ज् *bhrajj*, to fry. As to स्वप् *svap*, स्यम् *syam*, and व्ये *vye*, see § 393, note ||.

ग्रह् *grah*; Ben. गृह्यात् *grihyát*; Pass. गृह्यते *grihyáte*; Part. गृहीत: *grihítáh*; Ger. गृहीत्वा *grihítvá*; Int. जरीगृह्यते *jarígrihyáte*.

§ 395. शास् *śás*, to rule, substitutes शिष् *śish* in the benedictive, passive, participle, gerund, intensive, also in the second aorist. (Pân. VI. 4, 34.)

Ben. शिष्यात् *śishyát*; Pass. शिष्यते *śishyáte*; Part. शिष्ट: *śishtáh*; Ger. शिष्ट्वा *śishtvd*; Aor. अशिषत् *áśishat*.

Roots ending in consonants preceded by a nasal (which is really written as belonging to the root) lose that nasal before weakening terminations (Kit, Ṅit, Pân. VI. 4, 24). Thus

---

* This term comprises the six roots डुदाञ्, दाण्, दो, देङ्, डुधाञ्, and धेट्, all varieties of the radicals दा *dá* and धा *dhá*; but not दाप् and दैप्, i. e. दाति *dáti*, he cuts, and दायति *ddyati*, he cleans (Pân. I. 1, 20). Hence दीयते *díyate*, it is given; but दायते *ddyate*, it is cleaned.

† In other roots, ending in आ *d* or diphthongs, and beginning with more than one consonant, the change into ए *e* in the benedictive Par. is optional (Pân. VI. 4, 68). ग्लै *glai*, to wither; ग्लेयात् *gleydt* or ग्लायात् *gláydt*. ख्या *khyá*, to call; ख्यायात् *khydydt* or ख्येयात् *khyeydt*.

‡ स्वाप् *svdp*, to send to sleep, takes Samprasârana in the reduplicated aorist (Pân. VI. 1, 18). असूषुपत् *asúshupat*.

|| स्वप् *svap*, to sleep, स्यम् *syam*, to sound, and व्ये *vye*, take Samprasârana in the intensive also (Pân. VI. 1, 19); सोषुप्यते *soshupyáte*, सेसिम्यते *sesimyáte*, वेवीयते *vevíyáte*. श्वि *śvi* takes Samprasârana optionally in the intensive (Pân. VI. 1, 30); शोशूयते *śośúyáte* or शेश्वीयते *śeśvíyáte*. ह्वे *hve* forms Int. जोहूयते *johúyáte* (Pân. VI. 1, 33). In the intensive चाय् *cháy* forms चेकीयते *chekíyáte* (Pân. VI. 1, 21); प्याय् *pyáy*, पेपीयते *pepíyáte* (Pân. VI. 1, 29).

from संस् *sraṁs*, Part. स्रस्त: *srastáḥ*, Pass. स्रस्यते *srasyáte*, Ben. स्रस्यात् *srasyát*, Ger. स्रस्वा *srastvá*, Int. सनीस्रस्यते *sanísrasyáte*, Aor. अस्रसत् *ásrasat*; from रञ्ज् *raňj*, Ben. रज्यात् *rajyát*, Pass. रज्यते *rajyáte*, Part. रक्त: *raktáḥ*, Ger. रक्त्वा *raktvá* (or रङ्क्त्वा *raṅktvá*, Pâṇ. vi. 4, 32).

§ 396. With regard to the benedictive Âtm. see the general rules as to the strengthening of the base, § 344, and particularly § 348 seq. Remember, that if the benedictive Âtm. does not take intermediate इ *i*, penultimate इ *i*, उ *u*, ऋ *ri* are left unchanged, whereas in other strengthening tenses they take Guṇa (§ 344). Final ऋ *ri*, too, remains unchanged, and ॠ *rî* becomes ईर् *ir*, or, after labials, ऊर् *úr*. क्षिप् *kship*, to throw, क्षिप्सीय *kshipsíyá*; पॄ *prî*, to fill, पूर्षीय *púrshíyá*.

Benedictive.

PARASMAIPADA.

1. बुध्यासं *budhyásam*	बुध्यास्व *budhyásva*	बुध्यास्म *budhyásma*
2. बुध्या: *budhyáḥ*	बुध्यास्तं *budhyástam*	बुध्यास्त *budhyásta*
3. बुध्यात् *budhyát*	बुध्यास्तां *budhyástám*	बुध्यासु: *budhyásuḥ*

ÂTMANEPADA.

1. बोधिषीय *bodhishíyá*	बोधिषीवहि *bodhishívahi*	बोधिषीमहि *bodhishímahi*
2. बोधिषीष्ठा: *bodhishíshṭháḥ*	बोधिषीयास्थां *bodhishíyásthám*	बोधिषीध्वं *bodhishídhvám*
3. बोधिषीष्ट *bodhishíshṭá*	बोधिषीयास्तां *bodhishíyástám*	बोधिषीरन् *bodhishírán*

CHAPTER XV.

PASSIVE.

§ 397. The passive takes the terminations of the Âtmanepada.

Special Tenses of the Passive.

§ 398. The present, imperfect, optative, and imperative of the passive are formed by adding य *yá* to the root. This य *ya* is added in the same manner as it is in the Div verbs, so that the Âtmanepada of Div verbs is in all respects (except in the accent) identical with the passive.

Âtm. नह्यते *náhyate*, he binds; Pass. नह्यते *nahyáte*, he is bound.

§ 399. Bases in अय *ay* (Chur, Caus. Denom. &c.) drop अय *ay* before य *ya* of the passive.

बोधय *bodháy*, to make one know; बोध्यते *bodh-yáte*, he is made to know.

चोरय *choráy*, to steal; चोर्यते *chor-yáte*, he is stolen.

Intensive bases ending in य् *y* retain their य् *y*, to which the य *ya* of the passive is added without any intermediate vowel.

लोलूय *lolúy*, to cut much; लोलूय्यते *lolúyyáte*, he is cut much.

Intensive bases ending in य् *y*, preceded by a consonant, drop their य् *y*.

वेभिद् *bebhidy*, to sever; वेभिद्यते *bebhidyáte*, it is severed.

दीधी *dídhí*, to shine, वेवी *veví*, to yearn, दरिद्रा *daridrá*, to be poor, drop their final vowel, as usual.

दीधी *dídhí*, दीध्यते *dídhyáte*, it is lightened, i. e. it lightens.

§ 400. As to the weakening of the base, see the rules given for the benedictive, § 389 seq.

Passive.

SINGULAR.

	1.	2.	3.
Pres.	भूये *bhúyé*	भूयसे *bhúydse*	भूयते *bhúydte*
Impf.	अभूये *ábhúye*	अभूयथाः *ábhúyathdh*	अभूयत *ábhúyata*
Opt.	भूयेय *bhúyéya*	भूयेथाः *bhúyéthdh*	भूयेत *bhúyéta*
Imp.	भूये *bhúyaí*	भूयस्व *bhúydsva*	भूयतां *bhúydtdm*

DUAL.

Pres.	भूयावहे *bhúydvahe*	भूयेथे *bhúyéthe*	भूयेते *bhúyéte*
Impf.	अभूयावहि *ábhúydvahi*	अभूयेथां *ábhúyethdm*	अभूयेतां *ábhúyetdm*
Opt.	भूयेवहि *bhúyévahi*	भूयेयाथां *bhúyéydthdm*	भूयेयातां *bhúyéydtdm*
Imp.	भूयावहै *bhúydvahai*	भूयेथां *bhúyéthdm*	भूयेतां *bhúyétdm*

PLURAL.

Pres.	भूयामहे *bhúydmahe*	भूयध्वे *bhúyddhve*	भूयते *bhúydnte*
Impf.	अभूयामहि *ábhúydmahi*	अभूयध्वं *ábhúyadhvam*	अभूयंत *ábhúyanta*
Opt.	भूयेमहि *bhúyémahi*	भूयेध्वं *bhúyédhvam*	भूयेरन् *bhúyéran*
Imp.	भूयामहै *bhúydmahai*	भूयध्वं *bhúyddhvam*	भूयंतां *bhúydntdm*

General Tenses of the Passive.

§ 401. In the general tenses of the passive, य *yá* is dropt, so that, with certain exceptions to be mentioned hereafter, there is no distinction between the general tenses of the passive and those of the Âtmanepada. The य *ya* of the passive is treated, in fact, like one of the conjugational class-marks (*vikáranas*), which are retained in the special tenses only, and it differs thereby from the derivative syllables of causative, desiderative, and intensive verbs, which, with certain exceptions, remain throughout both in the special and in the general tenses.

Reduplicated Perfect.

The reduplicated perfect is the same as in the Âtmanepada.

Periphrastic Perfect.

The periphrastic perfect is the same as in the Âtmanepada, but the auxiliary verbs अस् *as* and भू *bhú* must be conjugated in the Âtmanepada, as well as कृ *kri*. (§ 342.)

Aorist.

§ 402. Verbs may be conjugated in the three forms of the first aorist which admit of Âtmanepada, and without differing from the paradigms given above, except in the third person singular.

The second aorist Âtmanepada is not to be used in a purely passive sense*.

§ 403. In the third person singular a peculiar form has been fixed in the passive, ending in इ *i*, and requiring Vriddhi of final, and Guṇa of medial vowels (but अ *a* is lengthened), followed by *one* consonant.

Thus, instead of अलविष्ट *álavishṭa*, we find अलावि *áláv-i*. ⎫
अबोधिष्ट *abodhishṭa*, — अबोधि *abodh-i*. ⎬ First Form.

अक्षिप्त *akshipta*, — अक्षेपि *akshep-i*. ⎫
अनेष्ट *aneshṭa*, — अनायि *anây-i*. ⎪
अकृत *akrita*, — अकारि *akâr-i*. ⎪
अदित *adita*, — अदायि *adây-i*. ⎬ Second Form.
अस्तीर्ष्ट *astírshṭa*, — अस्तारि *astâr-i*. ⎪
असृष्ट *asrishṭa*, — असर्जि *asarj-i*. ⎪
अदग्ध *adagdha*, — अदाहि *adâh-i*. ⎭

अदिक्षत *adikshata*, — अदेशि *adeś-i*. ⎫
अघुक्षत *aghukshata*, — अगूहि *agúh-i*. ⎪
अलिक्षत *alikshata*, — अलेहि *aleh-i*. ⎬ Fourth Form.
अधुक्षत *adhukshata*, — अदोहि *adoh-i*. ⎪
अधिक्षत *adhikshata*, — अदेहि *adeh-i*. ⎭

§ 404. Verbs ending in आ *á* or diphthongs, take य *y* before the passive इ *i*.

दा *dá*, अदायि *adáyi*, instead of अदित *adita*.

§ 405. Verbs ending in अय् *ay* (Chur, Caus. Denom. &c.) drop अय् *ay* before the passive इ *i*, though in the general tenses, after the dropping of the passive य *ya*, the original अय् *ay* may reappear, i.e. the Âtm. may be used as passive.

बोधय् *bodhay*, अबोधि *abodhi;* चोरय् *choray*, अचोरि *achori;* राजय् *rájay*, अराजि *arâji*.

In the other persons these verbs may either drop अय् *ay* or retain it, being conjugated in either case after the first form of the first aorist.

भावय् *bhávay:* अभाविषि *abhávishi*, अभाविष्ठाः *abhávishṭháh*, अभावि *abhávi;* or अभावयिषि *abhávayishi*, अभावयिष्ठाः *abhávayishṭháh*, अभावि *abhávi*.

§ 406. Intensive bases in य *y* add the passive इ *i*, without Guṇa.

Int. बोभूय् *bobhúy*, अबोभूयि *abobhúyi*.

Intensive bases ending in य *y*, preceded by a consonant, drop य *y*, and refuse Guṇa.

Int. बेभिद् *bebhidy;* Aor. अबेभिदि *abebhidi*.

Desiderative bases, likewise, refuse Guṇa.

Des. बुबोधिष् *bubodhish;* Aor. अबुबोधिषि *abubodhishi*.

---

* This would follow if *kartari* extends to Pâṇ. III. 1, 54, 56.

§ 407. The following are a few irregular formations of the 3rd pers. sing. aorist passive :

रभ् *rabh*, to desire, forms अरंभि *arambhi*. (Pâṇ. VII. 1, 63.)   See § 345, [10].

रध् *radh*, to kill,   —   अरंधि *arandhi*. (Pâṇ. VII. 1, 61.)

जभ् *jabh*, to yawn,   —   अजंभि *ajambhi*. (Pâṇ. VII. 1, 61.)

भंज् *bhañj*, to break, —   अभंजि *abhañji* or अभाजि *abháji*. (Pâṇ. VI. 4, 33.)

लभ् *labh*, to take,   —   अलंभि *alambhi* or अलाभि *aldbhi*. (Pâṇ. VII. 1, 69.)

       With prepositions लभ् *labh* always forms अलंभि *alambhi*.

जन् *jan*, to beget,   —   अजनि *ajani*. (Pâṇ. VII. 3, 35.)

बध् *badh*, to strike, —   अबधि *abadhi*. (Pâṇ. VII. 3, 35.)

§ 408. Roots ending in अम् *am*, which admit of intermediate इ *i* (§ 332, 16), do not lengthen their radical vowel. (Pâṇ. VII. 3, 34.)

शम् *śam*, अशमि *aśami;* तम् *tam*, अतमि *atami;* but यम् *yam*, अयामि *ayámi*.
Pâṇini excepts आचम् *ácham*, to rinse, which forms आचामि *áchámi*.   Others add कम् *kam*,
वम् *vam*, नम् *nam* (Pâṇ. VII. 3, 34, vârt.).

§ 409. Thus the paradigms given in the Âtmanepada may be used in the passive of the aorist, with the exception of the 3rd pers. sing. (See p. 182.)

अलविषि *alavishi*   अलविष्वहि *alavishvahi*   अलविष्महि *alavishmahi*
अलविष्ठाः *alavishṭháḥ*   अलविषाथां *alavishdthám*   अलविध्वं or °ढुं *alavidhvam* or -ḍhvam
अलावि *alávi*   अलविषातां *alavishátám*   अलविषत *alavishata*

The Two Futures, the Conditional, and the Benedictive Passive.

§ 410. These formations are identically the same in the passive as in the Âtmanepada.   Hence

       Fut. बोधिष्ये *bodhishyé*, I shall be known.
       Cond. अबोधिष्ये *ábodhishye*, I should be known.
  Periphr. Fut. बोधिताहे *bodhitáhe*, I shall be known.
       Bened. बोधिषीय *bodhishíyá*, May I be known !

*Secondary Form of the Aorist, the Two Futures, the Conditional, and
Benedictive of Verbs ending in Vowels.*

§ 411. All verbs ending in vowels, in अय् *ay*, and likewise हन् *han*, to strike, दृश् *dṛiś*, to see, ग्रह् *grah*, to take, may form a secondary base (really denominative), being identical with the peculiar third person singular of the aorist passive, described before.   Thus from लू *lú* we have अलावि *alávi*, and from this, by treating the final इ *i* as the intermediate इ *i*, we form,

Sing. 1. pers. अलाविषि *alávi-shi*,   by the side of अलविषि *alávi-shi*.
       2.   अलाविष्ठाः *alávi-shṭháḥ*,   —   —   अलविष्ठाः *alávi-shṭháḥ*.
       3.   अलावि *alávi*,   —   —   अलावि *alávi*.

Dual 1. pers. अलाविष्वहि *alávi-shvahi*, by the side of अलविष्वहि *alăvi-shvahi*.

2.　　　अलाविषाथां *alávi-sháthám*, —　— अलविषाथां *alăvi-sháthám*.

3.　　　अलाविषातां *alávi-shátám*, —　— अलविषातां *alăvi-shátám*.

Plur. 1. pers. अलाविष्महि *alávi-shmahi*, by the side of अलविष्महि *alăvi-shmahi*.

2.　　　अलाविध्वं *alávi-dhvam* or °ढ्-ढ्वम् — अलविध्वं *alăvi-dhvam* or °ढ्.

3.　　　अलाविषत *alávi-shata*,　. —　— अलविषत *alăvi-shata*.

Fut. लाविष्ये *lávi-shye*,　　　by the side of लविष्ये *lăvi-shye*.

Cond. अलाविष्ये *alávi-shye*, —　— अलविष्ये *alăvi-shye*.

Per. Fut. लाविताहे *lávi-táhe*, —　— लविताहे *lăvi-táhe*.

Ben. लाविषीय *lávi-shíya*, —　— लविषीय *lăvi-shíya*.

From चि *chi*, to gather, 3rd pers. sing. Aor. Pass. अचायि *acháyi*; hence

Aor. अचायिषि *acháyishi*, besides अचेषि *acheshi*, &c.

Fut. चायिष्ये *cháyishye*, — चेष्ये *cheshye*.

Cond. अचायिष्ये *acháyishye*, — अचेष्ये *acheshye*.

Per. Fut. चायिताहे *cháyitáhe*, — चेताहे *chetáhe*.

Ben. चायिषीय *cháyishíya*, — चेषीय *cheshíya*.

From घ्रा *ghrá*, to smell, 3rd pers. sing. Aor. Pass. अघ्रायि *aghráyi*; hence

Aor. अघ्रायिषि *aghráyishi*, besides अघ्रासि *aghrási*.

Fut. घ्रायिष्ये *ghráyishye*, — घ्रास्ये *ghrásye*.

Cond. अघ्रायिष्ये *aghráyishye*, — अघ्रास्ये *aghrásye*.

Per. Fut. घ्रायिताहे *ghráyitáhe*, — घ्राताहे *ghrátáhe*.

Ben. घ्रायिषीय *ghráyishíya*, — घ्रासीय *ghrásíya*.

From ध्वृ *dhvṛi*, to hurt, 3rd pers. sing. Aor. Pass. अध्वारि *adhvári*; hence

Aor. अध्वारिषि *adhvárishi*, besides अध्वृषि *adhvṛishi* or अध्वारिषि *adhvărishi*.

Fut. ध्वारिष्ये *dhvárishye*, — ध्वरिष्ये *dhvărishye*.

Per. Fut. ध्वारिताहे *dhváritáhe*, — ध्वर्ताहे *dhvărtáhe*.

Ben. ध्वारिषीय *dhvárishíya*, — ध्वृषीय *dhvṛishíya* or ध्वरिषीय *dhvărishíya**.

From हन् *han*, to kill, 3rd pers. sing. Aor. Pass. अघानि *aghání*; hence

Aor. अघानिषि *aghánishi*, besides (अवधिषि *avadhishi*). Pân. vi. 4, 62 †.

Fut. घानिष्ये *ghánishye*, — हनिष्ये *hanishye*.

Per. Fut. घानिताहे *ghánitáhe*, — हन्ताहे *hantáhe*.

Ben. घानिषीय *ghánishíya*, — (वधिषीय *vadhishíya*).

From दृश् *dṛiś*, to see, 3rd pers. sing. Aor. Pass. अदर्शि *adarśi*; hence

Aor. अदर्शिषि *adarśishi*, besides अदृक्षि *adṛikshi*.

Fut. दर्शिष्ये *darśishye*, — द्रक्ष्ये *drakshye*.

Per. Fut. दर्शिताहे *darśitáhe*, — द्रष्टाहे *drashṭáhe*.

Ben. दर्शिषीय *darśishíya*, — दृक्षीय *dṛikshíya*.

---

* See § 332, 5.

† Siddh.-Kaum. vol. ii, p. 270, seems to allow अकासि *akasi*.

From ग्रह् *grah*, to take, 3rd pers. sing. Aor. Pass. अग्राहि *agráhi;* hence

>Aor. अग्राहिषि *agráhishi,* besides अग्रहीषि *agrahíshi.*
>
>Fut. ग्राहिष्ये *gráhishye,*   —   ग्रहीष्ये *grahíshye.*
>
>Per. Fut. ग्राहिताहे *gráhitáhe,*   —   ग्रहीताहे *grahítáhe.*
>
>Ben. ग्राहिषीय *gráhishíya,*   —   ग्रहीषीय *grahíshíya.*

From रमय् *ramay*, to delight, Caus. of रम् *ram*, 3rd pers. sing. Aor. Pass. अरमि *arami* or अरामि *arámi;* hence

>Aor. अरमिषि *aramishi* or अरामिषि *arámishi,* besides अरमयिषि *aramayishi.*

§ 412. Certain verbs of an intransitive meaning take the passive इ *i* in the 3rd pers. sing. Aor. Âtm. Thus उत्पद्यते *utpadyate* (3rd pers. sing. present of the Âtmanepada of a Div verb), he arises, becomes उदपादि *udapádi,* he arose, he sprang up; but it is regular in the other persons, उदपत्सातां *udapatsátám,* they two arose, &c. (Pâṇ. III. 1, 60.)

§ 413. Other verbs of an intransitive character take the same form optionally (Pâṇ. III. 1, 61):

दीप् *díp* (दीप्यते *dípyate,* he burns, Div, Âtm.), अदीपि *adípi* or अदीपिष्ट *adípishṭa.*

जन् *jan* (जायते *jáyate,* he is born, he is, Div, Âtm.; it cannot be formed from जन् *jan* (Hu, Par.), to beget), अजनि *ajani* or अजनिष्ट *ajanishṭa.*

बुध् *budh* (बुध्यते *budhyate,* he is conscious, Div, Âtm.), अबोधि *abodhi* or अबुद्ध *abuddha.*

पूर् *púr* (पूरयति *púrayati,* he fills, Chur.), अपूरि *apúri* or अपूरिष्ट *apúrishṭa.*

ताय् *táy* (तायते *táyate,* he spreads, Bhû, Âtm.; really Div form of Tan), अतायि *atáyi* or अतायिष्ट *atáyishṭa.*

प्याय् *pyáy* (प्यायते *pyáyate,* he grows), अप्यायि *apyáyi* or अप्यायिष्ट *apyáyishṭa.*

CHAPTER XVI.

PARTICIPLES, GERUNDS, AND INFINITIVE.

§ 414. The participle of the present Parasmaipada retains the Vikaraṇas of the ten classes. It is most easily formed by taking the 3rd pers. plur. of the present, and dropping the final इ *i.* This gives us the Aṅga base, from which the Pada and Bha base can be easily deduced according to general rules (§ 182). The accent remains in the participle on the same syllable where it was in the 3rd pers. plur. If the accent falls on the last syllable of the participle, and if that participle does not take a nasal, then all Bha cases and the feminine suffix receive the accent. (Pâṇ. VI. 1, 173.) Thus

भवंति	भवंत्	Nom. S. भवन्	Acc. भवंतं	Instr. भवता &c.
bhávanti	*bhávant*	*bhávan*	*bhávantam*	*bhávatá*
तुदंति	तुदंत्	तुदन्	तुदंतं	तुदता &c.
tudánti	*tudánt*	*tudán*	*tudántam*	*tudatá*
दीव्यंति	दीव्यंत्	दीव्यन्	दीव्यंतं	दीव्यता &c.
dívyanti	*dívyant*	*dívyan*	*dívyantam*	*dívyatá*

		Nom. S.	Acc.	Instr.
चोरयंति *choráyanti*	चोरयंत् *choráyant*	चोरयन् *choráyan*	चोरयंतं *choráyantam*	चोरयता &c. *choráyatá*
सुन्वंति *sunvánti*	सुन्वंत् *sunvánt*	सुन्वन् *sunván*	सुन्वंतं *sunvántam*	सुम्वता &c. *sunvatá*
तन्वंति *tanvánti*	तन्वंत् *tanvánt*	तन्वन् *tanván*	तन्वंतं *tanvántam*	तन्वता &c. *tanvatá*
क्रीयंति *kríṇánti*	क्रीयंत् *kríṇánt*	क्रीयन् *kríṇán*	क्रीयंतं *kríṇántam*	क्रीयता &c. *kríṇatá*
अदंति *adánti*	अदंत् *adánt*	अदन् *adán*	अदंतं *adántam*	अदता &c. *adatá*
जुह्वति *júhvati*	जुह्वत् *júhvat*	जुह्वत् *júhvat*	जुह्वतं *júhvatam*	जुह्वता (§ 184) *júhvatá*
रुंधंति *rundhánti*	रुंधंत् *rundhánt*	रुंधन् *rundhán*	रुंधंतं *rundhántam*	रुंधता &c. *rundhatá*
बोभुवति Intens. *bóbhuvati*	बोभुवत् *bóbhuvat*	बोभुवत् *bóbhuvat*	बोभुवतं *bóbhuvatam*	बोभुवता (§ 184) *bóbhuvatá*

§ 415. The participle of the future is formed on the same principle.

		Nom. S.	Acc.	Instr.
भविष्यंति *bhavishyánti*	भविष्यंत् *bhavishyánt*	भविष्यन् *bhavishyán*	भविष्यंतं *bhavishyántam*	भविष्यता *bhavishyatá*

§ 416. The participle of the reduplicated perfect may best be formed by taking the 3rd pers. plur. of that tense. This corresponds, both in form and accent, with the Bha base of the participle, only that the स् *s*, as it is always followed by a vowel, is changed to ष् *sh*. Having the Bha base, it is easy to form the Aṅga and Pada bases, according to § 204. In forming the Aṅga and Pada bases, it must be remembered,

1. That roots ending in a vowel, restore that vowel, which, before उः *uḥ*, had been naturally changed into a semivowel.

2. That, according to the rules on intermediate इ *i*, all verbs which, without counting the उः *uḥ*, are monosyllabic in the 3rd pers. plur., insert इ *i*. (See Necessary इ *i*, § 338, 1 ; Optional इ *i*, § 337, 8.)

3rd P. Plur.	Instr. Sing.	Nom. Sing.	Acc. Sing.	Instr. Plur.
बभूवुः *babhúvuḥ*	बभूवुषा *babhúvushá*	बभूवान् *babhúván*	बभूवांसं *babhúvámsam*	बभूवद्भिः *babhúvádbhiḥ*
निन्युः *ninyúḥ*	निन्युषा *ninyúshá*	निनीवान् *niníván*	निनीवांसं *ninívámsam*	निनीवद्भिः *ninívádbhiḥ*
तुतुदुः *tutudúḥ*	तुतुदुषा *tutudúshá*	तुतुदवान् *tutudván*	तुतुदवांसं *tutudvámsam*	तुतुदवद्भिः *tutudvádbhiḥ*
दिदिवुः *didivúḥ*	दिदिवुषा *didivúshá*	दिदिवान् (§ 143) *did99ván*	दिदिवांसं *didivámsam*	दिदिवद्भिः *didivádbhiḥ*
चोरयामासुः *chorayámásuḥ*	चोरयामासुषा *chorayámásushá*	चोरयामासिवान् *chorayámásiván*	चोरयामासिवांसं *chorayámásivámsam*	चोरयामासिवद्भिः *chorayámásivádbhiḥ*

3rd P. Plur.	Instr. Sing.	Nom. Sing.	Acc. Sing.	Instr. Plur.
सुशुवुः *sushuvúḥ*	सुशुवुषा *sushuvúshá*	सुशुवान् *sushuvān*	सुशुवांसं *sushuvāṁsam*	सुशुवद्भिः *sushuvádbhiḥ*
तेनुः *tenúḥ*	तेनुषा *tenúshá*	तेनिवान् *tenivān*	तेनिवांसं *tenivāṁsam*	तेनिवद्भिः *tenivádbhiḥ*
चिक्रियुः *chikriyúḥ*	चिक्रियुषा *chikriyúshá*	चिक्रीवान् *chikrívān*	चिक्रीवांसं *chikrívāṁsam*	चिक्रीवद्भिः *chikrívádbhiḥ*
आदुः *ādúḥ*	आदुषा *ādúshá*	आदिवान् *ādivān*	आदिवांसं *ādivāṁsam*	आदिवद्भिः *ādivádbhiḥ*
जुहुवुः *juhuvúḥ*	जुहुवुषा *juhuvúshá*	जुहुवान् *juhuvān*	जुहुवांसं *juhuvāṁsam*	जुहुवद्भिः *juhuvádbhiḥ*
रुरुधुः *rurudhúḥ*	रुरुधुषा *rurudhúshá*	रुरुध्वान् *rurudhvān*	रुरुध्वांसं *rurudhvāṁsam*	रुरुध्वद्भिः *rurudhvádbhiḥ*

§ 417. In five verbs, where the insertion of इ *i* before वस् *vas* is optional (§ 337, 8), we get the following forms :

	3rd P. Plur.	Instr. Sing.	Nom. Sing.	Acc. Sing.	Instr. Plur.
गम् *gam*	जग्मुः *jagmúḥ*	जग्मुषा *jagmúshá*	जग्मिवान् or जगन्वान्* *jagmivān or jaganvān*	जग्मिवांसं *jagmivāṁsam*	जग्मिवद्भिः *jagmivádbhiḥ*
हन् *han*	जघ्नुः *jaghnúḥ*	जघ्नुषा *jaghnúshá*	जघ्निवान् or जघन्वान् *jaghnivān or jaghanvān*	जघ्निवांसं *jaghnivāṁsam*	जघ्निवद्भिः *jaghniváddbhiḥ*
विद् *vid*	विविदुः *vividúḥ*	विविदुषा *vividúshá*	विविद्वान् or विविदिवान् *vividvān or vividivān*	विविद्वांसं *vividvāṁsam*	विविद्वद्भिः *vividvádbhiḥ*
विश् *viś*	विविशुः *viviśúḥ*	विविशुषा *viviśúshá*	विविश्वान् or विविशिवान् *viviśvān or viviśivān*	विविश्वांसं *viviśvāṁsam*	विविश्वद्भिः *viviśvádbhiḥ*
दृश् *dṛś*	ददृशुः *dadṛiśúḥ*	ददृशुषा *dadṛiśúshá*	ददृश्वान् or ददृशिवान् *dadṛiśvān or dadṛiśivān*	ददृश्वांसं *dadṛiśvāṁsam*	ददृश्वद्भिः *dadṛiśvádbhiḥ*

§ 418. The participle of the reduplicated perfect Âtmanepada is formed by dropping इरे *ire*, the termination of the 3rd pers. plur. Âtm., and substituting आन *ána*.

बभूविरे *babhūviré*— बभूवानः *babhūvānáḥ*

चक्रिरे *chakriré*— चक्राणः *chakrāṇáḥ*

ददिरे *dadiré*— ददानः *dadānáḥ*

§ 419. The participle present Âtmanepada has two terminations,— मान *mâna* for verbs of the First Division (§ 295), आन *âna* for verbs of the Second Division.

In the First Division we may again take the 3rd pers. plur. present Âtm., drop the termination न्ते *nte*, and replace it by मानः *mânaḥ*.

In the Second Division we may likewise take the 3rd pers. plur. present Âtm., drop the termination अते *ate*, and replace it by आनः *ânaḥ*.

---

* The same optional forms run through all the Pada and Bha cases.

<table>
<tr><td></td><td>First Division.</td><td>Second Division.</td></tr>
<tr><td></td><td>भवंते bháva-nte—भवमान: bháva-mánaḥ</td><td>सुन्वते sunv-áte—सुन्वान: sunv-ánáḥ</td></tr>
<tr><td></td><td>तुदंते tudá-nte—तुदमान: tudá-mánaḥ</td><td>आप्नुवते ápnuv-áte—आप्नुवान: ápnuv-á</td></tr>
<tr><td></td><td>दीव्यंते dívya-nte—दीव्यमान: dívya-mánaḥ</td><td>तन्वते tanv-áte—तन्वान: tanv-ánáḥ</td></tr>
<tr><td></td><td>चोरयंते choráya-nte—चोरयमाण: choráya-mánaḥ</td><td>क्रीणते krín-áte—क्रीणान: krín-ánáḥ</td></tr>
<tr><td>Pass.</td><td>तुद्यंते tudyá-nte—तुद्यमान: tudyá-mánaḥ</td><td>अदते ad-áte—अदान: ad-ánáḥ</td></tr>
<tr><td>Caus.</td><td>भावयंते bhávdya-nte—भावयमान: bhávdya-mánaḥ</td><td>जुह्वते júhv-ate—जुह्वान: júhv-ánaḥ</td></tr>
<tr><td>Des.</td><td>बुभूषंते búbhúsha-nte—बुभूषमाण: búbhúsha-mánaḥ</td><td>रुंधते rundh-áte—रुंधान: rundh-ánáḥ</td></tr>
<tr><td>Int.</td><td>बोभूयंते bodhúyá-nte—बोभूयमान: bobhúyá-mánaḥ</td><td></td></tr>
</table>

§ 420. The participle of the future in the Âtmanepada is formed by adding मान: mánaḥ in the same manner.

> भविष्यंते bhavishyá-nte—भविष्यमाण: bhavishyá-mánaḥ
> नेष्यंते neshyá-nte—नेष्यमाण: neshyá-mánaḥ
> तोत्संते totsyá-nte—तोत्स्यमान: totsyá-mánaḥ
> एधिष्यंते edhishyá-nte—एधिष्यमाण: edhishyá-mánaḥ

§ 421. The participles of the present and future passive are formed by adding मान: mánaḥ in the same manner.

<table>
<tr><td>भूयंते bhúyá-nte—भूयमान: bhúyá-mánaḥ</td><td>भाविष्यंते—भाविष्यमाण:
bhávishyá-nte—bhávishyá-mánaḥ</td></tr>
<tr><td>बुध्यंते budhyá-nte—बुध्यमान: budhyá-mánaḥ</td><td></td></tr>
<tr><td>स्तूयंते stúyá-nte—स्तूयमान: stúyá-mánaḥ</td><td>नायिष्यंते—नायिष्यमाण:
náyishyá-nte—náyishyá-mánaḥ</td></tr>
<tr><td>क्रियंते kriyá-nte—क्रियमाण: kriyá-mánaḥ</td><td>Or like the Part. Fut. Âtm.</td></tr>
<tr><td>भाव्यंते bhávyá-nte—भाव्यमान: bhávyá-mánaḥ</td><td></td></tr>
</table>

The Past Participle Passive in त: tá{ḥ} *and the Gerund in* त्वा tvá.

§ 422. The past participle passive is formed by adding त: táḥ or न: náḥ to the root. कृ kri, कृत: kritáḥ, done, masc.; कृता kritá, fem.; कृतं kritám, neut. लू lú, लून: lúnáḥ, cut.

This termination त ta is, as we saw, most opposed to the insertion of intermediate इ i, so much so that verbs which may form any one general tense with or without इ i, always form their past participle without it. The number of verbs which must insert इ i before त ta is very small. (§ 332, D.)

Besides being averse to the insertion of intermediate इ i, the participial termination त ta, having always the Udâtta, is one of those which have a tendency to weaken verbal bases. (See § 344.)

§ 423. The gerund of simple verbs is formed by adding त्वा tvá to the root. कृ kri, कृत्वा kritvá, having done. पू pú, पूत्वा pútvá or, from पूङ् púṅ, पवित्वा pavitvá, having purified.

The rules as to the insertion of the intermediate इ i before त्वा tvá have been given before. With regard to the strengthening or weakening of the base, the general rule is that त्वा *tvá* without intermediate इ *i* weakens, with intermediate इ *i* strengthens the root (Pâṇ. I. 2, 18). It always has the Udâtta. In giving a few more special rules on this point, it will be convenient to take the terminations त *ta* and त्वा *tvd* together, as they agree to a great extent, though not altogether.

I. तः *táḥ* and त्वा tvá, *with intermediate* इ i.

§ 424. If तः *taḥ* takes intermediate इ *i*, it may in certain verbs produce Guṇa. In this case the Guṇa before त्वा *tvd* is regular.

शी *śí*, to lie down, शयितः *śayitáḥ* (Pâṇ. I. 2, 19); शयित्वा *śayitvd*.

स्विद् *svid*, to sweat, स्वेदितः *sveditáḥ* or स्विन्न: *svinndḥ*; स्वेदित्वा *sveditvd*.

मिद् *mid*, to be soft, मेदितः *meditáḥ*; मेदित्वा *meditvd*.

क्ष्विद् *kshvid*, to drip, क्ष्वेदितः *kshveditáḥ*; क्ष्वेदित्वा *kshveditvd*.

धृष् *dhṛish*, to dare, धर्षितः *dharshitáḥ*; धर्षित्वा *dharshitvd*.

मृष् *mṛish*, to bear, मर्षितः *marshitáḥ* (patient), (Pâṇ. I. 2, 20); मर्षित्वा *marshitvd*.

पू *pú*, to purify, पवितः *pavitáḥ* (Pâṇ. I. 2, 22); पवित्वा *pavitvd*, from पूञ् *púñ*. See No. 156.

§ 425. Verbs with penultimate उ *u* may or may not take Guṇa before त *ta* with intermediate इ *i*, if they are used impersonally.

द्युत् *dyut*, to shine, द्युतितं *dyutitám* or द्योतितं *dyotitám*, it has been shining. (Pâṇ. I. 2, 21.)

§ 426. If त्वा *tvd* takes intermediate इ *i*, it requires, as a general rule, Guṇa (Pâṇ. I. 2, 18), or at all events does not produce any weakening of the base. वृत् *vṛit*, to exist, वर्तित्वा *vartitvd*. स्रंस् *srams*, to fall, स्रंसित्वा *sraṁsitvd* (Pâṇ. I. 2, 23). पू *pú* (i. e. पूञ् *púñ*), to purify, पवित्वा *pavitvd* (Pâṇ. I. 2, 22).

Verbs, however, beginning with consonants, and ending in any single consonant except य *y* or व *v*, preceded by इ, ई *í* or उ, ऊ *ú*, take Guṇa optionally (Pâṇ. I. 2, 26): द्युत् *dyut*, to shine, द्योतित्वा *dyotitvd* or द्युतित्वा *dyutitvd*. The same option applies to तृष् *tṛish*, to thirst; मृष् *mṛish*, to bear; कृश् *kṛiś*, to attenuate (Pâṇ. I. 2, 25); तृषित्वा *tṛishitvd* or तर्षित्वा *tarshitvd*.

§ 427. Though taking intermediate इ *i*, त्वा *tvd* does not produce Guṇa, but, if possible, weakens the base, in रुद् *rud*, to cry, रुदित्वा *ruditvd* (Pâṇ. I. 2, 8); विद् *vid*, to know, विदित्वा *viditvd*; मुष् *mush*, to steal, मुषित्वा *mushitvd*; ग्रह् *grah*, to take, गृहीत्वा *grihítvd*; मृद् *mṛid*, to delight, मृदित्वा *mṛiditvd* (Pâṇ. I. 2, 7); मृद् *mṛid*, to rub, मृदित्वा *mṛiditvd*; गुध् *gudh*, to cover, गुधित्वा *gudhitvd*; क्लिश् *kliś*, to hurt, क्लिशित्वा *kliśitvd*; वद् *vad*, to speak, उदित्वा *uditvd*; वस् *vas*, to dwell, उषित्वा *ushitvd*.

§ 428. Roots ending in थ *th* or फ *ph*, preceded by a nasal, may or may not drop the nasal before त्वा *tvd* (Pâṇ. I. 2, 23); ग्रन्थित्वा *granthitvd* or ग्रथित्वा *grathitvd*, having twisted. The same applies to the roots वञ्च् *vañch*, to cheat, and लुञ्च् *luñch*, to pluck (Pâṇ. I. 2, 24); वञ्चित्वा *vañchitvd* or वचित्वा *vachitvd*.

II. तः *táḥ* and त्वा tvá, *without intermediate* इ i.

§ 429. Roots ending in nasals lengthen their vowel before तः *taḥ* and त्वा *tvd* (Pâṇ. vi. 4, 15). शम् *śam*, to rest, शान्तः *śántáḥ*, शान्त्वा *śántvd*.

क्रम् *kram*, to step, may or may not lengthen its vowel before त्वा *tvd* (Pâṇ. vi. 4, 18). क्रम् *kram*, क्रान्तः *krántáḥ*, क्रान्त्वा *krántvd* or क्रन्त्वा *krantvd*; also क्रमित्वा *kramitvd*.

§ 430. The following roots, ending in nasals, drop them before तः *taḥ* and त्वा *tvd*. (Pâṇ. vi. 4, 37.)

यम् *yam*, to check, यतः *yatáḥ*, यत्वा *yatvá**; रम् *ram*, to sport, रतः *ratáḥ*, रत्वा *ratvá*; नम् *nam*, to bend, नतः *natáḥ*, नत्वा *natvá*; हन् *han*, to kill, हतः *hatáḥ*, हत्वा *hatvá*; गम् *gam*, to go, गतः *gatáḥ*, गत्वा *gatvá*; मन् *man*, to think, मतः *matáḥ*, मत्वा *matvá*; वन् *van*, to ask; तन् *tan*, to stretch, ततः *tatáḥ*, तत्वा *tatvá*; and the other verbs of the Tan class, ending in न् *n*.

Note—Of the same verbs those ending in न *n* drop the nasal before the gerundial य *ya* and insert त् *t*: प्रमत्य *pramátya* (Pâṇ. VI. 4, 38): those ending in म *m* may or may not drop the nasal before the gerundial य *ya*: प्रगत्य *pragátya* or प्रगम्य *pragámya*.

§ 431. The following verbs drop final न् *n*, and lengthen the vowel.

जन् *jan*, to bear, जातः *játaḥ*, जात्वा *játvá*; सन् *san*, to obtain, सातः *sátaḥ*, सात्वा *sátvá*; खन् *khan*, to dig, खातः *khátaḥ*, खात्वा *khátvá*.

1. Roots ending in छ् *chh*, or व् *v*, substitute इ *i* and ऊ *ú*. (Pâṇ. VI. 4, 19.)

प्रछ् *prachh*, to ask, पृष्टः *prishṭaḥ* (§ 125), पृष्ट्वा *prishṭvá*; दिव् *div*, to play, द्यूनः *dyúnaḥ*, द्यूत्वा *dyútvá*.

2. Roots ending in ऋछ् *rchh*, or र्व् *rv*, drop their final consonant. (Pâṇ. VI. 4, 21.)

मुर्छ् *murchh*, to faint, मूर्तः *múrtaḥ*; तुर्व् *turv*, to strike, तूर्णः *túrṇaḥ*.

§ 432. The following verbs change their व् *v* with the preceding or following vowel into ऊ *ú*. (Pâṇ. VI. 4, 20.)

ज्वर् *jvar*, to ail, जूर्णः *júrṇaḥ*, जूर्त्वा *júrtvá*; त्वर् *tvar*, to hasten, तूर्णः *túrṇaḥ*, तूर्त्वा *túrtvá*; श्रिव् *sriv*, to dry, स्रूतः *srútaḥ*, स्रूत्वा *srútvá*; अव् *av*, to protect, ऊतः *útaḥ*, ऊत्वा *útvá*; मव् *mav*, to bind, मूतः *mútaḥ*, मूत्वा *mútvá*.

§ 433. Roots ending in ऐ *ai* substitute आ *á*: ध्यै *dhyai*, to meditate, ध्यातः *dhyátaḥ*, ध्यात्वा *dhyátvá*: or ई *í*; गै *gai*, to sing, गीतः *gítaḥ*, गीत्वा *gítvá*. Final ए *e* and आ *á*, too, are changed to ई *í*; पा *pá*, to drink, पीतः *pítaḥ*, पीत्वा *pítvá*; धे *dhe*, to suck, धीतः *dhítaḥ*, धीत्वा *dhítvá*.

§ 434. The following roots change their final vowel into इ *i*.

दो *do*, to cut, दितः *ditaḥ*, दित्वा *ditvá* (Pâṇ. VII. 4, 40); सो *so*, to finish, सितः *sitaḥ*, सित्वा *sitvá*; मा *má*, to measure, मितः *mitaḥ*, मित्वा *mitvá*; स्था *sthá*, to stand, स्थितः *sthitaḥ*, स्थित्वा *sthitvá*; धा *dhá*, to place, हितः *hitaḥ*, हित्वा *hitvá* (Pâṇ. VII. 4, 42); हा *há*, to leave (हीनः *hínaḥ*), हित्वा *hitvá* (Pâṇ. VII. 4, 43).

§ 435. शो *so*, to sharpen, and छो *chho*, to cut, substitute इ *i*, or take the regular आ *á*.

शो *so*, शितः *sitaḥ* or शातः *sátaḥ*, शित्वा *sitvá* or शात्वा *sátvá* (Pâṇ. VII. 4, 41).

§ 436. Exceptional forms:

दा *dá*, to give, forms दत्तः *dattaḥ*†, दत्त्वा *dattvá* (Pâṇ. VII. 4, 46).

स्फाय् *spháy*, to grow, forms स्फीतः *sphítaḥ* (Pâṇ. VI. 1, 22).

स्त्यै *styai*, to call (with प्र *pra*), forms प्रस्तीतः *prastítaḥ* (Pâṇ. VI. 1, 23) and प्रस्तीमः *prastímaḥ* (Pâṇ. VIII. 2, 54).

ष्यै *syai*, to curdle, forms श्ीनः *sínaḥ*, and शीतः *sítaḥ*, cold; but संश्यानः *saṁsyánaḥ*, rolled up (Pâṇ. VI. 1, 24, 25).

प्याय् *pyáy*, to grow, forms पीनः *pínaḥ*; but प्यानः *pyánaḥ* after certain prepositions (Pâṇ. VI. 1, 28).

§ 437. The verbs which take Samprasáraṇa before तः *taḥ* and त्वा *tvá* have been mentioned

---

in § 393, as undergoing the same change in the benedictive and passive. वच् *vach*, to speak, उक्तः *uktaḥ*, उक्त्वा *uktvá*, &c.

§ 438. Roots which can lose their nasal (§ 345,[10]) lose it before त: *taḥ* and त्वा *tvá*. स्रंस् *sraṁs*, to tear, स्रस्त: *srastaḥ*, स्रस्त्वा *srastvá*.

But स्कन्द् *skand*, to stride, forms its gerund स्कन्त्वा *skantvá*, and स्यन्द् *syand*, to flow, स्यन्त्वा *syantvá* (Pâṇ. vi. 4, 31), although their न् *n* is otherwise liable to be lost. Part. स्कन्न: *skannaḥ*, स्यन्न: *syannaḥ*.

नश् *naś*, to perish, and roots ending in ज् *j*, otherwise liable to nasalization, retain the nasal optionally before त्वा *tvá* (Pâṇ. vi. 4, 32). नंष्ट्वा *naṁshṭvá* or नष्ट्वा *nashṭvá* (but only नष्ट: *nashṭaḥ*); रङ्क्त्वा *raṅktvá* or रक्त्वा *raktvá* (but only रक्त: *raktaḥ*); मज्ज् *majj*, to dive, मंक्त्वा *maṅktvá* or मक्त्वा *maktvá* (Pâṇ. vii. 1, 60).

§ 439. Causal verbs form the participle after rejecting अय *aya*; कारयति *kârayati*, कारित: *kâritaḥ*, but कारयित्वा *kârayitvá*.

§ 440. Desiderative verbs form the participle and gerund regularly; चिकीर्षति *chikîrshati*, चिकीर्षित: *chikîrshitaḥ*, चिकीर्षित्वा *chikîrshitvá*.

§ 441. Intensive verbs Âtm. of roots ending in vowels form the participle and gerund regularly; चेक्रीयते *chekrîyate*, चेक्रीयित: *chekrîyitaḥ*, चेक्रीयित्वा *chekrîyitvá*. After roots ending in consonants the intensive य् *y* is dropt; बेभिद्यते *bebhidyate*, बेभिदित: *bebhiditaḥ*, बेभिदित्वा *bebhiditvá*.

Intensive verbs Par. form the participle and gerund regularly; चर्कर्ति *charkarti*, चर्कृत: *charkritaḥ*, चर्करित्वा *charkaritvá*.

न: *náḥ instead of* त: *táḥ in the Past Participle*.

§ 442. Certain verbs take न: *náḥ* instead of त: *táḥ* in the past participle passive, provided they do not take the intermediate इ *i*.

1. Twenty-one verbs of the Krî class, beginning with लू *lû*, to cut, लून: *lûnaḥ* (Dhâtupâṭha 31, 13; Pâṇ. viii. 2, 44). The most important are, धून: *dhûnaḥ*, shaken; जीन: *jînaḥ*, decayed. Some of them come under the next rule.

2. Twelve verbs of the Div class, beginning with सू *sû* (Dhâtupâṭha 26, 23–35; Pâṇ. viii. 2, 45). The most important are, दून: *dûnaḥ*, pained; दीन: *dînaḥ*, wasted; प्रीण: *prînaḥ*, loved.

3. Verbs ending in ऋ *ṛi*, which is changed into ईर् *îr* or ऊर् *ûr*. स्तृ *stṛi*, स्तीर्ण: *stîrṇaḥ*, spread; शीर्ण: *śîrṇaḥ*, injured; दीर्ण: *dîrṇaḥ*, torn; जीर्ण: *jîrṇaḥ*, decayed.

4. Verbs ending in द् *d*; भिद् *bhid*, भिन्न: *bhinnaḥ*, broken; छिद् *chhid*, छिन्न: *chhinnaḥ*, cut. But मद् *mad*, मत्त: *mattaḥ*, intoxicated. In नुद् *nud*, to push, विद् *vid*, to find, and उन्द् *und*, to wet, the substitution is optional (Pâṇ. viii. 2, 56); नुन्न: *nunnaḥ* or नुत्त: *nuttaḥ*.

5. Verbs which native grammarians have marked in the Dhâtupâṭha with

·E e

an indicatory ओ *o;* भुज् *bhuj* (भुजो *bhujo,* Dhâtupâṭha 28, 124), to bend, भुग्न: *bhugnaḥ.*

6. Verbs beginning with a double consonant, one of them being a semivowel, and ending in आ *â,* or ए *e,* ऐ *ai,* ओ *o,* changeable to आ *â* (Pân. VIII. 2, 43); ग्लै *glai,* ग्लान: *glânaḥ,* faded. Except ध्यै *dhyai,* to meditate, ध्यात: *dhyâtaḥ* (Pân. VIII. 2, 57); ख्या *khyâ,* to proclaim, ख्यात: *khyâtaḥ.* In त्रै *trai,* to protect, घ्रा *ghrâ,* to smell, the substitution is optional; त्राण: *trâṇaḥ* or त्रात: *trâtaḥ* (Pân. VIII. 2, 56.)

7. Miscellaneous participles in न: *naḥ:* पूर्ण: *pûrṇaḥ,* only if derived from पूर् *pûr,* and then with an optional form पूरित: *pûritaḥ* (Pân. VII. 2, 27); while the participle of पृ *pṛ* is said to be पूर्त: *pûrtaḥ* (Pân. VIII. 2, 57); क्षीण: *kshîṇaḥ,* from क्षि *kshi,* to waste; द्यून: *dyûnaḥ,* from दिव् *div,* to play, (not to gamble, where it is द्यूत: *dyûtaḥ*)*; लग्न: *lagnaḥ,* from लग् *lag,* to be in contact with (Pân. VII. 2, 18); also from लज् *laj,* to be ashamed; शीन: *śînaḥ* and श्यान: *śyânaḥ,* coagulated, but शीत: *śîtaḥ,* cold; ह्रीण: *hrîṇaḥ* or ह्रीत: *hrîtaḥ,* ashamed (Pân. VIII. 2, 56).

§ 443. Native grammarians enumerate certain words as participles which, though by their meaning they may take the place of participles, are by their formation to be classed as adjectives or substantives rather than as participles. Thus पक्व: *pakvâḥ,* ripe; शुष्क: *śushkaḥ,* dry (Pân. VI. 1, 206); क्षाम: *kshâmâḥ,* weak; कृश: *kṛiśâḥ,* thin; प्रस्तीम: *prastîmâḥ,* crowded; फुल्ल: *phullâḥ,* expanded; क्षीव: *kshîvâḥ,* drunk, &c.

§ 444. By adding the possessive suffix वत् *vat* (§ 187) to the participles in त *ta* and न *na,* a new participle of very common occurrence is formed, being in fact a participle perfect active. Thus कृत: *kṛitâḥ,* done, becomes कृतवान् *kṛitâvân,* one who has done, but generally used as a definite verb. स कटं कृतवान् *sa kaṭam kṛitavân,* he has made the mat; or in the feminine सा कृतवती *sâ kṛitavatî,* and in the neuter तत्कृतवत् *tat kṛitavat.* They are regularly declined throughout like adjectives in वत् *vat.*

Gerund in य ya.

§ 445. Compound verbs, but not verbs preceded by the negative particle अ *a,* take य *ya* (without the accent), instead of त्वा *tvâ.* Thus, instead of भूत्वा *bhûtvâ,* we find संभूय *sambhûya;* but अजित्वा *ajitvâ,* not having conquered.

§ 446. Verbs ending in a short vowel take त्य *tya* instead of य *ya.* जि *ji,* to conquer, जित्वा *jitvâ,* having conquered; but विजित्य *vijîtya.* भृ *bhṛi,* to carry, भृत्वा *bhṛitvâ;* but संभृत्य *sambhṛitya,* having collected. Except क्षि *kshi,* which forms प्रक्षीय *prakshîya,* having destroyed (Pân. VI. 4, 59).

---

* Pân. VIII. 2, 49, allows द्यून *dyûna* in all senses of the root दिव् *div,* except in that of gambling; see Dhâtupâṭha 26, 1. द्यून *dyûna* and परिद्यून *paridyûna,* pained, come from different root, दिव् *div,* to pain, Dhâtupâṭha 33, 51.

§ 447. Causative bases with short penultimate vowel, keep the causative suffix अय् *ay* before य *ya* (Pâṇ. VI. 4, 56): संगमयति *saṅgamáyati*, संगमय्य *saṅgamáyya*, having caused to assemble. Otherwise the causative suffix is, as usual, dropt: तारयति *táráyati*, प्रतार्य *pratárya*, having caused to advance. प्रापयति *prápáyati* forms प्राप्य *prápya* and प्रापय्य *prápáyya*, having caused to reach (Pâṇ. VI. 4, 57).

§ 448. The verbs called घु *ghu* (§ 392*), मा *má*, to measure, स्था *sthá*, to stand, गा *gá*, to sing or to go, पा *pá*, to drink or to protect, हा *há*, to leave, सो *so*, to finish, take आ *á*, not ई *í* (Pâṇ. VI. 4, 69). दो *do*, to cut, अवदाय *avaddya;* स्था *sthá*, प्रस्थाय *prasthdya*. But पा *pá*, to drink, may form प्रपाय *prapáya* or प्रपीय *prapíya* (Sâr.).

§ 449. Verbs ending in म् *m*, which do not admit of intermediate इ *i*, may or may not drop their म् *m*. Ex. नम् *nam*, to bow, प्रणम्य *praṇámya* or प्रणत्य *praṇátya;* गम् *gam*, to go, आगम्य *ágámya* or आगत्य *ágátya*. Other verbs ending in nasals, not admitting of intermediate इ *i*, or belonging to the Tan class, always drop their final nasal. Ex. हन् *han*, प्रहत्य *prahátya;* तन् *tan*, प्रतत्य *pratátya*†. खन् *khan* and जन् *jan* form खन्य *khánya* or खाय *khádya*, जन्य *jánya* or जाय *jádya*.

§ 450. Verbs ending in ऋ *ṛi* change it to ईर् *ír*, and, after labials, into ऊर् *úr*. Ex. वितीर्य *vitírya*, having crossed; संपूर्य *sampúrya*, having filled.

§ 451. Certain verbs are irregular in not taking Samprasâraṇa. Thus वे *ve*, to weave, forms प्रवाय *praváya;* ज्या *jyá*, to fail, उपज्याय *upajyáya;* व्ये *vye*, to cover, प्रव्याय *pravyáya*, but after परि *pari* optionally परिव्याय *parivyáya* or परिवीय *parivíya* (Pâṇ. VI. I, 41—44).

§ 452. Some verbs change final इ *i* and ई *í* into आ *á*. Thus मी *mí*, मीनाति *mínáti*, he destroys, and मि *mi*, मिनोति *minóti*, he throws, form निमाय *nimáya;* दी *dí*, to destroy, उपदाय *upadáya;* ली *lí*, to melt, optionally विलाय *viláya* or विलीय *vilíya* (Pâṇ. VI. I, 50—51).

CHAPTER XVII.

VERBAL ADJECTIVES.

Verbal Adjectives in तव्य: távyaḥ (*or* tavyâḥ), अनीय: aníyaḥ, *and* य: yáḥ
(*or* yâḥ *and* yaḥ).

§ 453. These verbal adjectives (called *Kṛitya*) correspond in meaning to the Latin participles in *ndus*, conveying the idea that the action expressed by the verbs ought to be done or will be done. कर्तव्य: *kartavyaḥ*, करणीय: *karaṇíyaḥ*, कार्य: *káryaḥ* ‡, faciendus. Ex. धर्मस्त्वया कर्तव्य: *dharmas tvayá kartavyaḥ*, right is to be done by thee.

---

† Versus memorialis of these verbs : रमियेमिनमी हंतिरनुदात्ता गमिमेनि: । तनु अयू च्यिच्
च्युकृणु यनु मनु तृणु मृणु ॥

‡ Another suffix for forming verbal adjectives is एलिम: *elímaḥ*, which is, however, of rare occurrence; पच् *pach*, to cook, पचेलिमा माषा: *pachelimá máshâḥ*, beans fit to cook; भिदेलिम: *bhidelimaḥ*, brickle, fragile. (Pâṇ. III. I, 96, vârt.)

§ 454. In order to form the adjective in तव्य: *tavyaḥ*, take the periphrastic future, and instead of ता *tá* put तव्य: *tavyaḥ*.

Thus दा *dá*, to give	दाता *dátá*	दातव्य: *dátávyaḥ*	दानीय: *dáníyaḥ*	देय: *déyaḥ*
गै *gai*, to sing	गाता *gátá*	गातव्य: *gátavyaḥ*	गानीय: *gáníyaḥ*	गेय: *geyaḥ*
जि *ji*, to conquer	जेता *jetá*	जेतव्य: *jetavyaḥ*	जयनीय: *jayaníyaḥ*	जेय: *jeyaḥ*
भू *bhú*, to be	भविता *bhavitá*	भवितव्य: *bhavitavyaḥ*	भवनीय: *bhavaníyaḥ*	भव्य: *bhávyaḥ*
कृ *kri*, to do	कर्ता *kartá*	कर्तव्य: *kartavyaḥ*	करणीय: *karaníyaḥ*	कार्य: *káryaḥ*
जॄ *jrí*, to grow old	जरिता *jarítá*	जरितव्य: *jaritavyaḥ*	जरणीय: *jaraníyaḥ*	जार्य: *járyaḥ*
क्ष्विद् *kshvid*, to sweat	क्ष्वेदिता *kshveditá*	क्ष्वेदितव्य: *kshveditavyaḥ*	क्ष्वेदनीय: *kshvedaníyaḥ*	क्ष्वेद्य: *kshvedyaḥ*
बुध् *budh*, to know	बोधिता *bodhitá*	बोधितव्य: *bodhitavyaḥ*	बोधनीय: *bodhaníyaḥ*	बोध्य: *bodhyaḥ*
कृष् *krish*, to draw	कर्ष्टा or क्रष्टा [1]	कर्ष्टव्य: or क्रष्टव्य: [2]	कर्षणीय: *karshaníyaḥ*	कृष्य: *krishyaḥ* [3]
कुच् *kuch* [4], to squeeze	कुचिता *kuchitá*	कुचितव्य: *kuchitavyaḥ*	कुचनीय: *kuchaníyaḥ*	कुच्य: *kuchyaḥ* [4]
मिह् *mih*, to sprinkle	मेढा *medhá*	मेढव्य: *medhavyaḥ*	मेहनीय: *mehaníyaḥ*	मेह्य: *mehyaḥ*
गम् *gam*, to go	गंता *gantá*	गंतव्य: *gantavyaḥ*	गमनीय: *gamaníyaḥ*	गम्य: *gamyaḥ*
दृश् *driś*, to see	द्रष्टा *drashtá*	द्रष्टव्य: *drashtavyaḥ*	दर्शनीय: *darśaníyaḥ*	दृश्य: *driśyaḥ*
दंश् *daṁś*, to bite	दंष्टा *daṁshtá*	दंष्टव्य: *daṁshtavyaḥ*	दंशनीय: *daṁśaníyaḥ*	दंश्य: *daṁśyaḥ*
Caus. भावय् *bhávay*, to cause to be	भावयिता *bhávayitá*	भावयितव्य: *bhávayitavyaḥ*	भावनीय: *bhávaníyaḥ*	भाव्य: *bhávyaḥ*
Des. बुभूष् *bubhúsh*, to wish to be	बुभूषिता *bubhúshitá*	बुभूषितव्य: *bubhúshitavyaḥ*	बुभूषणीय: *bubhúshaníyaḥ*	बुभूष्य: *bubhúshyaḥ*
Int. बोभूय् *bobhúy*	बोभूयिता *bobhúyitá*	बोभूयितव्य: *bobhúyitavyaḥ*	बोभूयनीय: *bobhúyaníyaḥ*	बोभूय्य: *bobhúyyaḥ*
Int. बोभू *bobhú*	बोभविता *bobhavitá*	बोभवितव्य: *bobhavitavyaḥ*	बोभवनीय: *bobhavaníyaḥ*	बोभव्य: *bobhavyaḥ*
Int. बेभिद्य् *bebhidy*	बेभिदिता *bebhiditá*	बेभिदितव्य: *bebhiditavyaḥ*	बेभिदनीय: *bebhidaníyaḥ*	बेभिद्य: *bebhidyaḥ*

§ 455. In order to form the adjective in अनीय: *aníyaḥ*, it is generally sufficient to take the root as it appears before तव्य: *tavyaḥ*, omitting, however, intermediate इ *i*, and putting अनीय: *aníyaḥ* instead. Guṇa-vowels before अनीय: *aníyaḥ* have, of course, the semivowel for their final element, and there can be no occasion for the intermediate इ *i*. The अय् *ay* of the causative and the य् *y* after consonants of intensives and other derivative verbs are, as usual, rejected. बुध् *budh*, बोधयति *bodhayati*, बोधनीय: *bodhaníyaḥ*; भिद् *bhid*, बेभिद्यते *bebhidyate*, बेभिदनीय: *bebhidaníyaḥ*.

§ 456. In order to form the adjective in य: *yaḥ* (ख्यत् *ṇyat*, &c.) it is

---

[1] *karshtá* or *krashtá*.   [2] *karshtavyaḥ* or *krashtavyaḥ*.   [3] § 456, 3.

[4] Never takes Guṇa (§ 345, note), except before terminations which have न् *ṅ* or इ *i*. This termination is ख्यत् *ṇyat*.

generally sufficient to take the adjective in अनीय: *aníyah* and to cut off अनी *ani*. Thus भवनीय: *bhav-aní-yah* becomes भव्य: *bhavyah*; चेतनीय: *chet-aní-yah*, चेत्य: *chetyah*; वयनीय: *vay-aní-yah*, वेय: *veyah*; बोधनीय: *bodh-aní-yah*, बोध्य: *bodhyah*. A few more special rules, however, have here to be mentioned :

1. Final आ *â*, ए *e*, ऐ *ai*, ओ *o*, become ए *e*. दा *dâ*, to give, देय: *deyah*; गै *gai*, to sing, गेय: *geyah*. (Pân. III. 1, 98; VI. 4, 65.)

2. Final इ *i* and ई *í* take Guṇa, as before अनीय *aníya*; जि *ji*, जेय: *jeyah*, to be conquered, different from जय्य: *jayyah*, conquerable; क्षि *kshi*, to destroy, क्षेय: *ksheyah*, different from क्षय्य: *kshayyah*, destructible (Pân. VI. 1, 81). Final उ *u* and ऊ *û*, under the same circumstances, are changed to अव् *av*, or, after अवश्य *avaśya*, when a high degree of necessity is expressed, to आव् *âv*; भव्य: *bhavyah* or अवश्यभाव्य: *avaśya-bhâvyah*; विप्रेण शुचिना भाव्यं *vipreṇa śuchinâ bhâvyam*, a Brâhman must be pure. Final उ *u* if it appears as उव् *uv* before अनीय *aníya*, appears as ऊ *û* before य *ya*; गु *gu*, to sound, गुवनीय *guvaníya*, गूय *gûya*.

3. Final ऋ *ṛi* and ॠ *ṛí* before य: *yah*, but not before अनीय: *aníyah*, take Vṛiddhi instead of Guṇa. कार्य: *kâryah*; पार्य: *pâryah*. (Pân. III. 1, 120, 124.)

4. Penultimate ऋ *ṛi*, which takes Guṇa before अनीय: *aníyah*, does not take Guṇa before य: *yah*, with few exceptions; वृध्य: *vṛidhyah*, दृश्य: *dṛiśyah* (Pân. III. 1, 110). But कृप् *kṛip*, to do, forms कल्प्य: *kalpyah*; चृत् *chṛit*, to kill, चर्त्य: *chartyah* (Pân. III. 1, 110); वृष् *vṛish*, to sprinkle, वृष्य: *vṛishyah* or वर्ष्य: *varshyah* (Pân. III. 1, 120). Penultimate ॠ *ṛí* becomes ईर् *ír*; कृत् *kṛit*, कीर्त्य: *kírtyah*.

5. Penultimate इ *i* and उ *u* take Guṇa before य: *yah*, as before अनीय: *aníyah*; विद् *vid*, वेद्य: *vedyah*; शुष् *śush*, शोष्य: *śoshyah*.

6. Penultimate अ *a*, prosodially short, before य: *yah*, but not before अनीय: *aníyah*, is lengthened, unless the final consonant is a labial (Pân. III. 1, 98; 124); हस् *has*, to laugh, हास्य: *hâsyah*; वह् *vah*, वाह्य: *vâhyah*. But शप् *śap*, to curse, शप्य: *śapyah*; लभ् *labh*, लभ्य: *labhyah*. The अ *a* remains likewise short in शक्य: *śakyah*, from शक् *śak*, to be able; in सह्य: *sahyah*, from सह् *sah*, to bear (Pân. III. 1, 99), and some other verbs*. खन् *khan* forms खेय: *kheyah* (Pân. III. 1, 111), which, however, may be derived from खै *khai*, to dig; हन् *han*, वध्य: *vadhyah* or घात्य: *ghâtyah*.

---

* Pânini (III. 1, 100) mentions only गद् *gad*, मद् *mad*, चर् *char*, यम् *yam*, if used without preposition. The Sârasvatî (III. 7, 7) includes among the Śakâdi verbs, शक् *śak*, सह् *sah*, गद् *gad*, मद् *mad*, चर् *char*, यम् *yam*, तक् *tak*, शस् *śas*, चत् *chat*, यत् *yat*, पत् *pat*, जन् *jan*, हन् *han*, (वध् *vadh*), शल् *śal*, रुच् *ruch*.

§ 457. The following are a few derivatives in य: *yah*, formed against the general rules:

गुह् *guh*, to hide, may form गुह्य: *guhyah* or गोह्य: *gohyah* (Pân. III. 1, 109, Kâśikâ); जुष् *jush*, to cherish, जुष्य: *jushyah;* ग्रह् *grah*, to take, गृह्य: *grihyah*, after प्रति *prati* and अपि *api;* वद् *vad*, to speak, उद्य: *udyah*, in composition (Pân. III. 1, 106; 114. ब्रह्मोद्या कथा *brahmodyâ kathâ*, a story told by a Brâhman); भू *bhû*, to be, भूय *bhûya*, in composition (Pân. III. 1, 107. ब्रह्मभूयं गत: *brahmabhûyam gatah*, arrived at Brahmahood); शास् *śâs*, to rule, शिष्य: *śishyah*, pupil.

We find त् *t* inserted before य: *yah*, in analogy to the gerunds in य *ya*, in the following verbs:

इ *i*, to go, इत्य: *ityah;* स्तु *stu*, to praise, स्तुत्य: *stutyah;* वृ *vri*, to choose, वृत्य: *vrityah;* दृ *dri*, to regard, दृत्य: *drityah;* भृ *bhri*, to bear, भृत्य: *bhrityah;* कृ *kri*, to do, कृत्य: *krityah*. But many of these forms are only used in certain senses, and must not be considered as supplanting the regular verbal adjectives. Thus गुह्य: *guhyah* and गोह्य: *gohyah* both occur; दुह्य: *duhyah* and दोह्य: *dohyah*, &c.

§ 458. Verbs ending in च *ch* or ज *j* change their final consonant into क *k* or ग *g* if the following य *ya* (*nyat*) requires the lengthening of the vowel. पच् *pach*, पाक्यं *pâkyam;* भुज् *bhuj*, to enjoy, भोग्यं *bhogyam*, but भोज्यं *bhojyam*, what is to be eaten (Pân. VII. 3, 69).

There are, however, several exceptions. Verbs beginning with a guttural do not admit the substitution of gutturals. Likewise the following verbs: यज् *yaj*, याच् *yâch*, रुच् *ruch*, प्रवच् *pravach*, रिच् *rich*, त्यज् *tyaj*, पूज् *pûj*, अज् *aj*, व्रज् *vraj*, वंच् *vañch* (to go). Thus याज्यं *yâjyam*, याच्यं *yâchyam*, रोच्यं *rochyam*, प्रवाच्यं *pravâchyam*, अर्च्यं *archyam*, त्याज्यं *tyâjyam*, पूज्यं *pûjyam* (Prakriyâ-Kaumudî, p. 55 b).

Infinitive in तुं *tum.*

§ 459. The infinitive is formed by adding तुं *tum*, which has no accent. The base has the same form as before the ता *tâ* of the periphrastic future, or before the तव्य: *tâvyah* of the verbal adjective. बुध् *budh*, बोधितुं *bódhitum*. (See § 454.) Ex. कृष्णं द्रष्टुं व्रजति *krishnam drashtum vrajati*, he goes to see Krishna; भोक्तुं काल: *bhoktum kâlah*, it is time to eat.

Verbal Adverb.

§ 460. By means of the unaccentuated suffix अं *am*, which, as a general rule, is added to that form which the verb assumes before the passive इ *i* (3rd pers. sing. aor. pass., § 403), a verbal adverb is formed. From भुज् *bhuj*, to eat, भोजं *bhójam;* from पा *pâ*, to drink, पायं *pâyam*. Ex. अग्रे भोजं व्रजति *agre bhojam vrajati*, having first eaten, he goes. This verbal adverb is most frequently used twice over. Ex. भोजं भोजं व्रजति *bhójam bhojam vrajati*, having eaten and eaten, he goes (Pân. III. 4, 22). It is likewise used at the end of compounds; द्वैधंकारं *dvaidhamkâram*, having divided; उच्चै:कारं *uchchaihkâram*, loudly.

CHAPTER XVIII.

CAUSATIVE VERBS.

§ 461. Simple roots are changed into causal bases by Guṇa or Vṛiddhi of their radical vowel, and by the addition of a final इ *i*. The root is then treated as following the Bhû class, so that इ *i* appears in the special tenses as अय *aya*. Thus भू *bhú* becomes भावि *bhávi* and भावयति *bhávayati*, he causes to be; बुध *budh* becomes बोधि *bodhi* and बोधयति *bodháyati*, he causes to know. The accent is on the *á* of *áya*.

§ 462. The rules according to which the vowel takes either Guṇa or Vṛiddhi are as follows:

1. Final इ *i* and ई *í*, उ *u* and ऊ *ú*, ऋ *ṛi* and ॠ *ṛí* take Vṛiddhi.

Thus स्मि *smi*, to laugh, स्माययति *smáyayati*, he makes laugh.

    नी *ní*, to lead, नाययति *náyayati*, he causes to lead.

    प्लु *plu*, to swim, प्लावयति *plávayati*, he makes swim.

    भू *bhú*, to be, भावयति *bhávayati*, he causes to be.

    कृ *kṛi*, to make, कारयति *kárayati*, he causes to make.

    कॄ *kṛí*, to scatter, कारयति *kárayati*, he causes to scatter.

2. Medial इ *i*, उ *u*, ऋ *ṛi*, ऌ *ḷi*, followed by a single consonant, take Guṇa; ॠ *ṛí* becomes ईर् *ír*.

Thus विद् *vid*, to know, वेदयति *vedayati*, he makes know.

    बुध *budh*, to know, बोधयति *bodhayati*, he makes know.

    कृत् *kṛit*, to cut, कर्तयति *kartayati*, he causes to cut.

    कॢप् *kḷip*, to be able, कल्पयति *kalpayati*, he renders fit.

3. Medial अ *a* followed by a single consonant is lengthened, but there are many exceptions.

    सद् *sad*, to sit, सादयति *sádayati*, he sets.

    पत् *pat*, to fall, पातयति *pátayati*, he fells.

Exceptions:

I. Most verbs ending in अम् *am* do not lengthen their vowel:

    गम् *gam*, to go, गमयति *gamayati*, he makes go.

    क्रम् *kram*, to stride, क्रमयति *kramayati*, he causes to stride.

Verbs in अम् *am* which do lengthen the vowel are,

कम् *kam*, to desire, कामयते *kámayate*, he desires; Caus. कामयति *kámayati*, he makes desire.

अम् *am*, to move, अमति *amati*, he moves; Caus. आमयति *ámayati*, he makes move.

चम् *cham*, to eat, चमति *chamati*, he eats; Caus. चामयति *chámayati*, he makes eat.

शम् *śam*, if it means to see, शाम्यति *śámyati*, he sees; Caus. शामयति *śámayati*, he shows; but शामयति *śamayati*, he quiets.

यम् *yam*, unless it means to eat, यच्छति *yachchhati*; Caus. यामयति *yámayati*, he extends; but यमयति *yamayati*, he feeds.

नम् *nam*, to bend, optionally lengthens its vowel if it is used without a preposition; नामयति *nâmayati* or नमयति *namayati*, he bends. If preceded by a preposition, the vowel always ought to remain short (Dh. P. 19, 67).

वम् *vam*, to vomit, optionally lengthens its vowel if it is used without a preposition; वामयति *vâmayati* or वमयति *vamayati*, he makes vomit. If preceded by a preposition, the vowel always ought to remain short (Dh. P. 19, 67)*.

II. A class of verbs collected by native grammarians, and beginning with घट् *ghaṭ* (Dh. P. 19, 1), do not lengthen their vowel. The same verbs may optionally retain their short vowel in the 3rd pers. sing. aorist of the causative passive (§ 405). The following list contains the more important among these verbs:

CAUSATIVE.

Root.	3rd Pers. Sing. Pres. Par.	3rd Pers. Sing. Aor. Passive.
1. घट् *ghaṭ*, to strive	घटयति *ghaṭayati*	अघटि or अघाटि *aghâṭi*
2. व्यथ् *vyath*, to fear	व्यथयति *vyathayati*	अव्यथि or अव्याथि *avyâthi*
3. प्रथ् *prath*, to be famous	प्रथयति *prathayati*	अप्रथि or अप्राथि *aprâthi*
4. मृद् *mrad*, to rub	मदयति *mradayati*	अमदि or अमादि *amrâdi*
5. क्रप् *krap*, to pity	क्रपयति *krapayati*	अक्रपि or अक्रापि *akrâpi*
6. त्वर् *tvar*, to hurry	त्वरयति *tvarayati*	अत्वरि or अत्वारि *atvâri*
7. ज्वर् *jvar*, to burn with fever	ज्वरयति *jvarayati*	अज्वरि or अज्वारि *ajvâri*
8. नट् *naṭ*, to dance	नटयति *naṭayati*	अनटि or अनाटि *anâṭi*
9. श्रथ् *śrath*, to kill	श्रथयति *śrathayati*	अश्रथि or अश्राथि *aśrâthi*
10. वन् *van*, to act †	प्रवनयति *pravanayati*	प्रावनि or प्रावानि *prâvâni*
11. ज्वल् *jval*, to shine †	प्रज्वलयति *prajvalayati*	प्राज्वलि or प्राज्वालि *prâjvâli*
12. स्मृ *smṛi*, to regret	स्मरयति *smarayati*	अस्मरि or अस्मारि *asmâri*
13. दृ *dṛi*, to respect, (not to tear)	दरयति *darayati*	अदरि or अदारि *adâri*
14. श्रा *śrâ*, to boil	श्रपयति *śrapayati*	अश्रपि or अश्रापि *aśrâpi*
15. ज्ञा *jñâ*, to slay, to please, to sharpen (?), to perceive	ज्ञपयति *jñapayati*	अज्ञपि or अज्ञापि *ajñâpi*
16. चल् *chal*, to tremble	चलयति *chalayati*	अचलि or अचालि *achâli*
17. मद् *mad*, to rejoice, &c.	मदयति *madayati*	अमदि or अमादि *amâdi*
18. ध्वन् *dhvan*, to sound, to ring	ध्वनयति *dhvanayati*	अध्वनि or अध्वानि *adhvâni*
19. दल् *dal*, to cut	दलयति *dalayati* (optional)	अदलि or अदालि *adâli*
20. वल् *val*, to cover	वलयति *valayati* (optional)	अवलि or अवालि *avâli*
21. स्खल् *skhal*, to drop	स्खलयति *skhalayati* (optional)	अस्खलि or अस्खालि *askhâli*
22. त्रप् *trap*, to be ashamed	त्रपयति *trapayati*	अत्रपि or अत्रापि *atrâpi*
23. क्षै *kshai*, to wane	क्षपयति *kshapayati*	अक्षपि or अक्षापि *akshâpi*

---

* Dhâtupâṭha 19, 67. ज्वल ह्वल ज्वल नमां अनुपसर्गाद्वा (मित्) (ज्वलह्वलेत्यनुपसृष्टस्यैव वैकल्पिकमित्त्वमीषणाम् राजारामशास्त्री). It seems indeed that the verbs without prepositions only, are optionally *mit* (i.e. short-voweled), while with prepositions they are *mit*, and nothing else. See, however, Colebrooke, Sanskrit Grammar, p. 317, note.

† Without a preposition, and optionally with a preposition. See note *.

24. जन् *jan* (Div), nasci — जनयति *janayati* — अजनि or अजानि *ajăni*
25. जॄ *jṛí* (Div), to grow old — जरयति *jarayati* — अजरि or अजारि *ajări*
26. रञ्ज् *rañj* (Bhû), to hunt, to dye* — रञ्जयति or रञ्° *rajayati* or *rañja-* — अरजि or अराजि *arăji*
27. ग्ला *glát* or ग्लै *glai*, to fade — ग्लपयति or ग्लापयति *glăpayati* — अग्लपि or अग्लापि *aglăpi*
28. स्ना *snát*, to wash — स्नपयति or स्नापयति *snăpayati* — अस्नपि or अस्नापि *asnăpi*
29. वन् *van†*, to cherish — वनयति or वानयति *vănayati* — अवनि or अवानि *avăni*
30. फण *phaṇ*, to go — फणयति or फाणयति(?) *phăṇayati* — अफणि or अफाणि *aphăṇi*

Note—Some of these verbs are to be considered as *mit*, i. e. as having a short vowel in the causative, if employed in the sense given above; while if they occur again in other sections of the Dhâtupâṭha and with different meanings, they may be conjugated likewise as ordinary verbs.

§ 463. Some verbs form their causative base anomalously:

I. Nearly all verbs ending in आ *á*, and most ending in ए *e*, ऐ *ai*, ओ *o*, changeable to आ *á*, insert प् *p* before the causal termination. (Pâṇ. VII. 3, 36.)

Thus दा *dá*, to give, ददाति *dadáti*, he gives; दापयति *dápayati*, he causes to give.

दे *de*, to pity, दयते *dayate*, he pities; दापयति *dápayati*, he causes pity.

दो *do*, to cut, दाति *dáti* or द्यति *dyati*, he cuts; दापयति *dápayati*, he causes cutting.

दै *dai*, to purify, दायति *dáyati*, he purifies; दापयति *dápayati*, he causes to purify.

II. Other irregular causatives are given in the following list. Their irregularity consists chiefly in taking प् *p* with Guṇa or Vṛiddhi of the radical vowel; sometimes in lengthening the vowel instead of raising it to Guṇa; and frequently in substituting a new base.

1. इ *i*, to go, in अधीते *adhíte*, he reads; Caus. अध्यापयति *adhyápayati*, he teaches ‡. (Pâṇ. VI. 1, 48.)
2. ऋ *ṛi*, to go, ऋच्छति *ṛichchhati*; Caus. अर्पयति *arpayati*, he places. (Pâṇ. VII. 3, 36.)
3. क्नूय् *knúy*, to sound, क्नूनाति *knúnáti*; Caus. क्नोपयति *knopayati*, he causes to sound.
4. क्री *krí*, to buy, क्रीणाति *kríṇáti*; Caus. क्रापयति *krápayati*, he causes to buy.
5. क्ष्माय् *kshmáy*, to tremble, क्ष्मायते *kshmáyate*; Caus. क्ष्मापयति *kshmápayati*, he causes to tremble. (Pâṇ. VII. 3, 36.)

---

* If the causative means to hunt, the न् *n* is rejected; रजयति मृगान् *rajayati mṛigán*, he hunts deer; रञ्जयति वस्त्राणि *rañjayati vastráṇi*, he dies clothes. We may also form अरजि *arañji*, but अराजि *ardñji* is wrong, अकारस्योपधात्वाभावेन दीर्घाप्राप्ते: (पा° ६. ४. ९३).

† With a preposition, but optionally without a preposition. The usage of the best writers varies, and Indian grammarians vary in their interpretation of Dhâtupâṭha 19, 67–68. See note (on preceding page).

‡ प्रति + इ *prati+i*, to approach, forms its causal regularly when it means to make a person understand, प्रत्याययति *pratyáyayati*. Otherwise the causative of इ *i* is formed from गम् *gam*.

6. चि *chi*, to collect, चिनोति *chinoti*; Caus. चापयति *châpayati*, or regularly चाययति *châyayati*, he causes to collect. (Pân. VI. 1, 54.)

7. छो *chho*, to cut, छ्यति *chhyati*; Caus. छाययति *chhâyayati*, he causes to cut.

8. जागृ *jâgri*, to be awake, जागर्ति *jâgarti*; Caus. जागरयति *jâgarayati*, he rouses.

9. जि *ji*, to conquer, जयति *jayati*; Caus. जापयति *jâpayati*, he causes to conquer.

10. दरिद्रा *daridrâ*, to be poor, दरिद्राति *daridrâti*; Caus. दरिद्रयति *daridrayati*, he makes poor.

11. दीधी *dîdhî*, to shine, दीधीते *dîdhîte*; Caus. दीधयति *dîdhayati*, he causes to shine.

12. दुष् *dush*, to sin, दुष्यति *dushyati*; Caus. दूषयति *dûshayati*, he causes to sin; also दोषयति *doshayati*, he demoralizes. (Pân. VI. 4, 91.)

13. धू *dhû*, to shake, धूनोति *dhûnoti*; Caus. धूनयति *dhûnayati*, he causes to shake.

14. पा *pâ*, to drink, पिबति *pibati*; Caus. पाययति *pâyayati*, he causes to drink; also पै *pai*, पायति *pâyati*, to be dry.

15. पा *pâ*, to protect, पाति *pâti*; Caus. पालयति *pâlayati*, he protects.

16. प्री *prî*, to love, प्रीणाति *prîṇâti*; Caus. प्रीणयति *prîṇayati*, he delights.

17. भ्रज्ज् *bhrajj*, to roast, भृज्जति *bhṛijjati*; Caus. भ्रज्जयति *bhrajjayati*, he makes roast, or भर्जयति *bharjjayati*, from भृज् *bhṛij*.

18. भी *bhî*, to fear, बिभेति *bibheti*; Caus. भापयते *bhâpayate* or भीषयते *bhîshayate*, he frightens; also regularly भाययति *bhâyayati*. (Pân. VI. 1, 56.)

19. मि *mi*, to throw, मिनोति *minoti*, and मी *mî*, to destroy, मिनाति *minâti*, form their Caus. like मा *mâ*.

20. री *rî*, to flow, or to go, रीयते *rîyate*; Caus. रेपयति *repayati*, he makes flow.

21. रुह् *ruh*, to grow, रोहति *rohati*; Caus. रोहयति *rohayati*, रोपयति *ropayati*, he causes to grow. (Pân. VII. 3, 43.)

22. ली *lî*, to adhere, लिनाति *linâti* and लीयते *lîyate*; Caus. लीनयति *lînayati*, लापयति *lâpayati*, and लाययति *lâyayati*; and, if the root takes the form ला *lâ*, also लालयति *lâlayati* (Pân. VII. 3, 39). The meaning varies; see Pân. VI. 1, 48; 51.

23. वा *vâ*, to blow, वाति *vâti*; Caus. वाजयति *vâjayati*, if it means he shakes.

24. वी *vî*, to obtain, वेति *veti*; Caus. वापयति *vâpayati* or वाययति *vâyayati*, if it means to make conceive. (Pân. VI. 1, 55.)

25. वे *ve*, to weave, वयति *vayati*; Caus. वाययति *vâyayati*, he causes to weave.

26. वेवी *vevî*, to conceive, वेवीते *vevîte*; Caus. वेवयति *vevayati*.

27. व्ये *vye*, to cover, व्ययति *vyayati*; Caus. व्याययति *vyâyayati*, he causes to cover.

28. वॄ *vṛî*, to choose, वृिनाति *vṛinâti*; Caus. वेपयति *vlepayati*, he causes to choose.

29. शद् *śad*, to fall, शीयते *śîyate*; Caus. शातयति *śâtayati*, he fells; but not, if it means to move. (Pân. VII. 3, 42.)

30. शो *śo*, to sharpen, श्यति *śyati*; Caus. शाययति *śâyayati*, he causes to sharpen.

31. सिध् *sidh*, to succeed, सिध्यति *sidhyati*; Caus. साधयति *sâdhayati*, he performs; but सेधयति *sedhayati*, he performs sacred acts.

32. सो *so*, to destroy, स्यति *syati*; Caus. साययति *sâyayati*, he causes to destroy.

33. स्फुर् *sphur*, to sparkle, स्फुरति *sphurati*; Caus. स्फारयति *sphárayati* and स्फोरयति *sphorayati*, he makes sparkle.

34. स्फाय् *sphây*, to grow, स्फायते *sphâyate*; Caus. स्फावयति *sphâvayati*, he causes to grow.

35. स्मि *smi*, to smile, स्मयते *smayate*; Caus. स्मापयते *smâpayate*, he astonishes; also स्माययति *smâyayati*, he causes a smile by something. (Pân. vi. 1, 57.)

36. ह्री *hrî*, to be ashamed, जिह्रेति *jihreti*; Caus. ह्रेपयति *hrepayati*, he makes ashamed. (Pân. vii. 3, 36.)

37. ह्वे *hve*, to call, ह्वयति *hvayati*; Caus. ह्वाययति *hvâyayati*, he causes to call.

38. हन् *han*, to kill, हंति *hanti*; Caus. घातयति *ghâtayati*, he causes to kill.

§ 464. As causative verbs are conjugated exactly like verbs of the Chur class, there is no necessity for giving here a complete paradigm. Like Chur verbs they retain अय् *ay* throughout, except in the reduplicated aorist and the benedictive Parasmaipada; and they form the perfect periphrastically. The only difficulty in causative verbs is the formation of their bases, and the formation of the aorist. Thus कृ *kri*, as causative, forms Pres. Par. and Âtm. कारयति, °ते, *kârayati, -te*; Impf. अकारयत्, °त, *akârayat, -ta*; Opt. कारयेत्, °त, *kârayet, -ta*; Imp. कारयतु, °तां, *kârayatu, -tâm*; Red. Perf. कारयांचकार, °चक्रे, *kârayâñchakâra, -chakre* (§ 342); Aor. अचीकरत्, °त, *achîkarat, -ta*; Fut. कारयिष्यति, °ते, *kârayishyati, -te*; Cond. अकारयिष्यत्, °त, *akârayishyat, -ta*; Per. Fut. कारयिता *kârayitâ*; Ben. कार्यात् *kâryât*; कारयिषीष्ट *kârayishîshta*.

§ 465. If a causative verb has to be used in the passive, अय् *ay* is dropt (§ 399), but the root remains the same as it would have been with अय् *ay*. Hence Pres. कार्यते *kâryate*, he is made to do; रोप्यते *ropyate*, from रुह् *ruh*, he is made to grow. The imperfect, optative, and imperative are formed regularly. The perfect is periphrastic with the auxiliary verbs in the Âtmanepada.

§ 466. In the general tenses, however, where the य *ya* of the passive disappears (§ 401), the causative अय् *ay* may or may not reappear, and we thus get two forms throughout (see Colebrooke, p. 198, note):

Fut. भावयिष्ये *bhâvayishye* or भाविष्ये *bhâvishye*.

Cond. अभावयिष्ये *abhâvayishye* or अभाविष्ये *abhâvishye*.

Per. Fut. भावयितहे *bhâvayitâhe* or भावितहे *bhâvitâhe*.

Ben. भावयिषीय *bhâvayishîya* or भाविषीय *bhâvishîya*.

First Aor. I. 1. p. अभावयिषि *abhâvayishi* or अभाविषि *abhâvishi*.

2. p. अभावयिष्ठाः *abhâvayishthâh* or अभाविष्ठाः *abhâvishthâh*.

3. p. अभावि *abhâvi*.

CHAPTER XIX.

DESIDERATIVE VERBS.

§ 467. Desiderative bases are formed by reduplication, the peculiarities of which will have to be treated separately, and by adding स् *s* to the root. Thus from भू *bhú*, to be, बुभूष् *búbhúsh*, to wish to be. The accent is on the reduplicative syllable.

§ 468. These new bases are conjugated like Tud roots. बुभूषामि *bubhú-shámi*, बुभूषसि *bubhúshasi*, बुभूषति *bubhúshati*, बुभूषावः *bubhúshávah*, &c.

§ 469. The roots which take the intermediate इ *i* have been given before (§ 331, 340), as well as those which take intermediate ई *í*. Thus from विद् *vid*, to know, विविदिष् *vividish*, to wish to know; from तॄ *trí*, to cross, तितरिष् *titarish* or तितरीष् *titaríish*, to wish to cross.

§ 470. As a general rule, though liable to exceptions, it may be stated that bases ending in one consonant may be strengthened by Guṇa, if they take the intermediate इ *i*. Thus बुध् *budh* forms बुबोधिषति *bubodhishati*; दिव् *div*, दिदेविषति *didevishati*: also कृ *kṛí*, चिकरिषति *chikarishati*; दृ *dṛí*, दिदरिषति *didarishati*. But भिद् *bhid*, Des. बिभित्सति *bibhitsati* (Pâṇ. I. 2, 10); गुह् *guh*, जुघुक्षति *jughukshati* (Pâṇ. VII. 2, 12). In fact, no Guṇa without intermediate इ *i*.

§ 471. But there are important exceptions. In many cases the base of the desiderative is neither strengthened nor weakened; रुद् *rud*, रुरुदिषति *rurudishati*. Other bases may be strengthened optionally; द्युत् *dyut*, दिद्युतिषते *didyutishate* or दिद्योतिषते *didyotishate*. Certain bases which do not take intermediate इ *i* are actually weakened; स्वप् *svap*, सुषुप्सति *sushupsati*.

1. Verbs which do *not* take Guṇa, though they have intermediate इ *i*.

रुद् *rud*, to cry, रुरुदिषति *rurudishati*; विद् *vid*, to know, विविदिषति *vividishati*; मुष् *mush*, to steal, मुमुषिषति *mumushishati*. (Pâṇ. I. 2, 8.)

2. Verbs which may or may not take Guṇa, though they have intermediate इ *i*.

Verbs beginning with consonants, and ending in any single consonant, except य् *y* or व् *v*, and having इ *i* or उ *u* for their vowel. (Pâṇ. I. 2, 26.)

द्युत् *dyut*, दिद्युतिषते *didyutishate* or दिद्योतिषते *didyotishate*.

But दिव् *div*, दिदेविषति *didevishati* or, without इ *i*, दुद्यूषति *dudyúshati* (Pâṇ. VII. 2, 49); वृत् *vṛit*, विवर्तिषते *vivartishate* or विवृत्सति *vivṛitsati*.

3. Verbs ending in इ *i* or उ *u*, not taking intermediate इ *i*, lengthen their vowel; final ऋ *ṛi* and ॠ *ṛí* become ईर् *ír*, and, after labials, ऊर् *úr*. (Pâṇ. VI. 4, 16.)

जि *ji*, to conquer, जिगीषति *jigíshati*; यु *yu*, to mix, युयूषति *yuyúshati*.

कृ *kṛi*, to do, चिकीर्षति *chikírshati*; तॄ *tṛí*, to cross, तितीर्षति *titírshati*.

मृ *mṛi*, to die, मुमूर्षति *mumúrshati*; पॄ *pṛí*, to fill, पुपूर्षति *pupúrshati*.

If, however, they take intermediate इ *í*, they likewise take Guṇa.

स्मि *smi*, to smile, सिस्मयिषते *sismayishate*; पू *pú*, to purify, पिपविषते *pipavishate*; गॄ *gṛí*, to swallow, जिगरिषति *jigarishati*; दृ *dṛi*, to respect, दिदरिषते *didarishate*.

4. गम् *gam*, to go, as a substitute for इ *i*, to go, and हन् *han*, to kill, lengthen their vowel before the स् *s* of the desiderative. (Pâṇ. VI. 4, 16.)

गम् *gam*, अधिजिगांसते *adhijigâṁsate*, he wishes to read; but जिगमिषति *jigamishati*, he wishes to go.

हन् *han*, जिघांसति *jighâṁsati*, he wishes to kill.

5. तन् *tan*, to stretch, lengthens its vowel optionally. (Pâṇ. V. 4, 17.)

तन् *tan*, तितांसति *titâṁsati* or तितंसति *titaṁsati*; but also तितनिषति *titanishati*. (Pâṇ. VII. 2, 49, vârt.)

6. सन् *san*, to obtain, drops its न् *n* and lengthens the vowel before the स् *s* of the desiderative. (Pâṇ. VI. 4, 42.)

सन् *san*, सिषासति *sishâsati*; but सिसनिषति *sisanishati*.

7. ग्रह् *grah*, to take, स्वप् *svap*, to sleep, and प्रछ् *prachh*, to ask, shorten their bases by Samprasâraṇa. (Pâṇ. I. 2, 8.) .

ग्रह् *grah*, जिघृक्षति *jighṛikshati*.   स्वप् *svap*, सुषुप्सति *sushupsati*.

प्रछ् *prachh*, पिपृच्छिषति *pipṛichchhishati*.

8. The following verbs shorten their vowel to इ *i* before the स् *s* of the desiderative, insert त् *t* (Pâṇ. VII. 4, 54), and reject the reduplication.

मी *mî* (मीनाति *mînâti*, to destroy, and मिनोति *minoti*, to throw), Des. मित्सति *mitsati*.

मा *mâ* (माति *mâti*, to measure, मिमीते *mimîte*, to measure, मयते *mayate*, to change), Des. मित्सति *mitsati*, मित्सते *mitsate*.

दा *dâ* (ददाति *dadâti*, to give, *dâṅ*, Dh. P. 25, 9, *dâṇ*, Dh. P. 22, 32; द्यति *dyati*, to cut, *do*, Dh. P. 26, 39; but not दाति *dâti*, to cut, *dâp*, Dh. P. 24, 51, because it is not *ghu*, cf. § 392; दयते *dayate*, to pity, *deṅ*, Dh. P. 22, 66), Des. दित्सति *ditsati*, दित्सते *ditsate*.

धा *dhâ* (दधाति *dadhâti*, to place, धयति *dhayati*, to drink), Des. धित्सति *dhitsati*.

9. Other desideratives formed without reduplication:

रभ् *rabh*, to begin (रभते *rabhate*), Des. रिप्सते *ripsate*.

लभ् *labh*, to take (लभते *labhate*), Des. लिप्सते *lipsate*.

शक् *śak*, to be able (शक्नोति *śaknoti*, शक्यति *śakyati*), Des. शिक्षति *śikshati*.

पत् *pat*, to fall (पतति *patati*), Des. पित्सति *pitsati*.

पद् *pad*, to go (पद्यते *padyate*), Des. पित्सते *pitsate*.

आप् *âp*, to obtain (आप्नोति *âpnoti*), Des. ईप्सति *îpsati*.

ज्ञप् *jñap*, to command (ज्ञपयति *jñapayati*), Des. ज्ञीप्सति *jñîpsati*.

ऋध् *ṛidh*, to grow (ऋध्नोति *ṛidhnoti*), Des. ईर्त्सति *îrtsati*.

दंभ् *dambh*, to deceive (दभ्नोति *dabhnoti*), Des. धीप्सति *dhîpsati* or धिप्सति *dhipsati*.

मुच् *much*, to free (मुंचति *muñchati*), Des. मोक्षते *mokshate* or मुमुक्षते *mumukshate*, he wishes for spiritual freedom.

राध् *râdh*, to finish (राध्यति *râdhyati*), Des. प्रतिरित्सति *prati-ritsati*, in the sense of injuring (Pâṇ. VII. 4, 54, vârt.), otherwise रिरात्सति *rirâtsati* (not रिरित्सति *riritsati*).

§ 472. Certain verbs which are commonly considered to belong to the Bhû class are really desiderative bases.

किल् *kit*, चिकित्सते *chikitsate*, he cures.   गुप् *gup*, जुगुप्सते *jugupsate*, he despises.

तिज् *tij*, तितिक्षते *titikshate*, he bears.   मान् *mân*, मीमांसते *mîmâṁsate*, he investigates.

वध् *badh*, बीभत्सते *bíbhatsate*, he loathes.   दान् *dán*, दीदांसते *dídámsate*, he straightens.

शान् *śán*, शीशांसते *śíśámsate*, he sharpens.

Reduplication in Desideratives.

§ 473. Besides the general rules of reduplication given in § 302–319*, the following special rules with regard to the vowel of the reduplicative syllable are to be observed in forming the desiderative base:

Radical अ *a* and आ *á* are represented by इ *i* in the reduplicative syllable (Pân. VII. 4, 79).

पच् *pach*, पिपक्षति *pipakshati*; स्था *sthá*, तिष्ठासति *tishṭhásati*.

§ 474. अव् *av* and आव् *áv*, standing as Guṇa or Vṛiddhi of radical उ *u* or ऊ *ú*, are represented by इ *i* in the reduplicative syllable, provided they be preceded by प *p*, फ *ph*, ब *b*, भ *bh*, म *m*, य *y*, र *r*, ल *l*, व *v*, ज *j* (Pân. VII. 4, 80).

पू *pú*, पिपावयिषति *pipávayishati*, (Red. Aor. अपीपवत् *apípavat*.) See § 375.

भू *bhú*, बिभावयिषति *bibhávayishati*, (Red. Aor. अबीभवत् *abíbhavat*.)

यु *yu*, यियविषति *yiyavishati*, and Caus. Desid. यियावयिषति *yiyávayishati*.

जु *ju*, जिजावयिषति *jijávayishati*, (Red. Aor. अजीजवत् *ajíjavat*.)

But नु *nu*, नुनावयिषति *nunávayishati*, (Red. Aor. अनूनवत् *anúnavat*.) See § 375†.

§ 475. Roots स्रु *sru*, to flow, श्रु *śru*, to hear, द्रु *dru*, to run, प्रु *pru*, to approach, प्लु *plu*, to swim, च्यु *chyu*, to fall, may under similar circumstances optionally take इ *i* or उ *u* in the reduplicative syllable.

स्रु *sru*, सिस्रावयिषति *sisrávayishati* or सुस्रावयिषति *susrávayishati*; but the simple desiderative सुस्रूषति *susrúshati* only.

स्वापय् *svápay*, the Caus. of स्वप् *svap*, forms सुष्वापयिषति *sushvápayishati*.

§ 476. Roots beginning with a vowel have a peculiar kind of internal reduplication, to which allusion was made in § 378. Thus (Pân. VI. 1, 2)

अश् *aś* forms अशिश् + इषति *aśiś + ishati*.

अट् *aṭ* forms अटिट् + इषति *aṭiṭ + ishati*.

अक्ष् *aksh* forms अचिक्ष् + इषति *achiksh + ishati*.

उच्छ् *uchchh* forms उचिच्छ् + इषति *uchichchh + ishati*.

§ 477. If the root ends in a double consonant, the first letter of which is स् *s*, द् *d*, or र् *r*, then the second letter is reduplicated.

अर्च् *arch*, अर्चिचिषति *archich-ishati*.   उन्द् *und*, उंदिदिषति *undid-ishati*.

उब्ज् *ubj*, उब्जिजिषति *ubjij-ishati*.

In ईर्ष्य् *írshy* the last consonant is reduplicated.

ईर्ष्य् *írshy*, ईर्ष्यियिषति *írshyiy-ishati* or ईर्ष्यिषिषति *írshyish-ishati*. (Pân. VI. 1, 3, vârt.)

In the verbs beginning with कंडूयति *kaṇḍúyati* (§ 498) the final य् *y* is reduplicated.

कंडूय् *kaṇḍúy*, कंडूयियिषति *kaṇḍúyiy-ishati*.

---

* Exceptional reduplication occurs in चिकीषति *chikíshati*, besides चिच्छीषति *chichíshati*, from चि *chi* (Pân. VII. 3, 58); in जिघीषति *jighíshati* from हि *hi* (Pân. VII. 3, 56), &c.

CHAPTER XX.

INTENSIVE VERBS.

§ 478. Intensive, or, as they are sometimes called, frequentative bases are meant to convey an intenseness or frequent repetition of the action expressed by the simple verb. Simple verbs, expressive of motion, sometimes receive the idea of tortuous motion, if used as intensives. Some intensive bases convey the idea of reproach or disgrace, &c.

§ 479. Only bases beginning with a consonant, and consisting of one syllable, are liable to be turned into intensive bases. Verbs of the Chur class cannot be changed into intensive verbs. There are, however, some exceptions. Thus अट् *at*, to go, though beginning with a vowel, forms अटाट्यते *atâţyate*, he wanders about; अश् *aś*, to eat, अशाश्यते *aśâśyate;* ऋ *ri*, to go, अरार्यते *arâryate* and अरार्ति *ararti* (Siddh.-Kaum. vol. II. p. 216); ऊर्णु *úrṇu*, to cover, अर्णोनूयते *úrṇonúyate* (Pâṇ. III. 1, 22).

§ 480. There are two ways of forming intensive verbs:

1. By a peculiar reduplication and adding य *yá* at the end. This *yá* has the accent.

2. By the same peculiar reduplication without any modification in the final portion of the base. The latter form occurs less frequently. It has the accent on the reduplicative syllable.

Bases formed in the former way admit of Âtmanepada only.

Ex. भू *bhú*, बोभूयते *bobhúyáte*.

Bases formed in the latter way admit of Parasmaipada only, though, according to some grammarians, the Âtmanepada also may be formed.

Ex. भू *bhú*, बोभवीति *bóbhavíti* or बोभोति *bóbhoti*.

The Âtmanepada would be बोभूते *bobhúte*.

Roots ending in vowels retain the य *ya* of the intensive base in the general tenses; roots ending in consonants drop it. Hence बोभूयिता *bobhúyitá*, but सोसूचिता *sosúchitá*. (Pâṇ. VI. 4, 49.)

§ 481. When य *ya* is added, the effect on the base is generally the same as in the passive and benedictive Par. (§ 389). Thus final vowels are lengthened: चि *chi*, to gather, चेचीयते *chechíyate;* श्रु *śru*, to hear, शोश्रूयते *śośrúyate*. आ *â* is changed to ई *í:* धा *dhâ*, to place, देधीयते *dedhíyate*. ऋ *ri* becomes ईर् *ír*, or, after labials, ऊर् *úr:* तृ *tri*, to cross, तेतीर्यते *tetíryate;* पृ *pri*, to fill, पोपूर्यते *popúryate*. Final ऋ *ri*, however, when following a simple consonant, is changed to री *rí*, not to रि *ri:* कृ *kri*, to do, चेक्रीयते *chekríyate*. When following a double consonant it is changed to अर् *ar:* स्मृ *smri*, to remember, सास्मर्यते *sásmaryate*. These intensive bases are conjugated like bases of the Div class in the Âtmanepada. It should be observed, however, that in the general tenses roots ending in vowels retain य *y* before the intermediate इ *i*, while roots ending in consonants throw off the य *ya* of the special tenses altogether. Thus from बोभूय *bobhúya*, बोभूयिता *bobhú-y-itá*; from बेभिद्य *bebhidya*, बेभिदिता *bebhiditá*.

§ 482. When य *ya* is not added, the intensive bases are treated like bases of the Hu class. The rules of reduplication are the same. Observe, however, that verbs with final or penultimate ऋ *ri* have peculiar forms of their own (§ 489, 490), and verbs in ऋ *rí* start from a base in अर् *ar*, and therefore have आ *á* in the reduplicative syllable. तॄ *tṛí*, तर् *tar*, तातर्मि *tátarmi*; 3rd pers. plur. तातिरति *tátirati*.

§ 483. According to the rules of the Hu class, the weak terminations require Guṇa (§ 297). Hence from बोबुध् *bobudh*, बोबोध्मि *bobodhmi*; but बोबुध्मः *bobudhmaḥ*. From बोभू *bobhú*, बोभोमि *bobhomi*, बोभवानि *bobhavání*; but बोभूमः *bobhúmaḥ*. Remark, however, that in 1. 2. 3. p. sing. Pres., 2. 3. p. sing. Impf., 3. p. sing. Imp. इ *í* may be optionally inserted:

बोबोध्मि *bobodhmi* or बोबुधीमि *bobudhími*; बोभोमि *bobhomi* or बोभवीमि *bobhavími*. And remark further, that before this intermediate इ *í*, and likewise before weak terminations beginning with a vowel, intensive bases ending in consonants do not take Guṇa (Pâṇ. vii. 3, 87). Hence बोबुधीमि *bobudhími*, बोबुधानि *bobudháni*, अबोबुधं *abobudham*. From विद् *vid*,

PRESENT.	IMPERFECT.	IMPERATIVE.
वेवेद्मि or वेविदीमि	अवेविदं	वेविदानि
vevedmi or *vevidími*	*avevidam*	*veviddni*
वेवेत्सि or वेविदीषि	अवेवेत् or अवेविदीः	वेविद्धि
vevetsi or *vevidíshi*	*avevet* or *avevidíḥ*	*veviddhi*
वेवेत्ति or वेविदीति	अवेवेत् or अवेविदीत्	वेवेत्तु or वेविदीतु
vevetti or *vevidíti*	*avevet* or *avevidít*	*vevettu* or *vevidítu*
वेविद्वः *vevidvaḥ*, &c.	अवेविद्व *avevidva*	वेविदाव *vevidáva*

Rules of Reduplication for Intensives.

§ 484. The simplest way to form the peculiar reduplication of intensives, is to take the base used in the general tenses, to change it into a passive base by adding य *ya*, then to reduplicate, according to the general rules of reduplication, and lastly, to raise, where possible, the vowel of the reduplicative syllable by Guṇa (Pâṇ. vii. 4, 82), and अ *a* to आ *á* (Pâṇ. vii. 4, 83).

चि *chi*, to gather, चीय *chíya*, चेचीयते *chechíyate*; चेचेति *checheti*.

क्रुश् *kruś*, to abuse, क्रुश्य *kruśya*, चोक्रुश्यते *chokruśyate*; चोक्रोष्टि *chokroshṭi*.

त्रौक् *trauk*, to approach, त्रौक्य *traukya*, तोत्रौक्यते *totraukyate*; तोत्रौक्ति *totraukti*.

रेक् *rek*, to suspect, रेक्य *rekya*, रेरेक्यते *rerekyate*; रेरेक्ति *rerekti*.

कृ *kri*, to do, क्रिय *kriya*, चेक्रीयते *chekríyate* (Pân. VII. 4, 27); चर्कर्ति *charkarti*.

कृ *krí*, to scatter, कीर्य *kírya*, चेकीर्यते *chekíryate*; चाकर्ति *chákarti*. (§ 482.)

पृ *pri*, to fill, पूर्य *púrya*, पोपूर्यते *popúryate*; पापर्ति *páparti*.

स्मृ *smri*, to remember, स्मर्य *smarya*, सास्मर्यते *sásmaryate*; सर्स्मर्ति *sarsmarti* *.

दा *dâ*, to give, दीय *díya*, देदीयते *dedíyate*; दादाति *dádáti*.

ह्वे *hve*, to call, हूय *húya*, जोहूयते *johúyate*; जोहोति *johoti*.

§ 485. The roots वंच् *vañch*, संस् *srams*, ध्वंस् *dhvams*, भ्रंस् *bhrams*, कस् *kas*, पत् *pat*, पद् *pad*, स्कंद् *skand*, place नी *ní* between the reduplicative syllable and the root. (Pân. VII. 4, 84.)

    वंच् *vañch*, to go round, वनीवच्यते *va ní vachyate*; वनीवंचीति *vanívañchíti*.

    संस् *srams*, to tear, सनीस्रस्यते *sa ní srasyate*; सनीस्रंसीति *sanísramsíti*.

    ध्वंस् *dhvams*, to fall, दनीध्वस्यते *da ní dhvasyate*; दनीध्वंसीति *danídhvamsíti*.

    भ्रंस् *bhrams*, to fall, वनीभ्रस्यते *ba ní bhrasyate*; वनीभ्रंसीति *baníbhramsíti*.

    कस् *kas*, to go, चनीकस्यते *cha ní kasyate*; चनीकसीति *chaníkasíti*.

    पत् *pat*, to fly, पनीपत्यते *pa ní patyate*; पनीपतीति *panípatíti*.

    पद् *pad*, to go, पनीपद्यते *pa ní padyate*; पनीपदीति *panípadíti*.

    स्कंद् *skand*, to step, चनीस्कद्यते *cha ní skadyate*; चनीस्कंदीति *chaniskandíti*.

§ 486. Roots ending in a nasal, preceded by अ *a*, repeat the nasal in the reduplicative syllable (Pân. VII. 4, 85). The repeated nasal is treated like म् *m*, and the vowel, being long by position, is not lengthened.

    गम् *gam*, to go, जंगम्यते *jangamyate*; जंगमीति *jangamíti*.

    भ्रम् *bhram*, to roam, बंभ्रम्यते *bambhramyate*; बंभ्रमीति *bambhramíti*.

    हन् *han*, to kill, जंघन्यते *janghanyate*; जंघनीति *janghaníti*.

§ 487. The roots जप् *jap*, to recite, जभ् *jabh*, to yawn, दह् *dah*, to burn, दंश् *dams*, to bite, भंज् *bhañj*, to break, पश् *pas*, to bind, insert a nasal in the reduplicative syllable. (Pân. VII. 4, 86.)

    जप् *jap*, जंजप्यते *jañjapyate*; जंजपीति *jañjapíti*. ·

    दंश् *dams*, दंदश्यते *damdasyate*; दंदशीति *damdasíti*.

§ 488. The roots चर् *char* and फल् *phal* form their intensives as,

    चंचूर्यते *chañchúryate* and चंचुरीति *chañchuríti* or चंचूर्ति *chañchúrti*.

    पंफुल्यते *pamphulyate* and पंफुलीति *pamphulíti* or पंफुल्ति *pamphulti*. (Pân. VIII. 4, 87.)

§ 489. Roots with penultimate ऋ *ri* insert री *rí* in their reduplicative syllable. (Pân. VII. 4, 90.)

    वृत् *vrit*, वरीवृत्यते *va rí vrityate*; वरीवृतीति *va rí vritíti*.

In the Parasmaipada these roots allow of six formations. (Pân. VII. 4, 91.)

ववृतीति *va r vritíti*.	वर्वर्ति *varvarti*.
वरिवृतीति *va ri vritíti*.	वरिवर्ति *varivarti*.
वरीवृतीति *va rí vritíti*.	वरीवर्ति *varívarti*.

---

* This form follows from Pân. VII. 4, 92, and is supported by the Mádhavíya-dhátuvritti. Other grammarians give सास्मर्ति *sásmarti*.

§ 490. The same applies to roots ending in कृ *ri*, if used in the Parasmaipada. (Pâṇ. VII. 4, 92.)

कृ *kri;*   चकरीति *cha r karîti.*   चर्केति *charkarti.*

चरिकरीति *cha ri karîti.*   चरिकर्ति *charikarti.*

चरीकरीति *cha rî karîti.*   चरीकर्ति *charîkarti.*

§ 491. A few frequentative bases are peculiar in the formation of their base *.

स्वप् *svap*, to sleep, सोषुप्यते *soshupyate;* but सास्वपि्त *sásvapti.* (Pâṇ. VI. 1, 19.)

स्यम् *syam*, to sound, सेसिम्यते *sesimyate;* but संस्यंति *samsyanti.*

व्ये *vye*, to cover, वेवीयते *veviyate;* but वाव्याति *vâvyáti;* or (§ 483) वाव्येति *vâvyeti.*

वश् *vas*, to desire, वावश्यते *vávasyate;* वावष्टि *vávashṭi.* (Pâṇ. VI. 1, 20.)

चाय् *cháy*, to regard, चेकीयते *chekiyate;* चेकेति *cheketi.* (Pâṇ. VI. 1, 21.)

प्याय् *pyáy*, to grow, पेपीयते *pepiyate;* पाप्याति *pápyáti.* (Pâṇ. VI. 1, 29.)

श्वि *svi*, to swell, शोशूयते *soshúyate* or शेश्वीयते *sesviyate;* शेश्वेति *sesveti.* (Pâṇ. VI. 1, 30.)

हन् *han*, to kill, जेघ्नीयते *jeghniyate;* जंघंति *jaṅghanti.* (Pâṇ. VII. 4, 30, vârt.)

घ्रा *ghrá*, to smell, जेघ्रीयते *jeghriyate;* जाघ्राति *jághráti.* (Pâṇ. VII. 4, 31.)

ध्मा *dhmá*, to blow, देध्मीयते *dedhmiyate;* दाध्माति *dádhmáti.* (Pâṇ. VII. 4, 31.)

गृ *grí*, to swallow, जेगिल्यते *jegilyate;* जागर्ति *jágarti.* (Pâṇ. VIII. 2, 20.)

शि *si*, to lie down, शाशय्यते *sásayyate;* शेशेति *seseti.* (Pâṇ. VII. 4, 22.)

§ 492. From derivative verbs new derivatives may be formed, most of which, however, are rather the creation of grammarians, than the property of the spoken language. Thus from भावयति *bhávayati*, the causal of भू *bhú*, he causes to be, a new desiderative is derived, बिभावयिषति *bibhávayishati*, he wishes to cause existence. So from the intensive बोभूयते *bobhúyate*, he exists really, is formed बोभूयिषति *bobhúyishati*, he wishes to exist really; then a new causative may be formed, बोभूयिषयति *bobhúyishayati*, he causes a wish to exist really; and again a new desiderative, बोभूयिषयिषति *bobhúyisha-yishati*, he wishes to excite the desire of real existence.

---

* The formation and conjugation of the Intensive in the Parasmaipada, or the so-called Charkarîta, have given rise to a great deal of discussion among native grammarians. According to their theory यङ् *yaṅ*, the sign of the Intensive Âtmanepada, has to be suppressed by लुक् *luk*. By this suppression the changes produced in the verbal base by यङ् *yaṅ* would cease (Pâṇ. I. 1, 63), except certain changes which are considered as Anaṅgakârya, changes not affecting the base, such as reduplication. Changes of the root that are to take place not only in the Intens. Âtm., but also in the Intens. Par., are distinctly mentioned by Pâṇini, VII. 4, 82—92. About other changes, not directly extended to the Intens. Par., grammarians differ. Thus the Prakriyâ-Kaumudî forms सोषोप्ति *soshopti*, because Pâṇ. VI. 1, 19, prescribes सोषुप्यते *soshupyate;* other authorities form only सास्वप्ति *sásvapti* or सास्वपीति *sásvapîti.* Colebrooke allows चेकेति *cheketi* (p. 332), because Pâṇ. VI. 1, 21, prescribes चेकीयते *chekiyate*, and the commentary argues in favour of चेकेति *cheketi.* But Colebrooke (p. 321) declines to form सेसिंते *sesinte*, because it is in the Âtm. only that Pâṇ. VI. 1, 19, allows सेसिम्यते *sesimyate.* Whether the Perfect should be periphrastic or reduplicated is likewise a moot point among grammarians; some forming बोभवांचकार *bobhavâñchakára*, others बोभूव *bobhúva*, others बोभाव *bobháva.*

CHAPTER XXI.

DENOMINATIVE VERBS.

§ 493. There are many verbs in Sanskrit which are clearly derived from nominal bases*, and which generally have the meaning of behaving like, or treating some one like, or wishing for or doing whatever is expressed by the noun. Thus from श्येन *śyena*, hawk, we have श्येनायते *śyenáyáte*, he behaves like a hawk; from पुत्र *putra*, son, पुत्रीयति *putríyáti*, he treats some one like a son, or he wishes for a son. Some denominatives are formed without any derivative syllable. Thus from कृष्ण *krishṇá*, कृष्णति *krishṇáti*, he behaves like Krishṇa; from पितृ *pitṛi*, father, पितरति *pitárati*, he behaves like a father.

These denominative verbs, however, cannot be formed at pleasure; and many even of those which would be sanctioned by the rules of native grammarians, are of rare occurrence in the national literature of India. These verbs should therefore be looked for in the dictionary rather than in a grammar. A few rules, however, on their formation and general meaning, may here be given.

Denominatives in य yá, Parasmaipada.

§ 494. By adding य yá to the base of a noun, denominatives are formed expressing a wish. From गो *go*, cow, गव्यति *gavyati*, he wishes for cows. These verbs might be called nominal desideratives, and they never govern a new accusative.

§ 495. By adding the same य ya, denominatives are formed expressing one's looking upon or treating something like the subject expressed by the noun. Thus from पुत्र *putra*, son, पुत्रीयति शिष्यं *putríyati śishyam*, he treats the pupil like a son. By a similar process प्रासादीयति *prâsâdíyati*, from प्रासाद *prâsâda*, palace, means to behave as if one were in a palace; प्रासादीयति कुट्यां भिक्षु: *prâsâdíyati kuṭyâm bhikshuḥ*, the beggar lives in his hut as if it were a palace.

§ 496. Before this य *ya*,

1. Final अ *a* and आ *á* are changed to ई *í*: सुता *sutá*, daughter, सुतीयति *sutíyati*, he wishes for a daughter†.

2. इ *i* and उ *u* are lengthened; पति *pati*, master, पतीयति *patíyati*, he treats like a master; कवि *kavi*, poet, कवीयति *kavíyati*, he wishes to be a poet.

---

* They are called in Sanskrit लिधु *lidhu*, from लिंग *liṅga*, it is said, a crude sound, and धु *dhu*, for धातु *dhátu*, root. (Carey, Grammar, p. 543.)

† Minute distinctions are made between अशनीयति *aśaníyati*, he wishes to eat at the proper time, and अशनायति *aśanáyati*, he is ravenously hungry; between उदकीयति *udakíyati*, he wishes for water, and उदन्यति *udanyati*, he starves and craves for water; between धनायति *dhanáyati*, he is greedy for wealth, and धनीयति *dhaníyati*, he asks for some money. (Pâṇ. VII. 4, 34.)

3. ऋ *ṛi* becomes रौ *rî*, ओ *o* becomes अव् *av*, औ *au* becomes आव् *âv*; पितृ *pitṛi*, father, पित्रीयति *pitrîyati*, he treats like a father; नौ *nau*, ship, नाव्यति *nâvyati*, he wishes for a ship.

4. Final न् *n* is dropt, and other final consonants remain unchanged; राजन् *râjan*, king, राजीयति *râjîyati*, he treats a man like a king; पयस् *payas*, milk, पयस्यति *payasyati*, he wishes for milk; वाच् *vâch*, speech, वाच्यति *vâchyati* (Pân. I. 4, 15); नमस् *namas*, worship, नमस्यति *namasyati*, he worships (Pân. III. 1, 19).

Denominatives in य *yá, Âtmanepada.*

§ 497. A second class of denominatives, formed by adding य *yá*, has the meaning of behaving like, or becoming like, or actually doing what is expressed by the noun. They differ from the preceding class by generally following the Âtmanepada*, and by a difference in the modification of the final letters of the nominal base. Thus

1. Final अ *a* is lengthened; श्येन *śyena*, hawk, श्येनायते *śyenâyate*, he behaves like a hawk; शब्द *śabda*, sound, शब्दायते *śabdâyate*, he makes a sound, he sounds; भृश *bhṛiśa*, much, भृशायते *bhṛiśâyate*, he becomes much; कष्ट *kashṭa*, mischief, कष्टायते *kashṭâyate*, he plots; रोमंथ *romantha*, ruminating, रोमंथायते *romanthâyate*, he ruminates. The final ई *î* of feminine bases is generally dropt, and the masculine base taken instead; कुमारी *kumârî*, girl, कुमारायते *kumârâyate*, he behaves like a girl. (Pân. VI. 3, 36–41.)

2 and 3. Final इ *i* and उ *u*, ऋ *ṛi*, ओ *o*, औ *au* are treated as in § 496; शुचि *śuchi*, pure, शुचीयते *śuchîyate*, he becomes pure.

4. Final न् *n* is dropt, and the preceding vowel is lengthened; राजन् *râjan*, king, राजायते *râjâyate*, he behaves like a king; उष्मन् *ushman*, heat, उष्मायते *ushmâyate*, it sends out heat.

Some nominal bases in स् *s* and त् *t* may, others must (Pân. III. 1, 11) be treated like nominal bases in अ *a*. Hence from विद्वस् *vidvas*, wise, विद्वस्यते *vidvasyate* or विद्वायते *vidvâyate*, he behaves like a wise man; from पयस् *payas*, milk, पयस्यते *payasyate* or पयायते *payâyate*, it becomes milk; from अप्सरस् *apsaras*, अप्सरायते *apsarâyate*, she behaves like an Apsaras; from बृहत् *bṛihat*, great, बृहायते *bṛihâyate*, he becomes great. (Pân. III. 1, 12.)

§ 498. Some verbs are classed together by native grammarians as Kaṇḍvâdi's, i.e. beginning with Kaṇḍû. They take य *ya*, both in Parasmaipada and Âtmanepada, and keep it through the general tenses under the restrictions applying to other denominatives in य *ya* (§ 501). Nouns ending in अ *a* drop it before य *ya*. Thus from अगद *agada*, free from

---

* Those that may take both Parasmaipada and Âtmanepada are said to be formed by क्यष् *kyash*, the rest by क्यङ् *kyaṅ*. Thus from लोहित *lohita*, red, लोहितायति or °ते *lohitâyati* or -*te*, he becomes red. (Pân. III. 1, 13.)

illness, अगदयति *agadyati*, he is free from illness; from सुख *sukha*, pleasure, सुख्यति *sukhyati*, he gives pleasure; from कंडू *kaṇḍú*, scratching, कंडूयति or °ते *kaṇḍúyati* or -*te*, he scratches.

Denominatives in स्य *sya*.

§ 499. Certain denominative verbs, which express a wish, take स्य *sya* instead of य *ya*. Thus from क्षीर *kshíra*, milk, क्षीरस्यति *kshírasyati*, the child longs for milk; from लवण *lavaṇa*, salt, लवणस्यति *lavaṇasyati*, he desires salt. Likewise अश्वस्यति *aśvasyati*, the mare longs for the horse; वृषस्यति *vrishasyati*, the cow longs for the bull (Pâṇ. vii. 1, 52). Some authorities admit स्य *sya* and अस्य *asya*, in the sense of extreme desire, after all nominal bases. Thus from मधु *madhu*, honey, मधुस्यति *madhusyati* or मध्वस्यति *madhvasyati*, he longs for honey.

Denominatives in काम्य *kâmya*.

§ 500. It is usual to form desiderative verbs by compounding a nominal base with काम्य *kâmya*, a denominative from काम *kâma*, love. Thus पुत्रकाम्यति *putrakâmyati*, he has the wish for a son; Fut. पुत्रकाम्यिता *putrakâmyitâ*. Here the य *y*, it is said, is not liable to be dropt. (Siddh.-Kaum. vol. ii. p. 222.)

§ 501. The denominatives in य *ya* are conjugated like verbs of the Bhû class in the Parasmaipada and Âtmanepada. Pres. पुत्रीयामि *putríyâmi*, Impf. अपुत्रीयं *aputríyam*, Imp. पुत्रीयाणि *putríyâṇi*, Opt. पुत्रीयेयं *putríyeyam*. Pres. श्येनाये *śyenâye*, Impf. अश्येनाये *aśyenâye*, Imp. श्येनावै *śyenâyai*, Opt. श्येनायेय *śyenâyeya*. In the general tenses the base is पुत्रीय् *putríy* or श्येनाय् *śyenây*; but when the denominative य *y* is preceded by a consonant, य *y* may or may not be dropt in the general tenses (Pâṇ. vi. 4, 50). Hence, Per. Perf. पुत्रीयामास *putríyâmâsa* (§ 325, 3), Aor. अपुत्रीयिषं *aputríyisham*, Fut. पुत्रीयिष्यामि *putríyishyâmi*, Per. Fut. पुत्रीयिता *putríyitâ*, Ben. पुत्रीयासं *putríyâsam*.

From श्येनायते *śyenâyate*, Per. Perf. श्येनायामास *śyenâyâmâsa*, Aor. अश्येनायिषि *aśyenâyishi*, Fut. श्येनायिष्ये *śyenâyishye*, &c.

From समिध् *samidh*, fuel, समिध्यति *samidhyati*, he wishes for fuel; Per. Fut. समिध्यिता *samidhyitâ* or समिधिता *samidhitâ*, &c. (Pâṇ. vi. 4, 50).

Denominatives in अय *aya*.

§ 502. Some denominative verbs are formed by adding अय *aya* to certain nominal bases. They generally express the act implied by the nominal base. They may be looked upon as verbs of the Chur class. They are conjugated in the Parasmaipada and Âtmanepada, some in the Âtmanepada only. They retain अय् *ay* in the general tenses under the limitations that apply to verbs of the Chur class and causatives (viz. benedictive Par., reduplicated aorist, &c.), and their radical vowels are modified according to the rules applying to the verbs of the Chur class (§ 296, 4).

Thus from पाश *pâśa*, fetter, विपाशयति *vipâśayati*, he unties; from वर्मन् *varman*, armour, संवर्मयति *samvarmayati*, he arms, (the final न् *n* being dropt); from मुंड *muṇḍa*, shaven, मुंडयति *muṇḍayati*, he shaves; from शब्द *śabda*, sound, शब्दयति *śabdayati*, he makes a sound (Dhâtupâṭha 33, 40); from मिश्र *miśra*, mixed, मिश्रयति *miśrayati*, he mixes (Pâṇ. iii. 1, 21; 25).

Some of these verbs are always Âtmanepada. Thus from पुच्छ *puchchha*, tail, उत्पुच्छयते *utpuchchhayate*, he lifts up the tail (Pân. III. 1, 20).

If अय *aya* is to be added to nouns formed by the secondary affixes मत् *mat*, वत् *vat*, मिन् *min*, विन् *vin*, these affixes must be dropt. From स्रग्विन् *sragvin*, having garlands, स्रजयति *srajayati*.

If अय *aya* is added to feminine bases, they are generally replaced by the corresponding masculine base. From श्येनी *syenî* (§ 247), white, श्येतयति *syetayati*, he makes her white (Pân. VI. 3, 36).

Certain adjectives which change their base before इष्ठ *ishtha* of the superlative, do the same before अय *aya*. मृदु *mridu*, soft, मृदयति *mradayati*, he softens ; दूर *dûra*, far, दवयति *davayati*, he removes.

Some nominal bases take आपय *âpaya*. Thus from सत्य *satya*, true, सत्यापयति *satyâpayati*, he speaks truly; from अर्थ *artha*, sense, अर्थापयति *arthâpayati*, he explains.

Denominatives without any Affix.

§ 503. According to some authorities every nominal base may be turned into a denominative verb by adding the ordinary verbal terminations of the First Division, and treating the base like a verbal base of the Bhû class. अ *a* is added to the base, except where it exists already as the final of the nominal base; other final and medial vowels take Guṇa, where possible, as in the Bhû class.

Thus from कृष्ण *krishṇa*, कृष्णति *krishṇati*, he behaves like Krishṇa; from माला *mâlâ*, garland, मालाति *mâlâti*, it is like a garland, Impf. अमालात् *amâlât*, Aor. अमालासीत् *amâlâsît*; from कवि *kavi*, poet, कवयति *kavayati*, he behaves like a poet; from वि *vi*, bird, वयति *vayati*, he flies like a bird; from पितृ *pitṛi*, father, पितरति *pitarati*, he is like a father; from राजन् *râjan*, king, राजानति *râjânati*, he is like a king (Pân. VI. 4, 15).

CHAPTER XXII.

PREPOSITIONS AND PARTICLES.

§ 504. The following prepositions may be joined with verbs, and are then called *Upasarga* in Sanskrit (Pân. I. 4, 58—61 ; § 148).

अति *ati*, beyond.   अधि *adhi*, over (sometimes धि *dhi*).   अनु *anu*, after. अप *apa*, off.   अपि *api*, upon (sometimes पि *pi*).   अभि *abhi*, towards. अव *ava*, down (sometimes व *va*).   आ *â*, near to.   उद् *ud*, up.   उप *upa*, next, below.   दुः *duḥ*, ill.   नि *ni*, into, downwards.   निः *niḥ*, without. परा *parâ*, back, away.   परि *pari*, around.   प्र *pra*, before.   प्रति *prati*, back.   वि *vi*, apart.   सं *sam*, together.   सु *su*, well.   They all have the *udâtta* on the first syllable except अभि *abhî*.

§ 505. Certain adverbs, called *Gati* in Sanskrit, a term applicable also to the *Upasargas* (Pân. I. 4, 60), may be prefixed, like prepositions, to certain verbs, particularly to भू *bhû*, to be, अस् *as*, to be, कृ *kṛi*, to do, and गम् *gam*, to go.

अच्छ *achchha*; e. g. अच्छगत्य *achchhagatya*, having approached (§ 445); अच्छोद्य *achchhodya*, having addressed. अद: *adaḥ*; e. g. अद:कृत्य *adaḥkritya*, having done it thus. अंतर् *antar*; e.g. अंतरित्य *antaritya*, having passed between. अलं *alam*; e. g. अलंकृत्य *alaṅkritya*, having ornamented. अस्तं *astam*; e. g. अस्तंगत्य *astaṅgatya*, having gone to rest, having set. आविः *âviḥ*; e. g. आविर्भूय *âvirbhûya*, having appeared. तिरः *tiraḥ*; e. g. तिरोभूय *tirobhûya*, having disappeared. पुर: *puraḥ*; e. g. पुरस्कृत्य *puraskritya*, having placed before (§ 89, II. 1). प्रादु: *prâduḥ*; e.g. प्रादुर्भूय *prâdurbhûya*, having become manifest. सत् *sat* and असत् *asat*, when expressing regard or contempt; e. g. असत्कृत्य *asatkritya*, having disregarded. साक्षात् *sâkshât*; e. g. साक्षात्कृत्य *sâkshâtkritya*, having made known. Words like शुक्ली *suklî*, in शुक्लीकृत्य *suklîkritya*, having made white. (Here the final अ *a* of शुक्ल *sukla* is changed to ई *î*. Sometimes, but rarely, final अ *a* or आ *â* is changed to आ *â*. Final इ *i* and उ *u* are lengthened; ऋ *ri* is changed to री *rî*; final अन् *an* and अस् *as* are changed to ई *î*; e.g. राजीकृत्य *râjîkritya*, having made king.) Words like अरी *ûrî*, in अरीकृत्य *ûrîkritya*, having assented. Words like खात् *khât*, imitative of sound; e.g. खात्कृत्य *khâtkritya*, having made *khât*, the sound produced in clearing one's throat.

§ 506. Several of the prepositions mentioned in § 503 are also used with nouns, and are then said to govern certain cases. They are then called *Karmapravachanîya*, and they frequently follow the noun which is governed by them (Pâṇ. 1. 4, 83).

The accusative is governed by अति *ati*, beyond; अभि *abhi*, towards; परि *pari*, around; प्रति *prati*, against; अनु *anu*, after; उप *upa*, upon. Ex. गोविंदमति नेश्वर: *govindam ati nesvaraḥ*, Isvara is not beyond Govinda; हरं प्रति हलाहलं *haram prati halâhalam*, venom was for Hara; विष्णुमन्वर्च्यते *vishnumanvarchyate*, he is worshipped after Vishṇu; अनु हरिं सुरा: *anu harim surâḥ*, the gods are less than Hari.

The ablative is governed by प्रति *prati*, परि *pari*, अप *apa*, आ *â*. Ex. भक्ते: प्रत्यमृतं *bhakteḥ praty amritam*, immortality in return for faith; आ मृत्यो: *â mrityoḥ*, until death; अप त्रिगर्तेभ्यो वृष्टो देव: *apa trigartebhyo vrishṭo devaḥ*, it has rained away from Trigarta, or परि त्रिगर्तेभ्य: *pari trigartebhyaḥ*, round Trigarta, without touching Trigarta.

The locative is governed by उप *upa* and अधि *adhi*. Ex. उप निष्के कार्षापणं *upa nishke kârshâpaṇam*, a Kârshâpaṇa is more than a Nishka; अधि पंचालेषु ब्रह्मदत्त: *adhi pañchâleshu brahmadattaḥ*, Brahmadatta governs over the Pañchâlas.

§ 507. There are many other adverbs in Sanskrit, some of which may here be mentioned.

1. The accusative of adjectives in the neuter may be used as an adverb.

Thus from मंद: *mandaḥ*, slow, मंदं मंदं *mandam mandam*, slowly, slowly; शीघ्रं *śighram*, quickly; ध्रुवं *dhruvam*, truly.

2. Certain compounds, ending like accusatives of neuters, are used adverbially, such as यथाशक्ति *yathâśakti*, according to one's power. For these see the rules on composition.

3. Adverbs of place :

अंतर् *antar*, within, with loc. and gen.; between, with acc. अंतरा *antarâ*, between, with acc. अंतरेण *antareṇa*, between, with acc.; without, with acc. आरात् *ârât*, far off, with abl. बहि: *vahiḥ*, outside, with abl. समया *samayâ*, near, with acc. निकषा *nikashâ*, near, with acc. उपरि *upari*, above, over, with acc. and gen. उच्चै: *uchchaiḥ*, high, or loud. नीचै: *nîchaiḥ*, low. अध: *adhaḥ*, below, with gen. and abl. अव: *avaḥ*, below, with gen. तिर: *tiraḥ*, across, with acc. or loc. इह *iha*, here. पुरा *purâ*, before. समक्षं *samaksham*, साक्षात् *sâkshât*, in the presence. सकाशात् *sakâśât*, from. पुर: *puraḥ*, before, with gen. अमा *amâ*, सचा *sachâ*, साकं *sâkam*, समा *samâ*, सार्धं *sârdham*, together, with instr. अभित: *abhitaḥ*, on all sides, with acc. उभयत: *ubhayataḥ*, on both sides, with acc. समंतात् *samantât*, from all sides. दूरं *dûram*, far, with acc., abl., and gen. अंतिकं *antikam*, near, with acc., abl., and gen. ऋधक् *ṛidhak*, पृथक् *prithak*, apart.

4. Adverbs of time :

प्रातर् *prâtar*, early. सायं *sâyam*, at eve. दिवा *divâ*, by day. अह्नाय *ahnâya*, by day. दोषा *doshâ*, by night. नक्तं *naktam*, by night. उषा *ushâ*, early. युगपद् *yugapad*, at the same time. अद्य *adya*, to-day. ह्य: *hyaḥ*, yesterday. पूर्वेद्यु: *pûrvedyuḥ*, yesterday. श्व: *śvaḥ*, to-morrow. परेद्यवि *paredyavi*, to-morrow. ज्योक् *jyok*, long. चिरं *chiram*, चिरेण *chireṇa*, चिराय *chirâya*, चिरात् *chirât*, चिरस्य *chirasya*, long. सना *sanâ*, सनात् *sanât*, सनत् *sanat*, perpetually. अरं *aram*, quickly. शनै: *śanaiḥ*, slowly. सद्य: *sadyaḥ*, at once. संप्रति *samprati*, now. पुनर् *punar*, मुह: *muhuḥ*, भूय: *bhûyaḥ*, वारं *vâram*, again. सकृत् *sakṛit*, once. पुरा *purâ*, formerly. पूर्वं *pûrvam*, before. ऊर्ध्वं *ûrdhvam*, after. सपदि *sapadi*, immediately. पश्चात् *paśchât*, after, with abl. जातु *jâtu*, once upon a time, ever. अधुना *adhunâ*, now. इदानीं *idânîm*, now. सदा *sadâ*, संततं *santatam*, अनिशं *aniśam*, always. अलं *alam*, enough, with dat. or instr.

5. Adverbs of circumstance :

मृषा *mrishâ*, मिथ्या *mithyâ*, falsely. मनाक् *manâk*, ईषत् *îshat*, a little. तूष्णीं *tûshṇîm*, quietly. वृथा *vṛithâ*, मुधा *mudhâ*, in vain. सामि *sâmi*, half. अकस्मात् *akasmât*, unexpectedly. उपांशु *upâmśu*, in a whisper. मिथ: *mithaḥ*, together. प्राय: *prâyaḥ*, frequently, almost. अतीव *atîva*, exceedingly. कामं *kâmam*, जोषं *josham*, gladly. अवश्यं *avaśyam*, certainly.

किल *kila*, indeed.   खलु *khalu*, certainly.   विना *vinâ*, without, with acc., instr., or abl.   ऋते *ṛite*, without, with acc. or abl.   नाना *nânâ*, variously. सुष्ठु *sushṭhu*, well.   दुष्ठु *dushṭhu*, badly.   दिष्ट्या *dishṭyâ*, luckily.   प्रभृति *prabhṛiti*, et cetera, and the rest, with abl.   कुवित् *kuvit*, really? कच्चित् *kachchit*, really?   कथं *katham*, how?   इति *iti*, इत्थं *ittham*, thus. इव *iva*, as;   हरिरिव *harir iva*, like Hari.   वत् *vat*, enclitic;   हरिवत् *harivat*, like Hari.

Conjunctions and other Particles.

§ 508. अथ *atha*, अथो *atho*, now then.   इति *iti*, thus.   यदि *yadi*, when. यद्यपि *yadyapi*, although.   तथापि *tathâpi*, yet.   चेत् *chet*, if.   न *na*, नो *no*, not.   च *cha*, and, always enclitic, like *que*.   किंच *kimcha*, and.   मा *mâ* or मा स्म *mâ sma*, not, prohibitively.   वा *vâ*, or.   वा—वा *vâ—vâ*, either—or.   अथवा *athavâ*, or.   एव *eva*, even, very; (स एव *sa eva*, the same.)   एवं *evam*, thus. नूनं *nûnam*, doubtlessly.   यावत्—तावत् *yâvat—tâvat*, as much—as.   यथा— तथा *yathâ—tathâ*, as—so.   येन—तेन *yena—tena*, यद्—तद् *yad—tad*, and other correlatives, because—therefore.   तथाहि *tathâhi*, thus, for.   तु *tu*, परं *param*, किंतु *kintu*, but.   चित् *chit*, चन *chana*, subjoined to the interrogative pronoun किं *kim*, any, some; as कश्चित् *kaśchit*, some one;   कथंचन *kathañchana*, anyhow.   हि *hi*, for, because.   उत *uta*, उताहो *utâho*, or.   नाम *nâma*, namely. प्रत्युत *pratyuta*, on the contrary.   नु *nu*, perhaps.   ननु *nanu*, Is it not? स्वित् *svit*, किंस्वित् *kimsvit*, perhaps.   अपि *api*, also, even.   अपि च *api cha*, again.   नूनं *nûnam*, certainly.

Interjections.

§ 509. हे *he*, भो *bho*, vocative particles.   अये *aye*, हये *haye*, Ah!   धिक् *dhik*, रे *re*, अरे *are*, Fie!

CHAPTER XXIII.

COMPOUND WORDS.

§ 510. The power of forming two or more words into one, which belongs to all Aryan languages, has been so largely developed in Sanskrit that a few of the more general rules of composition claim a place even in an elementary grammar.

As a general rule, all words which form a compound drop their inflectional terminations, except the last. They appear in that form which is called their base, and when they have more than one, in their Pada base (§ 180). Hence देवदास: *deva-dâsaḥ*, a servant of god; राजपुरुष: *râjapurushaḥ*, a king's man; प्रत्यग्मुख: *pratyagmukhaḥ*, facing west.

H h

§ 511. Sometimes the sign of the feminine gender in the prior elements of a compound may be retained. This is chiefly the case when the feminine is treated as an appellative, and would lose its distinctive meaning by losing the feminine suffix: कल्याणीमाता *kalyânîmâtâ*, the mother of a beautiful daughter (Pân. vi. 3, 34); कठीभार्यः *kathîbhâryaḥ*, having a Kathî for one's wife (Pân. vi. 3, 41). If the feminine forms a mere predicate, it generally loses its feminine suffix; शोभनभार्यः *sobhanabhâryaḥ*, having a beautiful wife (Pân. vi. 3, 34; 42).

The phonetic rules to be observed are those of external Sandhi with certain modifications, as explained in § 24 seq.*

§ 512. Compound words might have been divided into substantival, adjectival, and adverbial. Thus words like तत्पुरुषः *tatpurushaḥ*, his man, नीलोत्पलं *nîlotpalam*, blue lotus, द्विगवं *dvigavam*, two oxen, अग्निधूमौ *agnidhûmau*, fire and smoke, might have been classed as substantival; बहुव्रीहिः *bahuvrîhiḥ*, possessing much rice, as an adjectival; and यथाशक्ति *yathâsakti*, according to one's strength, as an adverbial compound.

Native grammarians, however, have adopted a different principle of division, classing all compounds under six different heads, under the names of *Tatpurusha, Karmadhâraya, Dvigu, Dvandva, Bahuvrîhi*, and *Avyayîbhâva.*

I. *Tatpurusha* is a compound in which the last word is determined by the preceding words, for instance, तत्पुरुषः *tat-purushaḥ*, his man, or राजपुरुषः *râja-purushaḥ*, king's man.

As a general term the *Tatpurusha* compound comprehends the two subdivisions of *Karmadhâraya* (I *b*) and *Dvigu* (I *c*). The Karmadhâraya is in fact a Tatpurusha compound, in which the last word is determined by a preceding adjective, e. g. नीलोत्पलं *nîlotpalam*, blue lotus. The component words, if dissolved, would stand in the same case, whereas in other Tatpurushas the preceding word is governed by the last, the man of the king, or fire-wood, i. e. wood for fire.

The *Dvigu* again may be called a subdivision of the Karmadhâraya, being a compound in which the first word is not an adjective in general, but always a numeral: द्विगवं *dvigavam*, two oxen, or द्विगुः *dviguḥ*, bought for two oxen.

---

* Occasionally bases ending in a long vowel shorten it, and bases ending in a short vowel lengthen it in the middle of a compound; उदक *udaka*, water, पाद *pâda*, foot, हृदय *hridaya*, heart, frequently substitute the bases उदन् *udan* (i.e. उद *uda*), पद् *pad*, and हृद् *hrid*. हृद्रोगः *hridrogaḥ*, heart-disease, or हृदयरोगः *hridayarogaḥ*. (Pân. vi. 3, 51—60.)

The particle कु *ku*, which is intended to express contempt, as कुब्राह्मणः *kubrâhmaṇaḥ*, a bad Brâhman, substitutes कद् *kad* in a determinative compound before words beginning with consonants: कदुष्ट्रः *kadushtrah*, a bad camel. The same takes place before रथ *ratha*, वद *vada*, and तृण *trina:* कद्रथः *kadrathaḥ*, a bad carriage; कत्तृणं *kattrinam*, a bad kind of grass. The same particle is changed to का *kâ* before पथिन् *pathin* and अक्ष *aksha:* कापथः *kâpathaḥ*, and optionally before पुरुष *purusha*. (Pân. vi. 3, 101—107.)

These three classes of compounds may be comprehended under the general name of *Determinative Compounds*, while the Karmadhâraya (I *b*) may be distinguished as *appositional* determinatives, the Dvigu (I *c*) as *numeral* determinatives.

II. The next class, called *Dvandva*, consists of compounds in which two words are simply joined together, the compound taking either the terminations of the dual or plural, according to the number of compounded nouns, or the terminations of the singular, being treated as a collective term : अग्निधूमौ *agni-dhûmau*, fire and smoke ; शशकुशपलाशा: *śaśa-kuśa-palâśâḥ*, nom. plur. masc. three kinds of plants, or शशकुशपलाशं *śaśa-kuśa-palâśam*, nom. sing. neut. They will be called *Collective Compounds*.

III. The next class, called *Bahuvrîhi* by native grammarians, comprises compounds which are used as adjectives. The notion expressed by the last word, and which may be variously determined, forms the predicate of some other subject. They may be called *Possessive Compounds*. Thus बहुव्रीहि: *bahu-vrîhiḥ*, possessed of much rice, scil. देश: *deśaḥ*, country ; रूपवद्भार्य: *rûpavad-bhâryaḥ*, possessing a handsome wife, scil. राजा *râjâ*, king.

Determinative compounds may be turned into possessive compounds, sometimes without any change, except that of accent, sometimes by slight changes in the last word.

The gender of possessive compounds, like that of adjectives, conforms to the gender of the substantives to which they belong.

IV. The last class, called *Avyayîbhâva*, is formed by joining an indeclinable particle with another word. The resulting compound, in which the indeclinable particle always forms the first element, is again indeclinable, and generally ends, like adverbs, in the ordinary terminations of the nom. or acc. neut.: अधिस्त्रि *adhi-strî*, for woman, as in अधिस्त्रि गृहकार्याणि *adhistri grihakâryâṇi*, household duties are for women. They may be called *Adverbial Compounds*.

I. *Determinative Compounds.*

§ 513. This class (Tatpurusha) comprehends compounds in which generally the last word governs the preceding one. The last word may be a substantive or a participle or an adjective, if capable of governing a noun.

1. Compounds in which the first noun would be in the Accusative : कृष्णाश्रित: *krishna-śritaḥ*, m. f. n. gone to Krishṇa, dependent on Krishṇa, instead of कृष्णं श्रित: *krishṇam śritaḥ*. दु:खातीत: *duḥkha-atîtaḥ*, m. f. n. having overcome pain, instead of दु:खमतीत: *duḥkham atîtaḥ*. वर्षभोग्य: *varsha-bhogyaḥ*, m. f. n. to be enjoyed a year long. ग्रामप्राप्त: *grâma-prâptaḥ*, m. f. n. having reached the village, instead of ग्रामं प्राप्त: *grâmam*

práptah : it is more usual, however, to say श्राम्प्राप्तः *práptagrámah* (Pâṇ. ii. 2, 4). Similarly are formed determinatives by means of adverbs or prepositions, such as अतिगिरि *atigiri,* past the hill, used as an adverb, or as an adjective, अतिगिरि: *atigirih,* ultramontane; अभिमुखं *abhimukham,* facing, &c.

2. Compounds in which the first noun would be in the Instrumental :

धान्यार्थः *dhánya-arthah,* m. wealth (*arthah*) (acquired) by grain (*dhányena*). शंकुलाखंड: *śankulá-khandah,* m. a piece (*khandah*) (cut) by nippers (*śankuládbhih*). दात्रच्छिन्न: *dátra-chchhinnah,* m. f. n. cut (*chhinnah*) by a knife (*dátrena*). हरित्रातः *hari-trátah,* m.f. n. protected (*trátah*) by Hari. देवदत्तः *deva-dattah,* given (*dattah*) by the gods (*devaih*), or as a proper name with the supposed auspicious sense, may the gods give him (*Dieu-donné*). पितृसमः *pitri-samah,* m. f. n. like the father, i. e. *pitrá samah.* नखनिर्भिन्न: *nakha-nirbhinnah,* m. f. n. cut asunder (*nirbhinnah*) by the nails (*nakhaih*). विश्वोपास्य: *viśva-upásyah,* m. f. n. to be worshipped by all. स्वयंकृत: *svayam-kritah,* m. f. n. done by oneself.

3. Compounds in which the first noun would be in the Dative :

यूपदारु *yúpa-dáru,* n. wood (*dáru*) for a sacrificial stake (*yúpáya*). गोहित: *go-hitah,* m.f.n. good (*hitah*) for cows (*gobhyah*). द्विजार्थः *dvija-arthah,* m.f.n. object (*artha*), i. e. intended for Bráhmans. Determinative compounds, when treated as possessive, take the terminations of the masc., fem., and neut.; e. g. द्विजार्था यवागू: *dvijárthá yavágúh,* fem. gruel for Bráhmans.

4. Compounds in which the first noun would be in the Ablative :

चोरभयं *chora-bhayam,* n. fear (*bhayam*) arising from thieves (*chorebhyah*). स्वर्गपतित: *svarga-patitah,* m.f. n. fallen from heaven. अपग्राम: *apa-grámah,* m. f. n. gone from the village.

5. Compounds in which the first noun would be in the Genitive :

तत्पुरुष: *tat-purushah,* m. his man, instead of *tasya,* of him, *purushah,* the man*. राजपुरुष: *rája-purushah,* m. the king's man, instead of *rájñah,* of the king, *purushah,* the man. राजसख: *rája-sakhah,* m. the king's friend. In these compounds *sakhi,* friend, is changed to *sakhah.* कुम्भकार: *kumbha-kárah,* a maker (*kárah*) of pots (*kumbhánám*). गोशतं *go-śatam,* a hundred of cows.

6. Compounds in which the first noun would be in the Locative :

अक्षशौंड: *aksha-śaundah,* m. f. n. devoted to dice. उरोज: *uro-jah,* m. f. n. produced on the breast.

---

* Most words ending in तृ *tri* or क *ka* are not allowed to form compounds of this kind. Hence कटस्य कर्ता *katasya kartá,* maker of a mat, not कटकर्ता *katakartá;* पुरां भेत्ता *purám bhettá,* breaker of towns. There are, however, many exceptions, such as देवपूजक: *deva-pújakah,* worshipper of the gods, &c.

§ 514. Certain Tatpurusha compounds retain the case-terminations in the governed noun.

सहसाकृत: *sahasâ-kritaḥ*, done suddenly (Pâṇ. VI. 3, 3). आत्मनाषष्ठ: *âtmanâ-shashṭhaḥ*, the sixth with oneself (Pâṇ. VI. 3, 6). परस्मैपदं *parasmai-padam*, a word for the sake of another, i. e. the transitive form of verbs (Pâṇ. VI. 3, 7, 8). कृच्छ्रालब्धं *krichchhrâl-labdham*, obtained with difficulty. स्वसु:पुत्र: *svasuḥ-putraḥ*, sister's son (Pâṇ. VI. 3, 23). दिवस्पति: *divas-patiḥ*, lord of heaven. वाचस्पति: *vâchas-patiḥ*, lord of speech. देवानांप्रिय: *devânâm-priyaḥ*, beloved of the gods, a goat, an ignorant person. गेहेपण्डित: *gehe-paṇḍitaḥ*, learned at home, i. e. where no one can contradict him. खेचर: *khecharaḥ*, moving in the air. सरसिज: *sarasi-jaḥ*, born in a pond, water-lily. हृदिस्पृश् *hṛidi-spṛiś*, touching the heart. युधिष्ठिर: *yudhishṭhiraḥ*, firm in battle, a proper name (Pâṇ. VI. 3, 9).

§ 515. To this class a number of compounds are referred in which the governing element is supposed to take the first place. Ex. पूर्वकाय: *pûrva-kâyaḥ*, the fore-part of the body, i. e. the fore-body; पूर्वरात्र: *pûrva-râtraḥ*, the first part of the night, i. e. the fore-night; राजदंत: *râjadantaḥ*, the king of teeth, lit. the king-teeth, i. e. the fore-teeth (Pâṇ. II. 2, 1). They would better be looked upon as Karmadhârayas; cf. § 517.

§ 516. If the second part of a determinative compound is a verbal base, no change takes place in bases ending in consonants or long vowels, except that diphthongs, as usual, are changed to आ *â*. Hence जलमुच् *jalamuch*, water-dropping, i. e. a cloud; सोमपा *soma-pâ*, Soma-drinking, nom. sing. सोमपा: *somapâḥ* (§ 239).

Bases ending in short vowels generally take a final त् *t*: विश्वजित् *viśvajit*, all-conquering, from जि *ji*, to conquer. Other suffixes used for the same purpose are अ *a*, इन् *in*, &c.

I b. *Appositional Determinative Compounds.*

§ 517. These compounds (Karmadhâraya) form a subdivision of the determinative compounds (Tatpurusha). In them the first portion stands as the predicate of the second portion, such as in *black-beetle*, *sky-blue*, &c.

The following are some instances of appositional compounds:
नीलोत्पलं *nîla-utpalam*, neut. the blue lotus. परमात्मा *parama-âtmâ*, masc. the supreme spirit. शाकपार्थिव: *śâka-pârthivaḥ*, masc. a S'âka-king, explained as a king such as the S'âkas would like, not as the king of the S'âkas. सर्वरात्र: *sarva-râtraḥ*, masc. the whole night, from *sarva*, whole, and *râtriḥ*, night. *Râtriḥ*, fem., is changed to *râtra*; cf. पूर्वरात्र: *pûrva-râtraḥ*, masc. the fore-night; मध्यरात्र: *madhya-râtraḥ*, masc. midnight; पुण्यरात्र: *puṇya-râtraḥ*, masc. a holy night. द्विरात्रं *dvi-râtram*, neut. a space of two nights, is a numeral compound (Dvigu). महाराज: *mahâ-râjaḥ*, masc. a great king. In these compounds महत् *mahat*, great, always becomes महा *mahâ* (Pâṇ. VI. 3, 46), and राजन् *râjan*, king, राज: *râjaḥ*; as परमराज: *parama-râjaḥ*, a supreme king: but सुराजा *su-râjâ*, a good king, किंराजा *kiṁrâjâ*, a bad king (Pâṇ. V. 4, 69, 70). प्रियसख: *priya-sakhaḥ*, masc. a dear friend. सखि *sakhi* is changed to सख: *sakhaḥ*. परमाह: *parama-ahaḥ*, masc. the highest day. In these compounds अहन् *ahan*, day, becomes

अह *aha;* cf. उत्तमाहः *uttamáhaḥ,* the last day. Sometimes अह्न *ahna* is substituted for अहन् *ahan;* पूर्वाह्णः *púrváhṇaḥ,* the fore-noon. कुपुरुषः *ku-purushaḥ,* masc. a bad man, or कापुरुषः *kápurushaḥ.* प्राचार्यः *pra-ácháryaḥ,* masc. a hereditary teacher, i. e. one who has been a teacher (*áchárya*) before or formerly (*pra*). अब्राह्मणः *a-bráhmaṇaḥ,* masc. a non-Bráhman, i.e. not a Bráhman. अनश्वः *an-aśvaḥ,* masc. a non-horse, i.e. not a horse. घनश्यामः *ghana-śyámaḥ,* m. f. n. cloud-black, from *ghana,* cloud, and *śyáma,* black. ईषत्पिंगलः *íshat-piṅgalaḥ,* m. f. n. a little brown, from *íshat,* a little, and *piṅgala,* brown. सामिकृतः *sámi-kritaḥ,* m. f. n. half-done, from *sámi,* half, and *krita,* done.

§ 518. In some appositional compounds, the qualifying word is placed last. विप्रगौरः *vipragauraḥ,* a white Bráhman; राजाधमः *rájádhamaḥ,* the lowest king; भरतश्रेष्ठः *bharata-śreshṭhaḥ,* the best Bharata; पुरुषव्याघ्रः *purusha-vyághraḥ,* a tiger-like man, a great man; गोवृंदारकः *govrindárakaḥ,* a prime cow.

I c. *Numeral Determinative Compounds.*

§ 519. Determinative compounds, the first portion of which is a numeral, are called *Dvigu.* The numeral is always the predicate of the noun which follows. They are generally neuters, or feminines, and are meant to express aggregates, but they may also form adjectives, thus becoming possessive compounds, with or without secondary suffixes.

If an aggregate compound is formed, final अ *a* is changed to ई *í,* fem., or in some cases to अं *am,* neut. Final अन् *an* and आ *á* are changed to ई *í* or अं *am.*

पंचगवं *pancha-gavam,* neut. an aggregate of five cows, from *panchan,* five, and *go,* cow. गो *go* (in an aggregate compound) is changed to गव *gava* (Pâṇ. II. 1, 23), and नौ *nau* to नाव *náva.* पंचगुः *pancha-guḥ,* as an adjective, worth five cows (Pâṇ. v. 4, 92). द्विनौः *dvinauḥ,* bought for two ships. द्व्यंगुलं *dvy-aṅgulam,* neut. what has the measure of two fingers, from *dvi,* two, and *aṅguliḥ,* finger; final *i* being changed to *a.* द्व्यहः *dvy-ahaḥ,* masc. a space of two days; *ahan* changed to *ahaḥ* (Pâṇ. II. 1, 23). पंचकपालः *pancha-kapálaḥ,* m. f. n. an offering (*purodáśaḥ*) made in a dish with five compartments, from *panchan,* five, and *kapálam,* neut. (Pâṇ. II. 1, 51, 52; IV. 1, 88). त्रिलोकी *tri-lokí,* fem. the three worlds : here the Dvigu compound takes the fem. termination to express an aggregate (Pâṇ. IV. 1, 21). त्रिभुवनं *tri-bhuvanam,* neut. the three worlds : here the Dvigu compound takes the neuter termination. दशकुमारी *daśa-kumárí,* fem. an assemblage of ten youths. चतुर्युगं *chatur-yugam,* neut. the four ages.

§ 520. The following rules apply to the changes of the final syllables in determinative compounds. Very few of them are general as requiring a change without any regard to the preceding words in the compound. The general rules are given first, afterwards the more special, while rules for the formation of one single compound are left out, such compounds being within the sphere of a dictionary rather than of a grammar.

1. ऋच् *rich*, verse, पुर् *pur*, town, अप् *ap*, water, धुर् *dhur*, charge, पथिन् *pathin*, path, add final अ *a* (Pân. v. 4, 74); अर्धर्चः *ardharchaḥ*, a half-verse. This is optional with पथिन् *pathin* after the negative अ *a ;* अपथं *apatham* or अपंथाः *apanthâḥ*.

2. राजन् *râjan*, king, अहन् *ahan*, day, सखि *sakhi*, friend, become राज *râja*, अह *aha*, सख *sakha ;* महाराजः *mahârâjaḥ*. (Pân. v. 4, 91.)

3. उरस् *uras*, if it means chief, becomes उरस *urasa ;* अश्वोरसं *aśvorasam*, an excellent horse (Pân. v. 4, 93). Likewise after प्रति *prati*, if the locative is expressed ; प्रत्युरसं *pratyurasam*, on the chest (Pân. v. 4, 82).

4. अक्षि *akshi*, eye, becomes अक्ष *aksha*, if it ceases to mean eye. गवाक्षः *gavâkshaḥ*, a window ; but ब्राह्मणाक्षि *brâhmaṇâkshi*, the eye of a Brâhman. (Pân. v. 4, 76.)

5. अनस् *anas*, cart, अश्मन् *aśman*, stone, अयस् *ayas*, iron, सरस् *saras*, lake, take final अ *a* if the compound expresses a kind or forms a name. कालायसं *kâlâyasam*, black-iron ; but सदयः *sadayaḥ*, a piece of good iron. (Pân. v. 4, 94.)

6. ब्रह्मन् *brahman* becomes ब्रह्म *brahma*, if preceded by the name of a country ; सुराष्ट्रब्रह्मः *surâshṭrabrahmaḥ*, a Brâhman of Surâshṭra (Pân. v. 4, 104). After कु *ku* and महा *mahâ* that substitution is optional (Pân. v. 4, 105).

7. तक्षन् *takshan* takes final अ *a* after ग्राम *grâma* and कौट *kauṭa ;* ग्रामतक्षः *grâmatakshaḥ*, village carpenter. (Pân. v. 4, 95.)

8. श्वन् *śvan*, dog, takes final अ *a* after अति *ati*, and after certain words, not the names of animals, with which it is compared ; आकर्षश्वः *âkarshaśvaḥ*, a dog of a die, a bad throw (?). (Pân. v. 4, 97.)

9. अध्वन् *adhvan* becomes अध्व *adhva* after prepositions ; प्राध्वः *prâdhvaḥ*. (Pân. v. 4, 85.)

10. सामन् *sâman*, hymn, and लोमन् *loman*, hair, become साम *sâma* and लोम *loma* after प्रति *prati*, अनु *anu*, and अप *ava ;* अनुलोमः *anulomaḥ*, regular ; अनुलोमं *anulomam*, adv. with the hair or grain, i. e. regularly. (Pân. v. 4, 75.)

11. तमस् *tamas* becomes तमस *tamasa* after अव *ava*, सं *sam*, and अंध *andha ;* अंधतमसं *andhatamasam*, blind darkness. (Pân. v. 4, 79.)

12. रहस् *rahas* becomes रहस *rahasa* after अनु *anu*, अप *ava*, and तप्त *tapta ;* अनुरहसः *anurahasaḥ*, solitary. (Pân. v. 4, 81.)

13. वर्चस् *varchas* becomes वर्चस *varchasa* after ब्रह्म *brahma* and हस्ति *hasti ;* ब्रह्मवर्चसं *brahmavarchasam*, the power of a Brâhman. (Pân. v. 4, 78.)

14. गो *go* becomes गव *gava*, except at the end of an adjectival Dvigu. पंचगवं *pañchagavam*, five cows ; but पंचगुः *pañchaguḥ*, bought for five cows. (Pân. v. 4, 92.)

15. नौ *nau*, ship, becomes नाव *nâva*, if it forms a numerical aggregate ; पंचनावं *pañchanâvam*, five ships : not when it forms a numerical adjective ; पंचनौः *pañchanauḥ*, worth five ships. (Pân. v. 4, 99.)

16. नौ *nau*, ship, after अर्ध *ardha*, becomes नाव *nâva ;* अर्धनावं *ardhanâvam*, half a ship. (Pân. v. 4, 100.)

17. खारी *khârî*, a measure of grain, becomes खार *khâra* as an aggregate ; द्विखारं *dvikhâram :* also after अर्ध *ardha ;* अर्धखारं *ardhakhâram*. (Pân. v. 4, 101.)

18. अंजलि *añjali*, a handful, after द्वि *dvi* or त्रि *tri*, may, as an aggregate, take final अ *a ;* द्व्यंजलं *dvyañjalam* or द्व्यंजलि *dvyañjali*, two handfuls. (Pân. v. 4, 102.)

19. अंगुलि *anguli*, finger, after numerals and indeclinables, becomes अंगुल *angula;* ड्यंगुलं *dvyangulam*, a length of two fingers. (Pân. v. 4, 86.)

20. सक्थि *sakthi*, thigh, becomes सक्थ *saktha* after उत्तर *uttara*, मृग *mriga*, and पूर्व *pûrva;* पूर्वसक्थं *pûrvasaktham*. (Pân. v. 4, 98.)

21. रात्रि *râtri*, night, after सर्व *sarva*, after partitive words, after संख्यात *sankhyâta*, पुण्य *punya*, likewise after numerals and indeclinables, becomes रात्र *râtra;* सर्वरात्रः *sarva-râtrah*, the whole night; पूर्वरात्रः *pûrvarâtrah*, the fore-night; द्विरात्रं *dvirâtram*, two nights. (Pân. v. 4, 87.)

22. अहन् *ahan*, day, under the same circumstances, becomes अह्न *ahna;* सर्वाह्णः *sarvâhnah*, the whole day : but not after a numeral when it expresses an aggregate ; द्यहः *dvyahah*, two days. Except also पुण्याहं *punyâham*, a good day, and एकाहं *ekâham*, n. and m. a single day. (Pân. v. 4, 88–90.)

II. *Collective Compounds.*

§ 521. Collective compounds (Dvandva) are divided into two classes. The first class (called इतरेतर *itaretara*) comprises compounds in which two or more words, that would naturally be connected by *and*, are united, the last taking the terminations either of the dual or the plural, according to the number of words forming the compound. The second class (called समाहार *samâhâra*) comprises the same kind of compounds but formed into neuter nouns in the singular. हस्त्यश्वौ *hasty-aśvau*, an elephant and a horse, is an instance of the former, हस्त्यश्वं *hastyaśvam*, the elephants and horses (in an army), an instance of the latter class. Likewise शुक्लकृष्णौ *śukla-krishnau*, white and black ; गवाश्वं *gavâśvam*, a cow and a horse.

If instead of a horse and an elephant, हस्त्यश्वौ *hastyaśvau*, the intention is to express horses and elephants, the compound takes the terminations of the plural, हस्त्यश्वाः *hastyaśvâh*.

§ 522. Some rules are given as to which words should stand first in a Dvandva compound. Words with fewer syllables should stand first : शिवकेशवौ *śiva-keśavau*, Śiva and Keśava; not केशवशिवौ *keśavaśivau*. Words beginning with a vowel and ending in अ *a* should stand first : ईशकृष्णौ *îśa-krishnau*, Îśa and Krishna. Words ending in इ *i* (gen. एः *eh*) and उ *u* (gen. ओः *oh*) should stand first : हरिहरौ *hari-harau*, Hari and Hara ; also भोक्तृभोग्यौ *bhoktri-bhogyau*, the enjoyer and the enjoyed. Lastly, words of greater importance should have precedence : देवदैत्यौ *deva-daityau*, the god and the demon ; ब्राह्मणक्षत्रियौ *brâhmaṇa-kshatriyau*, a Brâhman and a Kshatriya ; मातापितरौ *mâtâ-pitarau*, mother and father, but in earlier Sanskrit पितरामातरा *pitarâ-mâtarâ*, father and mother. (Pân. vi. 3, 33.)

§ 523. Words ending in ऋ *ri*, expressive of relationship, or sacred titles, forming the first member of a compound, and being followed by another word ending in ऋ *ri*, or by पुत्र *putra*, son, change their ऋ *ri* into आ *â* (Pân. vi. 3, 25). मातृ *mâtri* + पितृ *pitri* form मातापितरौ *mâtâpitarau*, father and mother ; पितृ *pitri* + पुत्र *putra* form पितापुत्रौ *pitâputrau;* होतृ *hotri* + पोतृ *potri* form होतापोतारौ *hotâpotârau*, the Hotri and Potri priests.

§ 524. When the names of certain deities are compounded, the first sometimes lengthens its final vowel (Pân. vi. 3, 26). Thus मित्रावरुणौ *mitrâvaruṇau*, Mitra and Varuṇa; अग्नीषोमौ *agnîshomau*, Agni and Soma. Similar irregularities appear in words like

द्यावापृथिव्यौ *dyâvâ-prithivyau*, heaven and earth; उषासानक्तं *ushâsâ-naktam*, dawn and night (Pân. VI. 3, 29–31).

§ 525. If the compound takes the termination of the singular, then final च् *ch*, छ् *chh*, ज् *j*, झ् *jh*, ड् *d*, ष् *sh*, and ह *h* take an additional अ *a*. वाच् *vâch* + त्वच् *tvach* form वाक्त्वचं *vâktvacham*, speech and skin (Pân. v. 4, 106). अहन् *ahan*, day (see § 90, 196), and रात्रि *râtri*, night, form the compound अहोरात्र: *ahorâtrah*, a day and night, a νυχθήμερον (Pân. v. 4, 87).

§ 526. भ्रातरौ *bhrâtarau* may be used in the sense of brother and sister; पुत्रौ *putrau* in the sense of son and daughter; पितरौ *pitarau* in the sense of father and mother; श्वशुरौ *śvaśurau* in the sense of father and mother-in-law. Man and wife may be expressed by जायापती *jâyâ-patî*, जंपती *jampatî*, or दंपती *dampatî*.

III. *Possessive Compounds.*

§ 527. Possessive compounds (Bahuvrîhi) are always predicates referring to some subject or other. A determinative may be used as a possessive compound by a mere change of termination or accent. Thus नीलोत्पलं *nîla-utpalam*, a blue lotus, is a determinative compound (Tatpurusha, subdivision Karmadhâraya); but in नीलोत्पलं सर: *nîlotpalam sarah*, a blue lotus lake, *nîlotpalam* is an adjective and as such a predicative or possessive compound; (see Pân. II. 2, 24, com.) In the same manner अनश्व: *anaśvah*, not-a-horse, is a determinative, अनश्वो रथ: *anaśvo rathah*, a cart without a horse, a horseless cart, a possessive compound.

Examples: प्राप्तोदको ग्राम: *prâpta-udako grâmah*, a water-reached village, a village reached by water. ऊढरथोऽनड्वान् *ûḍha-ratho 'naḍvân*, a bull by whom a cart (*rathah*) is drawn (*ûḍha*). उपहृतपशू रुद्र: *upahṛita-paśû rudrah*, Rudra to whom cattle (*paśuh*) is offered (*upahṛita*). पीतांबरो हरि: *pîta-ambaro harih*, Hari possessing yellow garments. प्रपर्ण: *pra-parṇah*, leafless, i. e. a tree from which the leaves are fallen off. अपुत्र: *a-putrah*, sonless. चित्रगु: *chitra-guh*, possessed of a brindled cow. रूपवद्भार्य: *rûpavad-bhâryah*, possessed of a beautiful wife. द्विमूर्ध: *dvi-mûrdhah*, two-headed: here *mûrdha* stands for *mûrdhan*. द्विपाद् *dvi-pâd*, two-legged: here *pâd* stands for *pâda*. सुहृद् *su-hṛid*, having a good heart, a friend. भक्षितभिक्ष: *bhakshita-bhikshah*, one who has eaten his alms. नीलोज्ज्वलवपु: *nîla-ujjvala-vapuh*, having a blue resplendent body.

§ 528. Bahuvrîhi compounds frequently take suffixes. The following rules apply to the changes of the final syllables in possessive compounds :

1. सक्थि *sakthi*, thigh, and अक्षि *akshi*, eye, if they mean really thigh and eye, take final अ *a*; कमलाक्ष: *kamalâkshah*, lotus-eyed. (Pân. v. 4, 113.)

2. अंगुलि *aṅguli*, finger, substitutes final अ *a* if it refers to wood; द्व्यंगुलं दारु *dvyaṅgulam dâru*, a piece of wood with two prongs*. (Pân. v. 4, 114.)

---

* अंगुलिसदृशावयवं धान्यादिविक्षेपणकाष्ठं, Prakriyâ-Kaumudî.

3. मूर्धन् *múrdhan*, head, substitutes final अ *a* after द्वि *dvi* and त्रि *tri;* द्विमूर्धः *dvimúrdhaḥ*, having two heads. (Pâṇ. v. 4, 115.)

4. लोमन् *loman*, hair, substitutes final अ *a* after अन्तर् *antar* and वहिः *vahiḥ;* अन्तर्लोमः *antar-lomaḥ*, having the hairy part inside. (Pâṇ. v. 4, 117.)

5. नासिका *násiká*, nose, becomes नस *nasa*, if it stands at the end of a name; गोनसः *gonasaḥ*, cow-nosed, i. e. a snake; but not after स्थूल *sthúla;* स्थूलनासिकः *sthúla-násikaḥ*, large-nosed, i. e. a hog. The same change takes place after prepositions; उन्नसः *unnasaḥ*, with a prominent nose. (Pâṇ. v. 4, 118, 119.)

6. After अ *a*, दु: *duḥ*, or सु *su*, हलि *hali*, furrow, and सक्थि *sakthi*, thigh, may substitute final अ *a;* अहलः *ahalaḥ* or अहलिः *ahaliḥ*. (Pâṇ. v. 4, 121.)

7. After the same particles, प्रजा *prajá*, progeny, and मेधा *medhá*, mind, are treated like nouns ending in अस् *as;* दुर्मेधाः *durmedháḥ*. (Pâṇ. v. 4, 122.)

8. धर्म *dharma*, law, preceded by one word, is treated like a noun ending in अन् *an;* कल्याणधर्मा *kalyáṇadharmá*. (Pâṇ. v. 4, 124.)

9. जंभा *jambhá*, jaw, after certain words, becomes जंभन् *jambhan;* सुजंभा *sujambhá*.

10. जानु *jánu*, knee, after प्र *pra* and सं *sam*, becomes जु *jñu;* प्रज्ञुः *prajñuḥ* (Pâṇ. v. 4, 129). This is optional after ऊर्ध्व *úrdhva* (Pâṇ. v. 4, 130).

11. अधस् *údhas*, udder, becomes अधन् *údhan;* कुंडोधनी *kuṇḍodhní*. (Pâṇ. v. 4, 131.)

12. धनुस् *dhanús*, bow, becomes धन्वन् *dhanvan;* पुष्पधन्वा *pushpadhanvá*, having a bow of flowers (Pâṇ. v. 4, 132). In names this is optional.

13. जाया *jáyá*, wife, becomes जानि *jáni;* शुभजानिः *śubhajániḥ*. (Pâṇ. v. 4, 134.)

14. गंध *gandha*, smell, substitutes गंधि *gandhi* after certain words; सुगंधिः *sugandhiḥ*. (Pâṇ. v. 4, 135–137.)

15. पाद *páda*, foot, becomes पाद् *pád* after certain words; व्याघ्रपाद् *vyághrapád*. (Pâṇ. v. 4, 138–140.)

16. दंत *danta*, tooth, becomes दत् *dat* after many words; द्विदन् *dvidan*, having two teeth, (sign of a certain age); fem. द्विदती *dvidatí*. (Pâṇ. v. 4, 141–145.)

17. ककुद *kakuda*, hump, becomes ककुद् *kakud* after certain words and in certain senses; अजातककुद् *ajátakakud*, a young bull before his humps have grown. (Pâṇ. v. 4, 146–148.)

18. उरस् *uras* and other words belonging to the same class add final क *ka;* व्यूढोरस्कः *vyúḍhoraskaḥ*, broad-chested. (Pâṇ. v. 4, 151.)

19. Words in इन् *in* add final क *ka* in the feminine; बहुस्वामिका *bahusvámiká*, having many masters, from स्वामिन् *svámin*, master. (Pâṇ. v. 4, 152.)

20. Feminine words in ई *í*, like नदी *nadí*, and words in ऋ *ṛi*, add final क *ka;* बहुकुमारीक *bahukumáríkaḥ*, having many maidens; बहुभर्तृक *bahubhartṛikaḥ*, having many husbands. (Pâṇ. v. 4, 153.)

21. Most other words may or may not add final क *ka;* बहुमालकः *bahumálakaḥ* or बहुमालाक *bahumálákaḥ* or बहुमालः *bahumálaḥ*. (Pâṇ. v. 4, 154.)

IV. *Adverbial Compounds.*

§ 529. Adverbial or indeclinable compounds (Avyayîbhâva) are formed by joining an indeclinable particle with another word. The resulting compounds, in which the indeclinable particle forms always the first element, are again indeclinable, and generally end, like adverbs, in the ordinary terminations of the nom. or acc. neut.

Examples : अधिहरि *adhi-hari*, upon Hari, instead of अधि हरौ *adhi harau*, loc. sing. अनुविष्णु *anu-vishnu*, after Vishṇu, instead of अनु विष्णुं *anu vishṇum*, acc. sing. उपकृष्णं *upa-krishṇam*, near to Krishṇa. निर्मक्षिकं *nir-makshikam*, free from flies, flylessly. अतिहिमं *ati-himam*, past the winter, after the winter, instead of अति हिमं *ati himam*, acc. sing. प्रदक्षिणं *pradakshiṇam*, to the right. अनुरूपं *anu-rûpam*, after the form, i. e. accordingly, instead of अनु रूपं *anu rûpam*, acc. sing. यथाशक्ति *yathâ-śakti*, according to one's ability, instead of शक्तिर्यथा *śaktir yathâ*. सतृणं *sa-triṇam* with the grass; सतृणमत्ति *satriṇam atti*, he eats (everything) even the grass, instead of तृणेन सह *triṇena saha*, with the grass. यावच्छ्लोकं *yâvach-chhlokam*, at every verse. आमुक्ति *âmukti*, until final delivery. अनुगंगं *anu-gangam*, near the Gangâ. उपशरदं *upa-śaradam*, near the autumn; from शरद् *śarad*, autumn (Pâṇ. v. 4, 107). उपजरसं *upa-jarasam*, at the approach of old age; from जरस् *jaras*, old age (§ 167). उपसमित् *upa-samit* or उपसमिधं *upa-samidham*, near the fire-wood; from समिध् *samidh*, fire-wood. उपराजं *upa-râjam*, near the king; from राजन् *râjan*, king.

§ 530. There are some Avyayîbhâvas the first element of which is not an indeclinable particle. Ex. तिष्ठद्गु *tishṭhad-gu*, at the time when the cows stand to be milked; पंचगंगं *pañcha-gangam*, at the place where the five Gangâs meet, (near the Mâdhav-râo ghât at Benares); प्रत्यग्ग्रामं *pratyag-grâmam*, west of the village.

§ 531. The following rules apply to the changes of the final syllables in adverbial compounds :

1. Words ending in mutes (*k, kh, g, gh, ch, chh, j, jh, ṭ, ṭh, ḍ, ḍh, t, th, d, dh, p, ph, b, bh*) may or may not take final अ *a :* उपसमिधं *upasamidham* or उपसमित् *upasamit*, near the fire-wood. (Pâṇ. v. 4, 111.)

2. Words ending in अन् *an* substitute final अ *a :* अध्यात्मं *adhyâtmam*, with regard to one-self. (Pâṇ. v. 4, 108.)

3. But neuters in अन् *an* may or may not; उपचर्मं *upacharmam* or उपचर्म *upacharma*, near the skin. (Pâṇ. v. 4, 109.)

4. नदी *nadî*, पौर्णमासी *paurṇamâsî*, आग्रहायणी *âgrahâyaṇî*, and गिरि *giri* may or may not take final अ *a :* उपनदि *upanadi* or उपनदं *upanadam*, near the river. (Pâṇ. v. 4, 110, and 112.)

5. Words belonging to the class beginning with शरद् *śarad* take final अ *a :* उपशरदं *upaśaradam*, about autumn. (Pâṇ. v. 4, 107.)

APPENDIX I.

DHÂTUPÂTHA OR LIST OF VERBS.

Explanation of some of the Verbal Anubandhas or Indicatory Letters.

ब *a* is put at the end of roots ending in a consonant in order to facilitate their pronunciation.

Accent.—The last letter of a root is accented with the acute, the grave, or circumflex accent, in order to show that the verb follows the Parasmaipada, the Âtmanepada, or both forms.

The roots themselves are divided into *udátta*, acutely accented, and *anudátta*, gravely accented, the former admitting, the latter rejecting the intermediate इ *i*.

आ *á* prohibits the use of the intermediate इ *i* in the formation of the Nishṭhâs (§ 333, D. 2), Pân. VII. 2, 16. Ex. फुल्ल: *phullaḥ* from निफला *ñiphalá*.

इ *i* requires the insertion of a nasal after the last radical vowel, which nasal is not to be omitted where a nasal that is actually written would be omitted (§ 345,[10]), Pân. VII. 1, 58; VI. 4, 24. Ex. नंदति *nandati* from नदि *nadi*, Pass. नंद्यते *nandyate*; but from मंथ् or मन्थ् *manth*, Pres. मंथति *manthati*, Pass. मथ्यते *mathyate*.

इर् *ir* shows that a verb may take the first or second aorist in the Parasmaipada (§ 367), Pân. III. 1, 57. Ex. अच्युतत् *achyutat* or अच्योतीत् *achyotít* from च्युतिर् *chyutir*.

ई *í* prohibits the use of the intermediate इ *i* in the formation of the Nishṭhâs (§ 333, D. 2), Pân. VII. 2, 14. Ex. उन्न: *unnaḥ* from उंदी *undí*.

उ *u* renders the admission of the intermediate इ *i* optional before the gerundial त्वा *tvá* (§ 337, II. 5), Pân. VII. 2, 56; and therefore inadmissible in the past participle (Pân. VII. 2, 15). Ex. शमित्वा *śamitvá* or शान्त्वा *śántvá* from शमु *śamu*; but शांत: *śántaḥ*.

ऊ *ú* renders the admission of the intermediate इ *i* optional in the general tenses before all consonants but य *y* (§ 337, I. 2), Pân. VII. 2, 44; and therefore inadmissible in the past participle (Pân. VII. 2, 15). Ex. सेद्धा *seddhá* or सेधिता *sedhitá* from सिधू *sidhú*; but सिद्ध: *siddhaḥ*.

ऋ *ṛi* prevents the substitution of the short for the long vowel in the reduplicated aorist of causals (§ 372*), Pân. VII. 4, 2. Ex. अलुलोकत् *alulokat* from लोकृ *lokṛi*.

ऋ *ḷi* shows that the verb takes the second aorist in the Parasmaipada (§ 367), Pân. III. 1, 55. Ex. अगमत् *agamat* from गम् *gamḷi*.

इ *e* forbids Vṛiddhi in the first aorist (§ 348*), Pân. VII. 2, 5. Ex. अमथीत् *ama-thít* from मथे *mathe*.

ओ *o* indicates that the participle is formed in न *na* instead of त *ta* (§ 442, 5), Pân. VIII. 2, 45. Ex. पीन: *pínaḥ* from ओप्यायी *opyáyí*.

ङ *n̄* shows that the verb follows the Âtmanepada (Pân. I. 3, 12).

ञ *ñ* shows that the verb follows both the Âtmanepada and Parasmaipada, the former if the act reverts to the subject (Pân. I. 3, 72).

फि *ñi* shows that the past participle has the power of the present (Pân. III. 2, 187). Ex. फुल्ल: *phullaḥ*, blown, from फिफुल्ला *ñiphalá*.

म् *m* shows that the vowel is not lengthened in the causative (§ 462, note), Pân. VI. 4, 92; and that the vowel is optionally lengthened in the aorist of the passive (Pân. VI. 4, 93).

Bhû Class (Bhvâdi, I Class).
I. Parasmaipada Verbs.

1. भू *bhú*, to be.

Parasmaipada : P. 1. भवामि *bhávámi*, 2. भवसि *bhávasi*, 3. भवति *bhávati*, 4. भवाव: *bhávávaḥ*, 5. भवथ: *bhávathaḥ*, 6. भवत: *bhávataḥ*, 7. भवाम: *bhávámaḥ*, 8. भवथ *bhávatha*, 9. भवंति *bhávanti*, I. 1. अभवं *ábhavam*, 2. अभव: *ábhavaḥ*, 3. अभवत् *ábhavat*, 4. अभवाव *ábhaváva*, 5. अभवतं *ábhavatam*, 6. अभवतां *ábhavatám*, 7. अभवाम *ábhaváma*, 8. अभवत *ábhavata*, 9. अभवन् *ábhavan*, O. 1. भवेयं *bháveyam*, 2. भवे: *bháveḥ*, 3. भवेत् *bhávet*, 4. भवेव *bháveva*, 5. भवेतं *bhávetam*, 6. भवेतां *bhávetám*, 7. भवेम *bhávema*, 8. भवेत *bháveta*, 9. भवेयु: *bháveyuḥ*, I. 1. भवानि *bhávání*, 2. भव *bháva*, 3. भवतु *bhávatu*, 4. भवाव *bháváva*, 5. भवतं *bhávatam*, 6. भवतां *bhávatám*, 7. भवाम *bháváma*, 8. भवत *bhávata*, 9. भवंतु *bhávantu* ‖ Pf. 1. बभूव *babhúva*† (see p. 175), 2. बभूविथ *babhúvitha*, 3. बभूव *babhúva*, 4. बभूविव *babhúvivá*, 5. बभूवथु: *babhúváthuḥ*, 6. बभूवतु: *babhúvátuḥ*, 7. बभूविम *babhúvimá*, 8. बभूव *babhúvá*, 9. बभूवु: *babhúvúḥ*, II A. 1. अभूवं *ábhúvam* (see p. 188), 2. अभू: *ábhúḥ*, 3. अभूत् *ábhút*, 4. अभूव *ábhúva*, 5. अभूतं *ábhútam*, 6. अभूतां *ábhútám*, 7. अभूम *ábhúma*, 8. अभूत *ábhúta*, 9. अभूवन् *ábhúvan*, F. 1. भविष्यामि *bhavishyámi*, 2. भविष्यसि *bhavishyási*, 3. भविष्यति *bhavishyáti*, 4. भविष्याव: *bhavishyávaḥ*, 5. भविष्यथ: *bhavishyáthaḥ*, 6. भविष्यत: *bhavishyátaḥ*, 7. भविष्याम: *bhavishyámaḥ*, 8. भविष्यथ *bhavishyátha*, 9. भविष्यंति *bhavishyánti*, C. 1. अभविष्यं *ábhavishyam*, 2. अभविष्य: *ábhavishyaḥ*, 3. अभविष्यत् *ábhavishyat*, 4. अभविष्याव *ábhavishyáva*, 5. अभविष्यतं *ábhavishyatam*, 6. अभविष्यतां *ábhavishyatám*, 7. अभविष्याम *ábhavishyáma*, 8. अभविष्यत *ábhavishyata*, 9. अभविष्यन् *ábhavishyan*,

---

† The reduplicative syllable ब *ba* is irregular, instead of बु *bu*. The base, too, is irregular (Pân. I. 2, 6); the regular form would have been बुभाव *bubháva*.

P. F. 1. अवितास्मि *bhavitásmi*, 2. अवितासि *bhavitási*, 3. अविता *bhavitá*, 4. अवितास्वः *bhavitásvah*, 5. अवितास्थः *bhavitásthah*, 6. अवितारौ *bhavitárau*, 7. अवितास्म: *bhavitásmah*, 8. अवितास्थ *bhavitástha*, 9. अवितार: *bhavitárah*, B. 1. भूयासं *bhúyásam*, 2. भूया: *bhúyáh*, 3. भूयात् *bhúyát*, 4. भूयास्व *bhúyásva*, 5. भूयास्तं *bhúyástam*, 6. भूयास्तां *bhúyástám*, 7. भूयास्म *bhúyásma*, 8. भूयास्त *bhúyásta*, 9. भूयासु: *bhúyásuh* ॥ Part. Pres. भवन् *bhávan*, Perf. बभूवान् *babhúván*, Fut. भविष्यन् *bhavishyán*, Ger. भूत्वा *bhútvá* or °भूय -*bhúya*, Adj. अवितव्य: *bhavitávyah*, अवनीय: *bhavaníyah*, अव्य: *bhávyah* (§ 456).

Âtmanepada*: P. 1. भवे *bháve*, 2. भवसे *bhávase*, 3. भवते *bhávate*, 4. भवावहे *bhávávahe*, 5. भवेथे *bhávethe*, 6. भवेते *bhávete*, 7. भवामहे *bhávámahe*, 8. भवध्वे *bhávadhve*, 9. भवन्ते *bhávante*, I. 1. अभवे *ábhave*, 2. अभवथा: *ábhavatháh*, 3. अभवत *ábhavata*, 4. अभवावहि *ábhavávahi*, 5. अभवेथां *ábhavethám*, 6. अभवेतां *ábhavetám*, 7. अभवामहि *ábhavámahi*, 8. अभवध्वं *ábhavadhvam*, 9. अभवन्त *ábhavanta*, O. 1. भवेय *bháveya*, 2. भवेथा: *bhávetháh*, 3. भवेत *bháveta*, 4. भवेवहि *bhávevahi*, 5. भवेयां *bháveyáthám*, 6. भवेयातां *bháveyátám*, 7. भवेमहि *bhávemahi*, 8. भवेध्वं *bhávedhvam*, 9. भवेरन् *bháveran*, I. 1. भवै *bhávai*, 2. भवस्व *bhávasva*, 3. भवतां *bhávatám*, 4. भवावहै *bhávávahai*, 5. भवेथां *bhávethám*, 6. भवेतां *bhávetám*, 7. भवामहै *bhávámahai*, 8. भवध्वं *bhávadhvam*, 9. भवन्तां *bhávantám* ॥ Pf. 1. बभूवे *babhúvé* (see note †, page 245), 2. बभूविषे *babhúvishé*, 3. बभूवे *babhúvé*, 4. बभूविवहे *babhúviváhe*, 5. बभूवाथे *babhúváthe*, 6. बभूवाते *babhúváte*, 7. बभूविमहे *babhúvimáhe*, 8. बभूविध्वे or °ढ्वे *babhúvidhvé* or -*dhvé* (see § 105), 9. बभूविरे *babhúviré*, I A. 1. अभविषि *ábhavishi*, 2. अभविष्ठा: *ábhavishtháh*, 3. अभविष्ट *ábhavishta*, 4. अभविष्वहि *ábhavishvahi*, 5. अभविषाथां *ábhavisháthám*, 6. अभविषातां *ábhavishátám*, 7. अभविष्महि *ábhavishmahi*, 8. अभविध्वं or °ढ्वं *ábhavidhvam* or -*dhvam*, 9. अभविषत *ábhavishata*, F. भविष्ये *bhavishyé* &c., C. अभविष्ये *ábhavishye* &c., P. F. 1. भविताहे *bhavitáhe*, 2. भवितासे *bhavitáse*, 3. भविता *bhavitá*, 4. भवितास्वहे *bhavitásvahe*, 5. भवितासाथे *bhavitásáthe*, 6. भवितारौ *bhavitárau*, 7. भवितास्महे *bhavitásmahe*, 8. भविताध्वे *bhavitádhve*, 9. भवितार: *bhavitárah*, B. 1. भविषीय *bhavishíyá*, 2. भविषीष्ठा: *bhavishíshtháh*, 3. भविषीष्ट *bhavishíshtá*, 4. भविषीवहि *bhavishíváhi*, 5. भविषीयास्थां *bhavishíyásthám*, 6. भविषीयातां *bhavishíyátám*, 7. भविषीमहि *bhavishímáhi*, 8. भविषीध्वं or °ढ्वं *bhavishídhvám* or -*dhvám*, 9. भविषीरन् *bhavishírán* ॥ Part. Pres. भवमान: *bhávamánah*, Perf. बभूवान: *babhúvánáh*, Fut. भविष्यमाण: *bhavishyámánah*.

Passive: P. 1. भूये *bhúyé*‡, 2. भूयसे *bhúyáse*, 3. भूयते *bhúyáte*, 4. भूयावहे *bhúyávahe*, 5. भूयेथे *bhúyéthe*, 6. भूयेते *bhúyéte*, 7. भूयामहे *bhúyámahe*, 8. भूयध्वे *bhúyádhve*, 9. भूयन्ते *bhúyánte*, I. अभूये *ábhúye* &c., O. भूयेय *bhúyéya* &c., I. भूयै *bhúyai* &c. ॥

---

* भू *bhú* may be used in the Âtmanepada after certain prepositions. Even by itself it is used in the sense of obtaining : स श्रियं भवते *sa śriyam bhavate*, he obtains happiness. (Sâr. p. 4, l. 3.)

‡ भू *bhú* with अनु *anu* means to perceive, and may yield a passive.

Pf. बभूवे *babhúvé* &c., like Âtmanepada, I A. 1. अभविषि or अभाविषि *ábhávishi*,
2. अभविष्ठा: or अभाविष्ठा: *ábhávishthâḥ*, 3. अभावि *ábhávi*, 4. अभविष्वहि *ábhávishvahi*
&c., like Âtmanepada, F. भविष्ये or भाविष्ये *bhávishyé* &c., C. अभविष्ये or अभाविष्ये
ábhávishye &c., P. F. भवितार्हे or भावितार्हे *bhávitdhe* &c., B. भविषीय or भाविषीय
bhávishíyá &c. ॥ Part. Pres. भूयमान: *bhúyámánaḥ*, Fut. भविष्यमाण: *bhávishyá-*
mánaḥ, Past भूत: *bhútáḥ*.

Causative, Parasmaipada : P. भावयामि *bhâváyámi*, I. अभावयं *ábhávayam*,
O. भावयेयं *bhâváyeyam*, I. भावयानि *bhâváyáni* ॥ Pf. भावयांचकार *bhávaydñchakára*,
II A. अबीभवं *ábíbhavam*, F. भावयिष्यामि *bhâvayishyámi*, C. अभावयिष्यं *ábhávayi-*
shyam, P. F. भावयितास्मि *bhávayitásmi*, B. भाव्यासं *bhávyásam*.

Causative, Âtmanepada : P. भावये *bhâváye*, I. अभावये *ábhávaye*, O. भावयेय
bhâváyeya, I. भावयै *bhâváyai* ॥ Pf. भावयांचक्रे *bhávaydñchakre*, II A. अबीभवे
ábíbhave, F. भावयिष्ये *bhâvayishyé*, C. अभावयिष्ये *ábhávayishye*, P. F. भावयितार्हे
bhávayitádhe, B. भावयिषीय *bhávayishíyá*.

Causative, Passive : P. भाव्ये *bhávyé*, I. अभाव्ये *ábhávye*, O. भाव्येय *bhávyéya*,
I. भाव्यै *bhávyai* ॥ Pf. भावयांचक्रे, ॰बभूवे, ॰आसे, *bhávaydñchakre, -babhúve, -áse*,
I A. अभावयिषि *ábhávayishi* or अभाविषि *ábhávishi*, F. भावयिष्ये *bhávayishyé* or
भाविष्ये *bhávishyé*, C. अभावयिष्ये *ábhávayishye* or अभाविष्ये *ábhávishye*, P. F.
भावयितार्हे *bhávayitádhe* or भावितार्हे *bhávitádhe*, B. भावयिषीय *bhávayishíyá* or
भाविषीय *bhávishíyá*.

Desiderative, Parasmaipada : P. बुभूषामि *búbhúshámi*, I. अबुभूषं *ábubhú-*
sham, O. बुभूषेयं *búbhúsheyam*, I. बुभूषाणि *búbhúsháni* ॥ Pf. बुभूषांचकार *bubhúshdñ-*
chakára, I A. अबुभूषिषं *ábubhúshisham*, F. बुभूषिष्यामि *bubhúshishyámi*, C. अबुभूषिष्यं
ábubhúshishyam, P. F. बुभूषितास्मि *bubhúshitásmi*, B. बुभूष्यासं *bubhúshyásam*.

Desiderative, Âtmanepada : P. बुभूषे *búbhúshe*, I. अबुभूषे *ábubhúshe*, O. बुभूषेय
búbhúsheya, I. बुभूषै *búbhúshai* ॥ Pf. बुभूषांचक्रे *bubhúshdñchakre*, I A. 1. अबुभूषिषि
ábubhúshishi, 2. अबुभूषिष्ठा: *ábubhúshishthâḥ*, 3. अबुभूषिष्ट *ábubhúshishta*, F. बुभूषिष्ये
bubhúshishyé, C. अबुभूषिष्ये *ábubhúshishye*, P. F. बुभूषितार्हे *bubhúshitdhe*, B.
बुभूषिषीय *bubhúshishíyá*.

Desiderative, Passive : P. बुभूष्ये *bubhúshyé*, I. अबुभूष्ये *ábubhúshye*, O. बुभूषेय
bubhúshyéya, I. बुभूष्यै *bubhúshyai* ॥ Pf. बुभूषांचक्रे *bubhúshdñchakre*, I A. 1. अबुभूषिषि
ábubhúshishi, 2. अबुभूषिष्ठा: *ábubhúshishthâḥ*, 3. अबुभूषि *ábubhúshi* (see § 406),
F. बुभूषिष्ये *bubhúshishyé*, C. अबुभूषिष्ये *ábubhúshishye*, P. F. बुभूषितार्हे *bubhúshitdhe*,
B. बुभूषिषीय *bubhúshishíyá*.

Intensive, Âtmanepada : P. 1. बोभूये *bobhúyé*, 2. बोभूयसे *bobhúyáse*, 3. बोभूयते
bobhúyáte, 4. बोभूयावहे *bobhúydvahe*, 5. बोभूयेथे *bobhúyéthe*, 6. बोभूयेते *bobhúyéte*,
7. बोभूयामहे *bobhúydmahe*, 8. बोभूयध्वे *bobhúyádhve*, 9. बोभूयंते *bobhúyánte*, I. 1. अबोभूये
ábobhúye, 2. अबोभूयथा: *ábobhúyathâḥ*, 3. अबोभूयत *ábobhúyata*, 4. अबोभूयावहि *ábo-*
bhúyávahi, 5. अबोभूयेथां *ábobhúyethám*, 6. अबोभूयेतां *ábobhúyetám*, 7. अबोभूयामहि
ábobhúyámahi, 8. अबोभूयध्वं *ábobhúyadhvam*, 9. अबोभूयंत *ábobhúyanta*, O. बोभूयेय

bobhúyéya &c., I. 1. बोभूये *bobhúyai,* 2. बोभूयस्व *bobhúyásva,* 3. बोभूयतां *bobhúyátám,*
4. बोभूयावहै *bobhúyávahai,* 5. बोभूयेथां *bobhúyéthâm,* 6. बोभूयेतां *bobhúyétâm,*
7. बोभूयामहै *bobhúyámahai,* 8. बोभूयध्वं *bobhúyádhvam,* 9. बोभूयंतां *bobhúyántâm* ।
Pf. बोभूयांचक्रे *bobhúyáṁchakre,* I A. 1. अबोभूयिषि *ábobhúyishi,* 2. अबोभूयिष्ठाः *ábobhú-yishthâh,* 3. अबोभूयिष्ट *ábobhúyishṭa,* 4. अबोभूयिष्वहि *ábobhúyishvahi,* 5. अबोभूयिषाथां *ábobhúyishâthâm,* 6. अबोभूयिषातां *ábobhúyishâtâm,* 7. अबोभूयिष्महि *ábobhúyishmahi,*
8. अबोभूयिध्वं or ॰ध्वं *ábobhúyidhvam* or *-ḍhvam,* 9. अबोभूयिषत *ábobhúyishata,*
F. बोभूयिष्ये *bobhúyishyé,* C. अबोभूयिष्ये *ábobhúyishye,* P. F. बोभूयिताहे *bobhúyitáhe,*
B. बोभूयिषीय *bobhúyishíyá.*

Intensive, Parasmaipada : P. 1. बोभोमि *bóbhomi* or बोभवीमि *bóbhavími,*
2. बोभोषि *bóbhoshi* or बोभवीषि *bóbhavíshi,* 3. बोभोति *bóbhoti* or बोभवीति *bóbhavíti,*
4. बोभूवः *bobhúváḥ,* 5. बोभूथः *bobhúthâḥ,* 6. बोभूतः *bobhútâḥ,* 7. बोभूमः *bobhúmáḥ,*
8. बोभूथ *bobhúthá,* 9. बोभुवति *bóbhuvati,* I. 1. अबोभवं *ábobhavam,* 2. अबोभोः *ábobhoḥ*
or अबोभवीः *ábobhavíḥ,* 3. अबोभोत् *ábobhot* or अबोभवीत् *ábobhavít,* 4. अबोभूव *ábo-bhúva,* 5. अबोभूतं *ábobhútam,* 6. अबोभूतां *ábobhútâm,* 7. अबोभूम *ábobhúma,* 8. अबोभूत *ábobhúta,* 9. अबोभवुः *ábobhavuḥ,* O. बोभूयां *bobhúyám,* I. 1. बोभवानि *bóbhavâni,*
2. बोभूहि *bobhúhí,* 3. बोभोतु *bóbhotu* or बोभवीतु *bóbhavítu,* 4. बोभवाव *bóbhavâva,*
5. बोभूतां *bobhútâm,* 6. बोभूतां *bobhútâm,* 7. बोभवाम *bóbhavâma,* 8. बोभूत *bobhútá,*
9. बोभुवतु *bóbhuvatu* ॥ Pf. 1. बोभवांचकार *bobhavâṁchakâra,* 4. बोभवांचकृव *bobha-vâṁchakriva,* 7. बोभवांचकृम *bobhavâṁchakrima;* also 1. बोभाव *bobhâva* or बोभूव *bobhúva,* 2. बोभूविथ *bobhúvitha,* 3. बोभाव *bobhâva* or बोभूव *bobhúva,* 4. बोभूविव *bobhúvivá**, 5. बोभूवथुः *bobhúváthuḥ,* 6. बोभूवतुः *bobhúvátuḥ,* 7. बोभूविम *bobhúvimá,*
8. बोभूव *bobhúvá,* 9. बोभूवुः *bobhúvúḥ,* II A. 1. अबोभूवं *ábobhúvam,* 2. अबोभूः *ábobhúḥ*
or अबोभूवीः *ábobhúvíḥ,* 3. अबोभूत् *ábobhút* or अबोभूवीत् *ábobhúvít,* 4. अबोभूव *ábo-bhúva,* 5. अबोभूतं *ábobhútam,* 6. अबोभूतां *ábobhútâm,* 7. अबोभूम *ábobhúma,* 8. अबोभूत *ábobhúta,* 9. अबोभूवुः *ábobhúvuḥ* (not अबोभूवन् *ábobhúvan*), I A. 1.† अबोभाविषं *ábobhâvisham,* 4. अबोभाविष्व *ábobhâvishva,* 7. अबोभाविष्म *ábobhâvishma,* F. बोभविष्यामि *bobhavishyámi,* C. अबोभविष्यं *ábobhavishyam,* P. F. बोभविताम्मि *bobha-vitásmi,* B. बोभूयासं *bobhúyásam.*

Note—Grammarians who allow the intensive without य *ya* to form an Âtmanepada, give
the following forms : Pres. बोभूते *bobhúté,* Impf. अबोभूत *ábobhúta,* Opt. बोभुवीत *bóbhuvíta,*
Imp. बोभूतां *bobhútâm,* Per. Perf. बोभवांचक्रे *bobhavâṁchakre,* Aor. अबोभाविष्ट *ábobhavishṭa,*
Fut. बोभविष्यते *bobhavishyáte,* Cond. अबोभविष्यत *ábobhavishyata,* Per. Fut. बोभविता *bobha-vitá,* Ben. बोभविषीष्ट *bobhavishíshṭá.* (See Colebrooke, p. 194.)

---

* The form बोभुविव *bobhuviva* is not sanctioned by any rule of Pâṇini.

† The first aorist is the usual form for intensives, but in भू *bhú* it is superseded by the
second aorist, this being enjoined for the simple verb. Some grammarians, however, admit
the first aorist optionally for भू *bhú* (Colebr. p. 193). The conflicting opinions of native
grammarians on the conjugation of intensives are fully stated by Colebrooke, p. 191 seq.

2. चित् *chit*, to think, (चिती.)

The Anubandha ई *î* shows that the participle in त: *tah* takes no intermediate इ *i*.

P. चेतति, I. अचेतत्, O. चेतेत्, I. चेततु ॥ Pf. 1. चिचेत, 2. चिचेतिथ, 3. चिचेत, 4. चिचितिव, 5. चिचितिषु:, 6. चिचिततु:, 7. चिचितिम, 8. चिचित, 9. चिचितु:, I A. 1. अचेतिषं, 2. अचेती:, 3. अचेतीत्, 4. अचेतिष्व, 5. अचेतिषं, 6. अचेतिष्टां, 7. अचेतिष्म, 8. अचेतिष्ट, 9. अचेतिषु:, F. चेतिष्यति, C. अचेतिष्यत्, P. F. चेतिता, B. चित्यात् ॥ Pt. चित:, चिचितवान्, Ger. चेतित्वा or चितित्वा, °चित्य, Adj. चेतितव्य:, चेतनीय:, चेत्य: ॥ Pass. चित्यते, Aor. अचेति, Caus. चेतयति, Aor. अचीचितत्, Des. चिचेतिषति or चिचितिषति, Int. चेचित्यते, चेचेति.

3. च्युत् *chyut*, to sprinkle, (च्युतिर्.)

The Anubandha इर् *ir* shows that the verb may take the first and second aorist.

P. च्योतति, I. अच्योतत्, O. च्योतेत्, I. च्योततु ॥ Pf. 1. चुच्योत, 2. चुच्योतिथ, 4. चुच्युतिव, I A. 1. अच्योतिषं, 2. अच्योती:, 3. अच्योतीत्, 9. अच्योतिषु:, or II A. 1. अच्युतं, 2. अच्युत:, 3. अच्युताम्, 9. अच्युतन्, F. च्योतिष्यति, C. अच्योतिष्यत्, P. F. च्योतिता, B. च्युत्यात् ॥ Pt. च्युतित: or च्योतित:, चुच्युतवान्, Ger. च्योतित्वा or च्युतित्वा, Adj. च्योतितव्य: ॥ Pass. च्युत्यते, Caus. च्योतयति, Aor. अचुच्युतत्, Des. चुच्योतिषति or चुच्युतिषति, Int. चोच्युत्यते, चोच्योति.

4. श्च्युत् *śchyut*, to flow, (च्युतिर्.)

P. श्च्योतति, I. अश्च्योतत्, O. श्च्योतेत्, I. श्च्योततु ॥ Pf. 1. चुश्च्योत, 9. चुश्च्युतु:, I A. 1. अश्च्योतिषं, 2. अश्च्योती:, or II A. 1. अश्च्युतं, F. श्च्योतिष्यति, C. अश्च्योतिष्यत्, P. F. श्च्योतिता, B. श्च्युत्यात् &c.

Note—This verb is sometimes written च्युत्.

5. मन्थ् *manth*, to shake.

P. मंथति ॥ Pf. 1. ममंथ, 2. ममंथिथ, 3. ममंथ, 7. ममंथिम, 8. ममंथु: (Pân. I. 2, 5) or, less correctly, ममन्थु: (§ 328, 4), I A. अमंथीत्, F. मंथिष्यति, P. F. मंथिता, B. मथ्यात् (§ 345, [10]) ॥ Pt. मथित:, ममंथान् or मेथिवान् (cf. § 395, note), Ger. मंथित्वा or मथित्वा (Pân. I. 2, 23; § 428), °मथ्य, Adj. मंथितव्य:, मंथनीय:, मंथ्य: ॥ Pass. मथ्यते, Caus. मंथयति, Des. मिमंथिषति, Int. मामथ्यते, मामंथि or मामंथीति, Impf. 3. अमामन्थत्.

Note—Roots ending in consonants preceded by a nasal, lose the nasal before weakening (*kit*, *ṅit*) terminations (Pân. VI. 4, 24); but not roots written with Anubandha इ. The terminations of the reduplicated perfect in the dual and plural are weakening (*kit*), except after roots ending in double consonants (Pân. I. 2, 5). According to some, however, the weakening is allowed even after double consonants: केचिदिति । प्रबोधोदयवृत्तिकारादय: । तथा च प्रबोधोदयवृत्तावुक्तं । संयोगादिश्च किङ्ङ । ररन्थु: ररन्थुरिति ॥ Roots, however, which thus drop the penultimate nasal in the perfect, need not take ए instead of reduplication: न्लोपिनो नेति केचित् ममन्थु: । Prakriyâ-Kaumudî, p. 7 b.

Native grammarians admit a verb मथति (*mathe*), and another मथ्नाति, which supply a variety of verbal derivatives.

6. कुन्थ् *kunth*, to strike, (कुथि.)

Roots marked in the Dhâtupâṭha by technical final इ *i* keep their penultimate nasal throughout. This root can take no Guṇa, on account of its final conjunct consonant.

P. कुंथति, I. अकुंथात्, O. कुंथेत्, I. कुंथतु ॥ Pf. 1. चुकुंथ, 2. चुकुंथिथ, 9. चुकुंथु:, I A.

अकुंपीत्, 9. अकुंपिषु:, F. कुंपिष्यति, P. F. कुंपिता, B. कुंप्यात्, (प्रनिकुंप्यात्, § 99, not with lingual ण, as Carey gives it) ॥ Pt. कुंपित:, चुकुंपान्, Ger. कुंपित्वा, °कुंप, Adj. कुंपितव्य: ॥ Pass. कुंप्यते, Caus. कुंपयति, Des. चुकुंपिषति, Int. चोकुंप्यते, चोकुंपि.

7. षिध् *sidh*, to go (षिध्), and षिध् *sidh*, to command (षिधू).

P. सेधति (निसेधति*), I. असेधत् ॥ Pf. 1. सिषेध, 2. सिषेधिथ, 9. सिषिधु:, I A. असेधीत्, F. सेधिष्यति, P. F. सेधिता, B. सिध्यात्.

In the sense of commanding or ordaining, this root is marked by technical ऋ (षिधू), and hence the intermediate इ may be omitted. Thus Pf. 2. सिषेधिथ or सिषेद्ध, 4. सिषिधिय or सिषिद्ध &c., F. सेधिष्यति or सेत्स्यति, P. F. सेधिता or सेद्धा, I A. असेधीत् (as before), or 1. असेत्सं, 2. असेत्सी:, 3. असेत्सीत्, 4. असेत्स्व, 5. असैत्स्वं, 6. असैद्ध्वं, 7. असेत्स्म, 8. असेद्ध, 9. असेत्सु: ॥ Pt. सिद्ध:, Ger. सेधित्वा or सिद्ध्वा, °सिध्य, Adj. सेधितव्य: or सेद्धव्य: ॥ Pass. सिध्यते, Caus. सेधयति, Des. सिसेधिषति or सिषित्सति (§ 103), Int. सेधिध्यते, सेषेद्धि.

8. खद् *khad*, to be steady, to kill, to eat.

P. खदति ॥ Pf. 1. चखाद (ă), 2. चखादिथ, 3. चखाद, 4. चखदिथ, 5. चखदु:, 6. चखदथु:, 7. चखदिम, 8. चखद, 9. चखदु:, I A. अखादीत् or अखदीत् (ă), (Pân. VII. 2, 7; § 348), F. खदिष्यति, P. F. खदिता, B. खद्यात् ॥ Pt. खदित:, चखद्वान्, Ger. खदित्वा, °खद्य, Adj. खदितव्य: ॥ Pass. खद्यते, Caus. खादयति, Des. चिखदिषति, Int. चाखद्यते, चाखत्ति.

9. गद् *gad*, to speak.

P. गदति (प्रणिगदति), I. अगदत् (प्रत्यगदत्), O. गदेत्, I. गदतु ॥ Pf. 1. जगाद (ă), 2. जगदिथ, 9. जगदु:, I A. अगादीत् or अगदीत् (ă), (Pân. VII. 2, 7; § 348), F. गदिष्यति, C. अगदिष्यत्, P. F. गदिता, B. गद्यात् ॥ Caus. गादयति, Des. जिगदिषति, Int. जागद्यते, जागत्ति.

10. रद् *rad*, to trace, to scratch.

P. रदति ॥ Pf. 1. रराद (ă), 2. रेदिथ, 9. रेदु:, I A. अरदीत् or अरदीत् (ă), (§ 348.)

11. नद् *nad*, to hum, (णद्.)

P. नदति (प्रणदति, प्रणिनदति) ॥ Pf. 1. ननाद (ă), 2. नेदिथ, 9. नेदु:, I A. अनादीत् or अनदीत् (ă).

12. अर्द् *ard*, to go, to ask, to pain.

P. अर्दति, I. आर्दत् ॥ Pf. 1. आनर्द, 2. आनर्दिथ, 9. आनर्दु:, I A. आर्दीत्, F. अर्दिष्यति ॥ Pt. अर्दित:, not आर्त:, see also p. 166 ॥ Caus. अर्दयति, आर्दिदत्, Des. अर्दिदिषति.

13. इन्द् *ind*, to govern, (इदि.)

P. इन्दति, I. ऐन्दत्, O. इन्देत्, I. इन्दतु ॥ Pf. इन्दाञ्चकार (§ 325) or इन्दामास or इन्दाबभूव,

---

* The change of स into ष is forbidden by Pânini VIII. 3, 113, when षिध् means to go. It is admitted by the Sâr. The Anubandha ऋ is sometimes added to षिध् to go, but is explained to be for the sake of pronunciation only. Colebrooke marks it as erroneous. Its proper meaning would be that intermediate इ is optional in the gerund, and forbidden in the past participle (§ 337, II. 5). The forms without intermediate इ belong properly only to षिध् to command. This verb *must* change its initial स after prepositions; निषेधति.

IA. 1. एंदिषं, 2. एंदी:, F. इंदिष्यति, C. एंदिष्यात्, P. F. इंदिता, B. इंद्यात् ॥ Pt. इंदित:, Perf. ईदांचकृवान् or बभूवान् or आसिवान्, Perf. Pass. ईदांचक्राण: or बभूवान: or आसान:.

14. निंद् *nind*, to blame, (णिदि.)

P. निंदति (प्रनिंदनं or प्रणिंदनं, § 98, 8, 2) ॥ Pf. निनिंद, I A. अनिंदीत्, F. निंदिष्यति, P. F. निंदिता, B. निंद्यात्.

15. निक्ष् *niksh*, to kiss, (णिक्ष.)

P. निक्षति (प्रणिक्षति, not प्रनिक्षति, § 98, 8, 2) ॥ Pf. निनिक्ष, I A. अनिक्षीत्, F. निक्षिष्यति, P. F. निक्षिता, B. निक्ष्यात्.

16. उख् *ukh*, to go.

P. ओखति (ओखति, § 43), I. ओखत् ॥ Pf. 1. उवोख (§ 314), 2. उवोखिथ, 3. उवोख, 7. ऊखिम, I A. ओखीत्, F. ओखिष्यति, C. ओखिष्यात्, P. F. ओखिता, B. उख्यात् ॥ Pass. उख्यते, Caus. ओखयति, Des. ओखिखिषति.

17. अंच् *añch*, to go, to worship, (अंचु and अचि.)

The Anubandha उ *u* of अंचु *añchu* allows the option of intermediate इ *i* in the gerund, अंचित्वा *añchitvá* or अक्त्वा *aktvá*, and its nasal remains, except before weakening forms (see *manth*, No. 5); but the Anubandha इ *i* of अचि *achi* requires the nasal throughout (Dhâtupâtha 7, 6).

P. अंचति ॥ Pf. 1. आनंच (§ 313), 9. आनंचु: (but see No. 5, note), I A. आंचीत्, F. अंचिष्यति, C. आंचिष्यात्, P. F. अंचिता, B. अंच्यात् (may he worship), अच्यात् (may he go), § 345, [10].

Pass. अच्यते and अंच्यते, Caus. अंचयति, Des. अंचिचिषति.

Distinguish between अंचित: worshipped, Ger. अंचित्वा having worshipped, and अक्त: moved (Pân. VII. 2, 53; VI. 4, 30); अंच् never seems to lose its nasal when it means to honour: Pass. अंच्यते he is honoured, अच्यते he is moved. The two roots, however, are not always kept distinct.

18. आंछ् *áñchh*, to stretch, (आछि.)

P. आंछति ॥ Pf. आनांछ or आंछ (§ 313), I A. आंछीत्, F. आंछिष्यति ॥ Caus. आंछयति, Des. आंछिच्छिषति.

19. म्रुच् *mruch*, to go, (म्रुचु.)

म्रोचति ॥ This and other verbs enumerated § 367 take optionally the first or second aorist; अम्रोचीत् or अम्रुचत् ॥ Pt. म्रुक्त:, Perf. मुम्रुचवान्, Ger. म्रुचित्वा, म्रोचित्वा (Pân. I. 2, 26), or म्रुक्त्वा.

20. हुर्छ् *hurchh*, to be crooked, (हुर्छा.)

P. हूर्छति (§ 143) ॥ Pf. जुहूर्छ, I A. अहूर्छीत् ॥ Pt. हूर्छित: or हूर्ण: (§ 431, 2).

21. वज् *vaj*, to go.

P. वजति ॥ Pf. 1. ववाज (*á*), 2. ववजिथ (§ 328), I A. अवजीत् or अवाजीत्, F. वजिष्यति.

22. व्रज् *vraj*, to go.

P. व्रजति ॥ Pf. 1. ववाज (*á*), 2. ववजिथ, I A. अव्राजीत् (§ 348*) ॥ Pt. व्रजित: ॥ Caus. व्राजयति, Des. विव्राजिषति, Int. वाव्रज्यते, वाव्रक्ति.

23. अज् aj, to go, to throw.

P. अजति, I. आजत् ॥ वी must be substituted in the general tenses before terminations beginning with vowels. Before all consonants except य (Pân. II. 4, 56, vârt.) this substitution is optional, i. e. both अज् and वी may be used ॥ Pf. 1. विवाय (â), 2. विवेय or विवयिय (§ 335, 3), [आजिय], 3. विवाय, 4. विविय (§ 334), [आजिय], 5. विव्ययुः, 6. विव्यतुः, 7. विव्यिय [आजिम], 8. विव्य, 9. विव्युः, I A. अवेयीत् [आजीत्], 9. अवेयुः, F. वेष्यति (§ 332, 3), C. अवेयत्, P. F. वेता, B. वीयात् [F. अजिष्यति, C. आजिष्यत्, P. F. अजिता] ॥ Pt. वीतः [अजितः], Perf. विवीवान् [आजिवान्], Ger. वीत्वा [अजित्वा], ०वीय, Adj. वेतव्यः [अजितव्यः], वयनीयः, वेयः ॥ Pass. वीयते, Caus. वायवति, Des. विवीषति [अजिजिषति], Int. वेवीयते (वेवेति is not sanctioned by Pânini).

24. क्षि kshi, to wane, *trans.* to diminish, (Colebrooke.)

P. क्षयति ॥ Pf. 1. चिक्षाय (â), 2. चिक्षेय or चिक्षयिय, 9. चिक्षियुः, I A. अक्षेयीत्, F. क्षेष्यति, B. क्षीयात् (§ 390) ॥ Pt. क्षितः or क्षीणः ॥ Pass. क्षीयते, Caus. क्षाययति, Des. चिक्षीषति, Int. चेक्षीयते, चेक्षेति. The Caus. क्षपयति belongs to क्षि (§ 462, II. 23) *.

25. कट् kaṭ, to rain, to encompass, (कटे.)

The Anubandha ए e prevents the lengthening of the vowel in the aorist.

P. कटति ॥ Pf. चकाट, I A. अकटीत् (no Vṛiddhi, § 348†).

26. गुप् gup, to protect, (गुपू.)

The verbs गुप् gup, to guard, धूप् dhúp, to warm, विच्छ richh, to go, पण paṇ, to traffic, पन paṇ, to praise, take आय âya in the special tenses, and take it optionally in the rest. (Pân. III. 1, 28; 31.)

P. गोपायति, I. अगोपायत्, O. गोपायेत्, I. गोपायतु ॥ Pf. गोपायांचकार (§ 325, 3) or जुगोप, I A. अगोपायीत्, अगोपीत्, or अगौप्सीत् (§ 337, I. 2), 6. अगौप्ताम्, F. गोपायिष्यति, गोपिष्यति, or गोप्स्यति, P. F. गोपायिता, गोपिता, or गोप्ता, B. गोपाय्यात् or गुप्यात् ॥ Pt. गोपायितः or गुप्तः, Ger. गोपायित्वा, गोपित्वा, or गुप्त्वा, Adj. गोपायितव्यः, गोपितव्यः, or गोप्यः ॥ Caus. गोपयति or गोपाययति, Des. जुगुप्सति, जुगुपिषति, जुगोपिषति, or जुगोपायिषति, Int. जोगुप्यते, जोगोपि.

27. धूप् dhúp, to warm.

P. धूपायति ॥ Pf. धूपायांचकार or दुधूप (no Guṇa, because the vowel is long), I A. अधूपायीत् or अधूपीत्.

28. तप् tap, to burn, (§ 332, 14.)

P. तपति ॥ Pf. 1. तताप (â), 2. ततप्य or तेपिय (§ 335, 3), 3. तताप, I A. 1. अताप्, 2. अताप्सीः, 3. अताप्सीत्, 6. अतापाम् (§ 351), F. तप्स्यति, P. F. तप्ता, B. तप्यात् ॥ Pt. तप्तः,

---

* The causative cannot have short *a*, and though both Westergaard and Boehtlingk-Roth give the short *a*, they produce no authority for it. The participle वृबितः is equally impossible, and should always be changed into वृपितः.

तेपिवान्, Ger. तप्ता, Adj. तप्तव्य:, तप्य: (short, because it ends in य, § 456, 6) ॥
Pass. तप्यते, Caus. तापयति, Des. तितप्सति, Int. तातप्यते, तातप्ति.

Note—With certain prepositions तप् takes the Âtmanepada (Pâṇ. 1. 3, 27); उत्तपते, वितपते it shines. It has an active sense in the passive (i.e. Div Âtm.), if it refers to तप: austere devotion; तप्यते तपस्तापस: the devotee performs austere devotion. In the sense of regretting (being burnt) it forms the Aor. अतप्त; अन्वतप्त पापेन कर्मणा he was distressed by a sinful act. (Colebr.)

<h3 style="text-align:center">29. चम् cham, to eat, (चमु.)</h3>

The following verbs lengthen their vowel in the special tenses (Pâṇ. vii. 3, 75, 76): चम् cham, if preceded by आ â, to rinse, आचामति âchâmati; ष्ठिव् shṭhiv, to spit, ष्ठीवति shṭhîvati (see No. 35); क्रम् kram, to stride, क्रामति krâmati (see No. 30); क्लम् klam, to tire, क्लामति klâmati. गुह् guh, to hide, गूहति gûhati, follows a different rule, lengthening its vowel throughout, instead of taking Guṇa, when a vowel follows. (Pâṇ. vi. 4, 89.)

P. चमति, but after the prep. आ, आचामति ॥ Pf. 1. चचाम (å), 2. चेमिथ &c., I A. अचमीत् (§ 348*) ॥ Pt. चांत: (§ 429), Ger. चांत्वा or चमित्वा, Adj. चमितव्य:, चाम्य: (Pâṇ. iii. 1, 126) ॥ Caus. चामयति (§ 462).

<h3 style="text-align:center">30. क्रम् kram, to stride, (क्रमु.)</h3>

क्रमु kram, to stride, भ्राशृ bhrâś, to shine, भ्लाशृ bhlâś, to shine, भ्रमु bhram, to roam, क्लमु klam, to fail, त्रसी tras, to tremble, त्रुट् truṭ, to cut, लष lash, to desire, may take य ya in the special tenses. Hence भ्राम्यति bhrâmyati or भ्रमति bhramati. (Pâṇ. iii. 1, 70.)

P. क्रामति or क्राम्यति, I. अक्रामत् or अक्राम्यत् ॥ Pf. चक्राम, I A. अक्रमीत् (§ 348*), F. क्रमिष्यति, P. F. क्रमिता, B. क्रम्यात् ॥

क्रम् lengthens its vowel in the general tenses (śit) of the Parasmaipada (Pâṇ. vii. 3, 76). Hence क्रामति, but क्रमते. It takes no intermediate इ in the Âtm.; Fut. क्रंस्यते, P. F. क्रंता, Aor. अक्रंस्त; but some grammarians admit intermediate इ.

Pt. क्रांत:, Perf. चक्रमवान्, Ger. क्रांत्वा (å) or क्रमित्वा (§ 429), Adj. क्रमितव्य: ॥ Pass. क्रम्यते, Caus. क्रमयति, § 461, (after prep. also क्रामयति), Des. चिक्रमिषति or चिक्रंसते, Int. चंक्रम्यते, चंक्रंति.

Note—It has been doubted whether क्रम् in the Div class also lengthens its vowel. It is not one of the eight Śam verbs (Pâṇ. vii. 3, 74); and in Pâṇ. vii. 3, 76, śyan is no longer valid. The Prasâda gives क्राम्यति; but adds, क्रमते तु श्यन्यपि दीर्घ: क्राम्यतीति। The Sârasvatî decides for क्राम्यति, giving the general rule (ii. 1, 145) शमादीनां दीर्घो भवति यकारे परे। and enumerating as शमादि, शम दम अम धम अम क्रम मद्. But क्रम् is not a Śamâdi at all, and instead of अम we ought to read क्रम्. Târânâtha in the Dhâturûpadarśa gives क्राम्यति, Râjârâmaśâstrî supports क्राम्यति.

<h3 style="text-align:center">31. यम् yam, to stop.</h3>

The roots गम् gam, to go, यम् yam, to cease, and इष् ish, to wish, substitute छ chchha for their final in the special tenses. (Pâṇ. vii. 3, 77.)

P. यच्छति, I. अयच्छत् ॥ Pf. 1. ययाम (å), 2. ययंथ or येमिथ, 9. येमु:, I A. अयंसीत् (§ 359), F. यंस्यति, P. F. यंता, B. यम्यात् ॥ Pt. यात:, येमिवान्, Ger. यत्वा, °यम्य or °यत्य, Adj.

यंतव्यः, यम्यः (नियाम्यः) ॥ Pass. यम्यते, Caus. यमयति (å), (§ 461), II A. अयीयमत्,
Des. यियंसति, Int. यंयम्यते or यंयंति.

Note—यम् may be used in the Âtm. with the prep. आ, if it is either intransitive,
आयच्छते तरुः the tree spreads, or governs as its object a member of the agent's body;
आयच्छते पाणिं he puts forth his hand. Likewise with the prep. आ, सं, उद्, if it is used
reflectively; संयच्छते व्रीहीन् he heaps together his own rice. Likewise after उप, when it
means to espouse; रामः सीतामुपायंस्त Râma married Sîtâ: here the Aor. may also be उपायत;
like उदायत he divulged another's faults. (§ 356.)

32. नम् *nam*, to bow, (णम्.)

P. नमति ॥ Pf. 1. ननाम (å), 2. ननंथ or नेमिथ, 9. नेमुः, I A. अनंसीत् (§ 359), F.
नंस्यति, P. F. नंता, B. नम्यात् &c., like यम्.   On the Causative, see § 461.

Note—नम् may be conjugated in the Âtmanepada. (Pâṇ. III. 1, 89.)
The Anubandha उ given to it by some grammarians is declared wrong by others.

33. गम् *gam*, to go, (गम्ॢ.)

P. गच्छति ॥ Pf. 1. जगाम (å), 2. जगमिथ or जगंथ, 3. जगाम, 4. जग्मिव (§ 328, 3),
5. जग्मुः &c., II A. अगमत् (§ 367), F. गमिष्यति (§ 338, 2), P. F. गंता, B. गम्यात् ॥
Pt. गतः, Perf. जग्मिवान् or जगन्वान्, Ger. गत्वा, °गम्य or °गत्य, Adj. गंतव्यः, गम्यः ॥
Pass. गम्यते, Caus. गमयति, Aor. अजीगमत्, Des. जिगमिषति, Int. जंगम्यते or जंगंति.

Note—With prep. सं it follows the Âtm., if intransitive.   The Caus. too, with the prep.
आ, may follow the Âtm., if it means to have patience; आगमयस्व तावत् wait a little.   In
the Âtm. the final म् may be dropt in the Aor. and Ben.; समगत or समगंस्त, संगसीष्ट or संगंसीष्ट.
(See § 355.)

34. फल् *phal*, to burst, (त्रिफला.)

P. फलति ॥ Pf. 1. पफाल (å), 2. फेलिथ (§ 336, II. 2), 3. पफाल, 4. फेलिथ,
I A. अफालीत् (§ 348*), F. फलिष्यति ॥ Pt. फुल्लः (Pâṇ. VIII. 2, 55), Ger. फलित्वा ॥
Pass. फल्यते, Caus. फालयति, Aor. अपीफलत्, Des. पिफलिषति, Int. पंफुल्यते, पंफुल्ति.
(Pâṇ. VII. 4, 87—89.)

35. ष्ठिव् *shṭhiv*, to spit, (ष्ठिवु.)

P. ष्ठीवति ॥ Pf. तिष्ठेव or टिष्ठेव, I A. अष्ठेवीत्, F. ष्ठेविष्यति ॥ Pt. ष्ठ्यूतः ॥ Pass.
ष्ठीव्यते (§ 143), Caus. ष्ठेवयति, Des. तिष्ठीविषति or तुष्ठ्यूषति (Pâṇ. VII. 2, 49), Int.
तेष्ठीव्यते.   No Intensive Parasmaipada.

Vowel lengthened in special tenses (see No. 29).   Initial sibilant unchangeable (§ 103).

36. जि *ji*, to excel.

P. जयति ॥ Pf. 1. जिगाय (å), 2. जिगेथ or जिगयिथ, 3. जिगाय, 4. जिग्यिव, 5. जिग्यव,
6. जिग्युः, 7. जिगियव, 8. जिग्य, 9. जिग्युः, I A. अजैषीत् (§ 350), F. जेष्यति, P. F. जेता,
B. जीयात् ॥ Pt. जितः, Perf. जिगिवान्, Ger. जित्वा, Adj. जेतव्यः, जयनीयः, जेयः, and
जय्यः (§ 456, 2), जित्यः only with हिंस् (Pâṇ. III. 1, 117) ॥ Pass. जीयते, Aor.
अजायि, Caus. जापयति, Aor. अजीजपत्, Des. जिगीषति, Int. जेजीयते, जेजेति.   It
follows the Âtmanepada with the prepositions परा and वि.

The change of ज् into ग् in the reduplicated perfect is anomalous (§ 319).   It does not take place in ज्या to wither (जिनाति), although the rule of Pâṇini might seem to comprehend that root after it has taken Samprasâraṇa. ज्या forms its reduplicated perfect जिज्यौ.

37. अक्ष् *aksh*, to obtain, (अक्षू.)

अक्ष् *aksh* follows also the Su class, अक्ष्णोति *akshṇoti* &c.

P. अक्षति ॥ Pf. 1. आनक्ष, 2. आनक्षिथ or आनष्ठ, 3. आनक्ष, 4. आनक्षिव or आनक्ष्व, 5. आनक्षुव:, 6. आनक्षथु:, 7. आनक्षिम or आनष्म, 8. आनक्ष, 9. आनक्षु:, I A. 1. आक्षिषं or आक्षं, 2. आक्षी:, 3. आक्षीत्, 4. आक्षिष्व or आक्ष्व, 5. आक्षिष्टं or आष्टं, 6. आक्षिष्टां or आष्टां, 7. आक्षिष्म or आक्ष्म, 8. आक्षिष्ट or आष्ट, 9. आक्षिषु: or आक्षु:, F. अक्षिष्यति or अक्ष्यति, P. F. अक्षिता or अष्टा ॥ Pt. अष्ट:, Ger. अष्ट्वा or अक्षित्वा ॥ Pass. अक्ष्यते, Caus. अक्षयति, Aor. आचिक्षत्, Des. आचिक्षिषति (§ 476).

तक्ष्, to hew, follows अक्ष् throughout, also in the optional forms of the Su class.

38. कृष् *krish*, to drag along, to furrow.

P. कर्षति ॥ Pf. 1. चकर्ष, 2. चकर्षिथ, 3. चकर्ष, 4. चकृषिव (§ 335, 3), I A. 1. अकार्षं, 2. अकार्षी:, 3. अकार्षीत्, 4. अकार्ष्व, 5. अकार्ष्टं, 6. अकार्ष्टां, 7. अकार्ष्म, 8. अकार्ष्ट, 9. अकार्षु:; or अक्राक्षं &c., or I A. 4. अकृक्षं &c. If used in the Âtmanepada, the two forms would be,

I A. 2. 1. अकृक्षि,	2. अकृष्ठा:,	3. अकृष्ट,
I A. 4. 1. id.	2. अकृक्षथा:,	3. अकृक्षत,
I A. 2. 4. अकृष्वहि,	5. अकृषाथां,	6. अकृषातां,
I A. 4. 4. अकृक्षावहि,	5. id.	6. id.
I A. 2. 7. अकृष्महि,	8. अकृढ्वं,	9. अकृषत,
I A. 4. 7. अकृक्षामहि,	8. अकृक्षध्वं,	9. अकृक्षत.

F. क्रक्ष्यति or कर्ष्यति, P. F. क्रष्टा or कर्ष्टा ॥ Pt. कृष्ट:, Ger. कृष्ट्वा ॥ Pass. कृष्यते, Caus. कर्षयति, Aor. अचकर्षत् or अचीकृषत्, Des. चिकृक्षति, Int. चरीकृष्यते, चरीकर्षि or चरीकृषि.

The peculiar Guṇa and Vṛiddhi of ऋ, viz. र and र, instead of अर् and आर्, take place necessarily in सृज्, to emit, and दृश्, to see (Pâṇ. vi. 1, 58); स्रष्टा, द्रष्टा, असार्क्षीत्, and अद्राक्षीत्: optionally in verbs with penultimate ऋ, which reject intermediate इ (Pâṇ. vi. 1, 59); तृप् to rejoice, तर्प्ता or तर्प्ता, Aor. अतार्प्सीत्, अत्राप्सीत् or अतृपत्.

39. रुष् *rush*, to kill.

P. रोषति ॥ Pf. 1. रुरोष, 2. रुरोषिथ, 9. रुरुषु:, I A. अरोषीत्, F. रोषिष्यति, P. F. रोषा or रोषिता (§ 337, II. 1).

40. उष् *ush*, to burn.

P. ओषति, I. ओषत् ॥ Pf. 1. ओषांचकार or उवोष (§ 326), 2. उवोषिथ, 3. उवोष, 4. अषिव &c., I A. औषीत्, F. ओषिष्यति, P. F. ओषिता, B. उष्यात् ॥ Pt. उषित: or ओषित: (§ 425) ॥ Des. ओषिषिषति.

41. मिह् *mih*, to sprinkle.

P. मेहति ॥ Pf. 1. मिमेह, 2. मिमेहिथ, I A. अमिक्षत् (§ 360), F. मेक्ष्यति, P. F. मेढा ॥

Pt. मीढः, Perf. मीढ्वान् (मिमिह्वान्), Ger. मीढ्वा ॥ Caus. मेहयति, अमीमिहत्, Des. मिमिक्षति,
Int. नेमिह्यते, नेमेढि, (नेमिहि, Westerg.)

42. दह् *dah*, to burn.

P. दहति ॥ Pf. 1. ददाह (å), 2. देहिथ or ददग्ध, F. धक्ष्यति (§ 118), P. F. दग्धा, B.
दह्यात्, I A. 1. अधाक्षं, 2. अधाक्षीः, 3. अधाक्षीत्, 4. अधाक्ष्व, 5. अदाग्ध्वं, 6. अदाग्धां, 7. अधाक्ष,
8. अदाग्ध्वं, 9. अधाक्षुः (see p. 185) ॥ Pt. दग्धः ॥ Caus. दाहयति, Aor. अदीदहत्, Des.
दिधक्षति, Int. दंदह्यते, दंदग्धि.

43. ग्लै *glai*, to droop; also म्लै *mlai*, to fade.

P. ग्लायति, O. ग्लायेत् ॥ Pf. 1. जग्लौ (§ 329), 2. जग्लिथ or जग्लाथ, 3. जग्लौ,
4. जग्लिथ, 5. जग्लथुः, 6. जग्लतुः, 7. जग्लिम, 8. जग्ल, 9. जग्लुः, I A. 1. अग्लासिषं (§ 357),
2. अग्लासीः, 3. अग्लासीत्, 4. अग्लासिष्व, 5. अग्लासिष्टं, 6. अग्लासिष्टां, 7. अग्लासिष्ट,
8. अग्लासिष्ट, 9. अग्लासिषुः, F. ग्लास्यति, P. F. ग्लाता, B. ग्लायात् or ग्लेयात् (§ 392†) ॥
Pt. ग्लानः, Ger. ग्लात्वा, °ग्लाय, Adj. ग्लातव्यः, ग्लानीयः, ग्लेयः ॥ Pass. (impers.)
ग्लायते, Caus. ग्लापयति or ग्लपयति (Dh. P. 19, 68), Des. जिग्लासति, Int. जा-
ग्लायते, जाग्लाति.

44. गै *gai*, to sing; also रै *rai*, to bark, कै *kai*, to croak.

P. गायति ॥ Pf. जगौ, I A. अगासीत्, F. गास्यति, P. F. गाता, B. गेयात् (§ 392).
Mark the difference between गै and ग्लै in the Bened. ॥ Pt. गीतः, Ger. गीत्वा,
°गाय, Adj. गातव्यः, गानीयः, गेयः ॥ Pass. गीयते, Aor. अगायि, Caus. गापयति, Aor.
अजीगपत्, Des. जिगासति, Int. जेगीयते, जागाति.

45. श्यै *shyai*, to sound, to gather; also स्त्यै *styai*, the same. (§ 103.)

P. श्यायति (§ 103), I. अश्यायत् ॥ Pf. शश्यौ, I A. अश्यासीत्, F. श्यास्यति, P. F. श्याता,
B. श्यायात् or श्येयात् ॥ Pt. श्यानः, प्रस्तीनः, प्रस्तीमः (§ 443).

Note—With regard to the initial lingual sibilant, the Prasâda quotes the Vârttika to
Pân. vi. 1, 64, as सुश्राद्रुष्वेभ्यश्छन्दसिवां सत्वनिषेधः । A marginal note says, सुश्राद्रुष्णुभ्यश्छन्द-
तीनामिदातुनिकर्यंपे प्रक्रियाकौनुखादौ सुश्राद्रुष्वेभ्यश्छन्दसिवामिति ज्ञे श्रष्टसंघातयोरिति पक्ष्यते ।
तदयुक्तं । भाष्णीयायां धातुवृत्तौ तथा युक्तिमद्दर्शनात्पदमंजरीकारादिभिरस्मृतत्वाच ॥

46. दै *dai*, to cleanse, (देप्.)

This verb is distinguished by a mute प् *p* from other verbs, like दा *dâ* &c. It is therefore
not comprised under the घु *ghu* verbs (§ 392*); it takes the first aorist (3rd form),
and does not substitute ई *i* or ए *e* for आ *â*.

P. दायति ॥ Pf. ददौ, I A. 1. अदासिषं, 2. अदासीः &c., F. दास्यति, P. F. दाता, B.
दायात् ॥ Pt. दातः ॥ Pass. दायते, Caus. दापयति, Des. दिदासति, Int. दादायते, दादाति.

47. धे *dhe*, to drink, (धेट्.)

This verb is one of the six so-called घु *ghu* roots (§ 392), roots which in the general tenses
have for their base दा *dâ* or धा *dhâ*.

P. धयति ॥ Pf. 1. दधौ, 2. दधिथ or दधाथ, 3. दधौ, 4. दधिव, 5. दधुः, 6. दधुः, 7. दधिम,
8. दध, 9. दधुः. It admits I A. 3. (§ 357), II A. (§ 368), and Red. II A. (§ 371):

1. अभासिषं,	2. अभासीः,	9. अभासिषुः,
1. अधाः,	2. अधाः,	9. अधुः,
1. अदधं,	2. अदधः,	9. अदधन्.

F. धास्यति, P. F. धाता, B. धेयात् ॥ Pt. धीतः, Ger. धीत्वा, °धाय ॥ Pass. धीयते, Caus. धापयति (Âtm. °ते to swallow), Aor. अदीधपत्, Des. धित्सति, Int. देधीयते, दाधाति, or, with the always optional ई, दाधेति.

<h3 style="text-align:center">48. दृश dṛiś, to see, (दृशिर्.)</h3>

This root substitutes पश्य paśya in the special tenses.

P. पश्यति, I. अपश्यत्, O. पश्येत्, I. पश्यतु ॥ Pf. 1. ददर्श, 2. ददर्शिथ or ददृष्ठ (§ 335), 3. ददर्श, 4. ददृशिव, 5. ददृशषुः, 6. ददृशथुः, 7. ददृशिम, 8. ददृश, 9. ददृशुः, I A. 1. अद्राक्षं, 2. अद्राक्षीः, 3. अद्राक्षीत्, 4. अद्राक्ष्व, 5. अद्राष्ट, 6. अद्राष्टां, 7. अद्राक्ष्म, 8. अद्राष्ट, 9. अद्राक्षुः (§ 360, 364); or II A. 1. अदर्शं, 9. अदर्शन्, F. द्रक्ष्यति, P. F. द्रष्टा, B. दृश्यात् ॥ Pt. दृष्टः, Ger. दृष्ट्वा, °दृश्य, Adj. द्रष्टव्यः, दर्शनीयः, दृश्यः ॥ Pass. दृश्यते, F. दर्शिष्यते or द्रक्ष्यते (§ 411), P. F. दर्शिता or द्रष्टा, B. दर्शिषीष्ट or दृक्षीष्ट, Aor. अदर्शि, Caus. दर्शयति, Aor. अदीदृशत् or अददर्शत्, Des. दिदृक्षते (Âtm.), Int. दरीदृश्यते, दर्दर्षि.

दृश and सृज take र and रा, instead of अर् and आर्, as their Guṇa and Vṛiddhi before consonantal terminations (Pân. VI. 1, 58). See No. 38.

Other verbs which substitute different bases in the special tenses (Pân. VII. 3, 78): ऋ forms ऋच्छति; सृ, धावति; शद्, शीयते (Âtm.); सद्, सीदति; पा, पिवति; घ्रा, जिघ्रति; ध्मा, धमति; स्था, तिष्ठति; म्ना, मनति; दा, यच्छति.

<h3 style="text-align:center">49. ऋ ṛi, to go.</h3>

P. ऋच्छति (उपार्छति, § 44), I. आर्छत् ॥ Pf. 1. आर, 2. आरिथ (§ 338, 7), 3. आर, 4. आरिव, 5. आरुः, 6. आरतुः, 7. आरिम, 8. आर, 9. आरुः, I A. 1. आर्षं, 2. आर्षीः, 3. आर्षीत्, 9. आर्षुः; the Second Aor. आरत् is generally referred to the ऋ of the Hu class, ऋणति; F. अरिष्यति (§ 338, 2), C. आरिष्यत्, P. F. अर्ता, B. अर्यात् (§ 390) ॥ Pt. ऋतः or ऋणः, Ger. ऋत्वा, °ऋत्य ॥ Pass. अर्यते, Caus. अर्पयति, Des. अरिरिषति, Int. अरार्यते, अरर्ति, अरियर्ति, अरर्तीति, अरियर्तीति (exceptional intensive, § 479, with the sense of moving tortuously).

<h3 style="text-align:center">50. सृ sṛi, to go.</h3>

P. धावति always means to run, while सरति is used likewise in the sense of going ॥ Pf. 1. ससार (ă), 2. ससर्थ (§ 335, 3), 3. ससार, 4. ससृव, 5. ससृषुः, 6. ससृतुः, 7. ससृम, 8. ससृ, 9. ससृुः, I A. 1. असार्षं, 2. असार्षीः, 3. असार्षीत्; the Second Aor. असरत् is generally referred to the सृ of the Hu class; F. सरिष्यति, P. F. सर्ता, B. स्रियात् (§ 390) ॥ Pt. सृतः ॥ Caus. सारयति, Des. सिसीर्षति, Int. सेसीर्यते, ससर्ति (§ 490).

<h3 style="text-align:center">51. शद् śad, to wither, (शद्.)</h3>

The special tenses take the Âtmanepada.

P. शीयते, I. अशीयत, O. शीयेत, I. शीयतां ॥ Pf. 1. शशाद (ă), 2. शशन्थ or शेदिथ,

L l

9. शेधुः, II A. अशदत्, F. शास्यति, P. F. शस्ता, B. शस्यात् ॥ Caus. शास्रयति (शादयति he drives), Des. शिशासति, Int. शाशद्यते, शाशत्ति.

52. सद् sad, to perish, (षद्.)

P. सीदति (निषीदति) ॥ Pf. 1. ससाद (ā), 2. सेदिव or ससत्थ, 9. शेधुः, II A. असदत् (न्यषदत्), F. सत्स्यति, P. F. सत्ता, B. सद्यात् ॥ Pt. सन्नः ॥ Pass. सद्यते, Aor. असादि, Caus. सादयति, Aor. असीषदत्, Des. सिषत्सति, Int. सासद्यते, सासत्ति.

53. पा pá, to drink.

P. पिबति ॥ Pf. 1. पपौ, 2. पपिव or पपाथ, 9. पपुः, II A. अपात्, F. पास्यति, P. F. पाता, B. पेयात् (§ 392) ॥ Pt. पीतः, Ger. पीत्वा, °पाय, Adj. पातव्यः, पानीयः, पेयः ॥ Pass. पीयते, Aor. अपायि, Caus. पाययति (or °ते to swallow), Aor. अपीप्यत् (Pâṇ. VII. 4, 4), Des. पिपासति, Int. पेपीयते, पापाति.

54. घ्रा ghrá, to smell, to perceive odour.

P. जिघ्रति, I. अजिघ्रत्, O. जिघ्रेत्, I. जिघ्रतु ॥ Pf. 1. जघ्रौ, 2. जघ्रिथ or जघ्राथ, 9. जघ्रुः, II A. अघ्रात्, or I A. अजिघ्रत् (§ 368, 357), F. घ्रास्यति, P. F. घ्राता, B. घ्रायात् or घ्रेयात् (§ 392†) ॥ Pt. घ्रातः or घ्राणः, Ger. घ्रात्वा ॥ Pass. घ्रायते, Aor. अघ्रायि, Caus. घ्रापयति, अजिघ्रपत् or अजिघ्रिपत् (Pâṇ. VII. 4, 6), Des. जिघ्रासति, Int. जेघ्रीयते, जाघ्राति.

55. ध्मा dhmá, to blow.

P. धमति ॥ Pf. दध्मौ, I A. अध्मासीत्, F. ध्मास्यति, B. ध्मायात् or ध्मेयात् ॥ Pt. ध्मातः ॥ Pass. ध्मायते, Aor. अध्मायि, Caus. ध्मापयति, Aor. अदिध्मपत्, Des. दिध्मासति, Int. देध्मीयते, दाध्माति.

56. स्था sthá, to stand, (ष्ठा.)

P. तिष्ठति ॥ Pf. तस्थौ (अधितस्थौ), II A. अस्थात् (न्यष्ठात्), 9. अस्थुः, F. स्थास्यति, B. स्थेयात् (§ 392) ॥ Pt. स्थितः, स्थित्वा, °स्थाय, Adj. स्थातव्यः, स्थानीयः, स्थेयः ॥ Pass. स्थीयते, Aor. अस्थायि, Caus. स्थापयति, Aor. अतिष्ठिपत्, Des. तिष्ठासति, Int. तेष्ठीयते, तास्थाति.

Note—After सं, अव, प्र, and वि, स्था is used in the Âtm.; also after आ, if it means to affirm; with उद्, if it means to strive, not to rise; or with उप, if it means to worship, &c.: Pres. तिष्ठते, Red. Perf. तस्थे, Aor. अस्थित, 9. सस्थिषत, Fut. स्थास्यते, Ben. स्थासीष्ट.

57. म्ना mná, to study.

P. मनति ॥ Pf. 1. मम्नौ, 2. मम्निथ or मम्नाथ, 9. मम्नुः, I A. अम्नासीत्, B. म्नायात् or म्नेयात् ॥ Pt. म्नातः ॥ Pass. म्नायते, Caus. म्नापयति, Aor. अमिम्नपत्, Des. मिम्नासति, Int. माम्नायते, माम्नाति.

58. दा dá, to give, (दाञ्.)

P. यच्छति* (प्रतियच्छति) ॥ Pf. ददौ, II A. अदात्, B. देयात् (§ 392) ॥ Pt. दत्तः, Ger. दत्त्वा (see No. 200, Pâṇ. VII. 4, 46), °दाय, Adj. दातव्यः, दानीयः, देयः ॥ Pass. दीयते, Caus. दापयति, Des. दित्सति, Int. देदीयते, दादाति.

59. ह्वृ hvṛi, to bend.

P. ह्वरति ॥ Pf. 1. जह्वार (ā), 2. जह्वर्थ (§ 335), 3. जह्वार, 4. जह्वरिव (§ 330, 334),

---

* After the preposition सं it may be used in the Âtmanepada.

9. नह्रुः, I A. अह्वापीत्, 9. अह्वापुः, F. ह्वरिष्यति (§ 338), P. F. ह्वर्ता, B. ह्वर्यात् (§ 390) ॥ Pt. हृतः, Ger. हृत्वा, °हृत्य, Adj. हर्तव्यः, हरणीयः, हार्यः ॥ Pass. ह्रियते, Caus. ह्वारयति, Des. जुहूर्षति, Int. जाह्वर्यते, जरीहर्ति.

60. स्कंद् *skand*, to approach, (स्कंदिर्.)

P. स्कंदति (परिस्कंदति or परिष्कंदति, Pâṇ. VIII. 3, 73, 74) ॥ Pf. 1. चस्कंद, 2. चस्कंदिथ or चस्कंत्थ, 9. चस्कंदुः or चस्कदुः (see भंज, No. 5), I A. अस्कांत्सीत्, 6. अस्कांतां, 9. अस्कांत्सुः; or II A. अस्कदं, F. स्कंत्स्यति, P. F. स्कंता, B. स्कद्यात् (§ 345, [10]) ॥ Pt. स्कनः (§ 103, 6), Ger. स्कंत्वा (§ 438) ॥ Pass. स्कद्यते, Caus. स्कंदयति, Aor. अचस्कंदत् (§ 374), Des. चिस्कंत्सति, Int. चनीस्कद्यते (§ 485), चनीस्कंति.

61. तॄ *tṛî*, to cross.

P. तरति ॥ Pf. 1. ततार (â), 2. तेरिथ, 3. ततार, 4. तेरिव, I A. अतारीत्, F. तरिष्यति or तरीष्यति (§ 340), P. F. तरिता or तरीता, B. तीर्यात्. In the Âtmanepada we generally find the verb used as Tudâdi, P. तिरते, Pf. तेरे, Aor. अतरिष्ट or अतरिष्ट or अतरीष्ट, F. तरिष्यते (î), B. तरिषीष्ट or तीर्षीष्ट ॥ Pt. तीर्णः, Ger. तीर्त्वा, °तीर्य ॥ Pass. तीर्यते, Aor. अतारि, Caus. तारयति, Des. तितरिषति or तितरीषति or तितीर्षति, Int. तेतीर्यते, तर्तर्ति.

62. रंज् *rañj*, to tinge.

This verb and दंश् *daṃś*, to bite, संज् *sañj*, to stick, and स्वंज् *svañj*, to embrace (Pâṇ. VI. 4, 25, 26), drop the penultimate nasal in the special tenses (§ 345, [10]) and in the weakening forms (§ 344, 395, note).

P. रजति, I. अरजत्, O. रजेत्, I. रजतु ॥ Pf. 1. ररंज, 2. ररंजिथ or ररंक्थ, 3. ररंज, 4. ररंजिव, 9. ररंजुः, I A. अरांक्षीत्, F. रंक्ष्यति, P. F. रंक्ता, B. रज्यात्. Also used in the Âtmanepada: P. रजते, Pf. 1. ररंजे, 2. ररंजिषे, I A. 3. अरंक्त, 9. अरंक्षत ॥ Pt. रक्तः, Ger. रक्त्वा or रंक्त्वा (Pâṇ. VI. 4, 31, § 438) ॥ Pass. रज्यते (Pâṇ. III. 1, 90), Caus. रंजयति or रजयति to hunt (§ 462, 26), Aor. अरीरजत् or अररंजत्, Des. रिरंक्षति, Int. रारज्यते, रारंक्ति.

63. किट् *kiṭ*, to cure, (किट.)

This and some other verbs which are referred to the Bhû class always take the desiderative terminations, if used in certain senses. किट् *kiṭ*, if it means to dwell, belongs to the Chur class, or, according to Vopadeva, it may be regularly conjugated as a Bhû verb; but if it means to cure, it is चिकित्सति *chikitsati*.

P. चिकित्सति, I. अचिकित्सत् &c. ॥ Pf. चिकित्सांचकार, I A. अचिकित्सीत्, F. चिकित्सिष्यति, P. F. चिकित्सिता.

In the same way are conjugated (§ 472):

1. गुप् (to conceal), जुगुप्सते he despises.
2. तिज् (to sharpen), तितिक्षते he endures.
3. मान् (to revere), मीमांसते he investigates.
4. बध् (to bind), बीभत्सते he loathes.
5. दान् (to cut), दीदांसति he straightens.
6. शान् (to sharpen), शीशांसति he sharpens.

64. पत् *pat*, to fall, (पतॢ.)

P. पतति (प्रक्षिपतति) ॥ Pf. 1. पपात, 9. पेतुः, II A. अपप्तं (§ 366), F. पतिष्यति ॥ Pt. पतितः ॥ Pass. पत्यते, Aor. अपाति, Caus. पातयति, Des. पिपतिषति or पित्सति (§ 337, II. 3).

65. वस् *vas*, to dwell.

P. वसति ॥ Pf. 1. उवास (ā̆), 2. उवसिथ or उवस्थ, 3. उवास, 4. ऊषिव, 5. ऊषु:, 6. ऊषतुः, 7. ऊषिम, 8. ऊष, 9. ऊषुः, I A. 1. अवात्सं (§ 132), 2. अवात्सीः, 3. अवात्सीत्, 6. अवात्सां (§ 351), F. वत्स्यति, P. F. वस्ता, B. उष्यात् ॥ Pt. उषितः, Ger. उषित्वा, °उष्य ॥ Pass. उष्यते, Aor. अवासि, Caus. वासयति, Aor. अवीवसत्, Des. विवत्सति, Int. वावस्यते, वावस्ति.

66. वद् *vad*, to speak.

P. वदति ॥ Pf. 1. उवाद (ā̆), 2. उवदिथ, 9. ऊदुः, I A. अवादीत्, F. वदिष्यति, B. उद्यात् ॥ Pt. उदितः, Ger. उदित्वा ॥ Pass. उद्यते, Aor. अवादि, Caus. वादयति, Aor. अवीवदत्, Des. विवदिषति, Int. वावद्यते, वावत्ति.

67. श्वि *śvi*, to swell, (टुओश्वि.)

P. श्वयति ॥ Pf. 1. शुश्वाव (ā̆) or शिश्वाय (ā̆), 2. शुश्वविथ or शिश्वयिथ, 3. शुश्वाव or शिश्वाय, 4. शुशुविव or शिशिव्यियिव, 5. शुशुवुः or शिशिव्ययुः, 9. शुशुवुः or शिशिव्युः, I A. अश्वयीत्, II A. अश्वत् or अशिश्वियत् and अश्वूयत्, F. श्वयिष्यति, P. F. श्वयिता, B. शूयात् ॥ Pt. शूनः ॥ Pass. शूयते, Caus. श्वाययति, Aor. अशिश्वयत्, Des. शिश्वयिषति, Int. शेश्वीयते or शोश्वूयते.

II. Âtmanepada Verbs.

68. एध् *edh*, to grow.

P. एधते, I. एधत, O. एधेत, I. एधतां ॥ Pf. एधांचक्रे*, F. एधिष्यते, C. एधिष्यत, P. F. एधिता, I A. 1. एधिषि, 2. एधिष्ठाः, 3. एधिष्ट, 4. एधिष्वहि, 5. एधिषाथां, 6. एधिषातां, 7. एधिष्महि, 8. एधिध्वं or °ध्वं, 9. एधिषत, B. एधिषीष्ट ॥ Pt. एधितः ॥ Pass. एध्यते, Aor. एधि, Caus. Pres. एधयति, °ते, Perf. एधयामास, F. एधयिष्यति, °ते, Cond. एधयिष्यत्, °त, P. F. एधयिता, II A. एदिधत्, °त, B. एधयिषीष्ट, Des. एदिधिषते.

69. ईक्ष् *îksh*, to see.

P. ईक्षते, I. ऐक्षत, O. ईक्षेत, I. ईक्षतां ॥ Pf. ईक्षांचक्रे, I A. ऐक्षिष्ट, F. ईक्षिष्यते, C. ऐक्षिष्यत, P. F. ईक्षिता, B. ईक्षिषीष्ट ॥ Pt. ईक्षितः ॥ Caus. ईक्षयति, Aor. ऐचिक्षत्, Des. ईचिक्षिषते.

70. दद् *dad*, to give.

P. ददते, I. अददत, O. ददेत, I. ददतां ॥ Pf. 3. दददे (§ 328, 1), 6. दददाते, 9. दददिरे (Pâṇ. vi. 4, 126), I A. अददिष्ट, F. ददिष्यते, P. F. ददिता, B. ददिषीष्ट ॥ Pt. ददितः ॥ Pass. दद्यते, Aor. अददि, Caus. ददयति, Aor. अदीददत्, Des. दिददिषते, Int. दादद्यते, दादत्ति.

---

* आस and बभूव are used in the Parasmaipada, चक्रे in the Âtmanepada. It is only in the passive that आस and बभूव take Âtmanepada terminations.

71. ष्वष्क् *shvashk*, to go.

P. ष्वष्कते, I. अष्वष्कत ॥ Pf. पष्वष्क्के, I A. अष्वष्किष्ट, F. ष्वष्किष्यते, P. F. ष्वष्किता,
B. ष्वष्किषीष्ट.

Note—The initial ष् is not liable to become स्. (See No 45; Pâṇ. VI. 1, 64, 1. Colebrooke, p. 219.)

72. ऋज् *rij*, to go, to gain, &c.

P. अर्जते, I. आर्जत ॥ Pf. आनृजे, I A. आर्जिष्ट, F. अर्जिष्यते, P. F. अर्जिता, B. अर्जि-
षीष्ट ॥ Pass. ऋज्यते (प्रार्ज्यते), Caus. अर्जयति, Aor. आर्जिजत्, Des. अर्जिजिषते.

73. स्वञ्ज् *svañj*, to embrace.

दंश् *damś*, सञ्ज् *sañj*, स्वञ्ज् *svañj* drop their nasal in the special tenses (Pâṇ. VI. 4, 25). See No. 62.

P. स्वजते, I. अस्वजत ॥ Pf. सस्वंजे or सस्वजे (Pâṇ. I. 2, 6, vârt.), I A. 1. अस्वंक्षि,
2. अस्वंक्थाः, 3. अस्वंक्त, 4. अस्वंक्ष्वहि, 5. अस्वंक्ष्वाथां, 6. अस्वंक्षातां, 7. अस्वंक्ष्महि, 8. अस्वंग्ध्वं,
9. अस्वंक्षत, F. स्वंक्ष्यते, B. स्वंक्षीष्ट ॥ Pass. स्वज्यते, Caus. स्वंजयति, Des. सिस्वंक्षते,
Int. सास्वज्यते, सास्वंक्ति.

74. त्रप् *trap*, to be ashamed, (त्रपूष्.)

P. त्रपते, I. अत्रपत ॥ Pf. 3. त्रेपे (Pâṇ. VI. 4, 122), 6. त्रेपाते, 9. त्रेपिरे, I A. 1.
अत्रपिषि or अत्रप्सि, 2. अत्रपिष्ठाः or अत्रप्थाः, 3. अत्रपिष्ट or अत्रप्त, F. त्रपिष्यते or त्रप्स्यते,
B. त्रपिषीष्ट or त्रप्सीष्ट.

75. तिज् *tij*, to forbear.

P. तितिक्षते ॥ Pf. तितिक्षांचक्रे, I A. अतितिक्षिष्ट, F. तितिक्षिष्यते, B. तितिक्षिषीष्ट ॥
Caus. तेजयति.

Note—See No. 63. The simple verb is said to form तेजते he sharpens.

76. पण् *paṇ*, to praise.

P. पण्यायते, I. अपण्यायत ॥ Pf. पण्यायांचक्रे or पेणे (without आय्). Thus likewise
Aor. अपण्यायिष्ट or अपणिष्ट, F. पण्यायिष्यते or पणिष्यते, B. पण्यायिषीष्ट or पणिषीष्ट ॥ Caus.
पाणयति, Aor. अपीपणत्, Des. पिपणिषते, Int. पंपण्यते.

Note—This verb (see No. 26) takes आय, but, as it is mentioned by Pâṇini III. 1, 28, together with पन्, with which it shares but the meaning of to praise, it is argued that it does not take आय, unless it means to praise. It is likewise argued that पण्, if it takes आय, does not follow the Âtmanepada, because the Anubandha, requiring the Âtmanepada, applies only to the simple verb, पण्, पणते he traffics. Other grammarians, however, allow both the Parasmaipada and Âtmanepada. The suffix आय may be kept in the general tenses. (Pâṇ. III. 1, 31.)

77. कम् *kam*, to love, (कमु.)

P. कामयते, I. अकामयत ॥ Pf. कामयांचक्रे or चकमे, I A. अचीकमत or (without अय्)
अचकमत (Pâṇ. III. 1, 48, vârt.), F. कमिष्यते or कामयिष्यते, B. कमिषीष्ट or कामयिषीष्ट ॥
Pass. कम्यते (â), Aor. अकामि (Pâṇ. VII. 3, 34, vârt.), Caus. कामयति, Des. चिकमिषते
or चिकामयिषते, Int. चंकम्यते.

Note—This verb in the special tenses takes अय, like a verb of the Chur class, and Vṛiddhi (Pâṇ. III. 1, 30). In the general tenses अय is optional. Or, if we admit two roots, the one कम् would be defective in the special tenses, while the other कामय is conjugated all through.

78. अय् *ay*, to go.

P. अयते, I. आयत ॥ Pf. अयांचक्रे (Pâṇ. iii. 1, 37), I A. 1. आयिषि, 2. आयिष्ठाः, 3. आयिष्ट, 4. आयिष्वहि, 5. आयिधार्म, 6. आयिधातां, 7. आयिध्वहि, 8. आयिध्वं or °ढ्वं, 9. आयिषत, F. अयिष्यते, B. अयिषीष्ट ॥ Caus. आययति, Des. अयियिषते.

With परा it forms पलायते he flees (Pâṇ. viii. 2, 19), Ger. पलाय्य; with प्र, प्रायते; and with परि, पर्ययते.

79. ईह् *îh*, to aim.

P. ईहते, I. ऐहत ॥ Pf. ईहांचक्रे, I A. ऐहिष्ट, F. ईहिष्यते, B. ईहिषीष्ट ॥ Caus. ईहयति, Aor. ऐजिहत्, Des. ईजिहिषते.

80. काश् *kâś*, to shine, (काशृ.)

P. काशते ॥ Pf. चकाशे or काशांचक्रे (§ 326), I A. अकाशिष्ट, F. काशिष्यते ॥ Caus. काशयति, Aor. अचकाशत्, Des. चिकाशिषते, Int. चाकाश्यते, चाकाशि.

81. कास् *kâs*, to cough, (कासृ.)

P. कासते ॥ Pf. कासांचक्रे (§ 326) ॥ Caus. कासयति, Aor. अचकासत् (§ 372*).

82. सिव् *siv*, to serve, (षेवृ.)

P. सेवते (परिसेवते) ॥ Pf. सिषेवे, I A. असेविष्ट, F. सेविष्यते ॥ Caus. सेवयति, Aor. असिषेवत्, Des. सिषेविषते, Int. सेषेव्यते.

83. गा *gâ*, to go, (गाङ्.)

P. 3. गाते, 6. गाते, 9. गाते, 1st pers. sing. गै, I. गातां, 1st pers. sing. गै, O. गेत, I. अगात ॥ Pf. 3. गगे, 6. जगाते, 9. जगिरे, I A. 1. अगासि, 2. अगास्याः, 3. अगास्त &c., F. गास्यते, B. गासीष्ट ॥ Pass. गीयते, Aor. अगायि, Caus. गापयति, Aor. अजीगपत्, Des. जिगासते, Int. जेगीयते.

84. रु *ru*, to go, to kill (?), to speak, (रुङ्.)

P. रवते ॥ Pf. 3. रुरुवे, 6. रुरुवाते, 9. रुरुविरे, I A. अरविष्ट ॥ Caus. रावयति, Aor. अरीरवत् (§ 474 and § 375†).

85. दे *de*, to protect, (देङ्.)

P. दयते ॥ Pf. 1. दिग्ये (Pâṇ. vii. 4, 9), 2. दिग्यिषे, 3. दिग्ये, I A. 1. अदिषि, 2. अदिधाः, 3. अदित, F. दास्यते, B. दासीष्ट ॥ Pt. दत्तः ॥ Pass. दीयते, Caus. दाययति, Des. दित्सते, Int. देदीयते.

Note—It is one of the पु verbs; दै, to protect, forms दायते in the present, but follows दे in the general tenses.

86. द्युत् *dyut*, to shine, (द्युत्.)

P. द्योतते ॥ Pf. दिद्युते (Pâṇ. vii. 4, 67), I A. अद्योतिष्ट or अद्युतत् (§ 367: Pâṇ. i. 3, 91; iii. 1, 55), F. द्योतिष्यते, B. द्योतिषीष्ट ॥ Caus. द्योतयति, Aor. अदिद्युतत्, Des. दिद्युतिषते or दिद्योतिषते, Int. देद्युत्यते, देद्योति.

Note—The verbs beginning with द्युत् optionally admit the II Aor. Parasmaipada (§ 367).

87. वृत् *vṛit*, to be, (वृतु.)

P. वर्तते ॥ Pf. ववृते, I A. अवर्तिष्ट or अवृतत्, F. वर्तिष्यते or वर्त्स्यति, B. वर्तिषीष्ट ॥ Caus.

वानेयति, Aor. अवीवृताम् or अववर्तम् (Pân. VII. 4, 7), Des. विवर्तिषते or विवृत्सति, Int. वरीवृत्यते.

Note—The verbs beginning with वृत्, i.e. वृत्, वृध्, गृध्, स्यंद्, कृप्, are optionally Parasmaipada in the aorist, future, conditional, desiderative (Pân. I. 3, 91—93). The same verbs do not take इ in their Parasmaipada tenses (Pân. VII. 2, 59); as to कृप्, see Pân. VII. 2, 60, and I. 3, 93.

88. स्यंद् *syand*, to sprinkle or drop, (स्यंदू.)

P. स्यंदते ॥ Pf. 1. सस्यंदे, 2. सस्यंदिषे or सस्यंत्से, 4. सस्यंदिवहे or सस्यंद्ध्वे, I A. 3. असस्यंदिष्ट, 6. अस्यंदिषातां; or असस्यंत्त (6. अस्यंत्सातां), or II A. अस्यदत् (not अस्यंदत्), F. स्यंदिष्यते or स्यंत्स्यते or स्यंत्स्यति (Pân. VII. 2, 59; see No. 87), B. स्यंदिषीष्ट or स्यंत्सीष्ट ॥ Pt. स्यन्न:, Ger. स्यंदित्वा or स्यंत्वा (Pân. VI. 4, 31) ॥ Caus. स्यंदयति, Des. सिस्यंदिषते or सिस्यंत्सते or सिस्यंत्सति.

89. कृप् *krip*, to be able, (कृपू.)

P. कल्पते ॥ Pf. चकृपे, I A. 3. अकल्पिष्ट or अकृप्त, 6. अकृप्सातां, 9. अकृप्त, or II Aor. Par. अकृपत्, F. कल्पिष्यते or कल्प्स्यते or कल्प्स्यति, P. F. 2. कल्पितासे or कल्पासे or कल्प्तासि, B. कल्पिषीष्ट or कृप्सीष्ट ॥ Pt. कृप्त: ॥ Caus. कल्पयति, Des. चिकल्पिषते or चिकृप्सति, Int. चलीकृप्यते or चलिकल्प्यते or चकल्प्यते.

90. व्यथ् *vyath*, to fear, to suffer pain.

P. व्यथते ॥ Pf. विव्यथे (Pân. VII. 4, 68), I A. अव्यथिष्ट, F. व्यथिष्यते ॥ Pass. व्यथ्यते, Aor. अव्यथि (तां), (§ 462), Caus. व्ययथति, Des. विव्यथिषते, Int. वाव्यथ्यते, वाव्यथि.

91. रम् *ram*, to sport, (रमु.)

P. रमते; with वि, आ, परि, उप, optionally Parasmaipada; विरमति (Pân. I. 3, 83) ॥ Pf. रेमे, I A. अरंस्त, after prepositions अरंसीत्, F. रंस्यते ॥ Pt. रत:, Ger. रत्वा, °रम्य or °रत्य ॥ Caus. रमयति, Aor. अरीरमत्, Des. रिरंसते, Int. रंरम्यते, रंरमीति.

92. त्वर् *tvar*, to hurry, (भित्वरा.)

The verbs ज्वर् *jvar*, त्वर् *tvar*, स्रिव् *sriv*, अव् *av*, मव् *mav*, substitute जूर् *júr*, तूर् *túr*, स्रू *srú*, ऊ *ú*, मू *mú* (Pân. VI. 4, 20) before weakening terminations beginning with consonants, except semivowels, and if used as monosyllabic nominal bases. Hence जूर्ण: *júrṇaḥ*, तूर्ण: *túrṇaḥ*, स्रूत: *srútaḥ*, ऊत: *útaḥ*, मूत: *mútaḥ*.

P. त्वरते ॥ Pf. तत्वरे, I A. 3. अत्वरिष्ट, 8. अत्वरिध्वं or अत्वरिद्वं, F. त्वरिष्यते ॥ Pt. तूर्ण: (§ 432) or त्वरित: ॥ Caus. त्वरयति (§ 462, II. 6), Aor. अतत्वरत् (§ 375†), Des. तित्वरिषति, Int. तात्वर्यते, तोतूर्ति.

93. सह् *sah*, to bear, (षह.)

P. सहते ॥ Pf. सेहे, I A. असहिष्ट, F. सहिष्यते, P. F. सहिता or सोढा (§ 337, II. 2) ॥ Pt. सोढ:, Adj. सह्य: (§ 456, 6) ॥ Pass. सह्यते, Caus. साहयति, Aor. असीषहत्, Caus. Des. सिसाहयिषति, Des. सिसहिषते, Int. सासह्यते, सासोढि.

Note—सह् and वह् change अ into ओ when ष would be followed by ढ, the result of the amalgamation of ह with a following dental (§ 128). Pân. VI. 3, 112.

III. Parasmaipada and Âtmanepada Verbs.

94. राज् *ráj*, to shine, (राजृ.)

P. राजति, °ते ॥ Pf. रराज, रराजे or रेजे (Pân. VI. 4, 125), I A. अराजीत्, अराजिष्ट,

F. राजिष्यति, °ते, B. राज्यात्, राजिषीष्ट ॥ Caus. राजयति, Aor. अररराजत्, Des. रिराजिषति, °ते, Int. रारज्यते, रारजि.

95. खन् *khan*, to dig.

P. खनति* ॥ Pf. 3. चखान, 6. चख्नुः, 9. चख्नुः ($ 328, 3), I A. अखनीत् (å), ($ 348), but Âtm. अखनिष्ट only, F. खनिष्यति, B. खन्यात् or खायात् ($ 391) ॥ Pt. खात:, Ger. खात्वा or खनित्वा, Adj. खेय: ($ 456, 6) ॥ Pass. खन्यते or खायते ($ 391), Caus. खानयति, Aor. अचीखनत्, Des. चिखनिषति, °ते, Int. चंखन्यते or चांखाय्यते ($ 391), चंखंति.

96. हृ *hri*, to take, (हृम्.)

P. हरति ॥ Pf. 1. जहार (å), 2. जहर्थ, 9. जहुः, I A. अहार्षीत्, Âtm. अहृत ($ 351), F. हरिष्यति, P. F. हर्ता, B. ह्रियात् ॥ Pt. हृत:, Ger. हृत्वा, Adj. हार्य: ॥ Pass. ह्रियते, Aor. अहारि, Caus. हारयति, Des. जिहीर्षति, °ते, Int. जेहृीयते, जर्हर्ति &c.

97. गुह् *guh*, to hide, (गुहू.)

गुह् *guh* takes ऊ *ū* before terminations beginning with vowels that would ordinarily require Guṇa.

P. गूहति ॥ Pf. 1. जुगूह, 2. जुगूहिथ or जुगोढ, 3. जुगूह, 4. जुगुहिव, 5. जुगुहुः &c., Âtm. 1. जुगुहे, 2. जुगुहिषे or जुगुहिषे &c., I Aor. see $ 362, F. गूहिष्यति or घोक्ष्यति, P. F. गूहिता or गोढा, Ben. Âtm. गूहिषीष्ट or घुक्षीष्ट ($ 345) ॥ Pt. गूढ:, Adj. गुह्य: or गोह्य: ($ 457) ॥ Pass. गुह्यते, Aor. अगूहि, Caus. गूहयति, Aor. अजूगुहत्, Des. जुघुक्षति ($ 470), Int. जोगुह्यते, जोगोढि.

98. श्रि *śri*, to go, to serve, (श्रिम्.)

P. श्रयति ॥ Pf. 1. शिश्राय (å), 2. शिश्रयिथ, 3. शिश्राय, 4. शिश्रियिव, 5. शिश्रियुः, II A. अशिश्रियत् ($ 371), F. श्रयिष्यति, B. श्रीयात् ॥ Pass. श्रीयते, Aor. अश्रायि, Caus. श्राययति, Aor. अशिश्रयत्, Des. शिश्रयिषति or शिश्रीषति ($ 471, 3; $ 337, II. 3), Int. शेश्रीयते.

99. यज् *yaj*, to worship.

P. यजति ॥ Pf. 1. इयाज (å), ($ 311), 2. इयजिथ or इयष्ठ ($ 335, 3), 4. ईजिव, 5. ईजुः, 6. ईजतुः, 7. ईजिम, 8. ईज, 9. ईजुः, I A. 1. अयाक्षं, 2. अयाक्षीः, 3. अयाक्षीत्, 4. अयाक्ष्व, 5. अयाष्टं, 6. अयाष्टां, 7. अयाष्म, 8. अयाष्ट, 9. अयाक्षुः, I Aor. Âtm. 1. अयक्षि, 2. अयष्ठाः, 3. अयष्ट, 4. अयक्ष्वहि, 5. अयक्षाथां, 6. अयक्षातां, 7. अयक्ष्महि, 8. अयद्ध्वं (not अयग्ध्वं), 9. अयक्षत, F. यक्ष्यति, P. F. यष्टा ($ 124), B. इज्यात् ($ 393) ॥ Pt. इष्ट:, Ger. इष्ट्वा, °इज्य ॥ Pass. इज्यते, Caus. याजयति, Aor. अयीयजत्, Des. यियक्षति, Int. यायज्यते, यायजि.

100. वप् *vap*, to sow, to weave, (डुवप्.)

P. वपति ॥ Pf. 1. उवाप (å), 2. उवपिथ or उवप्थ, 9. ऊपुः, I A. अवाप्सीत्, Âtm. अवप्त, F. वप्स्यति, P. F. वप्ता, B. उप्यात् ॥ Pt. उप्त: ॥ Pass. उप्यते.

---

* The Âtmanepada forms will in future only be given when they have peculiarities of their own, or are otherwise difficult.

101. वह् *vah*, to carry.

P. वहति ॥ Pf. 1. उवाह (*ă*), 2. उवहिथ or उवोढ, 3. उवाह, 4. ऊहिव, 5. ऊहुः, 6. ऊहतुः, 7. ऊहिम, 8. ऊह, 9. ऊहुः, I A. 1. अवाक्षं, 2. अवाक्षीः, 3. अवाक्षीत्, 4. अवाक्ष, 5. अवोढं, 6. अवोढां, 7. अवाक्ष्म, 8. अवोढ, 9. अवाक्षुः, I Aor. Âtm. 1. अवक्षि, 2. अवोढाः, 3. अवोढ, 4. अवक्ष्वहि, 5. अवक्षार्थां, 6. अवक्षातां, 7. अवक्ष्महि, 8. अवोढ्वं, 9. अवक्षत, F. वक्ष्यति, P. F. वोढा, B. उह्यात् ॥ Pt. ऊढः, Adj. वाह्यः ॥ Pass. उह्यते, Caus. वाहयति, Aor. अवीवहत्, Des. विवक्षति, Int. वावह्यते, वावोढि.

102. वे *ve*, to weave, (वेञ्.)

P. वयति ॥ Pf. 3. ववौ, 6. ववुः (or ऊवुः), 9. ववुः (or ऊवुः); or 3. उवाय, 6. ऊयतुः, 9. ऊयुः (§ 311), I A. 1. अवासिषं, 2. अवासीः, 3. अवासीत्, Âtm. अवास्त, F. वास्यति, P. F. वाता, B. ऊयात्, Âtm. वासीष्ट ॥ Pt. उत: (Pân. VI. 4, 2) ॥ Pass. ऊयते, Caus. वाययति, Des. विवासति, Int. वावाय्यते, वावाति.

103. ह्वे *hve*, to emulate, to call, (ह्वेञ्.)

P. ह्वयति ॥ Pf. 1. जुहाव (*ă*), 2. जुहविथ or जुहोथ, 3. जुहाव, 4. जुहुविव, II A. अह्वत् (§ 363), Âtm. अह्वत, or I A. अह्वास्त, F. ह्वास्यति, B. हूयात् ॥ Pt. हूत:, Ger. °हूय ॥ Pass. हूयते, Aor. अह्वायि, Caus. ह्वाययति, Aor. अजूहवत् (§ 371), Des. जुहूषति, Int. जोहूयते, जोहोति.

Tud Class (Tudâdi, VI Class).

I. Parasmaipada and Âtmanepada Verbs.

104. तुद् *tud*, to strike.

P. तुदति ॥ Pf. तुतोद, F. तोत्स्यति, P. F. तोत्ता, I A. अतौत्सीत्, Âtm. अतुत्त ॥ Pt. तुन्न:, Ger. तुत्त्वा ॥ Pass. तुद्यते, Caus. तोदयति, Aor. अतूतुदत्, Des. तुतुत्सति, Int. तोतुद्यते, तोतोत्ति.

105. भ्रज्ज् *bhrajj*, to fry, (भ्रस्ज्.)

भ्रस्ज् *bhrajj* takes Samprasâraṇa before weakening terminations, the same as ग्रह् *grah*, ज्या *jyâ*, वय् *vay*, व्यध् *vyadh*, वश् *vaś*, व्यच् *vyach*, व्रश्च् *vraśch*, प्रछ् *prachh* (Pân. VI. 1, 16). The terminations of the special tenses of Tud verbs are never strengthening, but weakening, if possible.

P. भृज्जति ॥ Pf. 1. बभर्ज्ज, 2. बभर्जिथ or बभ्रष्ट, 9. बभ्रज्जुः (Pân. I. 2, 5), or बभर्ज्जे &c. (Pân. VI. 4, 47), I A. अभार्क्षीत् or अभ्राक्षीत्, Âtm. अभ्रष्ट or अभर्ष्ट, F. भ्रक्ष्यति or भर्क्ष्यति, P. F. भ्रष्टा or भर्ष्टा, B. भृज्ज्यात्, Âtm. भृक्षीष्ट or भर्क्षीष्ट ॥ Pt. भृष्ट: ॥ Pass. भृज्ज्यते, Caus. भर्ज्जयति, Aor. अवभर्ज्जत् or अवभ्रज्जत्, Des. विभ्रज्जति or विभर्क्षति, Int. वरीभृज्ज्यते.

106. कृष् *kṛish*, to draw a line. (See No. 38.)

P. कृषति ॥ Pf. चकर्ष, I A. अकार्क्षीत् or अक्राक्षीत्, Âtm. अकृष्ट or अकृष्ट, F. कर्क्ष्यति or क्रक्ष्यति, P. F. कर्ष्टा or क्रष्टा, B. कृष्यात्, Âtm. कृक्षीष्ट ॥ Pt. कृष्ट: ॥ Pass. कृष्यते, Caus. कर्षयति, Aor. अचकर्षत् or अचीकृषत्, Des. चिकृक्षति, Int. चरीकृष्यते.

107. मुच् *much*, to loosen, (मुचॢ.)

Certain verbs beginning with मुच् *much* take a nasal in the special tenses. They are, मुच् *much*, लुप् *lup*, to cut, विद् *vid*, to find, लिप् *lip*, to paint, सिच् *sich*, to sprinkle, कृत् *krit*, to cut, खिद् *khid*, to pain, पिश् *piś*, to form. (Pân. VII. 1, 59.)

P. मुंचति ॥ Pf. मुमोच, I A. अमुचत्, Âtm. अमुक्त (§ 367), Des. मुमुक्षति or मोक्षते (§ 471, 9).

108. विद् *vid*, to find, (विदॢ.)

P. विंदति ॥ Pf. विवेद, II A. अविदत्, Âtm. अविद्ध, F. वेत्स्यति or वेदिष्यति (§ 332, 11) ॥ Pt. विन्न:.

109. लिप् *lip*, to paint.

P. लिंपति ॥ Pf. लिलेप, II A. अलिपत् (§ 367), Âtm. II A. अलिपत or I A. अलिप्त (§ 367).

II. Parasmaipada Verbs.

110. कृत् *krit*, to cut, (कृती.)

P. कृंतति (see No. 107) ॥ Pf. चकर्त, I A. अकर्तीत्, F. कर्तिष्यति or कर्त्स्यति (§ 337, II. 2), P. F. कर्तिता, B. कृत्यात् ॥ Pt. कृत्त: ॥ Pass. कृत्यते, Caus. कर्तयति, Aor. अचकर्तत् or अचीकृतत्, Des. चिकर्तिषति or चिकृत्सति (§ 337, II. 2), Int. चरीकृत्यते.

111. कुट् *kut*, to be crooked, to bend.

Certain verbs beginning with कुट् *kut* (Dhâtupâṭha 28, 73–108) do not admit of Guṇa or Vṛiddhi, except in the reduplicated perfect, the causative, and the intensive Parasmaipada. (Pân. I. 2, 1; § 345, note.)

P. कुटति ॥ Pf. 1. चुकोट, 2. चुकुटिष, I A. अकुटीत्, F. कुटिष्यति, P. F. कुटिता ॥ Caus. कोटयति, Int. चोकुट्यते, चोकोट्टि.

112. व्रश्च् *vraśch*, to cut, (ओव्रश्चू.)

P. वृश्चति (see No. 105) ॥ Pf. 1. ववर्श्च, 2. ववृश्चिष or ववर्ष्ट, I A. अव्रश्चीत् or अव्राक्षीत् (§ 337, I. 2), F. व्रश्चिष्यति or व्रक्ष्यति, B. वृश्च्यात् ॥ Pt. वृक्ण:.

113. कृ *krī*, to scatter.

P. किरति ॥ Pf. 3. चकार, 6. चकरतु:, 9. चकरु: (Pân. VII. 4, 11), I A. अकारीत्, F. करिष्यति or करीष्यति (§ 340), B. कीर्यात् ॥ Pt. कीर्ण: ॥ Pass. कीर्यते, Caus. कारयति, Des. चिकरिषति.

Note—After उप and प्रति, कृ takes an initial स् if it means to cut or to strike: उपस्किरति he cuts, उपस्कार; प्रतिस्किरति he cuts or he strikes (Pân. VI. 1, 140, 141). Also अपस्किरते he drops (Pân. VI. 1, 142).

114. स्पृश् *spriś*, to touch.

P. स्पृशति ॥ Pf. पस्पर्श, I A. अस्प्राक्षीत् or अस्पार्क्षीत् or अस्पृक्षत्, F. स्प्रक्ष्यति or स्पर्क्ष्यति, B. स्पृश्यात् ॥ Pt. स्पृष्ट: ॥ Des. पिस्पृक्षति, Int. परीस्पृश्यते, परीस्पर्ष्टि.

115. प्रछ् *prachh*, to ask.

P. पृछति (see No. 105) ॥ Pf. 1. पप्रच्छ, 2. पप्रच्छिष or पप्रष्ट, 9. पप्रच्छु: (§ 328), I A. अप्राक्षीत्, F. प्रक्ष्यति, B. पृच्छ्यात् ॥ Pt. पृष्ट: ॥ Pass. पृच्छ्यते, Caus. प्रच्छयति, Des. पिपृच्छिषति, Int. परीपृच्छ्यते.

116. सृज् *srij*, to let off.

P. सृजति ॥ Pf. 1. ससर्ज, 2. ससर्जिथ or ससृष्ट (see No. 48), I A. अस्राक्षीत्, F. स्रक्ष्यति ॥ Pt. सृष्ट:.

117. मज्ज् *majj*, to sink, (मस्जो.)

मज्ज् *majj* and नश् *naś* (Div) insert a nasal before strengthening terminations beginning with consonants, except nasals and semivowels. (Pân. VII. 1, 60.)

P. मज्जति ॥ Pf. 1. ममज्ज, 2. ममज्जिथ or ममंक्थ, I A. 3. अमांक्षीत् (§ 345), 6. अमांक्त्, 9. अमांक्षु:, F. मंक्ष्यति, P. F. मंक्ता ॥ Pt. मग्न:, Ger. मंक्त्वा or मक्त्वा (§ 438) ॥ Caus. मज्जयति, Aor. अममज्जत्, Des. मिमंक्षति, Int. मामज्ज्यते, मामंक्ति.

118. इष् *ish*, to wish, (इषु.)

P. इच्छति (see No. 31), I. एष्यात् ॥ Pf. 1. इयेष, 2. इयेषिथ, 3. इयेष, 4. ईषिव, 5. ईषयु:, 6. ईषयु:, 7. ईषिम, 8. ईष, 9. ईषु:, I A. ऐषीत्, F. एषिष्यति, P. F. एष्टा or एषिता (§ 337, II. 1) ॥ Pt. इष्ट: Ger. इष्ट्वा or एषित्वा ॥ Pass. इष्यते, Aor. एषि, Caus. एषयति, Aor. ऐषिषत्, Des. एषिषिषति.

III. Âtmanepada Verbs.

119. मृ *mri*, to die, (मृङ्.)

मृ *mri*, to die, though an Âtmanepada verb, takes Âtmanepada forms only in the special tenses, the aorist, and benedictive. (Pân. I. 3, 61.)

P. त्रियते*, I. अत्रियत, O. त्रियेत, I. त्रिये ॥ Pf. 1. ममार, 2. ममर्थ, 3. ममार, 4. मम्रिव, 5. मम्रयु:, I A. 1. अमृषि, 2. अमृषा:, 3. अमृत, F. मरिष्यति, P. F. मर्तासि, B. म्रिषीष्ट ॥ Pt. मृत: ॥ Pass. त्रियते, Caus. मारयति, Des. मुमूर्षति, Int. मेम्रीयते.

120. दृ *dri*, to observe, (दृङ्.)

P. द्रियते ॥ Pf. दद्रे, I A. अदृत, F. दरिष्यते, P. F. दर्ता, B. दृषीष्ट ॥ Pass. द्रियते, Caus. दारयति, Des. दिदरिषते (§ 332, 5). It is chiefly used with the preposition आ to regard, to consider.

Div Class (*Divâdi, IV Class*).

I. Parasmaipada Verbs.

121. दिव् *div*, to play, (दिवु.)

P. दीव्यति (§ 143) ॥ Pf. दिदेव, I A. अदेवीत्, F. देविष्यति, P. F. देविता, B. दीव्यात् ॥ Pt. द्यून: or द्यूत: (§ 442, 7), Ger. द्यूत्वा (§ 431, 1) or देवित्वा ॥ Caus. देवयति, Des. दिदेविषति or दुद्यूषति (§ 474), Int. देदीव्यते.

122. नृत् *nrit*, to dance, (नृती.)

P. नृत्यति ॥ Pf. 3. ननर्त, 9. ननृतु:, I A. अनर्तीत्, F. नर्तिष्यति or नर्त्स्यति (§ 337, II. 2) ॥ Pt. नृत्त: ॥ Caus. नर्तयति, Aor. अननर्तत् or अनीनृतत्, Des. निनर्तिषति or निनृत्सति.

---

* Final ऋ is changed to रि (§ 110) in the special tenses of Tud verbs, likewise before the य of the passive and benedictive (Pân. VII. 4, 28). Afterwards रि again becomes रिय्, according to Pân. VI. 4, 77.

123. नॄ *jṛí*, to grow old, (मॄ.)

P. जीर्यति* ॥ Pf. 3. जजार, 9. जजरुः (Guṇa, § 330) or जेरुः (§ 328, 2), I A. अजारीत् or II A. अजरत् (§ 367), F. जरिष्यति or जरीष्यति (§ 340), B. जीर्यात् ॥ Pt. जीर्णः ॥ Caus. जरयति (§ 462, 25), Des. जिजरिषति or जिजीर्षति (§ 337, II. 3).

124. ष्णो *śo*, to sharpen.

Verbs ending in ओ *o* drop ओ *o* before the य *ya* of the Div class (Pâṇ. vii. 3, 71); e. g. छो *chho*, to cut, सो *so*, to finish, दो *do*, to cut.

P. श्यति, I. अश्यात्, O. श्येत्, I. श्यतु ॥ Pf. शशौ (§ 329), I A. अशासीत् or II A. अशात्, F. शास्यति, P. F. शाता, B. शायात् (§ 392) ॥ Pt. शातः or शितः (§ 435) ॥ Pass. शायते, Caus. शाययति, Des. शिशासति, Int. शाशायते.

125. सो *so*, to finish.

P. स्यति ॥ Pf. ससौ, I A. असासीत्, II A. असात्, F. सास्यति, P. F. साता, B. सेयात् (§ 392) ॥ Pt. सितः, Ger. °साय ॥ Pass. सीयते (§ 392), Caus. साययति, Des. सिसासति, Int. सेसीयते.

126. व्यध् *vyadh*, to strike.

P. विध्यति (see No. 105) ॥ Pf. 3. विव्याध (§ 311), 9. विविधुः, I A. 1. अव्यात्सं, 2. अव्यात्सीः, 3. अव्यात्सीत्, 4. अव्यात्स्व, 5. अव्यात्सं, 6. अव्यात्स्वा, 7. अव्यात्स्म, 8. अव्याद्ध, 9. अव्यात्सुः, F. व्यत्स्यति, P. F. व्यद्धा, B. विध्यात् ॥ Pt. विद्धः ॥ Pass. विध्यते, Caus. व्याधयति, Des. विव्यत्सति, Int. वेविध्यते.

127. तृप् *tṛip*, to delight.

P. तृप्यति ॥ Pf. 1. ततर्प, 2. ततर्पिथ or ततर्प्थ or तत्रप्थ, 3. ततर्प, 4. ततृपिव or तत्रृप्व, I A. अतर्पीत् or अतार्प्सीत् (§ 337, I. 3) or अत्राप्सीत् (see No. 38) or II A. अतृपत्, F. तर्पिष्यति or तर्प्स्यति or त्रप्स्यति, P. F. तर्पिता, तर्प्ता or त्रप्ता, B. तृप्यात् ॥ Pt. तृप्तः ॥ Pass. तृप्यते, Caus. तर्पयति, Aor. अतीतृपत् or अततर्पत्, Des. तितृप्सति or तितर्पिषति, Int. तरीतृप्यते.

128. मुह् *muh*, to be foolish.

P. मुह्यति ॥ Pf. 1. मुमोह, 2. मुमोहिथ or मुमोग्ध or मुमोढ, II A. अमुहत् (§ 367, पुषादि)†, F. मोक्ष्यति or मोहिष्यति, P. F. मोग्धा or मोढा (§ 129) or मोहिता ॥ Pt. मुग्धः or मूढः ॥ Pass. मुह्यते, Caus. मोहयति, Des. मुमुक्षति, मुमोहिषति or मुमुहिषति, Int. मोमुह्यते, मोमोहि or मोमोढि.

---

* Final ॠ, changed to इर्, and lengthened before य.

† The Sârasvatî gives besides the second aorist the optional forms of the first aorist अमोहीत् or अमौक्षीत् (§ 337, I. 3, रधादि) or अमुक्षत् (§ 360). According to Pâṇ. iii. 1, 55 (§ 367), the forms of the first aorist are allowed in the Âtmanepada only; but later grammarians frequently admit forms as optional which are opposed to the grammatical system of Pâṇini. Sometimes the evasion of the strict rules of Pâṇini may be explained by the admission of different roots, as, for instance, in No. 130, where the first aorist Parasmaipada अझमीत्, given in the Sârasvatî, which is wrong in the Div class, might be referred to the Krí class.

129. नश् *naś*, to perish, (णश्.)

P. नश्यति ॥ Pf. 3. ननाश, 9. नेशुः, II A. अनशत् (पुषादि) or अनेशत् (§ 366), F. नशिष्यति or नंक्ष्यति (see No. 117) ॥ Pt. नष्टः, Ger. नष्ट्वा or नंष्ट्वा (§ 438).

130. शम् *śam*, to cease, (शमु.)

Eight Div verbs, शम् *śam*, तम् *tam*, दम् *dam*, श्रम् *śram*, भ्रम् *bhram*, क्षम् *ksham*, क्लम् *klam*, मद् *mad*, lengthen their vowel in the special tenses. (Pâṇ. VII. 3, 74.)

P. शाम्यति ॥ Pf. 3. शशाम, 9. शेमुः, II A. अशमत्, F. शमिष्यति, P. F. शमिता ॥ Pt. शांतः (§ 429), Ger. शांत्वा or शमित्वा ॥ Pass. शम्यते, Caus. शमयति (§ 462) he quiets, but शामयते or °ति he sees. (Dhâtupâṭha 19, 70.)

131. मिद् *mid*, to be wet, (निमिदा.)

मिद् *mid* takes Guṇa in the special tenses. (Pâṇ. VII. 3, 82.)

P. मेद्यति ॥ Pt. मिन्नः wet, or मेदितः (§ 333, D. 2*).

II. Âtmanepada Verbs.

132. जन् *jan*, to spring up, (जनी.)

जन् *jan* substitutes जा *jâ* in the special tenses. (Pâṇ. VII. 3, 79.)

P. जायते ॥ Pf. जज्ञे (§ 328, 3), I A. अजनिष्ट or अजनि (§ 413), F. जनिष्यते, P. F. जनिता, B. जनिषीष्ट ॥ Pt. जातः, Caus. जनयति, Des. जिजनिषते, Int. जाजायते or जंजन्यते.

133. पद् *pad*, to go.

P. पद्यते ॥ Pf. पेदे, I A. 3. अपादि (§ 412), 6. अपत्साताम्, 9. अपत्सत, F. पत्स्यते, P. F. पत्ता, B. पत्सीष्ट ॥ Pt. पन्नः ॥ Caus. पादयति, Aor. अपीपदत्, Des. पित्सते (§ 471, 9), Int. पनीपद्यते (§ 485).

134. बुध् *budh*, to perceive.

P. बुध्यते ॥ Pf. बुबुधे, I A. 1. अभुत्सि, 2. अबुद्धाः, 3. अबुद्ध or अबोधि, 4. अभुत्स्वहि, 5. अभुत्सायां, 6. अभुत्सातां, 7. अभुत्स्महि, 8. अभुद्ध्वं, 9. अभुत्सत, F. भोत्स्यते, P. F. बोद्धा, B. भुत्सीष्ट ॥ Pt. बुद्धः ॥ Caus. बोधयति, Aor. अबूबुधत्, Des. बुभुत्सते (बुध् of the Div class can *never* take intermediate इ, see § 332, 12; see also Kuhn, Beiträge, vol. VI. p. 104), Int. बोबुध्यते.

III. Parasmaipada and Âtmanepada Verbs.

135. नह् *nah*, to bind, (णह्.)

P. नह्यति or °ते ॥ Pf. 1. ननाह, 2. ननद्ध (§ 130) or नेहिथ, Âtm. नेहे, I A. 1. अनात्सं, 2. अनात्सीः, 3. अनात्सीत्, 4. अनात्स्व, 5. अनाद्ध्वं, 6. अनाद्धां, 7. अनात्स्त, 8. अनाद्ध, 9. अनात्सुः, Âtm. 1. अनत्सि, 2. अनद्धाः, 3. अनद्ध, 4. अनत्स्वहि, 5. अनत्सावहि, 6. अनत्सातां, 7. अनत्स्महि, 8. अनद्ध्वं, 9. अनत्सत, F. नत्स्यति, P. F. नद्धा ॥ Pt. नद्धः, Ger. नद्ध्वा, °नह्य ॥ Pass. नह्यते, Aor. अनाहि, Caus. नाहयति, Des. निनत्सते, Int. नानह्यते.

Chur Class (Churâdi, X Class).

Parasmaipada Verbs only.

136. चुर् *chur*, to steal.

P. चोरयति ॥ Pf. चोरयांचकार, I A. अचूचुरत्, F. चोरयिष्यति, P. F. चोरयिता, B. चोर्यात् (§ 386) ॥ Pt. चोरितः, Ger. चोरयित्वा ॥ Pass. चोर्यते, Caus. चोरयति, Des. चुचोरयिषति. No Intensive (§ 479).

137. चि *chi*, to gather, (चिञ्.)

The changes which roots undergo as causatives, take likewise place if the same roots are treated as Chur verbs. Hence according to § 463, II. 6, चि, as a Chur verb, may form P. चपयति or चपयति, the vowel, however, remaining short because, as a Chur verb, चि is said to be चिङ् (§ 462, note) ॥ I A. अचीचपत् or अचीचयत्, B. चप्यात् or चय्यात्.

Note—Several Chur verbs are marked as चिङ्, i. e. as not lengthening their vowel, some of which were mentioned in § 462, among the causatives. Such are ज्ञप् to know, to make known; चप् to pound; चह् to pound; यम्, if it means to feed; चल् to live.

138. कृत् *krît*, to praise.

P. कीर्तयति (§ 462, 2) ॥ I A. अचीकृतत् or अचिकीर्तत् (§ 377).

Su Class (Svâdi, V Class).

I. Parasmaipada and Âtmanepada Verbs.

139. सु *su*, to distil, (षुञ्.)

P. सुनोति, I. 2. सुनु (§ 321 *) ॥ Pf. सुषाव, Âtm. सुषुवे, I A. असावीत् (§ 332, 4); the Sârasvatî allows also असौषीत् (but against Pâṇ. VII. 2, 72), Âtm. असोष्ट; the Sâr. allows also असविष्ट (but see Pâṇ. VII. 2, 72); F. सोष्यति, P. F. सोता, B. सूयात् ॥ Pass. सूयते, Aor. असावि, Caus. सावयति, Aor. असूषवत्, Des. सुसूषति, Int. सोषूयते.

Note—The उ of नु may be dropt before terminations beginning with व or म, and not requiring Guṇa; but this is not the case if नु is preceded by a consonant. This explains the double forms सुनुमः and सुन्वः, सुनुमः and सुम्मः, असुनुव and असुन्व, असुनुव and असुम्म; and Âtm. सुनुवहे or सुन्वहे, सुनुमहे or सुम्महे, असुनुवहि or असुन्वहि, असुनुमहि or असुम्महि. The same rule applies to the Tan verbs.

140. चि *chi*, to collect, (चिञ्.)

P. चिनोति ॥ Pf. 3. चिचाय or चिकाय, 2. चिचेय or चिकेय or, according to Bharadvâja (§ 335, 3), चिचियिय or चिकियिय, 9. चिच्युः or चिक्युः, Âtm. चिच्ये or चिक्ये (Pâṇ. VII. 3, 58), I A. अचैषीत्, Âtm. अचेष्ट, F. चेष्यति, P. F. चेता, B. चीयात् ॥ Pass. चीयते, Caus. चाययति or चापयति (§ 463, II. 6, and No. 137), Des. चिचीषति or चिकीषति (Pâṇ. VII. 3, 58), Int. चेचीयते.

141. स्तृ *strî*, to cover, (स्तृञ्.)

P. स्तृणोति ॥ Pf. तस्तार, Âtm. तस्तरे, I A. अस्तारीत्, Âtm. अस्तरिष्ट (not अस्तृत,

if स्वादि) or खभूत (§ 332, 5, a rule which applies to the Âtmanepada only),
F. स्तरिष्यति (§ 332, 5), P. F. स्तरीता, B. स्तर्यात्, Âtm. स्तृषीष्ट or स्तरिषीष्ट (§ 332, 5) ॥
Pass. स्तर्यते, Caus. स्तारयति, Des. तिस्तीर्षति, Int. तास्तर्यते.

142. वृ *vṛi*, to choose, (वृञ्.)

P. वृणोति ॥ Pf. 1. ववार (å), 2. ववरिथ*, 3. ववार, 4. ववृव, 5. ववृप्रुः, 6. ववृतुः,
7. ववृम, 8. ववृ, 9. ववृः, I A. अवारीत् (§ 332, 5), Âtm. अवरिष्ट or अवृत (§ 340) or
अवृत (§ 337, II. 4), F. वरिष्यति or वरीष्यति, P. F. वरिता or वरीता, B. व्रियात्, Âtm.
वरिषीष्ट (not वरीषीष्ट, Pâṇ. vii. 2, 39) ॥ Pass. व्रियते, Aor. अवारि, Caus. वारयति,
Des. विवरिषति, विवरीषति or वुवूर्षति, Int. वेवूर्यते.

II. Parasmaipada Verbs.

143. हि *hi*, to go, to grow.

P. हिनोति ॥ Pf. जिघाय (Pâṇ. vii. 3, 56), I A. अहैषीत्, F. हेष्यति, P. F. हेता,
B. हीयात् ॥ Caus. हाययति, Aor. अजीहयत् (Pâṇ. vii. 3, 56), Des. जिघीषति, Int.
जेहीयते.

144. शक् *śak*, to be able, (शक्नु.)

P. शक्नोति ॥ Pf. 3. शशाक, 9. शेकुः, I A. अशकत्, F. शक्ष्यति, P. F. शक्ता ॥ Pt. शक्तः ॥
Pass. शक्यते (कर्तुं शक्यते it can be done), Caus. शाकयति, Aor. अशीशकत्, Des.
शिक्षति, Int. शाशक्यते.

145. शु *śru*, to hear.

This verb is by native grammarians classed with the Bhû verbs, though as irregular. It
substitutes शृ *śṛi* for शु *śru* in the special tenses.

P. 3. शृणोति, 6. शृणुतः, 9. शृण्वन्ति; 4. शृणुवः or शृण्वः ॥ Pf. 1. शुश्राव (å), 2. शुश्रोथ
(§ 334, 8), 3. शुश्राव, 4. शुश्रुव, 5. शुश्रुवुः, 6. शुश्रुवतुः, 7. शुश्रुम, 8. शुश्रुव, 9. शुश्रुः,
I A. अश्रौषीत्, F. श्रोष्यति, P. F. श्रोता, B. श्रूयात् ॥ Pass. श्रूयते, Aor. अश्रावि, Caus.
श्रावयति, Aor. अशुश्रवत् or अशिश्रवत् (§ 475), Des. शुश्रूषते (Pâṇ. i. 3, 57), Int. शोश्रूयते.

146. आप् *âp*, to obtain, (आप्नु.)

P. 3. आप्नोति, 4. आप्नुवः, 9. आप्नुवन्ति, I. आप्नोत्, O. आप्नुयात्, I. 3. आप्नोतु, 2. आप्नुहि ॥
Pf. आप, Aor. आपत्, F. आप्स्यति, P. F. आप्ता ॥ Pt. आप्तः ॥ Pass. आप्यते, Caus. आपयति,
Aor. आपिपत्, Des. ईप्सति.

III. Âtmanepada Verbs.

147. अश् *aś*, to pervade, (अशू.)

P. 3. अश्नुते, 6. अश्नुवाते, 9. अश्नुवते, 4. अश्नुवहे, I. 1. आश्नुवि, 2. आश्नुयाः, 3. आश्नुत,
4. आश्नुवहि, 5. आश्नुवार्या, 6. आश्नुवाता, 7. आश्नुमहि, 8. आश्नुध्वं, 9. आश्नुवत, O. अश्नुवीत,
I. 1. अश्नवै, 2. अश्नुध्वम्, 3. अश्नुतां, 4. अश्नवावहै, 5. अश्नुवार्यां, 6. अश्नुवातां, 7. अश्नवामहै,
8. अश्नुध्वं, 9. अश्नुवतां ॥ Pf. 1. आनशे, 2. आनशिषे or आनशे, I A. 1. आशि, 2. आशाः,

---

* According to Pâṇ. vii. 2, 13, we might form ववर्थ; but Pâṇ. vii. 2, 63, would sanction
ववरिथ. The special restriction, however, of ववर्थ to the Veda in Pâṇ. vii. 2, 64, is sufficient
to fix ववरिथ as the proper form in ordinary Sanskrit.

3. आह, 4. आह्लहि, 5. आख्यायां, 6. आख्यातां, 7. आह्लहि, 8. आहृध्वं, 9. आख्यत; or 1. आशिषि, 2. आशिष:, 3. आशिष्ट, P.F. अश्ट or अशिष्टा, F. अख्स्यते or अशिष्यते, B. अष्ठीष्ट or अशिषीष्ट ॥ Pt. अष्ट: ॥ Pass. अश्यते, Aor. आशि, Caus. आश्रयति, Aor. आशिश्रत्, Des. अशिशिषते, Int. अशाश्यते.

Tan Class (Tanvâdi, VIII Class).

All verbs belonging to this class are Parasmaipada and Âtmanepada Verbs.

148. तन् *tan,* to stretch, (तनु.)

P. तनोति, I. अतनोत्, O. तनुयात्, I. तनोतु; Âtm. P. तनुते, I. अतनुत, O. तन्वीत, I. तनुतां ॥ Pf. 3. ततान, 9. तेनु:, I A. अतानीत् or अतनीत् (§ 348), Âtm. 3. अतनिष्ट or अतत (§ 369), 2. अतनिष्ठा: or अतथा:, F. तनिष्यति, P. F. तनिता, B. तन्यात्, Âtm. तनिषीष्ट ॥ Pt. तत:, Ger. तत्वा or तनित्वा ॥ Pass. तायते or तन्यते (§ 391), Caus. तानयति, Aor. अतीतनत्, Des. तितनिषति or तितांसति, Int. तंतन्यते.

Note—Verbs of the Tan class may raise their penultimate short vowel by Guṇa; चुद् to go, अर्चोति or चुणोति. तनादेरुपधाया गुणो वा पिति, Sâr. II. 11, 3.

149. क्षण् *kshaṇ,* to kill, (क्षणु.)

P. क्षणोति ॥ Pf. चक्षाण, I A. अक्षणीत् (§ 348*), Âtm. 3. अक्षविष्ट or अक्षत, 2. अक्षविष्ठा: or अक्षथा:.

150. क्षिण् *kshiṇ,* to kill.

P. क्षिणोति or क्षेणोति ॥ I A. अक्षेणीत्, Âtm. अक्षेविष्ट or अक्षित.

151. सन् *san,* to obtain, (सनु.)

P. सनोति ॥ Pf. ससान, Âtm. सेने, I A. असानीत् (â), Âtm. असनिष्ट or असात (Pâṇ. II. 4, 79; VI. 4, 42).

152. कृ *kṛi,* to do, (डुकृञ्.)

कृ *kṛi* before weak terminations becomes कर् *kar,* but before strong terminations कुर् *kur.* Before व् *v* and म् *m,* and the य् *y* of the optative, the Vikaraṇa उ *u* is rejected, but the radical उ *u* is not lengthened.

P. 1. करोमि, 2. करोषि, 3. करोति, 4. कुर्व:, 5. कुरुष:, 6. कुरुत:, 7. कुर्म:, 8. कुरुथ, 9. कुर्वंति, I. 1. अकरवं, 2. अकरो:, 3. अकरोत्, 4. अकुर्व, 5. अकुरुतां, 6. अकुरुतां, 7. अकुर्म, 8. अकुरुत, 9. अकुर्वन्, O. 1. कुर्यां, 9. कुर्यु:, I. 1. करवाणि, 2. कुरु, 3. करोतु, 4. करवाव, 5. कुरुतां, 6. कुरुतां, 7. करवाम, 8. कुरुत, 9. कुर्वंतु ॥ Pf. 1. चकार (â), 2. चकर्थ, 3. चकार, 4. चकृव, 5. चक्रुष:, 6. चक्रतु:, 7. चकृम, 8. चक्र, 9. चक्रु:, I A. 1. अकार्षं, 2. अकार्षी:, 3. अकार्षीत्, 4. अकार्ष्व, 5. अकार्ष्ट, 6. अकार्ष्टां, 7. अकार्ष्म, 8. अकार्ष्ट, 9. अकार्षु:, F. करिष्यति, P. F. कर्ता, B. 1. क्रियासं, 2. क्रिया:, 3. क्रियात्, 4. क्रियास्व, 5. क्रियास्तं, 6. क्रियास्तां, 7. क्रियास्म, 8. क्रियास्त, 9. क्रियासु:.

Âtmanepada: P. 1. कुर्वे, 2. कुरुषे, 3. कुरुते, 4. कुर्वहे, 5. कुर्वाथे, 6. कुर्वाते, 7. कुर्महे, 8. कुरुध्वे, 9. कुर्वते, I. 1. अकुर्वि, 2. अकुरुथा:, 3. अकुरुत, 4. अकुर्वहि, 5. अकुर्वाथां, 6. अकुर्वातां, 7. अकुर्महि, 8. अकुरुध्वं, 9. अकुर्वत, O. 1. कुर्वीय &c., I. 1. करवै, 2. कुरुष्व, 3. कुरुतां, 4. करवावहै, 5. कुर्वाथां, 6. कुर्वातां, 7. करवामहै, 8. कुरुध्वं, 9. कुर्वतां ॥ Pf. 1. चक्रे, 2. चकृषे, 3. चक्रे,

4. ववृवहे, 5. वक्राथे, 6. वक्राते, 7. ववृमहे, 8. ववृद्वे, 9. वक्रिरे, I A. 1. अकृषि, 2. अकृथाः, 3. अकृत, 4. अकृव्वहि, 5. अकृवाथां, 6. अकृवातां, 7. अकृष्महि, 8. अकृद्वं, 9. अकृषत, F. करिष्यते, B. 3. कृषीष्ट, 8. कृषीद्वं ॥

Pt. कृतः, Ger. कृत्वा ॥ Pass. क्रियते, Aor. अकारि, Caus. कारयति, Aor. अचीकरत्, Des. चिकीर्षति, Int. चेक्रीयते, चर्कर्ति &c., or चर्करीति &c. (§ 490).

Krî Class (Kryâdi, IX Class).

I. Parasmaipada and Âtmanepada Verbs.

153. क्री *krî*, to buy, (डुक्रीञ्.)

P. क्रीणाति ॥ Pf. 1. चिक्राय (*ā̂*), 2. चिक्रयिथ or चिक्रेथ, 3. चिक्राय, 4. चिक्रियिव, 5. चिक्रियुः, 6. चिक्रियतुः, 7. चिक्रियिथ, 8. चिक्रिय, 9. चिक्रियुः, I A. अक्रैषीत्, Âtm. अक्रेष्ट, F. क्रेष्यति, P. F. क्रेता, B. क्रीयात्, Âtm. क्रेषीष्ट ॥ Pt. क्रीतः ॥ Pass. क्रीयते, Caus. क्रापयति, Des. चिक्रीषति, Int. चेक्रीयते.

154. मी *mî*, to kill, (मीञ्.)

The roots मी *mî*, मि *mi* (Su), and दी *dî* (Div) take final आ *â* whenever their ई *î* or इ *i* would be liable to Guṇa or Vṛiddhi, and in the gerund in य *ya* (§ 452). Pâṇ. VI. 1, 50.

P. मीनाति ॥ Pf. 1. ममौ, 2. ममाथ or ममिथ, 3. ममौ, 4. मिमिथिव, 5. मिम्युः, 6. मिम्यतुः, 7. मिमियथ, 8. मिम्य, 9. मिम्युः, I A. अमासीत् (§ 353), Âtm. अमास्त (§ 353), F. मास्यति, P. F. माता, B. मीयात्, Âtm. मासीष्ट ॥ Pt. मीतः, Ger. मीत्वा, °माय ॥ Pass. मीयते, Caus. मापयति (§ 463, II. 19), Des. मित्सति (§ 471, 8), Int. मेमीयते.

155. स्तम्भ *stambh*, to support, (स्तम्भु.)

The verbs स्तम्भ *stambh*, स्तुम्भ *stumbh*, स्कम्भ *skambh*, स्कुम्भ *skumbh*, and स्कु *sku* may be conjugated as Krî or as Su verbs.

P. स्तभ्नाति or स्तभ्नोति &c., I. अस्तभ्नात्, O. स्तभ्नीयात्, I. 1. स्तभ्नानि, 2. स्तभान*, 3. स्तभ्नातु, 4. स्तभ्नाव, 5. स्तभ्नीत, 6. स्तभ्नीतां, 7. स्तभ्नाम, 8. स्तभ्नीत, 9. स्तभ्नन्तु ॥ Pf. तस्तम्भ, I A. अस्तम्भीत् or II A. अस्तभत् (§ 367), F. स्तम्भिष्यति, P. F. स्तम्भिता, B. स्तभ्यात् ॥ Pt. स्तब्धः, Ger. स्तम्भित्वा or स्तब्ध्वा ॥ Pass. स्तभ्यते, Caus. स्तम्भयति, Des. तिस्तम्भिषति, Int. तास्तभ्यते.

156. पू *pû*, to purify, (पूञ्.)

The Krî verbs beginning with पू *pû* shorten their vowel in the special tenses (Pâṇ. VII. 3, 80). They stand Dhâtupâṭha 31, 12—32. The more important are, लू *lû*, to cut, स्तृ *strî*, to cover, वृ *vrî*, to choose, धू *dhû*, to shake, पृ *prî*, to fill, दृ *drî*, to tear, जृ *jrî*, to wither.

P. पुनाति, Âtm. पुनीते ॥ Pf. पुपाव, Âtm. पुपुवे, I A. अपावीत्, Âtm. अपविष्ट, F. पविष्यति, P. F. पविता ॥ Pt. पूतः, Ger. पूत्वा (पवितः and पवित्वा (§ 424) belong to पूङ्, पवते (Bhû class), see § 333. D) ॥ Pass. पूयते, Caus. पावयति, Aor. अपीपवत्, Des. पुपूषति (पिपविषते belongs to पूङ्, पवते, Bhû class, Pâṇ. VII. 2, 74), Int. पोपूयते.

---

* Krî verbs ending in consonants form the 2nd pers. sing. imperative in आन; § 321, note 2.

157. ग्रह् *grah*, to take.

This root takes Samprasâraṇa in the special tenses and before other weakening terminations.
(Pâṇ. VI. 1, 16.)

P. गृह्णाति, Âtm. गृह्णीते, I. अगृह्णात्, Âtm. अगृह्णीत, O. गृह्णीयात्, Âtm. गृह्णीत, I. गृह्णातु (2. गृहाण), Âtm. गृह्णीताम् ॥ Pf. 1. जग्राह (â), 2. जग्राहिथ, 3. जग्राह, 4. जगृहिव, 5. जगृहथुः, 6. जगृहुः, 7. जगृहिम, 8. जगृह, 9. जगृहुः, I A. 1. अग्रहीषम् (§ 341 and § 348*), 2. अग्रहीः, 3. अग्रहीत्, Âtm. 1. अग्रहीषि, 2. अग्रहीषाः, 3. अग्रहीष्ट, F. ग्रहीष्यति, P. F. ग्रहीता, B. गृह्यात्, Âtm. ग्रहीषीष्ट ॥ Pt. गृहीतः, Ger. गृहीत्वा ॥ Pass. गृह्यते, Aor. अग्राहि, Fut. ग्रहीष्यते or ग्राहिष्यते &c., Caus. ग्राहयति, Des. जिघृक्षति, Int. जरीगृह्यते, जाग्राहि (not जाग्राहि).

II. Parasmaipada Verbs.

158. ज्या *jyâ*, to grow weak.

This root takes Samprasâraṇa in the special tenses and before other weakening terminations.
(See No. 157.)

P. जिनाति, I. अजिनात्, O. जिनीयात्, I. जिनातु ॥ Pf. 1. जिज्यौ, 2. जिज्ञिय or जिज्यिव, 3. जिज्यौ, 4. जिज्ञिय, I A. अज्यासीत्, F. ज्यास्यति, B. जीयात् ॥ Pt. जीनः (जीतः as participle would be wrong, see Pâṇ. VIII. 2, 44; but it occurs in the sense of old (Am. Kosha, ed. Loisel. p. 135), and in the Vedic Sanskrit; see Kuhn, Beiträge, vol. VI. p. 104), Ger. जीत्वा, °ज्याय ॥ Caus. ज्यापयति, Des. जिज्यासति, Int. जेजीयते.

159. ज्ञा *jñâ*, to know.

This verb substitutes जा *jâ* in the special tenses. (Pâṇ. VII. 3, 79.)

P. जानाति, I. अजानात्, O. जानीयात्, I. जानातु ॥ Pf. जज्ञौ, I A. अज्ञासीत्, F. ज्ञास्यति, P.F. ज्ञाता, B. ज्ञायात् or ज्ञेयात् ॥ Pt. ज्ञातः ॥ Pass. ज्ञायते, Aor. अज्ञायि, Caus. ज्ञपयति (â), (see § 462, II. 15), Aor. अजिज्ञपत्, Des. जिज्ञासते, Int. जाज्ञायते.

160. बन्ध् *bandh*, to bind.

P. बध्नाति, I. अबध्नात्, O. बध्नीयात्, I. बध्नातु ॥ Pf. 1. बबन्ध, 2. बबन्धिथ or बबन्ध or बबन्ध, I A. 1. अभांत्सम्, 2. अभांत्सीः, 3. अभांत्सीत्, 4. अभांत्स्व, 5. अभांत्स्वं, 6. अभांत्स्त, 7. अभांत्स्त, 8. अभांत्स्त, 9. अभांत्सुः, F. भन्त्स्यति, P. F. बन्द्धा, B. बध्यात् ॥ Pt. बद्धः, Ger. बद्ध्वा ॥ Pass. बध्यते, Caus. बन्धयति, Aor. अबबन्धत्, Des. बिभन्त्सति, Int. बाबध्यते, बाबन्धि.

III. Âtmanepada Verbs.

161. वृ *vṛi*, to cherish, (वृ.)

P. वृणीते, I. अवृणीत, O. वृणीत, I. वृणीताम् ॥ Pf. ववृे, I A. अवरिष्ट or अवरीष्ट or अवृत, F. वरिष्यते or वरीष्यते, P. F. वरिता or वरीता, B. वरिषीष्ट or वृषीष्ट ॥ Pt. वृतः ॥ Pass. व्रियते, Caus. वारयति (â), Des. विवरिषते or विवरीषते, Int. वेवरीयते, वर्वर्ति &c. Contracted forms of the Des. and Int., वुवूर्षति and वोवूर्यते.

Ad Class (*Adâdi, II Class*).

I. Parasmaipada Verbs.

162. अद् *ad*, to eat.

P. 1. अत्मि, 2. अत्सि, 3. अत्ति, 4. अद्गः, 5. अत्यः, 6. अद्मः, 7. अद्यः, 8. अत्थ, 9. अदन्ति, I. 1. आदं, 2. आदः (Pâṇ. VII. 3, 100)*, 3. आदत्, 4. आत्तं, 5. आत्तं, 6. आत्तां, 7. आद्म, 8. आत्त, 9. आदन्, O. अद्यात्, I. 1. अदानि, 2. अद्धि†, 3. अत्तु, 4. अदाव, 5. अत्तं, 6. अत्तां, 7. अदाम, 8. अत्त, 9. अदन्तु ॥ Pf. 1. आद, 2. आदिथ &c., or substituting घस् ॥, 1. अघास (ఆ̆), 2. अघसिथ, 3. अघास, 4. अक्षिव, 5. अक्षुः, 6. अक्षतुः, 7. अक्षिम, 8. अक्ष, 9. अक्षुः, II A. 1. अक्षं, 2. अक्षः, 3. अक्षत्, F. अत्स्यति, P. F. अत्ता, B. अद्यात् ॥ Pt. जग्धः¶, Ger. जग्ध्वा, °जग्य (Pâṇ. II. 4, 36) ॥ Pass. अद्यते, Caus. आदयति, Aor. आदिदत्, Des. जिघत्सति.

163. घ्सा *psâ*, to eat.

P. घ्साति, I. 3. अघ्सात्; 9. अघ्सान् or अघ्सुः (§ 322‡), O. घ्सायात्, I. घ्सातु ॥ Pf. पघ्सौ, I A. अघ्सासीत्, F. घ्सास्यति, P. F. घ्साता, B. घ्सायात् or घ्सेयात् ॥ Pass. घ्सायते, Caus. घ्सापयति, Des. पिघ्सासति, Int. पाघ्सायते.

164. मा *mâ*, to measure.

P. माति, I. 3. अमात्, 9. अमान् or अमुः, O. मायात्, I. मातु ॥ Pf. ममौ, I A. अमासीत्, F. मास्यति, P. F. माता, B. मेयात् ॥ Pt. मितः, Ger. मित्वा, °माय ॥ Pass. मीयते, Aor. अमायि, Caus. मापयति, Aor. अमीमपत्, Des. मित्सति, Int. मेमीयते, मामाति or मामेति.

165. या *yâ*, to go.

P. याति, I. 3. अयात्, 9. अयान् or अयुः, O. यायात्, I. यातु ॥ Pf. ययौ, I A. अयासीत्, F. यास्यति, P. F. याता, B. यायात् ॥ Pt. यातः ॥ Pass. यायते, Caus. यापयति, Aor. अयीयपत्, Des. यियासति, Int. यायायते.

166. ख्या *khyâ*, to proclaim.

P. ख्याति, I. अख्यात्, O. ख्यायात्, I. ख्यातु ॥ Pf. चख्यौ, II A. अख्यत्, F. ख्यास्यति, P. F. ख्याता, B. ख्यायात् or ख्येयात् ॥ Pt. ख्यातः ॥ Pass. ख्यायते, Aor. अख्यायि, Caus. ख्यापयति, Aor. अचिख्यपत्, Des. चिख्यासति, Int. चाख्यायते.

167. वश् *vaś*, to desire.

This root takes Samprasâraṇa before the strong terminations of the special tenses, and in the weakening forms generally.

P. 1. वश्मि, 2. वक्षि (§ 125, 120), 3. वष्टि, 4. उश्वः, 5. उश्थः, 6. उष्टः, 7. उश्मः, 8. उष्ठ, 9. उशन्ति, I. 1. अवशं, 2. अवट्, 3. अवट्, 4. औश्व, 5. औष्टं, 6. औष्टां, 7. औश्म, 8. औष्ट, 9. औशन्, O. उश्यात्, I. 1. वशानि, 2. उड्ढि, 3. वष्टु, 4. वशाव, 5. उष्टं, 6. उष्टां, 7. वशाम,

---

* अद् inserts अ before terminations consisting of one consonant.

† When हि is added immediately to the final consonant of a root, it is changed to धि (Pâṇ. VI. 4, 101); § 321, note 1.

‖ In the tenses where अद् is deficient, घस् is used instead.

¶ This is formed from जग्ध् to eat, a reduplicated form of घस्. (Pâṇ. II. 4, 36.)

8. उष, 9. उषंतु ॥ Pf. 3. उवाश, 9. ऊषुः, I A. औवाशीत् (å), F. वशिष्यति, P. F. वशिता, B. उश्यात् ॥ Pass. उश्यते, Caus. वाशयति, Des. विवशिषति, Int. वावश्यते, वावष्टि.

<h3 style="text-align:center">168. हन् han, to kill.</h3>

This verb drops its final न् n before the strong terminations of the special tenses, and in the weakening forms generally, if the terminations begin with any consonant except nasals or semivowels (Pâṇ. VI. 4, 37). Before strong terminations beginning with vowels, हन् han becomes घ्न ghn (Pâṇ. VII. 3, 54). In the aorist and benedictive वध vadh is substituted. The desiderative, intensive, and the aorist passive are derived from घन ghan, the causative from घात ghat.

P. 1. हन्मि, 2. हंसि, 3. हंति, 4. हन्वः, 5. हथः, 6. हतः, 7. हन्मः, 8. हथ, 9. घ्नंति, I. 1. अहनं, 2. अहन्, 3. अहन्, 4. अहन्व, 5. अहतं, 6. अहतां, 7. अहन्म, 8. अहत, 9. अघ्नन्, O. हन्यात्, I. 1. हनानि, 2. जहि (Pâṇ. VI. 4, 36), 3. हंतु, 4. हनाव, 5. हतं, 6. हतां, 7. हनाम, 8. हत, 9. घ्नंतु ॥ Pf. 1. जघान (å), (Pâṇ. VII. 3, 55), 2. जघनिथ or जघंथ, 3. जघान, 4. जघ्निव, 5. जघ्निमुः, 6. जघ्नतुः, 7. जघ्निम, 8. जघ्न, 9. जघ्नुः, I A. अवधीत्, F. हनिष्यति, P. F. हंता, B. वध्यात् ॥ Pt. हतः, Ger. हत्वा, °हत्य (§ 449) ॥ Pass. हन्यते, Aor. अघानि or अवधि (§ 407), Caus. घातयति, Aor. अजीघतत्, Des. जिघांसति, Int. जंघन्यते or जेघ्रीयते (Pâṇ. VII. 4, 30, vârt., he kills), जंघंति.

<h3 style="text-align:center">169. यु yu, to mix.</h3>

Verbs of this class ending in उ u take, in the special tenses, Vṛiddhi instead of Guṇa before weak terminations beginning with consonants. (Pâṇ. VII. 3, 89.)

P. 1. यौमि, 2. यौषि, 3. यौति, 4. युवः, 5. युषः, 6. युतः, 7. युमः, 8. युथ, 9. युवंति, I. 1. अयवं, 2. अयौः, 3. अयौत्, 4. अयुव, 5. अयुतं, 6. अयुतां, 7. अयुम, 8. अयुत, 9. अयुवन्, O. युयात्, I. 1. यवानि, 2. युहि, 3. यौतु, 4. यवाव, 5. युतं, 6. युतां, 7. यवाम, 8. युतं, 9. युवंतु ॥ Pf. 3. युयाव, 9. युयुवुः, I A. अयावीत्, F. यविष्यति, P. F. यविता, B. यूयात् ॥ Pt. युतः ॥ Pass. यूयते, Aor. अयावि, Caus. यावयति, Des. युयूषति or यियविषति, Int. योयूयते, योयोति.

<h3 style="text-align:center">170. रु ru, to shout.</h3>

The verbs तु tu, रु ru, स्तु stu may take ई i before all terminations of the special tenses beginning with consonants. (Pâṇ. VII. 3, 95.)

P. 1. रौमि or रवीमि, 2. रौषि or रवीषि, 3. रौति or रवीति, 4. रुवः or रुवीवः, 5. रुयः or रुवीयः, 6. रुतः or रुवीतः, 7. रुमः or रुवीमः, 8. रुथ or रुवीथ, 9. रुवंति, I. 1. अरवं, 2. अरौः or अरवीः, 3. अरौत् or अरवीत्, 4. अरुव or अरुवीव, 5. अरुतं or अरुवीतं, 6. अरुतां or अरुवीतां, 7. अरुम or अरुवीम, 8. अरुत or अरुवीत, 9. अरुवन्, O. रुयात् or रुवीयात्, I. 1. रवाणि, 2. रुहि or रुवीहि, 3. रौतु or रवीतु, 4. रवाव, 5. रुतं or रुवीतं, 6. रुतां or रुवीतां, 7. रवाम, 8. रुत or रुवीत, 9. रुवंतु ॥ Pf. 3. रुराव, 9. रुरुवुः, I A. अरावीत्, F. रविष्यति, P. F. रविता, B. रूयात् ॥ Pt. रुतः ॥ Pass. रूयते, Caus. रावयति, Des. रुरूषति, Int. रोरूयते.

Note—The Sârasvatî gives अरौवीत्, रोरवीति, and रोता; but see § 332, 4. It likewise extends the use of ई to नु to praise.

<h3 style="text-align:center">171. इ i, to go.</h3>

P. 1. एमि, 2. एषि, 3. एति, 4. इवः, 5. इथः, 6. इतः, 7. इमः, 8. इथ, 9. यंति, I. 1. आयं,

2. एे:, 3. एेत्, 4. एेव, 5. एेतं, 6. एेतां, 7. एेम, 8. एेत, 9. आयन्, O. इयात्, I. 1. अयानि, 2. इहि, 3. एतु, 4. अयाव, 5. इतं, 6. इतां, 7. अयाम, 8. इत, 9. यंतु ॥ Pf. 1. इयाय (å), 2. इययिथ or इयेथ, 3. इयाय, 4. ईयिव, 5. ईयुप्, 6. ईयतुः, 7. ईयिम, 8. ईय, 9. ईयुः, I A. 1. अगां (Pâṇ. ii. 4, 45), 2. अगाः, 3. अगात्, 4. अगाव, 5. अगातं, 6. अगातां, 7. अगाम, 8. अगात, 9. अगुः (§ 368), F. एष्यति, P. F. एता, B. इयात् ॥ Pt. इतः, Ger. इत्वा, ॰इत्य ॥ Pass. ईयते, Aor. अगायि (§ 404), Caus. गमयति (Pâṇ. ii. 4, 46), Des. जिगमिषति (Pâṇ. ii. 4, 47). But see § 463, II. 1, and § 471, 4, with regard to this and cognate verbs if preceded by prepositions.

172. विद् *vid*, to know.

P. 1. वेद्मि, 2. वेत्सि, 3. वेत्ति, 4. विद्वः, 5. वित्थः, 6. विदः, 7. विद्मः, 8. वित्थ, 9. विदंति, I. 1. अवेदं, 2. अवेः or अवेत् (Pâṇ. viii. 2, 75), 3. अवेत् (§ 132*), 4. अविद्व, 5. अवितं, 6. अविदां, 7. अविद्म, 8. अवित्त, 9. अविदन् or अविदुः, O. विद्यात्, I. 1. वेदानि (or विदांकरवाणि &c., Pâṇ. iii. 1, 41), 2. विद्धि, 3. वेत्तु, 4. वेदाव, 5. वित्तं, 6. वित्तां, 7. वेदाम, 8. वित्त, 9. विदंतु ॥ Pf. विवेद or विदांचकार (§ 326), I A. अवेदीत्, F. वेदिष्यति, P. F. वेदिता, B. विद्यात् ॥

Another form of the Present is, 1. वेद, 2. वेत्थ, 3. वेद, 4. विद्व, 5. विदथुः, 6. विदतुः, 7. विद्म, 8. विद, 9. विदुः ॥ Pt. विदितः, Ger. विदित्वा ॥ Pass. विद्यते, Aor. अवेदि, Caus. वेदयति, Aor. अवीविदत्, Des. विविदिषति (Pâṇ. i. 2, 8), Int. वेविद्यते, वेवेत्ति.

173. अस् *as*, to be.

P. 1. अस्मि, 2. असि, 3. अस्ति, 4. स्वः, 5. स्थः, 6. स्तः, 7. स्मः, 8. स्थ, 9. संति, I. 1. आसं, 2. आसीः, 3. आसीत्, 4. आस्व, 5. आस्तं, 6. आस्तां, 7. आस्म, 8. आस्त, 9. आसन्, O. 1. स्यां, 2. स्याः, 3. स्यात्, 4. स्याव, 5. स्यातं, 6. स्यातां, 7. स्याम, 8. स्यात, 9. स्युः, I. 1. असानि, 2. एधि, 3. अस्तु, 4. असाव, 5. स्तं, 6. स्तां, 7. असाम, 8. स्त, 9. संतु ॥ Pf. 1. आस, 2. आसिथ, 3. आस, 4. आसिव, 5. आसयुः, 6. आसतुः, 7. आसिम, 8. आस, 9. आसुः ; Âtm. 1. आसे, 2. आसिषे, 3. आसे, 4. आसिवहे, 5. आसाथे, 6. आसाते, 7. आसिमहे, 8. आसिध्वे, 9. आसिरे †.

174. मृज् *mṛij*, to cleanse, (मृजू.)

This verb takes Vṛiddhi instead of Guṇa (Pâṇ. vii. 2, 114); it may take Vṛiddhi likewise before terminations that would not require Guṇa, if the terminations begin with a vowel (Siddh.-Kaum. vol. ii. p. 122).

P. 1. मार्ज्मि, 2. मार्षि, 3. मार्ष्टि (§ 124), 4. मृज्वः, 5. मृष्ठः, 6. मृष्टः, 7. मृज्मः, 8. मृष्ट, 9. मृजंति or मार्जंति, I. 1. अमार्जं, 2. अमार्ट्, 3. अमार्ट्, 4. अमृज्व, 5. अमृष्टं, 6. अमृष्टां, 7. अमृज्म, 8. अमृष्ट, 9. अमृजन् or अमार्जन्, O. मृज्यात्, I. 1. मार्जानि, 2. मृड्ढि, 3. मार्ष्टु, 4. मार्जाव, 5. मृष्टं, 6. मृष्टां, 7. मार्जाम, 8. मृष्ट, 9. मृजंतु or मार्जंतु ॥ Pf. 1. ममार्ज, 2. ममार्जिथ or ममार्ष्ठ, 3. ममार्ज, 4. ममृजिव or ममार्जिव, 5. ममृजुः or ममार्जुः, 6. ममृजतुः or ममार्जतुः, 7. ममृजिम or ममार्जिम, 8. ममृज or ममार्ज, 9. ममृजुः or ममार्जुः, I A. अमार्जीत् or अमार्क्षीत्, F. मार्जिष्यति or मार्क्ष्यति, P. F. मार्जिता or मार्ष्टा, B. मृज्यात् ॥ Pt. मृष्टः, Ger. मार्जित्वा or मृष्ट्वा, ॰मृज्य, Adj. मार्जितव्यः or

---

† The perfect both in the Parasmaipada and Âtmanepada is chiefly used at the end of the periphrastic perfect.

माङ्क्ष्यः, मृग्यः or माग्यैः (Pâṇ. III. 1, 113) ॥ Pass. मृज्यते, Aor. अमार्जि, Caus. मार्जयति, Des. मिमृक्षति or मिमार्जिषति, Int. मरीमृज्यते, मर्मार्ति.

175. वच् *vach*, to speak.

P. 1. वच्मि, 2. वक्षि, 3. वक्ति, 4. वच्वः, 5. वक्थः, 6. वक्ति, 7. वच्मः, 8. वक्थ, 9. वदंति or ब्रुवंति*, I. 1. अवचं, 2. अवक्, 3. अवक्, 4. अवच्व, 5. अवक्तं, 6. अवक्तां, 7. अवच्म, 8. अवक्त, 9. अवदन्*, O. उच्याम्, I. 1. वचानि, 2. वग्धि, 3. वक्तु, 4. वचाव, 5. वक्तं, 6. वक्तां, 7. वचाम, 8. वक्त, 9. वदंतु* ॥ Pf. 3. उवाच, 9. ऊचुः, II A. अवोचत् (§ 366), F. वक्ष्यति, P. F. वक्ता, B. उच्यात् ॥ Pt. उक्तः ॥ Pass. उच्यते, Aor. अवाचि, Caus. वाचयति, Aor. अवीवचत्, Des. विवक्षति, Int. वावच्यते.

176. रुद् *rud*, to cry, (रुदिर्.)

The verbs रुद् *rud*, स्वप् *svap*, श्वस् *śvas*, अन् *an*, जक्ष् *jaksh* take इ *i* before the terminations of the special tenses beginning with consonants, except य *y* (Pâṇ. VII. 2, 76). Before weak terminations consisting of one consonant, ई *î* is inserted (Pâṇ. VII. 3, 98); or, according to others, अ *a* (Pâṇ. VII. 3, 99).

P. 1. रोदिमि, 2. रोदिषि, 3. रोदिति, 4. रुदिवः, 9. रुदंति, I. 1. अरोदं, 2. अरोदीः or अरोदः, 3. अरोदीत् or अरोदत्, 4. अरुदिव, 9. अरुदन्, O. रुद्यां, I. 1. रोदानि, 2. रुदिहि, 3. रोदितु, 4. रोदाव, 5. रुदितं, 6. रुदितां, 7. रोदाम, 8. रुदित, 9. रुदंतु ॥ Pf. रुरोद, I A. अरोदीत् or अरुदत्, F. रोदिष्यति, P. F. रोदिता, B. रुद्यात् ॥ Pt. रुदितः ॥ Pass. रुद्यते, Aor. अरोदि, Caus. रोदयति, Aor. अरुरुदत्, Des. रुरुदिषति or रुरोदिषति, Int. रोरुद्यते.

177. जक्ष् *jaksh*, to eat, to laugh‖.

Seven verbs, जक्ष् *jaksh*, जागृ *jâgri*, to wake, दरिद्रा *daridrâ*, to be poor, चकास् *chakâs*, to shine, शास् *śâs*, to rule, दीधी *dîdhî*, to shine, वेवी *vevî*, to obtain, are called अभ्यस्त *abhyasta* (reduplicated). They take अति *ati* and अतु *atu* in the 3rd pers. plur. present and imperative, and उः *uḥ* instead of अन् *an* in the 3rd pers. plur. imperfect (§ 321†).

P. 3. जक्षिति, 9. जक्षति, I. अजक्षीत् or अजक्षत्, O. जक्ष्यात्, I. 3. अजक्षीत् or अजक्षत्, 9. अजक्षुः (§ 321‡) ॥ Pf. जजक्ष, I A. अजक्षीत्, F. जक्षिष्यति.

178. जागृ *jâgri*, to wake. (Pâṇ. VI. 1, 192, accent.)

P. 1. जागर्मि, 2. जागर्षि, 3. जागर्ति, 4. जागृवः, 5. जागृथः, 6. जागृतः, 7. जागृमः, 8. जागृथ, 9. जाग्रति, I. 1. अजागरं, 2. अजागः, 3. अजागः, 4. अजागृव, 5. अजागृतं, 6. अजागृतां, 7. अजागृम, 8. अजागृत, 9. अजागरुः; O. जागृयात्, I. 1. जागराणि, 2. जागृहि, 3. जागर्तु, 4. जागराव, 5. जागृतं, 6. जागृतां, 7. जागराम, 8. जागृत, 9. जाग्रतु ॥ Pf. 3. जजागार or जागरांचकार (Pâṇ. III. 1, 38), 9. जजागरुः, I A. अजागरीत् (see preface, p. ix), F. जागरिष्यति, P. F. जागरिता, B. जाग्र्यात् ॥ Pt. जागरितः ॥ Pass. जाग्र्यते, Aor. अजागारि, Caus. जागरयति, Des. जिजागरिषति. No Intensive.

---

* The 3rd pers. plur. present of वच् does not occur (Siddh.-Kaum. vol. II. p. 120); according to others the whole plural is wanting; according to some no 3rd pers. plur. is formed from वच्.

‖ जक्ष् to eat, from घस्; जक्ष् to laugh, from हस्.

179. दरिद्रा *daridrá*, to be poor. (Pâṇ. vi. 1, 192, accent.)

In दरिद्रा *daridrá* the final आ *á* is replaced by इ *i* in the special tenses before strong terminations beginning with a consonant (Pâṇ. vi. 4, 114). Before strong terminations beginning with vowels the आ *á* is lost (Pâṇ. vi. 4, 112).

P. 1. दरिद्रामि, 2. दरिद्रासि, 3. दरिद्राति, 4. दरिद्रिवः, 9. दरिद्रति, I. 3. अदरिद्रात्, 6. अदरिद्रां, 9. अदरिद्रुः, O. दरिद्रियात्, I. 1. दरिद्राणि, 2. दरिद्रिहि, 3. दरिद्रातु, 4. दरिद्राव, 5. दरिद्रां, 6. दरिद्रातां, 7. दरिद्राम, 8. दरिद्रात, 9. दरिद्रतु ॥ Pf. ददरिद्रौ or दरिद्रांचकार (Siddh.-Kaum. vol. ii. p. 125), I A. अदरिद्रीत् or अदरिद्रासीत् (Siddh.-Kaum. vol. ii. p. 126), F. दरिद्रिष्यति (Pâṇ. vi. 4, 114, vârt.), P. F. दरिद्रिता (not दरिद्राता).

180. शास् *śás*, to command, (शासु.) (Pâṇ. vi. 1, 188.)

शास् *śás* is changed to शिष् *śis* before weakening terminations beginning with consonants, and in the second aorist. (Pâṇ. vi. 4, 34.)

P. 1. शासिम, 2. शासिस, 3. शासित, 4. शिष्वः, 9. शासति, I. 1. अशासं, 2. अशाः or अशात्, 3. अशात् (§ 132), 4. अशिष्व, 5. अशिष्टं, 6. अशिष्टां, 7. अशिष्व, 8. अशिष्ट, 9. अशासुः, O. शिष्यात्, I. 1. शासानि, 2. शाधि (§ 132), 3. शास्तु, 4. शासाव, 5. शिष्टं, 6. शिष्टां, 7. शासाम, 8. शिष्ट, 9. शासतु ॥ Pf. शशास, II A. अशिषत्, F. शासिष्यति, B. शिष्यात् ॥ Pt. शिष्टः ॥ Pass. शिष्यते, Caus. शासयति, Des. शिशासिषति, Int. शेशिष्यते.

II. Âtmanepada Verbs.

181. चक्ष् *chaksh*, to speak, (चक्षिङ्.)

P. 1. चक्षे, 2. चक्षे, 3. चष्टे, 4. चक्ष्वहे, 5. चक्षाथे, 6. चक्षाते, 7. चक्ष्महे, 8. चड्ढे, 9. चक्षते, I. 3. अचष्ट, 9. अचक्षत, O. चक्षीत, I. चष्टां ॥ Pf. चचक्षे.

The other forms are supplied from ख्या or ख्ञा, the Red. Perf. optionally, (Pâṇ. ii. 4, 54, 55): Pf. चख्यौ ॥ II A. अख्यत् or °त, F. ख्यास्यति or °ते, B. ख्यायात् or ख्येयात्, or Âtm. ख्यासीष्ट.

182. ईश् *íś*, to rule.

The root ईश् *íś* takes इ *i* before the 2nd pers. sing. present and imperative (Pâṇ. vii. 2, 77). ईड् *íḍ* and जन् *jas* do the same, and likewise insert इ *i* before the 2nd pers. plur. present, [imperfect,] and imperative (Pâṇ. vii. 2, 78). The commentators, however, extend the latter rule to ईश् *íś*. See notes to Pâṇ. vii. 2, 78.

P. 1. ईशे, 2. ईशिषे, 3. ईष्टे, 8. ईशिध्वे, I. 3. ऐष्ट, 8. ऐशिध्वं or ऐड्ढ्वं, O. ईशीत, I. 1. ईशै, 2. ईशिष्व, 3. ईष्टां, 8. ईशिध्वं or ईड्ढ्वं ॥ Pf. ईशांचक्रे, I A. ऐशिष्ट.

183. आस् *ás*, to sit.

P. आस्ते, I. आस्त, O. आसीत, I. आस्तां ॥ Pf. आसांचक्रे (part. आसीनः, Pâṇ. vii. 2, 83), I A. आसिष्ट, F. आसिष्यते.

184. सू *sú*, to bear, (सूङ्.)

P. सूते, I. असूत, O. सुवीत, I. 1. सुवै (Pâṇ. vii. 3, 88), 2. सूष्व, 3. सूतां, 4. सुवावहे, 5. सुवाथां, 6. सुवातां, 7. सुवामहे, 8. सूध्वं, 9. सुवतां ॥ Pf. सुषुवे, I A. असविष्ट or असोष्ट

(§ 337, I. 1), F. सविष्यते or सोष्यते, B. सविषीष्ट or सोषीष्ट ॥ Pt. सून: (Pâṇ. VIII. 2, 45) ॥ Pass. सूयते, Aor. असावि, Caus. सावयति, Aor. असूषवत्, Des. सुसूषते (Pâṇ. VIII. 3, 61), Int. सोषूयते.

185. शी *śî*, to lie down, to sleep, (शीङ्.)

The verb शी *śî* takes Guṇa in the special tenses (Pâṇ. VII. 4, 21), and inserts र *r* in the 3rd pers. plur. present, imperfect, and imperative.

P. 1. शये, 2. शेषे, 3. शेते, 4. शेवहे, 5. शयाथे, 6. शयाते, 7. शेमहे, 8. शेध्वे, 9. शेरते (Pâṇ. VII. 1, 6), I. 1. अशयि, 2. अशेषाः, 3. अशेत, 4. अशेवहि, 5. अशयाथां, 6. अशयातां, 7. अशेमहि, 8. अशेध्वं, 9. अशेरत, O. शयीत, I. 1. शये, 2. शेष्व, 3. शेतां, 4. शयावहै, 5. शयाथां, 6. शयातां, 7. शयामहै, 8. शेध्वं, 9. शेरतां ॥ Pf. शिश्ये, I A. अशयिष्ट, F. शयिष्यते, B. शयीष्ट ॥ Pt. शयित: ॥ Pass. शय्यते (Pâṇ. VII. 4, 22), Aor. अशायि, Caus. शाययति, Des. शिशयिषते, Int. शाशय्यते, शेशेति.

186. इ *i*, to go, (इण्.) (Pâṇ. VI. 1, 186, accent.)

This verb is always used with अधि *adhi*, in the sense of reading. (Siddh.-Kaum. vol. II. p. 118.)

P. अधीते, I. 3. अध्यैत, 6. अध्यैयातां (Sâr. II. 5, 8), 9. अध्यैयत, O. अधीयीत, I. 1. अध्यये, 2. अधीष्व, 3. अधीतां, 4. अध्ययावहै, 5. अधीयाथां, 6. अधीयातां, 7. अध्ययामहै, 8. अधीध्वं, 9. अधीयतां ॥ Pf. अधिजगे (Pâṇ. II. 4, 49), I A. 3. अध्यैष्ट, 6. अध्यैषातां, 9. अध्यैषत, or 3. अध्यगीष्ट (Siddh.-Kaum. vol. II. p. 119), 6. अध्यगीषातां, 9. अध्यगीषत, F. अध्येष्यते, Cond. अध्यैष्यत or अध्यगीष्यत, P. F. अध्येता, B. अध्येषीष्ट ॥ Pt. अधीत: ॥ Pass. अधीयते, Aor. अध्यगायि or अध्यायि, Caus. अध्यापयति, Aor. अध्यापिपत् or अध्यजीगपत्, Des. अधीषिषति or अधिजिगांसते.

III. Parasmaipada and Âtmanepada Verbs.

· 187. द्विष् *dvish*, to hate.

P. 1. द्वेष्मि, 2. द्वेक्षि, 3. द्वेष्टि, 4. द्विष्वः, 9. द्विषन्ति, I. 1. अद्वेषं, 2. अद्वेट्, 3. अद्वेट्, 4. अद्विष्व, 9. अद्विषन् or अद्विषुः (§ 321‡), O. द्विष्यात्, I. 1. द्वेषाणि, 2. द्विड्ढि, 3. द्वेष्टु, 4. द्वेषाव, 5. द्विष्व, 6. द्विष्टं, 7. द्वेषाम, 8. द्विष्ट, 9. द्विषन्तु ॥ Pf. दिद्वेष, I A. अद्विक्षत्, F. द्वेक्ष्यति, P. F. द्वेष्टा, B. द्विष्यात्, Âtm. द्विक्षीष्ट ॥ Pt. द्विष: ॥ Pass. द्विष्यते, Aor. अद्वेषि, Caus. द्वेषयति, Aor. अदिद्विषत्, Des. दिद्विक्षति, Int. देद्विष्यते, देद्वेष्टि.

188. दुह् *duh*, to milk.

P. 1. दोह्मि, 2. धोक्षि, 3. दोग्धि, 4. दुह्वः, 5. दुग्धः, 6. दुह्मः, 7. दुग्धः, 8. दुग्ध, 9. दुहन्ति, I. 1. अदोहं, 2. अधोक्, 3. अधोक्, 4. अदुह्व, O. दुह्यात्, I. 1. दोहानि, 2. दुग्धि, 3. दोग्धु, 4. दोहाव, 5. दुग्धं, 6. दुग्धां, 7. दोहाम, 8. दुग्ध, 9. दुहन्तु ॥ Pf. दुदोह, I A. अदुधत् &c. (see § 362), F. धोक्ष्यति.

189. स्तु *stu*, to praise, (ष्टुञ्.)

P. 1. स्तौमि or स्तवीमि (see No. 170), 2. स्तोषि or स्तवीषि, 3. स्तौति or स्तवीति, 4. स्तुवः or स्तुवीवः, 9. स्तुवन्ति, I. 1. अस्तवं, 2. अस्तोः or अस्तवीः, 3. अस्तोत् or अस्तवीत्, 4. अस्तुव or अस्तुवीव, 9. अस्तुवन्, O. स्तुयात्, Âtm. स्तुवीत, I. 1. स्तवानि, 2. स्तुहि or स्तुवीहि, 9. स्तो

or स्तवीतु ॥ Pf. 3. तुष्टाव, 2. तुष्टोष, 6. तुष्टुवु:, 9. तुष्टुवु:, I A. अस्तावीत् (§ 338, 3), Âtm. अस्तोष्ट, F. स्तोष्यति, P. F. स्तोता, B. स्तूयात्, Âtm. स्तोषीष्ट ॥ Pt. स्तुत: ॥ Pass. सूयते, Aor. अस्तावि, Caus. स्तावयति, Aor. अतुष्टवत्, Des. तुष्टूषति, Int. तोष्टूयते, तोष्टोति.

190. ब्रू *brú*, to speak, (ब्रूञ्.)

This verb takes इ *i* before weak terminations beginning with consonants in the special tenses (Pâṇ. vii. 3, 93). The perfect आह *âha* may be substituted for five of the persons of the present (Pâṇ. iii. 4, 84). It is defective in the general tenses, where वच् *vach* (No. 175) is used instead.

P. 1. ब्रवीमि, 2. ब्रवीषि or आत्थ, 3. ब्रवीति or आह, 4. ब्रूव:, 5. ब्रूथ: or आहतु:, 6. ब्रूत: or आहतु:, 7. ब्रूम:, 8. ब्रूथ, 9. तुवंति or आहु:, I. 1. अब्रवं, 2. अब्रवी:, 3. अब्रवीत्, 4. अब्रूव, 5. अब्रूतां, 6. अब्रूतां, 7. अब्रूम, 8. अब्रूत, 9. अब्रुवन्, O. ब्रूयात्, I. 1. ब्रवाणि, 2. ब्रूहि, 3. ब्रवीतु, 4. ब्रवाव, 5. ब्रूतां, 6. ब्रूतां, 7. ब्रवाम, 8. ब्रूत, 9. तुवंतु.

191. ऊर्णु *úrṇu*, to cover, (ऊर्णुञ्.)

This verb may take Vṛiddhi instead of Guṇa before weak terminations beginning with consonants (Pâṇ. vii. 3, 90, 91), except before those that consist of one consonant only. It takes the reduplicated perfect against § 325, and reduplicates the last syllable (Pâṇ. vi. 1, 8). In the general tenses the final उ *u*, before intermediate इ *i*, may or may not take Guṇa (Pâṇ. i. 2, 3).

P. 3. ऊर्णोति or ऊर्णोति, 9. ऊर्णुवति, I. और्णोत्, O. ऊर्णुयात्, I. ऊर्णोतु or ऊर्णोतु ॥ Pf. 1. ऊर्णुनाव (â), 2. ऊर्णुनविथ or ऊर्णुनुविथ, 3. ऊर्णुनाव, 4. ऊर्णुनुविव, 5. ऊर्णुनुवु:, 6. ऊर्णुनुवु:, 7. ऊर्णुनुविम, 8. ऊर्णुनुव, 9. ऊर्णुनुवु:, I A. और्णावीत् or और्णुवीत् or और्णावीत् (Pâṇ. vii. 2, 6), F. ऊर्णविष्यति or ऊर्णुविष्यति, B. ऊर्णूयात् ॥ Pass. ऊर्णुयते, Caus. ऊर्णावयति, Aor. और्णुनवत्, Des. ऊर्णुनूषति or ऊर्णुनविषति or ऊर्णुनुविषति, Int. ऊर्णोनूयते, ऊर्णोनोति.

Hu Class (*Juhotyâdi, III Class*).

I. Parasmaipada Verbs.

192. हु *hu*, to sacrifice. (Pâṇ. vi. 1, 192, accent.)

P. जुहोति, I. अजुहोत्, O. जुहुयात्, I. जुहोतु ॥ Pf. जुहाव or जुहवांचकार (§ 326), I A. अहौषीत्, F. होष्यति, P. F. होता, B. हूयात् ॥ Pt. हुत: ॥ Pass. हूयते, Caus. हावयति, Aor. अजूहवत्, Des. जुहूषति, Int. जोहूयते, जोहोति.

193. भी *bhí*, to fear, (ञिभी.) (Pâṇ. vi. 1, 192, accent.)

This verb may shorten the final ई *i* before strong terminations beginning with consonants in the special tenses. (Pâṇ. vi. 4, 115.)

P. 3. बिभेति, 6. बिभीत: or बिभित:, 9. बिभ्यति, I. 3. अबिभेत्, 6. अबिभीतां or अबिभितां, 9. अबिभयु:, O. बिभीयात् or बिभियात्, I. बिभेतु ॥ Pf. बिभाय or बिभयांचकार (§ 326), I A. अभैषीत्, F. भेष्यति, P. F. भेता, B. भीयात् ॥ Pt. भीत: ॥ Pass. भीयते, Aor. अभायि, Caus. भाययति or भापयते or भीषयते (see § 463, II. 18), Des. बिभीषति, Int. बेभीयते, बेभेति.

194. ह्री *hrî*, to be ashamed. (Pân. VI. 1, 192, accent.)

P. 3. जिह्रेति, 6. जिह्रीतः, 9. जिह्रियति (§ 110), I. अजिह्रेत्, O. जिह्रीयात्, I. जिह्रेतु ।
Pf. 3. जिह्राय, 6. जिह्रियतुः, 9. जिह्रियुः or जिह्रयांचकार, I A. अह्रैषीत्, F. ह्रेष्यति, P. F. ह्रेता,
B. ह्रीयात् ॥ Pt. ह्रीयः or ह्रीतः (Pân. VIII. 2, 56) ॥ Pass. ह्रीयते, Caus. ह्रेपयति,
Aor. अजिह्रिपत्, Des. जिह्रीषति, Int. जेह्रीयते.

195. पृ *prî*, to fill, to guard.

This verb, and others in which final ऋ *ri* is preceded by a labial, changes the vowel into
उर् *ur*, except where the vowel requires Guṇa or Vṛiddhi. (Pân. VII. 1, 102.)

P. 1. पिपर्मि, 2. पिपर्षि, 3. पिपर्ति, 4. पिपूर्वः, 5. पिपूर्यः, 6. पिपूर्मः, 7. पिपूर्मः, 8. पिपूर्त,
9. पिपुरति, I. 1. अपिपरं, 2. अपिपः (or अपिपर्, Sâr.), 3. अपिपः (or अपिपर्त्), 4. अपिपूर्व,
5. अपिपूर्म, 6. अपिपूर्तां, 7. अपिपूर्म, 8. अपिपूर्त, 9. अपिपरुः, O. पिपूर्यात्, I. 1. पिपरानि,
2. पिपूर्हि, 3. पिपर्तु, 4. पिपराव, 5. पिपूर्म, 6. पिपूर्तां, 7. पिपराम, 8. पिपूर्त, 9. पिपुरतु ॥ Pf. 1.
पपार (ă), 2. पपरिथ, 3. पपार, 4. पपरिव, 5. पपरुः or पपरुः, 6. पपरुः or पपरुः, 7. पपरिम,
8. पपर, 9. पपरुः or पपरुः (Pân. VII. 4, 11, 12), I A. अपारीत्, F. परिष्यति (ई), P. F.
परिता or परीता, B. पूर्यात् ॥ Pt. पूर्तः (Pân. VIII. 2, 57), पूर्यः, and पूरितः are referred
to पूर् (§ 442, 7), Ger. पूर्त्वा, °पूर्य ॥ Pass. पूर्यते, Caus. पारयति, Aor. अपीपरत्, Des.
पुपूर्षति or पिपरिषति (ई), Int. पोपूर्यते, पापर्ति.

Several optional forms are derived from another root पृ, with short ऋ.
Thus, P. 3. पिपर्ति, 6. पिपृतः, 9. पिप्रति, I. 3. अपिपः, 6. अपिपृतां, 9. अपिपरुः, O. पिपृयात् ॥
I A. अपारीत्, B. प्रियात् ॥ Pass. प्रियते (§ 390), Int. पेप्रीयते (§ 481).

196. हा *hâ*, to leave, (ओहाक्.)

Reduplicated verbs ending in आ *â* (except the घु *ghu* verbs, see § 392 *) substitute ई *î* for आ *â*
before strong terminations beginning with consonants (Pân. VI. 4, 113). The verb हा *hâ*,
however, may also substitute इ *i* (Pân. VI. 4, 116).

P. 1. जहामि, 2. जहासि, 3. जहाति, 4. जहीवः (ई), 5. जहीयः (ई), 6. जहीतः (ई), 7. जहीमः
(ई), 8. जहीत (ई), 9. जहति, I. 1. अजहां, 2. अजहाः, 3. अजहात्, 4. अजहीव (ई), 9. अजहुः,
O. जह्यात् (Pân. VI. 4, 118), I. 1. जहानि, 2. जहीहि (ई) or जहाहि (Pân. VI. 4, 117),
3. जहातु, 4. जहाव, 5. जहीतं (ई), 6. जहीतां (ई), 7. जहाम, 8. जहीत (ई), 9. जहतु ॥ Pf. 1. जहौ,
2. जहिथ or जहाथ, 3. जहौ, 4. जहिव, 5. जहुः, 6. जहतुः, 7. जहिम, 8. जह, 9. जहुः, I A.
अहासीत्, F. हास्यति, P. F. हाता, B. हेयात् ॥ Pt. हीनः, Ger. हित्वा (Pân. VII. 4, 43),
°हाय ॥ Pass. हीयते, Caus. हापयति, Aor. अजीहपत्, Des. जिहासति, Int. जेहीयते.

197. ऋ *ri*, to go.

P. 3. इयर्ति, 6. इयृतः, 9. इयृति, I. 3. ऐयः (or ऐयर्त्), 6. ऐयृतां, 9. ऐयरुः, O. इयृयात्,
I. 1. इयरानि, 2. इयृहि, 3. इयर्तु, 4. इयराव, 5. इयृतं, 6. इयृतां, 7. इयराम, 8. इयृत, 9. इयृतु ॥
Pf. 1. आर, 2. आरिथ, I A. आरत्, 9. आरन् (§ 364), F. अरिष्यति, P. F. अर्ता, B. अर्यात्.

II. Âtmanepada Verbs.

198. मा *mâ*, to measure, (माङ्.)

P. 1. मिमे, 2. मिमीषे, 3. मिमीते, 4. मिमीवहे, 5. मिमाथे, 6. मिमाते, 7. मिमीमहे, 8. मिमीध्वे,

9. मिमते, I. 1. अमिमि, 2. अमिमीथाः, 3. अमिमीत, 4. अमिमीवहि, 5. अमिमाथां, 6. अमिमातां, 7. अमिमीमहि, 8. अमिमीध्वं, 9. अमिमत, O. मिमीत, I. 1. मिमे, 2. मिमीथ्व, 3. मिमीतां, 4. मिमावहै, 5. मिमाथां, 6. मिमातां, 7. मिमामहै, 8. मिमीध्वं, 9. मिमतां ॥ Pf. 1. ममे, 2. ममिषे, 3. ममे, 4. ममिवहे, 5. ममाथे, 6. ममाते, 7. ममिमहे, 8. ममिध्वे, 9. ममिरे, I A. 1. अमासि, 2. अमास्याः, 3. अमास्त, 4. अमास्वहि, 5. अमासाथां, 6. अमासातां, 7. अमास्महि, 8. अमाध्वं, 9. अमास्त, F. मास्यते, P. F. माता, B. मासीष्ट ॥ Pt. मितः, Ger. मित्वा, °माय (not मीय, Pân. vi. 4, 69) ॥ Pass. मीयते, Aor. अमायि, Caus. मापयति, Des. मित्सते, Int. मेमीयते.

III. Parasmaipada and Âtmanepada Verbs.

199. भृ *bhṛi*, to carry, (डुभृञ्.)

P. 1. विभर्मि, 2. विभर्षि, 3. विभर्ति, 4. विभृवः, 5. विभृथः, 6. विभृतः, 7. विभृमः, 8. विभृथ, 9. विभ्रति, Âtm. 1. विभ्रे, 2. विभृषे, 3. विभृते, I. 3. अविभः, 6. अविभृतां, 9. अविभरुः, Âtm. 3. अविभृत, 6. अविभ्रातां, 9. अविभ्रत, O. विभृयात्, Âtm. विभ्रीत, I. 1. विभराणि, 2. विभृहि, 3. विभर्तु ॥ Pf. 1. बभार (ă), 2. बभर्थ, 3. बभार, 4. विभृ (§ 334; Pân. vii. 2, 13) or विभरांचकार, I A. अभार्षीत्, Âtm. अभृत, F. भरिष्यति, P. F. भर्ता, B. भ्रियात्, Âtm. भृषीष्ट ॥ Pt. भृतः ॥ Pass. भ्रियते, Caus. भारयति, Des. बुभूर्षति, or विभरिषति, if it follows the Bhû class (Pân. vii. 2, 49), Int. बेभ्रीयते, बर्भर्ति.

200. दा *dâ*, to give, (डुदाञ्.)

The घु *ghu* verbs (§ 392 *) drop आ *â* before strong terminations, when other reduplicated verbs (see No. 196) change आ *â* to इ *i*. (Pân. vi. 4, 112, 113.)

P. 1. ददामि, 2. ददासि, 3. ददाति, 4. दद्वः, 5. दत्थः, 6. दत्तः, 7. दत्थः, 8. दत्थ, 9. ददति, Âtm. 1. ददे, 2. दत्से, 3. दत्ते, 4. दद्वहे, 5. ददाथे, 6. ददाते, 7. दद्महे, 8. दद्ध्वे, 9. ददते, I. 1. अददां, 2. अददाः, 3. अददात्, 4. अदत्त, 5. अदत्तं, 6. अदत्तां, 7. अदत्त, 8. अदत्त, 9. अददुः, Âtm. 1. अददि, 2. अदत्थाः, 3. अदत्त, 4. अदद्वहि, 5. अददाथां, 6. अददातां, 7. अदद्महि, 8. अदद्ध्वं, 9. अददत, O. दद्यात्, Âtm. ददीत, I. 1. ददानि, 2. देहि (Pân. vi. 4, 119), 3. ददातु, 4. ददाव, 5. दत्तं, 6. दत्तां, 7. ददाम, 8. दत्त, 9. ददतु, Âtm. 1. ददै, 2. दत्स्व, 3. दत्तां, 4. ददावहै, 5. ददाथां, 6. ददातां, 7. ददामहै, 8. दद्ध्वं, 9. ददतां ॥ Pf. 1. ददौ, 2. ददिथ or ददाथ, 3. ददौ, 4. ददिव, 5. ददुः, 6. ददुः, 7. ददिम, 8. ददे, 9. ददुः, Âtm. 1. ददे, 2. ददिषे, 3. ददे, 4. ददिवहे, 5. ददाथे, 6. ददाते, 7. ददिमहे, 8. ददिध्वे, 9. ददिरे, II A. 1. अदां, 9. अदुः, Âtm. अदिषि (see p. 184), F. दास्यति, °ते, P. F. दाता, B. देयात्, Âtm. दासीष्ट ॥ Pt. दत्तः (§ 436), Ger. दत्त्वा, °दाय ॥ Pass. दीयते, Aor. अदायि, Caus. दापयति, Aor. अदीदपत्, Des. दित्सति, Int. देदीयते, दादाति.

201. धा *dhâ*, to place, (डुधाञ्.)

This verb is conjugated like दा. It should be remembered, however, that the aspiration of the final ध, if lost, must be thrown forward on the initial द; hence 2nd pers. dual Pres. धत्थः &c. (§ 118, note). The Pt. is हितः, Ger. हित्वा, °धाय.

202. निज् *nij*, to cleanse, (णिजिर्.)

The verbs निज् *nij*, विज् *vij*, to separate, and विष् *vish*, to embrace, take Guṇa in their reduplicative syllable. (Pâṇ. VII. 4, 75·)

Reduplicated verbs (*abhyasta*, § 321 †) having a short medial vowel do not take Guṇa before weak terminations beginning with vowels in the special tenses. (Pâṇ. VII. 3, 87.)

P. 1. नेनेक्मि, 2. नेनेषि, 3. नेनेक्ति, 9. नेनिजति, I. 1. अनेनिजं, 2. अनेनेक्, 3. अनेनेक्, 7. अनेनिज्म, 9. अनेनिजुः, O. नेनिज्यात्, I. 1. नेनिजानि, 2. नेनिगिष, 3. नेनेक्तु ॥ Pf. निनेज, I A. अनैक्षीत् or II A. अनिजत्, F. नेक्ष्यति, P. F. नेक्ता, B. निज्यात्, Âtm. निक्षीष्ट ॥ Caus. नेजयति, Aor. अनीनिजत्, Des. निनिक्षति, Int. नेनिज्यते, नेनेक्ति.

Rudh Class (*Rudhâdi, VII Class*).

I. Parasmaipada and Âtmanepada Verbs.

203. रुध् *rudh*, to shut out, (रुधिर्.)

P. रुणद्धि, I. अरुणत्, O. रुंध्यात्, I. रुणद्धु ॥ Pf. 1. रुरोध, 2. रुरोधिथ, 3. रुरोध, 7. रुरुधिम, 9. रुरुधुः, IA. अरौत्सीत् or II A. अरुधत्, Âtm. रुरुधे, F. रोत्स्यति, P. F. रोद्धा, B. रुध्यात्, Âtm. रुत्सीष्ट ॥ Pt. रुद्धः, Ger. रुद्ध्वा, °रुध्य ॥ Pass. रुध्यते, Aor. अरोधि, Caus. रोधयति, Des. रुरुत्सति, Int. रोरुध्यते, रोरोद्धि.

II. Parasmaipada Verbs.

204. शिष् *śish*, to distinguish, (शिषॢ.)

P. 1. शिनश्मि, 2. शिनक्षि, 3. शिनष्टि, 4. शिंष्वः, 5. शिंष्ठः, 6. शिंष्टः, 7. शिंष्वः, 8. शिंष्ठ, 9. शिंषंति, I. 1. अशिनशं, 2. अशिनट्, 3. अशिनट्, 4. अशिंष्व, 5. अशिंष्टं, 6. अशिंष्टां, 7. अशिंष्म, 8. अशिंष्ट, 9. अशिंषन्, O. शिंष्यात्, I. 1. शिनशानि, 2. शिंद्धि (or शिंढि), 3. शिनष्टु ॥ Pf. शिशेष, II A. अशिषत्, F. शेक्ष्यति, P. F. शेष्टा, B. शिष्यात् ॥ Pt. शिष्टः ॥ Pass. शिष्यते, Caus. शेषयति, Des. शिशिक्षति, Int. शेशिष्यते, शेशेष्टि.

205. हिंस् *hiṁs*, to strike, (हिसि.)

P. हिनस्ति, I. 1. अहिनसं, 2. अहिनः or अहिनत्, 3. अहिनत् (§ 132), 4. अहिंस्व, 5. अहिंसं, 6. अहिंस्तां, 7. अहिंस्म, 8. अहिंस्त, 9. अहिंसन्, O. हिंस्यात्, I. 1. हिनसानि, 2. हिंधि, 3. हिनस्तु ॥ Pf. जिहिंस, I A. अहिंसीत्, F. हिंसिष्यति, P. F. हिंसिता, B. हिंस्यात् ॥ Pt. हिंसितः ॥ Pass. हिंस्यते, Caus. हिंसयति, Aor. अजिहिंसत्, Des. जिहिंसिषति, Int. जेहिंस्यते, जेहिंस्ति.

206. भंज् *bhañj*, to break, (भन्जो.)

P. भनक्ति, I. अभनक्, O. भंज्यात्, I. भनक्तु ॥ Pf. बभंज, I A. अभांक्षीत्, F. भंक्ष्यति, P. F. भंक्ता, B. भज्यात् ॥ Pt. भग्नः ॥ Pass. भज्यते, Aor. अभांजि or अभाजि (§ 407), Caus. भंजयति, Des. बिभंक्षति, Int. बंभज्यते, बंभंक्ति.

207. अंज् *añj*, to anoint, (अंजू.)

P. अनक्ति, I. आनक्, O. अंज्यात्, I. अनक्तु ॥ Pf. आनंज, I A. आंजीत्, F. अंजिष्यति or अंक्ष्यति, B. अज्यात् ॥ Pt. अक्तः, Ger. अंजित्वा or अंक्त्वा or अक्त्वा (Pâṇ. VI. 4, 32; § 438), °अज्य ॥ Pass. अज्यते, Aor. आंजि, Caus. अंजयति, Aor. आंजिजत्, Des. अंजिजिषति.

208. तृह् *tṛih*, to kill, (तृह.)

This verb inserts नो *ṇe* instead of न *ṇa* before weak terminations beginning with consonants.
(Pân. vii. 3, 92.)

P. 1. तृणेढि, 2. तृणोषि, 3. तृणेढि, 4. तृंढः, 5. तृंढः, 6. तृंढः, 7. तृंढः, 8. तृंढ, 9. तृंहति,
I. 1. अतृणहं, 2. अतृणेद्, 3. अतृणेद्, 4. अतृंढ, 5. अतृंढं, 6. अतृंढां, 7. अतृंढ, 8. अतृंढ, 9. अतृंहन्,
O. तृंह्यात्, I. 1. तृणहानि, 2. तृंढि, 3. तृणेढु ॥ Pf. ततर्ह, I A. अतर्हीत् or अतृक्षत्, F. तर्हिष्यति
or तर्क्ष्यति, P. F. तर्हिता or तर्ढा, B. तृह्यात् ॥ Pt. तृढः ॥ Pass. तृह्यते, Aor. अतर्हि, Caus.
तर्हयति, Aor. अततर्हत् or अतीतृहत्, Des. तितर्हिषति or तितृक्षति, Int. तरीतृह्यते, तरीतर्ढि.

III. Âtmanepada Verbs.

209. इन्ध् *indh*, to kindle, (निइंधी.)

P. इन्धे or इद्धे, I. ऐन्ध or ऐद्ध, O. इन्धीत, I. 1. इनधै, 2. इत्स्व, 3. इन्धां or इद्धां ॥ Pf.
ईधांचक्रे (or इधे, Pân. 1. 2, 6), I A. ऐन्धिष्ट, F. इन्धिष्यते, P. F. इन्धिता, B. इन्धिषीष्ट ॥
Pt. इद्धः ॥ Pass. इध्यते, Caus. इन्धयति, Des. इन्दिधिषते.

APPENDIX II.

On the Accent in Sanskrit.

§ 1. Although in Sanskrit the accent is marked in works belonging to the Vedic period only, yet its importance as giving a clue to many difficult points of grammar is now so generally acknowledged that even an elementary grammar would seem imperfect without at least the general outlines of the system of Sanskrit accentuation. I determined therefore in this new edition of my grammar to mark the accent in all cases where it seemed to be practically useful, but in order not to perplex the beginner with the marks of accent, I have added them in the transliterated words only, so that a student may still learn his grammar and his paradigms in Devanâgarî, unconcerned about the accents, until the accents themselves attract his notice, and enable him at a glance to see cause and effect in grammatical operations which otherwise would remain unintelligible. Thus if we look at *tráyaḥ*, tres, but *tribhíḥ*, tribus, and *tṛitíya*, tertius; at *émi*, I go, but *imáḥ*, we go; at *bódhâmi*, I know, but *tudámi*, I strike; at *váktum*, to speak, but *uktáḥ*, spoken, we see at once how the position of the accent, either on the radical syllable or on the termination, influences the strengthening or weakening of the base, and how this strengthening and weakening rested originally on a rational and intelligible principle.

§ 2. The accent is called in Sanskrit *Svara*, i. e. tone, and according to the description of native grammarians there can be no doubt that it was really musical. It meant the actual rising and falling of the voice, produced by the tension, the relaxation, and the wide-opening of the vocal chords; it was a musical modulation peculiar to each word, and it corresponded to what we call the singing or the *cantilena* of the speaker, which, though in modern languages most perceptible in whole sentences, may also be clearly perceived in the utterance of single words.

Ex. *María!* [music] , but *Máry!* [music] .
Ma ri a   Ma ry.

Whatever the accent became in later times, its very name of *prosodia, accentus*, i. e. by-song, shows that in Greek and Latin, too, it was originally musical, that *tonos* meant pitch, *oxys*, high pitch, *barys*, low pitch, and that *perispómenos*, drawn round, did not refer originally to the sign of the circumflex, but to the voice being drawn up and down in pronouncing a circumflexed syllable.

§ 3. For grammatical purposes we have to distinguish in Sanskrit two accents only, the *udâtta* and the *svarita*. The *udâtta* is pronounced by raising the voice, the *svarita* by a combined raising and falling of the voice. All vowels which have neither of these accents are called *anudâtta*, i. e. without *udâtta*, though they might with equal justice be called *asvarita*, without the *svarita*. The *anudâtta*, immediately preceding an *udâtta* or *svarita* vowel, is sometimes called *anudâttatara* or *sannatara**. (Pâṇ. i. 2, 29–31.)

---

* Bopp, following Professor Roth (Nir. p. LVIII), calls this accent *sannatatara*, as if from *sannata*, depressed; it is, however, derived from *sanna*, the participle of *sad*, to sink.

In transliterated words I mark the *udâtta* by the acute, the original *svarita* by the circumflex.

Every syllable without either the mark of *udâtta* or *svarita* has to be considered as grammatically unaccented; and an unaccented syllable before an *udâtta* or original *svarita*, as phonetically *anudâttatara*. If the *anudâtta* must be marked in transliterated words, it can be marked by the *gravis*. Thus in *té àvardhanta*, they grew, *té* has the *udâtta*, *à* the *anudâtta*. If the two words coalesce into *te 'vardhanta*, then *e* takes the *svarita*, *tê 'vardhanta*. Similarly, *sruchí+ìva* become *sruchîva; trí+àmbakam* become *tryâmbakam*.

§ 4. In Sanskrit the accents are indicated in the following way :

The *udâtta* is never indicated at all, but only the *svarita*, (whether original or dependent,) and the *anudâttatara (sannatara)*, i. e. the *anudâtta* immediately preceding an *udâtta* or *svarita* syllable. The sign of the *svarita* is ⊥, that of the *anudâttatara* is ⸗.

Whenever we find a syllable marked by ⸗, the sign of the *anudâttatara*, we know that the next syllable, if left without any mark, is *udâtta*; if marked by ⊥, it is *svarita*. Hence अग्निः is *agníḥ*, कन्या is *kanyâ*.

A monosyllabic word, if *udâtta*, has no mark at all. Ex. यः *yáḥ*, नु *nú*.

A monosyllabic word, if *anudâtta*, is marked by ⸗. Ex. वः *vaḥ*, नः *naḥ*.

A monosyllabic word, if *svarita*, is marked by ⊥. Ex. स्वः *svâḥ*.

§ 5. As a general rule every word has but one syllable either *udâtta* or *svarita*, the rest of the syllables being *anudâtta*. Any syllable may have the accent. But if an *udâtta* syllable is followed by an *anudâtta* syllable, its *anudâtta* is changed into what is called the dependent *svarita*. Ex. अग्निना *agnínâ*. Here अग् *ag*, originally *anudâtta*, is pronounced and marked as *anudâttatara;* नि *ni* is *udâtta*, and is therefore without any mark; ना *nâ*, originally *anudâtta*, becomes *svarita*, and is marked accordingly. In transliteration this dependent *svarita* need not be marked, nor the *anudâttatara*. Both may be treated as *anudâtta*, i. e. without grammatical accent, while their exact pronunciation in Sanskrit, to be described hereafter, is of importance to Vedic scholars only.

§ 6. If a word standing by itself or at the head of a sentence begins with several *anudâtta* syllables, they have all to be marked by the sign of *anudâttatara*. Ex. आप्नुवानः *âpnuvânaḥ;* हृदय्यया *hṛidayyâyâ*.

§ 7. By observing these simple rules, no doubt can remain as to the grammatical accent of any word in Sanskrit. The following is a list of the principal classes of accented words in Sanskrit :

1. A word consisting of one syllable which has the *udâtta*, is called *udâtta*. Ex. यः *yáḥ*, नु *nú*, कं *kâm*.

2. A word which has the *udâtta* on the last syllable, is called *antodâtta*. Ex. अग्निः *agníḥ*, जनिता *janitâ*.

3. A word which has the *udâtta* on the first syllable, is called *âdyudâtta*. Ex. इंद्रः *índraḥ*, होता *hótâ*.

4. A word which has the *udâtta* on the middle syllable, is called *madhyodâtta*. Ex. अग्निना *agnínâ*, अग्निभिः *agníbhiḥ*.

5. A word consisting of one syllable which has the original *svarita*, is called *svarita*. Ex. क्वा *kvâ*, स्वः *svâḥ*.

6. A word which has the original *svarita* on the last syllable, is called *antasvarita*. Ex. कन्या *kanyâ*.

7. A word which has the original *svarita* on the middle syllable, is called *madhyasvarita*. Ex. हृदुय्यंया *hridayyāyā*.

8. A word which has the original *svarita* on the first syllable, is called *ādisvarita*. Ex. खंबौरे *svārpare*.

9. A word without *udātta* or *svarita*, is called *sarvānudātta*. Ex. व: *vah*, न: *nah*.

10. A word with two *udātta* syllables, is called *dvirudātta*; बृहस्पतिः *brihaspátih*. Here the first syllable is *udātta*, and is therefore not marked at all. The second syllable is *anudátta*, and according to rule would become *svarita*. But as the next syllable is *udátta* again, the *anudátta* becomes *anudáttatara*, and is marked accordingly. The third syllable is *udátta*, and the last, originally *anudátta*, becomes *svarita*.

In मित्रावरुणौ *mitrávárunau*, the first syllable is *anudátta*, but becomes *anudáttatara*, because an *udátta* follows. The second syllable is *udátta*, so is the third, and hence neither of them has any mark. The fourth syllable, being *anudátta*, becomes *svarita*, because it follows an *udátta*. The last syllable is *anudátta* and, as nothing follows, is left without a mark.

11. A word with three *udátta* syllables, is called *trirudátta*; इंद्राबृहस्पती *índrábrihaspátí*.

§ 8. If words come together in a sentence, the same rules apply to them as to single words. Thus if a word ending in *udátta* is followed by a word beginning with an *anudátta* syllable, the *anudátta* syllable is pronounced as *svarita*. Thus य: + च, i. e. *yáh + chá*, become यश्च *yáśchā*, where the mark of the dependent *svarita* on च *cha* shows that य *ya* has the *udátta*.

If a word ending in an *anudátta* is followed by a word beginning with an *udátta* or *svarita*, the *anudátta* becomes *anudáttatara*. Ex. अजनयत् *ájanayat* + तं *tám* become अजनयत्तं *ájanayat tám*.

If a word ending in a *svarita*, which replaces an original *anudátta*, is followed by another word having the *udátta* on the first syllable, the general rule requires the *svarita*, being originally an *anudátta*, to become *anudáttatara*, so that we have to write यश् तत् *yáś cha tát*. Here we see that य: *yáh* has the *udátta*, because otherwise, at the beginning of a sentence, it would have to be marked with *anudáttatara*. As च *cha* has the *anudáttatara*, we see that it was originally *anudátta*, and became *anudáttatara*, because the next syllable तत् *tát* has the *udátta*, which need not be marked.

If instead of तत् *tát*, which has the *udátta*, we put ह्यः *hyáh*, which has the *svarita*, we should have to write यश् ह्यः *yáś cha hyáh*, the sign of the *svarita* on ह्यः *hyáh* showing first, that ह्यः *hyah* cannot be *udátta*, for in that case it would have no mark, and would require *svarita* on the next following syllable; and secondly, that it cannot be *anudátta*, for in that case it could not be preceded by an *anudáttatara*.

If an original *svarita* follows after a final *udátta*, it retains the sign of the *svarita*, but it is then impossible to say whether that sign marks the original or the dependent *svarita*. Ex. आत्मा क्वा *átmá + kvá* (Rv. I. 164, 4). Only, if an *udátta* followed after क्वा *kvá*, its *svarita* would remain (see § 9), while the dependent *svarita* would become *anudáttatara*.

If a word such as अरुणायुग्भिः *arunayúgbhih*, having the *udátta* on *yúg*, stands by itself, it must have the *anudáttatara* sign, not only under या *ya*, which immediately precedes the *udátta* syllable, but likewise under ण *a* and रु *ru*. But if preceded by अग्निः *agníh*, which has *udátta* on the last, the first syllable takes the *svarita*, the second requires no mark at all, and the third keeps its *anudáttatara* mark; अग्निरुरुणायुग्भिः *agnír arunayúgbhih*.

If instead of वग्निः *agníḥ* we put इंद्रं *índram*, which has the dependent *svarita* on the last, *udátta* on the first syllable, then we write इंद्रमरुणयुग्भिः *índram aruṇayúgbhiḥ*, because there is no necessity for marking the *anudátta* after a syllable which has the dependent *svarita*.

§ 9. If an original *svarita* is followed by an *udátta* or by another original *svarita*, it would be difficult to mark the accent. Thus if क्वा *kvá*, which has the original *svarita*, is followed by तत्र *tátra*, we could not write either क्वा तत्र or क्वा तत्र. In the former case we should lose the *anudáttatara* required before every *udátta* and independent *svarita;* in the latter, the sign of the original *svarita* being dropt, क्व *kva* would be taken for an *anudátta* syllable. To obviate this, the numeral १ is inserted, which takes both the *svarita* and the *anudáttatara* marks *, क्वा १ तत्र, and thus enables us to indicate what was wanted, viz. that *kvá* is *svarita*, and *tá* in *tátra* is *udátta*. Ex. युक्ष्मां + उर्वः become युक्ष्म १ युर्वः; ख: + वर्व become ख १ र्व (Rv. I. 105, 3).

If the vowel which has the original *svarita* is long, the numeral ३ is used instead of १, and the *anudáttatara* is marked both beneath the vowel and the numeral. Thus Rv. I. 105, 7. वाध्यः + पृकः become वाध्यो ३ पृकः. Rv. I. 157, 6. रथ्या + रथ्येभिः = रथ्या ३ राथ्येभिः †.

Rv. x. 116, 7. पक्वः + अग्नि + इंद्रु become पक्वो ३ अग्निंद्रु. Here *kvó* and *’ddhíu* have the *svarita*, the first is marked by पक्वो ३, the second by ३ अग्नि.

Rv. x. 144, 4. यः + अध्वः become यो ३ ध्वः ‡. This sinking of the voice, as here indicated, from the highest *svarita* to the lowest *anudáttatara* pitch is called *kampa*, shaking.

§ 10. If two vowels at the end and beginning of words coalesce into a new vowel, their respective accents are changed according to the following rules :

1. *Udátta*+*udátta*=*udátta* (Prát. 197). Ex. जुषाणा + उप = जुषाणोप *jusháṇá*+*úpa*= *jusháṇópa*. अप्सु + आ = अप्सा *apsú*+*á*= *apsvá*.

2. *Udátta*+*anudátta*=*udátta*. Ex. आ + इहि = एहि *á*+*ihi*= *éhi*. See exception *b*.

3. *Anudátta*+*anudátta*=*anudátta* (Prát. 198). Ex. मधु + उदकं = मधूदकं *mádhu*+*udakám*= *mádhúdakam*. प्रति + अद्रिश्रन् = प्रत्यद्रिश्रन् *práti*+*adriśran*= *prátyadriśran*.

4. *Anudátta*+*udátta*=*udátta*. Ex. इंद्रु + आ = इंद्रा *índra*+*á*= *índrá*. धेहि + आक्षितं = धेह्याक्षितं *dhehi*+*ákshitam*= *dhehyákshitam*.

5. *Svarita*+*udátta*=*udátta*. Ex. क्वा + इत् = क्वेत् *kvá*+*ít*= *kvét*. अध्यूत्ये + द्वासे = अध्यूत्ये ३ द्वासे *adyútyé*+*dvase*= *adyútyé ’vase* (Rv. I. 112, 24).

6. *Svarita*+*anudátta*=*svarita*. Ex. क्वा + इव = क्वेव *kvá*+*iva*= *kvéva*. क्वा + इदानीं = क्वे ३ दानीं *kvá*+*idáním*= *kvédáním* (Rv. I. 35, 7).

There are, however, some exceptions :

a. If *udátta i* coalesces with *anudátta i*, the long *í* takes *svarita* (Prát. 188, 199). Ex. सुचि + इव = सुचीव *sruchí*+*iva*= *sruchíva*. If, however, the first or second *i* is long, the contraction takes *udátta*. Ex. हि + ई = हीं *hí*+*ím*= *hím* (Rv. x. 45, 4).

b. If an *udátta* vowel becomes semivowel before an *anudátta* vowel, the *anudátta* vowel becomes *svarita* (Prát. 188). Ex. योज + नु + इंद्रु = योजा न्विंद्रु *yója*+*nú*+*indra*= *yójá*

---

* Some MSS. write क्वा १ तत्र.

† Professor Bopp (Grammatik, § 30, 5) gives this as an instance of a *svarita* followed by *anudáttatara* and *svarita*. In this case we should have to write रथ्या राथ्येभिः. But the fact is that in *ráthyebhiḥ* the first syllable has the *udátta*.

‡ The statement of Professor Benfey (Grammar, 2nd ed., p. 11) that the second *svarita* is not marked is against the authority of the MSS.

nvíndra. एव + हि + अस्य = एवा ह्यस्य *evá+hí+asya = evá hyásya* (Rv. 1. 8, 8). Also, नदी *nadí*, plur. नद्ः: *nadyáḥ*, but gen. sing. नद्याः: *nadyáḥ*, because in the former the termination is originally *anudátta*, in the latter *udátta*.

c. If an *udátta e* or *o* coalesces with an (elided) *anudátta a*, it takes *svarita* (Prát. 188). Ex. ते + अवर्धन्त = ते ऽवर्धन्त *té+avardhanta = té 'vardhanta.*

According to Máṇḍúkeya all *udátta* vowels coalescing with another *anudátta* vowel, become *svarita.* This is also the case in certain Bráhmaṇas; see Kielhorn, Bháshika-sútra, I. 5.

The accents produced by the coalescence of vowels have the following technical names, taken from the name of the Sandhi that gave rise to them :

1. *Praślishṭa*, the accent of two vowels united into one (*samávesa, ekíbháva*).

2. *Abhinihita*, the accent of two vowels of which the second is the elided *a*.

3. *Kshaipra*, the accent of two vowels of which the first has been changed into a semivowel.

4. *Tairovyañjana*, the *svarita*, replacing an *anudátta*, if separated by consonants from the preceding *udátta*. Ex. अग्निमीळे *agním íle*.

5. *Vaivṛitta* (or *pádavṛitta*), the *svarita*, replacing an *anudátta*, if separated by an hiatus from the preceding *udátta* (Prát. 204). Ex. य इंद्र *yá indra* *.

6. *Játya*, the *svarita* in the body of a word, also called *nitya*, inherent. It is always preceded by either *y* or *v*, and points to a period in the history of Sanskrit in which these semivowels retained something of their vowel nature. It may, in fact, be treated as medial *kshaipra;* and it is important that where the peculiar pronunciation of the different *svaritas* is described, that of the *játya* and the *kshaipra* is said to be identical (Váj. Prát. I. 125).

§ 11. By applying these rules we can with perfect certainty discover which syllable in each word has the grammatical accent, whether *udátta* or *svarita*. Unfortunately many words lose their accent in a sentence, particularly the verb which, in a direct sentence, is considered as a mere enclitic of the noun to which it belongs. Only in relative and conditional sentences, or when a verb begins a sentence, and under some other restrictions which are fully described by native grammarians, does the verb retain its independent accent. Vocatives also lose their accent, except at the beginning of a sentence, when they have the accent on the first syllable†. With these exceptions, however, every student, by following the rules here given, will be able to determine what is the real grammatical accent of any

---

* Besides the *tairovyañjana* and the *vaivritta*, which we should call the dependent *svarita*, other subdivisions are mentioned by some authorities. Thus if compound words are divided (in the Padapáṭha) by the *avagraha*, the *tairovyañjana* is called *tairoviráma*. Ex. गोऽपतौ *gó 'patau.* If a word is divided in the Padapáṭha, the first half ending in a *svarita* preceded by an *udátta*, and the second half beginning with an *udátta*, the *svarita* is called *táthábhávya.* Ex. तनूऽनपात्. Here *ta* is *udátta*, *nú* is *svarita*, then follows the *avagraha* or pause of division, and after that *na*, which is again *udátta*. Here a kind of *kampa* takes place, and the *svarita* is marked accordingly. Though the name *táthábhávya* is not mentioned in the first Prátisákhya, the peculiar accent which it is meant for is fully described in Sútra 212. In the commentary on the Váj. Prát. (120) it would perhaps be better to write *asaṁhitávat* instead of *svasaṁhitávat;* Weber, Ind. Stud. vol. IV. p. 137.

† See Bháshika-sútra, ed. Kielhorn, II. 1–31; Whitney, in Beiträge zur vergleichenden Sprachforschung, vol. I. p. 187.

word occurring in the hymns of the Rig-veda. The system of marking the *udâtta* and
svarita in the S'atapatha-Brâhmaṇa is slightly different, as may be seen from Professor
Weber's introductory remarks, and particularly from Dr. Kielhorn's learned notes on the
Bhâshika-sûtras.

§ 12. Quite different from the determination of the grammatical accent is the question
how the accents should be pronounced or intoned in a sentence, and particularly in the
hymns and Brâhmaṇas of the principal Vedas. This question concerns the student of the
Veda only, and different authorities differ on this point. The following short remarks must
be sufficient. According to the Rig-veda-Prâtisâkhya (187 seq.), the *udâtta* is high, the
anudâtta low; of the *svarita* one portion is higher than *udâtta*, the rest like *udâtta*, except
if an *udâtta* or *svarita* follows, in which case the voice sinks down to the *anudâtta* pitch.
This sinking down is called *kampa*, shaking. All *anudâtta* syllables, following after *svarita*
(whether original or dependent) are pronounced with *udâtta* pitch (195), except the last, which
is followed again by either *udâtta* or *svarita*, and takes the low pitch of *anudâtta* (196). This
pronunciation of *anudâtta* syllables with *udâtta* pitch is called the *Prachaya* accent (205).
We have therefore only three kinds of pitch, (no special *anudâttatara* pitch being recognised
in the Prâtisâkhya,) which in their relative position may be represented by

Thus in मादयस्व स्वर्णरे *mâdáyasva svârṇare*, मा *mâ* is *anudâtta*, द *da* is *udâtta*, य *ya* is *svarita*,
स्व *sva* is *anudâtta*, स्वर् *svâr* is *svarita*, णरे *ṇare*, both *anudâtta*, but pronounced like *udâtta*.

In अदब्धप्रमतिर्वसिष्ठः: *ádabdhapramatir vásishṭhaḥ*, अ *a* is *udâtta*, दब् *dab* is *svarita*,
धप्रम *dhaprama* are *anudâtta*, but pronounced like *udâtta*, ति *ti* is *anudâtta*, व *va* is *udâtta*,
सिष् *sish* is *svarita*, ठः *ṭhaḥ* is *anudâtta*, but pronounced as *udâtta*.

Other S'âkhâs vary in the pronunciation of the accents, as may be seen from their respective
Prâtisâkhyas. Much confusion has been caused by mixing up these different systems, and,
in particular, by trying to reconcile the rules of the Rig-veda-Prâtisâkhya with the rules
of Pâṇini. According to Pâṇini (1. 2, 29 seq.) the *udâtta* is high, the *anudâtta* low, but the
svarita is half high and half low, and the *anudâttas* following after *svarita* (original or
dependent) are pronounced monotonously (*ekasruti*), while the last of them, immediately

---

* Long after this was written I saw Dr. Haug's description of the accents in the
Zeitschrift der D. M. G. vol. XVII. p. 799. He gives the intervals much smaller, so that if
the *anudâtta* is *c*, the *udâtta* would be *d*, and the *svarita* would rise to *e*. This is no doubt
right, and it will be easy to transcribe my own notation accordingly. I only retain it because
it is clearer to the eye. What is very important, as confirming my view, is Dr. Haug's
remark that in listening to the recitation of the Pandits he could not perceive any difference
between the *udâtta* and the *anudâttas* if pronounced with *prachaya svara*.

preceding a new *udâtta* or *svarita*, is lower than *anudâtta*, and hence called *sannatara* or, by the commentators, *anudâttatara*. This system, too, though different from the former, gives us only three kinds of musical pitch, which may be approximately represented by

Ekaśruti is described as without any definite pitch (*traisvaryâpavâda*), and might therefore be intended for mere monotonous *recitative**.

---

* It is commonly used as synonymous with *prachita;* e. g. *udâttamayam prachitam ekaśrutti paryâyaḥ*, Vâj. Prât. iv. 138.

INDEX OF NOUNS.

NOTE—The figures refer to the §, not to the page.

í, mother, 238.

ši, eye, 234.

agnimath, fire-kindling, 157.

tichamú, better than an army, 227.

atilakshmí, better than Lakshmí,

tistri, better than a woman, m.f., 229.

í, eating, 182.

191.

aḍud, ox, 210.

tarvan, without a foe, 189.

tehas, time, 168.

vach, following, 181.

ater, 211.

mbiká, mother, 238.

ís, fire, 149.

yaman, name of a deity, 201.

ut, horse, 189.

tn, hurting, foe, 189.

vayáj, priest, 163.

ích, south, 180.

f. not desiring, 225.

t, blood, 214.

ij, blood, 161, 214.

ši, bone, 234.

n, n. day, 196.

n, day, at the end of a compound, 98.

argaṇa, month, 196.

man, soul, self, 191, 192.

आप: *ápaḥ*, water, 149, 211.

आशिस् *áśis*, blessing, 172.

आसन् *ásan*, face, 214.

आस्य *ásya*, face, 214.

°इन् *-in*, 203.

ईदृश *ídṛiś*, such, 174.

°ईयस् *-íyas*, 206.

उक्यशास् *ukthaśás*, reciter of hymns, 177.

उदक *udaka*, water, 214.

उदच् *udach*, upward, northern, 181.

उदन् *udan*, water, 214.

उन्नी *unní*, leading out, 221.

उपानह् *upánah*, shoe, 174.

उशनस् *uśanas*, nom. prop., 169.

उष्णिह् *ushṇih*, a metre, 174.

ऊर्ज् *úrj*, strength, 161.

ऋत्विज् *ṛitvij*, priest, 161.

ऋभुक्षिन् *ṛibhukshin*, Indra, 195.

ककुभ् *kakubh*, region, 157.

कति *kati*, how many, 231.

करभू *kárabhú*, nail, 221.

कवि *kavi*, poet, 230.

कान्त *kánta*, beloved, 238.

कान्ता *kántá*, fem. beloved, 238.

कियत् *kiyat*, How much? 190.

किर् *kir*, scattering, 164.

कुधी *kudhí*, m. f. a bad thinker, 221.

कुमारी *kumárí*, m. girlish, 227.

क्री *krí*, m. f. buying, 220.

क्रुञ्च *kruñch*, curlew, 159.

क्रोष्टु *kroshṭu*, jackal, 236.

खंज *khañj*, lame, 163.

गरीयस् *garīyas*, heavier, 206.

गिर् *gir*, voice, 164.

गुप् *gup*, guardian, 157.

गुह् *guh*, covering, 174.

गो *go*, ox, 218.

गोरक्ष *goraksh*, cowherd, 174.

ग्रामणी *grāmaṇí*, leader of a village, 221.

चकास् *chakās*, splendid, 172.

चकासत् *chakāsat*, shining, 184.

चिकीर्ष *chikīrs*, desirous of acting, 172.

चित्रलिख *chitralikh*, painter, 156.

जक्षत् *jakshat*, eating, 184.

जगत् *jagat*, world, 184.

जगन्वस् *jaganvas*, having gone, 205.

जग्मिवस् *jagmivas*, having gone, 205.

जघन्वस् *jaghanvas*, having killed, 205.

जघ्निवस् *jaghnivas*, having killed, 205.

जरा *jarā*, old age, 166.

जलक्री *jalakrī*, m. f. a buyer of water, 221.

जलमुच् *jalamuch*, cloud, 158.

जाग्रत् *jāgrat*, waking, 184.

तक्ष् *taksh*, paring, 174.

तक्षन् *takshan*, carpenter, 191.

तति *tati*, so many, 231.

तंत्री *tantrī*, f. lute, 225.

तरी *tarí*, f. boat, 225.

तिर्यच् *tiryach*, tortuous, 181.

तुरासाह् *turāsāh*, Indra, 175.

त्वच् *tvach*, skin, 158.

त्विष् *tvish*, splendour, 174.

दत् *dat*, tooth, 214.

ददत् *dadat*, giving, 184.

दधि *dadhi*, curds, 234.

दधृष् *dadhrish*, bold, 174.

दंत *danta*, tooth, 214.

दरिद्रत् *daridrat*, poor, 184.

दातृ *dātṛi*, giver, 235.

दामन् *dāman*, rope, fem., 179, 193.

दारा: *dārāḥ*, wife, 149.

दिधक्ष *didhaksh*, desirous of burning, 174.

दिव् *div* and द्यु *dyu*, sky, 213.

दिश् *diś*, showing, 174.

दिश् *diś*, country, 174.

दुह् *duh*, milking, 174.

दुहितृ *duhitṛi*, daughter, 235.

दृन्भू *dṛinbhú*, thunderbolt, 221.

दृश् *dṛiś*, seeing, 174.

देवेज् *devej*, worshipper, 162.

दोषन् *doshan*, arm, 214.

दोष् *dos*, arm, 172, 214.

द्यु *dyu* and दिव् *div*, sky, 213.

द्यो *dyo*, sky, 219.

द्रुह् *druh*, hating, 174.

द्वार् *dvār*, door, 164.

द्विदाम्नी *dvidāmní*, having two ropes, 194.

द्विष् *dvish*, hating, 174.

धनिन् *dhanin*, rich, 203.

धातृ *dhātṛi*, n. providence, 235.

धी *dhí*, m. f. thinking, 220.

धी *dhí*, f. intellect, 224.

धीवरी *dhīvarí*, wife of a fisherman, 193.

ध्वस् *dhvas*, falling, 173.

नदी *nadí*, f. river, 225.

नप्तृ *naptṛi*, grandson, 235.

नश् *naś*, destroying, 174.

नस् *nas*, nose, 214.

नह् *nah*, binding, 174.

नामन् *nāman*, name, 191.

नासिका *nāsikā*, nose, 214.

निनीवस् *ninīvas*, having led, 205.

निर्जर *nirjara*, ageless, 167.

नृ *nṛi*, man, 237.

नृतू *nṛitú*, m. f. dancer, 222.

नौ *nau*, ship, 217.

न्यच् *nyach*, low, 181.

पंगु *paṅgu*, m., पंगू *paṅgú*, fem. lame, 230.

पति *pati*, lord, 233.

पथिन् *pathin*, m. path, 195.

', foot, 214.

pt, m. f. protector, 222.

paramant, m. f. best leader, 221.

परिव्राज् parivráj, mendicant, 162.

parṇadhvas, leaf-shedding, 173.

arvan, joint, 191.

ṇdu, m. f. n. pale, 230.

vád, foot, 207.

'da, foot, 214.

piṇḍagras, lump-eater, 170.

tṛi, father, 235.

pipaksh, desirous of maturing, 174.

pipaṭhis, wishing to read, 171.

tlu, m. n. a tree and its fruit, 230.

pívan, fat, fem. पीवरी pívarí, 194.

punarbhú, re-born, 221.

n, man, (pums), 212.

', town, 164.

purudamśas, Indra, 168.

puroḍáś, an offering, 176.

úshan, name of a deity, 201.

t, army, 214.

vṛitand, army, 214.

ṛishat, deer, 185.

pechivas, having cooked, 205.

prajápati, lord of creatures, 233.

pratidivan, sporting, 192.

pratyach, western, 181.

radhí, m. f. thinking eminently, 221.

adhí, fem., 223.

praśám, quieting, 178.

rách, eastern, 180.

ráchh, asking, 160, 174.

ráñch, worshipping, 159.

ıdi, dark fortnight, 149.

bahurájan, having many kings, 194.

bahuśreyasí, auspicious, 227.

bahúrj, very strong, 161.

dh, knowing, 157.

ṛihat, great, 185.

ब्रह्मन् brahman, creator, 192.

भवत् bhavat, Your Honour, 188.

भिषज् bhishaj, physician, 161.

भी bhí, f. fear, 224.

भू bhú, being, 221.

भू bhú, f. earth, 224.

भूर् bhúr, atmosphere, 149.

भृज्ज् bhrijj, roasting, 162.

भ्राज् bhráj, shining, 162.

भ्रातृ bhrátri, brother, 235.

भ्रू bhrú, f. brow, 224.

मघवन् maghavan, Indra, 200.

मज्ज् majj, diving, 161.

°मत् -mat, 187.

मति mati, thought, 230.

मथिन् mathin, churning-stick, 195.

मधुलिह् madhulih, bee, 174.

°मन् -man, 191.

महत् mahat, great, 186.

मांस् máms, meat, 214.

मांस mámsa, meat, 214.

मातृ mátri, mother, 235.

मास् más, month, 214.

मुह् muh, confounding, 174.

मूर्धन् múrdhan, head, 191.

मृज् mrij, cleaning, 162.

मृदु mridu, m. f. n. soft, 230.

यकन् yakan, liver, 214.

यकृत् yakrit, liver, 214.

यज् yaj, sacrificing, 162.

यज्वन् yajvan, sacrificer, 192.

यति yati, as many, 231.

ययी yayí, f. road, 222.

युवन् yuvan, young, 199.

यूष yúsha, pea-soup, 214.

यूषन् yúshan, pea-soup, 214.

राज् ráj, shining, 162.

राजन् rájan, king, 191.

राज्ञी rájñí, queen, 193.

रुच् ruch, light, 158.

रुज् *ruj*, disease, 161.

रुरुद्वस् *rurudvas*, crying, 204.

रुष् *rush*, anger, 174.

रै *rai*, wealth, 217.

लक्ष्मी *lakshmí*, f. goddess of prosperity, 225.

लघु *laghu*, m. f. n. light, 230.

लिह् *lih*, licking, 174.

लू *lú*, m. f. cutting, 220.

वणिज् *vaṇij*, merchant, 161.

°वत् *-vat*, 187.

वधू *vadhú*, f. wife, 225.

°वन् *-van*, 191.

वर्षा: *varshá́ḥ*, rainy season, 149.

वर्षाभू *varshá́bhú*, frog, 221.

°वस् *-vas*, part. perfect, 204.

वाच् *vách*, speech, 158.

वातप्रमी *vátapramí*, antelope, 222.

वार् *vár*, water, 164.

वारि *vári*, water, 230.

°वाह् *-váh*, carrying, 208.

विद्वस् *vidvas*, knowing, 205.

विपाश् *vipáś*, a river, 174.

विप्रुष् *viprush*, drop of water, 174.

विभ्राज् *vibhrá́j*, resplendent, 162.

विवक्ष् *vivaksh*, desirous of saying, 174.

विविक्ष् *viviksh*, wishing to enter, 174.

विश् *viś*, entering, 174.

विश्वपा *viśvapá*, all-preserving, 239.

विश्वराज् *viśvará́j*, universal monarch, 162.

विश्वसृज् *viśvasṛij*, creator, 162.

विष् *vish*, ordure, 174.

विष्वच् *vishvach*, all-pervading, 181.

वृक्षलू *vṛikshalú́*, tree-hewer, 222.

वृश्च् *vṛiśch*, cutting, 159.

शकन् *śakan*, ordure, 214.

शकृत् *śakṛit*, ordure, 214.

शंखध्मा *śaṅkhadhmá́*, shell-blower, 239.

शासत् *śásat*, commanding, 184.

शुचि *śuchi*, m. f. n. bright, 230.

शुद्धधी *śuddhadhí*, thinking pure things, 221.

शुद्धधी *śuddhadhí*, a pure thinker, 221.

शुश्रुवस् *śuśruvas*, having heard, 205.

शुष्की *śushkí*, 222.

श्री *śrí*, f. happiness, 224.

श्वन् *śvan*, dog, 199.

श्वेतवाह् *śvetavá́h* and श्वेतवस् *śvetavas*, 209.

संवत् *saṁvat*, year, 149.

सक्थि *sakthi*, thigh, 234.

सखि *sakhi*, friend, 232.

सजुस् *sajus*, friend, 172.

सध्र्यच् *sadhryach*, accompanying, 181.

सम्यच् *samyach*, right, 181.

सम्राज् *samrá́j*, sovereign, 162.

सर्वषक् *sarvaṣak*, omnipotent, 155.

सानु *sánu*, ridge, 214.

सामि *sámi*, half, 149.

सिकता: *sikatá́ḥ*, sand, 149.

सुखी *sukhí*, wishing for pleasure, 222.

सुगण *sugaṇ*, ready reckoner, 154.

सुचक्षुस् *suchakshus*, having good eyes, 165.

सुज्योतिस् *sujyotis*, well-lighted, 165.

सुती *sutí*, wishing for a son, 222.

सुतुस् *sutus*, well-sounding, 170.

सुधी *sudhí*, m. f. having a good mind, 226.

सुपिस् *supis*, well-walking, 170.

सुभ्रू *subhrú*, m. f. having good brows, 226.

सुमनस् *sumanas*, well-minded, 165.

सुश्री *suśrí*, well-faring, 221.

सुसखि *susakhi*, a good friend, 232.

सुहिंस् *suhiṁs*, well-striking, 172.

सुहृद् *suhṛid*, friendly, 157.

सृज् *sṛij*, creating, 162.

सोमपा *somapá*, Soma drinker, 239.

स्त्री *strí*, woman, 228.

स्निह् *snih*, loving, 174.

स्नु *snu*, ridge, 214.

स्नुह् *snuh*, spueing, 174.

स्पृश् *spṛiś*, touching, 174.

स्रज् *sraj*, a garland, 161.

स्रस् *sras*, falling, 173.

स्रुच् *sruch*, ladle, 158.

स्वयं *svayam*, self, 149.

स्वयंभू *svayambhú*, self-existing, 221.

स्वर् *svar*, heaven, 149.

स्वसृ *svasṛi*, sister, 235.

स्वाप् *sváp*, having good water, 211.

हन् *han*, killing, 202.

हरित् *harit*, green, 157.

हाहा *háhá*, 240.

हृद् *hṛid*, heart, 214.

हृदय *hṛidaya*, heart, 214.

ह्री *hrí*, f. shame, 224.

INDEX OF VERBS.

NOTE—The number refers to the number of each verb in the Appendix.

अक्ष् *aksh*, to pervade, 37.

अज् *aj*, to go, to throw, (वी *ví*), 23.

अंच् *añch*, to go, to worship, 17.

अंज् *añj*, to anoint, 207.

अद् *ad*, to eat, 162.

अन् *an*, to breathe, 176.

अय् *ay*, to go, 78.

अर्द् *ard*, to go, to pain, 12.

अव् *av*, to help, 92.

अश् *aś*, to pervade, 147.

अस् *as*, to be, 173.

आंछ् *áñchh*, to stretch, 18.

आप् *áp*, to obtain, 146.

आस् *ás*, to sit, 183.

आह *áha*, to speak, 190.

इ *i*, to go, 171.

इ *i*, to go; अधी *adhí*, to read, 186.

इंद् *ind*, to govern, 13.

इंध् *indh*, to kindle, 209.

इष् *ish*, to wish, 118, 31.

ईक्ष् *íksh*, to see, 69.

ईश् *íś*, to rule, 182.

ईह् *íh*, to aim, 79.

उख् *ukh*, to go, 16.

उष् *ush*, to burn, 40.

ऊर्णु *úrṇu*, to cover, 191.

ऋ *ṛi*, to go, (ऋच्छति *ṛichchhati*), 49.

ऋ *ṛi*, to go, 197.

ऋज् *ṛij*, to gain, 72.

एध् *edh*, to grow, 68.

कट् *kaṭ*, to rain, to encompass, 25.

कम् *kam*, to love, 77.

काश् *káś*, to shine, 80.

कास् *kás*, to cough, 81.

किंत् *kit*, to cure, (चिकित्सति *chikitsati*), 63.

कुट् *kuṭ*, to bend, 111.

कुंथ् *kunth*, to strike, 6.

कृ *kṛi*, to do, 152.

कृत् *kṛit*, to cut, 110, 107.

कृप् *kṛip*, to be able, 89, 87.

कृष् *kṛish*, to furrow, 38.

कृष् *kṛish*, to trace, 106.

कृ *kṛí*, to scatter, 113.

कृत *kṛít*, to praise, 138.

क्रम *kram*, to stride, 30, 29.

क्री *krí*, to buy, 153.

क्लम *klam*, to tire, 29, 30, 130.

क्षण *kshaṇ*, to kill, 149.

क्षम *ksham*, to bear, 130.

क्षि *kshi*, to wane, to diminish, 24.

क्षिण *kshiṇ*, to kill, 150.

खद् *khad*, to eat, 8.

खन् *khan*, to dig, 95.

खिद् *khid*, to vex, 107.

ख्या *khyá*, to proclaim, 166.

गद् *gad*, to speak, 9.

गम् *gam*, to go, 33, 31.

गा *gá*, to go, 83.

गुप् *gup*, to protect, 26, 63.

गुह् *guh*, to hide, 97, 29.

गै *gai*, to sing, 44.

ग्रह् *grah*, to take, 157, 105.

ग्लै *glai*, to droop, 43.

घु *ghu*-class, 46, 47, 200.

घ्रा *ghrá*, to smell, 54.

चकास् *chakás*, to shine, 177.

चक्ष् *chaksh*, to speak, 181.

चप् *chap*, to pound, 137.

चम् *cham*, to eat, 29.

चह् *chah*, to pound, 137.

चि *chi*, to collect, 137, 140.

चित् *chit*, to think, 2.

चुर् *chur*, to steal, 136.

च्युत् *chyut*, to sprinkle, 3.

छो *chho*, to cut, 124.

जक्ष् *jaksh*, to eat, 177, 176.

जन् *jan*, to spring up, 132.

जागृ *jágṛi*, to wake, 178, 177.

जि *ji*, to excel, 36.

जृ *jṛí*, to grow old, 123, 156.

ज्ञप् *jñap*, to know, to make known, 137.

ज्ञा *jñá*, to know, 159.

ज्या *jyá*, to grow weak, 158, 36, 105.

ज्वर् *jvar*, to suffer, 92.

तक्ष् *taksh*, to hew, 37.

तन् *tan*, to stretch, 148.

तप् *tap*, to burn, 28.

तम् *tam*, to languish, 130.

तिज् *tij*, to forbear, (तितिक्षते *titikshate*), 75, 6;

तु *tu*, to grow, 170.

तुद् *tud*, to strike, 104.

तृप् *tṛip*, to delight, 127, 38.

तृह् *tṛih*, to kill, 208.

तृ *tṛí*, to cross, 61.

त्रप् *trap*, to be ashamed, 74.

त्रस् *tras*, to tremble, 30.

त्रुट् *truṭ*, to cut, 30.

त्वर् *tvar*, to hurry, 92.

दंश् *daṁś*, to bite, 62, 73.

दद् *dad*, to give, 70.

दम् *dam*, to tame, 130.

दरिद्रा *daridrá*, to be poor, 179, 177.

दह् *dah*, to burn, 42.

दा *dá*, to give, 58.

दा *dá*, to give, 200.

दान् *dán*, दीदांसति *dídáṁsati*, to straighten, 63.

दिव् *div*, to play, 121.

दी *dí*, to decay, 154.

दीधी *dídhí*, to shine, 177.

दुह् *duh*, to milk, 188.

दृ *dṛí*, to observe, 120.

दृश् *dṛiś*, to see, (पश् *paś*), 48, 38.

दृ *dṛí*, to tear, 156.

दे *de*, to protect, 85.

दै *dai*, to cleanse, 46.

दै *dai*, to protect, 85.

दो *do*, to cut, 124.

द्युत् *dyut*, to shine, 86.

द्विष् *dvish*, to hate, 187.

धा *dhá*, to place, 201.

धू *dhú*, to shake, 156.

धूप् *dhúp*, to warm, 27.